D0899042

People's Names

People's Names

A Cross-Cultural Reference Guide
to the Proper Use of Over 40,000
Personal and Familial Names
in Over 100 Cultures

HOLLY INGRAHAM

McFarland & Company, Inc., Publishers
Jefferson, North Carolina, and London

British Library Cataloguing-in-Publication data are available

Library of Congress Cataloguing-in-Publication Data

Ingraham, Holly, 1953–
    People's names : a cross-cultural reference guide to the proper
use of over 40,000 personal and familial names in over 100 cultures /
Holly Ingraham.
        p.   cm.
    Includes index.
    ISBN 0-7864-0187-7 (library binding : 50# alk. paper) ∞
    1. Names, Personal.   I. Title.
CS2305.I54   1997
929.9'7 — dc20   96-28638
                                                                           CIP

Manufactured in the United States of America

*McFarland & Company, Inc., Publishers
  Box 611, Jefferson, North Carolina 28640*

For my sister, Trini,
who started me off,
in names as in so many things

Acknowledgments

My deepest thanks go to Patrick, who not only kept up my spirits when making the sale and finishing the work, but provided technical expertise to boost the word processing, and even grueling secretarial labor.

Thanks also to the reference librarians at the Hawaii State Library Main Branch, especially in Language, Literature, and History, for their help answering questions over the phone and on site; and to those in the Inter-Library Loan Unit who found those copies of obscure texts and brought them in so quickly.

Special thanks to Donald E. and Lorna Touryan Miller, authors of *Survivors: An Oral History of the Armenian Genocide* (1993), for contributing extra Armenian female names, and catching a couple of my mistakes in that section.

With Chaucer, I beg that "if you find anything in here that displeases you, then impute it to my want of ability, and not to my will, who had very gladly done better." If you have better information, please do write me in care of the publisher.

Table of Contents

Introduction

The modern, international multiculturalism is a challenge to any of us, young and old. We are each a creature of our own culture. Not only is it sometimes difficult to adapt to others' habits, but if information about what those habits are is lacking, it is almost impossible.

The most basic courtesy we can extend to anyone is to use their names in what they perceive as a proper manner. At some time, someone must have mispronounced your name, or called you by the wrong name. At best it is irksome. If you feel it was done out of sheer carelessness, you are nettled that someone thinks you worthless, not worth the trouble to exert a little attention. Done on purpose, say, after the third correction? Imagine your simmering anger.

On the other hand, if you have a name which is often mispronounced simply because it is spelled in its own, idiosyncratic manner (like mine), you know what a rare but warm pleasure it is when a stranger addresses you, and gets it right without your first having to correct him or her. "This is an intelligent person," you can't help thinking, "someone sharper than most," simply because they recognized and used your name properly.

As this is written in English, I will assume that you are part of the Anglo-American community. You know that people have a first name, a last name, and often a middle name. You also know that they will share the last name with other members of their family. That's what last names are for!

A Chinese contact of yours from Taiwan also has a first, middle, and last name — say, Wong Chun Hoon. So you call him Mr. Hoon.

Wrong. His "last name" comes first. You just called him the equivalent of Mr. Joe. His *family name* is Wong, making him Mr. Wong. You never call him just Chun, either. If the two of you are on a "first name basis," then you call him Chun Hoon. It is a compound name, and might be written Chun-hoon, or Chunhoon.

As this worst-case scenario shows, the very words you normally use to describe names are so culturally narrow as to guarantee confusion and mistakes.

People can be just as offended on behalf of their entire ethnic group, especially when decades or centuries of cultural insensitivity have left them with raw nerves. As a business person, you might offend a few Chinese with your lack of information; as they are in contact with you, they may correct you. As a writer, you can offend thousands of people with a single book or play, and never know you are doing anything wrong. They will not write. They will simply blacklist you with all their friends as an ignorant clod, even though they have done nothing to make their naming habits accessible to you.

Everyone has been needing a single book that will familiarize them with other peoples' way of building and using names all around the planet. As a shopkeeper, a teacher, or an office worker, you need to be able to recognize foreign names, perhaps well enough to tell a Thai from a Cambodian at a glance, or an Estonian from a Latvian. Your situation is that people hand you a strange name, and you need to pronounce it right, and know which parts to use to address them.

Writers have it much worse. At long last, publishers will look at stories about characters who are not WASP, and you are ready to expand your horizons. But naming a character from an unfamiliar country is like trying to name your baby when you have complete ignorance of all the rules. No one helps out by handing you a name — or maybe you are given a multicultural baby-name book for Anglo-American babies. Even if this has accurate spellings and does not put men's names in the pink section, it still offers no help with all the rules for family names. You cannot count on "they wouldn't know any more about it than I do." Today's readers are better read, more sophisticated, and better travelled than ever. The people who used to consume the cheapest, sloppiest fiction now just watch television.

In this book, you will find everything you need as a general user: the paralegal or medical assistant handed a folder with a strange bunch of letters across the top, where the client's name goes; the school teacher who knows that mispronouncing the immigrant child's name on his or her first day in an American school can be crushing; the business person who wants to please and impress by addressing a client properly; the personnel manager wanting to enhance the company's diversity; the assignments manager who wants to avoid ethnic conflicts; the publisher who wants to index foreign authors correctly; the researcher trying to find the original rather than Anglicized name of an historical figure; the traveller who wants to be a welcome guest in foreign countries, simply by trying to fit in a little.

Because of the special and oft-ignored needs of fiction writers — novelists, screenwriters, playwrights, and all the tribe — never addressed even by the best of etiquette books and diplomatic preps, I have structured this book especially for their use. If you are a writer, this is probably the only book for names you will need for an entire career.

The name lists are very large. As a general user, you can read these to familiarize yourself with the look and feel of a culture's group of names (technically, an *onomasticon*). Nonetheless, the lists are sometimes very small compared to the entire known onomasticon; so while all the names in here are appropriate and suitable, there may be other equally authentic names which had to be left out for lack of space. An encyclopedia in a print format of all the world's known people's names might take fifty feet of bookshelf.

There is a large section on English language names because, first, you may be in the United States, speaking and writing in English, and yet not be totally familiar with the place, and second, family names and titles of address are in a state of flux. If you live in a conservative community, you may be unaware of the controversy being argued a short ways down the road.

A Few Necessary Technical Terms

A *personal name* is the one that belongs to the individual, distinguishing him or her from the other members of the family. It may be a "first name," or it may be the last name in a string, if the naming culture puts family names first. "First name" as personal name applies only to a limited number of cultures. A personal name may be an only name.

An *eke-name* is given to the individual in place of or in addition to the personal name ("eke"=also). In the name Nata Redmaene, "Nata" (Nathan) is the personal name and "Redmaene" (Redhair), the eke-name. The latter is not a family name if Nata's father is Peir Blac, or Nata Blac. Eke-names are used to separate different people with the same personal name, since most people only know or use a few score names. Eke-names may refer to personal characteristics, to place of origin or present dwelling, or to memorable events.

The *family name* refers only to a name that is inherited from generation to generation, regardless of where the person dwells or what offices they may hold. Family names may have originated as patronymics, place-names, titles, or eke-names, but they now live a life of their own. They may be gendered to show that the person is a son or daughter of the family, or has married into it, but the root remains the same.

A *surname* is literally an "after-name." Only sometimes is it a family name. In many cultures it is a title or an eke-name. It may also be an *honorific*, a kind of verbal medal awarded to the individual. In many cultures having inherited family names, that family name is not a surname, because the family name comes before the personal name or names. The two terms are not really interchangeable.

A *patronymic* is a "father-name" that changes between generations. Only after it ceases to change with the actual father's name is it a real family name. In many cultures, the middle name between the personal name and the family name may still be a patronymic, and must reflect the father. Less often there are *matronymics*, mother-names.

A *Christian name* is hallowed by being borne by a Catholic or Orthodox or similar saint, not just any old "first name." No Christianity, no Christian name. These may include names introduced to a culture after the coming of Christianity. Also, a Christian name may be that added by a convert, like Kamala Mahendra becoming Martha K. Mahendra after baptism, or Temua (nothing else) becoming John Temua. Closely related are *Biblical names*, which serve the same function for Protestants. Moslems also consider the use of an Islamic (Arabic) name to be a religious act, especially on conversion.

In some cultures, especially Polynesia and Japan, you will find *name-titles*. These are passed from one bearer to another, who need not be directly related in any set manner. Once the person has a name-title, it is used in all ways as if it were his or her individual name, often to the exclusion of any earlier name. Yet the name-title always indicates accomplishment or duties as well.

A *moniker* is a name, usually a personal name, which is treated simply as a sound-cluster that refers to a person, rather than having "a meaning." When Jennifer means "a white wave," it is a name, but not a moniker. When it means "pretty, fashionable girl" or "that woman over there," then it is just a moniker to the people using it.

Diminutives (dim.) indicate diminuation of formality or status, in some languages by making the name shorter (David becomes Dave), but more often by adding special endings: English Ann becomes Annie or Anniekins; French Jean becomes Jeannot; Yiddish Yosef becomes Yosseleh or Yosinkeleh.

A Comment About the Business World

Employers are no longer allowed to ask, either on forms or in interviews, an employee's race, ancestry, or religion; in such a way it is thought that bigotry in hiring or assignment can be lessened. Yet in dealing with this same employee, you must somehow show consideration and sensitivity to their ethnic and religious background. You cannot ask formally or put it in a personnel folder, but the person's name may still tell you. Knowing someone's background can be very helpful in avoiding conflicts or embarrassment, particularly when two or more persons of differing ethnicity are closely involved.

ESPECIALLY FOR FICTION WRITERS

Now that you have this book, you can save time while still naming your characters accurately and imaginatively. Very few pieces of fiction can survive with nameless characters and few more, with hackneyed names. You do not want a rep as the writer who "can't pick up a phone book." That phone book may serve as long as every story you write is set in the sort of area it represents, and you never need or want to mention another ethnic background.

Let us say you picked up a Taos phone book on your research trip. Now you are sitting down to your tale of old New Mexico, and you flip open the book...

Do you know if that last name is really Hispanic? Maybe it is Italian, or Portuguese. Some Cornish names look Spanish. The phone book is for *modern* New Mexico, and you find names from all over the world. Most phone book listings involve male first names, so you may have to dig for hours to find an Hispanic female name that is not Maria or Rosita. If you saw a first name like Visitacion or Trinidad, would you know it represented a woman?

You cannot *get* a phone book for Druidic Ireland, Periclean Athens, or the Roman Republic. Not even for Cromwell's London. Certainly not for the Minoans, whose language is still unknown. As for other planets... Yes, this book even gives you help for invented languages.

For the time being, let us assume your piece of fiction is a novel, set in the contemporary world.

Safety Basics

The most important point: **NEVER NAME A CHARACTER AFTER ANYONE YOU HAVE EVER KNOWN**, however slightly. You can get sued. Do not ransack your memory or school yearbooks at naming time. While you may use a first name, if it is not unique, using family names is chancy, unless they are dirt common. Using an actual person's full name is absolutely forbidden. (So is using an entire name out of a phone book.)

Using a real name for a character you consider admirable or sympathetic nevertheless provides no protection. Write a book about a noble Wiccan high priestess and if the person whose name was borrowed has become a devout Fundamentalist since you knew her, she might be outraged at the insult. Making a real-named character heterosexual can be offensive if the kid you knew back then is a now a gay activist. Yet you have to use real-world names. Unlike the Victorians, unless you are writing humor you cannot get away with naming someone "Uncle Pumplechook."

In this book you will not find "invented" names, like the exotica sometimes packed into baby-name books in order to make the promised 10,000. All of the names here have seen actual use. Also, there are what you may consider unattractive as well as pleasing names: You have both Cinderellas and villains to name.

One way to begin, with a modern-day work, is to check all the contemporary family names herein: If one is familiar, make yourself remember from where. An historical figure? A character in another book? Be cautious. You do not want to mislead your reader into thinking this is about that actual person or character — no westerns using "Earp" or "Hickock." You will want to avoid having yet another Regency romance with a villainous Lord Mandeville (a cowpoke or franctireur named Mandeville is another matter). Hidden fashions seem sometimes to exist among writers, lurking on a subconscious level, where a family name is suddenly in everyone's head. In two months I read three novels with two villains and a hero named Driscoll. Driscolls appeared by the handful for months, then disappeared.

If a family name summons up a person whom you knew, or merely heard of around town, do not use it. For you it is off-limits. Also avoid anything signalling current celebrities: if you recognize the name, so will your readers. Ten years from now, if you do not remember that "flash in the pan" any more, you can use the name. Do the same for the personal names of any group common in places you have known, eliminating those of any school classmates or fellow workers.

As an example, I knew a family named Smith pretty well, so I will never use the name for characters, no matter how common it may be.

"A Rose by Any Other Name Might Be a Gardenia"

The reader will note that, unlike the traditional baby-name book format, "meanings" have been omitted for names in most contemporary sections. Choosing names by these so-called meanings is one of the biggest mistakes a writer can make. No one ever stopped in the middle of a story to look up a character's name in a baby-name book. Most people do not even use those things for their babies. I have lost several good name books "borrowed" by expectant parents who then dubbed the boys Christopher and the girls Jennifer anyway. I do not believe that out of the hundreds or thousands of alternatives, all of them believed that nothing was more meaningful to them than "Christ Carrier" and "White Wave." They used the books simply as name lists, and after scanning the alternatives went with fashion after all.

The reason meanings are included is that in other cultures, especially those of the past, people might comment on a name's meaning or give a person a new name reflecting some event. This is often because the names are the same as meaningful words.

As Roger Price pointed out in his pioneering adult name book *What Not to Name the Baby*, people have preconceptions about the personalities attached to names. These have nothing whatsoever to do with those etymological "original meanings." Price acutely differentiates Tom from Tommy, Andrew from Andy, and Tony from Anthony.

"Gertie" or "Gert" sounds much stronger than the fluffy "Trudy" even if they all derive from Gertrude. Chris is stronger than Christopher, but Stevie is softer than Steve or Steven, which is firmer than Stephen. Yet within these groups, the "meanings" do not change!

As Bruce Lansky says of the name Ariel: "A lioness of God? Hardly! Ariel has a more ethereal image as a slim, pretty, princesslike girl who is smart and shy." His book *The Baby Name Personality Survey* is dedicated to these personality expectations, though for only a limited number of modern, mostly Anglo-American personal names. It does not give you the difference between Shin and Tajima, nor Thorhild and Ingeborg.

Fantasy writer Lin Carter covers the naming of names by pure sound especially well in Chapter Ten of *Imaginary Worlds*, "A Local Habitation and a Name: Some Observations on Neocognomina." He tries the difficult task of grafting the poet's ear onto a reader who may not possess one, so that when the names of places that never existed are created, they will have the proper sound for the things they represent. As he points out, "Stonehenge" has the right sort of ponderous, slow name for a megalithic mass, regardless of what the word means. "Piccadilly" is frivolous, light, and quick. In a well-invented world it would be completely wrong to use one for the other.

You must choose character names with the same ear. No matter what Percy or Algernon supposedly meant 500 or 1,000 years ago, to your reader a character with that name is going to sound like an interior decorator or maitre d'. It does not matter how glorious or romantic a name originally was if it sounds homely and dumb to the contemporary reader. No matter how bucolic the meaning of a name may be, if the reader does not know that virtually secret meaning, the character can sound jarringly country-club instead of family-farm. People do this sociological sizing-up subconsciously, but that means it is all the more powerful and dangerous. You fight it at your story's peril.

Odds are your reader is pretty much like you. Go down the list of names and decide for yourself which ones sound like dashing adventurers, which ones like clods, who is rich, who poor, who is rural, who urban. Equally, you know which names sound like a chummy granny or a forbidding grandmama, a work-flattened wait-person or a footloose scion of wealth, a successful professor or someone sweating for tenure.

Work fast, off your first impressions, and do not try to do too many at a sitting. When you have a strong reaction or image, write it down. You may even want to build some lists or a database of your own — "Eerie People," "Wimps and Marshmallows," "Growling Thugs," "Devious Masterminds," and so on — so that you can find that kind of name in a hurry, especially for secondary characters.

In sections where meanings are given, hold a card over the meanings as you work it for reactions.

Sound Traps

All cultures have favorite sounds. If you open your local telephone directory white pages, the largest section probably is for names starting with S. If you glance at the Japanese section in this book, you will see the letter B almost empty of names, while K, H, and Y would be even more dominant if not edited for variety.

Despite this, as a writer you have to scatter your characters' names across the alphabet. Names beginning with the same letter should be avoided. If possible, avoid even the same sounds; contrary to some theories, readers do not just see the names, they hear them — or try to. So not only should you avoid having one story with both Carl and Carmen, you should not have Carmen and Charlotte, or Cameron and Kim, or Cecilia and Sylvia.

Scriptwriters should pay more attention to sound-alikes than look-alikes.

However, if you are feeling starved for names, you can allow a minor,

walk-on sort of character to alliterate with a main character, *if* you make the
names very different otherwise. So if your Russian leading man is Anton, you may
make the minor role Aleksandr — longer, second sound different, ending different.

End sounds can be almost as confusing as initial sounds. You must choose
names for the hurried or distracted reader, not just the Ideal Reader settling in
for a leisurely day or two in a comfortable chair. Think "worst case scenario" —
reading a half-chapter on the commuter bus — and an imperfect memory.

Watch this with place-names, too. Do not have Gabrielle Brook and Derek
Gregory on Brick Lane and Durell Road in Glennville, Georgia. Not only would
you have the obvious front alliterations:

Gabrielle/Gregory/Glennville/Georgia
Brook/Brick
Derek/Durell

but there are terminal alliterations in:

Gabrielle/Durell/Glennville
Brook/Derek/Brick

and mid-sound R copies in:

Derek/Georgia/Durell/Gabrielle

In a fictional locale, there is no excuse; rename the town. In a real place,
choose the next street over or change the character's name.

Rhythms and Lengths

Too many writers fall into the "2-2" trap for characters, with two names each
having two syllables. Isaac Asimov did this in the Foundation trilogy, perhaps purposely to make the futuristic names still sound familiar and homey. So did Tolkien
for his hobbits: Fro-do Bag-gins, Bil-bo Bag-gins, Sam-wise Gam-gee. However,
it makes the names sound alike and harder to differentiate. Tolkien was poet
enough to shorten one to Sam. He also had Meriadoc Brandywine (4-3) and Peregrine Took (3-1), though shortened to Merry and Pippin.

Going 2-2 is one way to make your lead character fade into the wallpaper.
"Indiana Jones" (4-1) is more memorable than "Texas Johnson." So while you
might have used Roger Tamble, Kenneth Camden, Sandra Davits, and Megan
Winters, less regular rhythm will highlight names like Maribelle Wynn, Sylvia
Denisovich, Rod Thackery, and Kenneth Coops.

Keep a list of names. No descriptions attached, just a single line apiece so
that all the names in one work fit on one page. Have a column for the rhythm

count, so you can catch any repetitive bias. This also helps you track initials and alliteration.

Vary names as to overall length, too. Some can be curt — Juan Sol — others long — Epitacio Tolentino de Santa Rita. Silent letters and compound consonants make a name visually longer without adding syllables: Fridthjofs and Ari are both two syllables, and Norse, but clearly one is longer. "Glamour spellings," while looking Hollywood, often shorten a name, as when Dannie becomes Dani.

The Long Spell

Some people say your lead characters should always have short names, "so you won't get tired typing them." This is like saying your painting should always be largely of a color straight-out-of-the-tube so you will not get tired mixing it — bad advice!

The good news: just as a portraitist can mix up complex but common skin hues in advance and pack them in tubes, there are ways to make a twenty-letter name as easy to type as Lee. Anyone writing with the idea of publication should be using a word processor with a disk drive, if not a computer. You will no longer dread revisions, and thus fail to make them. You will also have no fear of long names.

Anything you use to type your manuscript should have "global search and replace." When you come to the long name, instead of typing "Agathangelos," type "A*." When you are through for the day, go to all the files you have changed or increased, and replace "A*" with "Agathangelos." This normally takes no more than a half-dozen keystrokes besides typing the name once.

With a more advanced machine, you can set up the name as a "macro" — your software manual will explain how. Then when you do something simple like hold down the Alternate key and hit A, "Agathangelos" appears. All those character names before each speech in scripts (for plays, movies, or graphic novels) can be inserted with the same tricks.

Note that longer names are often considered classier, or at least more distinguished. Having a name which takes time to deliver orally indicates that one can command other peoples' time, and that one will not be called for and expected to respond in haste, like a slave being ordered around.

Shortening a name is always a way of indicating familiarity or of lessening social status. So Rob Sawyer has a distinctly casual, chummy air, as opposed to Robert Sawyer, or more ponderously yet, Robert Johannsen Sawyer. Oddly enough, going by his initials as R. J. Sawyer makes the character even more remote: he has removed his name from the use of commoners, entirely.

In a setting where all the names are unfamiliar, say, Assyria about 4,000 years ago, keep the short, easy-to-remember names for characters who come and go in a hurry. You can use longer and stranger ones for your leads. The main characters' names are repeated so often, page after page and chapter after chapter, that the reader can get used to them. So make your male lead Asshurdurqali and your female lead Bellitsharrat, but make the two-chapter village chief Parutu, and his flirtatious daughter, Zabibie. The walk-ons, if named at all, are Bani and Mesaa.

Local Atmosphere

For some people, a little exoticism goes a long way; others need big doses of alien to feel that they have stepped out of their neighborhood. What seems "very foreign" to you may seem utterly mundane to your reader, and vice versa.

Better to err on the side of strangeness. Regardless of how common an English-looking name like Adam or Leon may actually be in a non–Anglo culture, you are abandoning a chance to make your foreign character or setting really *foreign* if you use it. Remember what your writing teacher said about your plot when you claimed that "it really happened that way!": "Mere facts are no excuse in fiction." Use Imre, Kazimiera, or Umberto, and you do not have to reiterate that your reader is no longer in Kansas.

To help you, I have noted here and there whether a name in a non–Anglo culture is popular or rare, despite its frequency among English speakers. All the foreign variations of "Christopher" that you find in baby-name books are nowhere near as common as the name is in English. The only names that seem popular across the world are variations on Mohammed, John, and Mary/Miriam.

However, those "just like English" names are very good for immigrants, who are now Something-Americans.

Erratic Names

Now, having lectured you on the ethnicity of your characters' names, I would like to point out the big smear across that neat graph. Since time immemorial, human beings have migrated, taking their names with them. Semites migrated into Sumeria before writing was invented. Israelites invaded the Levant, the Dorians invaded the Achaeans, the Pereset invaded the whole eastern Mediterranean. Germans move to France, and vice versa. All sorts of Europeans joined the invasion of the New World, and the Irish Wild Geese went everywhere.

Usually, the first generation or two keeps their ethnic names. The family name may be mutated to suit local pronunciation or spelling, like O'Donahue becoming O'Donaju in South America. A family may be considered acclimatized when the children are no longer Maeve and Liam O'Donaju, but Florita and Raimundo O'Donaju.

Similarly, Gustav von Saxe, if he moves to Holland may become Gustaf van Saxe, or Gustave de Saxe if he takes French citizenship. One has truly immigrated when one tries to fit the local forms. People who stick to Old Country forms signal the location of their hearts. While they may have to live *here*, they still think of this as an exile that may be ended, or out of which their descendants may be able to return *there*.

When providing ethnic diversity in a scene, in Europe always borrow names from the nearest countries first. For other places, you should try and find statistics on the ethnic breakdown. For example, in Hawaii, the most common names are not European or Hawai'ian. The single largest ethnic group is the Japanese. Equally, along the southern border of the United States you may find more Hispanic surnames than anything else. Minnesota is thick with Scandinavian names.

In North America, the racial mix is often quite random, and you should not stick entirely to the British Isles chapters. You should consider building names like Sean Esposito or Yvette Kazinczy. My high school graduating class included a genuine Johann Lopez. This is not exclusively an American phenomenon. After a couple of generations of intermarriage, is the Rodriguez family in Merthyr Tydfil considered Spanish or Welsh? They use English personal names. Trevisanos in England came out of Treviso, Italy, centuries ago, and British Victorian Pineros had been Pinheiros in Portugal only a century before. By the 19th century, Argentina had absorbed numerous Middle European families — and later, Chinese, who by now speak only Spanish. Brazil has its "Confederados," who fled the Reconstruction after the War Between the States.

In these cases the foreign names need not make the characters behave a bit differently than their neighbors. It can, however, provide you with name variety in your story — or even a required plot turn.

Setting the Clock

When your book or script is set in another age, you can lend temporal atmosphere by using period names. While the most common French names have been largely unchanged between the Middle Ages and the end of the 20th century, they only added the Classical names during the Renaissance. Be careful: a lot of names that may look Classical to you belong to early saints whom the French have memorialized right through the ages.

Remember that your main characters' names will wind up in the cover blurb; much of your other research will not. If you give a Regency lady the 1980s girl-name, "Ashley," you may think it looks as pretty as current mothers do, but you risk getting dropped back in the rack by the real Regency buff: back then, if used at all, it would go to a boy. The same goes for bestowing the name "Kelly" on any female before the middle of this century. It simply *feels* wrong, as if you had not immersed yourself in the period the way your best readers have.

On the other hand, "Gertrude" and "Matilda" were very popular in the late 19th century, when a mother wanted to give her daughter a name with strength and character; giving her a male name would be utterly unacceptable. Many modern baby-name books do not list these two any more than they do Rollo,

Homer, Wilbur, or Oscar for boys. A heroine named Gertrude will not sound modern, but it might be appropriate to her period.

The French began to develop a mania for variety in the 17th century, which the English did not catch until the 19th. Until then, most English babies were named from a list of a couple of dozen choices, rarely anything different. Using too many odd personal names for the upper classes in your Elizabethan swashbuckler is another kind of anachronism. This is where the habit of referring to people by their family names comes from: there are far more family names in use than personal ones.

Gender or Not

Some plots turn on a name's not being clearly male or female, or on being normally one, but usable for the other. In some places, like France or America, this is easy. In others it is impossible, as among classical Roman patricians, or Russians.

Where names are re-gendered, you will find the rules in this book, just in case you caught a nice name on your own and want to cook it properly. That work is already done for any name in this book. You can easily see how names for your female characters will look.

For some ethnic groups, there is no difference between male and female names. Except for a few "pretty-sweet" girl-names and "macho-strong" boy-names, most are unisex neutrals. Sometimes the boys get "pretty-sweet" names, too, and no one thinks twice about the warlord being named Soft Light of Dawn. In these cultures, people simply do not make rash assumptions about gender. Often parts of speech tell them who's what. If information is hazy, they will not be dumbfounded to find that the person is the unexpected sex, since it was always a possibility.

The foreigner from a "men are men, and women are women, and never the twain shall meet" culture is the one who gets knocked for a loop by these neuter names. He or she knows enough to figure that Hildegard means "battle fortress" and Beldeor is "beautiful deer." So this foreigner *knows* that the first must be a man and the second a woman. Kapow.

Western Europe

ENGLISH

The traditional English, as epitomized by the upper classes of the 18th century, were content with a dozen or two choices of personal name for each sex. But between the ambitious middle classes and Romanticism, the English — in the home Isles, in North America, and in Australia — novel, original, even exotic personal names became acceptable, even desirable.

Americans, followed by the Australians, seem to be the most likely to invent names out of the whole cloth, and mothers in the Deep South most of all. English and Canadians are most likely to borrow foreign names, especially French ones for girls.

Last names in these countries come from all over Europe. A lot of good British family names that have been in the country for four centuries are Italian or Spanish in origin. French name immigration dates back to the 11th century.

America is the most racially mixed, followed by Canada, then England; Australia and New Zealand least of all. Black Americans have broadened the range of names by adding African and pseudo–African names in the last half of the 20th century. This same group also invents many names from scratch.

Since the seventies, there has been a rise especially in neocognomina for girls based on "La-" or "Di-" followed by a nice-sounding syllable or two; also anything ending in "-elle" or "-ella": Shirelle, Lashirl, and Dimella are names I have heard mothers use. Other new names come from purposely re-spelling or re-pronouncing traditional names, though a certain number of these are *mis*-spellings and *mis*pronunciations, like putting "Cherie" on the birth certificate, but saying "Cherry." "Casino" can wind up pronounced "KAH-sih-no" by the culturally challenged.

An Americanism that could fairly be counted on during the 19th and early 20th centuries was giving the child a personal name, the mother's family name, and the father's family name. Thus, the mother's lineage was legally recorded, though the child normally only displayed the father's family name.

1

Family Names and Personal Titles

When my husband and I went to get married in the eighties, the formal paperwork included choosing among the following naming options:

(1) wife adopts husband's family name
(2) wife hyphenates husband's family name to hers
(3) husband and wife both hyphenate their names together
    (a) his first
    (b) hers first
    (c) she puts hers first, he puts his first
(4) husband hyphenates wife's family name to his
(5) husband adopts wife's family name
(6) both keep their family names, separately

This is not so much a result of the collapse of Miss and Mrs. into Ms., as a separate symptom of egalitarianism. If you feel obliged to write to me or about me, I am Ms. Holly Ingraham. Married, I can't be a Miss, and I'm not Mrs. because Ingraham is my natal name.

Culturally, "Miss" always indicated a never-married woman. "Mrs." was short for "mistress of—" and for the last couple of centuries was followed by, not the woman's personal name, but her husband's. Mrs. John Richards was his wife or widow. If Miss Ann Brown married Mr. John Richards, but divorced him, she might have called herself Mrs. Brown Richards. If he divorced her — that is, she were the "guilty party" — then she was Mrs. Ann Brown. She did not resume her "maiden name" with the Miss, because her status was no longer a maiden's.

When divorce was rare, and an unmarried woman outside the home rarer still, this worked well enough. Now, a woman needs the continuation of a name recognizable in her field as much as any man.

One painter wrote to an artist's magazine to ask help on resolving the crisis of changing names, and the replies were as interesting as the original letter. It is usual for a woman to begin a career under her natal name, get married and use his family name, get divorced and use both, remarry and go mad. One artist took the happy attitude that the signature changes would enable collectors of her work to tell at what time in her career the painting had been done. Another had phased out last names entirely, using her first name and a sigil. The original letter-writer had added to her woes by refusing to duplicate the name of her husband's brother's wife, who shared her first name, even though this in-law apparently was not also a painter.

In this circumstance, Ann Brown would sign her paintings Ann Richards when she married, then Ann Brown Richards after her divorce, then after remarriage Ann Richards White, or Ann Brown White, or Ann with a crescent, or flee back to Ann Brown.

Then there's the new discussion over what family name the kids get: the father's; a hyphenation of both parents'; or the boys get mom's and the girls get dad's. Interestingly, apparently to avoid a complete division of the sexes, almost no one ties the boys to dad's family and the girls to mom's.

So when Ann Brown and John Richards marry and have children, they may be Lisa Richards and Simon Miller, or Lisa Richards-Miller, or Simon Miller-Richards. As has been pointed out by many, hyphenating is all right in the first degree, but what will Simon Richards-Miller do when he marries Jennifer Warren-Boscovich? The computer databases only take so many letters in a last name. Personally, I think the future will bring the end of the family name. Before there was an aristocracy, there were no family names. In the postaristocratic society, there is no need for them either. We will each have a personal name, which parents will try to make distinctive rather than repetitive. Social Security numbers are now acquired in infancy and used for identification throughout one's life. A personal name, a number, and a fingerprint are more than enough to identify anyone in the age to come. Everyone first-names everyone else as soon as they meet, so it is not like we will lose our present dignity and reserve.

However, there is nothing to say that the personal name cannot be two-part, so that Simon and Jennifer's children may be Vincent Bronco, Henrietta Marie, and Kelly Blue.

The following personal names are hardly all those available. You can use any personal name from anywhere in the world, no matter how alien, and say the child was named for the kindly neighbor who drove Mom to the doctor while she was expecting. Then again, maybe Mom heard the name in passing and remembered it when naming-time came.

COMMON NAMES AND THEIR VARIANTS

Ann

Often it has been compounded with other names: Annalisa or Annalise (Anna + Lisa); Georganne or Georgianna (George + Anna); Annabelle (Anna + Belle).

Hannah; Anne, Anitra, Annie, Annia, Anya, Anetta, Anette, Annitta, Anni, Anny, Ani; Nan, Nancy, Hannie, Hattie, Nita, Ninon, Nanine, Nanna, Nanny, Ana, Annah, Annalie, Ayn, Anneth.

Charles

Charlie, Charley, Chuck, Chuckie, Chas, Carol, Carrol, Caroll, Caryl, Carl, Carle.

Feminine: Carol, Caroline, Carolin, Carolyn, Carolyne, Carolina, Charlotte, Charlotta, Charlene, Charli (extremely modern), Sharlene, Sharleen, Charleen, Carla, Carly.

Edward

Ed, Eddie, Eddy, Eddi, Ned, Neddy, Neddie, Ward.

Feminine: Nedda, Neddi, Edie, Edy, Edi, Edwina, Edwarda.

Elizabeth

Already common, this became so popular among English speakers in the wake of England's Elizabeth I that they worked out many variations, and have borrowed most of the foreign ones.

At the time of her reign (1558–1603), the common nickname was Bess. Poets devised names for her that fit their rhymes better than the long original, including Eliza, whence all the variations on that half of her name; and Gloriana, "the glorious one," which is the source of Gloria and Glory, when the last is not a religious-attribute name. Beth appears in the early 19th century, along with Lizzie and Betsy, Libby and Lib. Liz and Lisa arrived in the early 20th century, but Betty goes back to at least the middle of the 18th, among the lower classes. Lissa was very rare until the 1960s and is still uncommon.

Liza, Elsa, Elsie, Elissa, Ella, Elly, Ellie, Elysa, Elyse; Lissa, Bessie, Bettina, Lizbeth, Bette, Betta.

Masculine: El; any "El-" name might be used, like Elliot, in honor of rich Aunt Elizabeth.

George

Also used as a family name.

Gordy, Georgie, Georgy, Geo, Geordy (Scots).

Feminine: Georgia, Georgette, Georgina, Georgy, Georgelle.

Henry

So common that "every Tom, Dick, and Harry" meant "everyone." Hal is the distinctively Anglo diminutive. Hank is American, from the 19th century on.

Harri, Hari, Enry, Enri, Henny, Harry.

Feminine: Henriette, Henrietta, Harriet, Harriette.

John

This has been so common that it has been used to mean "man," as in "jack of all trades."

Johnny, Johnnie; Jack, Jacky, Jackie, Jon, Zane.

Feminine: Joan, Joanna, Jean (Scots), Jeanne, Yanna, Jane, Janey, Jan, Janie, Zaneta, Jenny, Janina, Janine, Janna, Ivanna, Johnine, Johnette, Jonine, Joanine, Jeanette, Jonnette, Jani, Jain, Jaine, Jayne, Janet, Janette.

Joseph

Joe, Jo, Seph, Joey.

Feminine: Joey, Josetta, Jo, Joelle, Joette, Joessa, Josepha.

Katherine

The popularity of this name has been steady, even in the Middle Ages when there were Crusades against the heretics called Cathars. Kate was the preferred nickname through the Renaissance, as testified by Shakespeare's *The Taming of the Shrew*; Cathy or Kathy seems to have emerged from the shadows in the late 18th century as a nickname that came out of Scotland into northern England.

Catharine, Cathy, Cat, Kitty, Kit, Katie, Kay; Cathaline, Lina, Linette, Linetta, Trina, Trinka, Catharina, Rina, Rena.

Masculine: Kitt.

Louis

Used by kings of France dating back to the sons of Charlemagne. From Louis XIV forward, it was felt giving a child this indicated political leanings in Europe. Up to the start of the 19th century, the feminine form you find is Louise, but after that Louisa becomes popular. Lois had a temporary popularity in the early 20th century.

Louie, Lou, Lew, Louey; Alouys, Aloycius, Lewis.

Feminine: Louisette, Louella.

Margaret

Margie, Margy, Maggie, Maggy, Maggi, Margi, Marge, Meg, Madge, Midge, Peg, Peggy, Peggi, Peggie, Margot.

Mary

Usually considered a female name, in honor of the Virgin Mary or the Saints Mary.

Marian is often considered to be a combination of Mary and Ann, but it can also be a development by misspelling or mispronouncing off Mariam, via the masculine Marion.

Maryam; Mariam, Miriam, Mirian, Miram; Myrrha, Mira, Myra, Mirra, Myria; Mally, Moll, Molly, Mame, Mamie, Mariana, Marianna, Marinda, Mia, Mirian, Mirianne, Miriama, Mirra, Mureen; Marietta, Marita, Maretta, Marette; Maren, Mairiah, Mariae, Marice, Marise, Maryse, Maridel, Mariel, Marielle, Mariela, Marilee, Marilyn, Marisa, Moya, Moyra, Marion.

Masculine: Marion, Marrion (Am), Merriam (Am); often any "Mar-" name can be so considered, like Martin or Martial.

Michael

Mike (Am), Mick (Brit/Aussie), Mikey, Mickey.

Feminine: Michelle, Michaella, Micki, Michael (rare, often considered backwoods).

Richard

Rich, Richie, Richy, Rick, Ricky, Ricki, Rikki, Dick, Dickon, Dicky, Dickie, Dikkon.

Feminine: Richarda, Richanda, Ricky, Ricki, Rikki, Ricka.

Robert

Rob, Robin, Bob, Bobby, Robbie, Robby, Bert, Bertie, Bobbin.

Feminine: Roberta, Robertina, Robbi, Bobbi, Berta, Robin, Robina, Robinette, Robinetta, Robinella, Bobina.

Thomas

While very popular, somehow it has avoided racking up many variations.

Tom, Tommy, Thom.

Feminine: Thomasina, Tommi, Thomasa, Thomasine.

William

Will, Willy, Willie, Willi, Bill, Billy, Bilikens, Wilsie.

Feminine: Willa, Wilma, Willimina, Wilhelmina, Wili, Willa, Billy, Billie, Billi, Bili.

LESS COMMON FEMALE NAMES

Many diminutives have independent lives, so that Trixie or Trudy is the name on the birth certificate, not Beatrice or Gertrude.

Abigail, Abbey, Abbie, Gail, Gale
Ada, Adah
Adalia, Adele, Adelle
Adora
Adria, Adriana, Adrea
Agatha, Aggie, Aggy
Agnes, Annis, Anyas, Nessa, Nessi, Nessie, Nesta, Neysa
Aimee
Alana, Allene

Alberta, Allie, Berta, Albertina, Elberta, Elbertine
Alexandra, Alexa, Alexine, Alexis, Lexie, Lexine, Zandra
Alice, Alicia, Alisha, Alicea, Alissa, Alithia, Alyce, Alys, Alison, Allison, Allie, Alli
Allegra
Althea, Alathea, Alethea, Aleta, Aletta

Alura
Alyssa
Amabelle, Amabel
Amanda, Mandy, Manda
Amaryllis
Amber
Ambrosine, Ambrosia — rare
Amelia, Amy, Emilia, Emmie, Emmy, Em, Amalea, Emeline, Emmelina

Amethyst — rare until recently
Amy, Amie, Ami
Andrea, Andria
Angela, Angie, Angy
Angelica
Annora, Anora
April
Ariella, Arielle, Ariel
Astra
Audrey, Audrie, Audry
Aura
Aurelie, Aura Lee, Aurelia
Azalea, Aza
Azure, Azura — extremely rare until the 1960s
Barbara, Barbra, Babs, Barbie, Barbi
Beatrice, Beatrix, Trixie, Trixy, Trixi, Bea, Bee
Belinda
Bernadette, Bernie, Berny, Bernadine
Bernice, Bernie, Berny
Beryl
Birdy, Birdie
Blanche
Blessing
Bliss
Blossom
Blythe, Blithe
Bonny, Bonnie, Bunnie, Bunni, Bunny
Brenda — very American
Candy, Candi, Candie, Candace, Candice
Celandine
Celeste, Celestine
Charity, Chari
Chastity, Chas
Cherie, Cherry, Cherrie, Cheri, Cher, Sherry, Sheri, Sher
Cheryl, Cherilyn, Sharyl
Christine, Christina, Christie, Christy, Chris — also Kristine, etc.
Cicily, Cecilia, Cecile, Celia, Cissy, Ceci
Cindy, Cindie, Cindi

Clara, Clarissa, Clarice; Claire
Claramae
Claudia
Colleen, Collene
Constance, Connie, Con — rare
Coral
Corrie, Corry, Cory, Cora
Crystal, Crysta, Crystalla — also with initial K; 1960s forward
Cynthia, Cynthie
Daniela, Daniella, Danielle
Daphne
Darlene, Darleen, Darline
Davida, Davette, Davina, Davinda
Dawn, Dawna, Dawny, Dawnie, Dawni, Dawnee
Deanna, Deanne
Deborah, Debora, Debra, Debbie, Debby, Debbi
Dee
Della
Delores, Dolores, Lorie
Denise
Diana, Diane, Dianna, Dianne, Dyanne, Dyanna, Dyan
Donna
Doreen, Dorene, Dorine, Dorina
Doris, Dorie
Dorothy, Dorthy, Dotty, Dottie, Dot, Dolly
Dove, Dovey
Edith, Edie, Edy, Edi
Edna
Eleanore, Elenore, Eleanora, Elenora, Ellen, Ellie, Elly, Nell
Elmira, Almira, Mira
Erica, Erika
Erin, Erinne, Erynn
Ertha, Eartha
Estelle
Esther, Ester

Etta
Eunice
Evangeline
Eve, Eva, Evie
Evelyn
Faith
Fawn
Fay, Fae
Felicia, Felice, Felicity
Fern
Fleur, Fleurette
Florence
Flower
Frances, Fran, Franny, Frannie, Fanny, Frankie
Freda, Frieda
Gail, Gaile, Gayle — since 1950s in US
Gemma
Geraldine, Gerry, Geri
Gertrude, Gert, Gertie, Gerty, Trudy, Trudie, Trudi
Gilda
Ginger
Gladys
Grace
Gwen, Gwendolyn
Hazel
Heather
Hedy
Helen, Hellen, Helene, Helena, Lena
Hilda
Holly, Hollie, Holli
Hope
Ida
Irene — ee-REE-nee in England, eye-REEN in America
Iris
Irma
Isabel, Isabelle, Isabella
Ivy
Jade
Janice
Janina
Jasmine, Jessamine
Jennifer, Jenny, Jen
Jessica, Jessie

Jill
Jody, Jodie, Jodi
Joy
Joyce
Judith, Judy, Judie
Julie, Julia
June
Karen — particularly
    1950s-60s babies
Kelly — since 1960s
Kerry — since 1960s
Kim, Kimberly, Kimber-
    ley
Lana, Lanna
Lara
Laraine, Lorraine, Lau-
    raine, Larraine
Lark
Laurel, Laura, Laurey,
    Laurie, Laurelle, Lau-
    rette, Lauretta, Lauren,
    Lora, Lorena, Laurina,
    Laurine, Lory, Lori,
    Loretta, Lorella,
    Lavinia, Lavinny, Vin-
    nie
Lee
Leona, Leonie
Leontine, Leontyne
Leslie, Lesley — since
    1950s
Liana, Lyana
Lily, Lillian, Lilian, Lili,
    Lilli, Lilly
Linda — very big in the
    1950s
Lucianna, Lucianne
Lucy, Lucinda, Cindy
Lydia
Lynn, Lynne
Madeline, Madelaine,
    Maddy, Maddie
Mahalia
Marcella
Marcia, Marsha, Marcy,
    Marcey
Marigold, Mari, Goldie
Marilyn, Marilin, Mary-
    lyn, Marylin
Marlene, Marlena, Mar-
    lina

Martha, Mattie, Matty,
    Martie, Marty
Maureen, Moreen
Mavis
Maxine, Maxene
May, Mae
Megan
Melanie, Melly, Mellie
Melinda, Malinda
Melissa, Malissa
Melody, Melodie, Melodi
Mercedes
Mercy
Meredith
Merle, Merleen, Merlene,
    Merline
Merry
Mildred, Millie, Milly
Mimi
Mindy
Mira, Myra
Miranda
Modesty
Monica
Morgana
Muriel
Myrna
Myrtle — rare in second
    half of 20th c.
Nadine
Naomi
Natalie
Nicole, Nichole, Nico-
    lette, Nikki
Noelle
Nola
Nona
Norah, Nora
Norma
Olive, Olivia
Oma
Ona
Opal
Oralia
Pamela, Pam, Pammie,
    Pammy, Pammi
Pansy, Pansie
Patricia, Patty, Patsy, Pat,
    Tricia, Trisha, Trish
Paula, Pauline, Paulette;
    Polly

Pearl
Penny, Penelope
Philippa — mostly British
Phyllis, Phillis
Portia, Porsche, Porsha
Priscilla, Cilla, Prissy
Prudence, Pru — mostly
    British and Australian
Rachel, Raquel
Rae
Rainbow — a hippy name
Ramona
Randi
Rebecca, Reba
Renata
Rose, Rosie, Rosalie
Rosemary, Rosemarie
Rowena
Roxanne, Roxanna
Ruby
Ruth, Ruthie
Ruthadele, Ruthadelle
Sabina, Sabine
Sabrina
Samantha, Sammi, Sam
Sapphira
Sarah, Sara, Sarie, Sally,
    Sal, Sadie (first half
    20th c.)
Selena, Selina, Selene
Selma, Anselma
Serena, Serina
Sharon, Sharron, Shar-
    onne, Sharin, Shari,
    Sharry, Sherry
Sheila
Shelley, Shellie
Shirley, Shirl — sometimes
    used for boys in the
    20th c.
Sibyl, Cybil, Sibella,
    Cybilla
Sophie, Sophia
Spring
Stacey, Stacy — since
    1950s
Stefanie, Steffie, Steffi,
    Steffy, Stephanie, Ste-
    vie, Steve
Stella
Storm, Stormy

Sunny, Sunnie
Sunshine — a hippy name
Susan, Suzanne, Susanna,
    Susannah; Susie, Suzy,
    Suzie, Suzi
Sylvia, Silvia
Tabitha — especially in
    1970s
Tallulah — American,
    from native; rare
Tammy, Tammie, Tammi
Tansy
Tara
Tempest, Temmy
Thelma
Theodora, Theo, Dora
Theresa, Teresa, Terry,
    Terrie, Terri, Teri,
    Tessa, Tessie, Tess

Tina
Topaz, Topaze
Tracy, Tracey — since
    1950s
Twyla — this is not
    unique to Ms. Tharpe
Una
Ursula
Valentina, Valentine
Valerie, Val, Valeria
Vanessa
Velda
Velvet
Vera
Verna
Veronica, Vonnie, Ronnie
Vesper
Victoria, Vicky, Vickie,
    Vikki, Tori, Toria

Vina, Vena
Violet
Virginia, Ginny, Ginnie
Vita
Vivian
Wanda
Wendy
Willow
Winifred, Winnie,
    Winny
Winona, Wennonah —
    one of few Native
    American names to
    catch on
Yolanda
Yvette
Yvonne, Evonne, Evon
Zelda
Zoe

LESS COMMON MALE NAMES

Aaron, Aron
Abraham, Abram, Abe,
    Abie, Bram
Ace, Acey
Adam, Adamm, Addam
Adrian
Alan, Allen, Allan
Alben, Albern
Albert, Al, Bert, Bertie
Aldous, Aldus, Aldis
Alexander, Alex, Alec,
    Aleck, Al
Alfred
Algernon
Allard
Almo, Elmo
Aloysius
Alvin
Ambrose
Andrew, Andy
Ansel, Ancel, Ansell,
    Anselm
Anthony, Tony
Arlo — American
Arnold, Arnie, Arney,
    Arni
Artemas
Arthur, Art, Artie

Ashbel
Aubrey
Audie, Audey
Augie, Auggy; August,
    Gus
Bard, Bardolf
Barney, Barnabas, Bar-
    naby
Bart, Bartel, Barth, Bat,
    Bartholomew
Basil
Benedict, Ben, Bennie
Benjamin, Ben, Bennie
Bernard, Barnard
Bertram — British; Bert,
    Bertie
Bishop
Blaine, Blane
Blythe
Bonar
Brad
Bran, Brand
Brick — American
Briton
Bruce
Bruno
Buck — American
Budd

Bull
Burl, Burle
Burt, Bert
Byron
Cain
Calvin
Cecil
Cedric, Cedrick
Chad
Chance
Christopher, Chris —
    occasionally spelled
    with initial K for Ch
Claire, Clare, Clarence
Clark
Clay
Clement
Cliff
Clive — very British
Clyde
Cole
Colin — usually British
Corey, Correy, Cory,
    Corry, Corrie
Craig, Craige
Curtis
Cyril — very British
Dale

Damon
Daniel, Dan, Danny
Darrel, Darrell, Daryl,
   Darryl
Darren
David, Dave, Davey
Dean
Delbert
Dennis, Denny
Derek, Derrick, Darrick
Dion
Dirk
Donald, Don, Donny
Dwayne, Duane, Duayn
Dylan, Dillon
Earle, Earl
Edwin, Ed
Egbert, Eggbert
Elliot, Eliot, Elliott,
   Eliott
Elmer
Elroy, Eleroy — (Am)
Elwood, Woody, El
Emmett, Emmet, Emmit
Emory, Amory
Eric, Erick, Aric, Rick
Erin
Ernest
Errol
Erwin
Faust
Felix
Flint, Flynt
Frances, Frank, Frankie
Fredrick, Fred, Freddy,
   Freddie, Rick — rare
Gabriel
Galen
Garth
Gary, Garry, Garrey,
   Garey
Gene, Eugene
Geoffrey, Geoff — British
Gerard
Gerold
Gerrit, Garrett
Gilbert, Gil
Giles
Glen, Glenn
Godfrey
Greg, Gregory

Griffin, Griff
Guy
Harlan
Harold, Hareld, Harry
Harvey
Herman
Herschel
Hiram
Hobart
Homer, Horatio — any-
   thing classical
Howard, Howie, Ward
Hubert
Hugh, Huey
Ike
Inigo
Irving
Ivon
Jared
Jason
Jasper, Jaspar
Jay — American
Jed
Jeffrey, Jeff, Jeffie —
   American
Jeremy, Jerome
Jerry — often freestand-
   ing; also short for
   many things
Jeter
Julius, Julian, Jules
Keith
Kenneth, Ken, Kenny
Key
Kip, Kipp
Lance
Lawrence, Laurence,
   Larry, Laurie
Lee
Leo, Leon
Leonard, Leon
Leroy
Lester
Lin, Lynn, Lynne
Link
Lionel
Luck
Malin — American
Mandell
Mark
Marshall

Martin, Marty
Marvin
Matthew, Matty, Mattie
Max, Maximilian, Maxim
Melvin
Meredith
Miron, Myron
Morris
Nathan, Nathaniel, Nat,
   Nate, Nattie, Natty
Nicholas, Nick, Nicky,
   Nickie, Nikki
Nigel — very British
Niles
Noble
Noel
Octavius
Odelle
Ogden
Oliver, Ollie
Omar
Oran
Orange
Orde
Orion
Orrick
Orson
Osborn
Oscar
Osgood
Oswald
Otis
Paget
Patrick, Pat, Rick
Paul
Percival, Percy
Peregrine
Perry, Pery
Peter, Pete, Petey
Philip, Phil
Phineas
Quentin
Quinto
Rafael, Rafe, Raphael
Ralph
Raymond, Ray
Red, Redd
Reed, Reede
Renny
Reuben
Reverdy

Rex
Ring, Ringgold
Rodger, Roger
Rodmond, Rod
Rodney, Rod, Roddy,
  Roddie
Roper
Ross
Roy
Rufus
Russ, Rust, Rusty
Samuel, Sam, Sammy
Scott, Scotty
Sebastian
Seth
Shane
Sidney, Sydney
Simon
Skip, Skipp, Skipper
Sol, Soloman
Sonny — American
Sparkey, Spark, Sparks

Squire
Stanley
Steven, Steve, Stevie; Ste-
  phen, Stephan, Stefan
Sylvester, Sy, Sly — since
  1960s, Silvester
Tadd
Thane
Theodore, Theo, Teddy,
  Ted
Thorn, Thorne
Torr
Travers
Tremaine, Tremayne
Trevor
Tully
Ty, Tye
Ulrich
Urban
Valentine, Val
Van
Vance

Vaughn
Vernon
Victor, Vic
Vincent, Vince, Vinny
Virgil
Wade
Walter, Walt, Wally
Ward
Warner
Warren
Wayne
Wendell
Wesley
West
Westel
Wilbur
Wilford
Willis
Wolf, Wolff, Wolfe
Woodrow
Worth

American children can be named for a State (Tex, Arkansas), for a city (Dallas, Boston — *not* two-parters like New York or Los Angeles), or for a native tribe (Shawnee, Cherokee). However, place-name personal names are most often nicknames indicating former residence. Family names as personal names were first used for boys in any number in the 19th century. By the beginning of the 20th, the New York and Boston "upper crust" was doing it for girls, too. This was the start of girls named Tracey and Kelly. Kelly, being an Irish family name, would almost always be an American girl, perhaps Canadian, probably born after World War II.

The English, and their descendants around the world, often have English place-names as family names, whether because their ancestors owned the place, or simply lived there. So scan your map of England for names like York, Bristol, Manchester, etc.

Black Americans, following emancipation, did not necessarily take the names of their old owners — sometimes anything but! On the whole they favored good, solid, British Isles names, often choosing Scottish names. Only around Louisiana did they go for French family names, then often in a Creole form.

FAMILY NAMES

The most common are often listed as: Smith, Jones, Williams, Taylor, Davies, Brown, Thomas, Evans, Roberts, and Johnson, though some come from Welsh.

Abbott, Abbot
Abington
Abney
Ackerley, Ackley
Acland
Adam, Adams, Adamson,
  Addams
Adcock
Addington, Addison
Adney, Adye, Ady
Aikin
Ainger
Airy, Airey
Alderson, Aldington
Aldridge
Alford
Allen
Alston
Amery
Amherst
Angell
Anson
Appleby, Appleton
Appold
Arber
Archer
Arkwright
Armstead, Armistead
Arne
Arnold
Arthur
Arydon
Asbury
Ashford
Ashhurst
Ashmead
Aston
Atchison, Atchkinson,
  Atkinson
Atherton
Atterbury
Atteridge
Attwood, Atwood
Atwater
Auden
Austen, Austin
Aveling
Averill, Averell
Avison
Aylesworth
Aylmer

Ayrton
Babbage
Babcock
Babington
Badham
Baffin
Bagley
Bailey, Baily, Bayley,
  Bayly
Bains, Baynes
Baker
Bakewell
Baldwin
Banks
Barlow, Barlowe
Barnard
Barnet
Barnfield
Barrett, Barret, Barett,
  Barratt
Barrow, Barrows
Bartlet, Bartlett
Barton
Battishill
Bax, Baxter
Bayliss
Baylor
Beach
Beal, Beale, Beales, Beall
Beazsey, Beasley
Beckford
Beckham
Beckwith
Beecham
Beecher, Beechey
Begbie
Beke
Belial
Bell, Belle
Bellew
Belsham
Belt
Bennet
Bensley
Benson
Bent
Bentham, Benthan
Benton
Beresford
Bethell
Betterton

Beverly, Beverley
Bewes
Bewick
Bickersteth
Biddle
Billings, Billington
Binney, Binns
Bird, Byrd
Birdwood
Birkbeck
Birkett
Birley
Birrel
Bishop
Black, Blacke
Blackburn
Blackett
Blackwood
Blake, Blakely, Blakey
Blakelock
Blamir
Blampied
Bland, Blandford
Blashfield
Blatch, Blatchford
Blenk
Blomfield, Bloomfield
Blunt, Blount
Blythe
Bodley
Bokenham, Bokenam
Bolt, Bolte, Bolton
Bondfield
Bonington
Bonner
Bonwick
Boole
Booth, Boothe
Boott
Borrow
Boscawen
Bosley
Botham
Bottome, Bottomley
Bouch
Boughton
Boulger
Boulton, Bolton
Bourdillon
Bourne
Bowell, Bowles

Bowerbank
Bowers
Bowman
Boydell
Brace
Braddock
Braddon
Bradford
Bradlaugh, Bradley
Branch
Brassey
Brathwaite, Brathwait, Brathwayte
Braxton
Bray
Brearley, Brearly
Brent
Brereton
Brewer, Brewerton
Brickwood
Bridge, Bridges, Bridger
Bridle
Brierley, Brierly
Briffault
Bright
Brind, Brindley, Brinsley
Britten, Britton
Broadbent
Broadhead
Broadwood
Brock, Brockedon
Broke
Brook, Brooke, Brooks
Broom, Broome
Broughton
Brown, Browne, Browning
Buckle
Bucklin, Buckford, Buckley
Buckstone
Budge
Bullard
Buller
Bullock
Bunbury
Bunting
Burder, Burdett
Burgon
Burke, Burkitt
Burleigh, Burley

Burnaby
Burnell
Burney
Burnham
Burr, Burrell
Burroughs, Burrows
Bury
Busby
Butler
Buxton
Byerly, Byers, Byrd, Byrley
Byles
Bywater
Calkin
Callcott
Callendar
Calverly
Cambronne
Canby
Caner
Cannan
Cannon
Canter
Canton
Capell
Capern
Carden
Carlile, Carlyle
Carrington
Carte, Carter
Castle, Castlebury
Cattermole
Cattley, Cautley
Caunt
Cave
Cayley
Chamier
Champneys
Chancellor
Chandler
Chantrey
Chapman
Chappell
Chares
Charnwood
Chase
Chatfield
Cheetham
Chenery, Cheney
Chesney

Chester, Chesterton
Chetwode
Chipman
Chisholm
Chittenden
Choate
Chorley
Chudley
Church
Clapham
Clapperton, Clapton
Clare, Claire
Claxton
Cleaveland
Clegg, Cleghorn
Coburn, Coburne
Coghill
Coldwater
Collier
Coningsby
Cory
Cosway
Cotes, Cotman
Cotsworth
Courthope
Courtney
Cousins, Cusins
Cowell, Cowles
Cowie
Cowley
Cox, Coxe, Coxey
Crabb, Crabbe
Cradock, Craddock
Craik
Cranch
Crandall
Crane
Creasy
Creighton
Crenshaw
Creswick
Crew, Crewe, Crews
Cribb
Crisamore
Cross
Crosswhite
Crowell
Crowninshield
Crozier
Culbert, Culbertson
Cureton

Curwen
Curwood
Cust
Cutler
Dalby
Dales
Dampier
Dana
Danforth
Daniel, Daniell, Daniels
Darnaby
Darts
Daubeny
Davidson, Davis
Dawkins, Dawson
Dealtry
Denham
Dennis, Dennison,
   Denny
Dent
Devie
Dibden
Dilke
Dines
Dobell
Dobson
Dodd, Dod — American,
   Dodsley
Doddridge
Dollond
Domett
Dorr, Dorrit, Dorret,
   Dorett
Doulton
Dowson
Drage
Draper
Drayton
Drinkwater
Driver
Drury
Duckworth
Duncombe
Dutton
Dyer
Dykes
Earle, Earlom
Easley
East, Easton
Eastlake
Eastman

Eddington
Edgar [EHD-ger]
Edger [EHD-jer]
Edmunds, Edmund-
   son
Edwards
Egerton
Egg, Eggleston
Eisley
Elgar
Ellicott
Ellis, Elliston
Ellsworth
Elwell
Ely
Emmons
Enfield
Estmont
Etty
Fairfield
Falconbridge
Farrington
Figg
Flower
Folkes
Fothergill
Frankland
Franks
Freeman
Frothingham
Froude, Frowd
Fryatt
Fulford
Fuller, Fullerton
Furnivall
Furse
Gaffey
Gaisford
Gale, Galton
Galvase
Gannon
Garbett
Gardner, Gardiner, Garner
Garnett
Garrett, Garret, Garret-
   son, Garrettson
Garvice
Garvin
Gary
Gates, Gatewood
Gell, Gellibrand

Geoffrey
Gibbon, Gibbons, Gibbs,
   Gibbson, Gibson
Gimbel, Gimble
Ginn
Gissing
Glaisher
Glanville
Glazebrook
Glover
Godfrey
Godkin
Godlee
Godwin, Godwine,
   Goodwin
Goff
Gomme
Goodale, Goodall
Gooderidge
Goodpaster
Goodspeed
Goossens
Gorst, Gort
Gorton
Gould
Gower
Granger
Grayson
Greathead
Green, Greene
Greenough
Greenwood
Greet
Gregory
Grenfell
Gretting
Grey, Gray
Griswold
Grose, Gross
Grossmith
Grote
Grove, Groves
Guest
Guild
Gull, Gully
Habington
Haddon, Haden
Hake
Hall, Halliwell
Hamerton
Hampden, Hampton

Hanaford, Hansford
Hannington
Hanson
Hapgood
Harden, Harding, Hardinge
Hardwick
Hare
Hargreaves
Harland
Harling
Harmsworth
Harper
Harraden
Harris, Harrison
Hartley, Harty
Harvey
Haskins
Hastings
Hatcher
Hatton
Havergal
Hawes
Haworth
Hayward
Hazlitt
Head
Heath, Heathcoat
Heaton
Heavysege
Henry
Henty
Hepworth
Herbert
Herford
Heseltine
Hichens, Hitchens
Hicks, Hickson
Higginson
Hill, Hilton
Hillhouse
Hobart
Hobbs, Hobbes, Hobson
Hockaday
Hocking
Hodge, Hodgkin, Hodgson
Hoigges
Holden
Hole, Holl
Holland

Hollis
Holloway
Holmyard
Holt
Holyoake
Hone
Hookham
Hopton
Hopwood
Horsley
Hough [HUHF]
Houghtailing [HUHF-tayl-ing]
Houghton [HOO-ton]
Howard
Howitt
Hudson
Huff, Huffe
Huffam, Huffham
Huggins
Hunt, Hunter, Huntsman
Huntingdon, Huntington
Hurd
Huskisson
Hyndman
Hyne
Inge, Ingelow
Ingleby, Inglesby
Inglefield
Inglis
Insley
Inswell
Iredell
Izard
Jackling, Jacks, Jackson
Jacobs
James, Jamison
Jane, Jayne
Jarret
Jay
Jeffers, Jefferson, Jefferies, Jeaffreson
Jeffrey, Jeffreys, Jeffery, Jeffries
Jenkins, Jenks, Jenckes, Jinks
Jenyns
Jervis
Johns, Johnson, Johnston
Jordan

Jowett
Judd, Judson
Juxon
Kemp, Kempe
Kennett
Kent
Kett
Kimberley
King
Kingdon — N, not M
Kinglake
Kingsbury
Kingsford
Kirby
Kitt, Kitson
Kitteridge, Kittredge
Kitton
Knapp
Knolles, Knowles
Knott
Lake
Lancer
Lande, Lander, Landor
Langeston
Langham
Langland
Larraby, Laraby
Lathrop
Latimer
Latrobe
Lawes, Lawson
Lawrence
Layard
Leaf
Leatham
Leathes
Ledyard
Lee, Leigh
Leftwich
Leland
Leonard
Lethbridge
Lewes, Lewis
Liddell
Lightbourn, Lightbourne, Lightburne, Lightborne, Lightburn
Lingard
Linton
Lister
Littlehale, Littlehales

Littleton
Livesay
Locke, Locker, Lockyer
Long, Longman
Longacre
Longbourne
Longley, Langeley
Longstreth
Lothrop
Lovelace
Lovell
Lowe, Low, Lowell, Lowson
Lowth
Lubbock
Lucas
Luckey
Lucy
Ludlow
Lugard
Lunn
Lutwidge
Lydekker
Lyne, Lynd, Lynn
Lyon
Lytton
Maddox
Madison
Madlock
Malaby
Malleson
Mallock
Manby
Manning
Mansel
Margoliouth
Markham
Marshall
Marshman
Martin
Marywight
Masefield
Maston
Matthews, Matthewson
Maurice
May, Maybrick
Maynard
Mead, Meade
Meakin
Medhurst
Meggs
Mercer

Merivale
Merriman
Merritt
Merwin
Metcalfe
Meynell
Michaels, Michaelson
Milburn
Mill, Mills
Milledge
Miller, Milman
Millsom
Milne, Milner
Minot
Mitchel, Mitchell —
    American, Mitchill,
    Michell
Mitford
Mivart
Moberly
Molesworth
Molland
Monkhouse
Monson
Moorcroft
Moore, More
Morfill
Morier
Morland
Morris, Morrisey, Morri-
    son
Morton
Moseley, Mozley
Moss
Moulton
Moxon
Muddock
Mulock
Munsby
Myres
Naden
Naismith, Naismyth,
    Nesmith, Nesmyth
Needham
Nell, Nelson
Nesbit, Nesbitt
Nevins, Nevinson
Newbolt
Newcliff
Newfield
Newnes

Nicholas, Nichols, Nich-
    olson
Niles
Norman, Normanby
Norris
North, Northcote
Norton
Norvell
Noyes
Nutt
Nutting, Nuttall
Oakley
Oastler
Ocheltree
Olcott
Oldham
Oldmixon
Oldys
Oliver, Olivers
Ollivant
Orcutt
Ord
Orford
Ormerod
Orton
Osborne, Osburn,
    Osbern, Osbourne
Osgood, Osgoode
Outram
Overton
Ovey
Oxenden
Oxenham
Oxley
Page, Paget
Paish
Pakenham
Paley
Palgrave
Palmer
Pares
Parke, Parkes, Parks, Par-
    kin, Parkins
Parker
Parmele
Parrinder
Parsons
Patteson, Pattison
Pauncefote
Paxson, Paxton
Peacock

Peake
Peale
Pearse, Pearson
Peartree
Peck
Pelham
Pemberton
Penman, Penson
Perkins, Perkin — rare
Peter, Peters
Petrie
Pharoh
Phelps
Phillimore
Phillips, Philips, Phil-
   lipps, Phipps
Phillpotts
Pinchback
Pinckney, Pinkney
Pinkstone
Pipes
Plowden
Pollack
Popham
Porter
Potter, Potts
Pound
Poynings
Pratt
Preble
Preston
Prestwich
Pretty, Pretyman
Prime
Pritchard
Pritchett
Proctor
Proud, Proudfit
Prynne
Pryor, Prior
Puddicombe
Pulteney
Pusey
Quain
Quaritch
Quarles
Quarterpath
Le Queux
Quincey
Radford
Rains, Rainsford

Ramsey
Randall, Randel, Run-
   dell, Randle — Ameri-
   can
Ransome
Rawdon
Rawling, Rawlins, Raw-
   linson
Rayleigh, Raleigh
Redfield
Redhouse
Reed, Read, Reade, Reid
Rice
Richards, Richardson
Ridgeway
Roberts, Robertson
Robins, Robbins, Robinson
Rooke
Rouse, Rous
Routh
Routledge, Rutledge
Rowbotham
Rowland, Rowlands,
   Rowlandson
Rowley
Royden
Rucker
Rumbold
Russel
Ryland
Sanford
Sass
Sawbridge
Scroggs
Seabrook
Seabury
Seaton, Seton
Sedleigh, Sedley
Sell, Sellers
Shedden
Sherard
Sherrington
Skeat
Skrine
Slack
Sladen
Slim
Slingsby
Sloane, Sloan — American
Small, Smallwood
Smeaton

Smith, Smithe, Smythe,
   Smyth, Smithson
Sneyd
Soddy
Souter
Southcott
Southerne, Sothern
Southey
Southwell
Southworth
Sowerby
Spalding
Spedding
Speed
Speke
Spofford
Stacey
Stanhope
Stannard
Stark, Starke, Starkey
Starling
Stead, Stedman
Stephen, Stephens, Ste-
   phenson, Steevens, Ste-
   vens, Stevenson
Stern, Sterne
Stewart, Steward, Seward,
   Stuart, Stuarte
Still, Stille
Stimson
Stockton
Stoddard
Stopes
Stopford
Stoppard
Storey — British, Story —
   American
Stothard
Stowe
Stratton
Street, Streeton
Strickland
Strutter, Strutt
Sturgeon
Sturt
Style, Styles
Suffolk, Suffolke
Summers
Sumter, Sunter
Sutherland
Sutton

Swann
Swanwick
Sweet, Sweetser
Swift, Swifte
Swinnerton
Swinton
Symonds
Taggart
Tailor, Taylor, Tayler
Tamble
Tarleton
Tasker
Terry
Tharpe, Thorpe
Thistlewaite
Thistlewood
Thompson, Thomsen,
  Thomson
Thore
Thornton
Thurston
Tichborne
Tillett
Tilstone
Titchener
Tizard
Todd
Toliver, Tolliver
Tomes
Tomline, Tomlinson,
  Tompkins
Tooke
Torriton
Tovey
Tower, Towers
Towne, Towneley
Tracey
Trimble, Trumbull
Trench
Tyler, Tiler
Underwood
Upton
Vernon
Vian
Vincent, Vinson
Vizetelly — probably Ital-
  ian origin, long ago
Vokes
Voysey

Wace
Waddington
Wade
Wadleigh
Wadsworth
Wainewright — British,
  Wainwright — American
Wait, Waite
Wake, Wakefield
Walford
Walker
Waller, Walling
Walston
Walters
Ward, Warden
Warren
Warter
Waterman
Waters
Waterton
Watkin, Watkins, Wat-
  son
Weatherford
Weatherly
Weaver, Webster
Weed
Weekes, Weeks
Weld
Weller
Wensleydale
Wentworth
Wesley
West, Westcott, Westma-
  cott, Westrin
Westlake
Wetherald
Wharton
Wheatley
Wheaton, Wheatston
Wheeler, Wheelton
Wheelwright
Whiston
Whitaker
Whitbread
Whitcher
White, Whiting
Whitefield, Whitfield
Whitehill
Whitgreave

Whitlock
Whitmer
Whitridge, Whittredge
Whitside
Whitson
Whittemore
Wickard
Wickliffe
Wight
Wilkins, Wilkinson
Willard
Williams, Williamson,
  Wilson
Winckworth
Windle
Winslow
Winthrop
Wise, Wiseman
Wister
Wither, Withers
Witherspoon
Woffington
Wolcot, Wolcott
Wold
Wollaston
Wood, Woods
Woodberry, Woodbury
Woodbridge
Woodfall
Woodford
Woodman
Woodward
Woodworth
Wool, Wooley
Woollcott, Woollett
Woolman
Woolson, Woolston
Workman
Worrel
Wraxhall
Wyatt
Wylie
Wyndham
Yarrell
Yates
Young, Yonge
Younghusband
Youngman

SCOTTISH

In the cold and broken Highlands, the clan system became a means of survival. The central, most powerful families have the clan name itself. Other families would be associated with such a family as "clients" or dependants of the clan — part of my family descends from a client clan of the Colquhouns, who would use the Colquhoun badge and tartan. In the Lowlands, the clan was not so important, but that's like saying eating is not as important as breathing.

There were 31 Highland clans, using 96 tartans. The rest are Lowlanders. The tartans were fixed before 1645, probably before 1600 — but the assignments are not much older than that. Don't be picky about plaid patterns before, say, 1550.

Authorities may say "surnames" became general in Scotland around the 12th century but this only means that patronymic surnames became general. Inheritable, unchanging family names arrived after another two centuries. The "mac-" is a son-word, the daughter-word being "nic-." If you are using patronymics still, rather than family names, be sure to gender that.

There is a certain silliness on the part of some books as to various Scottish personal names equalling English ones. Most Scottish names derive from Gaellic or Norse originals, and have no connection to Hebrew or Latin ones, as far as descent goes. All this equality means is that the Scottish name, say, Beathag, has the same meaning as the foreign Sophie; both mean "wisdom," or came from a similar source. To indicate, an equal sign has been used.

A distinctively Scottish spelling is QUH, as in Farquhar. It was used where an Englishman would use WH, as in "quher" for "where." It indicated an aspirated K, softer than the throat-clearing CH of loch. The MH was an M tending to V.

In practice, you can say QUH as KW, MH as M, and CH as hard K. Scottish names are so common in North America that they need little other comment.

Some Scottish diminutives crept over the border into Yorkshire by the 19th century, so that "Cathy" as the heroine of *Wuthering Heights* had a distinctively Northern sound in its day.

FEMALE NAMES

Ada, Adelaide, Adeline
Aenea
Agatha
Agnes
Ailsa=Elsa, also used
Alicia, Alison, Alice
Amilia=Emily; also

Aimil, Amy
Anabladh
Anders, Andra
Anna
Annabella=since at least
    1350
Aoirig, Eighrig

Arabella
Armorel
Barbara, Baubie
Beathag, Bethia
Beitris=Beatrice, also
    used
Bertha

Bevin
Blanche
Bride=Bridget, from
    Scandinavian saint
Cairistiona=Christina;
    Christine also used
Caitlin=Kathleen, also
    used
Caroline
Ceit=Kate
Charlotte=after 1600
Claudia
Clementine
Constance
Dalta
Daveen, Davena, Devene,
    Davelle, Davida
Deborah
Delia
Deonaid
Diana
Diorbhail, Diorbhoguil
Dorcas
Ealasaid=Elizabeth, also
    used; Elsie
Edith
Effric=Euphemia, Effie
Egidia
Eilidh
Eirene
Eleanor
Elspeth=Elizabeth;
    Elspet, Elspie
Emily
Emma, Emmeline
Esther
Ethel
Eugenia
Eva
Felicia
Fionnaghal
Flora, Floraidh
Florence
Frangang=Frances, Fanny,
    also used
Georgiana
Gertrude
Gillian
Giorsal=Grace, also used
Grizel=Griselda, Grishild,

also used
Hannah
Harriet
Helen
Henrietta
Honora
Ida
Iona
Iseabel=Isabel; also
    Isobal, Ishbel, Isabella
Isla
Ivana=John, fem.
Jacobina=James, fem.
Janet, Jonet
Jemima
Jessie
Joanna, Johan
Josephine
Katrine=Katharine, also
    used; Catriona
Kyla
Lachlanina
Laura
Letitia
Lileas, Lilias=Lillian
Liusaidh=Louise, Lucy,
    Louisa
Lorna
Lucretia, Lucy, Lucie
Mabel
Madeline, Magdalen
Mairghread=Margaret;
    also Maisie, Peigi,
    Maggie, Maxie, Mysie
Malai=Molly
Marcail, Marsali=Mar-
    jorie
Marion
Matilda, Maud
Mavis
Melicent
Mhairie=Mary, Maria,
    also used; Mairi,
    Mhaire, Mhairi,
    Mhari, Mharie, Moira,
    Moire, Muire
Miriam
Moibeal=Mabel, also
    used
Moireach=Martha, also

used
Morag=Sarah, also used
Moray
Morna
Muireall=Muriel
Murnia=Myrna, also used
Nairne
Nancy, Nannette
Nessie
Olivia
Pauline
Pearl
Phillipa
Phoebe
Priscilla
Raoghnailt, Raonaild,
    Raonaid=Rachel; actu-
    ally from Ragenhild
Rebecca
Regina
Rhoda
Robertina
Rosalie
Rosalind, Rossalyn, Ross-
    lyn
Rosamond
Rowena
Salaidh=Sally
Selma
Senga
Seonaid=Jane, also used
Shonah, Shone
Sileas=Cecilia or Julia,
    also used
Sine=Jane
Siubhan=Judith, also used
Sophia
Sorcha=Claire, Clara, also
    used
Suisadh=Susan; Siusan
Sybil
Tamarka, Tammy
Tatiana
Teresa
Theodosia
Una=Winifred, also used
Ursula
Viola
Virginia
Wilhelmina

MALE NAMES

Adhamh, Adam, Adam-
  nan
Aed
Aeneas
Ailbert=Albert
Ailean=Alan
Aindreas=Andrew, also
  used
Ainslie
Alastair=Alexander, also
  used; Alastare, Allister,
  Alasdair, Alaister, Alis-
  tar, Sandy — extremely
  popular
Allan
Alpin, Alpine
Angus
Anndra
Aoidh
Aongus — somewhat pop-
  ular; also Angus
Archibald — popular
Artair=Arthur
Athol
Aulay
Banquo
Baptist
Barclay
Bearnard
Beatham
Bhaltair
Brock
Broderick
Brody
Bruce
Cailean=Colin
Catan, Cattanch, Chattan
Colin, Cailean
Coll, Colley, Colla
Cosmo
Craig
Daibidh=David; popular
Domhnall=Donald
Dougal
Duff
Dugald
Duncan
Durell
Eanruig=Henry, also used

Ebenezar
Egidius
Eocha
Ewan
Farquhar, Fearchar
Feargus, Fergus
Fife
Fingal, Fionn, Fionnghal
Forbes
Gavin, Gawin
George, Geordie, Georas;
  Seoras, Seorsa, Deorsa
Gilleabart,
  Gillebride=Gilbert
Gillean
Gilleasbuig
Gillecriosd
Glenn
Goraidh=Godfrey
Grant, Grannd
Gregor, Griogair
Grig
Guinn, Gunn, Guinne,
  Gunnach=Norse Gunn
  and Gunnar
Hamish=James, which is
  more commonly seen
Harailt=Harald, Norse
Horatius
Hugh, Uisdean, Hisdean
Ian=John; Iaian, Eoin —
  popular
Inness, Innes, Innis
Jamie
Kathel, Cathal
Keddy
Keir
Keith
Kenneth, Kenny — very
  popular; from Coin-
  neach
Kentigern
Kerr
Labhruinn=Lawrence
Lachlan, Lachunn, Lach-
  lann — from Norse
Lachunn
Laird
Lamond=Layaman, Norse

for lawman
Lawrie
Lenox
Leslie
Lorne
Lucais=Luke, Lucas
Luthais=Louis
Lyle
Malcolm
Manius
Maolmuire=Maurice
Marmion
Martainn=Martin
Mata=Matt
Matthew
Maxwell
Micheil
Monroe, Munro
Morag
Morven
Muir
Mungo
Murdo
Murdoch, Muireach,
  Murchadh
Murray, Moirreach
Nairne
Neacail=Nicholas
Niall, Neil
Ninian
Padruig, Paruig,
  Para=Patrick
Parlan=Bartholomew
Peadair=Peter
Pol=Paul
Rab, Raby
Ranald, Ronald, Raonull
Reginald
Richie
Robert, Rob — very pop-
  ular; Raibeart; from
  Norman
Rory, Ruairich=Norse
  Rurik
Rothach
Sawney
Seadhgh, Shaw
Seamas, Shamus
Shim, Sim, Simon

Sholto	Tammas, Tamhas, Tomas	Norse Thorkl, Thor-
Sim	Tavis=Thomas; Tavish,	ketil
Somhairle=summer sailor,	Tevis	Tormoid, Tormod=Nor-
used for Samuel	Tearlach=Charles, also	man; actually Norse
Steaphan=Stephen	used	Thormund
Tam=Tom	Torcull, Torcall, Torquil=	Uilleam=William

Family Names

Highland Clans, Septs, and Dependents

Each of the names represents a family, but some are clustered because they are undoubtedly alternate spellings, Anglicizations, and shortenings within what was anciently one name. The name following "Clan ..." is the chief's family name.

Clan Buchanan: Dove, Dow, Dowe; Harper, Harperson; Lennie, Lenny; Macaldonich; Macandeoir; MacAslan, MacAuselan, MacAuslan, MacAusland, MacAuslane, McCausland; MacCalman, MacCalmont, MacCammond, MacColman, Colman; MacChruiter; MacCormack; MacDonleavy, Donleavy, Donlevy; MacGibbon, Gibb, Gibson, Gilbertson, MacGilbert; Macgrieusich; Maindeor, Macindoe; Mackinlay, Mackinley, Macinally; MacMaster; MacMaurice; MacMurchie, MacMurchy, Murchie, Murchison; Macnuyer; MacWattie, Watson, Watt; MacWhirter; Masterson; Risk, Ruskin; Sittal, Spittel; Yuill, Yuille, Yule

Clan Cameron: Chalmers; Kennedy; MacChlerich, MacChlery, Maclerie, Clark; MacGillonie; Macildowie; MacKail; MacMartin, Martin; MacOnie; MacOurlic; MacPhail, Macvail; MacSorley, Sorley; MacUlric, MacWalrick; Paul; Taylor

Clan Campbell: Bannatyne; Burns, Burnes, Burnett; Denoon, Denune; Harres, Harris; Haws, Hawson; MacConnechy, MacConochie, Connochie; MacGibbon; Macglasrich; MacIsaac; MacIver, MacIvor; MacKellar; MacKessock, MacKissock; MacLaws, MacLehose; MacNichol; Nichol, Nicol, Nicoll; MacOran; MacOwen; MacPhedran; MacPhun; MacTause, MacTavish, Tawesson; Mac-

Thomas, Thomas, Thomason, Thompson, Thomson; MacUre, Ure

Clan Campbell of Breadalbane: MacDearmid, MacDermid

Clan Campbell of Cawdor: Caddell; Calder

Clan Campbell of Loudoun: Hastings; Loudoun

Clan Chattan: Cattanach; Clark, Clarke, Clarkson, Clerk, MacChlerich, MacCurrach, MacChlery, Maclerie; MacFall; MacNiven; MacPhail, Macvail

Clan Colquhoun: also Calhoun; Kilpatrick, Kirkpatrick; Macachounich; MacCowan, Cowan

Clan Cumming: Buchan; Comine, Comyn; MacNiven, Niven; Russell

Clan Davidson: Dawson, Dow; Kay; Macdade, Macdaid, MacDavid, Davie, Davis

Clan Drummond — said to have a founder from Hungary; Grewar, Gruer; Maccrouther, Macgrewar, Macgrowther, Macgruder, Macgruther; MacRobbie

Clan Farquarson: Brebner; Coutts; Findlay, Findlayson, Finlay, Finlayson; Greusach; MacCaig, MacCuaig; MacCardney; MacEarachar; MacFarquhar, Farquhar; Machardie, Machardy, Hardie, Hardy; MacKerchar, MacKerracher; Mackindlay, Mackinlay; Reoch, Riach; Tawse

Clan Ferguson: MacAdie; MacFergus, Fergus, Ferries; MacKerras, MacKersey

Clan Forbes: Bannerman; Fordyce; Michie; Watson; Watt

Clan Fraser: Frissell, Frizell; Macimmey; MacGruer; MacKim, MacKimmie; MacShimes, MacSimon, MacSymon, Sim, Sime, Simson, Simpson, Syme, Symon; Tweedie

Clan Gordon: Adam; Adie, Edie; Crombie; Huntly; Milne; Todd

Clan Graham: Allardice; Bontein, Bontine, Buntain, Bunten, Buntine; MacGibbon; MacGilvernock; Macgrime; Menteith, Monteith

Clan Grant: MacGilroy, Macilroy, Gilroy

Clan Gunn: Gallie; Gaunson; Georgeson; Henderson; Jameson, Jamieson; Johnson; MacComas; MacCorkill, MacCorkle; MacIan; MacKames, MacKeamish; MacKean, Kean, Keene; MacRob; MacWilliam, Williamson, Wilson; Manson; Nelson; Robison, Robson; Sandison; Swanson

Clan Innes: Dinnes, Ennis, Innie; McRob; McTary; Marnoch; Mavor; Middleton; Mitchell; Reidfuird, Redford; Thain; Wilson

Clan Lamont: Black; Brown; Bourdon, Burdon; Lamb, Lambie, Lammie; Landers; Lyon; Macalduie; MacClymont; MacGilledow, MacGillegowie, Macilzegowie; Macilwhom; MacLamond, MacLymont, Lemond, Limond, Limont, Lamondson; MacLucas, Lucas, Luke; MacPatrick, Patrick; MacPhorich; MacSorley, Sorley; Meiklham; Toward, Towart; Turner; White

Clan Leslie: Bartholomew; Lang; More

Clan Lindsay: Crawford; Deuchar

Clan MacAllister: Alexander

Clan MacArthur: MacCartair, MacCarter, Arthur

Clan MacAulay: MacPhedron, MacPheidiran

Clan MacBean: Bean; MacBeath, MacBeth; Macilvain, MacVean

Clan MacDonald: Bowie; Darroch; Donald, Donaldson, Donilson, Donnelson; Hawthorn; Isles; MacBeth, MacBeath, MacBheath, Beath, Beaton, Beth-une; MacBride, Macilvride, Galbraith, Gilbride; MacCaishe, MacCash, MacCooish, MacCuish; MacCall, MacColl, Colson; MacCodrum; MacConnell, Connall, Connell; MacCook, MacCuag; MacCrain; MacDaniell; Macdrain, Drain, O'Drain; MacEachern, MacEachran; MacElfrish; MacElheran; MacGorrie, MacGorry, Gorrie, Gowrie; MacGoun, MacGowan, MacGown, Gowan; MacHugh, Hewison, Houstoun, Howison, Hughson; MacHutchen, MacHutcheon, Hutcheonson, Hutcheson, Hutchinson, Hutchison, MacCuithein, MacCutcheon; MacIan, MacKean; Macilreach, Macilriach, Macilleriach, Macilwraith, MacRaith, Reoch, Riach; Macilrevie, Revie; MacKellachie, MacKallaig, MacKelloch, MacCeallaich, Kellie, Kelly, Mac a'Challies; MacKiggan; MacKinnell, Kinnell; MacLairish; MacLardie, MacLardy, MacLarty; MacLaverty, MacLeverty; MacMurchie, Murchie, Murchison; MacMurdo, MacMurdoch, Murdoch, Murdoson; MacO'Shannaig, O'Shannaig; MacQuistan, MacQuisten; MacRorie, MacRory, MacRuer, MacRurie, MacRury, Rorison; MacShannachan, Shannon, O'Shannachan; MacSorley, Sorley; MacSporran, Sporran; MacSwan; MacWhannell, Whannel; Martin; O'May, May; O'Shaig; Purcell; Train

Clan MacDonald of Ardnamurchan: Johnson; Kean, Keene

Clan MacDonald of Clanranald: Mackechnie; MacKeochan, MacKichan; MacKessock, MacKissock; MacMurrich; MacVarish, Macvurrich, MacVurie

Clan MacDonald of Glencoe: Henderson; Johnson; MacHenry; MacIan; MacKean, Kean, Keene

Clan MacDonell of Glengarry: Alexander; Sanderson

Clan MacDonell of Keppoch: MacGillivantic; Macgilp, MacKillop, MacPhilip, Pilipson; Macglasrich; Ronald, Ronaldson

Clan MacDougall: Carmichael; Dougall; Livingston, Livingstone; MacConacher, Conacher; MacCowan, Cowan; MacCoul, MacHowell, Macoul, Macowl; MacCulloch; MacDulothe; MacKichan;

MacLucas, MacLugash, MacLulich; Mac-Namell

Clan MacDuff: Abernethy; Duff; Fife, Fyfe; Spence, Spens; Wemyss

Clan MacFarlane: Bartholomew; Galbraith; Gruamach; Kinnieson; Lennox; MacAindra; MacAllan, Allan, Allanson, McAllen; MacCaa, MacCause, MacCaw, Caw, MacGaw, MacGeoch; MacCondy; MacEoin; Macgreusich, Griesck; Macinstalker, Stalker; MacIock; MacJames; Mackinlay; MacNair, MacNeur; Mac-Nider, MacNiter; MacRob, MacRobb, Robb; MacWalter; MacWilliam; Miller; Monach; Napier; Parlane; Thomason; Weaver; Weir

Clan Macfie: Duffie, Duffy; Mac-Cuffie, Machaffie, McAfee

Clan MacGillivray: MacGillivour; MacGilroy, Gilroy, Macilroy; MacGilvra, MacGilvray, Macilvrae

Clan MacGregor: Black; Caird; Comrie; Dochart; Fletcher; Gregor, Gregorson, Gregory, Greig, Grigor; King; Leckie, Lecky; MacAdam; Macara, Macaree; MacChoiter; MacConachie; Maccrouther, Macgrowther, Macgruder, Macgruther; Macgrewar, Grewar, Grier, Grierson, Gruer; Macilduy; MacLeister; MacLiver; MacNee, MacNeish, MacNie, MacNish, Neish, Nish; MacPeter, MacPetrie, Peter; Malloch; White, Whyte

Clan Macinnes: MacAngus, Angus; MacCainsh, MacCansh; MacMaster

Clan Macintyre: MacTear, Tyre; Wright

Clan Mackay: Bain, Bayne; MacCay; MacCrie; Mackee, Mackie; MacPhail; Macquey; Macquoid; Macvail; Neilson; Paul, Polson; Williamson

Clan MacKenzie: Kenneth, Kennethson; MacBeolain; MacConnach; MacIver, MacIvor; MacKerlich; MacMurchie, MacMurchy, Murchie, Murchison; MacVanish, MacVinish

Clan Mackinnon: Love; Mackinney, Mackinning; Mackinven; MacMorran

Clan Mackintosh: Adamson; Crerar; Dallas, Doles; Elder; Esson; Glen, Glennie; MacAndrew; MacAy, Ayson, Mac-Hay; MacCardney; MacCombie, Mac-Combe, MacComie, Combie; M'Conchy;

Macglashan; Machardie, Machardy, Hardie, Hardy; Mackeggie; M'Killican; MacOmie; Macritchie, Ritchie; Mac-Thomas; Niven; Noble; Paul; Shaw; Tarrill; Tosh, Toshach

Clan MacLachlan: Lacklan, Lauchlan; MacEwan, MacEwen, Ewan, Ewen, Ewing; MacGilchrist, Gilchrist

Clan Maclaine of Lochbuie: Mac-Cormick; MacFadyen, MacFadzean, Mac-Phadden; MacGilvra, Macilvora

Clan MacLaurin: MacFater, Mac-Phater, MacFeat; MacPatrick, Paterson; MacGrory, MacRory

Clan Maclean: Black; Clanachan; Garvie; Lean; MacBeath, MacBheath, MacBeth, Beath, Beaton; Macilduy; MacLergain; MacRankin, Rankin; MacVeagh, MacVey

Clan Maclennan: Lobban, Logan

Clan Macleod of Harris: Beaton, Beton; MacCaig; MacClure; MacCrimmon; MacCuaig; MacHarold; Macraild; Norman

Clan Macleod of Lewis: Callum; MacAskill; MacAulay; MacCaskill; Mac-Lewis, Lewis; MacNicol; Tolmie

Clan Macmillan: Bell; Brown; Mac-Baxter, Baxter

Clan Macnab: Abbot, Abbotson; Dewar; Gilfillan; Macandeoir

Clan MacNaughton: Kendrick; Mac-Brayne; Maceol; MacHendrie, MacHendry, Hendrie, Hendry

Clan MacNeil: MacNeilage, Mac-Neiledge; MacNelly, Neal, Neil, Neill

Clan Macpherson: Currie; Fersen; Gillespie, Gillies; MacGowan, Gow; MacLeish, MacLise, Lees; MacMurdo, MacMurdoch, MaMurrich, MacVurrich, Murdoch, Murdoson

Clan Macquarrie: MacCorrie, Mac-Corry, MacGorrie, MacGorry; MacGuaran; MacGuire, Macquaire, Macquhirr, Macquire, MacWhirr, Wharrie

Clan Macqueen: MacCunn; Mac-Swan, MacSwen, MacSween, Swan; Mac-Swyde

Clan Macrae: Macara, Macra, Macrach, MacCraw; MacRaith, MacRath, Rae; Rae, McCrae, McCrea

Clan Malcolm: MacCallum, Malcomson
Mar Tribe: Marr; Morren; Strachan; Tough
Clan Mathieson: MacMath; MacPhun; Mathie
Clan Menzies: Dewar; Macindear; MacMenzies, Monzie; MacMinn, Means, Mein, Meine, Mennie, Meyners, Minn, Minnus; MacMonies
Clan Morison: Gilmore; MacBrieve, Brieve
Clan Munro: Dingwall; Foulis; MacCulloch; MacLulich; Vass, Wass
Clan Murray: MacMurray, Moray; Rattray; Small; Spalding
Clan Ogilvy: Airlie; MacGilchrist, Gilchrist; Milne
Clan Robertson: Colleir, Colyear; Inches; MacConachie, MacConnechy; MacDonachie, Donachie, Duncan, Duncanson, Dunnachie, Tonnochy; Macinroy, Roy; MacIver, MacIvor; Maclagan; MacRobbie, MacRobie, MacRobert; Reid; Stark

Clan Ross: Dingwall; Gillanders; MacAndrew, Anderson, Andrew; MacCullock; MacLulich; MacTaggart, Taggart; MacTear, MacTier, MacTire; Vass, Wass
Clan Sinclair: Caird; Clouston; Clyne; Linklater; Mason
Clan Skene: Cariston; Dis, Dyce; Hallyard; Norie
Clan Stewart: Boyd; Garrow; Menteith, Monteith; Carmichael; MacMichael
Clan Stewart of Appin: Carmichael; Livingston, Livingstone; MacCombich, Combich; Mackinlay; Maclae, Maclay, Maclea, Macleay; MacMichael
Clan Stewart of Atholl: Crookshanks, Cruickshank; Duilach; Gray; Macglashan
Clan Stuart of Bute: Bannatyne; Fullarton, Fullerton; Jameson, Jamieson; MacCamie; MacCloy; MacCaw; MacKirdy; MacLewis; MacMunn, Munn; MacMutrie
Clan Sutherland: Cheyne; Federith; Gray; Keith; Mowat; Oliphant

Family Names

These names are unaligned, late, and or Lowland.

Aiken, Aitken, Aiton, Akenside
Aless
Baikie
Baillie
Bainbridge, Banebrudge, Bainbrudge, Baynebridge
Baird
Bairnsfeather
Balios
Balnaves
Barbour
Barclay
Barrie
Beattie
Beilby
Bell, Bellenden
Berwick
Blackie, Blaikie
Blackwood
Blair
Bogue
Bower
Boyce
Braid
Brisbane
Brough
Brougham
Brownlee
Brymner
Cairns
Calderwood
Candlish
Cardus
Cargill
Caven
Christison
Clyde
Cochrane, Cochran
Cockburn
Colomb
Crockett
Cronin
Cruden
Cunningham, Cunninghame
Cushny
Dalzell, Dalziel
Deems, Deemster, Dempster
Dinwiddie
Doohan, Doone
Dunbar
Dundas, Dundee
Dunn, Dunne, Dunning
Eccles
Eckford
Edmonstone
Elder

Fairbairn
Falconer
Fenwick
Ferrier
Gairdner
Galloway
Galt
Geddes, Geddy
Geikie
Glass, Glas
Glendon
Graham
Gregory
Guthrie
Haig
Halkett
Herdman
Hogg
Imey
Inchbald
Inglis
Irvine
Ivory
Jebb
Ker
Kirk, Kirke, Kirkbride
Kirkaldy, Kirkcaldy
Kynynmound
Laird
Laughlin

Lawson
Legge
Lillie
Lipton
Lockhart
Lorimer
Lyall, Lyell
Lyte
Masson, Mauson
Melrose
Mill, Millar, Miller
Milligan
Milner
Moffat
Mollison
Moncrieff
Montrose
Motherwell
Muir, Muire, Murray
Muirhead
Nairn
Nasmyth
Nesbit, Nisbet, Nesbitt
Noel
Orchardson
Orr
Pasley — no i
Paterson
Pender
Preston

Primrose
Pringle
Quiller
Raeburn
Ramsay
Redpath
Renfrew, Rennie, Renwick
Sanderson
Semphill
Smiles
Smollett
Smybert, Smibert
Spenlove
Stirling, Sterling
Strange, Strang, Strangways
Tait
Tannahill
Tassie
Thom
Tolmie
Urquhart
Wardlaw
Wedderburn
Wilkie
Wishart, Wiseheart
Yarrow

All "mac" names may be spelled "mc" by some.

"Mac" followed by a vowel or a K-sound may be written without the second capital letter; as may many others.

McAdoo
McAleste, MacAlister,
    Macallister,
    Macalester, Macalister,
    McAllister
MacAlpin, McAlpine
McAneny

McCarren
MacChesney
McChord
McClernand
McClung
McClurg
McCosh

MacCracken
McCrady
McCrary
McCullers
MacLaren, Maclaren
Macnamara, MacNamara

IRISH

Irish personal names go into pre-history. Family names become common about 1200. Note that the spellings change. The long English occupation resulted in a simplification of Irish. The names also became "spelled as sounded" when the Wild Geese migrated to Russia, Germany, France, Italy, Spain, and the Americas. Very often, in America especially, the "mac" or "o" would be dropped from family names, though this happened in Ireland, too. These variations are included.

There are a lot of English and Scottish names to be found in the Emerald Isle, due to several centuries of occupation, some rather peaceful and at times downright friendly, like that of the Sean-ghalls. There are also a number of names from the Norse, who founded Dublin.

You should be careful about "typically Irish" names, when you are writing an historical. Mary, though its variants are used for about a quarter of the women in Ireland today, was very rare until the 17th century. Brigit was virtually unused until the 18th!

FEMALE NAMES

Many girls are given non–Celtic names like Ellen, Letitia, Grace, Rose, and so forth.

Abaigeal
Agata
Aideen
Aigneis
Ailis
Aindrea
Aingeal=Angel, not used
Alastriona
Allsun
Annabla
Aoiffe
Bevin
Blinnie
Bluinse
Brianna, Bryana
Brigit, Bridget, Brigid,
  Bride, Bridey; Biddy
Cathlin, Caitlin, Caitrin,
  Catraoine=Katherine
Colleen
Cristin, Cristiona
Damhnait=Dymphna
Dearbhail, Dervilia
Deirdre
Doireann
Doreen
Duana
Eadaoine
Edana
Eileen, Aileen, Alina,

Alena, Alinna, Alli,
  Lina; Eibhlinn
Eilis=Elizabeth
Eimile=Emily
Eister=Esther
Ena
Erinna, Erina, Erine
Ethna, Ethni
Evaleen
Fainche
Faoiltighearna
Fiadhnait
Fiona, Fionna
Fionnghuala=shortened
  to Nuala; also Fenella,
  Fionula
Gobnait
Gormfhlaith
Grainne, Granua, Gran-
  nia, Grania, Graine=
  Grace
Hilde
Ide
Iseabal, Isibeal, Sibeal —
  Anglo-Norman
Islean, Isleen
Ita
Kathleen — Anglicized;
  Irish doesn't use K
Labhaoise=Louisa

Lasairfhiona, Lassarina
Lean — pet of Eleanor
Lil, Lile
Luighseach
Maeve, Mave, Mab
Maible
Maighlin=Madeline
Maire, Mairona, Maura,
  Maureen, Moira,
  Muire=Mary
Mairghread=Margaret
Maitild, Tilde=Matilda;
  Norman
Malvina
Maureen
Meadhbh=Marjorie
Meara
Melva
Muirgheal=Muriel
Nabla, Naible
Nainseadh
Neill, Neilli — pet forms
  of Eibhlin
Noinin, Noirin — pet
  forms of Nora
Odharnait
Oilbhe
Onora, Nora — Anglo-
  Norman
Oona, Una

Orfhlait
Orna
Paili, Pails, Pal=Polly
Peig, Peigi=Peg, Peggy
Proinnseas, Proinseas
Rathnait
Richeal
Rioghna
Rois, Roise — Anglo-
    Norman
Sadhbh, Sadhbha=Sophie

Saidhbhin=Sabina
Saraid
Seosaimhthin — late
    adaptation for Jose-
    phine
Sheelagh, Sheila
Sibeal
Sile, Sisile=Cecilia
Sinead, Sheena, Shena=
    John
Siobhan, Siubhan

Sorcha
Sosanna=Susanna, Susan
Toireasa — after 16th c.
Traoine, Triona — from
    Catraoine
Treasa, Treise
Una
Ursula — 6th c. and after
Vevina — foreign

MALE NAMES

Perfectly good Irishmen have non-ethnic names like Eugene, John, Michael, Daniel, William, Henry, and Frank.

Aguistin
Aidan
Aindreas
Aineislis=Stanislaus
Alabhaois=Aloysius
Alair, Allare
Alan, Allen, Ailin
Alphonsus
Alsandair
Ambros
Amhlaobh, Auliffe
Anntoin
Aodh — Hugh
Aralt — Harald
Art, Artur
Bailintin — Valentine
Barry
Beartlaidh — Beartley
Brann
Brendan
Brian, Bryan, Bryant
Buadhach — Victor
Carroll, Carol, Caerbhaill
Colin
Conan
Conn
Connor
Darren
Denis
Dermit, Dermot,
    Diarmid, Darby

Domhnall-anchogaidh
Donchadh
Donough
Duane, Dwayne
Dubhdara
Dubhghall, Doyle
Egan, Eagan
Eoin, Seain, Seann,
    Shane=John
Fergus
Filib=Philip
Finian
Finn
Flann
Flynn
Galvin
Gearalt=Gerald
Gearard=Gerard
Gearoidh=Garrett
Gilibeirt=Gilbert
Gothfraidh=Godfrey
Greagir, Grioghar=Gre-
    gory
Guin
Hanraoi=Henry
Hoibeard=Hubert
Hoireabard=Herbert
Iomhar, Ivor
Kelvin
Kerwin
Kevin, Kavin

Kieran
Killian
Kyle
Labhras=Lawrence
Laval
Liam
Lugaidh
Luineach
Lusmore
Maghnus, Manus
Ned
Padraic, Paddy, Padraig=
    Patrick
Peadar
Phelim, Felim
Raghnall, Ranald
Riobard
Riocard
Riordan
Roderic
Rodhlann
Rory, Ruaidhri
Roy
Ruarc, Roarke
Sailbheastar=Sylvester
Sean, Shawn
Seumas, Shemus, Shamus
Siomonn
Solamh
Somhairle, Sorley
Ted, Teddy

Teig, Tadhg
Thaddeus, Thaddy, Tadd,
   Taddy
Tioboid=Tobias

Tiomoid=Timothy
Tomas
Turlough
Ualtair=Walter

Uilliam=William
Uillioc=Ulysses
Uinsionn=Vincent

FAMILY NAMES

"Mac" may also be "Mc" or even "M'" or "Ma-" with the root name attached without being capitalized. If you remember the Scottish were originally from Scotia (Ireland), these will not seem misplaced.

Adair	Eagan, Egan	Logue
Balfe	Emmet, Emmett	Lon, Lunn
Banim	Ferguson	Lovins
Banning	Ferris, Farris	McAuley
Blaine	Finley	McBride
Blakeny	Flynn, Flinn, Flynne	MacCarroll
Bourke	Forbes	MacCatharny
Bowie	Gallway, Galloway	M'Clintock, McClintock
Boyne	Gannon	McCloskey
Brodie	Gaynor	MacConmidhe
Byrne	Gilchrist	M'Corkle
Cairnes, Cairns	Gilligan	McCormick, McCormack
Caley	Gilmore	MacCowan
Carberry, Carbury	Gorman	McCreight
Carney, Carnay	Grattan	Maccurdy, McCurdy
Cavan, Cavanaugh,	Hagan	MacCutcheon
Cavanagh	Hanlon	MacDermotts
Cluny	Healy	MacDonoughs
Conolly	Hogan	MacElligott
Conway	Horrigan	MacGarry; Garry, Gary
Corcoran	Innis	MacGeoghegan; Mac-
Coughlin	Ireland	Geogan
Coyle	Kane, Kayne, Kain	MacGuire; Maguire
Cronan, Cronyn	Keefe	MacHugh
Cronohan	Keelan	MacKinley
Daly, Daley	Keeley	MacNeill; Neill, Neal
Darcy, Darcie, Darcey	Keith	MacOileverius
Dempsey	Keller	M'Rorey
Dermott	Kennedy	M'Shuttle
Derry	Kern	Maginn, Maginnis
Desmond	Kerr	Mahaffey
Devin	Kilpatrick	Mahone, Mahony
Devlin	Kinnard	Maryn
Dogherty, Doherty	Kyan	Mathew
Doolan	Lavery	Mayo
Dooley	Lawless	Meagher
Dowden	Leary	Moor, Moore
Duffy	Lever	Mulholland, Mulhullon

Mulready	O'Kevan	Rooney
Murray	O'Mahoney, O'Mahony	Rowan, Rowe
Nolan	O'Malley; Malley	Ryan
O'Brien; Bryant, Bryan,	O'Malloys; Malloy	Scully
Brian, Brien	O'Melaghlain	Shanahan
O'Callaghan; Callahan	O'More; Moore	Shannon
O'Casey; Casey	O'Neal, O'Nales, O'Neill;	Shea
O'Clery; Clery	Neil, Neal	Sheridan
O'Connor; O'Conor,	Oran	Skelly
Conner, Connor	O'Reilly; Riley	Sloan
O'Donnell	O'Shaughnessy	Strahan
O'Donoghue; Donahue	Ouseley	Stranahan
O'Donovan	Peate	Sullivan
O'Dwyer; Dwyer	Phelan	Sweeney
O'Faolain, O'Fallon; Fal-	Quan	Teague
lon	Queron	Thomond
O'Gara	Quill	Tierney
O'Geoghegans; Geogan	Quillan	Tighe
O'Grady; Grady, Gradey	Quinn	Tully
O'Halloran; Halloran	Rafferty	Tynan
O'Hart; Hart	Riddock	Wolfe
O'Houlighan	Riordan	
O'Hynes, O'Hines; Hines	Ronan	

Non-Celtic Irish Names

Many of these date from the first Norman invasions, or from the earlier Danish, or from overseas traders.

Doyle: of Norse origin
Fitzgerald: of Norman origin, as any Fitz
MacAulliffe: of Norse origin
MacIvors: of Norse origin
MacManus, McManus: of Norse origin

MacRanald: of Norse origin
MacSorley, M'Sorley: of Norse origin
Portingal: Portuguese
O'Rourke, O'Rorke; Rourke, Roarke, Rorke: of Norse origin

WELSH

Up through the 19th century at least, the Welsh were preserving the patronymic form, X ap-Y, and many do to this day. Though family names had been generally adopted by the 18th century, Thomas Jones' full name would be Thomas ap Gwyllim Jones, and his son would be Roger ap Thomas Jones. This is one way to make a lone Welshman stand out in your story.

According to Bardsley, a full 95 percent of Welsh family names derive from patronymics; "there is scarcely a trade name, only a few nicknames, no official surnames that I know of, just a sprinkling of local [place] surnames..." In addition, rather than using ap-William, the patronymic was frequently Anglicized as Williamson or Williams, making distinctively Welsh surnames rare.

Many of the "family names" started out as personal names *for men*, and can still be used so. The modern Welsh are as fond of saint-names and using family names as personal names as most of the British Isles.

Pronunciation

The Welsh double-L is nothing like the Hispanic double-L. The Welsh use it for a sound like an unvoiced L: tongue in that position, breath out hard to make a sound. This was often corrupted into FL or BL, so that Lloyd became Floyd, or Llud turned into Blud, later Blood.

Another signal that a name may be Welsh is the RH, which is a regular R softened by not quite bringing the lips together, and aspirating, blowing out, while saying it.

W is the U in "tune." The I is always short as in "hit," the long I as in "machine" represented by a Y. That's how Y as a vowel got into English. The common diphthong WY comes out "we" when you tighten the "oo-ee" into a single sound.

FEMALE NAMES

Aderyn
Adwyn
Aelwen
Aerona
Alys=Alice
Aneira
Angharad
Annwan, Angwen, Anwen
Anwyl
Arddun
Arianwen
Avonwy
Awel
Aylwen
Bedelia
Blanchefleur
Blodeyn, Blodyn
Blodwen
Brangwaine
Branwen
Bronwen, Bronwyn

Bryn, Brynn
Caron, Carrone
Caryl, Cary, Carrie, Carys
Catrin=Catherine;
   Catriona
Ceinwen
Ceri — from Caron;
   Cerri, Cerrie, Cerys
Cordelia, Corry, Delia
Delwyn, Delwin
Delyth
Derrine — from Deron
Eifiona — place-name
Eira
Eiralys, Eirlys
Eirian
Eirwen, Eirwyn
Elin
Eluned, Eiluned
Elvis
Elwy

Elwyn, Elwin, Elwina
Enid
Eryl
Essyllt=Isolde
Eurwen
Gladys=Claudia; Gwl-
   adys
Glenda
Glenys, Glenis
Glynis, Glyness, Glinys
Goewyn, Goewin
Gwen, Vanora
Gwendolyn, Gwen
Gwendydd, Gwenda
Gweneal
Gwenivere, Guinevere
Gwenllian
Gwennog
Gwennol
Gwynedd
Hafwen

Heulwen
Iestina=Justina
Iola — fem. Iorweth
Jestina=Justina
Joane
Llawela — fem. Llewellyn
Llinos
Lynwen
Mabyn
Mair=Mary; Mairwen
Meinwen
Meirionfa — place-name
Meirionwen — place-

name
Modwen, Modwenna
Morfydd, Morfudd,
   Morvydd
Morwenna
Myfanwy, Myfannwy
Nerys — lord, but women
   use it now
Nest, Nesta=Agnes
Olwen
Owena — fem. Owen
Rhian
Rhiannon — Goddess

name
Rhonda — a place-name
Rhonwen, Ronwen
Sian — John
Sulwen
Tegan, Tegen, Tegwen
Valma
Venetia
Wallis
Winifred, Winefride
Winne
Yseulte, Isolde

MALE NAMES

Alexander
Alun
Aneurin
Arthur
Bevan — surname
Bleddian, Bleddyn, Ble-
   dyn
Brynmor
Cade, Cadel
Cai, Caio, Caius
Caradwg, Caradog
Carr
Catesby — corrupted to
   Gatsby
Caw
Ceredig, Ceretic
Cole
Conwy
Cystennin=Constantine
Dafydd=David; Taffy,
   Daffy, Daffyd; very
   popular
Dee, Du
Deiniol
Dewi, Dewey
Drew
Dylan, Dillon, Dillan,
   Dilwyn
Dynand
Eddow
Edmwnd=Edmund
Eignion, Ennion, Eynon,
   Eygneun

Eilwyn, Elwin
Elian
Ellis
Emrys=Ambrose
Enan
Ermin
Errol
Evan, Ev — popular
Galvin
Gawain, Gavin, Gowan
Geraint
Gerwyn
Gethin
Glyn
Griffith
Guillym=William;
   Gwilym
Guinier
Gwenogvryn
Gwylfai
Gwyn, Gwynne, Gwynn
Gwynfor
Haydn
Hew, Huw=Hugh
Howel, Hywel, Howell
Iago
Idris
Idwal
Iestin=Justin, also used;
   Iestyn
Ieuan=John, also used
Ifor=Ivor
Inir

Iolo
Iorwen
Iorweth
Irfon
Isan
Ithel, Ithell
Jevan
Jone
Kay
Kenewrec
Kenn
Llewellyn, Lewlyn, Lewe-
   lyn
Lloyd
Llud
Llydewig — Celtic, not
   from German
Mabon
Maddox, Madoc
Maldwyn
Math
Meredith
Merion
Meurig
Morgan
Morven, Morvin, Merfin,
   Morfydd
Mostyn
Myfanwy
Newlin
Nye
Owen, Ewan, Ewen,
   Owein, Owain

Padarn
Penrod
Penwyn
Peredur
Rhett
Rhodri
Rhys, Rys
Richard
Rwrith [ROO-rith]

Siarl
Sion
Sulwyn
Taliesin
Tomos=Thomas
Trefor, Trevor
Tristan, also Tris
Tristram, Tris
Tudor, Tuddor, Tudir=

Theodore
Ultan
Urien
Wmffre=Humphrey
    [OOMF-freh]
Yestin
Yevan

FAMILY NAMES

Abadam — ap-Adam
Abethell — ab-Ithell
Ahern
Annan
Anwell
Anyon
Badams — ap-Adam
Bayly
Baynham — ap-Eignion/
    Ennion
Beddoe, Beddoes, Bed-
    dow, Beddows,
    Bedow — ap-Eddow
Bedward, Beddard —
    ab-Edward
Bellion — ap-Enion
Bellis, Bellis, Bellys, Bell-
    yse — ap-Ellis
Benyon, Bennion, Bin-
    yon — ap-Enyon
Bethall, Bethell, Bithell,
    Bythell — ap-Ithell
Bevan, Bevans — ap-Evan
Beynon, Baynon —
    ap-Eynon
Blethyn
Blevin, Bliven
Blood, Blud — ap-Llud
Bloyd — ap-Lloyd
Bowen — ap-Owen
Brangwyn
Bryce
Bryn
Caddock
Cade
Cadell
Cadfael

Cadogan
Cador
Cadwallader
Cardiff
Carew, Carey
Caron, Carron, Caronne
Carr
Carson — Carr's son
Caswall
Cerwyn
Coed, Coad, Coade
Craddock
Darren, Deron
Davids
Deverell
Dewey
Drew
Dugmore
Easton
Ellis
Ensor
Errol, Erryl
Evan, Evans
Ewan, Ewen
Flood, Flud
Floyd
Garnock
Glanmor
Glendower
Glyn, Glen, Glenn,
    Glynis, Glyness
Goch
Goscombe
Gower
Griffith, Griffin, Gryffith,
    Gryffin, Gryff, Gruffydd
Gwern

Gwyn, Gwynne, Guinne
Gwyneth
Haines
Heilyn
Howell, Howel, Hywel
Hugh, Hughes — son of
    Hugh
Ison, Isans, Izon, Izen —
    son of Isan
John
Jones — son of John
Kent
Kimball
Llewellyn
Lloyd, Loyd, Lloyds
Llyn, Lyn, Linn, Lynne
Maddox, Maddock,
    Maddoch, Madox
Map
Meredith
Methuen
Morgan, de Morgan
Nash
Newlin, Newlyn
Nye
Owen, Owens, Owain
Parry — ap-Harry
Peddowe — ap-Eddow
Penrhyn
Pinnion, Pinyon —
    ap-Enion
Powell — ap-Howell
Powelson
Powys
Prys
Radclyffe
Reece, Rhys, Reese, Rice

Renfrew	martin	Trevor, Trefor
Renno	Trahern, Trahurn, Trah-	Tudor
Rhondda	erne	Tudwal
Romney	Tremaine, Tremayne,	Vaughn
Sayers, Sayres	Tremane	Welsh, Welch
Tarrant, Tarent	Trevelyan, Trevelian	Wren, Ren
Throckmorton, Throg-	Trevithick	

CORNISH

Family names are found in Cornwall at least as early as rolls collected in 1327, probably since the early Middle Ages. An old rhyme runs:

By Ros-, Car-, Lan-, Tre-, Pol-, and Pen-
Ye may know most Cornishmen

Tre-, Pol-, and Pen- are the most popular out of those six. All are from eke-names based on where someone dwelt.

Car — fort or camp, also Ker-
Tre — homestead
Pol — pool
Pen — head or end
Ros — heath or promontory
Lan — enclosure
Bos — dwelling

Other family names developed from animal nicknames, occupations, and three forms of patronymic: Map-, the "son of" prefix; the father's name with the possessive S; and a diminutive of the father's name. If you would like to check the change over time, there are rolls for 1523, and from 1600 to 1812.

Cornwall was one of the corners of Britain where the Britons held out against Saxon and Norman influence. The Cornish language developed names off the same Celtic roots as the others, so there is independent overlap. If you name a character Kelly, though, even most of your Cornish readers will think "Irish." So those listed below are those that don't overlap, but are distinctly Cornish. Also omitted are all those with known Huguenot, Irish, Welsh, Saxon, etc., roots, even if they have been in Cornwall 400 or 1,000 years.

If you are thinking of stepping back to very early Cornwall, and using these as personal names, remember to check these as Celtic words, not Saxon. The name Blyth does not mean "happy"; it means "wolf." Best is not a superlative, but "moss," though certainly your readers will not know this unless you tell them. Even occupational names are tricky, as Dyer is the Cornish for a thatcher, not a cloth-colorer.

Nonetheless, by the 12th century, most Cornish speakers were using Norman personal names, especially the Big Four, William, Ralph, Richard, and John. Indeed, the last was borne by a quarter of all Cornishmen. The few known Celtic-rooted names were re-introductions brought over from Brittany with the Normans, like Ives, Sampson, and Alan.

The Cornish personal names below are suitable for use when the Britons are hassling with the English, or for contemporary Cornish, whose parents have revived the name in the modern quest for novelty and ethnicity. The Cornish versions of foreign names are usable up through at least the 19th century, though they became rarer after the 16th century.

One notable contrast of Cornish with English or Norman name choices: a penchant for Biblical names like Joseph and David, which are virtually unknown among the others until the Reformation.

FEMALE NAMES

Arghans, Arranz
Athwenna
Banallen
Barenwyn
Bennath
Berlewen
Beryan
Blejan
Blejennyk
Blejwyn
Bora, Borra
Bronnen
Bryluen
Caja
Cattran=Catherine
Columba
Conwenna
Crewenna
Cryda, Creeda
Delen, Dellen
Delennyk
Derowen
Derwa
Dywana
Ebrel
Elerghy
Elestren
Elowen
Endelyon
Enor
Eppow — dim. of Elizabeth

Esyld, Eseld — original
    form of Isolde/Ysolt
Eva=Eve
Ewa, Ewe
Feoca
Fyna, Feena
Glander
Glanna
Gonnetta — in 14th c.
Gwaynten
Gwenep
Gwenfrewi, Jenifry, Jene-
    fred, Jenifer — origi-
    nated here!
Gweniver
Gwennol
Gwiryon
Gwynder
Hebasca
Hedra
Heenah=Hannah
Jenna, Jedna, Jana=Jane
Jowna, Jowanet — dim.
    Joan
Kayna, Keyna, Keyn
Kekezza
Kelynen
Kensa
Kerensa, Kerenza
Keresen, Kerezen
Keresyk, Kerezik

Kerra
Kew, Kewa
Kewera, Keweraz
Lasek, Ladoc
Lowena, Lowenna
Lowenek
Mabena, Mabyn
Marya, Mareea=Mary
Melder
Meliora, Melyor, Mellear
Melwyn
Melyonen
Meraud, Merouda
Metheven
Morenwyn
Morgelyn
Morvoren
Morwenna
Morwennol
Nessa
Newlyna, Newlyn
Non, Nonna
Pasca, Pascatte, Pasces,
    Pascowes — Easter
Peswere, Pezwera
Redigan=Radagund
Richow — fem. Richard
Rosen, Rozen
Rosenwyn
Sidwell, Sativola
Sowena, Sowenna

Splanna
Steren, Sterennyk
Talwyn
Tamsyn — Thomasina
Tecca
Tegen

Tregereth
Tressa
Trueth
Ughella, Ewella
Vorva
Weneppa

Wenn, Wenna
Whecca
Whegyn
Ygerna, Igerna
Yselka
Zennor, Senara

Male Names

"-sek" diminutive endings are Middle Cornish, "-oc/-ok" Old Cornish

Alun, Alan
Angawd
Arthek, Arthyen, Arthien
Austell
Benesek, Bennet, Benedict
Boconnoc
Branoc, Branek
Branwalather
Brengy
Bryok, Breok
Budic
Buryan
Byrsige
Cadan, Cadon
Cadreth
Cadwur
Carasek, Caradok
Casek, Cadok
Caswal
Casworon
Caswyn
Cathno, Cathnow, Cathnoe
Cenue
Clemo, Clemow, Clemowwe — dim. of Clement
Clesek
Colyn=Nicholas
Corentyn
Crantok
Custentin, Costentyn= Constantine
Cyfel, Cyvel
Daoc
Daveth, Daddow, David, Dewi
De, Dey

Dewin
Dilly, Dili
Doniert, Donyerth, Donyarth
Drestan — original form of Tristan
Dungarth
Dynham
Elec
Eleder
Elli
Enoder
Enodok, Gwenedok, Wenedoc
Enyon
Erbyn
Eres
Ervan
Eval
Evan=John
Feok
Fryek, Fryok
Geach
Gerens=Gerent, or Geraint
Germo, Germow, Germoe
Gilgis
Glewas, Glewya
Gordhyans — honor
Gorheder
Gorneves
Goron
Gorthelyk
Gourgy
Gwendern
Gweri
Gwithyen
Gworyen

Gwydel
Gwynek, Gwyno, Gwynow, Gwynoe
Gwynhelek
Gwynwallo, Gwynwallow, Gwynwalloe
Gwystyl
Gwythenek, Wethinoc
Gyfel
Hedrek, Hedrok
Henna, Hendra — dim. of Henry
Hicca — short for Richard
Hocken — dim. Henry
Howel, Howell
Hyviu
Iahan, Jowan=John
Iunwith
Jacca, Jaco, Jacka=Jack
Jago=James
Jamma — dim. James
Jelbart, Jelbert — Gilbert
Jory — dim. George
Kenal
Kenbres
Kendern
Kengar
Kenhebres
Kenow
Kenver
Kenwal
Kenwyn, Kenwythen
Kevern
Kitto, Kittow, Kittoe — dim. of Christopher
Lalluwy, Lallow, Lallo, Lalloe
Leven

Lewyth
Litho
Lowthas
Luk — Luke
Lywci
Maban
Mael
Malscos
Margh=Mark
Massen
Mawgan, Malgen
Mayek, Mayok
Merin
Meryasek, Meriasek
Milian, Milyan
Milyek, Milyoc
Mor
Mychal, Myghal=
  Michael
Nadelek, Nadelack=
  Noel
Nectan
Nerth
Nicca — dim. of Nicholas
Oby — dim. of Osbert
Omffra, Omfra=

Humphrey
Padern
Pascoe, Pascow
Pawley, Pawle, Paulle=
  Paul
Pawlyn=Paul
Peder=Peter
Pedrek, Petherek, Pether-
  ick, Peddrick
Pencast=Pentecost
Peran
Petroc, Petrok — dim.
  Petherick
Pilcok
Rawe, Raw, Row,
  Rowe=Ralph or
  Radulphus
Rewan, Rumon
Ryel, Ryol
Ros
Rumun, Ruan
Ryual
Sadorn=Saturn, Satur-
  day
Salac
Santo, Sanders, Saun-

ders — Alexander
Seder
Selevan=Solomon
Sithny
Stephen — from 5th c.
Talan
Talek
Teudar, Tewdar
Tudwal, Tudy
Udy, Eda — common
  through 16th c.
Uny, Ewny
Ustoc
Uther —16th and 17th c.
Uthno
Vark=Mark
Vyvyan
Welet
Wella=William
Weryn
Worec, Worek
Yestin=Justus
Yllogan, Illogan
Ythgans
Ythno, Uthno

EKE-NAMES FOR EARLY PERIODS

Byhan — little
Chok — jackdaw, chat-
  terer
Cough — red
Du — black, dark
an Dyer — the thatcher
an Elergh — the swan

Galla — the Gaul
an Gell — the tawny
an Gof— the smith
an Gravyor — the carver,
  the sculptor
an Gref— the strong one
an Gwyn — the fair, the

white
an Hyr — the tall, the
  long
Saws — Saxon
Tek — fair, beautiful
an Ver — the short
whegoll — dearest

FAMILY NAMES

Allett
Ancell, Ansell
Andain, Andean, Endean
Andrewartha, Trewartha
Angear
Angilley
Angrave
Annan, Anning
Annear

Anstice, Anstiss, Enstice
Argall
Arscott
Bain, Bane, Bean
Baragwanath
Barnicoat, Barnecutt
Bedell, Bodell, Beadell,
  Biddle
Behenna

Beith
Benallack, Bonallack
Beney, Binney, Bunney,
  Bonney, Penney
Bennetto
Bersey
Berty, Burthy, Berth
Bescoby
Beskeen

Beswarick, Beswetherick
Bew, Bewes, Buse
Bice
Biddick
Blamey
Boase, Bose
Boden, Boaden
Bodiella
Bodinnar, Berdinnar
Bolitho
Bone
Bonython
Borlase, Burlase
Bosanko, Bosanketh,
  Bosanquet
Bosence
Bosustow, Bosisto
Botterell, Bottrell, Botral
Boundy
Bray
Britton, Britten, Briddon
Buzza, Buzzacott
Caddy
Calf, Calff
Carah, Cara
Carbines
Carbis
Cardell
Cardew
Cardy, Carty, Carthy
Carew
Carey
Cargeeg, Carkeek
Carkeet
Carloss
Carnall, Carnell
Carnsew
Carrick, Carrivick
Carveth
Casley, Causley
Cavell, Cavill
Challis, Callis, Collis
Charke
Chegwidden, Chegwin,
  Chegwyn
Chellew
Chenhall, Chenhalls
Chenoweth, Chynoweth
Chivell
Clegg
Clemmow, Clemo,

Climo, Clymo
Clinnick
Cloke, Clook
Clymas
Coath
Colenso
Colley, Collie, Colly,
  Colle
Colliver
Combellack
Congdon
Connock, Cunnack,
  Cunnick
Coombe, Coombes
Corin
Cossentine
Cottell, Cotell, Cottle
Cowls, Coules, Coulls
Craddock, Cradick
Crago, Craggs, Craig
Crebo, Creba
Creek
Croggan
Crowgey
Cundy
Curgenven
Curnow
Curtis, Courtis, Courtice,
  Corteys, Courties
Daddow
Denham, Dynham, Din-
  ham
Derry
Deveril, Deveral
Dew
Dilly
Dinner, Denner
Dobell, Doble
Dow, Dower
Dowling, Dowlyn
Drew
Dustow
Ead, Eade, Ede
Eathorne
Edyvean, Eddyvean
Ellacott, Ellicoat, Elcoat
Ellis
Ennis, Enys
Ennor
Eva, Evea
Faull

Found
Frayne
Freethy
Gale, Gall, Galley
Geach
Geake
Gerrans
Gew
Gillis
Glinn, Glynn
Gloyn, Gloyne
Gluyas
Godden, Gooden
Golley, Gollie
Gool, Gole
Goss
Govett
Gribbin, Gribben, Gripe
Gribble
Grylls, Grills
Gummow, Gummoe
Gwennap
Gwinnel
Hain, Hayne, Haines,
  Heynes
Hammill
Hannaford, Hannafore
Hannah, Hennah
Heale, Heal
Hellyer
Hender, Hendra
Hobba, Hobby
Hollow
Hosken, Hosking, Hos-
  kins
Huddy
Huthnance
Inch, Innes, Innis
Isbell
Ive, Ivey, Ivy
Jelbart, Jelbert
Jewell, Jewells
Joll, Jolliffe, Juleff, Jolly
Julian, Julyan
Keast, Keats
Keen, Keane
Keigwin
Kelynack
Kempthorne
Kersey
Kestle, Kestell, Kessell

Key
Kinber
Kinver
Kitto, Kittow
Kliskey
Knuckey
Lambourne
Lander, Launder, Ladner
Landeryou, Lenderyou
Lanfear
Lavin
Lawry, Lawrey, Lewry, Lowry, Lory
Leddra
Legassick
Legg, Leggo
Lethlean, Lelean
Lewarne, Lewin
Liddicoat
Lock, Locke
Lower, Lawer
Loze
Lukey, Lukeys
Luzmoor, Luzmore
Mabin, Mabane
Maddern, Madron
Maile, Male
Mannel, Manuel
Menadue
Menhenick, Menhinick, Menhenitt
Messa, Messer
Morcom, Morcomb, Morcum
Mounter
Mylor
Nancarrow
Nankervis
Nankivell, Nancekivell
Newth
Noall, Nowell, Noel
Noon
Oates, Oatey
Odgers
Olver, Olverman
Opie
Pascoe
Pellow, Pellew
Penaluna
Pendarves, Pendarvis
Penellum

Penglaze
Penhallow
Penprase, Penpraze
Penrice
Pentreath
Penwarden, Penwarne
Permewan
Perrow
Pezzack
Pinnick, Pinnock, Pennock
Polglaze
Polmear, Pelmear
Polwin
Praed
Prose, Prouse
Quick
Quintrell
Rescorla, Roscorla, Scholler
Restarick
Rodda
Roscarrock
Rosemayle
Rosemergy, Rosemurgy
Rosevear
Rosewarne
Rouse, Rowse, Rows
Ryall
Sallow, Sallis, Sallows
Sanders, Sauners
Scaddan
Scoble, Scobel
Scrase
Soady, Sawdey
Spargo
Spettigue
Talling, Tallon
Taskis
Thake
Thow
Tinney
Tossell
Trathen
Trebell
Tredrea, Tredray
Treffry
Treganowan
Tregea, Tregay
Tregellas, Tregelles
Tregenza

Treglown, Tregloan
Trehane
Trelease
Trembath, Tenbath, Trembeth
Tremearne
Tremenheere
Trenance
Trengove
Trenouth, Trenoweth
Trepress
Tresawne, Trezona
Trestain
Trethewey
Trevain, Trevains
Trevarth, Trevarthen, Trevarton, Treverton
Trevellick
Trevenen
Trevivian
Trew, True
Treweek
Trewhella
Treworgie
Trinick, Trinnick
Trounson
Trythall
Tyack
Tyzzer
Udy
Uren
Ustick
Varcoe, Vercoe, Varker
Vear
Vellacott
Vellanoweth
Venton
Vickery
Vinson
Vosper
Voss, Vos, Vose
Warne, Wearne
Weary, Wherry, Werry
Werring, Wearing, Werren
Wevel, Wivell
Widdon
Windle, Wintle
Withiel
Worden
Youren

FRENCH

The French feminine of a masculine name does not always end in "-ette" or "-ine." Sometimes a name is feminized simply by adding an E. But some male names end in E or double-E. You just have to know — and some baby-name books are not always careful on this. See:

Male	*Female*	*Male*	*Female*
René	Renée	Louis	Louise
Désire	Désirée	Germain	Germaine
Yvon	Yvonne	Yves	Yvette
Antoine	Antoinette	Charles	Charlotte
Clément	Clémentine, sometimes Clémence	Honoré	Honorine, sometimes Honorée

The French do not always regender saints' names. While other countries may give a boy a secondary name of Maria or Anita, France is notable for using them as *first* names for boys, and for using some *male* saints' names unisex. If you want to put your son or daughter under the protection of Saint Anne and Saint Steven, you can name him or her Anne Étienne. This dates back to the Middle Ages, when there were queens named Claude, and it has not died out yet.

So there can be easy confusions with Étienne Marie, Marguerite Richard, and the like. This may be why the French are so punctilious about including gender titles, whether "monsieur," "mademoiselle," or "madame." "Ms." has no equivalent; the Academy will fight it to the death, as they did "computer" (it is an "ordinateur").

So you may not be able to immediately give the sex of Lucie Simplice Camille Benoît Desmoulins without these titles.

The French are also distinctive for hyphenated first names. Anne-Marie and Jean-Marie are the most popular for women and men respectively.

The French follow standard Catholic nomenclature for the most part, giving a child approved saints' names at its Christening, followed by the father's family name. Often the particular names would match those of its godparents. It was not uncommon to have two godmothers and two godfathers. Amongst the nobility, a child could have half a dozen, and not always two-by-two. This custom is reflected in all the fairytales where the little princess has lots of fairy godmothers. At confirmation you get to add the saint's name of your choice.

In the 17th century the French began using Gallicized versions of classical Greek and Roman names, as Neo-Classicism became ubiquitous. Even so, the French had long kept a fondness for Romanesque names like Diane down the centuries. Often, like Hippolyte, they were early saints' names.

The French also began using a lot of Romantic names, too, as the century wore on. The English were usually a generation behind this fashion in girls' names, and rarely used such fancifulness for boys.

Also, do not be afraid to use an occasional German or Dutch or Spanish personal name — or family name. France has long been a magnet to foreigners. The centuries of the Irish Brigade left Frenchmen named Patrice de McMahon, too.

Titles of Nobility

Masculine	Feminine	English Equivalent
roi	reine	king, queen
dauphin	dauphine	French crown prince
prince	princesse	prince, princess
principicule		princeling
duc	duchesse	duke, duchess
marquis	marquise	marquis, marchioness
comte	comtesse	count, countess
vicomte	vicomtesse	viscount, viscountess
baron	baronne	baron, baroness
baronnet		baronet

A sieur holds a seigneury, which, with the title "sieur de [place-name]" is inherited by the eldest son. A great many of these were created in the New World in what is now Canada.

Pronunciation

It has seemed to many people who are not French that the language insists on pronouncing words differently from the way they are spelled. "Th" is the same as "t." Final sounds can change according to the next word out of your mouth. Final "-eaux" is sometimes "-oh" and sometimes "-eurz." Do not guess, if you want to rhyme properly: check a dictionary *and* a language tape. French is a spoken language more than it is a written one.

Because of this lack of mechanical regularity, I am including pronunciation in brackets on many names. Too often, names have crossed the water, and the way we pronounce them makes the French cringe. "Agnes" is the very pretty AH-nyes, not our harsh AG-ness. "Richard" is ree-SHARD, not RIH-churd.

Most vowels sound differently depending on, not only surrounding letters, but diacritical marks that do not appear on many word-processors and printers, notably the circumflex and the *accent grave* (grahv, not graiv). You can fake a final *accent ague* with a following apostrophe. Most troubling is the lack of the cedilla, which hangs under a C to tell you it is soft, as in François. If the lack of diacriticals bothers you, and your printer does not produce them, use the names that do not require them.

Unaccented final E is silent, as in English. Any vowel followed by an N is nasalized; there is no English equivalent. The sound is similar, it just comes out the nose instead of the mouth. Most of the vowels do not match the nearest English equivalent, anyway, which is why one has to work to acquire a decent accent, and why French speakers of English have just as much trouble shedding their accents.

Creole French sounds very different from the original, like the equivalent of pidgin English. The accent differences within France are not as strong as they were, but you can still tell a Norman from a southerner. For example, St. Martin is normally [SA- mahr-TAH-], but in Provence it is [SANG mahr-TANG].

GENERAL PRONUNCIATION

A — A in pasta
Ç — cydilla C, as S
CH — CH in machine
E — usually E in pen
É — E in hey; E with accent ague
È — E with accent grave; E in pen
Ê — E with circumflex; E in pen
EAU — O in flow
EI — A in mane
G — hard G in gun, except before E and I, when it is J-sound
GN — NY

H — silent
I — I in machine
J — Z in azure
O — O in hope
Ô — O with circumflex; now as O in hope, but not originally
OI — WA
QU — K in key
TH — T in tune
U — U in tune
˜ — nasal sound

Doubled consonants are hit a little harder and held a little longer.

Final S, T, Z, N, or R are silent when they immediately follow a vowel; Paris — [pah-RI]; Genet — [zhe-NAY]; tenez or tener — [teh-NAY].

FEMALE NAMES

* used without change for boys, too

Abrialle
*Adelaide, Adèle, Adelina
Adorée [ah-doh-RAY]
Adrienne
Agathe [ah-GAHT]
Agnes [AH-nyes]
Aimée [ay-MAY]
Albertine
Alette, Aletta
Alexandrine

Alice [AH-lees]
Alphonsine
Amandine [AH-ma--DEEN]
Amédée [ah-may-DAY]
Amélie [AH-may-lee]
Amourette
Anastasie [AH-nah-STAH-zee]
Andrée [ahn--DRAY] — rare
Andromède (Andromeda) [AHN-dro-MED]

Angèle
Angeline [an-zheh-LEEN],
Angélique [an-zhe-LEEK]
*Anne [AHNN]; Annette [ahn-NETT]; Nanette, Nina, Ninetta, Ninette, Nana
Antoinette [AHN-twah-NETT], Toinon [twa-NO~] (dim.), Antonie [AHN-to-NEE]
Arabelle
Arette
Ariane [AH-ree-AHN]
Armine [ar-MEEN]
Aubine
Augustine
Aurélie
Aurore [o-ROAR]
Bathilde [bah-TEELD]
Béatrice [BEY-ah-TREES]
Benoîte [ben-o-EET]
Bérénice [BAY-ray-NEES]
Bergette [ber-ZHETTE]
Bernadette, Bernadine
Bernarde, Bernadette
Berthe [BEHR-teh]
Berthilde [behr-TEELD]
Blaisotte [blay-SOHTT]
Brigide [bree-ZHEED], Brigitta, Brigitte
Calandre
Calanthe
Candide, Candida
Cassandre
Catant [kah-TA-T, nasal A]
*Catherine [KA-ter-EEN]
Cécile, Célie [say-SEEL]
*Céleste, Célestine
Célie [say-LEE], Céline
Cerise [seh-REES]
Césarine [say-zah-REEN]
Charlotte, Charlotta [shar-LOT, shar-LOT-ah]
*Claire, Clairette, Clarette, Clarisse
Claudette, Claudelle, Claudine [klow-DETT, -DELL, -DEEN]
Cléanthe [klay-AHNTH]
Clélie [klay-LEE]
Clémence [klay-MAHNS]
Clémentine [KLAY-mahn-TEEN]
Cléopatre [klay-oh-PAH-tr]
Clotilde [kloh-TEELD]

Colette, Collette, Coletta [ko-LETT, -LET-ta]
Colombe, Coulombe [koh-LOWM]
Constantine
Coralie [KO-rah-LEE]
Cordélie
Corinne [ko-REEN]
Cornélie
Crescence [kreh-SAH-NS]
Damienne [DAH-mee-EHN]
Danielle, Daniella [dahn-YELL, YEL-la]
Delphine [del-FEEN]
Denise [deh-NEES]
Diane [dee-AHN]
Doralice [DOR-ah-LEES]
Dorette [dor-ET]
Dorothée [DO-ro-TAY]
*Éléonore [EH-leh-o-NOR]
*Élisabeth; Élise [ay-LEES], Elisa, Lisette, Babette
Eloise
Emmanuelle
Ernestine
Estelle
Eugénie [YEW-zhe-NEE]
*Eulalie [YEW-lah-LEE]
Euphémie [YEW-fay-MEE]
Evaine [eh-VAYN]
Faustine [fow-STEEN]
Félicitée, sometimes Félicité
Fernande [fehr-NAH-D]
Flavère [flah-VAYR], Flavie [flah-VEE]
Fleur [FLUR], Fleurette
Flore [FLOOR], Flora
Florence [floh-RAHNS]
Fortunée [fohr-tu-NAY]
Françoise [frah~-SWAHZ], Francette, Francesca
Frédérique
Gabrielle
Genève [zhe-NEHV]
Geneviève [ZHEH~-vee-EHV]
Georgette [zhohr-ZHEHT]
Georgienne, Georgine
Géraldine
Germaine [zher-MAYN]
Gertrude [gayr-TROOD]
Gervaise [zher-VAYZ]
Ginette [zhee-NET]

Giselle, Gisele [zhee-ZELL]
Grazielle [GRAH-zee-EL]
Griselda [gree-SEHL-dah] — rare
Guillelmine, Guillemette [gee-yel-
   MEEN, hard G]
Hedvige [hehd-VEEG] — very rare
Hélène [ay-LEHN]
Héloise [ay-lo-IZ]
Henriette [ON-ree-ET]
Hippolyte — rare
Honorée [on-or-AY]
Honorine [ON-or-EEN],
Hortense [or-TE-NZ] — very Imperial
Ide [EED]
Irène [ee-RAYN]
Isabeau [EE-sa-BO]
Jaqueline [ZHA-keh-LEEN], Vanessa
Jeanne [ZHOHN], Jeannette [zhohn-
   NET],
Joëlle [zho-EL] — very modern
Joie [ZHWA]
Josephe [zho-SEF], Josèphe
Josephine [ZHO-se-FEEN], Fifi,
   Fifine
Josette [zho-ZET]
Judithe [zhu-DEETH], Judith
Julie [zhu-LEE], Juliette, Julietta
   [ZHU-lee-ET, -ET-tah]
Julienne [zhu-lee-EN]
Justine [zhu-STEEN]
Laure [LAWR], Laurette [lawr-ET],
   Lauriane
Léetice, Letizia
Léonie [LAY-o-NEE]
Lili
Lis [LEE]
Lissette, Lisette [lee-SET], Lissie
Lolotte [lo-LOT]
Loretta
Louise — very popular, Louisa; Loulou
Lourdes — only if born after 1860
Lucette, Lucie [lu-SET, lu-SEE]
Lucienne
Lucile
Lucrèce [lu-KRES]
Lydie [lih-DEE]
Lynette [lin-ET]
Mabelle [mah-BEHL]
Madeleine, Madelaine, Madelon
Manette, Manon (dim.)
Marcelle, Marcella, Marceline

Marcie
*Margaret
Marguerite [MAR-gyur-EET], Mar-
   got
Marianne [mah-ree-AHN]
*Marie, Manette, Manon, Marielle,
   Maryse, Mariette, Marietta Marthe
   [MAR-teh] — popular w/commoners
Martine [mar-TEEN]
Matilde, Mathilde [mah-TEELD]
Mavis [mah-VEES]
Michelle [mee-SHELL]
Mignot [mee-NYOH]
Modestine
Monique [moh-NEEK]
Nadia
Nadine [nah-DEEN]
Napoléonette — very rare
Nathalie [NAH-tah-LEE]
Nathanielle [na-TAHN-ee-EL]
Nicolette, Nicoletta
Noëlle
Octavie [OHK-tah-VEE]; Octavia
   [ohk-TAH-vee-ah] — rarer
Odelette
Odette
Odile [oh-DEEL]
Olive [oh-LEEV]
Olivia [oh-LEEV-ee-ah]
Olympe [oh-LEEMP]
Ophélie
Pascale [pah-SKAHL]
Paulette, Pauline, Paule
Perrine
Petronelle [peh-troh-NEHL]; Pétro-
   nille [pay-troh-NEEL]
Phèdre [FAY-dreh]
Pierrette [pyair-ETTE] — rare
Questa [KEH-sta]
Quiterie [KEE-teh-REE]
Rachelle [rah-SHELL]
Raoule [rah-OOL]
Rébeque [ray-BECK]
Reine [RAYN], Reinette
Renée [reh-NAY]
Robine — rare
Rolandine
Romaine [ro-MAYN]
Rosalie
Rose
Rosemarie [ROZ-mah-REE]

Rosemonde
Rosette
Roxanne [rok-SAHN]
Sabine [sah-BEEN]
Salomé
Sapho
Sara — unusual
Sarotte [say-ROHT]
Sébastienne
Sérafine [say-rah-FEEN]
Sibylle
Sidonie [SEE-doh-NEE]
Silvaine [seel-VAYN]
Simone [see-MOAN], Simonette, Simonetta
Solange [so-LAHNZH]
Sophie
Soulle [SOOL], Souline
*Suzanne [su-ZANN], Suzette, Suzetta, Susanne

Sylvie, Silvie
Tenille
*Thérèse, Thereson (dim.)
Thomasine, Thomasina
Trinnette
Ursule [oor-SYOOL]
Valérie
Venise [veh-NEES]
Verenice
Vérone
Véronique [VAY-ro-NEEK]
Victoire [veek-TWAR],
Victorine [veek-tor-EEN]
Violette, Violetta
Virginie
Vivienne
Yolande [yo-LAHND], Yolanda
Yvette, Ivette [ee-VET]
Yvonne, Ivonne [ee-VOHN]
Zénobie [ZAY-noh-BEE]

MALE NAMES

* used without change for girls, too

Abel
Absalon
Adolphe
Adoré
Adrien [ay-dree-a~] — ends in nasal E
Aignan
Alain, Allain [ah-LAYN]
Alcandre
Alexandre [AH-leks-AHN-dreh]
*Alexis [ah-LEKS-ee]
Alfred
Alphonse
Aluin [ah-LWEEN]
Amable, Aimable
Ambroise [ahm-BRWAZ]
Amédée [AH-may-day] (Amadeus)
Amour — rare, but actually used
Anatole
Andoche [ahn-DOHSH] — very rare
André
Annibal [AHN-nee-bal] (Hannibal)
Anthelme
Antoine [ahn-TWAHN]
Antonin

Apollinaire
Aralt
Archaimbaud [ar-shaym-BOW], Archambault [ar-sham-BOWLT]
Aristide
Armand [ahr-MAHND]
Arnaut [ar-NO], Arnault, Arnauld, Arnoult, Arnould, Arnaud
Arsène [ar-SAYN]
Artamène
Artus
Athanase [ah-tah-NAHS]
Aubert [o-BEYR]
Aubin [o-BA~] — ends in nasal I
Audric [O-dreek]
*Auguste [oh-GOOST]
Augustin
Aurèle [o-REL], Aurelien
Baltasar
Baptiste
Barnabé [BAR-nah-BAY]
Barthélmy [BAR-tell-mee], Barthélemy [bar-TAY-leh-mee], Bartholomé [bar-toe-low-MAY]

Basile [ba-SEEL]
Bénigne
Benjamin [BEN-zha-MEEN]
Benoît [behn-o-EE], Benoîst [behn-o-EEST]
Bernard, Bernardin
Blaise [BLAYZ], Blaize; Blaisot [blay-SO]
Blancart [blah-KAHR]
*Camille [kah-MEEL]
Certain [sehr-TA~]
César [say-ZAR]
Charles [SHARL]; Charlot (dim.) [shar-LO]
Chrétien [kray-TYE~]
Christophe [kree-STOWF]
*Claude [CLOWD]
Clément [klay-MA~]
Cléomine [KLAY-oh-MEEN]
Cléophas — rare
Conrade
Constant
Constantin — rare
Damien [DAH-mee-e~, nasal E]
Daniel [dah-nyel]
Delacroix [deh-lah-KRWAH]
Demetre [deh-MEH-tr`] (Demetrius)
Denis, Denys [dah-NEE]
Deodat
Désire [day-ZEER]
Dieudonné [dyur-dohn-NAY] — unusual
Dione [dee-OWN]
Donatien
Edmond
Édouard [ay-dou-ARD]
Éleuthère [ay-lyu-TAYR] — rare
Élie — not popular
*Elisée [EH-lee-ZAY] — very rare
Elme — rare
Elzear — rare
Émery
Émile [eh-MEEL]
Emmanuel, Emanuel
Ernest [ehr-NEST]
Esprit [eh-SPREE] very rare
*Étienne [ay-tee-EN], Tiennot (dim.) [tyen-O]
Eugène [yoo-ZHEN]
Eustache [yu-STAHSH]
Évariste [eh-vah-REEST]

Félicité [fay-LEE-see-TAY]
Félix [fay-LEEKS]
Ferdinand
Firmin [feer-MI~]
Flavian, Flavien
Florentin
Fortuné [for-tu-NAY]
Francisque [frahn-SEESK]
François [frahn-SWAH]
Frédéric
Gabriel
Gaspard
Gaston [gah-STO~, nasal O]
Geofroy, Geoffroy, Geoffroi [zhe-FROY]
Georges [ZHOR-zh]
Gérard [zhay-RAHRD]
Géraud [zhay-ROAD]
Germain [zher-MA~, nasal A]
Gervais [zher-VAY]
Gilles [ZHEEL]
Godefroi [GO-deh-froy], Godefroy
Gratien [grah-tee-E~, nasal E]
Guérard [gay-RAHRD]
Guibert [gee-BEHRT, hard G]
Guillaume [hard-g gee-YAWM]
Gustave [gu-STAHV]
Guy [hard-g GEE]
Hégésippe [ay-gay-SEEP]
Henri [on-REE]
Héraclius [ay-RAH-klee-us]
Hercule [er-KYOOL] (Hercules)
Hermès [ehr-MEHZ]
Hillaire [ee-LAYR]; Hilarion [ee-LAH-ree-o~] — rare
*Hippolyte [EE-po-LEET]
Honoré [on-or-AY]
Ignace [ig-NAHS]
Irenée [ee-reh-NAY], — St. Ireneaus
Isadore [EE-sah-dohr], Isidore, Isidor
Isambard [EE-sahm-bahrd]
Jean [ZHO~, nasal A] — better class, Jeannot (dim.) [zhohn-NO]; Jacques [ZHAK] — common, plebeian, Jacquet (dim.) [zhah-KAY]
Jean Baptiste [ZHO~ bahp-TEEST] — less popular
Jérôme [zher-OHM]
Joachim [zhwa-KEEM]
Joseph [ZHO-sef]
Jourdain [zhor-DA~, nasal A]

Jules [ZHUL]
Julien [ZHU-lee-E-, nasal E]
Justin, Just [zhu-STA-] [ZHOOST]
Lambert [LAHM-behr]
Laurent [low-RA-, nasal E]
Lazarre, Lazare
Léon [lay-O-, nasal O]
Léonard [LEH-o-NARD], Lienard
   [LEE-eh-NARD] — uncommon
Léopold
Louis [lu-EE]
Luc [LUWK]
Lucien, Luce [luh-see-E-] [LOOS]
Marcel, Marcellin (dim.) [mahr-SEL,
   MAR-seh-LA-]
Marin
Martial
Mathieu [ma-TEW]
Mathurin
Matthias
Maurice [mow-REES]
Maxime [mahk-SEEM]
Médard
Melchior
Michel [mee-SHEL], Michau, Michon
   (dim.)
Modeste
Napoléon —after you-know-who,
   not before
Narcisse [nahr-SEES]
Nathaniel [na-TAHN-ee-EL]
Nazaire
Népomucène
Néron [neh-RO-]
Nicolas [NEE-ko-la]
Nicole
Nicomède
Noël — rare, but used since at least 1760
Octave (Octavius)
Odilon
Offroy — rare
Olivie [oh-lee-VEE]
Olivier [oh-LEE-vee-ay]
Oscar
Pascal
Pasquier [pah-skee-AY]
*Patrice [pah-TREES]
Paul [PAOOWL]
Perceval
Pétrus — rare
Philarète [fee-lah-REHT] — very rare

Philippe, Phillipe [fee-LEEP]
*Pierre [PYAYR], Pierrot (dim.)
   [pyayr-O]
Placide [plah-SEED]
Polycarpe
Prosper [pro-SPAY]
Quennel [keh-NEL]
Quintien [ke--tee-EH-]
Raymond [ray-MOWND
Remi
René [reh-NAY]
Restif [reh-STEEF]
Reynard
*Richard [ree-SHARD]
Robert [ro-BEAR]
Roch [ROHSH]
Rodolphe
Roger [roh-ZHAY]
Romain
Savyn
Sébastien
Serge [SERZH]
Sidon, Si (dim.) [see-DO-, SEE]
Siffre [SEEF-r]
Silvain
Siméon
Simon [see-MO-], Simion [SEE-
   mee-O-]
Stanislas
Sulpice
Sylvain
Tancrède
Thadeé [tah-DAY]
Théobald [TAY-oh-BAHLD]
Théodore [TAY-oh-dor]
Théophile [tay-oh-FEEL]
Théophraste [TAY-o-frahst] — very rare
Thomas [to-MAS]
Tristan [tree-STAH-]
Urbain
Valérand
Valéry
Vernon
Victoir, Victoire [veek-TWA]
Victorien
Vincenz, Vincent
Virgile [veer-ZHEEL]
Xavier [zah-vee-AY]
Yves [EEVS]
Yvon [ee-VO-, nasal O]
Zacharie [ZAH-kah-REE]

HYPHENATED PERSONAL NAMES

Examples of two and three-part names.

Female	Male	
		Jean-Luc
		Jean-Marie
Anne-Louise	Anne-Jean-Marie-René	Jean-Michel
Anne-Marie	François-Marie	Jean-Paul
Lucile-Amandine-Aurore	Guillaume-François	Louis-Nicolas
Marie-Anne	Henri-Marie-Raymond	Louis-Prosper
Marie-Léonie	Jacques-Ange	Napoléon-Henri
	Jacques-Yves	René-Robert
	Jean-Claude	Pierre-Albert
	Jean-François	Pierre-Marie-Sébastien
	Jean-Jacques	Sylvestre-Antoine

FAMILY NAMES

Achard [ah-SHAR]
Aguesseau
Aimedieu [ai-meh-DYU]
Albanel
Allarmet
Altaroche
Amanzé [ah-mahn-ZAY]
d'Amboise [dahm-BWAHZ]
Amontons
d'Ancelet, Ancelot [dahn-seh-LAY]
Andrieux [ahn-dree-OOH]
Apollinaire [ah-POHL-ee-NAYR]
Argoud
Aubron [o-BRO~, nasal O]
Augereau [o-zher-O]
Augier [o-gee-AY]
d'Auteroche
Babeuf, Baboeuf [bah-BERF]
de Baif
Baillet, Baillot
Ballarger
Baltard
de Banville
Baratier
Barbaroux
Barberot [bar-ber-O]
Barbier
Baril [bah-REEL]
Barrande
Barranes [bahr-RAHN]

Barrière
Barrot [bahr-ROH]
Barthez, Barthes
Barthou [bar-TOE]
de Basseville
Bastiat
Bataille [bah-TAHY]
Battet [bat-TAY]
Baudin
Baudrillart
de Bausset
Bautain
Bazaine, Bazin
Bazancourt
Bazeries [BAH-zer-EE]
de Beaujeau
de Beauvais [boh-VAY]
Becque [BEHK]
Becquerel
Bedier
Belain
Belgrand
Bellange
du Bellay
Bellivier [bel-LEE-vee-AY]
Bellot, Belot [behl-LOH]
Bendalou
de Bénouville
de Béranger, Bérenger
Béraud

Bergaigne
Bergerat
Berjaud
Bernage
Berquin, de Berquin [behr-KANK-]
Berthelot, Berthollet
Berthier
Bessieres
Beule
Biard, Biart
Bibaud
Bichat
Bidault
du Bignon, Bignon [doo bee-NYO-]
Billet, Billot
Biot
Bisson
Bizot [bee-ZO]
Blanche, Blanchet
Blanqui [bla--KEE]
Blondel, Blondin
Blouet
Bochart
Boesset
Boileau [bwah-LO]
de Boisdeffre [bwah-DEFR]
Boissier [bwah-SAY]
de Boissieu [deh bwah-SOH]
Boissonade [BWAH-soh-NAHD]
Boivin
Bonnassieux
Bonnemère
de Bonneval
Bonnivet [bohn-nee-VAY]
Bonpland
Bonvalot [boh--vah-LO]
Bornet [bohr-NAY]
Bornier
Borras [bor-RAH]
Bosquet
Bouchardon
Boucher
Bouchette
Boudin
Boufflers
Bouguereau
Bouilhet
de Bouillé
Bouilly
Boulanger [boo-lahn-ZHAY]
Bourchier

Bourdaloue
Bourgelat
Bourgeois — a baronial family
Bourinot
de Bourmont
Bournonville [BOOR-no--VEEL]
Boursicot [boar-see-KO]
Boutroux
Bouvard, Bouvart
Brachet
Breal
Brianchon
Brieux
Brimbaudier [bram-BOW-dee-AY]
Brinon
Brodeur
Brosselet [BROS-seh-LAY]
Broussaid
Brune
Brunet [broo-NAY]
Brunetiere [broo-NEH-tee-AYR]
Brunot
Buchez [boo-SHAY]
Buchon
Buffier
Buisson
Cabet
de Cadoine
Caillavet
Callet, Callot [kahl-LEY, kahl-LO]
Caillie, Caille [kai-YEE, KAI]
Calmet, Calmette
Cambert
Cambronne
Campan
Capoul
Cardot [kar-DOE], Carnot [kar-NO]
Carpeaux
Carré [kar-RAY]
Carrel
Carrier
Casadesus
Casgrain
Cassas
de Castagny
de Castellane
Cathelineau [KAH-teh-lee-NO]
Cauchy
Cavaignac [KAH-vay-NYAHK]
Cerles

Chabaneau
de Chabannes
Chabot
Chabrier
du Chaillu
Chalier
Chambellan
Chamfort
Chamier
Chapais
Chapleau
Chappe
Charcot
Charlier
Charnay
Charton
Chartran
Chasseriau
Chastelard
Châtard
Chatrian [sha-tree-A~, nasal A]
Chaumette
de Chénier
des Cheriots [day shayr-ee-OH]
de la Chérois
Chevruel
Cheysson [shay-SO~, nasal O]
Chirac [shee-RAHK]
de Choiseul
Choquet
Chouat, Chouart [shoo-AT]
Chouteau
Christophile
Cladel
Clairaut, Clairault [kley-ROW]
Clarac
Cleary
Clérisse
de Cléron
des Cloizeaux [day klwah-ZOH]
Cochet [ko-SHAY]
de Colmieu [deh kohl-MYEW]
Considerant
Coppée [ko-PAY]
Cot, Cotin [KO]; from Hérault
Cottet
de Couder
Coulanges
de Coulomb
Couperin
Cournot

Court, Courtois
Couthon
Crevaux
Cros [KROW]
Cugnot [koo-NYOT]
Cuignet [quee-NYAY]
de Curel
de Custine
Dablon
Daguesseau
Dalmores
Dalou
Danican
Darboux
Darcet
Dassault
Daubenton, d'Aubenton
Daudet [dow-DAY]
Daunou
Daurignac [DOE-ree-NYAHK]
Debierne
Debraux
Deferre
Degoutte
Delaborde
Delage
Delambre
Delaunay
Delavigne
Delcassé [DEL-cahs-SAY]
Delessert
Delibes
Delorme, de l'Orme
Delorte
Demarteau
Demoivre
Deprez
Derain
Déroulède [DAY-roo-LED]
Desaguliers
Desargues
Desault
Descroizilles
Després
Dessaix
Detaille
Dides [DEED]
Dierx
Dimnet
Dorion
Doumer

Drevet
Drieu la Rochelle
Drouet
Drouet d'Erlon
Drumont
Duchenne
Duchez [doo-SHAY]
Ducrotay de Blainville
Dufaure
Dulong
Dupanloup
Dupark
Duperré
Duperrey
Dupille [doo-PEEL]
Dupuytren
Duret
Duruy
Duthiers
Duvernois, Duvernoy
Duveyrier
Enfantin
de l'Épée [duh lay-PAY]
d'Éprémesnil
Érard
Esber [es-BAY]
Esmenard
Espinas, Espinasse
Esquirol
Esterle
Estienne [EHS-tee-E~N], Fabre
   [FAHBR]
Étienne [EH-tee-E~N]
Fabry
Faguet
Faidherbe
de Failly
Falguière
de Faloux
Fauvert [fo-VAYR]
Fialin
Flandin
de Flavigny
Floquet [flo-KAY]
Foccart
Fourcaud
Fournier
Fourton
de Foy
Frechette
Fremiet, Fremiot

Freneau
Fréron
Frérot [fray-RO]
de la Fresnaye
Fromentin
Frossard
Gaboriau
Gachard
Gaillardet
Gallieni
Ganneau [gan-NO]
Garat
Garneau
Garreau
Gasquet
Gastineau
Gaubil
Gaudichaud
Gaudry
Gaumont
Gavarret [gah-vah-RAY]
Geffrard
Gemier
Gensonne
de Gerando
Gérard, Géraud
Géricault
Gérôme [zhay-ROHM]
Gigoux
Girard, Girardin [zhee-RARD], de
   Girard
Girardon
Giraud [zhee-ROWD]
Glasson
Godefroy
Gosselin
Goulin [goo-LI~]
Goupil
de Gourgaud
de Gramont
Granet
Gras
Gratry
Gravier
Gresset
Greuze
Grévy [gray-VEE]
Grignard
Groussard
Guadet
Guérin

Guesde
Guiche
de Guignes
Guillaume, Guillaumet, Guillemen
Guilmant
Guitry
Guollet [go-LEY]
Guyon [hard-g gee-O~, nasal O]
du Ha [du HAH]
Hadamard [ah-dah-MAHRD]
Hanataux, Hanotaux [ah-nah-
    TOW]
Harpignies [ahr-pee-NYEE]
Harrisse [ah-REESS]
Hauy [OWEE]
Havet [ah-VAY]
Héneault [eh-NAWLT]
Hervieu [her-VIEW]
Heurtaux [er-TOW]
Hoche [OHSH]
Houdard
Houdon
Houssaye
Hovelacque [O-veh-LAHK]
Husson
Ibert [ee-BAYR]
Imbot [eem-BO]
d'Indy
Isabey
Isouard
Jacqué
Jacquemart
Janet, Jannet [zhah-NAY]
Janin
Joffre
Joliot [ZHO-lee-O]
Jouffroy
Jouhaux
Joutel
de Jouvenel
Juchereau [zhewsh-RO]
de Julleville [deh ZHUHL-eh-
    VEEL]
Jurieu
Jusserand
Labat
de Laborde
Labrouste
Labrunie
de Lacaille
Lachaise

Lacordaire
de Lacretelle
Ladoux [lah-DOO]
Lafont
Lajard
de Lajarte
Lajeunesse
Lajoux [lah-ZHOO]
Lalemant, Lallemand
Lamercier [la-MER-see-AY],
    Limercier
de Lameth
Lancret
Langevin
de Langlade
Lannes
Latreille
Laugère [low-ZHEYR]
Laurencin
Lavedan
Laveran
Lavisse
Lebesgue [luh BEHG]
Leblanc
Lécestre [lay-SESTR]
Lecocq
Ledru-Rollin
Lefort
Léger
Legrain
Lejeune
Leleux [leh-LYER]
Lemaître
Lemelin
Lemieux
Lemonnier
Leneru
Lenoir
Leprohon
Leris [leh-REE]
Lesage
de Lesseps
Lesueur
Leverrier
Liard
Liguest
Linant
Littre
Loisy
Loubet [loo-BAY]
Lozeau

Luchaire [loo-SHAYR]
Lumière
Machault [mah-SHOW]
Maillol
de Malet
Malon, Malonet [ma-lo-NAY]
Malus
Mangin
Manoury
Marchand
Marcou, Marcoux [mar-COO]
de Marenches [deh mah-RONSH]
Maret
Marin
Maritain
de Mariveaux [duh mah-ree-VO]
Marmier
de Marolle [duh mah-ROL]
Marquey [mahr-KAY]
Martinaud [MAR-tee-NO]
Masqueray
Massillon
Maubert [mow-BAYR]
Maurel
Mauriac
Mazurier [mah-ZOO-ree-AY]
Méchain
Meillet
Meissonier
Mercier
Mermet [mayr-MAY]
Meryon [may-RYOH~]
du Mesnil [doo may-NEEL]
de la Mettrie
de Meulan
Mézières
Michaud, Michault
Michel [mee-SHEL], Michelet
Migne
Mignet
Millardet
Mirat
Mocquereau
Moissan [mwah-SA~]
Mollien
Monge
Monnier [mohn-nee-AY]
Monsigny
Monteson
de Montfaucon
de Montholon

de Monvel
Moréas
Moret
de Mornay
de Morny
Mossard
Motteaux
Mougeot [moo-ZHYO]
Mounet
Murger
Muselier [moo-SEH-lee-AY]
de Nancrède
Naquet
Nazaire
Nélaton
Néricault
Nicole, Nicolle, Nicollet, Nicot
Nisard
Nodier
de Noé
Nord
de la Noue
Noufflard
Nougues
Olier [OH-lee-AY]
Ollion
Orfila
Oudinot
Ouvrard
Paillole [pai-YOL]
Pajou
Panard
Papineau
Paques [PAK]
Pasdeloup
Patenotre [paht-NOH-tr]
Patraud [pah-TRO]
Pau [POH]
de Pauger
Peaucellier
Pégoud
Péguy [peh-GEE, hard G]
Pélabon
Pelissier
de la Peltrie
Pergaud
Péri
Permon
Peyre
Phélypeaux
Pineau [pee-NO]

Pingaud [pa--GO]
Planquette
Poquelin [poh-keh-LA-]
de la Porte
Préault
Pressence
Pridaux
Puiseux
Quatremère [KAH-treh-MAYR]
Quelés [keh-LAYS]
Quérard [kay-RARD]
Quesnel [keh-NEHL]
Quételet
Quicherat [KEE-shayr-A]
Quinet [kee-NAY]
Radisson
Radot
Ramadier [rah-MAH-dee-AY]
Raoux
Raspail
Ravignan
Réal [ray-AL]
Régnier
Rémy, de Rémy
Renan
Renaudel [reh-no-DEL]
Renouvier
Reybaud [ray-BOW]
de Riant
Ribault, Ribaut
Richer [ree-SHAY]
Richet [ree-SHAY]
Rotion
Risteau
Rivarol
Robidoux [roh-bee-DOO]
Rochet [roh-SHAY]
Rochette [roh-SHEHT]
Rolland [roh-YAND]
de Ronsard
de Rosny
Rouillan [ru-ee-YA-]
Roulier [ru-lee-AY]
Roumer
Roussilhe [ru-SEEL]
Sainte-Beuve [SANT-BEWV]
de Sainte-Maure
Saint-Simon [SA--see-MO-]
Sarrien
de Saulx
Savary

de Selves
Sembat [sehm-BAH]
Séquard [seh-KARD]
de Sivry
Soule
Soumet
Soustelle [su-STELL]
Suchet
Sudreau [su-DRO]
Surcouf
Surette
Tache
Taillandier [tai-YA--dee-AY]
Taine
Tallien
Tarde
Taschereau
Tercier [TAYR-see-AY]
Thery [tay-REE]
Theuriet
Thibaud, Thibaudet [tee-BOWD]
Thiers
Thorez [tow-RAY]
Thyraud [tee-ROE]
le Tonnelier
Tonnerre [ton-NEYR]
de la Tremoille
Valabrègue
Vater
Le Vau [luh VO]
Verdier [VAYR-dee-AY]
Vergier [ver-zhee-AY]
Verneuil [vayr-NWEEL]
Vernière [VAYR-nee-EYR]
Vétillart
Viardot
Viaud [vee-OWE]
Vidi [vee-DEE]
Vidocq [vee-DOK]
Vignaud
de Vigny [vee-NYEE]
Villemain
de Vivonne
Vollon
Vouet [VWAY]
Vuillemin [VWEE-yeh-MI-]
Watelet [vah-teh-LAY]
Weygand
Ximénèsa — Spanish import
Yriarte [EE-ree-AHRTT]
Yvon [ee-VO-]

DUTCH AND FLEMISH

Another European people whose names have more bearers abroad than in Holland, Dutch is the rootstock of the Boers or Afrikaaners of South Africa, as well as many old New York families. A Germanic language, though definitely not German, an English speaker with a supple mind can sometimes follow the gist of a conversation.

Of course, the Dutch borrow names from abroad like everyone else. There are plenty of good Dutch with French, Belgian, German, and even Irish names.

Do not mistake some of the spellings below for typos. Dutch is distinguished by the use of "van" as the "of" word, differing from the Germon "von." Also, A's are sometimes doubled, so that our "-ian" is rendered "-iaan." J is pronounced like our Y, not uncommon, but the Dutch use it in last syllables where we would use "-ine" as in Constantijn for Constantine.

By 1500, ordinary men were still known by a personal name and a patronymic, but those of a better class had begun to inherit place-names as family names as early as 1400. Even with family names, men frequently had a patronymic middle name. This was their father's personal name with "-szoon" attached. Later this was shortened to "-sz," about 1600. That lasted one or two centuries longer. So the son of Adriaen Lucaszoon Schalcken would be Jakob Adriaenszoon Schalcken, and his son might be Lucas Jacobsz Schalcken, if he falls on the shorter side of usage.

If you run into someone in your research called "Oom Jan" or the like, "Oom" simply means "uncle," and is used as a title of familiar respect.

FEMALE NAMES

Aleen, Alene, Alleen	Feltja, Felta	Louisa
Aloysia	Francisca	Margarete, Margaret
Amalia	Geertruida, Gertrud	Maria, Marie
Amaron	Helena	Marielle
Anna, Anneke, Annetje	Henrietta	Maryse
Beatrix	Irene	Mena
Betje	Isabella	Neltje
Christijna	Jenni	Sara
Cornelia	Johanna	Saskia
Dora	Josephine	Teresa
Elisabeth, Elsa, Ilsa, Else	Juliana	Thilly
Emma	Kenau	Wilhelmina

MALE NAMES

Some Dutch or Flemish Catholics use Anne or Marie as a middle name for a boy.

Aagje
Aart, Aert, Aernout
Abel
Abraham, Bram
Adam
Adriaan, Adriaen
Alexander
Allart, Aldert
Aloys
Andries
Anton
Arent
Arnold
Ate
Augier
Barend, Bernaert, Bernard, Bernhard
Bart, Barth, Barthild
Boetius
Bonaventure
Brandt
Campegius
Carel
Caspar
Christiaan
Christoph
Constantijn
Cornelis, Cornelius —
   very popular
David
Denis
Diderik, Didericus
Dierik, Dirk, Dirck
Eduard
Egide, Gilles
Eglon
Emanuel
Everardus, Everard, Everhardus
Ferdinand

Frans, Franciscus
Frederik
Fridolin
Gaspar
Geertgen, Gerhard, Gerhards, Gerrit, Gheerardt, Gheeraert, Gerard
Geisebrecht
Georg
Gerbrand
Ghislain, Ghiselin
Gilles
Gustaff
Harmen
Havick
Heike
Heironymus
Hendrik
Herman
Hubertus
Huig, Hugo — becomes
   Hugenszoon or
   Hugensz
Huilbrecht
Izaak
Jakob — popular
Jan — very popular
Jan Baptist, Jan Baptista
Jeremias
Jeroom
Johan, Johannes — popular
Joost, Just
Josse, Josquin
Jozef, Joseph, Josephus
Justus
Karel
Kees
Laurens

Leander
Lodewijk
Lucas
Ludolf
Maarten
Marcellus
Marinus
Mathys, Matthijs
Maurice
Menno
Michiel, Michael
Nandor
Nikolaas, Nicolaes, Nicolas
Otto
Paul
Philipps
Pieter — very popular;
   also Petrus
Quentin, Quinten
Rafel, Raphael
Regnier
Reinaerde
Reiner
Reinhart
Rembrandt
Rip
Roeloff
Roger
Rudolf
Scheltius
Simon
Steven
Theodor
Tobias
Valdemar
Valentyn
Willem
Wouter
Zeeman

Family Names

Adam
van Aeken
van Aelit
Aertsen, Aertszen
Alma
van Alstyne
van Ammers-Kuller
van Amstel
Bakhuizen van den
  Brink
Backhuysen, Bakhuisen,
  Bakhuysen
Beckx
Bega
van Beijeren
Bekker, Backer
Berchem, Berghem
van den Bergh
Bijns, Byns
Bilderdijk
van Binche
Bissen
Blaeu, Blaeuw, Blauw
Blauvelt
Bloemaert, Blomart
van Bloemen
Boerhaave
Bogaers
Bok
Bomberg
Bosboom
Bosch, Bos
Bosman
Brandt
Bredero
van Brederode
Bril, Brill
van den Brink, ten Brink
Brouwer, Brauwer
de Busbecq, Busbeck,
  Bousbecq, Bouse-
  becque
van Calcar, Kalkar,
  Kalcker
Calvaert, Calvart
Camphuysen
van Ceulen, van Keulen
Chastelain, Chastellain
Christiaanse

de Cooge
Coornhert
Cornelisz, Corneliszoon
Cort, de Cort
Couperus
van Coxie
de Crayer
Cuyler
Cuyp, Cuypers, Kuyper
Daendels
Dankerts
Davits, David
Dedel
Deken
Deterding
Deutz
van Dieren
van der Does, van der
  Dousa
Donders
Dorislaus
Dou, Dow, Douw
Drebbel
Droeshout
van Droogenbroeck
Duyckinck
Edelinck
van den Eeckhout
Eekhoud
van Egmont
Eijkman
Einthoven
Elzevir, Elzevier, Elsevier
Emants
van Erp, Erpinius
van Ess
Fabricius, Fabritius
van der Faes
Fodor
Frelinghuysen
Frijtom
Fyt, Feydt
Gallien
Geert, Geerts
Geulincx
Glauber
van der Goes
Gohl
Gossaert, Gossart

van Goyen, Goijen
de Graaf, de Graff
Gronov, Gronovius
Groote, Groot, Groete,
  de Groot, Grotius
van Haarlem
de Haas
van der Haegt, Verhaecht
Hals
de Heem
van Heemskerck
Heijermans
Hein, Heijn, Heinsius,
  Heyn
van Helmont
Hobbema
de Hondt
van Hoodstraeten
de Hoogh
Houbraken
de Houtman
Hudde
Huygens, Huyghens
Huysum, van Huysum
Ingenhousz
Isaac
Israels
Jans, Jansen, Janssen
Jongkind
Jordaens
Kalf
Kamerlingh
de Kempener, de Kempe-
  neer
van Kessel, Kessel
Kieft
Kleffius
van Koetsveld
de Koninck
Kremer
van Laar, van Laer
Langendijk
van Lennep
van Leuven
van Leyden
Lingelbach
Lorentz
Lutyens
Luzac

Maartens
van Maerlant
Maes, Maas
van Mander
Mappa
Matsys, Massys, Metsys, Messys
Memling, Memlinc
Mengelberg
Mesdag
de Meurs
Michaelis
van Mierevelt, van Miereveld
van Mieris
Mignon
Moeller van den Bruck
Mojert
Mulder
Mytens
Naundorf, Naundorff
Neefs, Neeffs, Nefs
van der Neer
Netscher
Nieuwenhuis
van Noort
van Nuyssen
Obrecht, Hobrecht
Oertel, Ortell
van Okeghem, van Ockeghem
Onnes

d'Ooge
Ooms
van Oost
van Oostsanen
van Ostade
Osterhout
Patinir
Petri
de Peyster
Philipse
van der Poorten
Pypelincx
van Rensselaer
van Riebeeck
van der Roe
Roelofs
Roggeveen
van Ruisdael, van Ruysdael
van Sant
Schalcken
van Schoorle
tot Sint Jans
de Sitter
Snayers
Snyder, Snyders
Steen
van Steenwijk, Steenwiyk
Stevin, Stevinus
Swammerdam
Swanevelt
Tanchel, Tanquelin

Tappan
Tefft
Ten Boom
Ten Kate
Terborch, ter Borch
Tiele
Tietjens
Toorop
Tserklaes
van Uijlenburgh
van Valkenburgh
van de Velde, van der Velder
Verplanck
Vesalius
Visscher
Vitringa
Volckertszoon
Vondel, van den Vondel
Vos, de Vos
van Vranken
van der Waals
van Wart
van der Werff
van der Weyden
Wijnants, Wynants
Willet
de Winter
van de Woestijne
Wyttenbach
Zelle

FRISIAN

Frisia on the Baltic was the staging ground for the Anglo-Saxon invasion of Britain (in fact, Angles, Saxons, and Frisians). Frisia is now split between Holland and Germany, but the names continue even where the language fails (like Catalan or Breton, it is one of the endangered languages of Europe). Frisian names have made it to the United States, even the personal ones like Mia, Wilt, Hoot, Dirk, and Elle, as well as many family names you may recognize.

Emigration, especially to the United States, results in a loss of all the diacriticals. Like Dutch, J is our Y. Final E's are all sounded. The endings "-je" and "-ke" are diminutive, as are "-chen" and "-chin."

Pronunciation

Most umlauted letters are as in German. The others follow.

A — A in pasta
Â — AU in tau
Ä — A in hay
E — E in get
Ê — E in hey
I — I in pin

Î — I in machine
J — Y in yes
O — O in hot
Ô — O in hole
U — U in putt
Û — U in tune

FEMALE NAMES

Adda
Afke, Efke, Eveke, Eva
Agatha, Agt, Agte
Albertje
Almôd, Almôth, Almt
Anna, Anke, Anken,
  Aennchen, Annechin,
  Annatje, Nâtje
Bauke, Bâwke, Bâfke,
  Bâvke
Bela
Benna
Brûnke, Brûntje
Deverke
Dirktje, Dirtje
Djurke, Jurke
Doda
Ebbe, Eveke
Eeltje
Eka, Eke, Ekea, Eckea
Ella
Elsbet
Emma

Eta, Etta, Ettje
Fia, Fiake, Fike — from
  Sofia
Fokka
Foletta
Fôlke, Fulke, Fulka, Ful-
  leke, Fulla, Folla
Gerdtje
Gerdût, Gädrût
Gêske, Gêsa
Grendelke, Grennelke
Harmke
Hebe, Hebeke, Hêbke,
  Hëpke
Hester
Hilke, Hille, Hilla, Hilda
Hima, Himke
Hiske
Idje, Itje, Ida
Ikke, Ikka, Ika
Immeke, Imke
Inka
Janna, Jantje

Jetta, Jettchen
Jurke
Kâtje
Lûitje
Lükke
Machelt, Machtild,
  Mechtild
Marê, Merêken, Marêke,
  Maike
Margrêta, Margrêt,
  Magrêta, Magrêt,
  Megrêt, Mergrêt,
  Grêta, Grêtje
Menna, Menje
Meta, Metta, Metje
Mia, Mîke, Mîtje
Okka
Onna
Peta, Peterke
Tale, Talea, Tâlke, Taletta
Tâtje, Tetta, Tetje
Wobbeke, Wobke
Wübke

MALE NAMES

Abbo
Adde
Ade
Aeilco
Agge
Aisso, Aisse, Eisse
Albert, Albarts, Albardus,
  Albertus
Alerk
Alle
Alt
Amel

Amke
Arend, Arnd, Arndt
Arjen, Arien
Arrel, Arl
Athe
Atte, Atto
Baino, Beino
Banno, Bantje
Bärend, Bêrend, Bernd
Bele, Behl, Beil, Bill;
  Beelke, Belke
Bêner

Benge
Benno
Bôdewîn, Boldewîn
Boko
Bôle, Boele, Bôleke,
  Bôlke, Bolkes
Bonno
Boys, Boye, Boy, Boyke
Brûno
Datter
Dedde
Dêtlêf

Detmer
Dever
Dîderik, Dîdrîk, Dîdrîch, Dîderk, Dierk, Dirk
Dîko, Dyko
Dîle, Diele
Djure
Djurelt, Durelt
Dodo
Ebbe, Ebbo, Ebo, Ebe, Eppo, Eve
Edde
Edo, Edje
Edsard
Egbert, Ebbert
Egge
Eibo, Eibe
Eiko, Eike
Eilert, Eilt
Eimo, Eime
Eint, Eent
Ele, Ehle
Elle
Eme, Emo, Ehme, Eimo, Emke
Emmo, Emme
Ernst
Esdert
Eve, Ewe, Aeve
Fauke
Fekko, Fêko, Feyko, Fekke
Feyke
Fimmo, Fimme
Fôke, Fouke
Fokke, Fokko
Folkerd
Folkmar
Folpmer
Folpt, Fulpt
Folrâd, Fulrâd
Fôlrîk, Fôlrîch, Fôlerk
Frërk, Frêrk, Frêrik
Fulbrand
Fulf
Fullo, Fulko
Galt, Gâlt, Garrelt, Arlt, Gerlt
Garbert
Garbrand
Garrelt, Gerrelt

Geiko, Gaiko, Gayko, Geike, Geio, Gayo
Gerd, Gerjet, Gêjert, Gert, Gerriet, Geert
Gerke
Gêso, Giso, Gisbert, Gijsbert
Grendel, Grennel
Habbo
Haddo, Hatto, Heddo, Hedde
Hagen
Hamke, Hamo
Hâro, Hâre
Harrell, Harle
Hayo, Heie, Hei
Heiko, Haiko
Hein, Heini, Heink
Heite, Heit
Helmer
Herman, Harm
Hêro, Hêre, Herre
Hibbo, Hibben
Hiddo, Hidde
Hillerd, Hillerk, Hillrich, Hillrik
Hillmer, Hilmer
Hinrich, Hinderk
Hoot, Hotbert
Ibo, Ibe, Ihbe
Ide, Idse, Itse, Idze
Igge
Iko, Ike
Imel
Imme, Immo
Ing, Ingo, Inguio
Ino, Ine, Ihno, Inge, Ihnke
Ippo, Ippe
Jabbo, Jabbe, Jabe
Jak, Jäkchen
Jakub, Jakup
Jan
Jasper
Jelle
Jellrich, Jellrik, Jellerk
Jibbo
Jimme
Jochem, Jofen
Joost, Juist, Just
Jürgen, Jürjen, Jürn, Görgen, Jörg

Karsten, Kersten, Karsen, Kassen, Kasjen, Kristjan
Kasper
Kês
Klâs, Niklâs
Lambert, Lampert, Lambrecht
Lanbert, Lanpert, Lantpert
Lindo
Lübbert
Lübbo, Lübke
Lûdo
Lûdowig, Lûdewig, Lûdwig
Lüitje
Lüke, Lüdeke, Ludeke, Liudeke
Lûks
Lüppo, Lübbo, Lüpke
Lûth, Lûtet
Mammo, Mamme
Manno, Manne
Meinert, Menêrt, Meint, Meent
Meino, Magino, Megino
Memmo, Me'mo, Me'me, Memke, Mêmke
Mêne
Menno, Menne, Menko, Menke
Mense, Mens
Mês, Mêwes
Michel
Mimke, Mimmke, Mimeken, Mimmeken
Mimste
Nanno, Nanne
Nôme, Nôm
Ode, Odo
Okko, Ocko, Okke
Ommo
Onno, Onke, Onneke, Ontje
Ordgîs, Ortgîs, Oortgies, Oorthgies, Oordgiese
Ortwin, Oorthwin, Ooordwin
Otte, Otto
Paul

Peter
Poppe, Popke, Popken
Reent
Reimer
Reiner
Reinhard
Reint
Rembold
Remmer
Rewert
Rikkerd, Rikkert
Rôlf
Rötger
Rummert, Rumke
Rumo, Rumke
Sebo
Sibet
Sibo

Sikko, Sikke
Swêerd, Swêert
Swîthert, Swittert, Switer
Tako, Tâks
Tammo, Tamme
Tanno
Tebbo, Tebbe
Têwes
Thado, Thade, Tado,
  Tade
Tjado, Tjade
Tjârd, Tjard, Tjârt
Tjarko
Tjetmer
Tönjes
Ubbo, Ubbe
Udo, Ude
Ufo, Ufe, Uvo, Uffo,

Uffe, Ufke
Uko, Üko, Uke
Ulerk, Ulrik
Ulferd, Ulfert
Warner, Warntje
Wêert
Wêt
Wilbert
Wildert, Wilt
Wilhelm, Wilm
Wilko, Wilke
Wît, Wiet, Witje, Wietje
Wîterd, Wîtherd, Wîthert
Wobbo, Wobbe, Wobbi
Wolbrecht
Wübbo

FAMILY NAMES

Abben, Abena
Adden
Aden, Adena
Aggen
Aissen, Eissen
Alberts, Albers
Alerks, Alers, Ahlers
Allen, Allena
Alts
Amels
Amke
Arends
Arjens, Ariens, Arjes
Arkonâ, Arkenâ
Arrel, Arl
Athen
Attena
Bainen, Beinen
Banjes
Bärends, Berend
Bavink
Bêners
Bengen
Bêninga, Bênenga
Bôlen, Bolema
Bonnen
Boyen, Boyinga, Boyink,
  Boyunga
Brûninga, Brûns, Bron-

sema, Brûnken
Dedden
Dielen
Diken, Dyken, Dikena,
  Dykena
Dirks, Dirksen, Dirken,
  Dierken
Djuren
Doden, Dodens, Dodena
Eben, Even, Eppen, Ebe-
  ling
Edden
Eden, Edinga
Edsards, Edzards, Esderts
Egberts, Egbers
Eggen
Ehlen
Eiben
Eilerts, Eilers, Eilts, Eils
Eimers
Eints
Ellen
Emen, Ehmen, Emminga,
  Emken
Emminga, Emmius
Epkema
Eppen
Fekken, Feyken, Feikena
Feyen

Feyken
Fimmen
Flame, Flam
Foken
Fokken, Fokkena
Folkerds, Folkers
Folpts
Folrichs, Fôlerks, Fôlers
Frërksen
Frese, Frêse
Garrelts, Garrels, Ger-
  relts, Gerrels
Geiken
Gerdes
Gerken
Gërman
Grôn
Grönefeld, Grönfeld
Gronewold, Gronwold
Habben, Habbinga
Haddinga
Hagena
Halbertsma
Haming
Hâren, Haringa, Har-
  ringa
Harms, Harmens
Hayung, Heyungs,
  Hayunga

Hedden, Heddinga
Heikens, Heiken, Hei-
  kena, Haiken, Hayken
Heine, Heinen
Heits
Helmers
Hêren, Herren
Hibben
Hidden
Hillern
Hillmers
Hinrichs, Hinnerks, Hin-
  ners, Hinnerssen,
  Hünerssen
Hoots, Hoting, Hooting
Iben, Ibben, Ibeling
Idsen, Itzen, Idsinga
Iggen, Iggena
Iken, Ikena
Imels
Immen
Inen, Ihnen
Ippen
Jabben
Jak
Jansen, Janssen, Jenssen
Japiks
Jaspers
Jellen, Jellena
Jibben
Jimmen
Jürgens, Jürjens, Jürns
Just
Karstens, Karsens, Kas-
  sens, Kasjens
Klûn, Kluin
Lübben, Lübbena, Lübkes

Lubberts, Lübbers
Lûdowigs, Lûdewigs,
  Lûdwigs
Luitjens
Lüken
Mammen, Memmen,
  Mamminga, Mem-
  minga
Manninga
Meinerts, Meiners, Meints,
  Meents
Memkes, Mêmkes, Mimkes
Mênen
Menken
Mennen, Menninga
Mensen, Mensinga
Nannen, Nanninga
Odens, Odenga, Odinga
Okken, Okkinga
Ommen, Omkes
Onkes, Onnekes
Onnen
Ontjes
Otten
Pauls, Paulsen
Peters, Petersen
Poppen, Poppinga
Reents
Reimers
Reiners
Reints
Remmers, Remmerssen
Rewerts
Rikkerts, Rikkers
Rôlfs
Rötgers
Rumkes

Rummerts, Rummers
Seba, Sebens
Siebens
Sikkens, Sikkinga
Swêerds, Swêerts, Swêers
Switers, Switters
Takes, Takens
Tammen, Tamminga
Tannen
Tebben
Thaden, Taden
Tjaden
Tjârds, Tjards, Tjârts
Tjarks
Tjetmers
Troelstra
Ubben, Ubbinga
Uden
Ufen, Uven, Uffen,
  Ufkes
Uken, Ukena
Ulerks, Ulers
Ulferds, Ulferts, Ulfers
Warners, Warntjes
Wêerts, Wêers, Weiers
Wêrda, Wiarda
Wêts
Wilberts, Wilbers
Wilken
Wilms
Wîts, Wiets, Wîtjes,
  Wietjes
Wobbena, Wobben
Wolbrechts, Wolbergs
Wübbens, Wubbena
Wumkes

GERMAN

The problem with German names on English word-processors and printers is that the machines often lack the O or U with umlaut, which should really then be rendered OE or UE, i.e., *Führer* becomes *Fuehrer*. You could perhaps show it as "u:" or "o:" with the two dots after being the closest to two dots over: *Fu:hrer*. The ß is easily and properly changed to SS, as in *Strasse*, street.

One family named Müller on coming to America became Miiller; in hand-writing, the umlauted U looked like two connected I's.

Remember, German is not spoken just in Germany. It is the language of Austria and some Swiss. German names have migrated with their owners, not just to North America, but to South America, Africa, and in Europe particularly to Holland, Belgium, France, Northern Italy, Russia, and Poland. It was these "ethnic Germans" that the Nazis were using to claim rights to all that real estate. Family names ending in "-mann" will look more Austrian if you drop one of the N's.

The prefix "von" to the family name indicates a level of nobility, if only the petty nobility. Germans are very picky about family names, and it takes the literal equivalent of an act of Congress, or the monarchial equivalent, to make any changes at any period. You must have legal permits showing good reason to hyphenate your family name with your spouse's.

A peculiar mark of honor voted to the men of the World War I ship *Emden* was that they could, if they wished, hyphenate the ship's name to their family name, to distinguish their descendants in perpetuity. Captain von Mueller did not (that should be Müller, umlauted U), though many others did, including a prince of the imperial Hohenzollern line who had the luck to serve aboard her. The "von" is always used when a family name that has a "von" is preceded by a personal name (Erich von Stroheim) or a title, like the captain above. Scholarly sources drop the "von" when using the last name alone, as when referring to Mueller's gentlemanly conduct. But it is more "pop" to keep the "von" attached, just as we usually keep the "van" in Dutch names, the "di" in Italian names, and the "de" in French ones. Face it, it sounds more Teutonic!

However, if you are short on names for commoners, you can always drop the "von." This was done by many immigrants who wanted to seem less Germanic, more "American."

German "pet names" are often made with the "-chen" ending, but also with "-el" or "-eli" or "-tzi." Some call "-chen" Northern (Prussian) and "vulgar," and the diminutive ending "-lein" Southern (Austrian) and "literary."

Current German law allows the registrar to protect newborn Germans from their parents, by refusing birth certificates with names which are bizarre, insulting, or uncertain in gender. The last can be fixed by adding a definitely male or female second name.

Titles of Nobility

Male	Female	English Equivalents
Kaiser	Kaiserin	emperor, empress
König	Königin	king, queen
Kron prinze	Kron prinzessin	crown prince, princess
Prinz	Prinzessin	prince, princess
Herzog	Herzogin	duke, duchess
Markgraf	Markgrafin	marquis, marchioness
Graf	Grafin	count, countess
Baron	Baronin `	baron, baroness

Pronunciation

You have to hear umlauted vowels to pronounce them; there's no handy way to write down the difference. AU sounds like OW in "how." Final E's have a small, unaccented sound, barely voiced at all, somewhere between EH and UH.

EI is pronounced long I as in "time." IE is long E as in "me." Easy to confuse; go by the second letter.

W is pronounced V. Vienna is written *Wien* in German, but the initial sound is the same. V's are still pronounced as in English, though. G is always hard, as in "gun."

TH comes out T, same as in French. Double T's are hit a little harder. CH is a back of the throat K, just as in Scottish or Yiddish. Yiddish, by the way, is a Germanic language with a heavy Hebrew vocabulary. Much of the phony German you hear in cartoons and other low comedy is actually Yiddish. When you realize this, the Hitler routines are even funnier.

Of course there are dialectical differences of accent in German, just as between Vermont and Tennessee. The Prussians are crisp and gutteral, more your classic "Cherman" accent. Bavarians have a softer sound: notably the W's V sound gets aspirated halfway to F. Prussian CH's clear out a lot more phlegm. Their H's are pretty hard, too.

FEMALE NAMES

Adelheid, Adele
Adelicia
Adriane
Agathe
Agnes
Alberta
Alexandra, Alexia, Alexis,
    Alix
Alice
Aloisa
Amalia, Amalie
Anastacie
Angelika, Geli
Anna, Anitte, Annchen
    (dim.), Anneli,
    Annette — popular
Antonie
Arabelle
Auguste, Augusta
Beatrix
Benedikta
Berta, Berthe
Bertita

Betti, Bettina
Bianka
Blanka
Brigitta
Camille
Christa, Christiane,
    Christine
Cilli
Clara
Clarissa, Klarissa — popular
Claudia
Clothilde, Klothilde
Constanza, Konstanze
Cordula, Kordula
Deboran
Dorle, Dorlisa
Dorothea, Dore, Dorchen
    (dim.) — popular
Editha
Elena
Eleonore
Elizabeth, Elise, Lise

Elke
Elsa, Ilsa, Else, Elschen
    (dim.)
Elvire
Emilia, Emmy
Ernestine
Eugenia
Euphemia — rare
Eva, Evchen (dim.)
Fanny — 19th c. and after
Florentia — rare
Franze, Franziska
Frida, Frieda — popular
Friederike, Fredi, Fritzi,
    Fritze, Fritzinn
Georgina
Gerhardine
Gertrud, Gertraud
Gisela
Grishilde, Griseldis
Gusta
Hanne, Hannele, Hanni
Hedwig, Hedda

Heinrika, Henrike
Helene
Helmine
Hetta
Hilda, Hilde
Hildegard, Hildegarde
Holde, Holle
Hortensia
Hulda
Hyacinthie
Ida
Imma, Emma
Inge
Irma
Isabelle
Jenny
Johanna
Josepha — popular
Juliane
Julie
Jutta
Kaethe
Karla
Karlotte, Lotte, Lottchen;
   Charlotte
Karoline — popular;
   Caroline
Katerine, Katrina, Katha-
   rina; Katti, Ketti;
   Katchen (dim.); Käthe,
Klara
Klarissa
Klementine
Kornelia
Kristina, Kristiana
Laura

Lena, Lene, Leni, Lina,
   Linchen
Lenore
Leonarda
Liesa, Liesal, Lieschen
   (dim.)
Lillian, Lilli, Lili, Lily —
   popular
Lola
Lucie
Lucretia
Ludmilla, Ludmila, Mila,
   Ludchen (dim.)
Ludovika
Luise
Luzi
Magdalene, Marlene,
   Madlen, Magda, Mady
Malkin
Margrete, Margarethe,
   Gretal, Grethal,
   Gretchen, Grete, Greta
   Maria, Marie — Mari-
   etta, rare
Marion
Marthe
Mathilde
Mechtilde
Meta
Mitzi
Monika
Natalia
Nele
Nette, Netchen
Olympie
Ottilie

Pauline
Petronille
Philippine
Rahel — likely to be con-
   sidered Jewish
Raimunde
Rebekka — likely to be
   considered Jewish
Regine
Renate
Ricarda
Rosa
Rosalinde
Rosamonde
Ruperta
Sabine
Sara
Sibylle
Sophia, Sophie — very
   popular
Stephanine
Susann
Therese, Tresa, Trescha
Trine, Trinchen
Ulla
Uta
Verona
Veronike
Victoria
Virginia
Wilhelmina, Wilhelmine,
   Mina, Minna, Mena —
   very popular
Zella
Zita

MALE NAMES

An occasional Catholic German will give a son the middle name Maria, but never as a first name.

Abalard, Abelard, Abilard
Adalbert
Adam
Adolf
Adrian
Ahren
Alaric
Albrecht

Alder
Alexander
Alois
Anastasius
Andreas
Anton
Arius
Armin

Arndt
Arno
Arnold
Artur
August — somewhat pop-
   ular
Baldwin, Balduin
Balthasar

Barthel, Bartol
Barthold
Barthololmäus
Basle
Benedikt
Benjamin
Benno
Bernhard, Bernd, Berend
Bertold, Bertel
Bruns, Bruno — not that
popular
Caspar
Christian
Christoph
Claus, Klaus
Clemens, Klemens
Dagobert
Dieter
Dietrich — popular
Dominik
Eduard — not unpopular
Edwin
Elert
Elman
Emanuel — fairly popular
Emil — popular
Emrich, Emmerich
Engelhard
Ephraim
Erdmann
Erich
Ernst — popular
Erwin
Eugen — popular
Ewald
Faber
Felix
Franz — popular, espe-
cially in Austria
Friedrich — very popular
Fritz, Fritzchen (dim.)
Gebhard
Georg — popular
Gerd
Gerhard
Gideon
Gottfried — not unpopu-
lar
Gotthelf, Gotthilf
Gotthold

Gottleib — popular
Gottlob
Gottwald
Guenther, Gunther,
Gunter
Gustav — very popular
Hans, Hansel (dim.) —
popular
Hasso
Heinrich, Heinz — very
popular
Helmuth, Helmut
Herbert, Heribert
Hermann — very popular
Heyderich
Heymann
Hubert
Hugo
Ignaz
Immanuel
Ingelbert
Jakob
Johann, Johannes — very
popular
Josef — popular
Julius
Jürgen
Justinus
Justus — rarely Just
Karl — extremely popular
Kaspar
Klaus — somewhat popu-
lar
Klemens
Konrad
Konstantin
Leberecht
Leo, Leonard
Leopold, Luitpold — not
unpopular
Lion
Lobegott
Lothar
Ludwig — popular; rarely
Chlodwig
Lujo
Manfred
Martin — popular with
Protestants
Matthäus

Maximilian, Max
(often a free-stand-
ing name)
Melchior
Michael
Moritz
Nepomuk
Nikolaus
Oskar
Oswald
Otfried — unusual
Otto — somewhat popular
Ottomar — unusual;
Ottmar
Paul
Philipp
Pieter
Reinecke, Reinke (dim.)
Reinhold
Reinmar
Richard — not unpopular
Rüdiger — unusual
Rudolf — fairly popular
Rupert, Ruprecht — not
unpopular; Robert
sometimes used
Sasha — currently on a
boom like our Jason
Sebastian
Seigmund — not unpopu-
lar
Selig
Siegmund
Theobold
Theodor — popular
Ulrich
Valentine
Viktor
Walther, Walter — some-
what popular
Werner
Wilfred
Wilhelm, Wilchen
(dim.) — very popu-
lar
Willibald
Woldemar
Wolfgang
Wülfing
Zephyrin

FAMILY NAMES

Abert
Abich
Abt
Achenbach
Achenwall
Ackermann
Adenauer
von Aehrenthal
Aepinius
Ahlefeldt
Ainmiller
Alsberg
Altgeld
von Alvensleben
Ambros
von Amerling
von Amsdorf
Anschutz
Anspacher
Apel
von Archenholz
von Aretin
Argelander
von Armansperg
von Arneth
Arnstein
von Aschbach
Ast
von Asten
Auenbrugger, von Auen-
   brugg
Auersperg
von Auffenberg
Aufrecht
Aurbacher
von Auwers
Avenarius
Ayrer
von Baader
Bahr
Baltzer
Barany
Bardt
Bartholdt
Basedow, von Basedow
von Baudissin
Bauer
von Bauernfeld
Baumgarten

Baur
Bebel
Becher
Bechstein
Becke, Becker
Beckmann
Behm
Behrends
Beissel
von Belling
Bemelmans
Bendemann
von Benedek
Benfey
Benndorf
Bennigsen, von Bennig-
   sen
Berendt
Bergius
Bergk
Bergmann, von Berg-
   mann
von Bernstorff
Bessel, Bessels
Bethe
von Bethmann
Betz
von Beust
von Bezold, Bezold
Biedermann
Biel
von Biela
Bierstadt
von Bilguer
Bimeler
Bischof, Bischoff
von Bissing
Blechen
Bleibtreu
Blenk, Blenker
Blind
Blitzstein
Blum
Blumenschein
Blumenthal, von Blu-
   menthal
Blumentritt
Bock, Bockh
Bode, von Bode

Boellmann
Bohlen, von Bohlen
Boldt
Boltzmann
Bothe
Bottiger
Bouterwek
Brachvogel
Brambach
Brandt, von Brandt
von Brauchitsch
Bredow, von Bredow
Brefeld
Brehm
Breisach
Breithaupt
Breitkopf
Brendel
Bretschneider, von
   Bretschneider
Briegleb
von Brockdorff-Rantzau
Brockes
Brockhaus
Bronn
von Bruck
Brucker, Bruckner
von Bruhl
Bruhns
Bucheler
Buchner
Buchrucker
Bulthaupt
von Bunge
von Buol-Schauensten
Busch
Busching
Butenant
Butschli
Cabanis
Cammerhoff
Camphausen
Capellen
von Carnall
Cassirer
Cauer
von Christ — short I,
   rhymes with twist
Christoffel

Clebsch
Conze
Corssen
Creuzer
Dahlmann
von Dalberg
Dalman
Damrosch
von Dannecker
Daub
von Dechen
von der Decken
Dedekind
von Defregger
Deger
Dehmel
Delitzsch
Denhardt, Denhart
Denner
Diels
Dieterici, Dieterich,
   Dietl, Dietrich
Dillmann
von Dingelstedt
Distler
Ditters von Dittersdorf—
   many old families with
   this pattern
Dobereiner
Dohrn
von Dollinger
Dorn, Dorner, Dornier
Draeseke
Dreyer
von Dreyse
Driesch
Duboc
Duhring
Dürbach, Duerbach
Ebeling
Eberlein, Eberlin
Ebers, Ebert, Eberth
Eckermann
Ehrenberg
Ehrle, Ehrlich
Eichhorn
Eichler
Eisner
Eller
Elze
von Emmich

Encke
Engelmann
von Engerth
Enghaus
Engler
von Epp
Erb
Erdmann
Ernst
Ertl
Esmarch, von Esmarch
Ettmuller
Ettwein
Eulenberg, zu Eulen-
   berg — occasionally
   instead of von
Euting
Exner
Eytelwein
Faber, von Faber
Falb
Falk, Falke
von Falkenhayn
Federmann
von Fernkorn
Francke, Frank
Frasch
Frauenstadt
von Fraunhofer
Freiligrath
Freund
Freundlich
Freytag
Fried
Friedel
Friedheim
Friedlander
Friedrich
von Fritsch
Frobenius
Froebel, Fröbel
Frommel
Froschammer
von Fuhrich
Fulda
von Furth
Furtwängler
von der Gabelentz
Gaedertz
Gaffky
von Galen

Gall, Galle
Gans, Ganz
Gauermann
von Gebhardt
Gegenbaur
Geibel
Geiler von Kaysersberg
Geinitz
von Geissel
Gellert
Genth
Gerhardt
Gericke
Gerland
Gerstacker
von Gerstenberg
Gesenius
Geyl
Gleim
Gmelin
von Goeben
von der Goltz
Gossen
Grabbe
Graebe
Graupner
Grein
Grell
Grillparzer
von Grolman
Grotefend
Groth, von Groth
Grün, Gruen
von Gudden
Guertner
Gussenbauer
Haas, Haase
Haber
Hahnemann
Halder
von Hammer
Hammerling
Harbach
von Hardenberg
Hardt
Hartmann, von Hart-
   mann
Haude
Haupt
Hauptmann
Haushofer

Hebbel, Hebel
Hecker
Heckewelder
Hedmondt
Heimsoeth
Heinicke, Heinkel
Heinrich, Heinse
Hell
Hellwig
Hempel, Hempl
Herbermann
Hergesheimer
von Herkomer
Hermann, von Hermann
von Hersfeld
von Hertling
Hertwig
Herwegh
Heussgen, Hussgen
Heyse
Hilferding
von Hillern
Hilprecht
Hittorf
Hitzig
Hofman, von Hofmann,
  Hoffman
von Hofmannsthal
Holderlin
Hossbach
von Hotzendorff
Huber, Hubner
Hugenberg
Hugo
Hümer
von Hutten
Immermann
Immisch
Jacobi
Jaegersvon
Jagow
Jank
Jülg, Juelg
Junghuhn
Kalb
Kalbeck
Karsch, Karschin
Kaufmann
Kaulbach, von Kaulbach
von Kaunitz
Kautzsch

von Ketteler
Kielhorn
Kienzl
Kiesler
Kinkel
Klaproth
Klengel
von Klenze
Klopp
Kluge, von Kluge
Knabb, Knabe
Knapp
Knaus
Kneipp
Kneisel
von dem Knesebeck
Knille
Knoop
Knortz
von Kobell, Kobell
Koester
Koffka
Kogel
Kohl, Kohler
Kohlrausch
Koldewey
Kolreuter, Koelreuter
Koppe
Korting
Kosegarten
Koser
Kostlin
Kraus, Krauss
Kreisler
Krenek
von Kretschmann
Kronecker
von Krudener
Kugler
Kummer
Kürnberger
Lachmann
Lamprecht
Langenscheidt
Lappenberg
Laudon, Loudon
Laufer
Leberecht
Lehmbruck
Leibl
Leichhardt

Leinsdorf
Lemnitzer
von Lenback
Lenel
Lenhartz
Lentz, Lenz
Leo
Leonarz
Leonhardt
Lessing
Leutze
Ley
Leypold, Leypoldt
Lieber
Liebknecht
Lima von Sanders
Lincke, Linke
von Lingg
Litolff
von Littrow
Loeffler
Loffler
von Lofftz
Loofs
von Lossow
Lotze
Lowie
Lubke
Lüdecke
Ludwig
Lummer
Magnus
Makart
Mann
Manteuffel
von Marr
Mattheson
von Max
Mehring
Meitner
Meltzer
Memminger
Menger, Mengs
von Menzel
Meyer, Mayer, von
  Mayer
Mielatz
Miller
Millocker
Mitscherlich
Mittermaier

von Mohl
Moldenke
von Mollendorf
Mond
Monn
Morgenstern
Mörike, Moerike
Morwitz
Moscheles
Most
von Mücke, Muecke;
  -Emden
von Müller, Mueller
Muhlenmann
Mundt
Muther
Nachtigal
Nagel
Natorp
Naumann
Nees von Esenbeck
Neisser
Nernst
Netscher
von Neuhof
Neukirch
von Neumayer
Niecks
Niemann
von Niemeyer
Nindemann
Nippold
Nissl
Nitze
Nitzsch
Noeggertath
Nottebohm
Nussbaum, von Nuss-
  baum
Oberhoffer
Oberholtzer
Ochs
Oertel
Oeser
Oesterley
Oetinger
Olbers
Olbrich
Older
Opitz
Orth

Ostwald
Ottendorfer
Otterbein
von Papen
Pauer
Paulsen
von Payer
Penck
von Perfall
Perthes
von Pettenkofer
Pfitzner
von Pflanzer-Baltin
Pflederer
Pfluger
Plücker, Pluecker
Poetsch
von Polentz
Postl
Prandtl, Prantl
Pregl
Preller
Priessnitz
Prutz
Pursch
Quantz
Quidde
Quincke
von Radowitz
Rahv
Raiffeisen
Ramberg
Raspe
Ratke, Ratich
Ratzel
Rau
von Raumer
Raupach
von Reber
Redlich
Reger
Reichardt
Reimensnyder
Reinecke
Reinhold
Rethel
Retzsch
von Reuenthal
Riedesel
Riemann
Rietschel

von Rintelen
Ritschl
Roediger
Roehde
Rohlfs
Rose
Rosegger
Rosen
von Rotteck
Rückert
Ruge
Ruhmkorff
von Rundstedt
Rupp
Rüstow
Scherfer
Schleirmacher
Schmidt
Schmidt von der Launitz
Schonemann
Schönkopf
Schramm
Schücking, Schuecking,
  Schucking
Schurz
von Schwarzenberg
Schweinfurth
Siebold
Siemering
Sigel
Slevogt
Sombart
von Soxhlet
Spangenberg
Speilhagen
Spitta
Spohr
Spurzheim
Steffeck
Stein, von Stein
Steinheil
Steinthal
Steinweg
Stinde
Stinnes
Stocker, Stoecker
Stoeckel
Stohmann
zu Stolberg
Storm
Strasburger

Streicher
Stresemann
von Struensee
von Struve
Stumpf
Sturm, von Sturm
Südfeld
Sutter
Tauchnitz
Tauscher
von Teuffel
van der Thann
Thesiger
von Thielmann
Thumann
von Thunen
Tieck
Tiedt
Tischbein
von Tischendorf
Todleben
Traugott
Trippenmeker
Uhland
Varnhagen von Ense
von Vicari
Viebig
von Vietinghoff
Vogel

Vogel von Falckenstein
Vogler
Volck
Volkmann, von Volk-
    mann
Voss, Vossius
Vulpius
Waagen
Waechter
von Waldersee
Waldmuller
Walsham
Walter, Walther
Wappaeus
Warburg
Wasmann
von Weber, Weber
Wedekind
Weizsäcker
Welker
Welser
Weyr
Wieland
Wiengatner
Willstatter
Windaus
zu Windisch-Graetz
Windthorst — [VINDT-
    horst]

von Winter
von Wissmann
Wolf, Wolff
Wullner
Yorck von Wartenburg
Zacharia, Zacharia von
    Lingenthal
Zacher
Zahn
von Zedlitz, Zedlitz
Zeigler
Zeiss
von Zeiten, von Ziethen
Zell, Zeller
von Zenker
Ziller
Zimmern
Zingerle
Zingerle von Sommers-
    berg
Zinnen
von Zinzendorf
von Zittel
Zockler
von Zoller
Zorn
Zschokke
Zumpt

INTRODUCTION TO
SCANDINAVIAN NAMING

This is the home of the Norse, and many personal names have been in use for a thousand years. Left over from the Norse patronymic are the many "-son" and "-sen" family names. On the whole, Swedes tend to use "-son," while the Danes and Norwegians use "-sen," but the area has been shuffling population so thoroughly for so long that a Peterssen family may have been in Sweden 300 years.

If you cannot find a personal name you like here, the character's parents can always have revived an old Norse one; see that chapter.

Pronunciation

Most keyboards do not have the ø/Ø used in Scandinavia; if yours does not, try @. And perhaps you could use a following quotation mark, " for an umlauted vowel. All of these are short, dull vowel sounds. Final E's are also short.

A grave accent following an A, A`/a`, can stand for Å; up until 1948 this was frequently written Aa or aa, standing for a sound halfway between the O's of "rote" and "pod." Đ or đ is the hard TH in then.

J is always pronounced like our Y.

Q, X, Z, hard C, PH, and PS indicate a foreign word or name.

DANISH

Denmark is the continental holding of the Norse, and often fought with the Russians and Germans over the Baltic coasts, as well as with Sweden. The vocabulary has been influenced over the centuries by German, over the Schleswig-Holstein border, a traditional division between the two people.

DANISH FEMALE NAMES

Adeline	Gerda	Luise
Agneta	Hedvig	Malena
Anna	Hortense	Margreta
Annelise	Inge, Inga, Ingrid	Marie
Astrid	Jana	Sara
Atti	Jensine	Sigrid
Bengta	Johanne	Sonja
Bodil	Karen, Karin	Sophie, Sophia
Dagmar	Kjelda	Thomasine
Elisabeth	Kristian, Christina,	Ulla
Elsa, Ilsa, Else	Christine	Valborg
Frederika	Lene	Viktoria
Gala	Leonora	Vita

DANISH MALE NAMES

Aabye, Åbye	Axel, Aksel	Edvard
Aage, Åge	Bardo	Egede
Adam	Bent	Ejnar
Albert	Bertel	Emanuel
Alfred	Bronnum	Emil
Anders, Andreas	Carl	Erasmus
Angul	Christian, Christiern	Erik
Arild	Christoffer	Ernst
Arnold	Clemens	Esaias
Asger	Conrad	Ferdinand
Asmus	Cornelius	Fini
August	David	Frants

Frederik, Frederic
Frits
Georg
Gottfred
Gottlob
Gustav
Hakon, Haakon, Håkon
Halfdan
Hans
Harald
Helge
Hendrik
Henrik
Herman
Hersleb
Hjalmar
Holger, Holgar
Hviid
Immanuel
Isak
Japetus
Jen, Jens
Jeppe
Jesper
Joakob
Joern
Johan
Johannes
Jørgen, Jörgen
Julius

Kaj
Karl
Kaspar
Knud, Knute. Knuth
Knudaage, Knudåge
Kristian
Lauritz
Leck
Leopold
Lewis
Lorens
Louis
Ludolf
Ludvig
Lyne
Malte
Martin
Mogens
Niels
Nikolaj
Nils
Ole
Orla — yes, masc.
Otto
Ove
Peder, sometimes Peter
Piet
Poul
Rasmus
Rikard

Robert
Rold
Rudolf
Sandođe
Schack
Sextus (Danish parents
   get Roman-happy,
   too)
Siegfred
Signius
Simon
Sophus
Søren
Steen
Styrbjørn
Svend
Terkel
Theodor
Thøger
Thomas
Thorkild
Troels
Tycho
Valdemar
Victor
Viggo
Vilhelm
Villads
Vitus

Danish Family Names

Aagesen, Aagessøn, Åges-
   søn, Ågesen
Aakjaer, Åkjaer
Aarestrup, Årestrup
Aarsbo, Årsbo
Abell
Abildgaard, Abildgård
Abrahamsen
Amberg
Andersen
Arrebo
Attrup
Axelson
Baggesen
Bajer [BUY-er]
Bang
Barnekow

Bartholdy, Bartholin
Bechgaard, Bechgård
Becker, Bekker
Behrend
Bendix
Bentzon
Berggreen
Bergstedt
Bering
Bersoe
Bille
Bjerregaard, Bjerregård
Blicher
Bødtcher
Bohlmann
Bohr
Borck

Bording
Børresen
Boye
Brahe
Brandes
Branner
Bredahl
Bregendahl
Brochmand
Brondal
Brondsted
Brunn
Buntzen
Carstens
Cibert, Cibber
Crumlin
Dalgas

Dalsgaard, Dalsgård
Dam
Danning
Dons
Drachmann
Eckersberg
Enna
Erichsen
Esmann
Estrup
Ewald
Fabricius
Fallingborg
Fibiger
Finecke
Finsen
Frølich, Frolich
Gade
Gelert
Gjellerup
Glass
Glistrup
Gram
Grandjean
Gravlund
Gronlund
Grundtvig
Gulberg
Güntelberg
Gyllembourg
Hamerik
Hansen
Hartmann
Hauch
Heiberg
Hein
Heise
Helgesen
Helsted
Hemming
Henningsen
Henriksen
Herbebred
Herdal
Herholdt
Hertz
Hjortđ
Holberg
Holme, Holm
Horneman
Hostrup

Hovgaard, Hovgård
Huitfeldt — noble family
Hvass
Hvidt
Ingemann
Isitt
Jacobsen
Jager
Jensen
Jerichau
Jespersen
Jorgensen
Juel
Kaalund, Kålund
Kalhauge
Kidde
Kingo
Kirk
Kjaerholm
Klim
Knudsen
Kristensen
Krogh
Krøyer
Krygell
Laale, Låle
Lange
Langgaard, Langgård
Larsen
Lassen
Lehmann
Lindgren
Løkken
Lumbye
Lund
Madvig
Malling
Matthison
Menved
Michaëlis
Mikkelsen
Miskow
Mølgaard, Mølgård
Møller
Müller
Munk
Nansen
Nexø
Nielsen
Nobel
Norden

Nordraak, Nordråk
Nørstad
Oehlenschläger
Oersted, Orsted
Olesen
Olrik
Orheim
Ørn
Paars, Pårs
Palladius
Paludan
Panum
Paulli
Pedersen
Petersen
Ploug
Pontoppidan
Pram
Qvistgaard, Qvistgård
Rafn
Rahbek
Rask
Rasmussen
Ravn
von der Recke
Richardt
Rode
Roesdahl
Romer
Rørdam
Rosenberg
Rosenfeld
Rubner
Rung
Rüsager
Ryberg
Rybner
Scavenius
Schack
Schumacher
Skeel — noble family
Sønderby
Sørensen
Soya
Stangeland
Steenberg
Steensen
Steenstrup
Steno
Stuckenberg
Tagg

Tausen	sen	Vedel
Tegnér	Thrane	Verner
Terkelsen	Thuren	Villumsen
Thaarup, Thårup	Tofft	Winding
Thorvaldsen, Thorwald-	Utzon	Winther

SWEDISH

Sweden was the powerhouse of the Scandinavian peninsula, and at one time controlled both of what are now Norway and Finland, as well as the Baltic trio of Estonia, Latvia, and Lithuania.

SWEDISH FEMALE NAMES

Aasa, Åsa	Eleonora	Klara
Agneta	Elisabet	Kolina
Alicia	Ellen	Kristina
Amata	Elsa	Lotta
Anki	Emilie	Lovisa
Anna, Anita, Anneka, Annika	Eva	Majvor
	Frederika	Malin
Antonetta	Freja, Freya	Margaret
Arriet	Greta	Margit
Astrid	Gunilla	Maria
Aurora	Hanna	Marianne
Barbro	Harriet	Olivia
Bibi	Hedvig	Ottiliana
Birgit, Brigitta, Brigit, Birgitta	Hertha	Rika
	Inga	Ruth
Bittan	Ingeborg	Selma
Blanka	Inger	Sofi
Blenda	Ingrid	Tyra
Britt, Britta, Brita	Johanna	Ulla
Celia	Kajsa, Kaysa, Kaj	Ulrika
Charlotta	Karin	Vilma
Chresta	Katarina	Wanja, Vanya
Christina	Kersten, Kerstin	Wera

SWEDISH MALE NAMES

Adolf	Allvar	Amadeus
Agne	Alrik	Anders — popular
Alfred	Alvar	Arne

Arnold
Arram
Artur
Arvid
Axel — Swedes use this far
  more than other Scan-
  dinavians
August
Barthelemy
Basilius
Basle
Bengt
Bernhard
Bertel
Birger
Bjorn
Christian
Christophe, Christopher
Dag
Daniel
Edvard
Elge'rus
Elias
Emil
Erik
Erland
Esais
Fabian
Folke
Frans
Frederik
Fritz
Gabriel
Gerhard

Gösta
Gries
Gunnar
Gunno, Gun
Gustaf— popular; also
  Gustav
Hadrian
Hans
Hansel
Hasselqvist
Hjalmar
Ingmar
Ivar
Jakob — popular
Jens
Jeremia
Johan
Jonam
Jonas — popular
Jöns
Jorgen
Josua
Karl — popular
Klas
Knut
Konrad
Krister
Kristoffer
Laris
Lars
Lauris
Lennart
Ludwig, Louis
Lukas

Magnus
Martin
Mathias
Mihlje
Mikael
Niklas
Nils — popular
Olaus
Olof, Olov
Oskar
Otto
Pär
Per — fairly popu-
  lar
Philipp
Rickard
Rolle
Sigvard
Simson
Stefan
Sten
Svante
Sven
Teodor
Thorsten, Torsten
Tor
Torbern
Torkel
Valdemar
Verner
Viktor
Vilhelm
Ville

Swedish Family Names

Alexanderson
Almqvist
Alstromer
Ambrosiani
Andersson
Andree
Angstrom
Armfelt
Arnoldson
Arrhenius
Artedi
Arwidsson
Attebom

Aulin
Backlund
Banér
Bellmann
Bergen
Bergman
Berling
Berzelius
von Beskow
Bexelius
Bildt
Björk, Björkman
Bjornsson

Bjornstrand
Bostrom
Branting
Bremer
Bretting
Brinell
von Brinkerman, von
  Brinckerman
Bystrom
Carlen
Cassel
Clausen
Cleve

Creutz
Cronstedt
Croon
Crusenstolpe
Dahl
Dahlberg, Dahlbergh
Dahlgren
Dahlstierna
Dalén
von Dalin
Dryander
Dybeck
Eberhart
Edgren
Edstrom
Ehrensvard
Ekborg
Ekman
Enquist
Estvall
Fagerlin
Fahlcrantz
Flygare
Fogelberg
Folkung, Folkungar
Foreshell
Forskal
Forssell
Franzen
Fredgaard, Fredgård
Fremstad
Fries
Froding
Fryxell
de Geer
Geijer
af Geijerstam
Göransson
Grane
Gronberg
Guggenberger
Gulbranson
Gullstrand
Gustafson, Gustaffson,
    Gustavsson
Gyllenborg
Gyllenstierna
Hägg
Hallen, Hallin

Hallgren
Hallstrom
Hammarskjold
Hedin
von Heidenstam
Helm
Hoas
Holgersson
Horn
Hyllested
Jacobsson
Jansen, Jansson
Kalm
Karlfeldt
Kebbe
Kellgren
Kessle
Klingspor
Konigsmark
Kreuger
Lagerkvist
Lagerlöf
Lagerman
Larsson
Leffler
Lenngren
Lenstrom
af Leopold
Lind
Lindbergh
Lindblom
Lindgren
Lindstrom
Ling
Lingegaard, Lingegård
Lundeberg
Lundgren
Lundkvist
Lundmark
Malmstedt
Michelsen
Mittag
Moberg
Myrdal
Nathorst
Niebuhr
Nilsson
Nordenberg
Nordenfeldt

Nordenflycht
Nordenskjöld
Nordgren
Nordquist
Nylen
Nyren
Ockerson
Ossian-Nilsson
Osterdahl
Ostergren
Oxenstierna
Palander
Palmaer
Palme
Pasche
Petri
Polhem
Printz
Rydberg
Rydqvist
Runeberg
Ruth
Scheele
Seashore
Sefstrom
Sellstedt
Siegbahn
Sjostrom
Snoilsky
Soderblom
Stål
Stävberg
Stoessel
Strindberg
Sture
Swensson
Tegner
Thorild
Thorvaldsen
Thulin
Torell
Torstenson, Torstensson
Villner
Waldenstron
Wallin
Wehtje
von Wrangel
Zorn

NORWEGIAN

Norway was long part of Denmark, after having been settled by the same Norse peoples, so that Norwegian and Danish names are not very different. Norwegian was everyday talk, while Danish was the literary language. Check the Danish listing for someone whose family may have crossed the border 40 or 400 years ago.

NORWEGIAN FEMALE NAMES

Aase, Åse	Fredrika	Kristine, Kristin
Agathe	Gina	Lona
Asta	Gressa	Martha
Astrup	Gunda	Ola
Aud	Hanna	Olea
Birgit	Hansine	Rane
Brit	Hedda	Signe
Camilla	Hedwig	Sigrid
Charlotte — French ori-	Helga	Solveig
gin, but heavily used	Helge	Sonja
since 18th c.	Inger	Synnöve
Cora	Jakobine	Terese
Dagny	Karena	Thora
Doris — foreign origin	Katla	Thordis
Dorte	Kirsten	Ursula

NORWEGIAN MALE NAMES

Aall, Åll	Audr	Egeberg
Absalon	Bert	Eilert
Aegot	Bjørn, Bjarne	Eilif
Aksel	Bjørnstjerne	Einar
Alexander	Bodil	Eivind
Alf	Bojer	Elseus
All	Bonnevie	Ernst
Amund	Catharinus	Eyolf
Andreas	Claes	Eyvind, Eivind
Anton	Claus	Fartein
Arild	Dag	Fridtjof
Arkin	David	Galt
Arne	Donalt	Geirr
Arnold	Dreng	Georg
Arnulf	Dyre	Gerhard
Artur	Edemil	Gregors
Arve	Edmund	Gunnar
Arvid	Edvard	Gustav

Halldis
Halvdan, Halfdan
Hans
Harald
Henrik
Herman
Hersleb
Hjalmar
Hjorth
Ingebret, Engebret
Ingolf
Ivar, Iver
Jakob
Jens
Johan
Jonas
Jørgen, Jörgen
Just
Kare
Kjell
Klaus
Knud, Knute, Knut

Krist, Kristian
Kristofer
Lars
Lauritz
Leif
Ludvig
Magnus, Magne
Matteus, Mathias
Mikkel, Michael
Morad
Nagel
Nicolai
Nils
Nordahl
Odd, Odo
Olaf, Olav — popular
Ole
Otto
Paal, Pål
Petter, Peter, Per, Peder
Rasmus
Rikard

Roald
Rudolf
Severin
Sigbjorn
Sigurd
Sigvard, Sigvardt, Sig-
    warth, Sigwardt
Siurt
Sophus
Sparre
Sten
Svend
Sverre
Tarjei
Thor
Thorbjörn
Thorvald
Tor, Tore
Trygve, Tryggve
Vilhelm
Waldemar

NORWEGIAN FAMILY NAMES

Aanrud, Ånrud
Aasen, Åsen
Abel
Alnaes
Amundsen
Andersen
Anker
Arneberg
Asbjornsen
Aspestrand
Astrup
Aukrust
Backer
Balchien
Bernick
Birkeland
Bjerkes, Bjerknes
Bjørkman
Bjørnsgaard, Bjørnsgård
Bjornson, Bjørnson
Blom
Bojer
Bonnevie
Borchgrevink
Borgstrøm

Borkman
Bormann
Boyeson
Braaten, Bråten
Brandes
Braunmann
Brekke
Brostrup
Brovik
Bruheim
Brun
Brustad
Brynie
Bugge
Bull
Claussøn
Cleve
Collett
Crøger
Dahl
Dass
Dietrichson
Døderlein
Dunn
Egede

Egge
Eggen
Ekdal
Elling
Elvsted
Engebretsen
Eyde
Fahlcrantz
Falkberget
Falsen
Fangen
Fasting
Fearnley
Finsen
Fitje
Flagstad
Flintenberg
Foyn
Fritzner
Fuglesang
Furuholmen
Gabler
Garborg
Geelmuyden
Gill

Gomnaes
Grieg
Grondahl
Groven
Gude
Haarklou, Hårklou
Hagerup
Halvorsen
Hamsun
Heiberg
Heine
Hektoen
Henrikson
Hiis
Hjelm
Hoel
Holberg
Holt, Holter
Hurum
Irgens
Jacobsen
Jaeger
Janson
Jensen
Johanson, Johansen
Jonsson
Jordan
Kielland
Kinck
Kjerulf
Kleven
Konow
Krag
Krog
Krohg
Lammers
Landstad
Lange
Larsen
Lassen
Lie
Lindeman
Løkke
Løland

Lövborg
Lunde
Michelsen
Moe
Moen, Mohn
Møller
Molvik
Munch
Nansen
Neupert
Nilsen
Nordraak, Nordråk
Nygaardsvold, Nygårds-
  vold
Obstfelder
Olsen
Ørjasaeter
Orvil
Ostenso
Øverland
Paulus
Pedersen, Pederssøn
Petersen, Petterson
Prytz
Qvigstad
Reidarson
Reiss
Relling
Resi
Revold
Riiser
Rolfsen
Roll
Rongen
Rosenkrone
Roverud
Rud
Rygh
Saeverud
Sandel
Sandemose
Sandvik
Sandvold
Schjelderup

Schjøtt
Segelcke
Selmer
Sinding
Sivle
Skarheim
Skjaeraasen, Skjaeråsen
Skouen
Solstad
Sørensen
Stamsø
Steffens
Stockmann
Styr
Svendsen
Sverdrup
Tellefsen
Thrane
Thygesen
Tordenskjold
Torjussen
Torson
Tullin
Tvedt, Tveit
Udbye
Ulvestad
Undset
Uppdal
Valen
Vesaas, Vesås
Vigeland
Vinje
Vogt
Waaktaar, Wåktår
Wangel
Welhaven
Wergeland
Werle
Wessel
Wildenvey
Wingar
Winge
Winter
Zetlitz

ICELANDIC

The Icelandic phonebooks list everyone in the order of their personal names. Just like their Norse ancestors, the Icelanders have never bothered with anything silly like family names. Eirik Magnusson's children are Halldor Eiriksson and Helga Eiriksdotter. They will be found in the phonebook under H, their father under E, and their grandfather, Magnus Eiriksson, under M. Women keep their birth-names.

To help answer "WHICH Eirik Eiriksson from the East Village?" people have eke-names, which might further distinguish the notable, like Eirik the Red or Eirik the Clumsy. In Norse culture, what we call eke-names may be called "by-names."

Pagan Names

The Icelanders are conservative. Besides speaking the next best thing to Old Norse, they still use the Thor names as often or more often than the saint names. Like so many people, they think of names as "just names," not any kind of description or dedication.

Because of this, you can use the Norse section for many Icelanders. For the rest, take Christian names from the other Scandinavian countries.

HISPANIC

In all the lands colonized by the Spanish, Catholicism predominates with its saint names, and in many cases Spanish itself remains the official spoken language. Besides naming a child after a saint, it is Hispanic to sometimes name it for various feast days, either the one on which it was born, or the one on which it was christened, like Visitación for the Feast of the Visitation. Then again, it may be named for Uncle Visitación who has all the money.

Many names are hidden references to the Virgin, like Marina for Mary, Star of the Sea (*Marina Stella Maris*), or all the Flor- names for the Virgin of the Flowers.

Because some feast or shrine names are used unchanged for both sexes, it is slightly possible to confuse a man's name with a woman's, as when it is written down somewhere free-standing, like a list. However, adjectives, particles, etc., have to be gendered to match a person's sex, so in a conversation or letter such mistakes are virtually impossible.

When boys are named for Santa María, in every example I have seen María was the second name, after Carlos, Juan, or something else indubitably masculine. However, while most parents also would use a "unisex" name as a girl's second name, I have met women known as Trinidad and Purificación.

How Many Names Where

Amongst those who follow Spanish nomenclature, first comes your personal baptismal names, which may be several. At your confirmation, you yourself choose one to add in honor of your chosen favorite saint. These are followed by your father's family name, an "y" (pronounced EE) and your mother's family name, as in Indalecio Prim y Prats. Women do not change their family name at marriage.

This results in some contretemps when Spaniards emigrate to, say, America. The immigration guy asks the *pater familias* what his name is: "Luis Pedro Rodríguez y García." "What's the kid's name?" "Miguel Alonzo Rodríguez y Rivera." And when the paperwork is done, the father now is officially Luis García, while his son is Miguel Rivera, even though the paternal family name is Rodríguez. It happened nearly like this in my family in 1920.

On top of this, a number of proud lines compound a family name as: father's family name, father's mother's family name, mother's family name *y* mother's mother's family name: Miguel Rodríguez García Rivera y Sorzano. Then, some drop one or the other grandmother's moniker if it is not a distinguished line. This sort of upper-class game helps identify the social climber who has not been raised on the complex genealogies. The *parvenu* can use it to claim female connections more easily, so it is two-edged.

The nobility add a place-name, "*de* Something." Choose a Spanish place-name as you would one for a titled person in a Regency Romance: preferably a fictitious place, or a real place that did not figure in a title, or a real place whose title was of a different degree. Only lastly or with good cause use a real title. Check your *Almanach de Gotha*, which is the *Burke's Peerage* for the whole continent.

Geographic Differences

Colonial Hispanics use a slightly different battery of personal names. For example, a Spaniard or Puerto Rican would never name a son Jesús [hay-ZOOS], but it is common in Mexico and the rest of Central America, though not in the Philippines. Many younger sons and impoverished nobles went out with the Conquistadors, so not everyone in the colonies has commoners' names. Some colonial names are very local, like Vicuña, in honor of the animal of the Andes. Also note that by the 19th century, there are Argentines of note like Juan Vucetich, whose family name is not Hispanic in the least. I have met Chinese-Argentines who did not speak a word of Chinese, too. Latin America is no more purely Iberian than North America is Anglo-Saxon.

In Latin America, most often a child has at least two personal names, followed by the father's family name, ending in the mother's maiden name. So the son of Esteban González and Catalina Camargo would be Ippolito María González Camargo, found in the phonebook under González. In Central America especially, there is a tendency to drop the "de" off Spanish names, as North Americans tend to shed "de" and "von" off French and German names.

Little Names and Big

Spanish speakers will nickname someone not only with a diminutive, a "little name," but with augmentatives, which add a sense of bigness. This is used for regular nouns, just not names. The word for man, *hombre*, can become *hombrazo*, "big man" or *hombracho* or *hombrachón*, meaning a massive, heavily built man, which use the male augmentatives, "-azo" and "-acho/-achon." The female augmentative is "-ona" as when *mujer*, "woman," becomes *mujerona*, "big woman" or "matron." The diminutives "-ito" and "-ico" for male things are friendly, positive, or even fond, but "-elo" has a sense of belittlement. The feminine diminutive is "-ita."

So Juan may be Juanito or Juanico to his family, but the guy who's trying to put him down will call him Juanelo. The equivalent of Big John is Juanazo (augmentative names are rare). His 200 pound mother, Carmela, may be Carmelona, but when she was 16 and half the mass, she was known as Carmelita. Of course, someone can get a diminutive or augmentative as an official name, so that Anita was never Anna, nor Carlito ever Carlo.

Titles of Nobility

What are castles in Spain without the romance of the noble families that built them? These are the Spanish titles of nobility, with their nearest English equivalents in the peerage.

Masculine	Feminine	English Equivalents
rey	reina	king, queen
infante	infanta	prince, princess
príncipe	princes	a foreign/reigning prince
principillo		princeling
duque	duquesa	duke, duchess
marqués	marquesa	marquis, marchioness
conde	condesa	count, countess
barón	baronesa	baron, baroness
baronet		baronet

Titles appear among commoners, often indicating those professions requiring education. Arquitecto Bello does not have the personal name Arquitecto; Sr. Bello is an architect. The few I have collected:

Masculine	Feminine	English Equivalent
arquitecto	arquitecta	architect
dr., doctor	dra., doctora	doctor
ingeniero	ingeniera	engineer
licenciado	licenciada	lawyer
prof., profesor	profa., profesora	professor

Finally, because I have seen them misused:

Señor, Sr.	any other man, outside the Church or military
Señorita, Sa.	a never-married woman
Señora, Sra.	any other woman — married, divorced, widowed

Pronunciation

Spanish is very regular. Once you get used to the cadence, you can sound pretty good reading text and not know a blessed thing you're saying.

Accent is usually but not always on the next to last syllable. This applies to all words ending in a vowel or diphthong (two vowels pronounced as one), or in N or S. If the word ends in any other consonant, then the default accent is on the last syllable. Note: "-io" is a diphthong, so Florencio or Rosario will be [flohr-EN-syo] and [roh-SAHR-yo]. Accented versions are due to dialectical variations.

An accent over a vowel does not change its sound, but tells you that this syllable bears the main accent for the word. Not every name need contain a written accent.

But just as a Cockney tout sounds different from a 23rd Baron, from a Georgia farmer, from a Sydney businessman, so there are different accents, even vocabularies, amongst Spanish speakers. The well-educated often adopt the Castilian accent, which is soft, sometimes called the Castilian lisp. Laborers and fishermen from the north of Spain have this by nature. I am told that the Mexicans sound harsh and choppy, South Americans clear, but "different." You try describing a Missouri accent to a Spanish speaker without demonstrating it!

A — short open a, as in pasta

C — hard C as in cat, before A, O and U; soft C as in city before I or E

D — the Castilian accent makes this a soft DHarma/THen sound, so that "diablo" can sound like "thee-AH-blow"; elsewhere, regular D

E — e as in hey, even at the end of a word

G — as in gun; before E or I, a hard H

H — silent

I — i in machine

J — h as in hot

LL — a palatized LY, so that "llama" sounds like "lyama," but NOT "lee-ama"

Ñ — NY, as in canyon, which in Spanish is cañon

O — long open o, as in go
P — as in panda, silent in right in front of a T
QU — Q alone, or K; as in palanquin/palankeen
S — normally S, or sometimes Z in the New World
U — long u, as in tutu
X — ks
Z — Z as in zero

There is no K.

Unisex Religious Names

Anunciación
Asunción
Concepción
Consuelo
Encarnación

Natividad
Pasión
Paz
Presentación
Purificación

Redención
Refugio
Rosario
Trinidad
Visitación

Female Names

Adelaida, Adelina, Adelita
Agnes
Agripina
Agueda
Aldonza
Alejandra, Alejandrina
Aleta, Aletea, Aleda, Alita
Aletea
Alicia
Aloisia
Alonza
Alma
Amalia
Amata, Amada
Ana, Anita, Anica, Aniceta
Angelita
Antonina, Antuca
Anunciata
Asela
Aventurada
Barbara
Beatriz
Belicia, Belica, Belita, Belia, Bebe
Benedicta, Benita, Benicia
Bernarda, Bernardina,

Bernardita
Betina
Blanca
Bonita
Brigida
Calandria
Calida
Camila
Caridad
Carla, Carlita, Carlota
Carmela, Carmelita
Carmena, Carmencita
Carolina
Casandra
Catalina, Catarina
Cecilla
Celestina
Chabela, Chabi
Chalina
Charita, Chara, Charo
Chela
Chica
Chila
Chimena, Ximena
Chofa, Chofi
Chumina
Clarisa, Clarita, Clareta
Conchita

Constancia, Constanza
Consuela, Sucla, Suelita
Cristina
Damita
Diogracias
Dolores, Dolorcitas, Doloritas
Dominga
Dorotea
Eduarda
Eleonor, Elenor
Elisa, Elsa
Elvira
Emilia
Engracia
Enriqueta
Erlinda
Ermelinda
Ernestina
Esmarelda, Esmerelda
Estralita
Eufemia
Eugenia
Eulalia
Eva, Evita
Fátima — only after WW1
Felicia
Fernanda

Filomena
Flocarfina
Flora, Florita
Florida [flor-I-da, not
    FLOR-i-da]
Francisca
Frasquita
Genoveva
Gianina
Gidita
Gina, Ginata, Ginia
Gisela
Gitana
Gracia
Graciana
Graciela
Guadelupe
Guillerma, Guilla
Hermina, Hermenia
    [er-MEE-nah, er-meh-
    NEE-ah]
Hilaria [ee-LAH-ree-ah]
Imelda
Inéz, Inés, Ynés, Ynéz;
    Inesita, Ynesita
Irenea
Isabella, Belita, Elisa,
    Ysabel, Isabel; Isabelita
Isola
Jacinta, Jacinda
Jada [HA-da]
Jandina [han-DEE-nah]
Jesusa [hey-SOO-sah] —
    Mexico primarily
Jorgina [hor-GEE-nah]
Juanita, Juana [hwah-
    NEE-tah, HWAH-
    nah]
Juliana
Julieta
Juno, Junita
Laureana
Leni
Leonor, Leonora
Leya
Licha, Lici
Lilia, Liliosa
Liseta
Lolita

Lorenza
Loretta
Lucía
Lucila
Lucita
Lucrezia
Luisa
Lupe
Luz
Magdelena, Magaly,
    Magda, Magola
Maita
Mamerta
Manuela
Margarita, Margara
María — ultimately popu-
    lar; Mariquita, Marita,
    ad infinitum
Mariana
Marina
Martina, Marta
Maruca, Maruja
Matilde
Melosa
Mema
Mercedes
Milagros
Morena, Mora
Nana
Narsisia, Narcisna
Necha
Nelia
Neneca
Neva
Ninita, Nita, Nina
Nuela
Ofelia
Pacita, Paca
Paloma
Pancha, Panchita
Paquita
Pasionária
Paulita
Pepita
Ponciona, Ponicía
Presca
Purita
Querida
Queta

Rafaela
Ramona
Raniona
Raquel, Roquel
Refuguia
Reina
Ría
Rita
Rosabel, Rosbel
Rosalia
Rosita, Rosa
Salomé, Salomena
Salustiana
Sanchia, Sanchita
Santana
Sarita, Saritia
Seraphina, Seraphima
Sevilla
Sofía, Soficita
Sol, Solana
Soledad, Soledá
Techa, Ticha
Teodora
Teresa, Teresita, Theresia,
    Tere
Tesaura
Tete
Tiana
Tiara
Tolivia
Tolasa
Tona
Trella
Trifónia
Udelfonsa
Ursulina
Valeriana
Victoriana, Victorina
Violanta, Violante
Violeta
Virida
Vitoria
Vivianna
Yolanda, Yolonda
Yoli
Zaida, Zeida
Zarita
Zenaida
Zita

MALE NAMES

Achileo
Adolfo
Agustín, Augustín
Alberto
Alejandro
Alfonse, Alfonso — popular
Alfredo
Alonzo
Álvaro
Amadeo, Amado
Ambrosio
Anastasio
Andrés
Aniceto
Anunciato
António — popular
Arcénio
Aristides
Armando
Arnaldo
Arturo
Augusto
Aurelio
Baldomero
Baltazar
Bartolomé
Basílio
Bautista
Beltrán
Benedito, Benito
Bernal
Bernardo, Bernardino —
   popular
Camilo
Carlos, Carlito
Catalino — rare
Celestino
Cirilo
Claudio
Cornelio
Cristóbal
Dalmacio
Dámaso
Danilo
Dejésus
Deorinio
Diego — popular
Dionicio, Dionisio
Domingo

Eduardo — popular
Eliodoro
Elisio
Emilio
Engracio
Enrique
Estanislao
Esteban
Ezequiel
Federico
Felipe — popular
Félix
Fermín
Fernando
Fidel
Florencio, Florendo, Flo-
   rentino, Floriano
Francisco, Cisco — popular
Gabriel
Gaspar
Gaudelio
Gaudencio
Gerónimo, Jerónimo
Giullen
Gomes, Gómez
Gonzalo
Gregorio
Guadelupe
Gualberto
Guillermo
Gustavo
Gutierre
Hermengildo [er-mehn-
   GEEL-doh]
Hermínio [er-MEE-nee-oh]
Hernando [er-NAN-doh]
Hernani [er-NAN-ee] —
   older form
Hilarión, Hilario [ee-lah-
   ree-OHN, ee-LAH-ree-
   oh]
Hipólito [ee-POH-lee-toh]
Honorato [OHN-oh-
   RAH-toh]
Iago
Ignacio
Ildefonso
Indalecio
Íñigo [EE-nyee-goh] —

from Basque
Irenio
Ismael
Jacinto [hah-SEEN-toh]
Jaime [HAY-meh]
Jerónimo [heh-ROH-
   nee-moh]
Jesús [hay-ZOOS] —
   more New World use
Joán [ho-AHN]
Joaquín [huah-KEEN]
Jorge [HOR-geh]
José, Joselito — very popular
Jovencio [hoh-VEHN-
   see-oh]
Juan, Juanito — very popular
Juan Bautista
Julián [hoo-lee-AHN]
Jusepe [hoo-SEH-peh]
Justo [HOO-stoh]
Largo
Laureano
Lázaro
Leonardo
Lope
Lorenzo
Lucas
Lucio
Luis
Macedonio
Manuel — popular
Marcello, Marcelino
Marco
Mariano
Marino
Mario
Martín
Matias
Matin
Mauricio
Melchior
Miguel, Miguelito — very
   popular
Modesto
Mónico
Narcisso, Narciso
Neftalí
Nepomuceno
Nicasio

Onofre
Orilio
Orlando
Orlino
Osanio
Óscar
Pablo, Pablito
Pancho, Panchito
Pánfilo
Pasqual, Pacho — also,
    Pascual
Patricio, Patrocinio
Paulino — rare
Pedro, Pepe — popular
Pero
Plácida (yes, -a), Plácido
Policarpo — rare
Ponciono
Primitivo
Rafael
Ramón

Redentor
Reynaldo
Ricardo
Rito
Roberto
Rodolfo
Rodrigo, Rodríguez
Rogelio
Rogue — Argentine
Rolito
Rosario
Rosito
Rufino
Salvador
Sancho
Sebastián
Serafín
Severino, Severo
Silvestre
Silvio
Simón, Simeón

Tadeo
Teodoro
Téodulo
Teotimo
Tiburcio
Tomás — popular
Uldarico
Ulises
Urbano
Valentin
Valeriano
Vasco
Venancio
Ventura
Victoriano
Vincente, Vicente
Vittorio
Ximénes
Yáñez

FAMILY NAMES

The source country is listed for you to use as you need. You may want a name particularly associated with Peru, or you may want to avoid the name of anyone notably Peruvian. "All" means that the name can be found anywhere. "Sp" means that I have found it only on Old World Spaniards. Any "Sp" name may have migrated to the New World. However, I am never dead certain that a New World name might not have been invented there, and so is improper for a Spaniard.

ABBREVIATION KEY

Arg	Argentina
Bol	Bolivia
CentAm	Central America
Col	Colombia
DomRep	Dominican Republic
Ecu	Ecuador
Guat	Guatemala

Nic	Nicaragua
NW	New World
Par	Paraguay
PR	Puerto Rico
SoAm	South America
Uru	Uruguay
Ven	Venezula

Abadía — Col
Acevedo — all
Achá — Bol
de Acuña — Sp
Agramonte — Cuba
Aguado — Sp
Agudo — Sp
Aguilar — Sp
Aguilera — Sp
de Aguirre — Unknown

Alaminos — Sp
de Alargón — Sp
Alberdi — Arg
de Albornoz — Sp
Alcántara — all
Alcayaga — Chile
de Almagro — Sp
Alonso — all
Altamira — Sp
Alva — Sp

de Alvarado — Sp
Álvarez — Sp
de Alvear — Arg
Ambrossiani — Peru
Arana — Unknown
Arboleda — Col
Arce — all
Arias de Avila — Col
Armaya — Bol
Armendáriz — Col

de Asbaje — Mexico
Azevedo — all
Bahamonde — Unknown
Balbuena — Par
Ballivián — Bol
Balmaceda — Chile
Balmes — Sp
Balta — Peru
Balvas — Sp
Baquerizo — Ecu
Barreda — Peru
Barros — Unknown
Barrundia — CentAm
Bastida — Sp
de Bastidas — Unknown
Basualto — Unknown
Bautista — Cuba
Becerra — Sp
Becquer — Sp
de Belalcázar — Col
Bello — SoAm
Bellvis — Unknown
Beltrán — Mexico
Belzú — Bol
Benavente, Benevente — Sp
Benavides — Peru
Berra — Mexico
Berruguete — Sp
Betanzos — Sp
Blasco — Sp
Borjia — Sp, for Borgia
Bravo — all
Bucareli — Sp
Bulnes — Chile
Bustamante, de Busta-
    mante — Mexico
Cabeza de Vaca — Sp
Cabrera — Sp
Cáceres — Peru
Cajigal de la Vega — Sp
de Caldas — Col
Calleja del Rey — Sp
Calles — Mexico
Calomarde — Sp
Calvo — Arg
Camacho — Mexico
de la Camara — Sp
Camargo — Col
Campero — Bol
Camposorio — Sp
Campuzano — Cuba

Canalejas — Sp
Cano, del Cano — Sp
Cánovas del Castillo — Sp
de Capmany Suris — Sp
Carballo — Unknown
Carcano — Arg
Carnicer — Sp
Caro — Col
Carpio — Mexico
Carranza — Mexico
Carreño — Sp
Carrera — Guat
de Carvajal — Sp
de Casal — Cuba
de las Casas — Sp
de Castaños — Sp
Castelar — Sp
Castilla — Peru
de Castillejo — Sp
Castillo — Arg, Mexico
Cavana — Sp
Cavanilles — Sp
Ceballos — Sp
Centeno — Sp
Cerro — Unknown
Cervera — Sp
dc Céspedes — all
de Cetina — Sp
Chanca — Sp
Chávez — Mexico
Chocano — Peru
de Cienfuegos — Sp
Cirera — Sp
Clavijero, Clavigero —
    Mexico
Codovilla — Arg
Concha — Col
Córdoba — Col
Córdova — Bol
Coronel — Sp
Correal — Mexico
Cortina — Mexico
Costilla — Mexico
Cota de Magaque — Sp
Covarrubias — Mexico
Crevea — Sp
de la Cruz — all
Cubero — Sp
Dávila — Chile
Daza — Bol
Delgado — Sp

Delmonte — DomRep
Diamante — Sp
Díaz — all
Domínguez — all
Drago — Arg
Durán — Sp
Echarte — Cuba
Echegaray — Sp
Echenique — Peru
Echeverría — Arg
Eizaguirre — Sp
Encalada — Chile
de Encina, de Enzina — Sp
Enríquez de Paz — Sp
Epejo — Unknown
Ercilla — Sp
Escobar — Sp
de Eslava — Sp
Espartero — Sp
de Espejo — Sp
Espinel — Unknown
Espínola — all
Espinosa, de Espinoza — all
de Espronceda — Sp
Estenssoro — Bol
Estévez — Unknown
de Ezpeleta — Col
Fajardo — Sp
de Falla — Sp
Ferández — Uru
Fernández — all; Fernández
    de Córdoba, marqués de
    Guadalcázar, etc.
Figueras — Unknown
Flores — Col
Fombona — Ven
Frauca — Unknown
Frías — Bol
Fuentes — Cuba, Mexico
Gali — Sp
Galindo — Bol
Gallego — Sp
de Gálvez — Sp
Gamarra — Peru
de Games — Sp
de Garay — Sp
García — all
Garcilaso — Sp
de Gayangos — Sp
Girón — Sp
de Gomara — Sp

Gómez — Col
de Góngora — all
González — all
González de Riancho — Sp
de Goya — Sp
Goyeneche — Chile
Gracián — Sp
de Grijalva — Sp
Grosolé — Bol
Gual — SoAm
Guerra — all
Guerrero — all
de Guevara — Sp
Güiraldes — Arg
Guiteras — Cuba
de Guridi — Sp
Gurrea — Sp
Gutiérrez — Bol
de Heredia — Cuba
Hernández — all
Herrán — Unknown
Herrera, de Herrera — all
Hidalgo — Mexico
de Hinojosa — Unknown
Holguín — Col
de Hostos — PR
Huerta — Mexico
Huidobro — Chile
Ibáñez — Sp
de Ibarbourou — Uru
Ibarruri — Sp
Icaza — Ecu
Ignacio — Mexico
Iniguez — Cuba
Irigoyen — Arg
de Isla — Sp
Iturbi, de Iturbi —
    Unknown
de Jáuregui — Sp
Jiménez — all
de Jovellanos — Sp
Jovellar — Sp
Lafuente — Sp
Laínez, Laynez — Sp
Lanzo — Bol
Lanzol — Sp
Larreta — Arg
Lavalleja — Uru
Leguía — Peru
León — all
Lerdo de Tejada — Mexico

Linares — Bol
Lleras — Col
Llorente — Sp
Lope de Rueda — Sp
López — all; López de
    Ayala — Sp; López de
    Legazpi — Sp; López de
    Mendoza, marqués — Sp
Lozada, Losada — Mexico
Lozano — all
Lucientes — Sp
de Madrazo — Sp
Maldonado — Mexico
Manrique — Sp
Marmol — Arg
Maroto — Sp
de Márquez, Márquez — Sp
Marroquín — Sp
Martínez — all; Martínez
    de Campo — Sp; Mar-
    tínez de la Rosa — Sp;
    Martínez Sierra — Sp
Medina — all
Meléndez — Sp; Meléndez
    Valdés — Sp
Melgarejo — Bol
Melzi — Sp
de Mena — Sp
Méndez — all
Mendieta — Cuba
Mendoza — all; de Men-
    doza — Sp
Mercador — Sp
Mérida — all
de Mesonero — Sp
Milanés — Cuba
Mina — Sp
de Miranda — Ven
Miró — Sp
Mola — Sp
Molina — Sp
de Molinos — Sp
Monagas — Ven
de Montalván — Sp
de Montalvo — Sp
Montefur — Cuba
Montenegro — Unknown
Montes — Unknown
de Montijo — Sp
Montoya — all
de Montpalau — Sp

Morages — Unknown
Moral — Sp
Morales, de Morales — all
Moratín, de Moratín — Sp
Morazán — CentAm
Moreto — Sp
Morillo — all
Morino — Ecu
Moyano — Sp
Murillo — all
Nabuco — Unknown
Najera — Mexico
Naón — Arg
Nariño — Col
de Naroña — Unknown
Narváez, de Narváez — Sp
Navarro — all
Nervo — Mexico
Niño — Sp
Núñez — all
de Obaldía — all
Obando — Col
Obregón — Mexico
de Ojeda — Sp
Olaya — Col
de Olid — Sp
Olmedilla — Sp
Olmedo — all
de Onante — all
Orbe — Sp
Orbegozo — Peru
Ordóñez de Montalvo —
    Unknown
de Orellana — Sp
Oropesa — Sp
Orozco — Mexico
Orrente — Sp
Ospina — Col
Otero — NW
de Ovando — Sp
Oviedo — all
Pacheco — all
Padilla, de Padilla — all
Páez — NW; tribe name too
Palma, Palmas — all
Pardo — Peru
Pareja — Sp
Pasarón — Sp
Pasquale — Unknown
Patiño — Bol
de Paula — Col

Pavón — Mexico
Paz — Bol
Peirola — Peru
Pelayo de Cordoba — Sp
Peñaranda — Unknown
de Pereda — Sp
Pérez — all
Pérez de Montalbán — Sp
de Piérola — Peru
Pinilla — Col
Pintos — Par
Pinzón — Sp
de Portola — Sp
Pradilla — Sp
Prieto — Sp
Quesada, de Quesada — all
de Quevedo — Sp
Quintana — Sp
Quintanilla — Bol
de Quiroga — Sp
Rabasa — Mexico
Restrepo — Col
Reyes — Col
Ribadeneira — Sp
de Ribalta — Sp
Ribera — Unknown
del Riego — Sp
Ripoll — Sp
Robledo — Col
Rocafuerte — Ecu
Rodríguez — all
de las Roelas — Sp
de Rojas, Rojas — Sp
de Romanos — Sp
de Rosas — Unknown
Rubio
Rubira — Sp
de Rute — Sp
Saavedra — Sp
Sáenz de Licona — Sp

Sala — Sp
Salcedo — Peru
Salinas — Par
Sanclemente — Col
Sandoval, de Sandoval — all
Sarmiento — Nic
Serra — Sp
Silvela — Sp
Siqueiros — Mexico
Sirvén — Sp
Solano — Par
Solar — Chile
Soler — Sp
de Solís — Sp; Solís — Col
Sorolla — Sp
Sorzano — Bol
Sosa — Par
Suárez — all
de Sucre — SoAm
Tamayo
Tejada — all
Téllez — Sp
de Timoneda — Sp
Topete — Sp
Torcuato — Arg
Torres — Col
Tuero — Sp
Turbay — Col
Urdaneta — Col
Urquiza — Arg
Urriolagoitia — Bol
Urrutia — Col
Ursua — Sp
Valcárcel — Sp
Valdés, Valdez — all
de Valera — Sp
Vallenilla — Ven
Vásquez de Coronado — Unknown
de la Vega — Sp

Vejador — Unknown
Venero de Leiva — Col
de Ventancurt — Sp; de Ventancour
Victoria — Sp
Vicuña — Chile; South America only
Vidaurri — Mexico
de la Vielleuze — Sp
Villagrán, Villagra — Unknown
Villarroel — Bol
Villazón — Bol
Villegas — Sp
Vizcaíno — Sp
de Xeres, de Xerez, de Jeres — Sp
Ximénez — Sp
Ximénez de Cisneros — Sp
Xuares — Par
Yanes — Ven
Yáñez de Oñez — Sp
de Yriarte, de Iriarte, Iriarte — Sp
Zaldívar — Cuba
Zamacois — Sp
Zamora, de Zamora — Sp
Zárate — Sp
Zavala — Nic
Zea — Col
Zeballos — Sp
Zelaya — Nic
Zorilla, Zorrilla — Sp
Zuloaga — all
de Zumárraga — Sp
Zúñiga, de Zúñiga — all
de Zurbarán — Unknown
Zurita — Sp

PORTUGUESE

One half of the population of South America speaks Portuguese, not Spanish. They are a far greater piece of humanity than the residents of Portugal. Though often of native or African descent, their naming practices are nearly the same as the Portuguese. In Hawaii, the "Pordagee" are one of the notable subpopulations. Even when they use other first names, you should have these family names handy when you bring your characters to Honolulu, as well as Recife.

Even when Portugal was under Spanish rule, the names were distinctive. It is only rarely, or among the high nobility, that they compound family names like the Spanish. When they do, the father's family name is followed by "e," not the Spanish "y," and the mother's family name. If both names have "de" or another prefix, it is dropped from the matronymic. So the son of João da Silva and Graca da Costa is Martinho da Silva e Costa. By the 1800s in Brazil the matronymic is retained, but the "e" is dropped; so he is Martinho da Silva Costa.

The "h" in Portuguese adds a Y sound, like the tilde (~) in Spanish. So "piranha" is pee-RAH-nyah, not the English pih-RAH-nah. The tilde above a vowel, followed by another, nasalizes the second one. If you took French, you know the sound. Consider it to create an invisible half-N after the second vowel. An accent over a vowel does not change its sound, but tells you which syllable to accent. The cedilla C sounds like S.

If you are setting your big saga in Brazil, rather than using only archetypal Portuguese names you should remember some of the other Europeans drawn to Brazil, with family names like Kubitschek and Lott following good Portuguese personal names. But if your Brazilians are few, they will not feel Brazilian to the reader with such Germanic or Slavic monikers.

FEMALE NAMES

Agueda	Eleonora — Old World	Marianna
Ailinn	Felipa — Old World	Natalia
Amelia — Old World	Graça — Old World	Raquel
Beatriz — Old World	Inés — Old World	Rebeca
Bernardina	Irina	Ritta
Branca — Old World	Isabel — Old World	Serafima
Carlota — Old World	Ivone	Tereza — Old World
Catarina — Old World	Joaquina	Vanda
Catharina	Judite	Vitoria
Celestina	Lianor — Old World	Zetta
Delfina	Margarida — Old World	
Diani	Maria — Old World	

MALE NAMES

Abílio — Old World	Alexander, Aleixo — Old World; Alexandre	Aniceto — Old World
Adão		Antero — Old World
Adolfo	Aluisio	António (or Antônio) — Old World
Afonso, Affonso, Alfonso — Old World; very popular	Alvaro — Old World	Aquilino — Old World
	Amador — Old World	Artur
Alão	Anfitriões — Old World; Amphitrion, very rare	Augusto

Bartolomeu
Basilio
Bernardim — Old World
Camilo — Old World
Césario
Claudio
Columbano — Old World
Conrado
Constant
Cristão, Cristiano, Cris-
    tovão — Old World
Dario
Davi
Delfim
Diani
Dinis, Diniz — Old
    World
Diogo — Old World;
    popular
Domingos — Old World
Duarte — Old World
Eduardo — popular
Egas — Old World
Emilio
Épitácio
Erico
Eugénio — Old World
Euriço
Evaristo
Feliciano — Old World
Fernám, Fernando, Fer-
    não — Old World
Filinto — Old World
Floriano
Fontes — Old World
Francisco — Old World;
    very popular
Gaspar — Old World

Gétulio
Gil — Old World
Gomes — Old World
Gregorio — Old World
Guilherme — Old World
Har — Oldo
Heitor — Old World; rare
Henrique — Old World
Hermes
Hernane
Humberto
Ignácio
Irineo
Jaco
Jayme
Jeremias
João — Old World and
    traditional; José — more
    New World, very pop-
    ular
Joaquim
Jorge — Old World
Josef
Júlio
Juscelino
Leão
Leonardo
Lourenço, Lourenco
Luiz — Old World
Manoel, Manuel — Old
    World
Marcos
Maria — as a first name,
    too
Martim
Martinho — popular
Mateus
Maximiliano

Mel
Mousinho — Old World
Nereu
Nicolau — New World;
    Nicolão — Old
    World
Nilo
Nuno — Old World; pop-
    ular
Patricio
Paulo
Pedro — Old World; pop-
    ular
Plinio
Prudente
Raimundo
Raúl — Old World
Rui, Ruy
Salvador
Sansão
Sebastião, Sebastiano —
    Old World
Serafim
Sergio — New World
Sighefredo
Simão
Tarquinio — Old World
Teófilo
Timoteo
Tomás, Tomaz, Tomé —
    Old World; popular
Tristão — Old World
Urbano
Valentin — Old World
Vicente
Vitor
Zacarias
Zeusef

FAMILY NAMES

de Aguiar — Old World
de Albuquerque — Old
    World
Alcoforado — Old World
de Alencar — New World
de Almeda — Old World
de Alvarenga
Alvares, Álvarez
Alves

Alves Lima — New World
Andrade
de Andrade — Old World
de Andrada e Silva —
    New World
de Anunciação — Old
    World
de Araíjo
de Araújo — Old World

Arrais — Old World
de Arriaga — Old World
de Assis
de Ávila
de Azevedo
Barbosa — Old World
Barboza — New World
Barreto — Old World
de Barros — Old World

Barroso — New World
Belo — Old World
Bernardes — Old World
Bernardes Pimenta — Old World
Biester — Old World
de Bocage — Old World
Bonifacio
Bordalo — Old World
Botelho
Braga — Old World
Branco — Old World
Brandão — Old World
Braulio
Braz
de Brito — Old World
Cabral — Old World
Cabrillo — Old World
de Camões — Old World
Capelo — Old World
Capistrano
Carmona — Old World
de Carvalho — Old World
de Castanheda — Old World
Castelo — Old World
Castelo Branco — Old World
de Castilho — Old World
de Castro — Old World; popular
Chagas — New World
Coelho — Old World
Coimbra da Luz
Correia — Old World
Correa da Serra — Old World
Corte-Real, Corterreal — Old World
da Costa — Old World
da Costa Cabral — Old World
Coutinho — Old World
do Couto — Old World
da Cruz — Old World
da Cunhaboth
Deodoro
de Deus — Old World
de Deus Ramos — Old World
Diasall

Duram, Durão — New World
Dutra
Eça de Queirós — Old World
Ennes — Old World
Feijó — Old World
Fernandes — Old World
Ferraz
Ferreira — Old World
Fialho — Old World
de Figueiredo — Old World
Filho
da Fonseca
de Fragoso — Old World
Freyre — New World
Furtado — New World
Fuzeta da Ponte — Old World
da Gamaboth
Garção — Old World
Gil — Old World
Gomes — Old World
Gomes de Costa — Old World; Gonçalves — Old World
Gonçalves de Magalhães — New World
Gonzaga — Old World
da Graça Aranha — New World
Guerra
Guimarães — New World
de Gusmão — Old World
Henriques
Herculano — Old World
Herculão de Carvalho — Old World
Ivens — Old World
Jobim
Junqueiro — Old World
Lacerda
Leitão — Old World
de Lima
Lisboa — "from Lisbon"
de Lobeira — Old World
Lobo — Old World
Lopes — Old World; popular
Machado
de Magalhães — Old

World
Malhão — Old World
Malheiro
Malta — Old World
Mangbeira
Martins — Old World
de Mattos, Matos
Medina — Old World; popular
de Melo — Old World
Mendes-Pinto — Old World
de Meneses — Old World
Miguel — Old World
de Miranda — Old World
Moniz — Old World
de Montemôr — Old World
de Moraes Barros — New World
de Morais — Old World
Moreira
da Mota — Old World
Muniz
Nabuco
do Nascimento — Old World
Nobre — Old World
de Oliveira — Old World
da Orta — Old World
Ortigão — Old World
Osorio — New World
Paranhos
Patricio — Old World
Pecanha
Peixoto — New World
Pena
Pereira — Old World; popular
Perestrello — Old World
Pessanha — Old World
Pessôa — Old World
Pinheiro — Old World
Pinto — Old World
Pompeia
da Ponte
Pôrto — Old World
Prestes
de Queiroz — Old World
de Quental — Old World
Quita — Old World

Ramalho — Old World
Ramos — Old World
dos Reis — Old World
de Resende — Old World
de Ribeiro, Ribeiro — Old
　World
Rocha Pitta — New World
Rodrigues
de Sá
Salazar — Old World
Sales
Salgado
do Salvador
de Santa Rita — Old

World
de Santa Ritta — New
　World
de Sequeira — Old World
da Silva — Old World;
　popular
de Sousa — all; popular
Taunay
Tavares
Távora
Teixeira
Tolentino — Old World
de Trinidade — Old
　World

Tristão — Old World
Vargas
de Vasconcelos — Old
　World
Vaz de Camões — Old
　World
Verde — Old World
de Verney — Old World
Viana — Old World
Vicente — Old World
Vieira — Old World
Xavier
de Zurara — Old World

ITALIAN

These follow the usual Euro-Catholic pattern of two or three given names, a chosen confirmation name, and the father's family name.

Some say that novelty is not highly valued by most Italians, who use a relatively small number of names, some dating back to the Roman empire. On the contrary, in my researches I found Italians to be fond of a great number of names, if not quite as novelty-mad as modern baby-name books. As a writer you cannot afford too many over-used names. However, neither do you need unreal exotica. Many solid Italian names are unfamiliar to an English-speaking audience.

Like many Catholics, boys may have Maria as a secondary name, but not as a primary personal name. Very occasionally Catarina will also show up as a male secondary name.

A moderate number of Italian parents are naming their children in alliterative sets. This can be simple alliteration — Caterina, Constantia, and Carlo — or a complete match of the first syllable — Ercole, Erico, and Ermanno. For most fiction this would be confusing, but you may find it useful to tie together characters in a very large work; best for brother and sister pairs.

Diminutives and Augmentatives

Like David can become Davy in English, Italian names can be changed by diminutive endings, which reference gender: -ino/-ina, -etto/-etta, -ello/-ella. The diminutive ending "-uccio/-uccia" can indicate a certain level of reproach, "-accio/-accia," real disgust. There is also the augmentative ending "-one." This applies to more than names. Take the word *casa*, "house":

cassetta, casina, or casella would be "a dear little cottage";
casone is "a big, impressive house";
casuccia is "an insignificant little place";
casaccia would be "a lousy little joint."
So depending on the feelings of the person talking, Gian can be adorably Gianetto, Giannino, or Gianello; dismissed as Gianuccio; loathed as Gianaccio; or be the equivalent of Big John as Gianone.

In titles, therefore, there are at least three ways to call someone a princeling: principino, principotto, and principuccio.

Titles of Nobility

Male	Female	English Equivalents
re	regina	king, queen
principe	principessa	prince, princess
duca	duchessa	duke, duchess
conteduca	conteduchessa	count-duke (rare)
marchese	marchessa	marquis, marchioness
conte	contessa	count, countess
visconte	viscontessa	viscount, viscountess
barone	baronessa	baron, baroness
baronetto		baronet
cavaliere		knight

Pronunciation

There are no silent letters — those final E's are pronounced.
A — A in pasta
C — hard as in cat, except before E and I
CC — CH in church
E — E as in pen; before R, as in person
G — G in gun; before E or I, as in gin
I — I in machine
O — O in hope
U — U in tune

FEMALE NAMES

Ada
Adelaida, Adelina
Adriana
Agata
Agne, Agnella, Agnesca,

Agnese, Agnesina,
Agnola
Albiera
Albinia
Alda

Alessandra, Alessia
Aletea
Allegra
Alma
Amadea

Amata
Amelia, Amalia
Amelita
Amica
Amina
Aminta
Angela
Angelica
Anna, Annetta, Annina
Anna Maria
Antonia, Antonieta
Artemisia
Beatrice
Bellanca
Benedetta
Bernardina
Bettina, Betta
Bianca
Bice
Brigada, Brigida
Camilla
Caprice
Carina
Carita
Carla, Carlotta
Carmela, Carmelina,
  Melina
Catarina, Caterina
Cecilia
Celestina
Chiara
Christina
Claire
Clara
Clarice, Clarissa
Claudia
Clementina
Clemenza
Concettina
Constantia, Constanza
Cristina
Daniela
Edetta, Edita
Eleonora

Elisabetta, Elisa
Eloisa
Emilia
Eusapia
Fiametta
Filiberta
Filipa, Pippa, Filippina
Filomena
Fiora, Fioretta
Francesca
Gabriela
Gaetana
Gemma
Gessica
Gia, Gianna
Gianina, Giovanna
Ginevra
Giordana
Gisela
Giuditta
Giulia, Giulietta
Grazia, Graziosa, Graz-
  iella
Guelfa
Hippolyta
Ilvia
Imelda
Innocenza
Isabella
Laura
Lavinia
Leonora
Letizia
Lidia
Liliana
Lina
Lisa
Lisettina
Lorenza
Luca, Lucia, Lucrezia
Luciana
Luigia
Luisa
Maddalena

Marcella, Cella
Margarita, Margherita
Maria, Mariella, Marietta
Maria Luisa
Marianna
Marisa
Marta
Matilde, Matilda
Maura
Michaella
Monica
Natalia
Nicoletta
Olinda
Olivia, Olivieta
Olympia
Oriana
Ortensia
Paolina
Patrizia
Pina
Porzia
Reina
Rosa
Rosalba
Rosetta
Rosina
Savina
Simonetta
Sofia
Teresa, Teresina, Theresa
Valencia
Valentina
Vannozza
Venezia
Viola
Violante
Violetta
Vittoria
Viviana
Zaira
Zola

MALE NAMES

Adamo
Adriano
Agostino

Alberto
Albino
Alcide

Aldo
Aleardo
Alessandro, Sandro

Alfredo
Alonso
Alphonse, Alfonso
Alvino
Ambrogio
Amedeo, Amadeo
Amico
Amilcare
Amintor
Angelo
Aniello
Antonio, Antonino
Apostolo
Araldo, Aroldo
Ariodante
Armando
Arnaldo
Aroldo
Arrigo
Arturo
Augusto
Aurelio
Baldassare
Barnaba
Bartolomeo
Basilio
Battista
Benedetto
Beniamino
Bernardo, Bernardino
Bettino
Biagio
Briano
Bruno
Camillo
Carlo, Carlino
Carmelo
Carmine
Carolo
Casimiro
Cesare
Cirillo
Claudio
Clemente
Cleofonte
Conrado
Constantino
Cornelio
Corrado
Cosimo
Crispino

Cristiano
Cristoforo
Damiano
Daniele
Davide
Demetrio
Dionigi
Dionisio
Domenico
Donati, Donato, Dona-
    tello
Edgardo
Edmondo
Eduardo, Edoardo
Emanuele
Emilio
Enrico, Rico
Enzio, Enzo
Ercole
Erico
Ermanno
Ettore
Eugenio
Ezio
Fabiano
Fabio
Fabrizio
Federico
Felice
Ferrucio
Filippo
Flavio
Fortunino
Francesco
Gabriele, Gabrielli,
    Gabriello
Gaetano
Galileo
Geremia
Geronimo
Giacchino
Giacobbe
Giacomo
Giacopo
Giambattista
Giamo
Gian, Gianetto, Gino
Giancarlo
Gianfranco
Gioacchino
Gioffredo

Giordano
Giorgio
Giotto
Giovanni
Girolamo
Giuseppe, Peppino
Giustino
Giusto
Graziano, Graziadio
Gregorio
Gualtiero
Guglielmo
Guido
Guntero
Gustavo
Ignazio
Ippolito
Isaia
Italo
Ivanoe — after Scott's
    Ivanhoe! — very rare
Jacopo
Leonardo, Lionardo
Lodovico
Lorenzo
Luciano
Luigi
Macedonio
Manfredo
Marcello
Marco
Mario
Martino
Masaccio
Massimiliano
Massimo — popular
Matteo
Mattia
Maurizio
Melchiorre
Menico
Menotti
Michele
Muzio
Natale
Nataniele
Nerone
Nicolo, Nicola
Olindo
Oreste
Orlando

Oronzo
Orsino
Otello
Ottone
Palmerino
Paolo, Paoli
Pasquale
Patrizio
Pellegrino
Peppe, Peppo
Pero, Piero
Pietro
Pino
Placide, Placido
Pompeo
Primo
Quirino
Rafael, Raffaele, Raffaello
Raimondo
Ranieri, Raniero
Renzo

Ricciotti
Roberto
Rocco
Rodolfo, Rudolfo
Rodrigo
Rolando
Rosario
Ruberto, Ruperto
Ruggerio, Ruggero
Salvatore
Samuele
Santo
Saverio
Secondo
Sem
Sergio
Sigefriedo
Silvio
Simone
Stanislao
Stefano

Taddeo
Taro
Tazio
Teodoro, Teodore
Thaddeo
Timoteo
Tito
Tomaso, Tommasso, Tommaso
Tullio
Ugo
Umberto
Urbano
Valentino
Vasco
Vilfredo
Vincenzo
Virginio
Vittore, Vittorio
Xaverio

Family Names

d'Abano
Abbate, Abbati, dell'Abbate
Acerbi
Agliardi
Agnello, Agnelli
Agnesi
Albani
Alberoni
Albinoni
Alboni
Alciati
Aldini
Alenio
Alfieri
Algardi
Algarotti
Alini
Alosa
Altieri
Aluzzo
Amabile
Amari
Amazzalorso
de Amicis
d'Ancona

Aniello
d'Annunzio
Antelami
Antommarchi
Antonelli
Appiani
Arici
Arrivabene
Ascoli
Assarino
Assarotti
Avellino
Avezzana
Azuni
Bacciocchi
Badoglio
Baini
Balbi
Balzani
Bandiera
Baratieri
Barberi
Barbirolli
Barezzi
Barilli
Barrili

Bartolini
Bartolozzi
Batoni, Battoni
Battisti
Bazzini
di Beccaria
Bellavitis
Bellincioni
Bellotto, Belloto
Beltrami
Belzoni
Benelli
Bentivogliio
Berchet
Bergami
Bergonzi
Bernini
Bertini
Bessani
Bettinelli
Bianconi
Biandrata
Blandrata
Blaserna
Boccanegra
Boccanera

Boccherini
Bodoni, Boddoni
Boggione
Boiardo
Boito
Boldini
Bonomi
Bononcini, Buononcini
Bonzano
Borelli
Borgese, Borghesi
Boschetti
Boselli
Bossi
Botta
Bottari
Braschi
Brocchi
Broschi
Brumidi
Bulgarelli
Buroni
Busoni
Cabrini
Cadorna
Caffarelli
Cagnoli
Cairoli
Calamatta
da Calzabigi
Camanini
Cambini
Cammarano
Campagna
Campanari
Camuccini
Canaletto
Caneva
Canina
Cantani
Cantu
Capuana
Caracciolo
Carcano
Carissimi
Carli-Rubbi
Carpuani — Sicilian
Carra
Carracci, Caracci
Carrera, Carriera
Carutti di Cantogno

Casati
Casazza
Casella
Castellani
Castelli
Castelvetro
Casti
Castiglione
Cavalcaselle
del Cavaliere
Cavallo
Cavedoni
di Cavour
Cecchetti
Ceconi
Cernuschi
Cerutti
Cesalpino
Cesarotti
Cesti
della Chiesa
di Chirico
Ciamician
Ciampi
Ciba
Cignani
Cimaroasa
Cipriani
Cirillo
Clementi
Consalvi
Conti
Costaggini
Cravatta
Craviotto
Credi, Credico
Cremona
Crescentini
Crescimbeni
Crescioni
Creta, Cretaro
Crisanti
Crispi
Cristiano
Crivellari, Crevelli
Crollalanza
Cubito
Cuccetta
Cuccovillo
Cuffia
Culicchia

Cultellaio
Cumello
Cuoco
Cuorvo
Cura
Curatolo
Curci, Curcione
Curti
Custulire
Cuzza, Cuzzale, Cuzzi
Danei
Deledda
Delvintisette
Denina
Depretis
Dolci, Dolce
Donizetti
Douhet
Dragonetti
Durand del la Penne
Duse
d'Ecclisso
Eduardi
Egitto
Einaudi
Elci
Elia
degli Elmi
Enea
d'Epiro
Episcopo
d'Eramo
Erasimi
Erbetti
Ermini, Ermitani
Espano
Esperto
Esposi
Esposite, Esposito
Ettori
Eusebio
Fabretti
Fabrizi
Fabrizio
Facciolati
Fagnani
Falcone, Falco
Fanti
Farinacci
Federzoni
Ferrero

Figarolla
Fiorito
Fochio
Gabrielli
Gaetano
Galimberti
Gallenga
Galli
Galvani
Ganganelli
Garofalo
Gasparri
Gattaro
Gavazzi
Gazzana
Genovesi
Giacosa
Giardino
Gioberti
Giolitti
Giotti
Girifalco, Grifalcon
Gnoli
Gozzi
Grassi
Graziani
Grisi
Grossi
Guardi
de Gubernatis
Guerrazzi
Guerrini
Iacabacci
Iacacci
Iacapraro
Iacoli
Iacobellis
Iaconissa
Ianara
Iannaro
Iapelli, Iappelli
Iavazzo
Ieraci
Ignasio
d'Ilario
Illuminati
Imazio
Imbonati
Imbriaco
Impallomeni
Impavido

Impicciati
Imriani
Incalcaterra
Incandela
Incani
Ingannamorte
Ingegno
Innocenti
Insalat, Inzalata
Invernio
Inzinga
de Ioanna
Iovino
Iozzi
Isoldi, Isotti
Iusillo
Izzo
Jaconissa
Jannigro
Jatta
Jemolo
Jenco
Lablache
Lambruschini
Lanciani
Lanfranco
Legrenzi
Leoncavallo
Leopardi
de'Ligouri
Lincio
Locatelli
Logroscino
Lombard
Longobardo
Lorenzini
Loria
Luini
Lulli
Luzzatti
Madesani
Magliabechi, Magliabec-
   chi
Maglione
Mai
Majocci
Malpighi
Mantegazza
Manzoni
Marchesi
Marinetti

Masaniello
Mascagni
Mastai-Ferretti
Matteotti
Matteucci
Mazarini
Mazzini
Mazzoni
Melloni
Menabrea
Mercantini
Mezzofanti
Milelli
Mimbelli
Montanelli
Montecuccoli, Montecuc-
   culi
Montefiore
Monteverde
Monti
Morgagni
Morghen
Morosini
Nanini, Nanino
Nardini
Niccolini
de Nicola
Nicotera
Nievo
Nota
Novati
Odascalchi
Ojetti
Operti
Oriai
Oriani
Orlando
Pacelli
Pacini
Pacinotti
Paer
Paisiello, Paesiello
Palladino
Pallavicino
Palma di Cesnola
Panizzi
de Paoli
Paone, Paonetti, Paonessa
Papini
Parini
Pascoli

Pasini, Pasinelli
Passaglia
Pavone, Pavona
Pellegrini
Pellico
Peluso
Pergolesi
Pignatelli
Pinelli di Sangro
Ponchielli
Praga
Prati, Preti
del Prete
Prezzolini
Primoli
Provesi
Pugnani
Quadraro
Quadretti
delle Quadri
Quaglia, Quaglio
Quagliri
Quarantotto
Quarelli
Quaresima
di Quattro
della Quercia
Quesada
Quillici
Quintarelli
Quinzio
Quirici
Quirini
Radicati
Ranieri
Rattazzi
Ratti
Rezzonico
Ricci
Riccoboni
Righi
Robotti
Romagnosi
Rosellini
Rosmini
Rossetti
Rudini
Ruffo
Russolo
de Sanctis
Sarto

Savorgnan di Brazza
Scamozzi
Schiaparelli
Secchi
Serao
Serbati
Severini
Spallanzani
Starabba di Rudini
Stefani
di Stefano da Fossano
Stradella
Sturzo
Sugana
Taglioni
Tamberlik
Taparelli
Tarteglia
Tedesco
Tiepolo
Tiraboschi
Tittoni
Togliatti
Tommasini
della Torre
Toscanini
Tranquilli
Trivulzio
Ubbriachi
Uccello, Ulcelli
Uda
Ulianich
Ulivetti
Ulloa
Umili
Unicorno
Urciuoli
Urso, d'Urso
Usignuolo
dell'Uva, d'Uva
Uvari
Uzielli, Uzziello
Vacchetta
Vagliavello
Valente
della Valentina
Valenziano
Valisari
Valle, Valletti
Valori
Valorosa

Vani
Varcadipane
Varchi
Vassalle, Vassallo
Vedovati
Vegliante
Veli, Velli
Vellotti, Velluti
Venerato
Venezia, Veneziani
Venosta
Ventresca
Ventura de Raulica
Verga
Verita
Vermigli, Vermiglioli
Vesci
Vespi, Vespoli
Vetrioli
Vezza, Vezzalli
Viapiana
Vicario, Viccari, del Vicario
de Vico
Videmari
Vigliano, Viglione
Vigo
Villani
Vinattieri
Violante
Viotti
Viscardi
Visibelli
Viterbo
Vittorangeli
Vitulo, Vitullo
Vivimpace
Vollpe
Volta, dalla Volta
Voltatorna
de Voto
Vullo
Vulpetti
Yacobone
Yacullo
Youngo
Zaccaria
Zamboni
Zanella
Zanotti
Zarlenga, Zarlinga

Zecca
Zendrini
Zetto
Zicaro
Ziella
Ziganto

Zini
Zirafi
Zoca, Zocco
Zocchi
Zolfanella
Zonari

Zondador
Zottoli
Zuccarelli, Zuccherelli
Zuccaro
Zuppetti
Zuricini

Eastern Europe

FINNISH

Finnish is very different from the other languages of Scandinavia. They are descended from Norse. Finnish is closer to Estonian and Hungarian. However, Finland was often a part of Sweden or Russia, which means there are many people in and of Finland who are not ethnic Finns. They retain many Norse but very few Russian family names, as well as those of many German immigrants, but nowadays they often have Finnish personal names, or adapt their names to look more Finnish: Henrik for the German Heinrich, for example. The Finnish national anthem was written by a Johan Ludvig Runeberg.

Name order is normal for Europeans: personal name first, family name last.

Pronunciation

Finnish names use more umlauted A's and O's, than the Norse, but don't use the circle-topped A, nor the non–Latin consonents. Frequent doubled letters are its greatest distinction: Aaneskoski, Kuusamo, Hameenlinna, Iisalmi, Mikkeli, Sippola, Siipyy, Tammisaari, etc., among place-names. While you are checking your map, it may not explain that *joki* means "river" and *jarvi* means "lake."

A — A as in arm
E — E as in egg
I — I as in in
O — O as in on
U — U as in pull
Y — UE as in rue
Ä — A as in man; you can write it "A:" if you need to
Ö — EU as in bleu; you could render it "O:"
Doubled vowels are just lengthened for a count; they do not sound different.
J — Y in yes
W — V as in vet

FEMALE NAMES

Aila, Aili	Kiputyttö	Minna
Ainikki	Kivutar	Mirjam
Aino	Kristia	Osmotar
Anna-Liisa — adapted	Kristiina	Päivätär
from abroad	Kustaa	Pihlajatar
Anni, Anniki, Annikki	Kuutar	Piltti
Eila	Kylli, Kyllikki	Rauni
Etelätär	Lokka	Sinetar
Hanni	Louhi	Suonetar
Heljä	Loviatar	Suovakko
Helli	Luonnotar	Suvetar
Hilkka	Lusa	Syöjätär
Hongatar	Maija, Maijii	Tammatar
Ilmatar	Maikki	Tellervo
Ilpotar	Manalatar	Terhenetar
Irma	Margarete	Tuometar
Kaarina	Maria	Tuonetar
Kalevatar	Marja, Marjatta	Tuulikki
Kankahatar	Melatar	Valma
Kanteletar	Mielikki	Vammatar
Katajatar	Mimerkki	Vellamo

MALE NAMES

Aarre	Filip	Kimmo
Aino	Frans	Kosti, Kusti
Aleksis	Fredrik	Kristian
Alvar	Georg	Kyösti
Andras	Göran	Lasse
Antero	Gustaf	Lauri
Armas	Hannes	Leevi
Arto	Hannu	Martti
Arvid, Arvo	Harald	Matti — popular
Aulus	Heikki	Mika, Mikko
Bengt — popular	Heino	Nilo
Bjarne	Iikka	Oke
Bo	Ilmari, Ilmar	Olavi
Carls	Jaakko, Jaako	Olof
Daniel	Jeremias	Oskari
Eemil	Joonas	Paavo
Eero	Joosef, Jooseppi, Seppo	Pehr
Eino	Jorma	Pekka
Elaias	Juhani, Juho	Pietari
Eliel	Jukka	Raimo
Emanuel	Jussi	Reku
Erkki	Kaarlo	Risto, Ristomatti
Evind	Kalevi, Kaleva, Calevi	Sakari

Selim
Sulho
Tapani
Tauno
Teemu
Tellarvo
Teuvo

Timo
Toivo — popular
Torvern
Tuomas, Tuomo
Urho
Uuno
Väinö

Veikko
Vilhelm
Viljo, Wiljo, Vilho
Vuokko
Yrjö
Zachris

FAMILY NAMES

Aalto
Ahlqvist
Andersson
Arwidsson
Asp
Aura
Bergman
Brofeldt
Canth
Carlson
Carpelan
Castren
Collan
Crusell
Damström
Edelfelt
Ehrström
Ekman
Eriksson
Estlander
Furuhjelm
Gadolin
Ganander
Genetz
Haapalainen
Haapanen
Hannikainen
Hedman
Hiltunen
Hyvönen
Ikonen
Ilaskivi
Ingelius
Jaatinen
Jacobsen
Järnefelt
Jokinen
Jotuni
Kaariainen
Kaivanto

Kajanus
Kalela
Kallio
Kaski
Kaukonen
Kekkonen
Kilpinen
Kivi
Klami
Klemetti
Klinge
Kohva
Koivunen
Kokkonen
Kontula
Koskenniemi
Koskinen
von Kothen
Kotilainen
Krohn
Kuula
Laine
Launis
Leino
Lindholm
Linko
Linna
Linnala
Linsen
Liukko
Lönnbohm
Lönnrot
Maasalo
Madetoja
Mäkelä
Mannerheim
Manninen
Markkanen
Melartin
Merikanto

Mielck
Myllyniemi
Niitemaa
Nurmii
Paasikivi
Paasonen
Pacius
Palmgren
Pekkanen
Piavarinta
Pohjola
Poijärvi
Porthan
Raitio
Ranta
Ratia
Relander
Rewall
Salonen
von Schantz
Setälä
Sibelius
Sillanpää
Similä
Snellman
Stahlberg
Stenberg
Sundman
Sundström
Suominen
Svenhufvud, Svinhufvud
Tahkolahti
Tarpila
Tegner
Teir
Tenovaara
Topelius
Törnudd
Tuominen
Turunen

Tyti	Valtari	Voutilainen
Väisänen	Vilen	Wegelius
Vala	Vilkuna	Wennerstrand
Valjakka	Viren	Yrjö
Väljas	Visa	

ESTONIAN

A lot of people in and from Estonia have German and Scandinavian names, with the occasional Russian. Estonia was under Teutonic and Danish rule from 1219 to 1559. It was then fought over by the Swedes, the Poles, and the Russians until Sweden triumphed in 1645. The native barons sided with Peter the Great in 1700, the country was ceded to Russia in 1712, and only freed itself in 1919.

However, the nobility were always referred to as "Baltic Germans." In Livland, Polish, Lithuanian and Swedish nobles moved in from the 1680s. Through the end of the 19th century, Estonian was dismissed as a peasant dialect, and only in the 20th has there been a strong push to use Estonian rather than other personal names. So your choice of names differs between a novel about Estonian pagans fighting the Teutonic Knights, when you should use very strongly ethnic, non–Christian names, and a tale of barons in the 1840s.

Family names appeared among Estonian-name users later than most places in Europe, since like most Russian-ruled peasants, they were enserfed.

FEMALE NAMES

Aino	Kaarin	Merja
Betti	Katharina, Kati, Katrin,	Olli
Daggi	Katri	Reet
Elda	Krista	Riina
Elina	Lea	Rutt — Ruth; Jewish
Elisabet	Lenni	Salme
Ellen	Liisa, Liisi	Tilda
Elli	Lydia	Uli
Elts	Marga	Urmi
Epp	Mari, Marye — the for-	Vera
Etti	eign Marie often used	
Hele	Meeri	

MALE NAMES

Aadu
Aarne
Ado — fairly popular
Aili
Alexander, Aleksei
Alo — fairly popular
Anatoli, Anatol
Andres, Andrus, Andi,
　Ando, Andu
Ants, Anton
Arno, Arnold
Artur — popular
Arvo
August
Bernard
Daniel
Eduard — popular
Eerik
Elmar
Endel
Enn
Ernst
Esmo
Evald
Friedebert
Friido
Gustav
Hando
Harald
Harri
Heino
Heldur
Helmi
Helmut
Ilmar
Ioosep

Jaagup, Jaak — obsolete,
　Jakkob and Jakkab
Juhan — when young,
　Juku, Juss, later
　Juhanes; in age, Juhan;
　Jaan — popular, Jaanus,
　Hannes, Hannus, Ants,
　Henn, Henno, Enn,
　Enno, Hanno — obso-
　lete, Hann
Juri, Jüri
Kaarel — Germanic, Karl
Kaido
Kalev
Kersti
Konstantin, Kostya
Kristian, Kristjan, Krists
Leks
Lembit
Lennart
Maimu
Mait
Marju
Mart, Märt
Mati
Mats
Mattias — rare, Madis —
　popular, Matt, Mati,
　Mats
Meelik
Meinhard
Mihkel
Mikk
Neeme
Nigol
Nikolai

Olavi, Olaf
Oskar
Otu, Otto
Pärtel, Pärtelmes, Pärt-
　mus, Pärt
Paul
Peet, Peeter — popular,
　Peedu (dim.), Päär —
　obsolete
Priit
Raimo
Rein
Riho
Riki, Riks
Rolli
Rudolf
Siimon, Siim
Sirje
Sulev
Teodor
Toe
Toivo — popular
Tõnis
Tõnu
Toomas
Tuudur
Üllar
Uno
Veljo
Vello
Viilip, Viilup, Vilpus —
　obsolete
Viivi
Viktor
Villem
Voldemar, Volemar

FAMILY NAMES

Aasa
Aau
Aavik
Alver
Arens
Arumäe
Eenpalu
Eliaser — Jewish

Gailit
Haav
Hint
Hion
Hyvämäki
Ibius
Ird
Jaanits

Järvesoo
Järvi
Jõeäär
Juhanson
Kaarmán
Kahu
Kallas
Kama

Kangro	Moora	Savisaar
Karindi	Müürisepp	Selter
Karjahärm	Nigol	Semper
Karma	Niit	Siilivask
Karotamm	Niklus	Siiras
Karu	Nõmm	Sirk
Kasemaa	Õisman	Sõrmus
Kelam	Oksa	Speek
Kerde	Olbrei	Suits
Kiik	Öpik	Taagepara
Kiin	Oras	Takkin
Kitzberg	Pacius	Talvik
Kivimäe	Palgi	Tambek
Konks	Palli	Tamman
Kontus	Panso	Tammsaare
Köörna	Parming	Tampere
Kross	Pärn	Tarmisto
Kruus	Päts	Tarvel
Kukk	Pennar	Teemant
Künnapas	Pihlak	Titma
Kuttunen	Piip	Toivonen
Kuuli	Piirimäe	Tõnisson
Kuusberg	Piliau	Tõnurist
Laaman	Põld, Põldmäe	Tooms, Toomus
Laar	Pullat	Tormis
Laasi	Püss	Traat
Laidoner	Raag	Tubin
Larka	Raamot	Tuglas
Laul	Raid	Üdi
Lauristin	Rätsep	Uibopuu
Leetmaa	Raud	Uluots
Ligi	Raudsepp	Unt
Liim	Raun	Uustalu
Liiv	Rei, Reino	Vahtre
Lippmaa	Ridala	Valgamai
Lõugas	Ristikivi	Valton
Luiga	Rummo	Vares
Luik	Runnel	Vassar
Luts	Rütli	Velner
Maamugi, Maamägi	Ruubel	Vesilind
Mäe, Mäelo	Rüütel	Veske
Mägi	Ruutsoo	Vetemaa
Mereste	Saar	Vettick
Meri	Saarepera	Vihalemm
Merilaas	Saarmaa	Viiding
Mesikäpp	Saat	Vilde
Metsanurk	Sabe	Vilms
Mikiver	Sallo	Vuorela
Miljan	Särgava	Warma

RUSSIAN

Russians always had two names, a personal name and a patronymic, versions of the father's personal name for sons and daughters. If you notice the similarity to the Viking/Icelandic custom, please also note that the Russ were Scandinavian explorers, traders, and colonists.

Later on, the better sorts added a family name based on the land they held. Everyone had a family name by the middle of the 19th century, and this, too, showed gender by its ending. A woman's name cannot be easily mistaken for a man's; she would have to adopt a male persona or pseudonym to cause confusion.

The noble class of names ends in "-ov," if you are writing pre–Revolution. Sometimes this was rendered in foreign languages as "-off," so you will find some writers using "Romanoff" rather than "Romanov," but this is quite passé, as well as making it difficult to properly gender the name. But it is common in the descendants of refugees to England, France, America, etc. Equally, "-ev" often became "-eff."

The male form of the patronymic ends in "-ovich," the female in "-ovna," though sometimes the male ending is shortened to "-ich." So the children of Aleksandr Ilich Simakov would be Andrei Aleksandrovich Simakov and Katarina Aleksandrovna Simakova. People are often called by both names the way Southerners use "Patty Sue," rather than just "Patty." People will commonly be referred to as Pavel Andreich, or Marya Pavlovna.

A married woman uses the feminine of her husband's family name, so that Bella Simonovna Durova who marries Rodion Vasilovich Zarubin becomes Bella Durova Zarubina. So while you cannot mistake gender, you may be able to make mistakes about a woman's marital status if, as is common, she is merely referred to as Bella Zarubina.

Periodically you will run into the name of a Russian that does not fit these rules. Russia was long a land of opportunity to the younger sons of the rest of Europe. You will find lots of names that are Polish, as well as Scottish, Swedish, German, Irish, French, Czech, Hungarian, etc., from those who took service under various Czars as soldiers, scholars, explorers, diplomats, and such. In the days of the USSR, you will find various types of subject peoples who are living in Russia, willingly or not. Ukrainian and Russian names have been found in each other's territories for centuries, in great numbers.

If the name has not been Russified, do not gender it, unless the "home" ethnic group genders names. Then, use their rules, not Russian ones.

Pronunciation

A as in pat
E as in tell

I as in pin, or as in machine
O as in top
U as in tune, not as in use or as in up
Y as in yes, or, at the end, — I as in machine
G as in gun, not as in gin
You can use X for any KS below: Aleksandr=Alexandr or Alexander; Maksim=Maxim. This often happened to emigrants.

FEMALE NAMES

Name; diminutive or alternate form

Adeliya
Agafia, Agafya; Agasha
Aleksandra; Aleksasha
Alena; Alenka
Alisa
Amaliya
Anastasia
Angelina
Anna; Annuska, Anouska,
    Anya, Anninka
Ariane; Arina, Arinka
Beatriks; Beatrisa
Bella
Celestyna
Danila; Dasha
Danilka
Dominika; Domka
Doroteya
Dusya
Ekaterina
Elena
Elisavetta
Eudoxia
Evdokiya
Fanya
Fyodora
Galina; Galinka, Galya,
    Galka, Gasha
Georgina [hard G's —
    gay-or-GEE-na]
Inessa; Inka
Ioanna
Irina
Irisa; Irisha
Ivanna
Izabella

Jelena
Jereni
Johana
Karina
Katerina; Katenka, Kate-
    rinka, Katya, Katyusha
Khristina; Khristya
Kira
Klara
Kostenka; Kostya,
    Kostyusha
Kotik; Kotinka
Larissa, Lara
Larochka
Lavra
Lenora, Lena, Lenka,
    Leka
Lera, Lerka
Lida; Lidka
Lilia
Lisenka
Lizavieta
Ludmilla
Luiza
Lydia
Magdalina
Manka, Manya
Mara
Marina
Marya; Masha, Mas-
    henka, Mashka,
    Marinka, Mariya,
    Maruska
Melaniya; Melashka
Milda
Nadezhda; Nasha, Nashka

Nadia; Nadka
Nastasya; Nastka
Natalya; Natasha,
    Natalka, Tasha, Tashka
Nelya
Nessia
Nina
Nyura; Nyusha
Olena; Olenka
Olga; Olka, Olya,
    Olyusha
Orina; Orya
Orlenda
Pavla
Pavlina; Pavlinka
Pelageya
Rakhil; Rakhila
Rosina
Ruzha
Selinka
Senta
Sofya; Sofka
Sonia, Sonya
Stefania; Stesha, Steshda
Svetlana, Svetla
Tamara; Tasha
Tataiana; Tanya, Tania,
    Tanka
Terezilya
Tomochka
Valya; Valka
Varvara
Vasilissa
Vera; Verasha, Verinka,
    Verka
Verusya

Viera   Yuliya; Yulinka, Yulka   Zilya
Yarina, Yaryna   Zenaida, Zenaide

MALE NAMES

Name	Son Form	Daughter Form	Diminutives, Notes
Adam	Adamovich	Adamovna	Adamka
Aleksandr	Aleksandrovich	Aleksandrovna	Sasha, Sashinka
Alexei	Alexeievich	Alexeievna	
Anastasi	Anastasovich	Anastasovna	Stas
Anatoli	Anatolovich	Anatolovna	
Andrei	Andreich/Andreievich	Andreiovna	Andreyka
Androniki	Andronikovich	Andronikovna	
Antin	Antinovich	Antinovna	Antinko
Arseni	Arsenovich	Arsenovna	
Artur	Arturovich	Arturovna	
Benedikt	Benediktovich	Benediktovna	
Berngards	Berngardovich	Berngardovna	
Boris	Borisovich	Borisovna	
Cheslav	Cheslavovich	Cheslavovna	Cheska
Christov	Christovich	Christovovna	
Damian	Damianovich	Damianovna	
Danya	Danovich	Danovna	
Denis	Denisovich	Denisovna	Denka, Denya
Dimitri	Dimitrovich	Dimitrovna	Dimka
Edmund	Edmundovich	Edmunovna	rare
Elie	Eliovich	Eliovna	
Eriks	Eriksovich	Eriksovna	
Eugeni	Eugenovich	Eugenovna	also Evgeni
Feliks	Feliksovich	Feliksovna	
Filipp	Filippovich	Filippovna	Filya
Fridrik	Fridrikovich	Fridrikovna	
Fyodor	Fyodorovich	Fyodorovna	Fedinka
Galaktion	Galaktionovich	Galaktionovna	Galya
Gaspar	Gasparovich	Gasparovna	
Gavril	Gavrilovich	Gavrilovna	Gavya
Gennadi	Gennadovich	Gennadovna	
Georgi	Georgovich	Georgovna	
Gotfrid	Gotfridovich	Gotfridovna	
Gregor	Gregorovich	Gregorovna	Gregori, Grisha
Igor	Igorovich	Igorovna	
Ikovle	Ikovlevitch	Ikovlevna	
Ilarion	Ilarionovich	Ilarionovna	
Ilya	Ilich	Ilovna	
Ioakim	Ioakimovich	Ioakimovna	
Ippolit	Ippolitovich	Ippolitovna	
Ivan	Ivanovich	Ivanovna	Ivanchik
Josef	Josevich	Josevovna	
Karl	Karlovich	Karlovna	
Kazimir	Kazimirovich	Kazimirovna	

Name	Son Form	Daughter Form	Diminutives, Notes
Kesar	Kesarovich	Kesarovna	
Kliment	Klimentovich	Klimentovna	Klimka
Kondrati	Kondratovich	Kondratovna	
Konstantin	Konstantinovich	Konstantinovna	
Lavr	Lavrovich	Lavrovna	
Lavrenti	Lavrentovich	Lavrentovna	
Lavro	Lavroovich	Lavrovna	
Leonid	Leonidovich	Leonidovna	
Luchok	Luchokovich	Luchokovna	
Luka	Lukovich	Lukovna	Lukasha
Maksim	Maksimovich	Maksimovna	Maksimka
Marka	Markovich	Markovna	Markusha
Matvei	Matveiovich	Matveiovna	
Mikhail	Mikhailovich	Mikhailovna	Misha
Mili	Milovich	Milovna	
Miron	Mironovich	Mironovna	
Modest	Modestovich	Modestovna	
Mstislav	Mstislavovich	Mstislavovna	grand-duke Kiev
Nikifor	Nikiforovich	Nikiforovna	
Nikolai	Nikolaiovich, Nikitich	Nikolaiovna	Nikita
Nil	Nilovich	Nilovna	Nilya
Oleg	Olegovich	Olegovna	
Onufri	Onufriyevich	Onufriyovna	
Osip	Osipovich	Osipovna	Osya
Pavel	Pavlovich	Pavlovna	Pasha, Pashka, Pavlik
Petr	Petrovich	Petrovna	Petinka, Petrusha
Porfiri	Porfirovich	Porfirovna	
Rodion	Rodionovich	Rodionovna	
Rollan	Rollanovich	Rollanovna	
Rostislav	Rostislavovich	Rostislavovna	Rostya, Rostik
Sergei	Sergeich	Sergeiovna	Sergeika
Slava	Slavovich	Slavovna	Slavik, Slavka
Stanislav	Stanislavovich	Stanislavovna	
Stefan	Stefanovich	Stefanovna	
Tadei	Tadeiovich	Tadeiovna	
Tanas	Tanasovich	Tanasovna	
Timofei	Timofeiovich	Timofeiovna	Timok, Tisha, Tishka, Tima, Timka
Tomas	Tomasovich	Tomasovna	
Tsezar	Tsezarovich	Tsezarovna	= Caesar
Urvan	Urvanovich	Urvanovna	
Ustin	Ustinovich	Ustinovna	
Valentin	Valentinovich	Valentinovna	
Valeri	Valerovich	Valerovna	
Vasil	Vasilovich	Vasilovna	
Vassili	Vassilovich	Vassilovna	Vasily, Vasili
Viktor	Viktorovich	Viktorovna	
Vissarion	Vissarionovich	Vissarionovna	
Vitali	Vitalovich	Vitalovna	

Name	Son Form	Daughter Form	Diminutives, Notes
Vladimir	Vladimirovich	Vladimirovna	
Vladislav	Vladislavovich	Vladislavovna	
Vsevolod	Vsevolodovich	Vsevolodovna	
Vyacheslav	Vyacheslavovich	Vyacheslavovna	
Yefim	Yefimovich	Yefimovna	
Yevgeni	Yevgenovich	Yevgenovna	
Yuri	Yurovich	Yurovna	Yusha
Zakhar	Zakharovich	Zakharovna	Zasha
Zhenka	Zhenkovich	Zhenkovna	Zheka
Zigfrids	Zigfridovich	Zigfridovna	
Zinon	Zinonovich	Zinonovna	

FAMILY NAMES

Masculine Form	Feminine Form	Notes
Abakumov	Abakumova	
Afanasiev	Afanasieva	
Agranov	Agranova	
Aitmatov	Aitmatova	
Aivazovsky	Aivazovskaya	
Akhmadulin	Akhmadulina	
Akhmatov	Akhmatova	
Aksakov	Aksakov	
Akulov	Akulova	
Aldanov	Aldanova	
Alekhin	Alekhina	
Aleksandrov	Aleksandrova	
Alekseyev	Alekseycva	
Alikhanov	Alikhanova	
Amirdzhanov	Amirdzhanova	
Andreyev	Andreyeva	
Andronikov	Andronikova	
Andropov	Andropova	
Antokolski	Antokolskaya	
Antonov	Antonova	
Arbatov	Arbatova	
Arensky	Arenskaya	
Argunov	Argunova	serfs
Artuzov	Artuzova	
Astafyev	Astafyeva	
Avdusin	Avdusina	
Bagirov	Bagirova	
Bakunin	Bakunina	
Balabanov	Balabanova	
Balakirev	Balakireva	
Balitsky	Balitskaya	
Baranov	Baranov	
Baratynsky	Baratynskaya	
Barkov	Barkova	
Baryatinsky	Baryatinskaya	princely family
Bekhterev	Bekhtereva	

Masculine Form	Feminine Form	Notes
Beloborodov	Beloborodova	
Belostotsky	Belostotskaya	
Beltov	Beltova	
Belyakin	Belyakina	
Berzin	Berzina	
Bessonov	Bessonova	
Bezlov	Bezlova	
Biryuzov	Biryuzova	
Bitov	Bitova	
Boborykin	Boborykina	
Bogomelov	Bogomelova	
Bondarev	Bondareva	
Borisov	Borisova	
Boyarsky	Boyarskaya	
Brechkovsky	Brechkovska	
Bredichin	Bredichina	
Breshkovsky	Breshkovskaya	
Brushkin	Brushkina	
Brusilov	Brusilova	
Bryukov	Bryukova	
Bugaev, Bugayev	Bugaeva, Bugayeva	
Bukharin	Bukharina	
Bulanov	Bulanova	
Bulgakov	Bulgakova	
Bunin	Bunina	
Bykov	Bykova	
Cancrin	Cancrina	
Chambov	Chambova	
Chelyuskin	Chelyuskina	
Cherakasov	Cherakasova	
Cherinov	Cherinova	
Chernavsky	Chernavskaya	
Chernov	Chernova	
Chetverakov	Chetverakova	
Chirikov	Chirikova	
Chlenov	Chlenova	
Chudov	Chudova	
Chukovsky	Chukovskaya	
Danilov	Danilova	
Danishevsky	Danishevskaya	
Dargomyzhsky	Dargomyzhskaya	
Dashkov	Dashkova	
Demichev	Demicheva	
Derzhavin	Derzhavina	
Diakonov	Diakonova	
Dragomanov	Dragomanova	
Dragomirov	Dragomirova	
Drosdov	Drosdova	
Dubovoy	Dubovoya	
Dubskiy	Dubskia	
Durov	Durova	

Masculine Form	Feminine Form	Notes
Dushenov	Dushenova	
Dzerzhinsky	Dzerzhinskaya	
Dzhamalbekov	Dzhamalbekova	
Efimov	Efimova	
Efremov	Efremova	
Egorov	Egorova	
Erbanov	Erbanova	
Evdokimov	Evdokimova	
Fadeyev	Fadeyeva	
Filipov	Filipova	
Fineyev	Fineyeva	
Frolov	Frolova	
Fyodorov	Fyodorova	
Gagarin	Gagarinaa	princely family
Gapon	Gapona	
Gerasimov	Gerasimova	
Glazunov	Glazunova	
Golenishchev	Golenishcheva	
Golitsyn	Golitsyna	
Golovnin	Golovnina	
Golovskin	Golovskina	counts
Golubkov	Golubkova	
Goncharov	Goncharova	
Gorchakov	Gorchakova	princes
Gordeyev	Gordeyeva	
Grebenshikov	Grebenshikova	
Grekov	Grekova	
Griboyadov	Griboyadova	
Guedenov	Guedenova	
Gutchakov	Gutchakova	
Ignatiev	Ignatieva	
Ippolitov	Ippolitova	
Ivanov	Ivanova	
Izvolsky	Izvolskaya	also Isvolsky
Kaletin	Kaletina	
Kalinin	Kalinina	
Kamenev	Kameneva	
Karamzin	Karamzina	
Karpov	Karpova	
Katkov	Katkova	
Kaznakov	Kaznakova	
Kheraskov	Kheraskova	
Khomyakov	Khomyakova	
Khrennikov	Khrennikova	
Kniazhnin	Kniazhnina	
Knigin	Knigina	
Kolchak	Kolchaka	
Kolontay	Kolontaia	
Koltsov	Koltsova	
Kondratiev	Kondratieva	
Konev	Koneva	

Masculine Form	Feminine Form	Notes
Konorov	Konorova	
Korobuin	Korobuina	
Korvin	Korvina	
Kostomarov	Kostomarova	
Koussevitsky	Koussevitskaya	
Kovalevsky	Kovalevskaya	
Kravchinsky	Kravchinskaya	
Krokhin	Krokhina	
Krotkov	Krotkova	
Krukovsky	Krukovskaya	
Krupsky	Krupskaya	
Krylov	Krylova	
Kunavin	Kunavina	
Kuprin	Kuprina	
Kuropatkin	Kuropatkina	
Kutuzov	Kutuzova	
Kutznetsov	Kutznetsova	
Kuznetchev	Kuznetcheva	
Laptev	Lapteva	
Lavrov	Lavrova	
Lebedev	Lebedeva	
Leonov	Leonova	
Lermoliev	Lermolieva	
Liadov, Lyadov	Liadova, Lyadova	
Likhachev	Likhacheva	
Linitsky	Linitskaya	
Litvinov	Litvinova	
Livanov	Livanova	
Lopatin	Lopatina	
Lopukhin	Lopukhina	
Lukin	Lukina	
Lunacharsky	Lunacharskaya	
Lvov	Lvova	
Lyalin	Lyalina	
Lyubimov	Lyubimova	
Makarov	Makarova	
Markovnikov	Markovnikova	
Mdivany	Mdivania	
Medvedev	Medvedeva	
Menshikov	Menshikova	
Merezhkovsky	Merezhkovskaya	
Metchnikov	Metchnikova	
Milyukov	Milyukova	
Milyutin	Milyutina	
Molchanov	Molchanova	
Mrachkovsky	Mrachkovskaya	
Muralov	Muralova	
Muraviev	Muravieva	
Muzakov	Muzakova	
Myasnikov	Myasnikova	
Narishkin	Narishkina	

Masculine Form	Feminine Form	Notes
Nekrasov	Nekrasova	
Nenashev	Nenasheva	
Neyolov	Neyolova	
Nikolaev	Nikolaeva	
Nitchkov	Nitchkova	
Novikov	Novikova	
Ognev	Ogneva	
Okudzhav	Okudzhava	
Orlov	Orlova	
Ostrogorsky	Ostrogorskaya	
Ostrovsky	Ostrovskaya	
Oumansky	Oumanskaya	
Parshikov	Parshikova	
Penovsky	Penovskaya	
Petchorin	Petchorina	
Petrov	Petrova	
Plekhanov	Plekhanova	
Pobedonostsev	Pobedonostseva	
Polozov	Polozova	
Pronin	Pronina	
Protopopov	Protopopova	
Provotorov	Provotorova	
Pyatakov	Pyatakova	
Radomislsky	Radomislskaya	
Ragozin	Ragozina	
Ratushinsky	Ratushinskaya	
Rebikov	Rebikova	
Repin	Repina	
Rokossovsky	Rokossovskaya	
Rosov	Rosova	
Rostopchin	Rostopchina	
Rostovtzev	Rostovtzeva	
Ryabakov	Ryabakova	
Rylev	Ryleva	
Safonov	Safonova	
Samoilov	Samoilova	
Sanin	Sanina	
Sapozhniov	Sapozhniova	
Savinkov	Savinkova	
Selivanov	Selivanova	
Serebryakov	Serebryakova	
Serpilin	Serpilina	
Shalyapin	Shalyapina	
Shebalin	Shebalina	
Shedrin	Shedrina	
Sheremetyev	Sheremetyeva	counts
Shuvalov	Shuvalova	
Simakov	Simakova	
Simonov	Simonova	
Skobelev	Skobeleva	
Snegov	Snegova	

Masculine Form	Feminine Form	Notes
Sobolevsky	Sobolevskaya	
Sokolov	Sokolova	
Soloviev	Solovieva	
Solovyov	Solovyova	
Speransky	Speranskaya	
Spetsivtsev	Spetsivtseva	
Stetsky	Stetskaya	
Stolyarov	Stolyarova	
Stolypin	Stolypina	
Strunsky	Strunskaya	
Subachev	Subacheva	
Suvorov	Suvorova	
Svetlov	Svetlova	
Svidigailov	Svidigailova	
Taneiev	Taneieva	
Teternikov	Teternikova	
Tolbukhin	Tolbukhina	
Tomsky	Tomskaya	
Travkov	Travkova	
Trepov	Trepova	
Trifonov	Trifonova	
Ulanov	Ulanova	
Ulyanov	Ulyanova	
Ustinov	Ustinova	
Vakhtangov	Vakhtangova	
Varyguin	Varyguina	
Vasiliev	Vasilieva	
Verestchagin	Verestchagina	
Vinogradov	Vinogradova	
Volkansky	Volkanskaya	a princely family
Volodin	Volodina	
Volokhov	Volokhova	
Volsky	Volskaya	
Voronov	Voronova	
Voroshilov	Voroshilova	
Voslensky	Voslenskaya	
Vyshinsky	Vyshinskaya	
Vysotsky	Vysotskaya	
Yadrintsev	Yadrintseva	
Yakovlev	Yakovleva	
Yefremov	Yefremova	
Yusupov	Yusupova	a princely family
Zagoskin	Zagoskina	
Zaharov	Zaharova	
Zarubin	Zarubina	
Zaslavsky	Zaslavskaya	
Zhukov	Zhukova	
Zhukovsky	Zhukovskaya	
Zinoviev	Zinovieva	
Zukermanov	Zukermanova	

GEORGIAN

The Caucasus provided a haven for a language no longer related to anything else. Therefore, the aboriginal names are unrelated to other name systems, too. However, since the 19th century conquest of the Caucasus by Russia, many Russian and other foreign names have been used in the area. There was also a back-wash of personal names. The female personal name Tamara originated in Georgia, then spread to Russian and Ukrainian use.

If you want purely Georgian names, simply compare to the list of Russian names. These will do nicely as a pick-list for the 20th century.

FEMALE NAMES

Anita
Daredian
Dularkukht
Emilia
Luba
Manana

Mellushkella
Nestan
Nino
Nunu
Pahatman, P'hatman
Salome

Tamar, Tamara — thence
    to Russian
Tinatin, T'hinat'hin
Vera

MALE NAMES

Abram
Arkady
Arsenna
Artash
Bessarion, Besso
Bijo
Challico
Chalvah
Chancho
Cucule
Cyrille
Davit
Dimitri
Eduard
Elia, Eliko

Geno
Gia
Giorgi, Gogio
Givi
Igor
Illarion
Ioseb
Irakli
Jacalo
Jano
Konstantin, Kosta
Lado
Merab
Onise
Otari

Petri, Petro
Sandro
Shot'ha
Soso
Teddo
Vactangi
Vallodia
Vanno, Vano
Vasso
Wardo
Zachara
Zaza
Zezva
Zviad

FAMILY NAMES

* very famous, or in the news

Ahaismelashvili
Amirejibi

Bagrationi
Bostoganashvili

Bugadze
Chkhaidze

Cholokashvili	Kakashvili	Pecswelashvili
*Gamsakhurdia	Kostava	*Rust'hveli
Gochilaidze	Lobjanidze	*Shevardnadze
Gudiashvili	Melaidze	
*Jughashvili	Papashvili	

UKRAINIAN

While many people in Ukraine (Ukrainia or the Ukraine, depending on the age of your reference) have Russian personal or family names, there are distinctly Ukrainian ones you may want to use. Don't forget that in some periods this area was part of Poland, so a certain number of those names, mutated or not, may show up.

Patronymic surnames appear at least as early as the military rolls of the 14th century. However, these may have been patronymic forenames.

Distinctively Ukrainian is the family name ending *-enko*, which can be traced to the second half of the 12th century, when it was -enok. Then -enko replaced -enok which was typical for the region of Kyjiv (Kiev) in the mid–1500s. By 1683, -enok had completely disappeared into -enko. As -ënak, -enok did live on as a Belorussian ending: Vasilënak, son of Vasil; Kavalënak, son of kaval, a blacksmith.

However, to chop things very finely, -enko belongs to eastern and central Ukraine. In western Ukrainia (Halyčyna and Vollyń), -uk, -juk, -śkyj, -ćkyj, and -źkyj prevail; no -enko.

Pronunciation

Accented vowels are like Spanish ones; the pronunciation does not change, it just tells you which syllable to accent. Apostrophes indicate a slight break in the word, so you do not hang the consonant on the wrong syllable; also that the word is more or less abbreviated.

No two sources put Ukrainian into English the same way; most were inconsistent.

A — A in pasta
Č— CH as in church
E — E in hey
Ě— E in pen
Ę— U in bun
I — I in machine; some use Y rather than doubling the I

J — Y in yes
Ĺ — palatized L, as in table
Ń —first N in onion, or NY in canyon
Š — SH in shush
X — KH, the CH in loch
Ž — as the Z in azure

PLACE-NAMES

Kyjiv — Kiev
Xarkiv, Kharkiv — Kharkov

FEMALE NAMES

Ahrypýna, Horpýna
Akylýna,
Alexandra
Chrystýna, Chrýstja
Danýlo
Dárija
Elena
Hafíja, Aháfija
Halína, Hálka
Hánna; Hanúuska,
　Hándzja, Hanúlja,
　Ganusják, Hanúsja,
　Gančák, Hánka
Hryńkó, Hryń
Jankó

Jarema
Jaylýna
Jevdokíya, Javdócha
Jevpráksija, Práksja
Juchýma, Chýmka
Jurkó
Juxýma, Xýma, Xýmka
　(dim.)
Katerýna, Cátrja
Ksénija, Ksénka
Kúz'má
Makrýna
Maĺana, Malánka
Margíta
Maríja, Marúsja

Melánija, Malánka
Motróna, Mótrja
Nastásija, Anastasíja,
　Nástja
Nátalia
Odárka — popular
Oksána
Ólha
Paláha
Sóphie
Tetjána
Varvára, Varka
Ženja

MALE NAMES

Adám, Odám
Anánij, Onánij, Onánko
　(dim.)
Andríj, Ondríj
Antioch
Artém, Artemius, Artemko
Bayda
Bohdan, Bogdan, Boh-
　dánko — divinely
　given
Borís'

Dančul
Danýl
Drahosláv, Dráhoš
Ermank, Ermak
Gregori
Hérman
Hryhórij
Ilarion, Larión
Ili
Isýdir, Sýdir
Iván — dim. Vańkó, Ivanko

Jan, Jankó
Jurei, Jurkó
Kazimir
Konstantýn, Kostjantýn,
　Kosť
Matvei
Mikhail
Nemýr — unfriendly
Oleksánder
Oleksíj, Olexnó (dim.),
　Oléško (dim.)

Opanás
Parxím
Pavló
Pédir, Xvédir
Pedór'
Petró, Petr
Pylýp
Semén

Serhíj
Stepán
Suprún
Svi
Taras
Thomy, Tomi
Tóma; Tomkó (dim.)
Tymísh

Vasilja, Vasilei, Vasýl;
    Vasýlko (dim.)
Volodymyr
Vovk — wolf
Xódor
Xomá, Chomá
Xoměk
Xvédir; Xvédkó (dim.)

FAMILY NAMES

Andrijéko
Ánnič
Apostol — a Cossack het-
    man
Artemenko
Artimovič
Babenko — baba, grand-
    mother
Beiko
Bělocerkovčenko
Bilocerkovčenko
Biloúščenko — biloús,
    white mustache
Bohun
Bondarenko — bondar,
    hooper
Boysenko
Bratunenko — bratun,
    dim. of brat, brother
Budyonny, Budyenny —
    Cossack
Buhdiańčič
Bulharinenko — bolhár,
    Bulgarian
Bulharowicz — bolhár,
    Bulgarian
Chmielnicki — Polish/
    Cossack
Chrístič
Čyženko, Čiženko
Darienko
Didenko — did, grand-
    father
Djačenko — djak, cantor
Dorošenko
Dovženko
Drahuševič
Elman

Gálkévič
Gandzévič
Haletchko
Haponenko
Hirmanovič
Hlúščenko — hluxý, deaf
    man
Holovátnko — holová, big
    head
Hončarenko — Horčár,
    potter
Horpynenko
Hrinčenko
Hryvénko — hrýva, mane,
    long, thick hair
Ivanénko
Ivanovyc, Ivanovič
Kantemir, Cantemir —
    Cossack
Kateríničh
Katrič
Kirděvič
Kirdievič
Kirkidij
Kněžni
Korněenko
Kornienja
Korótčenko — Korótkyj,
    short man
Kosjačénko — Kósyj,
    squint-eyed
Kostenko
Kostęntinovič
Kovalenko — koval,
    blacksmith
Kovbaščenko
Kramarenko — kramar,
    tradesman

Krávčenko — kravéc, tailor
Kravchuk
Kryvénko — kryvyj, lame
Kuhténko — kóhút, cock
    in Polish
Kulinenko
Kulinič
Kulýna, Kýlýna
Kuzmyč, Kuzmič, Kuz'
Kvitka-Osnovjanenko
Kyndeviča
Larionénk
Lěsy
Lifar — Kyjiv
Lisovič
Lojevyč
Lotyšenko
Margítič
Mátfějevič
Matfievvič
Matienko, Matěenko
Mótrenko
Movčanenko
Mudry
Mykyténko
Nátalič
Nemerič, Meirič, Meýryč
Neměryč, Neměrič
Nestęko
Nestěkovič, Nestękovič
Neumyvájčenko —
    neumyvájko, does not
    like to wash face
Odamenko
Odarčenko
Odárčenko
Oleksievič
Oleščenko

Olevčenko
Olexnovič
Olhirovič
Onančič
Ondrěevič
Opanasovič
Orendarenko
Parxomovič
Pavlénko
Pazničenko — from
   Páznyk, holiday
Pedorenko
Petrénko
Pěvnenko
Pilipovič
Pivnenko
Poénko — pip, priest
Pultavčenko — from
   poltavec, someone
   from Poltava
Rédko
Ruz
Sagaidachny
Samilovič — a Cossack
   hetman
Semenovič
Serhijénko
Sestryčenko — sestra, sis-
ter

Ševčenko
Sidorenko, Sidorovič
Siminenko
Skljarenko — skljar, glass-
   cutter
Skovaroda
Špylenko, Špilenko
Stariščyčev
Stepányč
Storoženko
Suprunenko
Suxovijenko
Švečénko — švec, shoe-
   maker
Sytnikovič, Sitničenko
Teslénko — téslja, carpenter
Tilibenko — telýcya,
   heifer
Tkačénko — tkač, weaver
Tolochko
Tomčenko
Tomofev — Cossack
Tomylenko
Tovstenko
Tymošénko
Vačkovič
Vasýlčenko
Veckovič
Věčkovič

Vęčkovičo
Velikiy
Venckovič
Vereščako
Věreščako
Vílxoveč
Voronínaja, Voroné-
   naja — vórna, crow
Vovčinko, Vóvčenko
Vyshnevtskyy
Wanczuk
Xanenko
Ximčenko
Xmelnýckyj, Xmelny-
   čenko
Xodorič
Xoměkovič
Xomič
Xrěbtovič
Xrebtoviča
Xrěbtoviča
Xvedorenko — from
   Chwedczenye
Zaleski — Polish origin
Zěnčenko
Zilboorg — Kyjiv
Zinčenko
Zinkovič
Žylenko, Žilenko

BELARUSAN

Many authorities hold Belarusan (Byelorussian, Bielorussan) to be a dialect of Russian, the two languages being at least as closely related as Spanish and Portuguese, or Urdu and Hindi.

The names may seem to be, for the most part, Russian names transliterated to Latin in a peculiar manner. For example, Zenon Paznyak is rendered in Belarusan specialty books as Zianon Paźniak, Vyacheslav Kebich as Viačaslaŭ Kiebič, and Stanislav Shushkevich as Stanislaŭ Šuškievič. This is because the Russian version is transliterated out of the Cyrillic alphabet into English. Belarusan is written with marked Roman letters, and is no more wrong, or unusual, than Czech or Spanish. In fact, once you know the diacriticals, it is a very logical pronunciation. You have your choice of writing names in Belarusan or in English (without diacriticals, but make the necessary changes).

From Russian there is a G-to-H shift. The Belarusan Hieorhi is the equivalent of the Russian Georgi. Ditto Siarhiej and Sergei, Halina and Galina. So do not just borrow any Russian personal name without checking some odd places for the equivalent.

There are also some very non–Russian names: Halšan, Ryhor, Rahnieda, and others. Also, the distinctively Belarusan "-enak/-ak" ending does set apart those who do not have Russian or Polish family names.

In some contexts Belarusans may put the family name first, followed by the personal name, as do the Lithuanians and Ukrainians.

Some family names are gendered, like Russian or Lithuanian names. Not all, though; those without a feminine version are unisex.

In 1989, the population of what is now Belarus broke down as 77.8 percent Belarusan; 13.2 percent Russian; 4.1 percent Polish; 2.9 percent Ukrainian; and various others, 2 percent. So just as not all American names are Anglo-American names, not all names in Belarus are Belarusan.

Pronunciation

A — A in pasta
C — TS in tsetse; change to TS for English version
Č— CH in church; change to CH for English version
E — E in pen
G — always hard G as in gun
H — H in have
I — I in machine
J — Y in yen; change to Y for English version
O — O in home
S — S in sun
Ś — palatized S; change to S for English version
Š — SH in shush; change to SH for English version
U — U in rule
Ŭ — W in how; change to W or V for English version
Y — Y in many; change to I for English version
Z — Z in zero
Ź — palatized Z; change to Z for English version
Ž — ZH, as the Z in azure; change to ZH for English version
CH — CH as in loch; change to KH for English version
DZ — DZ in adze
DŽ — J in jug; change to J for English version

FEMALE NAMES

Aleksandra	Branislava	Iziasava
Anastasia	Euphrosyne	Kazimira
Bračyslava	Halina	Lydia

Pradslava
Radaslava
Rahnieda
Sophia
Stanislava

Stefanija
Uladzimira
Usiaslava
Usiavalada
Valancina

Valantyna
Viačaslava
Volha
Zora

MALE NAMES

Belarusan	*English*
Adam	
Alaksandr	
Alaksiej	
Aleh, Aleš	Alesh
Alhierd	
Aloiza	
Anatol	
Anton	
Barys	
Bračyslaŭ	Brachislav
Branislaŭ	Branislav
Dzmitry	
Francišak — fairly popular	Francishak
Halšan	Halshan
Hienadź	
Hieorhi	
Ihar	
Ihnat	
Iosif	
Iziasaŭ	Iziasav
Jahaila	
Jakaŭ	Jakov
Janka, Jan	
Jaŭchim	Jovkhim
Jaŭhien — popular	Javhien
Jury, Juryj	
Kastuš	Kastush
Kazimir	
Keistut	
Kipryjan	
Kirill	
Kirlya	
Laŭren	Lavren
Lazar	
Lianid	
Leŭ	Lev
Maksim	
Michail	
Michaš	Mikhash
Mikalaj	
Mikola	

Belarusan	English
Mitrafan	
Nil	
Paval	
Piotr	
Radaslaŭ	Radaslav
Radzim	
Rahvalod	
Ryhor	
Sciapan	
Siarhiej — fairly popular	
Stanislaŭ	Stanislav
Stefan	
Svidryhaila	
Uladzimir, Uladzimier — very popular	
Usiaslaŭ	Usiaslav
Usievalad	
Vaclaŭ — popular	Vaclav
Valentyn	
Valeryjan	
Varfalomey	
Vasil', Vasilya	
Viačaslaŭ	Viachaslav
Vincuk	
Vitali	
Vitaŭt — fairly popular	Vitavt
Zair	
Zianon	
Źmitrok	Zmitrok
Žyhimont	Zhihimont

Family Names

Masculine	Feminine	Anglicized
Abecedarski	Abecedarskaja	
Adamovič		Adamovich
Aleksandrovič		Aleksandrovich
Aleksiutovič		Aleksiutovich
Aničenka		Anichenka
Astroŭski	Astroŭskaja	
Azhur		
Bahdanovič		Bahdanovich
Bahuševič		Bahushevich
Baradulin	Baradulina	
Baŭharyn	Baŭharyna	Bavgarin
Baŭharynovič		Bavgarinovich
Bazarevič		Bazarevich
Biadula		
Biarizkin	Biarizkina	
Bič		Bich

Masculine	Feminine	Anglicized
Bohša		Bohsha, Bogsha
Borushko		
Bulachaum		
Buraŭkin	Buraŭkina	Burovkina
Bykaŭ	Bykava	
Čakvin	Čakvina	Chakvin
Čaus		Chaus
Cierashkovich		
Cieraškovič		
Doŭnar		Dovnar
Harecki		
Harun		
Hierasimovič		Hierasimovich
Hilevič		Hilevich
Hrybanač	Hrybanava	
Hryc		
Hryckievič		Hryckievich
Hryniavicki		
Husoŭski	Husoŭskaja	Husovski
Ihnatoŭski	Ihnatoŭskaja	Ignatovsky
Ipataŭ	Ipatava	Ipatova/Ipatov
Jahoraŭ	Jahorava	Yahorov
Januškievič	Yanushkievich	
Jaraslavič		Yaraslavich
Jaŭmienaŭ	Jaŭmienava	Yavmienov
Jelizarjeŭ	Jelizarjeva	Yelizaryov
Jermalovič		Yermalovich
Jucho		Yukho
Kalinoŭski	Kalinoŭskaja	Kalinovski
Kamienski	Kamienskaja	
Karski	Karskaja	
Kaspiarovič		Kaspiarovich
Kavalenak		
Kazloŭski	Kazloŭskaja	Kazlovski
Kipel		
Kiseleŭ		Kiselev
Kisialoŭ	Kisialova	
Kolas		
Konan		
Kopysski		
Kraŭčanka		Kravchanka
Kryčeŭski	Kryčeŭskaja	Krichevski
Kryžanoŭski	Kryžanoŭskaja	Krizhanovski
Kupala		
Kupava		
Labyncaŭ	Labyncava	
Lastoŭski	Lastoŭskaja	Lastovski
Latyšonak		Latishonak
Lecka		
Litvak		

Masculine	Feminine	Anglicized
Lojka		
Lučanok		Luchanok
Luckievič		Luckievich
Lukašuk		Lukashuk
Lyakh		
Lysenko		
Maldzis		
Maračkin	Maračkina	Marchkin
Marcinkievič		Marcinkievic
Mašeraŭ	Mašerava	Masherov
Mikalajšanka		Mikalaychanka
Motyl		
Navumčyk		Navumchik
Novik		
	Parchomienka	
Paškievič		Pashkievic
Platonaŭ	Platonava	
Praškovič		Prashkovich
Rahojša		Rahoysha
Rahula		
Rasolka		
Rusak		
Sambuk		
Sapieha		
Šavel		Shavel
Šavzin	Šavzina	Shavzin
Šerech		Sherekh
Siaredzič		Siaredzich
Siarhiejeŭ	Siarhiejeva	Sergeiev
Skaryna		
Stankievič		Stankievich
	Staniuta	
Starčanka		Starchanka
Statkievič		Statkievich
Šukieloyts		Shukieloits
Šupa		Shupa
Sviontak		
Tarasaŭ	Tarasava	
Taraškievič		Tarashkievich
Tkačoŭ	Tkačova	Tkachov
Trusaŭ	Trusava	
Tryhubovič		Tryhubovich
Tumash		
Ulicionak		
Vakhromeyev		
Vasilenak		
Viarcinski	Viarcinskaja	
Volacič		Volacich
Yakovenko		
Yaroš		Yarosh

Masculine	Feminine	Anglicized
Yukho		
Zablocki		
Żboraŭ	Żaborava	Zaborov
Żylinski	Żylinskaja	Zhilinski

LITHUANIAN

Normal name order for Lithuanians is family name first, followed by personal name. Under Soviet rule, this would be followed by a patronymic:

Vedluga Benediktas Juozo (son of Joseph)

Svirelyte Marija Stepono (daughter of Stephan)

As usual, almost all English-language sources change the order to make it suit the Western concept of "first names and last names."

It seems that female names end in A or E, male names in S, rarely O. Last names gender according to the wearer. Married women end their husbands' family names in -iene. Girls, and never-married women of any age, end their father's family name in -aite, yte, -ute, and -(i)ute. So Ivanauskis' daughter will be Ivanauskaite, his wife Ivanauskiene.

The year 1400 is considered the dividing line between the old single-name system before family names, and the modern two-name system. Middle names are rare, but slowly becoming more common. Up until the 1920s, babies were named from a list of approved saints. Now, new names are being invented, making for middle saint names which appear only on the baptismal record, and are ignored later in life.

Pronunciation

The number of diacritical marks below is violently reduced from some of the more pedantic sources. My power word-processor is used by most publishing houses. If its software does not have the sign, the publisher will not want the expense to set up special graphics for a single novel. So rather than do three-quarters, none of which make grand differences to your ears, I have cut all but the most important. The macron vowels are gone, along with tildes, various accents, and dotted letters.

Since you are writing in English, not Lithuanian, you need only worry about:

Č — CH in church; in English, CH

Š — SH in shush; in English, SH

Ž — Z in azure; in English, ZH

These you can render with their English spellings.

All final E's are pronounced.

J — Y in yet

Agniya	Ale	Angele
Aldona	Aliute	Anikke, Annze

Audre, Audrone,
  Audrute — thunder-
  storm
Aušra — dawn
Birute
Bronislova, Brone
Egli — fir tree
Elzbieta
Igne
Jadwiga
Janina

Jievute
Julija
Jura — sea
Kofryna
Laime — good luck
Laimute
Margarita
Marija, Marijona
Maryte
Nastasya, Nastka, Nas-
  tusya, Stasya

Ona=Anne
Pelida
Ragana
Rasa — dew
Roze, Rozele, Rozyte
Ruta — rue plant
Sofija
Tasya, Taska, Tasenka
Veronika

Male Names

Adomas
Algirdas
Algirmantas
Andrius, Andrus
Antanas (very popular)=
  Anthony
Arune
Audris, Audrys, Audrius,
  Audronis, Audrutis —
  thunderstorm
Augustus
Bernardas
Beržas — birch tree
Danukas
Donatus
Dovidas
Emanuelis
Gediminas
Gintaras
Gregoras
Haroldas
Jecis

Jekebs
Jogailo
Jonas
Jonelis
Jonukas
Jonutis
Juozapas, Juozas
Jurgis
Justas
Justinas
Justukas
Kazimieras, Kazys
Kestutis
Kristijonas
Leonas
Liutas
Martinas
Mikalojus
Mindaugas
Motiejus
Petras
Petrelis

Petrukas
Povilas
Pranciškus, Pranas
Raulas
Raulo
Risardas
Rosertas
Rugys — rye
Samuelis
Skirhailas
Solomonas
Stanislovas
Tomas, Tomelis
Vacys
Valionis
Vanda
Vandele
Vilius
Vincas
Visvaldas
Vitrigailas
Vytautas

Family Names

Masculine	Feminine, Married	Feminine, Single
Alksninis	Alksniniene	Alksninaite
Alminauskis	Alminauskiene	Alminauskaite
Andriulis	Andriuliene	Andriulyte
Antanaitis	Antanaitiene	Antanaityte
Baranauskas	Baranauskiene	Baranauskaite
Basanavičius	Basanavičiene	Basanavičute
Baužas	Baužiene	Baužaite
Brazauskas	Brazauskiene	Brazauskaite

Masculine	Feminine, Married	Feminine, Single
Čekuolis	Čekuoliene	Čekuolyte
Çernius	Çerniene	Çernute
Čiurlionis	Čiurlioniene	Čiurlionaite
Degutis	Degutiene	Degutyte
Donelaitis	Donelaitiene	Donelaityte
Dovydenas	Dovydeniene	Dovydenaite
Dubauskas	Dubauskiene	Dubauskaite
Duonelaitis	Duonelaitiene	Duonelaityte
Grigonis	Grigoniene	Grigonyte
Ivanauskas	Ivanauskiene	Ivanauskaite
Ivinskis	Ivinskiene	Ivinskaite
Jasinskis	Jasinskiene	Jasinskaite
Jonynas	Jonyniene	Jonynaite
Juškevičius	Juškevičiene	Juškevičute
Kirkilas	Kirkiliene	Kirkilaite
Klimas	Klimiene	Klimaite
Krasauskas	Krasauskiene	Krasauskaite
Kreve	Kreviene	Krevaite
Kudirka	Kudirkiene	Kudirkaite
Landsbergis	Landsbergiene	Landsbergyte
Maciulevicius	Maciuleviciene	Maciulevicute
Maciulis	Maciuliene	Maciulyte
Maciunas	Maciuniene	Maciunaite
Malinauskas	Malinauskiene	Malinaukaite
Masionis	Masioniene	Masionyte
Mickevičius	Mickevičiene	Mickevičute
Morkunas	Morkuniene	Morkunaite
Paleckis	Paleckiene	Paleckyte
Papartis	Papartiene	Paparyte
	Paulekiene	Paulekiute
Peckauskas	Peckauskiene	Peckauskaite
Petraitis	Petraitiene	Petraityte
Petrauskas	Petrauskiene	Petrauskaite
Petrulis	Petruliene	Petulyte
Psiblilauskas	Psibilauskiene	Psibilauskaite
Račkus	Rackuviene	Račkute
Rimša	Rimšiene	Rimšaite
Salys	Saliene	Salyte
Silingas	Silingiene	Silingaite
Skardžius	Skarrdžiuviene	Skardžiute
Smetonas	Smetoniene	Smetonaite
Snieckus	Snieckiene	Sniedkute
Staugautis	Staugautiene	Staugautyte
Stitilis	Stitiliene	Stitilyte
Storasta	Storastiene	Storastaite
Stulgenskis	Stulgenskiene	Stulgenskiate
Svirelis	Svireliene	Svirelyte
Tumas	Tumiene	Tumaite
Vaiciunas	Vaiciuniene	Vaiciunaite
Valancius	Valanciene	Valancute

Masculine	*Feminine, Married*	*Feminine, Single*
Valionis	Valioniene	Valionyte
Vedluga	Vedlugiene	Vedlugaite
Voldemaras	Voldemariene	Voldemaraite
	Zemiene	Zemaite
Žilinskas	Žilinskiene	Žilinskaite
Zingeris	Zingeriene	Zingeryte
Zymantas	Zymantiene	Zymantaite

LATVIAN (LETTISH)

Notice how all male names end in S, female ones in E or A. Name order is like ours, personal name first, family name last. Family names gender, but it is difficult to find Latvian ones, rather than imports from surrounding countries. Three points for pronunciation: J is our Y, Š is SH, and final E's are sounded.

FEMALE NAMES

Anya, Anyuta	Irusya	Lucija
Asenka	Jana	Mare
Aska, Asya	Janina	Margrieta
Beatrise	Judite	Nadina
Brigita	Juliane	Nastasya, Nastka,
Cecilija	Kamila	Nastusya, Stasya,
Edite	Karina	Tasya
Elizabete	Karlene	Sarlote=Charlotte
Gerda	Krista	Tasenka, Taska
Gizela	Kristine	Urzula
Grieta	Liene	Viktoria
Henriette	Lisbete	Zanna
Irka	Lizina	

MALE NAMES

Aivars	Berngards	Fabius
Alberts	Bernhards	Filips
Albins	Brencis	Fridrichs
Aleksanders	Dainis	Gotfrids
Anatolijs	Daniels	Gothards
Andrejs	Edgars	Gregors
Ansis	Edmunds	Guntis
Antons	Eriks	Gustavs
Armands	Ervins	Haralds

Imants
Indriskis
Janis — popular; Jahnis
Jazeps
Jeks
Justins
Justs
Karlens
Karlis — popular
Kriss, Krists, Krisis

Labrencis
Leonhards
Leons
Leopolds
Lukas
Martins
Marts
Mikelis, Miks, Mikus
Milkins
Niklavs, Nikolais

Pauls
Pavils
Richards
Rihards
Roberts
Rudolfs
Stefans
Valters
Zigfrids

FAMILY NAMES

Masculine	*Feminine*
Baumanis	Baumana
Blaumanis	Blaumana
Gorbunovs	Gorbunova
Hartmanis	Hartmana
Ivans	Ivana
Jadlowker	
Knorins	Knorina
Kuzmins	Kuzmina
Ozolinsh	
Penikis	Penika
Poruks	Poruka
Pumpurs	Pumpura
Rozitis	Rozita
Škapars	Škapara
Stenders	Stendera
Strals	Strala
Ulmanis	Ulmana
Ziedonis	Ziedona

POLISH

Some books will tell you that there were Poles named Nicholas, Thaddeus, Casimir, Sigismund, Ladislas, and Sofia. Not true. At home they were Mikolaj, Tadeusz, Kazimierz, Zygmunt, Władysław, and Zofja. This is one more example of "civilizing" foreign names so they will seem more familiar and less "uncouth."

Polish uses a lot of diacritical marks to get 10 vowels and 35 consonants out of the Latin alphabet. Most of these can be dropped without bothering the English-speaking reader. In case you need to know how to pronounce things properly, we give the marked versions.

As a source of names, Poles seem fond not only of classical Latin (Julius, Vespasian, Fabian) and saints (Stephen, Ignace), but of French for an alternate source (Gabriella, Theophile, Christophe).

One of the Slavic languages, Polish uses different forms of the family name for men and women — most of the time — "-ski" becomes "-ska," and "-cki" is feminized to "-cka." The endings "-owa" and "-ina" indicate a wife; "-ówna" and "-anka" a daughter. Some names seem to use a neuter form for both. Where I cannot be fairly certain of the alternate form, I do not give it. So as not to reduce your name choices, there are some you will have to use only for male characters, a few only for female.

You will be delighted to hear that since 1973 this gendering has been optional. In a contemporary story, you can get away with the masculine form alone. Before then, you must use the differing forms.

The Polish language is hostile to gender-mistake plots. Verbs are so inflected that they indicate the sex of both the speaker and the person addressed.

Amongst proudly claimed Polish artists you will find Germanic names like Weyssenhoff and Strug (who used a Polish-sounding pseudonym). Remember, ethnic purity in Europe has been pretty mythical for centuries, in the cities and upper classes.

Where Polish names are used varies enormously from one century to another. In 1387, the grand duchy of Lithuania was joined to Poland in a powerful state, where the Polish aristocracy tried hard to erase the Lithuanians except as peasants. By 1610, the eastern border of Poland temporarily swept past Moscow! Then there were the partitions, the Republic of 1918 to 1939, the second disappearance during the Second World War, the westward roll of the borders afterwards. Poles and Polish names will be found in all these formerly Polish territories.

Pronunciation

A — French *on*, nasalized
Á — accented A, as in pasta
Ą — ogonek A
C — TS as in bits
Ć — TSH, unique to Polish
CH — CH in loch, strong uvular fricative
CZ — CH as in church
DZ — DG as in edge
E — French *in*, nasalized
Ę — ogonek E
I — I in machine
J — Y as in yes
Ł — Slavic "barrel L," almost a W, like the L in talk
Ń — NY, the French GN in champagne

RZ — RZH, as if azure were arzure
Ś — accented S
SZ — SH as in shush
W — V in viv
Y — German umlauted U, as in *Führer*
Ź — Z with accent
Ż — Z with overdot
Accent is almost always on next to last syllable.

FEMALE NAMES

Name	*Pronunciation*	*Notes and Alternatives*
Adelaidá		
Agatá		Agá, Agatká
Agnieszká	ahg-nee-EHSH-kah	
Albertyná	ahl-ber-TUE-nah	Albinká
Aleská		Alká, Alá
Amaliá		
Amelciá	ah-MEL-tsia	
Anná		Aniá, Anká
Antoniná		Antá, Atká
Bernardá		
Brygidá		Brygitká, Brygá
Cecyliá	tse-TSUE-lee-ah	
Celá	TSE-lah	Celek, Celinká, Celká
Cesiá	tse-SEE-ah	
Constantiá		
Dagá		
Danielká		Danká
Dorotá		Dorosiá, Dorká
Edytá	eh-DUE-tah	Eddá, Edká
Elá		
Elsie		
Elżbietá	elz-bee-EH-tah	Elizá, Elká, Elsbietká
Elzuniá		
Ewá	EH-vah	
Felciá	fehl-TSEE-ah	Felká, Felá
Felipá		Filpiná
Franciszká	frahn-TSEESH-kah	Franiá, Fraká
Frydá		
Gabrjelá	gab-RYEHL-ah	
Haná		Hanká
Heléná	he-LEHN-ah	
Henrietá		Henká, Heniá
Inká		
Inok		
Itká		

Iwoná	ee-VO-nah	Iwonká
Izabellá		Izabel, Izá
Name	*Pronunciation*	*Notes and Alternatives*
Jagá	YAH-gah	
Janá	YAH-nah	
Janiná		
Jasiá	yah-SEE-ah	
Joanká	yo-AHN-kah	
Joasiá	yo-ah-SEE-ah	
Jolantá	yo-LAHN-tah	Jolá
Jozefá		
Julciá	yul-TSEE-ah	Julá
Justiná	yuh-STEE-nah	Justá
Kamilá	kah-MEE-lah	Kamilká, Milá
Karoliná		Karolinká
Kasienká		Kasin, Kaská, Kasiá
Kazimierá	kah-zee-mee-EHR-ah	
Khrystyná		Krystá, Krystká, Krystynká, Krysiá
Klará		
Laurká		
Letyciá	leh-tue-TSEE-ah	
Lidá		Lidká
Lillá		Lilká
Lodoiská	loh-DOYSH-kah	
Lucyá	lu-TSUE-ah	
Ludwiká		Ludká
Magdá		Magiá
Marciá	mahr-TSEE-ah	
Margisiá		Margitá, Gitá
Mariná		
Marja	MAHR-yah	=Maria; most popular; Marii, Maciá, Manká, Marylá, Maryná, Masiá
Melciá	mehl-TSEE-ah	Melká, Melá
Minká		
Naciá	nah-TSEE-ah	
Nataliá		Natká, Natá
Nelá		Nelká
Olá		
Olesiá		
Pawliná	pahv-LEE-nah	
Pelciá	pehl-TSEE-ah	Pelá
Penelopá		Lopá
Polciá	pohl-TSEE-ah	Polá
Reniá		
Ritá		
Salciá	sahl-TSEE-ah	
Stanisławá	stah-nee-SWAH-vah	
Stefaniá		Stefciá, Stefká, Stefá
Tawiá	tah-VEE-ah	
Teklá		

Tereniá
Tereská

Name	Pronunciation	Notes and Alternatives
Tesá		Tesiá
Tilá		
Tolá		Tolsiá, Tosiá
Trudá		
Waleriá	vah-leh-REE-ah	Walá
Wanda	VAHN-dah	
Wanziá	vahn-ZEE-ah	
Werá	VEH-rah	
Wierá	vee-EHR-ah	Wierciá, Wierká
Wirá	VEE-rah	Wirke, Wisiá
Zannz		
Zochá		
Zofja	ZOH-fyah	=Sofia; popular; Zoshá
Zuzana		Zuzanká, Zuziá, Zuzká, Zusá
Zytká		

MALE NAMES

Name	Pronunciation	Notes and Alternatives
Adam		Adas
Adolf		Adok
Albin		Albek
Aleksander		popular 19th c.; Aleks
Alfred		
Alojzy	a-LOY-zeu	
Andrzej	ahn-DRZHEY	popular
Antoni	ahn-TOH-nee	Antonin, Antos, Antek, Tonek
Artur		Artek
Atanazy		Atek
Aureli		Aurek
Bartos		Bartek
Benedykt		Bendek, Benek
Biernat	bee-EHR-nat	
Bogomił	BOH-goh-meev	
Bohdan		
Bolesław	BOH-le-swahv	Sławek
Bonawenturá	boh-nah-ven-TU-rah	
Bozentá		
Bronisław	BROH-nee-swahv	Bronek, Sławek
Cezar		Cezary, Cezek
Cyprjan	TSEU-pryan	
Czesław	CHEH-swahv	
Donat		Donek
Dymitry		Dymek, Dyzek
Dyonizy	deu-o-NEE-zheu	
Edzio	ehdg-EE-oh	Edek

138 Contemporary Names

Name	Pronunciation	Notes and Alternatives
Fabjan	FAH-byahn	fairly popular; Fabek
Fil		Filipek
Name	*Pronunciation*	*Notes and Alternatives*
Franciszek	frant-SEE-shek	became popular 18th c.; Franek, Franio, Franus
Frycz	FREUCH	Frydek
Fryderyk		Fredek
Genio		Genek
Geron		Gerik, Garek
Gostae		
Grzegorz	GRZHE-gorzh	
Habdank		
Henier		Heniek
Henryk	HEHN-reuk	
Ignacy	ig-NAH-tseu	Ignac, Inek
Iwan	EE-vahn	
Jalu	YA-lu	
Jan	YAHN	very popular; Janko, Janek, Jankeil
Jędrzej	YED-rzhey	Jedrek, Jedrus
Jeryz	YE-reuzh	
Jerzy	YER-zheu	
Joachim	yoh-AH-kheem	
Józef		
Juljan	YUL-yahn	
Juljusz	YUL-yush	
Kaden		
Kajetan	kah-YEH-tahn	
Kamil	KAH-meel	
Karol		Karolek
Kazimierz	KAH-zee-MEE-erzh	fairly popular; Kazek, Kazik,Kazio
Klemens		Klimek
Kleofas		
Konstanty		
Kornel		
Krystian		Krys, Chrystian, Crystek
Krzysztof	KRZHEUSH-tof	
Leon		Leonek, Leos
Leszek	LEH-shehk	
Lucjan	LUHTS-yan	
Ludwik	LUD-veek	
Łukasz	LU-kahsh	
Maciej	ma-TSEE-ehy	
Marceli	mar-TSEH-lee	
Marcin	MAR-tseen	
Marjan	MAR-yan	
Mateusz	MAH-toosh	Matyas
Maurycy	mawr-REU-tseu	
Michał	MEE-khahw	Michak, Michalek
Mieczysław		
Miesko		Mietek
Mikołaj	mee-KOH-way	Mikolai, Milek

Natan		
Olęs	Olek	
Name	*Pronunciation*	*Notes and Alternatives*
Oskar		
Ossip		
Oswald	OS-vahld	
Otton		Otek
Piotr		Piotrek, Pietrek
Rafał		
Roman		
Ryszard	RUE-shard	Rysio, Rye
Sebastjan		
Sęp		
Sergiusz	ser-GEE-ush	Serg
Skarbek		
Stanisław	STAH-nee-swahv	Sławek
Stasio		Stasiek
Stefan		
Szymon	SHUE-mon	popular
Tadeusz	TAH-doosh	Tadek, Tadzio
Teodor		Teodorek, Teos
Teofil		
Titus		Titek, Tytus
Tomisław	TOH-mee-swahv	Tomek, Tomcio
Tymon		Tymek
Ursyn	OOR-suen	
Wacław	VAHK-wahv	
Wespazjan	vehs-PAHZ-yan	
Wiktor	VEEK-tohr	
Wilhelm	VEEL-helm	
Wincenty	vee-TSEHN-tue	Wicent, Wicus, Wicek
Władysław	VWA-due-swahv	popular
Włodzimierz	vwo-DGEE-meerzh	
Wojciech	VOY-tsee-ekh	
Zygfryd		Zygi
Zygmunt	ZHEUG-munt	Zygi

FAMILY NAMES

Masculine	*Pronunciation*	*Feminine: Wife/Daughter*
Adamowski		Adamowska
Asnyk	AHS-neuk	Asnykowa [ahs-neuk-OV-ah]
		Asnykówna
Bandrowski	bahn-DROV-skee	Bandrowska
Belcikowski		Belcikowska
Bem		Bemowa/Bemówna
Bendá		Bendowa/Bendówa
Beniowski	beh-nee-OV-skee	Beniowska
Berent		Berentowa/Berentówna

Masculine	Pronunciation	Feminine: Wife/Daughter
Bielski		Beilska
Birkowski	beer-KOV-skee	Birkowska
Bobrzyński	boh-BRZHUEN-skee	Bobrzyłska
Bogusławski	boh-guh-SWAHV-skee	Bogusławska
Boguszewski	boh-guh-SHEV-ska	Boguszewska
Borowski		Borowska
Borowy	bohr-OH-vee	Borowa/Borówna
Branicki		Branicka
Brodziński	broh-DGEEN-skee	Brodzińska
Broniewski	brohn-ee-EHV-skee	Broniewska
Bruchnalski		Bruchanalska
Bruski		Bruska
Brzozowski	brzho-ZOV-skee	Brzozowska
Budny	BUD-nue	Budna
Chlapowski		Chlapwska
Chlebowski	khleh-BOHV-skee	Chlebowska
Chlopicki		Chlopicka
Chmelnizki		Chmelnizka
Chmielowski	khmee-eh-LOV-skee	Chmielowska
Chodkiewicz		Chodkiewicza
Chodowiecki		Chodowiecka
Choromański		Chormanska
Ciechanowski	tsee-eh-khah-NOV-skee	Ciechanowska
Cwojdziński	kvoy-DGEEN-skee	Cwojdzińska
Cyrankiewicz	tsue-rahn-kee-EHV-eech	Cyrankiewsiczowa/
		Cyrankiewxiczówna
Czacki		Czackowa/Czackówna
Czartorski		Czartorska
Czartoryski		Czrtoryska
Czechowic	che-KHOHV-eets	Czechowicowa/Czechowicówna
Dábrowski	dah-BROHV-skee	Dábrowska
Dekert		Dekertową — deh-ker-TOH-vah
Dembinski		Dembinska
Długosz	DWU-gosh	Długoszowa/Długoszówna
Dmowski	DMOHV-skee	Dmowska
Dobrzycki	doh-BRZHEUTS-kee	Dobrzycka
Doświadczyński	dos-vee-ahd-CHUEN-skee	Doświadczyńska
Drużbacki		Drużbacka
Dvorski		Dvorska
Dyaboski		Dyaboska
Dyagasiński		Dyagasińska
Feliński		Felińska
Gabilowitsch		Gabilowischowa/Gabilowischówna
Gałecki		Gałecka
Gaszynski		Gaszynska
Gladkowski		Gladkowska
Głowacki	gwo-VATS-kee	Głowacka
Godowsky		Godowska
Gojawiczeński	go-ya-vee-CHEHN-skee	Gojawiczyńska
Goltz		Goltza

Masculine	Pronunciation	Feminine: Wife/Daughter
Gornicki		Gornicka
Gumplowicz		Gumplowiczowa/Gumplowiczówna
Halecki	hah-LETS-kee	Halecka
Heilprin		
Horsztyński	horsh-TEUN-skee	Horsztyńska
Hrdlicka		
Hussowski	hus-SOHV-skee	Hussowska
	eew-wah-KOHV-eech	Iłłakowicz
Irzykowski	eer-zhue-KOV-skee	Irzykowska
Janicki		Janicka
Jasnorzewski	yahs-nor-ZHEV-skah	Jasnorzewska
Jastrow	YAHS-trohv	Jastrowa/Jastrówna
Kadłubek		Kadłubekowa/Kadłubekówna
Karłowicz	kahr-WOH-veech	Karłowiczowa/Karłowiczówna
Karpiński		Karpińska
Kasprowicz	kah-SPROH-veech	Kasprowiczowa/Kasprowiczówna
Klonowic	kloh-NOH-veech	Klonowicowa/Klonowicówna
Kniaźnin		Kniaźnina/Kniaźnanka
Kochanowski	koh-khah-NOHV-skee	Kochanowska
Kochowski	koh-CHOHV-skee	Kochowska
Kołłątaj		
Komarnicki		Komarnicka
Komorowski	koh-moh-ROHV-skee	Komorowska
Konarski		Konarska
Konopnicki		Konopnicka
Kopernik		Koperniká— Copernicus
Korboński		Korbońska
Korzeniowski	kohr-zhen-ee-OV-skee	Korzeniowska
Korzybski		Korzybska
Kościuszko	koh-zkee-USH-koh	Kościuszka
Koźmian		
Krasicki		Krasicka
Krasiński		Krasińska
Kraszewski	krah-SHEV-skee	Kraszewska
Kryński		Kryńska
Krzycki	KRZHUETS-kee	Krzycka
Krzywicki	krzhue-VEETS-kee	Krzywicka
Krzyżanowski	krzhue-zhan-OV-skee	Krzyżanowska
Ksaweri	ksah-VEH-ree	Ksaweri
Kuncewicz	kuhn-TSEH-veech	Kuncewiczowa/Kuncewiczówna
Kuśnierz	kus-nee-erzh	
Landowsky		Landowska
Łaski		Łaska
Lechoń		
Lednicki		Lednicka
Ledochowsky		Ledoshowska; counts
Lelewel	leh-LEH-vehl	
Lenartowicz	leh-nahr-TOH-veech	Lenartowiczowa/Lenartowiczówna
Leszczyński	lesh-chuen-skee	Leszczyńska
Leszetycki		Leszetycka

Masculine	Pronunciation	Feminine: Wife/Daughter
Małachowski	mah-wah-KHOHV-skee	Małachowska
Małczewski	mahw-CHEV-skee	Małczewska
Małecki		Małecka
Malinowski	mah-lee-NOHV-skee	Malinowska
Markiewicz		Markiewiczowa/Markiewiczówna
Matuszewski	mah-tuh-SHEV-skee	Matuszewska
Mickiewicz	meets-kee-EH-veech	Mickeiwiczowa/Mickeiwiczówna
Mikołajczyk	mee-koh-WAY-chuek	Mikołajczykowa/Mikołajczykówna
Mitosz	MEE-tosh	Mitoszowa/Mitoszówna
Mochnacki		Mochnacka
Modrzejewski	moh-drzheh-YEV-skah	Modrzejewska
Modrzewski	moh-DRZHEV-ski	Modrzewska
Morsztyn	MORSH-tuen	Morsztyna
Moszkowski		Moszkowska
Nałkowski	nahw-KOHV-skee	Nałkowska
Naruszewicz	nah-ru-SHEV-ich	Naruszewiczowa/Naruszewiczówna
Niemcewicz	nee-ehm-TSEH-veech	Niemcewiczowa/Niemcewiczówna
Norwid	NOR-veed	
Noskowski		Noskowska
Ogiński		Ogińska
Opaliński		Opalińska
Orkan		
Orzeszk	OR-zheshk	Orzeszkową — or-zhesh-KOH-vah
Osiński		Osińska
Ossoliński		Ossolinska; princely
Ostrorog		
Paskewicz		Paskewiczowa/Paskewiczówna
Passow		Passowa/Passówna
Pawlikowski	pahv-lee-KOV-skah	Pawlikowska
Piwiński	pee-VEEN-skee	Piwińska
Polak		Polaka
Połaniecki	poh-wah-nee-EHTS-kee	Połaniecka
Poniatowski	poh-nee-ah-TOV-skee	Poniatowska
Potocki		Potocka
Potrzuski		Potrzuska
Przyboá	przhue-BOH-ah	
Przybyszewski	przue-bue-SHEV-skee	Przybyszewska
Przynski	PRZHUEN-skee	Przynska
Raczkiewicz		Raczkiewiczowa/Raczkiewiczówna
Raczyński		Raczyńska
Radziwiłł	rah-DGEE-veew	
Rej		
Rostworowski	rohst-vohr-OV-skee	Rostworowska
Rozwadowski	roz-vah-DOHV-skee	Rozwadowska
Rzewuski	rzhe-VUH-skee	Rzewuska
Sarbiewski	sahr-bee-EHV-skee	Sarbiewska
Seklucjan		
Serafinawicz	sehr-ah-fee-NAH-veech	Serafinawiczowa/Serafinawiczówna
Siedlicki	see-ehd-LEETS-kee	Siedlicka
Sienkiewicz	see-ehn-kee-EH-veech	Sienkiewiczowa/Sienkeiwiczówna

Masculine	Pronunciation	Feminine: Wife/Daughter
Sieroszewski	see-ehr-oh-SHEV-skee	Sieroszewska
Sikorski		Sikorska
Masculine	*Pronunciation*	*Feminine: Wife/Daughter*
Słonimski		Słonimska
Słowacki	swoh-VAHTS-kee	Słowacka
Smreczyński		Smreczyńska
Starowolski	stah-roh-VOHL-skee	Starowolska
Stojowski		Stojowska
Stokowski		Stokowska
Stypulkowski		Stypulkowska
Świętochowski	svee-eh-toh-KHOV-skee	Świętochowska
Szarzyński	shar-ZHUEN-skee	Szarzyńska
Szatkowski	shat-KOV-skee	Szatkowska
Szczucki	SHCHU-tskee	Szczucka
Szujski	SHUY-skee	Szujska
Szymonowic	sheu-mo-NO-veets	Szymonowicowa/Szymonowicówa
Tęczyński		Tęczyńska
Trembecki	trem-BETS-kee	Trembecka
Trzosinski	ter-so-SEEN-skee	Trzosinska
Twardowski	tvar-DOV-skee	Twardowska
Ujejski		Ujejska
Ulenowski	uh-leh-NOV-skee	Ulenowska
Voynicz		Voyniczowa/Voyniczówna
von Wasielewski		von Wasielewska
Wiersynski	vee-ehr-SUEN-skee	Wiersynska
Witkiewicz	veet-kee-EH-veech	Witkiewiczowa/Witkeiwiczówna
Wociechowski	voh-tsee-eh-KHOV-skee	Wocienchowska
Wodzinski		Wodzinska
Wojciechowski		Wojciechowska
Wrzodak		Wrzodaka
Wyspiański	veu-spee-AHN-skee	Wyspiańska
Wyzewski		Wyzewska
Zablocki		Zablocka
Zaleski		Zaleska
Zalinski		Zalinska
Załuski		Załuska
Zamojski		Zamojska
Zamoyski		Zamoyska
Zapolski		Zapolska
Zarembin		Zarembina/Zarembanka
Zawodziński	zah-voh-DGEEN-skee	Zawodzińska
Zborowski	zborh-ROHV-skee	Zborowska
Zbylitowski		Zbylitowska
Żeleński		Żeleńska
Żeromski		Żeromska
Zienliński		Zienlińska
Zimorowicz	zee-mo-RO-vich	Zimorowiczowa/Zimorowiczówna
Zoltowski	zohl-TOHV-skee	Zoltowska

HUNGARIAN

They call their own country Magyarország. The Magyars are the root ethnic tribe, vaguely related to the Finns, Estonians, and Turks, but only by linguistic traces. Names remain in common use that date back a thousand years or more, which were then borne by kings and princes of the Arpad dynasty.

For those interested in the period of a century or two ago, I have noted when I could family names belonging to the nobility. When you notice many have the Germanic "von" in them, remember the Austro-Hungarian Empire was dominated by the German-speaking Austrians.

Even though English-language works may name Hungarians in the mode of personal name followed by family name, this is not the Magyar way, any more than it is the Japanese way. If your story is actually set in Hungary, a character should not be introduced as Adam Nagy, but as Nagy Adam. This is one of those points on which you can be simply, utterly impressive, thereby winning the deep faith of your audience that you have done more than two days' research on Hungary. Omitting it may leave the knowledgeable reader wary and distant, afraid this is only a hasty potboiler.

Some vowels have an accent mark, others a double accent, sometimes printed as an umlaut. To indicate this in your manuscript, you might use a following apostrophe or quotation mark. In most cases, even a Hungarian will forgive you for leaving out the diacritical marks.

FEMALE NAMES

Adél	Gracia	Klara, Klarika
Ágota, Agotha	Gruzia	Kriska
Aliz, Alizka	Gyorci	Lenci
Amalia	Ila	Lidi
Anci	Ilka	Likszi
Annus, Ninacska,	Ilona	Lilike
Annuska, Anikó	Iluska	Linka
Boske, Boski	Iréne, Irenka	Liszka
Bózsi	Johanna	Magdolna
Dani	Jolán, Jolanka	Malcsi
Darda	Joli	Máli, Malinka
Duci	Juci, Jucika	Mara, Marcsa, Mariska
Erinn	Judit	Margit
Evi, Evike	Julianna, Julinka, Juliska	Mária
Ferike	Jutka	Martus, Martuska
Franci	Kamila	Neci
Frici	Kata, Katinka	Nusi
Gitta	Kató, Katoka	Onella
Gizi, Gizike, Gizus	Katus	Rebeka

Rezi
Riza, Rizus
Roza
Rozalia
Rozsi
Ruzsa
Sarika

Sarolta
Sasa
Teca
Tercsa
Teresa, Terez, Terezia,
    Terike, Teruska
Treska

Vica
Zigana
Zizi
Zsanett
Zsazsa

MALE NAMES

Ádorjan
Ágoston
Albert
Álmos
Andor, Andorás
András, Andris
Antal
Árpád
Artur
Aurele
Aurelius
Bálint
Ballas
Bazel
Béla — popular
Benedek, Benedik, Benke,
    Beno, Bence, Benci
Bernat
Bertalan
Bódog
Cezar
Dacso
Damján
Dániel
Dávid
Deco
Dénes, Dennes
Dezső
Domokos, Domonkos,
    Domó, Dome
Domotor, Domó
Edgard
Edvard
Elemér, Elek
Emeric
Endre
Ernő
Ferenc, Ferencz — popu-
    lar

Fűlőp
Gábor
Gáspár
Gellart
Gergely
Géza
Gusztáv
Győorgy — popular
Gyula, Gyala — very pop-
    ular
Ignaz
Illyes
Imre
István, Isti
Janczi
János, Janika — very pop-
    ular
Jenci, Jensi
Jenő, Jinő
József, Jóska — popular
Kálmán
Károly
Kásmér
Kelemen
Kerestel
Kobi
Koloman
Lajos
László
Lázár
Lenci
Loránd, Lóránt'
Lorinc
Makszi, Maks
Mano
Marci, Marcilka, Marcilki
Márkus
Máté
Mátyás

Micu
Mihály — very popular
Miklos, Miki, Miksa
Misi, Miska
Mór
Moritz
Niklos, Niki
Odi
Ődőn
Orbán
Pál, Páli, Palika
Péter
Rafael
Rendor
Rez, Rezső
Rikard, Riczi
Samie, Samu
Sándor, Sanyi
Szigfrid
Tabor
Tade
Tamás
Timót
Tivadar
Todor
Ulászló
Vazul
Vencel
Vidor
Viktor
Vili
Vilmos
Vinci
Zako
Zigfrid
Zoltán
Zsigmond
Zsolt

FAMILY NAMES

Ady
Andrassy
Angyal
Apponyi — noble; counts
Arany
Asboth
Babits
Bacsányi
Bajza
Ballagi
Bánffy
Baross
Bátory
Batthyány
Belcredi — noble
Benczur
von Beniowsky
Beothy
Berzsenyi
Bessenyey — noble, also
   Bessenyei
Bethlen — noble, Bethlen
   von Iktar in full
Boczkay — noble
Boehm
Bokanyi
Bolyai
von Burian von Rajecz
Császár
Csók
Csokonai
Csoma
Czuczor
Damjanich
Dávid
Deák
Dessewffy
von Doczi/Dóczy
Dohnányi
Dumany
Egressy
Endlicher
Eőtvős
Erdelyi
Erkl
Eszterházy — noble; since
   13th c.
Fadrusz
Fay

Fejer
Fejérváry — de Komlos-
   Keresztes, a baronial
   title
Fessler
Flesch
Goldmark
Goldziher
von Gombos
Gőrgey, von Gőrgey
Gratz
Gyongyosi
Harányi
Haraszthy de Mokcsa
Herczeg
von Hevesy
Hidas
Hollós
Hóman
Horthy; Horthy de
   Nagybanya
Horvath
Hubay; Hubay von Sza-
   latna
Illyeshazy — noble branch
   extinct in 1838
Iványi
von Janko
Jókai
Joseffy
von Josicka
Jurisics — noble
Justh
Kadar
von Kallay — noble
Kalnoky
Kármán
von Karman
Károlyi — noble
Kárpáthy
Kazinczy
Kemény
Kisfaludy
Kiss
Klaka
Kmety
Kodály
Koestler
Kőlcsey

Kolozsvári
Kőrmendi
Kornis
Kőrősi
Kossa
Kossuth
Kosztolányi
Krúdy
Kúeczky
Kun
Lengyel
Lotz
Madách
Maléter
Mányoki
Márai
Merse
Mészáros
Mikszáth
Mindszenty
Moholy-Nagy
Mólnar
Munkácsy
Nagy
Nikisch
Orczy
Paál
Pázmány
Petőfi
Pogányi
Prohászka
Rajk
Rákóczi, Rakoczy — noble
Rákosi
Remenyi
Reviczky
Rippl
Rónai
Salamon
Schick
Stibor
Szaalay
Széchenyi — noble
Széchy
Szegedy
Szekfű
von Szell
Szemere
Szenczi

Szent-Gyorgyi von Nagy-
  rapolt
Szerb
Szinyei
von Taaffe
Teleki — noble, also
  Telecki
Thőkőly — noble
Tisza, von Tisza — noble

Tollagi
Tompa
Vitáz
Vőrősmarty
Wekerle
Werbőczy
Ybl
Zach
Zápolya — noble,

sometimes Szapolyai
Zerffi
Zerhazy — noble
Zichy
Zilahy
Zolnay
Zrinyi — noble

ROMANIAN

In Romanian, the "-escu" ending is the equivalent of the north European "-son" or "-sen." A Romance language, rather than a Slavonic one, so you will not have to change family names to suit gender.

A — A in pasta
Â — A in cane
C — K as in kick
Ć — CH in church
S — S in sit
Ś — SH in shush

FEMALE NAMES

Alexandra
Amalia
Ana, Anicuta
Antonetta
Cecilia
Celine
Cornelia
Dol
Dora
Dorotthea
Elena
Elica

Ema
Euphrosyne — not usual
Francise
Helene
Ioan
Irina, Irini
Iulia
Jenica
Lucia
Magda
Maria
Maricara

Marussa
Militza
Mite
Nina
Nora
Olga
Reveca
Rodica
Sava
Ursule
Veronica
Zizi

MALE NAMES

Adrian
Alexandru — very popu-
  lar; Alecu

Andrei
Anton
Artur

Aurelian
Barbu, Barbo
Basarab

Bogdan
Camil
Caton
Cezar
Ćivu
Constantin — very popu-
   lar
Corneliu
Dic
Dimitrie, Demetrius
Duiliu
Eitel
Emil
Enric
Garabet
Gheorghe — popular
Giofroi
Godoired
Grigore — popular
Gustav
Horia

Iancu
Ilie
Ioan
Ion — popular
Ionel
Iosif
Iuliu
Karl
Konrad
Leca
Liviu
Lucian
Marius
Matei
Mihail — very popular
Mihas
Mircea
Miron
Neagoe
Nićofor
Nicolae — very popular

Noe
Octavian
Petru — popular;
   Petar
Pop
Radu — very popular
Râzvan
Reimond
Sabin
Sion
Sorin-Daniel
Ştefan
Taku
Teodor
Vasile
Victor
Vidra
Vlaciu
Vlad
Zaharia
Zamfira

Family Names

Alecsandri, Alexandrescu
Aman — Transylvanian
Andreescu
Anghel
Antonescu
Arbore
Ardelean
Asaki
Averescu
Babic
Bâlâcescu
Balcescu
Bârsan
Bercovici
Bibescu, Bibesco
Blaga
Bolinteneanu
Bolliac
de Boyescu
Brancoveanu
Brancuśi
Brâtianu
Bunescu
Câlinescu
Cantacusino
Cantemir

Caragiale
Cârlova
Catargi
Cercel
Cireseanu
Codreanu
Conaći
Constantinescu
Cosaceanu
Cośbuc
Cosmad
Costin
Crainic
Creangâ
Cristea
Cutzescu
Cuza
Dârâscu
Davila
Delavrancea
Dimitriscu
Dobre
Dobrogeanu
Duca
Eftimiu
Eliade

Emilian
Eminescu
Eminovici
Enesco, Enescu
Florescu
Gafencu
Ghica
Ghika
Gigurtu
Goga
Goma
Greaceânu
Grigorescu
Groza
Haiduci
Haśdeu
Hentzia
Iancu
Ibrâileanu
Ionescu
Iorga, Iorgalescu
Iosif
Kogâlniceanu
Kremnitz
Lazâr
Lecca

Lućian
Lupescu
Maior, Maiorescu
Mandaćem
Maniu
Manole
Marghiloman
Medrea
Micle
Micu
Mihailescu
Milescu
Miracovići
Mirea
Mironescu
Movilâ
Mureśianu
Neculce
Negruzzi, Nigruzzi
Negulici
Nottara
Odobescu

Paciurea
Pallady
Pâtrascu
Pauker
Penescu
Petrascu
Plesita
Pop, Popea, Popescu
Pordea
Râdelescu
Radescu
Ramniceanu
Rebreanu
Ressu
Romniceanu
Russo
Sadoveanu
Sanatescu
Sâulescu
Serbe
Sima
Śincai

Sirato
Slavici
Sorbul
Stâcescu
Staći
Stefânescu
Steriadi
Stoica
Sturdza
Tanase
Teodorescu
Theodorean
Titulescu
Tonitsa
Ureć
Vâcârescu
Vaida-Voevod — Transyl-
vanian
Valbudea
Vioescu
Zamfirescu

CZECH AND SLOVAK

Besides being close Slavonic languages, these peoples were joined in Czecho-slovakia. Their use of the Latin alphabet is thick with diacritical marks, and does not sound like it looks to us. Sometimes you wonder who left out all the vowels. I grew up around Slovaks, and I have to check the table of pronunciation constantly.

Most publishers and readers will accept Czech and Slovak names without the diacritical marks, so I have written that version first. You may also spell as sounded, transliterating into English pronunciation of the letters. In that case, "Safarik" (Šafařik) could become "Shuhfuhzheek," and "Alica" is "Uhleetsa."

Your choice of which way to write Czech and Slovak names is completely individual. In my entirely personal opinion, if I were doing non-fiction, say, a Czech history, I would include a pronunciation table in the prefatory material, and require diacriticals. If I were writing a novel set in the area, I would like dia-criticals, but otherwise transliterate. Using regular spelling without diacriticals does not allow anyone to pronounce it right. I would use it only in non-fiction where a single Czech's name in passing does not have to be right, but I think I would add a pronunciation in brackets at the first use.

Because of this, when necessary, I give first the in-between, because it is closer to what you will see in a lot of indexes. Second is the diacriticized version, the authentic. Third, is a transliteration.

Happily, you will find many names that do not have any diacriticals that you can use without any conflict at all! If the only diacritical is an accented final Y, you can skip it and most people will still get it right. Ditto accented E, A, U, or I; at least the reader won't be too far off.

On top of all this fun, women use a feminine version of the family name, like most Slavonic and Slavic languages. Unmarried, they add "-á," "daughter of," to the last consonant of their father's family name, "-ský" becomes "-ská"; the unaccented male "-a" becomes the accented and different-sounding "-á," which is added to names ending in consonants. Married, they use a feminine of their husband's family name — or their last husband's if divorced or widowed: the masculine "-ský" ending becomes "-sková, otherwise "-ová" is added to the last consonant.

So the daughter of Zikmund Petr Svoboda is Karolina Vorsila Svobodá (note the change to an accented A) who, if she marries Levoslav Václav Smrek, will be Karolina Smreková. If she married Otakar Antonín Tuma, she would be Karolina Tumová. Her daughter by Levoslav would be Ufžena Smreká; by Otakar, Jula Tumá.

I have listed most names under Czech, which was the dominant language until the 19th century. It was only during the mid-century nationalism that Slovak began being used literarily. Quite simply, it is often impossible for an outsider to identify a specifically Slovak name unless the source is so good as to separate them from the Czechs.

The "of" word is ze or just z, like the French de/du, the German von, Dutch van, or Italian di/da.

Pronunciation

Stress is always on the first syllable. The letters that do not sound like their English equivalents are:

A — U in butter
Á — A in rather
C — TS in pets
Č — CH in church
CH — Scottish CH in loch
D — dental D, tongue against the back of the teeth
DŽ — J in jump
E — E in get
É — E in they
Ě — YE
G — G in gun
H — voiced aspirative fricative; hard H
I — I in machine, but short
Í — I in machine, but long

J — Y in yes
Ň — palatized N, as in new
O — O in for
Ó — O in door, long
R — rolled R
Ř — Z in azure, S in measure
S — S in sit
Š — SH in shun
T — dental T
U — U in put
Ú — long U, as in prune
Y — I in it
Ý — long EE
Z — Z in zen
Ž — S in measure (yes, same as R)
Appearing only in Slovak are:
Ä — A in pasta
DZ — DZ in adze
Ĺ — L as in least, but softer
Ô — UO
Ŕ — long, rolled vocalized R
The foreign W is pronounced V.

SLOVAK FEMALE NAMES

Simple	Diacritical	Sounds like	Diminutives
Katarina	Katarína	Kuhtuhreenuh	
Maria	Mária	Mahreeuh	Márika
Marta		Muhrtuh	Martka
Veronika		Veroneekuh	Veronuška
Urzena	Uťžena	Urrzhennuh	Uťženka

SLOVAK MALE NAMES

Simple	Diacritical	Sounds like	Diminutives
Anton			
Boleslav			
Emil		Ehmeel	
Jan	Ján	Yahn	
Josef, Jozef		Yosef	
Juraj		Yuruhy	
Laco		Lutso	
Levoslav			
Milan			

Simple	Diacritical	Sounds like	Diminutives
Milo		Meelo	
Oldrich	Oldřich	Oldzheekh	
Pavel		Puhvel	
Pavol		Puhvol	
Petr		Petter	

Family Names

Simple	Diacritical	Sounds like	Feminines
Bartka			Bartá/Bartková
Bella		Belluh	Bellá/Bellová
Blaha	Bláha		Bláhá/Bláhová
Botto			Bottá/Bottova
Chlebovca		Khlehbohvtsuh	Chlebovcá/Chlebovcová
Ciliak	Čiliak	Cheeleeuhk	Čiliaká/Čiliaková
Grgas		Gurguts	Grgasá/Grgasová
Hrljac		Heraljats	Hrljacá/Hrljacová
Janosik	Jánošík	Yahnosheek	Jánošíká/Jánošíková
Jilemnický		Yeelemnitsky	Jilemnická/Jilemnicková
Kolenicka	Kolenička	Koleneechkuh	Koleničká/Koleničková
Kollar	Kollár	Kollar	Kollará/Kollarová
Lukac	Lucáč	Lutsach	Lucáčá/Lucáčov'
Mišura		Mishuruh	Mišurá/Mišurová
Novomedsky	Novomedský		Novomedská/Novomedsková
Orszagh	Országh	Orszagh	Orszaghá/Orszaghova
Paucula	Paučula	Pauchuluh	Paučulá/Paučuloá
Pivovarci	Pivovarči	Peehvovuhrchee	Pivovarčá/Pivovarčová
Razus	Rázus	Razus	Razusá/Razusová
Repka			Repká/Repková
Safarik	Šafařik	Shuhfuhzheek	Šafařiká/Šafařiková
Smrek		Semrek	Smreká/Smreková
Turosik	Turošík	Turosheek	Turošíká/Turošíkova
Urban			Urbaná/Urbanová
Vajansky	Vajanský	Vayansky	Vajanská/Vajanskvá
Zahorec	Záhorec	Zahhorets	Záhorecá/Záhorecová

If there are not enough listed here, borrow from the Czechs.

Czech Female Names

Simple	Diacritical	Sounds like	Diminutives
Ada	Áda	Aduh	
Adela	Ádela	Ahdeluh	Adelka
Agnesa	Ágnesa	Ahgnesuh	Agneska
Alzbeta	Alžběta	Ulzhbayta	Běta, Bětka, Betuška

Simple	Diacritical	Sounds like	Diminutives
Ana	Ána	Annuh	Aneška, Anežka, Anicka, Anuška
Andela	Anděla	Undayluh	
Andula			Andulka
Bara	Bára		
Barbora			Barborka
Baruska	Baruška	Barushkuh	
Bedriska	Bedřiška	Bedzhishkuh	
Blanka			
Blazena		Bluhzenna	Blaza
Bobina		Bobihna	
Bozena	Božena	Bozhennuh	
Brona	Broňa	Bronyuh	
Cile		Tsiyluh	Cilka
Dasa		Duhsuh	
Dela		Deluh	
Dita		Diytuh	Ditka
Doma		Domuh	
Dora		Doruh	Dorka
Dorota		Dorotuh	
Edita		Ediytuh	
Elena		Elenuh	Elenka, Eliška
Eliska	Eliška	Eliyshkuh	
Emmy			
Evicka	Evička	Eviychkuh	Evka
Evuska	Evuška	Evushkuh	
Fela			
Franca		Frantsuh	Francka, Frantiska
Franziska			
Gitka		Giytka	Gituška
Gizela		Giyzeluh	
Hana		Huhnuh	Hanicka, Hanka
Helena		Helenuh	Hela, Helenka, Heluška
Hera			
Iduska	Iduška	Idooshkuh	
Irena		Irenuh	Irenka, Irka
Izabella		Izabelluh	
Jana	Jána	Yanuh	Jánika, Jánka
Jenka		Yenkuh	
Jindraska	Jindraška	Yindrashka	
Jirina	Jiřina	Yizhinnuh	
Jitka		Yitka	
Jula	Júla	Yuluh	Júlka
Juliana	Júliana	Yulianuh	Júliška, Júlka
Karla	Kárlá	Karluh	Kárlika, Kárlinka
Karolina			Karola
Katarina			Katica, Katuška, Kata
Kristina			Krista, Kristinka
Kveta	Květa	Kvaytuh	Květka
Leka			

Simple	Diacritical	Sounds like	Diminutives
Lenka			
Magdelena, Magdalena			Magda
Marca		Martsuh	
Margita			
Marie		Marieh	
Mariena			Marienka
Marketa	Markéta	Markaytuh	Marka
Marticka		Martitskuh	
Matylda			Tylda
Milada			Milka
Natalia			Natasa
Olina		Oliynuh	
Olunka			Oluška
Pavla			
Pavlina			
Reza, Rezka			
Rose			
Ruza			
Ruzena	Rúžena	Ruezhenuh	
Ryba		Rihbuh	
Stasa			Staska
Stefania			Stefka
Teodora			
Tereza	Teréza	Terayzuh	Terézka
Trava			
Tyna		Tihnuh	
Vanda		Vunduh	
Vera	Věra	Vyeruh	Verka
Verona			Veronka
Vilma		Viylmuh	
Vorsila		Vorsiyluh	
Zelena		Zelenuh	Zelenka
Zofia	Žofia	Zhofiuh	Žofka
Zuzana			Zuzanka, Zuzka, Zusa

CZECH MALE NAMES

Simple	Diacritical	Sounds like	Diminutives
Adam			Adamko
Albinek			
Ales	Aleš	Alesh	
Alexander			
Andrej		Andrey	
Antonin	Antonín	Antoniyn	Antek
Arne			
Arnost			
Bazil			
Bedrich	Bedřich	Bedzhikh	

Simple	Diacritical	Sounds like	Diminutives
Bela			
Berno			Bernek
Bohuslav			
Boleslav			
Cenek		Tsehnehk	
Dalibor			
Dano			Danko
Dismas			
Dobroslav			
Edouard			
Egon			
Emil			
Eugen			
Evzen			
Frana	Fráňa	Franya	
Frantisek	František	Fruntyshek	
Frico		Fritso	
Gabo			Gabko
Georg			
Gustav	Gustáv		Gustik
Hanus	Hanuš	Hannush	
Havlicek	Havlíček	Huvlychek	
Holan			
Honza			
Hynek		Hinnek	
Ignát			
Ilja		Ilya	
Isa	Iša	Isha	
Jan	Ján	Yan	Janko
Jaromir	Jaromír	Yuromiɪ	
Jaroslav		Yaroslav	
Jiri	Jiří	Yyzhiy	
Josef		Yosef	Joska
Jur			Jurik
Juro			Jurko
Karasek	Karásek		
Karel			
Klement			Klemo
Konrad			
Kostka			
Kovar			
Kubes	Kubeš	Kubbesh	Kuba, Kubik
Ladislav			
Leksik			Lekso
Leos	Leoš	Leosh	Leoško
Lukas	Lukaš	Lukash	Luko
Matej	Matěj	Mateay	
Michal		Mikhal	
Michna		Mikhna	
Miroslav			

Simple	Diacritical	Sounds like	Diminutives
Miso			Misko
Nikola			
Otakar			Otik
Pavel			
Pepa			Pepik
Petr			
Prokop			
Rajmund		Raymund	
Rastislav			
Samo			Samko
Smil		Smihl	
Stanislav			Stano
Stefan			
Svatopluk			
Tomas	Tomáš	Tommash	
Tynek		Tinnek	Tynko
Vaclav	Václav	Vatslav	
Vasil		Vahsiyl	
Vilek		Viylek	
Vilem	Vilém	Villaym	Vilko
Vitezslav	Vítězslav	Viyteazslav	
Vladimir	Vladímir	Vladiymir	Vladko
Vojtech	Vojtěch	Voytyekh	
Xaver		Ksahver	
Zdenek	Zdeněk	Zdenyek	Zdenko
Zikmund		Zeekmund	

CZECH FAMILY NAMES

Simple	Diacritical	Sounds like	Feminine: Wife/Daughter
Ambros			Ambrosá/Ambrosová
Banta			Bantá/Bantová
Bartos	Bartoš	Bartosh	Bartosá/Bartová
Bencur	Bencúr	Bentsoor	Bencúrá/Bencúrová
Benda			Bendá/Bendová
Bendl			Bendlá/Bendlová
Benes			Benesá/Benesová
Bezruc	Bezruč	Bezruch	Bezručá/Bezručová
Blahoslav			Blahoslavá/Blahoslavová
Bolzano			Bolzaná/Bolzanová
Borkovec	Bořkovec	Bozhkovets	Bořkovecá/Bořkovecová
Borovský			Borovská/Borovsková
Brezina	Březina	Bzhezina	Březiná/Březinov'
Broucek	Brouček	Brouchek	Broučeká/Broučeková
Brozik			Broziká/Brozikóvá
Burian			Burianá/Burianová
Cech	Čech	Chekh	Čechá/Čechová
Celakovsky	Čelakovský	Chelakovsky	Čelakovská/Čelakovsková
Cep	Čep	Chep	Čepá/Čepová

Simple	Diacritical	Sounds like	Feminine: Wife/Daughter
Cernohorsky	Černohorský	Chernohorsky	Černohorská/
			Černohorsková
Chelcicky	Chelčický	Khelchitsky	Chelčická/Chelčicková
Chladni			Chladná/Chladnová
Chlubna		Khlubna	Chlubná/Chlubnová
Chod		Khod	Chodá/Chodová
Destinn			Destinná/Destinnová
Divisch	Divišch	Dyvyshkh	Divischá/Divischov'
Dobrofský			Dobrofská/Dobrofsková
Dreyschock			Dreyschocká/
			Dreyschocková
Drtina		Dertihnuh	Drtiná/Drtinová
Dubcek	Dubček	Dubchek	Dubčeká/Dubčeková
Durych		Duriykh	Durychá/Durychová
Dusík			Dusíká/Dusíková
Dyk			Dyká/Dyková
Dzban		Duzbun	Dzbaná/Dzbanová
Erben			Erbená/Erbenová
Fibich		Fibikh	Fibichá/Fibichová
Flaska	Flaška	Flashka	Fla šká/Flašková
Gregr		Grehger	Gregrá/Gregrová
Grund			Grundá/Grundová
Haba	Hába		Hábá/Hábová
Halas			Halasá/Halasová
Halek	Hálek		Háleká/Háleková
Hanka			Hanká/Hanková
Harant			Harantá/Harantová
Hasek	Hašek	Hashek	Hašeká/Hašeková
Havlicek	Havlíček	Huhvlichek	Havlíčeká/Havlíčeková
Helfert			Helfertá/Helfertová
Hlavacek	Hlaváček	Hlavachek	Hlaváčeká/Hlaváčeková
Hlinka			Hlinká/Hlinková
Hodin			Hodiná/Hodinová
Holacek	Holaček	Holachek	Holačeká/Holačeková
Holar			Holará/Holarová
Holub			Holubá/Holubová
Hora			Horá/Horová
Horak			Horaká/Horaková
Hostinský			Hostinská/Hostinsková
Hostovský			Hostovská/Hostovsková
Hrdlicka	Hrdlička	Hurdlichkuh	Hrdličká/Hrdličková
Hurben			Herbená/Herbenová
Hus			Husá/Husová
Husak	Husák	Husahk	Husaká/Husaková
Jakubec		Yukkubets	Jakubecá/Jakubecová
Janacek	Janáček	Yunnachek	Janáčeká/Janáčeková
Janauschek	Janáuschek	Yunnauskhek	Janauscheká/
			Janauschekova
Jebavý		Yebuvy	Jebavá/Jebavová
Jelínek			Jelíneká/Jelíneková

Simple	Diacritical	Sounds like	Feminine: Wife/Daughter
Jerabek			Jerabeká/Jerabeková
Jeremias	Jeremiáš	Yeremyash	Jeremiášá/Jeremiášová
Jezek	Ježek	Yezhek	Ježeká/Jezeková
Jirak	Jirák		Jiráká/Jiráková
Jirasek	Jirásek	Yirasek	Jiráseká/Jiráseková
Jirovec	Jírovec	Yiyrovets	Jírovecá/Jírovecová
Kabana			Kabaná/Kabanová
Kafenda			Kafendá/Kafendová
Kajetan	Kajetán		Kajetáná/Kajetánová
Kalik	Kálik		Káliká/Kaliková
Kaprál			Kaprálá/Kaprálová
Karel			Karelá/Karelová
Kolar			Kolará/Kolarová
Komenský			Komenská/Komensková
Kopta			Koptá/Koptová
Kovarovic	Kovařovic	Kovazhovits	Kovazhovicá/ Kovazhovicová
Kozeluh	Koželuh	Kozheluhh	Koželuhá/Koželuhová
Krasnohorsky	Krásnohorský		Krásnohorská/ Krásnohorsková
Kral		Krul	Kralá/Kralová
Krejci	Krejčí	Kreychiy	Krejčíá/Krejčova
Kricka	Křička	Kzhichkuh	Křičká/Křičkov'
Krizkovsky	Křížkovský	Kzhiyzhkovsky	Křížkovska/Křížkovsková
Kubelík			Kubelíká/Kubeliková
Kukucin	Kukučín	Kukuchin	Kukučíná/Kukučínová
Kupka			Kupká/Kupková
Kvapil			Kvapilá/Kvapilová
Langer			Langerá/Langerová
Lichnowsky		Lykhnovsky	Lichnowská/ Lichnowskayá
Linda			Lindá/Lindová
Lobkowitz			
Loebl			Loeblá/Loeblová
ze Lvovic		zeh Lvovits	Lvovicá/Lvovicová
Macha	Mácha	Makhuh	Máchá/Máchová
Machar		Makhar	Machará/Macharová
Majer		Muhyehruh	Majerá/Majerová
Masaryk			Masaryká/Masaryková
Mauthner			Mauthnerá/ Mauthnerová
Medek			Medeká/Mediková
Moyzes			Moyzesá/Moyzesová
Mraz	Mráz	Meraz	Mrázá/Mrázová
Mrstik	Mrštik	Mershtik	Mrštiká/Mrštiková
Myslivecek	Mysliveček	Myslivechek	Mysliveček/ Myslivečeková
Nejedlý		Neyedly	Nejedlá/Nejedlová
Neruda			Nerudá/Nerudová
Nezval			Nezvalá/Nezvalová

Simple	Diacritical	Sounds like	Feminine: Wife/Daughter
Novak	Novák		Nováká/Novaková
Novotný			Novotná/Novotnová
Orel			Orelá/Orelová
Ostrcil	Ostrčil	Osterchil	Ostrčilá/Ostrčilová
z Otradovic		Zotradovits	Otradovicá/Otradovicová
Palacky	Palacký	Palatsky	Palacká/Palacková
Petrzelka	Petrželka	Petterzhelka	Petrželká/Petrželková
Picha	Pícha	Pykha	Píchá/Píchová
Polivka	Polívka		Polivká/Polivková
Prazak	Pražák	Pruhzhak	Pražáká/Pražáková
Purkinje		Purkinye	Purkinjá/Purkinjová
Rais			Raisá/Raisová
Rejcha		Reykha	Rejchá/Rejchová
Ridky	Řidký	Zhidky	Řidká/Řidková
Rovenský			Rovenská/Rovenská
Rychnovský		Rikhnovsky	Rychnovská/Rychnovsková
Salda	Šalda	Shalda	Šaldá/Šaldová
Seegr			Seegrá/Seegrová
Skroup	Škroup	Shkroup	Škroupá/Škroupová
Sladek	Sládek		Sládeká/Sládeková
Slansky			Slanská/Slansková
Smetana			Smetaná/Smetanová
Sova			Sová/Sovová
Spurna			Spurná/Spurnová
Sramek	Šrámek	Shuhramek	Šrámeká/Šrámeková
Steyr			Steyrá/Steyrová
ze Stitneho	Štítného	Shtytnayho	Štítnéhá/Štítnéhová
Stitny	Štítny	Shtytny	Štítná/Štítnová
Suchon	Suchoň	Suchogn	Suchoňá/Suchoňová
Suk			Suká/Suková
Svehla			Svehlá/Svehlová
Světla		Svyetluh	Světlá/Světlová
Svoboda			Svobodá/Svobodová
Sykora		Sikoruh	Sykorá/Sykorová
Talich		Tuhlikh	Talichá/Talichová
Tomasek	Tomášek	Tomashek	Tomášeká/Tomášeková
Tranovsky	Třanovský	Tzhanovsky	Třanovská/Třanovsková
Tuma			Tumá/Tumarová
Turnovský			Turnovská/Turnovsková
Tusara			Tusará/Tusarová
Tyl		Tihl	Tylá/Tylová
Ujezd		Uhyezd	Ujezdá/Ujezdová
Vacek	Vaček	Vuhchek	Vačeká/Vačeková
Vancura	Vančura	Vuhnchura	Vančurá/Vančuroá
Vanhal	Vaňhal	Vanyal	Vaňhalá/Vaňalová
Vasek	Vašek	Vashek	Vašeká/Vašeková
Velazlavina	Velazlavína		Velazlavíná/Velaslavinová
Vlcek	Vlček	Vulchek	Vlčeká/Vlčeková

Simple	Diacritical	Sounds like	Feminine: Wife/Daughter
Vojtech	Vojtěch	Voytyekh	Vojtěchá/Vojtěchová
Vomacka	Vomáčka	Vomachka	Vomáčká/Vomáčková
Vorisek	Voříšek	Vozhiyshek	Voříšeká/Voříšeková
Vrchlický		Verchlicky	Vrchlická/Vrchlickova
Vycpalek	Vycpálek	Vitspalek	Vycpáleká/Vycpáleková
Zach		Zakh	Zachá/Zachová
Zahradnicek	Zahradníček	Zahradniychek	Zahradníčeká/
			Zahradníčeková
Zalenka			Zalenká/Zalenková
Zelinka			Zelinká/Zelinková
Zeman			Zemaná/Zemanová
Zenkl		Zehkehl	Zenklá/Zenklová
Zeyer			Zeyerá/Zeyerova
Zich		Zikh	Zichá/Zichová
Zvonar	Zvonař	Zvonazh	Zvonařá/Zvonařová
Zywny	Zywný	Zivny	Zywná/Zywnová

Eastern Mediterranean

SLOVINSKI

In the town where I grew up, "Free Croatia" was spray-painted across the back fence at the local supermarket for years. There was Yugoslav Hall and there was Croatian Hall, and every Croatian family had the red and white checkerboard arms (*Šahovnica*) displayed in the frontroom. So the divisive politics of the Balkans are not new.

However, politics not withstanding, Croats, Serbs, and Slovenes speak only different dialects of the same Slavic language. The Serbs have in recent times gone out of their way to be different by adding lots of loan words, but the names they use in common. This is sometimes called Yugoslavian ("southern Slavs") or now that that country is history, Slovinski, from the older days of history before outside forces encouraged "micro-nationalism" on the principle of "divide and conquer."

Macedonians, unless they are Serbian immigrants and their descendants, use Bulgarian-style names, not Slovinski.

If you set your story in the Slovinski areas, be sure to look into the extended family vocabulary. There are 50 different words for types of relatives. In place of our simple "son," they have:

sučic — baby son, under 5

sinak — child son, 5 to 10 years old

sinko — adolescent son, 10 to 18

sin — grown son, over 18

In the same sort of linguistic subtlety, by choosing a different ending for a noun, the speaker says whether he or she likes, dislikes, or is neutral about the subject. Nonetheless, I can find no evidence that family names have different endings for men and women. Among Slavs, this is unusual.

The Moslem Bosnians are the most different of the group. They use Moslem personal names in their Turkish versions — Ibrahim, Kemal, Murad, Fatima. Look in the Turkish and Arabic sections for more help there.

Pronunciation

Pronunciation is pretty much "WYSIWYS"—what you see is what you say—except for some diacritical marks. Note that Serbs use Cyrillic letters; by using Latin letters, everything immediately looks Croatian.

The C with the haček (Č)—you could use "c<" for manuscript purposes if you do not have international characters—is the same as the CH in "church."Ć (use C') is a soft CH as in "pitcher." In the common Slavic son-ending "-vić" is usually Anglicized to "-vich."

Š (you could use "S<") is the SH in "short." A Z with the same diacritical (Ž; use "Z<") is the Z in "azure." As in so many languages, J is the same as the Y in "yes."

R alone has come to stand for what was formerly ER. So "perst" is now "prst," "kerst" is "krst." The "Anglicized Spelling" column should help you with pronunciation.

FEMALE NAMES

	Group	Anglicized Spelling
Cvijeta		Sviyeta
Dobrica	Serb	
Draga	Serb	
Dragana	Serb	
Gordana		
Isidora		
Jelena		Yelena
Jula	Serb	Yula
Juliana	Serb	Yuliana
Liljana	Serb	Lilyana
Mara	Serb	
Maria	Serb	
Marija	Croat, Slovene	
Milena	Serb	
Milica	Yugo	
Milka		
Milunka	Serb	
Mina		
Mira	Yugo	
Mirjana	Serb	Miryana
Nada	Serb	
Oosood	Serb	
Paula	Croat	
Raviyoyla	Serb	
Roksanda	Croat	
Senada	Bosnian	
Slavenka	Serb	
Snezana		
Sophie	Serb	

	Group	Anglicized Spelling
Veela	Serb	
Vera	Yugo	
Vika	Serb	
Zofka		

MALE NAMES

	Group	Anglicized Spelling
Alexsa, Aleksandar	Serb	
Alija	Bosnian	Aliya
Andrej	Croat	Andre
Andrija		Andria, Andriya
Ante, Antun	Croat; popular	
Anton	Slovene	
Arkan	Serb	
Arsenije	Serb	Arseney
Bartholomaus, Bartel	Slovene	
Batele	Serb	
Blagoje	Serb	Blagoye
Bogić	Bosnian	Bogich
Bogoljub		Bogolyub
Borisav	Serb	
Boro		
Božidar		Bozhidar
Branimir	Croat	
Branislav	Serb; popular	
Branivoje		Branivoye
Branko	Serb; popular	
Brno		Berno, Burno
Budimir	Croat; Serb	
Dimitrija, Dimitrije	Serb	Dimitria, Dimitrie
Djordje	Croat	Georgie
Djuro	Serb	
Domentijan		Domentian
Dominik, Dinko		
Dositei		
Dragan	Serb	
Dragoljub	Serb	
Dragoslav	Serb	
Draža	Serb	
Dušan	Serb; popular	Dushan
Ejup	Bosnian	Eyup
Ekrem	Moslem Serb	
Eugen	Croat	
Fikret	Bosnian	
Franc		
Franjo	Croat	Franyo
Frederic	Slovene	

	Group	*Anglicized Spelling*
Gjuro	Croat	Giuro
Gojko	Croat	Goiko
Ivan	all	
Ivo	Croat	
Janez	Slovene	Yanez
Janko	Slovene	Yanko
Jerko	Bosnian	Yerko
Jernej	Slovene	Yerney
Josip	all	Yosip
Jovan	Serb, popular	Yovan, John
Jože	Serb	Yozhe
Kemal	Moslem Serb	
Ksaver		
Laza, Lazar	Serb	
Ljubomir	Serb	
Ljudevit	Croat	
Luka	Croat	
Marin		
Marko	Serb	
Mate	Croat	
Matija	Serb	Mattiya
Mihalj	Serb	
Milan, Miladin	all, very popular	
Milorad	Serb	
Miloš	Serb, Croat	Milosh
Milovan	Serb	
Milutin	Serb	
Miodrag	Serb	
Mirko	Serb	
Momir	Serb	
Nebojša	Serb	Neboysha
Nedeljko	Serb	Nedelyko
Neven	Croat	
Nikola	Serb	
Njegoš	Serb	Nyegosh
Oton	Slovene	
Pavle	Croat	
Petar	all	Peter
Predrag	Serb	
Primuž		Primuzh
Radenko		
Radmilo	Serb	
Radoman	Serb	
Radovan	Serb	
Rastko	Serb; Slovene	
Ratko	Serb; fairly popular	
Ratomir	Serb	
Sava	Serbian	
Sergej	Serb	
Silvije	Croat	Silvia

	Group	Anglicized Spelling
Sima	Serb	
Simon	Slovene	
Sinisa	Serb	
Šiško		Shishko
Slaven	Croat	
Slavko	Serb, Croat	
Slobodan	Serb; popular	
Srgjan	Croat	Sergian
Stanko	Slovene	
Stefan	Croat	
Stevan	Serbian	
Stipe	Croat	
Stjepan	Croat	Stepan
Stojan	Serb, Croat; popular	
Strahimir		
Svetozar	Serb	
Tihomir	Serb	
Tomislav	Croat	
Valentin		
Vatroslav	Croat	
Velimir	Yugo	
Velja, Veljko	Serb	
Vinko	Serb	
Vladimir	all	
Vladislav		
Vojislav	Serb; popular	
Vuk, Vukan	Serb	
Žarko	all; somewhat popular	Zharko
Zdravko	Bosnian	
Zlatko	Bosnian	
Zoran	Serb	

FAMILY NAMES

	Group	Anglicized Spelling
Abdić	Bosnian Moslem	Abdich
Adamić	Slovene	Adamich
Adžić	Serb	Adzhich
Ajduković		Adukovich
Andrić	Croat	Andrich
Arsić	Serb	Arsich
Aškerc	Slovene	Ashkerc
Avakumović	Serbian	Avakumovich
Babić	Serb	Babich
Ban	Serb	
Baraga	Slovene	
Basariček	Croat	Basarichek
Begović	Croat	Begovich

	Group	*Anglicized Spelling*
Bogdanović	Serb	Bogdanovich
Bogićević	Serb	
Bokan	Serb	
Boljkovac	Croat	
Bosković	Croat	Boskovich
Botic	Croat	Botich
Božović		
Branković		Brankovich
Broz/Brosovich	Croat	
Budihna	Serb	
Bulatović		
Cerović	Croat	
Copić		Copich
Ćorović	Serb	Chorovich
Ćosić	Serb	
Crnozemski	Macedonian	Cernozemski
Čurčin	Serb	
Cvetković		
Cvijan	Serb	
Davidović	Serb	
Degoricija	Croat	
Demeter	Croat	
Dimitrijević		
Dizdarević	Serb	
Djilas		Dilas, Dyilas
Doko	Bosnian	
Domljan	Croat	
Draculić	Serb	
Drašković	Serb	
Drnovšek	Slovene	
Držić		Derzich
Dučić	Serb	
Dušan	Serbian	
Elez	Serb	
Filipović	Bosnian Moslem	Filipovich
Frankopan	Croat	
Gaj	Croat	Gay
Ganić	Bosnian	Ganich
Gavrilivić	Serb	Gavrilivich
Glavaš	Croat	Glavash
Gorkić		Gorkich
Grahovac		
Grebo	Bosnian	
Gregorčić	Slovene	Gregorchich
Gregurić	Croat	Gregurich
Gundulić	Croat	Gundulich
Gustinčić		Gustinchich
Harambašić	Croat	Harambashich
Ilić	Serb	Ilich
Izetbegović	Bosnian	Izetbegovich

	Group	Anglicized Spelling
Jagić	Croat	Yagich
Jakšić	Serb	Yakshich
Jelačić	Croat	Yelachich
Jenko	Slovene	Yenko
Jevrić	Serb	Yevrich
Jokanović	Serb	Yokanovich
Jović	Serb	Yovich
Jurica	Croat	
Kadijević	Serb	
Kahrimanović	Moslem Serb	Kahrimanovich
Karadžić	Serb	Karadzhich
Karić	Serb	
Kljuić	Croat	
Knežević	Bosnian	
Kočić	Serb	
Koljević	Serb	
Kollar	Slovene	
Kopitar	Slovene	
Korošeć	Slovene	
Kosović	Serb	
Kostić	Serb	Kostich
Košutić	Serb	
Kozarac		
Kranjčević	Croat	Kranychevich
Kreso	Bosnian	
Krivec	Serb	
Krnarutić		Kernarutich
Ksaver	Slovene	
Kučan	Serb; Slovene	
Kukanjac	Serb	
Kumičić	Croat	
Kurspahić	Bosnian Moslem	
Kusturica	Bosnian	
Kveder		
Lazić		
Letica	Croat	
Lončar	Croat	Lonchar
Maček	Croat	
Macura	Serb	
Mandić	Serb	
Marcović	Serb	
Marinković		
Marković	Croat	
Martić	Serb	
Marulić		Marulich
Mashin	Serb	
Matavuli	Serb	
Mažuranić		
Menčerić		Menchetich
Mesić	Croat	

	Group	Anglicized Spelling
Mesko	Slovene	
Mičunović	Serb	
Mihajlović	Serb	
Mihanović		
Miklosić		
Milinović	Serb	
Miočić		Miochich
Mladić	Serb	
Močnik	Slovene	
Mugoša	Yugo	
Nazor	Croat	
Negovanović	Serb	
Nemanja	Serb	
Nikolić	Croat	
Nusić		
Obradović	Serb	
Obrenović	Serb	
Parčević		
Paroški	Serb	
Pašić	Serb	Pashich, Pashitch
Pavelić	Croat	
Pavičić	Croat	
Perović	Croat	
Perušić	Serb	
Petar	Croat	
Petrović	all	Petrovich
Pogačić		
Popović	Serb; Croat	
Presern		
Pribičević	Serb	
Protić	Serb	
Puhovski	Croat	
Pupovac	Serb	
Purić		
Račić		
Radicević		
Ranjina		Ranyina
Ranković	Serb	
Rašković	Serb	
Ristić	Serb	
Šabanović	Bosnian Moslem	Shabanovich
Šandor		Shandor
Šantić	Serb	Shantich
Sekulić		
Šenoa	Croat	Shenoa
Sepulavić		
Šestakov	Serb	Shestakov
Sidran	Bosnian	
Simonović		
Skerlić	Serb	

	Group	Anglicized Spelling
Sokolović	all	Sokolovich
Srškić		Sershkich
Stanković	Serb	
Starčević	Croat	Starchevich
Stefanović	Serb	
Stoinić	Yugo	
Stojadinović		
Šubašić		Shubashich
Sušak	Croat	Sushak
Tarbuk	Serb	
Tijanić	Serb	
Todorović		
Tomašević	Bosnian	Tomashevich
Tomašić	Croat	Tomashich, Tomasich
Topalović	Serb	Topalovich
Torbica	Serb	
Tresić	Croat	Tresich
Trnski	Croat	Ternski
Trubar		
Tus	Croat	
Tvrtko	Serb or Croat	
Unković	Serb	Unkovich
Uroš	Serbian	Urosh
Uzelac	Serb	
Uznović		Uznovich
Vasić	Croat	Vasich
Vico	Serb	
Vlahović		Vlahovich
Vraz	Slovene	
Vukčić	Bosnian	Vukchich
Vukičević		Vukichevich
Vukmanović	Serb	Vukmanovich
Zagorka		
Živković		Zhivkovich
Zlatarić		Zlatarich
Zrinski, Zrinyi	Croat	
Župančić	Slovene	Zhupantich
Zuzorić		Zuzorich

MEDIEVAL EKE-NAMES

Dečanski — for monastery of Dečani
Dragutin
Dušan — the mighty
Milutin
Prvovjenčani

Radoslav
Stevan — crowned
Uroš
Vladislav — glory of the Slavs

BULGARIAN AND MACEDONIAN

Bulgaria was built on a nation of Slavs who were conquered by the tribe known as the Bulgars. So while you will recognize many Slavic names and structures from Russian and the like, Bulgarian has its own idiosyncratic versions. It does gender the family name to indicate whether the bearer is male or female. The diminutives often lead an independent life, so that Dimcho is never called Dimitri, nor is Petko necessarily a Petr, any more than every Lisa or Beth is "really" an Elizabeth. You will also find versions of names like Jordan — Yordan — not often found in other Slavic countries.

Most Macedonians use Bulgarian-style names, rather than Slovinski-style ones. This shows in the "-ov" or "-ski" rather than "-ich" endings of family names, originally patronymics.

In 1981, in line with the long-term Bulgarization of family names in the country, those with Turkish or Moslem personal names were required to change them, also, so as to no longer stand out as a sub-group.

The one odd letter, the marked U, is pronounced long, as in tune.

FEMALE NAMES

Agnessa
Aleksi
Alisa
Anna — very popular
Annabel
Blaga
Ceciliia
Devora
Elena — popular
Elizabeta — popular

Emilia
Fani
Ginka
Kira
Klara
Liliana
Liudmila — popular
Lucine
Marketa
Paulina

Rahil
Sofronia
Stanka
Suzana
Tereza
Tsvetanka
Vangalia
Viktoria
Yudita

MALE NAMES

Aleko, Alekko
Aleksandŭr — very popular
Andrei
Angel
Anton
Artur
Asen, Assen
Atanas
Bogdan
Boian

Boris
Damyan
Dimcho, Dimi, Dimo
Dimitŭr — very popular
Djenyu
Dobri — somewhat popular
Dragan — somewhat popular
Feliks
Feodor

Franc
Ganyu
Gavril
Gelassi — unusual
Georgi, Georg — very popular; Macedonian, too; (dim.) Geo
Gotse
Grigor, Grigoi — popular; (dim.) Grisha
Henri

Henrim
Hrabr — rare, old
Hristo — popular
Hristofor, Hristopar
Ilia — unusual; =Elijah
Ioan
Ivan — popular
Kaiser — unusual
Kaloyan — old
Karl
Kazimir
Kimon — not unpopular
Kir, Kiril
Kliment
Konstantin — somewhat
  popular
Kosta — popular
Krŭstiu
Liuben — somewhat popular
  ular
Liubomir
Liudmil
Marko
Matei
Mihail — very popular,

sometimes Michail
Mincho
Minko
Mito
Neron — rare
Nikola, Nikolai — popu-
  lar
Nikolav — Macedonian
Paiisi — rare
Pentcho — popular
Petko — very popular
Petŭr — very popular
Racho
Radko
Radoi
Raicho
Raiko
Raphael
Sasho — Macedonian
Sava
Simeon
Sofroni
Stanko
Stefan
Stiliyan

Stoyan — very popular
Stoyko
Svetoslav
Timotei — unusual
Todor — very popular
Traicho
Tsanko
Tsvetko
Valeri
Vasil — very popular;
  Macedonian, also
Venelin
Venteslav
Veselin
Viktor
Vilhelm
Vladimir
Vŭlko
Yanko
Yonko
Yordan
Yosif
Zahari
Zdravko
Zhivko

FAMILY NAMES

Masculine	*Feminine*
Arnaudov	Arnaudova
Bagrianov	Bagrianova
Bakalov	Bakalova
Bakshev	Baksheva
Balabanov	Balabanova
Berov	Berova
Blagoev	Blagoeva
Boboshevski	Boboshevska
Bogorov	Bogorova
Bokov	Bokova
Bosilkov	Bosilkova
Botev	Boteva
Bozhilov	Bozhilova
Burov	Burova
Chankov	Chankova
Chervenkov	Chervenkova
Cheshmedjiev	Cheshmedjieva
Chilingirov	Chilingirova
Chintulov	Chintulova
Damyanov	Damyanova
Danev	Daneva

Masculine	*Feminine*
Daskalov	Daskalova
Debelyanov	Debelyanova
Delchev	Delcheva
Devedjiev	Devedjieva
Dimitrov	Dimitrova
Dimov	Dimova
Djagarov	Djagarova
Dmitriev	Dmitrieva
Dragiev	Dragieva
Dramaliev	Dramalieva
Drinov	Drinova
Durvingov	Durvingova
Filipov	Filipova
Filov	Filova
Gabrovski	Gabrovska
Ganev, Genov	Ganeva, Genova
Geshov	Geshova
Gichev	Gicheva
Giorgiev	Giorgieva
Girginov	Girginova
Gligorov	Gligorova
Haitov	Haitova
Hristoforov	Hristoforova
Hristov	Hristova
Isusov	Isusova
Ivanitsov	Ivanitsova
Ivanov	Ivanova
Kamenov	Kamenova
Karalichev	Karalicheva
Karavelov	Karavelova
Kazasov	Kazasova
Kioseivanov	Kioseivanova
Kolarov	Kolarova
Konstantinov	Konstantinova
Kostov	Kostova
Kosturkov	Kosturkova
Krŭstev	Krŭsteva
Kulishev	Kulisheva
Lazarov	Lazarova
Levchev	Levcheva
Levski	Levska
Liapchev	Liapcheva
Lukov	Lukova
Lulchev	Lulcheva
Malinov	Malinova
Marinov	Marinova
Marjanovsky	Marjanovska
Markov	Markova
Mihailov	Mihailova
Mihov	Mihova

Masculine	*Feminine*
Milev	Mileva
Muraviev	Muravieva
Mushanov	Mushanova
Mutafchiev	Mutafchieva
Mutafov	Mutafova
Mutkurov	Mutkurova
Naumov	Naumova
Neichev	Neicheva
Nemirov	Nemirova
Nikolov	Nikolova
Nikov	Nikova
Obbov	Obbova
Omarchevski	Omarchevska
Ordanoski	Ordanoska
Panchevski	Panchevska
Panov	Panova
Pastuhov	Pastuhova
Pavlov	Pavlova
Penev	Peneva
Petkov	Petkova
Petrov	Petrova
Protogerov	Protogerova
Rachev	Racheva
Radev	Radeva
Radoslavov	Radoslavova
Raichev	Raicheva
Rainov	Rainova
Rakitin	Rakitina
Rakovski	Rakovska
Ralin	Ralina
Sakŭzov	Sakŭzova
Sarafov	Sarafova
Savov	Savova
Sebek	Sebeka
Shipkov	Shipkova
Shishmanov	Shishmanova
Shopov	Shopova
Slaveikov	Slaveikova
Slavov	Slavova
Smirnenski	Smirnenska
Sobolev	Soboleva
Stamatov	Stamatova
Stamboliiski	Stamboliiska
Stambolov	Stambolova
Stanchev	Stancheva
Stoilov	Stoilova
Stoyanov	Stoyanova
Strashimirov	Strashimirova
Svintıla	Svintılova
Tanev	Taneva

Masculine	*Feminine*
Terpeshev	Terpesheva
Todorov	Todorova
Tomov	Tomova
Topencharov	Topencharova
Toshev	Tosheva
Traikov	Traikov
Tsanev	Tsaneva
Tsankov	Tsankova
Tunov	Tunova
Tupurkovski	Tupurkovska
Turlakov	Turlakova
Vankov	Vankova
Vaptsarov	Vaptsarova
Vasiliev	Vasilieva
Vasov	Vasova
Vassilev	Vassileva
Vazov	Vazova
Velchev	Velcheva
Velitchkov	Velitchkova
Velkov	Velkova
Veltchev	Veltcheva
Venedikov	Venedikova
Vlaikov	Vlaikova
Vŭlkov	Vŭlkova
Yavarov	Yavarova
Yovkov	Yovkova
Yugov	Yugova
Yurukov	Yurukov
Zabunov	Zabunova
Zagorchinov	Zagorchinova
Zaimov	Zaimova
Zankov	Zankova
Zhivkov	Zhivkova
Ziapkov	Ziapkova
Zlatarski	Zlatarska
Zlatev	Zlateva
Zograf	Zografa

ALBANIAN

Outside of Albania itself and the area adjoining in Serbia, there are large concentrations of Albanians in Massachusetts, in Epirus and especially in Kossovo and Macedonia. In 1478 the country became part of Ottoman Turkey, and remained so until 1912, so names have a strong Turkish flavor. The land-owning gentry usually had "Bey" or "Beg" after the male names, a title of superiority. Family names evolved after independence.

Ethnic Albanian names do not have any immediately recognizable tags, like the "-ian" and "-itsi" of Armenian, or the "-os" of Greek, but the general look of them can be strange to English-reading eyes — Zogu, Xoxe, Ypi, Djafer — a kind of cat-ran-across-the-keyboard look.

Because Albania has a Muslim majority, you will find personal Arabic names like Ahmed and Ismail. The Christian minority will often use familiar Christian names: Anton, Mark, Anna. Of course, some parents borrow abroad, from Serb, Croat, and Italian.

Name order is what you are used to: personal name first, followed by family name. Middle names are rare.

The only odd letter is Ç which has the sound of TS. All letters are sounded, including final E. LL is as in the Spanish llama. In some transliterations, X is used for K, as was Q, adding variety to your choices.

FEMALE NAMES

Adile	Kimete	Rita
Anna	Maxhide	Ruhije
Dafina	Muzejen	Senie
Domenika	Nafije	Sura
Flutra, Flutura	Raymonda	

MALE NAMES

Abbas, Abas	Chim	Harun
Abdyl	Demir	Hasan
Adem	Dilaver	Haxhi
Agaj	Djafer	Hysen — popular
Ahmed, Ahmet	Dusko	Ibrahim
Alexander	Enver — popular	Ihsan
Ali	Essad	Iliaz
Anton — fairly popular	Fidai	Imer
Arsem	Figri	Iskander
Avni	Gani — fairly popular	Ismail
Azem	Gaqi	Jani
Azis	Gjelosh	Kalem
Bame — fairly popular	Gjergj	Koci
Bardhok	Gjezgi	Kol
Bardhyl	Gjon	Llesh
Bashkim	Gramoz	Mara, Marash
Beqir	Hajrulla — fairly popular	Mark
Betas	Haki, Hakik	Mehmet, Muhamet
Bido	Halil — popular	Midhat
Blendi	Halim	Muharem
Çaush	Hamit — fairly popular	Murredin

Mustafa
Myftar
Myslim
Namzo
Naum
Nezir
Niko
Nuçi
Petrit — fairly popular
Pjerin
Preparim
Qazim, Kasem
Qemal, Kemal
Ramadan, Rama
Ramazan, Rama
Ramiz, Ramis

Rapush
Rexh, Rexhep
Riza
Rrok
Rusta
Ryfat
Sadik
Said, Seid
Sali — fairly popular
Samih, Sami — fairly
   popular
Sefer
Selim
Simon
Sotir — fairly popular
Suad

Tahir
Tati
Turhan
Vangel
Veli
Veton
Vlash
Xhelo
Xhemal — very popular
Xhetan
Zef
Zenel — fairly popular
Zeni
Zogoll

FAMILY NAMES

Alia
Aliko
Andoni
Aslani
Azis
Azizaj
Bajrami
Ballamci
Balluku
Bardha
Basho, Basha
Bega
Beqari
Berisha — often seen
Branica — often seen
Budo
Butka
Bylykbashi
Ceci
Cenaj
Cerova
Chekrezi
Daci
Dai
Dalipi
Daliu
Daver
Dhimo
Dilo
Doder
Doko

Dosti
Ermenji
Frasheri
Gaba
Gega
Gera
Gerveshi
Gjura
Gjurchu
Gjyle
Guzin
Hajdari
Hila
Hito
Hoxha — often seen
Isufi
Juba, Jubani
Kacuqi
Kaustic
Kelmendi
Kokoshi
Kombetar
Kosmaçi
Kota
Kotori
Kryeziu
Kuka
Kupi
Laci
Leka
Lepenica

Logoreci
Lusha
Malushi
Mançe
Manukaj
Matjani
Matuka
Morava — often seen
Muço
Ndou
Nerguti
Nikolla
Noli
Pali
Papajani
Pashko
Peza
Planeja
Prenci
Prifti
Qirjaqi
Ramadani
Riza
Rugova
Rustemi
Salku
Selmani
Shehu — often seen
Sheno
Sino
Sula

Surroi	Traga	Ypi
Terpeza	Tresova	Zavalani
Theodosi	Veli	Zeneli
Toptani	Xhabexhiu	Zyberi
Toshi	Xoxe	

GREEK

The Greeks have it neatly worked out. The first son is almost always named for his father's father, the second for the other grandfather. Ditto the daughters, after the grandmothers. The later offspring are usually named for other relatives.

These are the modern Greek names, and while you may still find boys named Socrates, you had best hold back on using Classic, Hellenic names. The saints of the Greek Church are much more popular. Girls are more likely to get Hellenic names.

Greek family names, when used by Greeks in Greece, have slightly different endings for men and women. These are often ignored by foreign writers and immigration officials, but you should not be so sloppy, any more than with Russians. In case you find a name on your own, and want to use it for the other gender:

Male	becomes	Female
-as		-a
-es		-e
-is		-i
-on		-on
-os		-o
-ou		-o

All vowels are pronounced, including final E.

FEMALE NAMES

Agathi, Agathe, Agatha, Aggi	Berenike, Berenice	Elpenike
Akrevoe	Charis, Charissa, Charisse	Evadne, Evadnie
Aleka, Alike	Despo	Fotina
Alverta	Dorothea	Hrisoula, Soula
Andronike	Dwora	Ioanna
Angelica, Angeliki	Efimia, Efi	Kalica, Kalyca
Anna — very popular	Eirini — for Irene	Katerini, Katina
Arete, Arethi	Elena, Eleni, Elenitsa, Nitsa — for Helen	Kostatina, Kosta
Berek		Lascarina
		Lilika

Margareta, Margaritis,
  Margaro, Ritsa
Marina, Marika
Maroula, Roula
Melina, Melita, Litsa
Moscho
Noula
Pelagia, Pelegia, Pelgia
Pinelopi — for Penelope

Pipitsa
Popi
Rasia
Rena
Sema
Sofi, Sophia
Sophronia
Stamatia
Tassis

Theodosia
Theophila
Triphena, Tryphana,
  Tryphene, Tryphenia,
  Tryphina
Voska
Xanthe
Xylia, Xylina
Zoë, Zoie

MALE NAMES

Alexandros, Alekos
Andreas
Antoniou, Antonios,
  Andonios, Andonis,
  Tonis
Apostolides
Aristides
Athansios
Belen
Binkentios
Demetrius
Dimitrios, Dimos
Dionusios, Dionyssios
Domenikos
Elis, Eliasz
Enrikos
Evangelinos, Evangelos
Georgios, Giorgis, Gior-
  gos
Giannes, Giannis, Gian-
  nos
Gregorios, Grigorios
Haralpos
Iakov, Ialovos, Iakobos

Ilias
Ioannes, Ioannis, Ion
Iosif
Khambis
Konstandinos, Konstanti-
  nos, Kotsos, Constanti-
  nos — popular
Korudon
Kristo, Kristos, Kristia-
  nos, Christianos, Chris-
  tos
Leonidas
Loukas
Manolis
Marinos
Markos
Martinos
Matthaios
Mihail, Mikhail, Mikha-
  lis, Mikhos
Nikolaos, Nikolos,
  Nikos — popular
Panagris, Panos
Petros, Petro, Pavlos

Phillipos, Philos
Pirro
Rihardos
Rouvin
Semon
Sergi, Sergios
Stamos
Stavros
Stefanos, Stefos, Stepha-
  nos — popular
Thanos
Theodoros, Theos
Timotheos, Timos
Urian
Vasilios, Vasilis, Vasilos,
  Vassos, Basilios
Vokos
Xenos
Xylon
Yannis, Yiannis
Zacceus, Zacchaeus, Zac-
  cheus

FAMILY NAMES

Masculine
Aliapoulios
Andonion
Andronikos
Apostolou
Argyropoulos
Armacolas
Belokas
Benizelos

Feminine
Aliapoulio
Andonion
Androniko
Apostolo
Argyropoulo
Armacola
Beloka
Benizelo

Masculine	Feminine
Bernardakis	Bernardaki
Bikelas	Bikela
Botsares, Botzaris	Botzari
Botssis	Botssi
Boubalinas	Boubalina
Bozzaris	Bozzari
Bryennios	Bryennio
Bulgaris	Bulgari
Canaris	Canari
Chadzidakis	Chadzidaki
Christopoulos	Christopoulo
Chrysoloras	Chrysolora
Contopoulos	Contopoulo
Delyannis	Delyanni
Dmitris	Dmitri
Dossas	Dossa
Dragoumis	Dragoumi
Eftimiades	Eftimiade
Emmanualides	Emmanualide
Gazes	Gaze
Gouskos	Gousko
Hatzidakis	Hatzidaki
Iliakis	Iliaki
Jannaris	Jannari
Kalomirakis	Kalomiraki
Kambites	Kambite
Kanaris, Kanares	Kanari, Kanare
Kapodistrias	Kapodistria
Katsimbras	Katsimbra
Katsirdakis	Katsirdaki
Kiskirdis	Kiskirdi
Klissouris	Klissouri
Kolokotrones	Kolokotrone
Kondyles, Kondylis	Kondyle, Kondyli
Koundouriotes, Koundouriotis,	Koundouriote, Koundourioti,
Kountouriotes, Kountouriotis	Kountouriote, Kountourioti
Koutselinis	Koutselini
Lagoudakis	Lagoudaki
Lambros	Lambro
Lascaris	Lascari
Loues	Loue
Macridis	Macridi
Macris	Macri
Makarios	Makario
Manzaros	Manzaro
Marinatos	Marinato
Maurogiannis	Maurogianni
Mavrocordatos, Maurocordatos	Mavrocordato, Maurocordato
Mavromichalis	Mavromichali
Metrapolous	Metrapolo

Masculine	Feminine
Miaoules, Miaulis	Miaoule, Miauli
Michalakopoulos	Michalakopoulo
Mylonas	Mylona
Pallis	Palli
Pangalos	Pangalo
Pangatos	Pangato
Papadiamantopulos	Papadiamantopulo
Pappadakis	Pappadaki
Pappelis	Pappeli
Perdicaris	Perdicari
Petros	Petro
Pitsios	Pitsio
Rhigas	Rhiga
Romaios	Romaio
Rufos	Rufo
Sakellarakis	Sakellaraki
Sapounas	Sapouna
Sgouros	Sgouro
Skouloudes	Skouloude
Solomos	Solomo
Sophocles	Sophocle
Spinoulas	Spinoula
Spyridion	Spyridio
Theotokopoulos	Theotokopoulo
Tomochichis	Tomochichi
Triandaphyllou	Triandaphyllo
Tricoupis	Tricoupi
Trypanis	Trypani
Tsaldaris	Tsaldari
Tsavdarolgou	Tsavdarolgo
Tsembaras	Tsembara
Tsolakoglou	Tsolakoglo
Tzavellas	Tzavella
Venizelos	Venizelo
Vlatakis	Vlataki
Xenos	Xeno
Ypsilantis	Ypsilanti
Zaimis, Zaimes	Zaimi, Zaime
Zalokostas	Zalokosta
Zenos	Zeno
Zervos	Zervo

TURKISH

Turks are not Arabs. They were originally the minority of the Avars which adopted Islam rather than Judaism. As a result, they were culturally drawn towards

Arab lands, coming in from the northeast and conquering the old Arabic empire a stretch at a time. This began quite a while ago: the Saladin who defended Outre-Mer from the Crusaders under Richard the Lion-Hearted was a Seljuk Turk.

Once the Turks began migrating into the Mideast, an earlier wave like the Seljuks would conquer, settle down, get Arabicized, and get conquered in turn by the next tribal wave off the steppes. The last were the Ottoman Turks, whose Ottoman Empire shrank into the present nation of Turkey.

The decree of Kemil Ataturk in 1928, requiring all Turks to choose and thereafter use inherited family names was not only to modernize in the European fashion, but to make possible registering people for accurate taxes and military draft. There were just too many Mehmet Ali's and Ali Mehmet's, who had only to change their village to suddenly seem someone else. Nonetheless, in earlier times members of a powerful family might be known by names that included their place of origin, like the Kuprili family.

Turkish rather than Arabic was made the country's official language by Ataturk. The Semitic Arabic language had been more useful as a lingua franca understood from one end of the vast Empire to the other, but the Altaic tongue, Turkish, was more common in the core left after North Africa and Syria and Persia were accepted as permanently lost.

Still, you can use Arabic names for many Turks, especially early in the 20th century. If the list of female names seems too short, use Arabic names to eke it out.

"Pasha" (Paşa) is a title, not a name, no more than "Sir" is amongst baronets. Turkish titles come after the man's name, indicating a district governor or a military commander. "Dey" is another title of respect. Originally meaning "mother's brother [uncle]" and used for any older man, it became the title of the commander of the Janissaries. "Beg" or "Bey" is inferior to a pasha. "Ghazi" is another military title. "Aga" or "Agha" (Ağa) is a local big shot.

Many Turks are referred to conversationally by a double name — Kara Ayshe, Ali Ziya — both of which are personal names, like Peggy Sue or Joe Bob. Family names are so new that they are inquired after only if necessary. Of course, rural dwellers are more inclined to ignore them than sophisticated cosmopolitans.

Pronunciation

ı — undotted I, for the "nothing" vowel, or schwa, like the U in bun; for manuscript purposes you could use \ or I* if your machine lacks it.

I — I in pit

Ç — CH in church; use C' or S*

Ş — SH in shush; use S' or S*

Ğ — Y in yes; use G< or G*

Ü — Ü in German führer; use U: or U*

Ö — Ö, the EU in French feu; use O: or O*

FEMALE NAMES

Ayshe
Azize
Bitki
Bulbul — nightingale
Cari
Chakir
Edip
Elma
Emine
Fatma
Ferhundeh
Güllü
Halide
Hasna

Hatije
Ibrishah
Kalyori
Kara
Karanfil
Leyla
Maya
Meryem
Nesrin
Nevin
Saide
Saril
Seher
Serap

Shadiye — popular
Sofya
Söğöt
Sunbul — ear of grain"
    Tahireh
Umay
Ümmü
Zehra
Zeliha
Zerdali
Zeynep — popular
Zeyno
Zübeyde

MALE NAMES

Abdülhak
Abidin
Adnan
Ahmet, Ahmad, Ahmed
Ali, Aali
Alp
Amurath, Murad, Murat
Arif
Arslan
Ateshoğlu
Aziz
Bajazet, Bayazid
Baki
Bedri
Behçet
Bülent
Cahit
Celâl
Cemal
Cetin
Cevdet
Daud
Davut
Dede
Direk
Djem, Jem, Zizim
Djemal
Djevdet
Edhem
Emin

Enver
Eren
Ertuğrul
Esat
Fahir
Fahri
Fahrünnisa
Faik
Fazıl, Fazil
Fethi
Feyhaman
Feyyaz
Fuat
Hacı
Hajador
Hakkı
Haldun — somewhat pop-
    ular
Halil
Halit
Hamit
Hikmet
Hüseyin
Hüsnü
Ibosh
Ibrahim
Ilhan
Ismat
Izzet
Jemali

Kadri
Kavafin
Kâzim
Kemal — very popular
Kiamil
Kilij
Kir
Kudret
Kül
Lemi
Lostromo
Mahmud, Mahmut —
    fairly popular
Malik
Melih
Memduh
Midhat
Muhsin
Mukhtar
Mustafa
Nabi, Nabizade
Namk
Nazım — popular
Necati
Necip
Nejad
Nevit
Nezihe
Niyazi
Nuri

Nurullah
Oktay
Ömer
Orhan — popular
Orkhan
Osman, Othman
Rahmi
Rauf
Recaizade
Recep
Refet
Refik
Rejeb
Reşat, Reshat
Reşit, Reshid, Rashid
Rifat
Sabahattin — somewhat
  popular

Sabri
Sait
Sakir
Salih
Samim
Samipaşazade
Selim
Seljuk
Şevket
Sezai
Shükrü
Sıtkı
Süleyman
Tabour
Tahsin
Talât, Talaat — popular
Talip
Tevfik

Togrul, Tugrul or Tugh-
  zil
Tulun
Ulvi
Veli
Vural
Vüs'at
Yahya
Yakub
Yakup
Yaşar, Yashar
Yücel
Zade
Zeki
Ziya
Zühtü
Zulkuf

FAMILY NAMES (AFTER 1928)

Abasıyanık, Abasiyanik
Adivar
Akbal
Aksal
Ali
Altan
Anday
Arel
Arikan
Ataç
Atlı
Aydemir
Aydınalp
Bairakdar
Balıkçısı
Baltacıoğlu
Bayar
Bayazit
Baysal
Bele
Berk
Beyatlı
Buyrukçu
Callı
Conker
Cumalı
Dağlarca
Devrim
Dino

Dormen
Duran
Edib
Ekrem
Erbil
Erkin
Erkut
Ersoy
Ertuğrul
Esen
Esendal
Eyüboğlu
Fikret
Gökalp
Göktulga
Güngör
Güntekin
Gürpınar
Gürsel
Haşim
Inönü
Iyem
Iz
Kanık
Karabekir
Karabulut
Karaosmanoğlu
Karasu
Karay

Karpat
Kayacan
Kayalıdere
Kemal
Kısakürek
Kocagöz
Kocamemi
Kodallı
Koman
Köprülü — of Kupril
Küçük
Kurmay
Makal
Makkemesi
Menderes
Meriç
Müridoğlu
Nayır
Necatigil
Nesin
Okyar
Onat
Orbay
Pakyürek
Paspati
Ran
Rasim
Rey
Rifat

Saclıoğlu	Tarus	Yalman
Saygun	Teoman	Yilderim — lightning; use
Seyfettin	Tollu	as eke-name in earlier
Siyavuşgil	Tonguç	periods
Tahir	Uşaklıgil	Yücel
Taner	Usmanbaş	Zeid
Tarancı	Vefik	
Tarhan	Yalçın	

OLDER EKE-NAMES, SOMEWHAT ARABICIZED

Alp Arslan — courageous lion
Djezzar — butcher
Katib Chelebi — noble secretary

ARMENIAN

Armenia is an ancient land, and an ancient language with its own 36-letter alphabet. The names in the following lists are transliterations into the Latin alphabet, so there may be alternate spellings.

By the age of Christian political dominance, the Armenians whose name are preserved are using a "Christian" name followed by a place-name, which ends in "-atsi" or some variation of it, sometimes merely the "-i." When known, the list below will give the place-name. More common at the present time is the equally old "-ian" ending, which is one of the signatures of an Armenian name. It is the inevitable "son of" ending. In the former Soviet areas, this is normally transliterated "-yan." "Hanem" is a female title of deference, like "lady" which, followed by the family name, should not be mistaken for a personal name.

Where Armenians have made themselves at home in the Orient, including India and Burma, patronyms and the family names derived from them have taken a different course. Instead of Khachikian, it is Catchick, Gregor instead of Gregorian, Arathoon instead of Harutuinian, Apcar for Abgarian, Pogose for Poghossian, Gasper for Gasparian, and Bagram for Bagramian. When in doubt, use the father's name without any ending.

While there are a good many Christian names — the Armenian equivalent of John, Thomas, Stephen, Margaret, etc. — there are many others not like anything else on Earth. If you did not tell where you got them, you could use most Armenian names in a fantasy world and most readers would think you made them up. They *look* swords-and-sorcery.

So if your more mundane character needs a touch of the truly exotic, consider making him or her Armenian, or of Armenian descent. In the early seventies, I used to watch Armenian-language shows broadcast out of San Diego, in order to catch the dancing. So there are plenty of Armenians out there.

FEMALE NAMES

Aghavni
Ana, Ani — for Anne
Anaguel
Anait, Anahit
Araxie
Arda
Arousiag
Arpi, Arpiné, Sirarpi —
    early morning sun
Ashkhen
Astghik
Azni
Baydzar
Dikranouhi
Dirouhi
Dzaghig
Emma
Ephtim
Ester
Fenya
Gayane
Geulania
Geuleta
Gilda

Gohar
Hanna
Hasmig
Hayastan
Herminé
Herout
Hripsimé
Irina
Isabel
Karina
Khatoun
Lucine — moon
Luisa
Margaret
Mariam — very popular;
    for Mary, too
Martha
Mayreni
Miriam
Nartouhie
Nazelli
Nevrieh
Nika
Nvart

Perus
Repega — for Rebecca
Salpi
Sara
Satenig
Seda, Seta
Shirin
Shnorig
Shoushan, Shushawn
Silva
Siroun
Sona — popular
Sossie
Tagun
Takoohi, Takouhi
Taline
Verzhine
Yebraksi
Yevnig
Yulia
Zabelle
Zarouhi
Zhenya
Zoulvisia

MALE NAMES

Abraham
Alekan
Ambartsum
Anak
Anania
Antranig, Andranik
Araik
Arak'el — popular
Aram
Ararat
Aristakes
Armen — popular
Armenag
Armig

Arno
Arpiar
Arsen
Arshavir
Arshile
Arthash
Artur
Artyom
Ashot
Avedis
Avetik
Aykhaz
Bedros
Benjamin

Berj
Bessak
Boghos
Constantine
Dikran — fairly popular
Dmitri
Elishey
Emik
Ervand
Eznik
Frik
Gabriel
Garabed
Garnik

Garo
Genrikh
Ghevont
Gostan
Gourgen
Grigor
Hacob
Hagop, Hacop, Hakop —
    very popular
Haig
Haroutioun, Harutiun,
    Arathoon (Orient)
Hetum
Hovagim
Hovhan, Hovhannes,
    Hovanes — very popu-
    lar
Hovnathan
Hovsep
Iskender
Kerop
K'erovbey
Kevork — fairly popular
Khachik
Khatchatour
Khoren
Kirakos
Komitas
Koriun
Lazar
Leva
Lewond
Malachia

Manoug, Manuk
Mardiros — fairly popular
Martros
Matteos
Megerdich, Mekertitch
Mekhitar
Melik'
Migran
Minas
Movses
Nahabed
Nalash
Narik
Nerses
Never, Nover
Nubar
Ovanes
Papken
Paroyr
Rafik
Razmik
Rhipsime
Rouben
Sahak
Salpi
Sambel
Samvel
Sarkis — fairly popular
Sargis
Sebeos
Sembat
Sergo
Serobey, Sero

Sharvash, Shavarsh
Shont
Shumavon
Shushanik
Simeon
Sirarpie
Soghomon
Sos
Stephanos, Stepan —
    fairly popular
Thoma — popular
Tigran
Tiran
Toros
Trdat
Vahakn
Vahan
Vahram
Vano
Varaztad
Vardan, Vartan — fairly
    popular
Varuzhan
Vasgen, Vazken
Vigen
Vosdanik
Vroyr
Yerwand
Zareh — fairly popular
Zenob
Zograt
Zori

FAMILY NAMES

Abajian
Abramyan
Adamian
Adoian
Afsharian
Agbashyan
Agojian
Ailanjian
Ajemian
Akopyan
Alboyadjian
Almoyan, Almoian
Althamartsi
Ambartsumyan

Amberdtsim
Amiralian
Apelian
Apkarian
Arakelian, Arakelyan
Arslanian
Arsruni
Arutunyan
Arzumanian
Asolik
Astourian
Atobikyan
Avakian, Avakyan
Aygektsi

Babagochian
Bagdasirian
Bagratuni
Bahadourian
Balayan
Balishetsi
Bandigian
Bardakjian
Barsegyan
Bartanyan
Basmajian
Bekzadian
Benlian
Berberian

Beshgaturian
Bosabalian
Boyajian
Buchakjian
Chilingirian
Chorabajian
Chulayetsi
Coumarian
Dadrian
Daghlian
Dakessian
Damadian
Darhanian
Darpinian
Dekmejian
Derderian
Dergazarian
Devedjian
Dulgerian
Edesatsi — of Edessa
Elmajian
Elmassian
Ephrikian
Erzenkatsi — of Erzincan
Essayan
Etoian, Etoyan
Eurejian
Ezenkatsi — of Erzincan
Galstyan
Garabedian
Garbyan
Gasparian
Gedikian
Ghazarian — often seen
Der Ghevondian
Giroyan, Giroian
Glak
Golbatsi — of Golp
Gubatyan
Guroian
Hadidian
Hagopian — frequent
Halajian
Haleblian
Hambartsumian
Haroutunian
Hartunian
Haygazian
Haytaian
Heratsi — of Her
Hovakimian

Hovannisian
Hovnatanian
Hovsepian
Iskenderian
Issahakian
Janjikian
Kalankatuatsi
Kandoian
Kaputikyan
Karapetyan
Karsh
Kazanjian
Kazaryan
Kerebian
Keshishian
Ketcharetsi
Ketchedjian
Ketenjian
Khachatryan
Khadjesari
Khanzadyan
Khorenatsi — of Chorene
Knunyants
Kochar
Kojoyan
Konsulian
Koundakjian
Koushnarian
Kouyoumdjian
Kuljian
K'utchak
Jivani
Lambronatsi — of Lam-
   bron
Laputikyan
Lastivertsi
Levonian
Libaridian
Maghakian
Malejian
Mamikonian
Manjikian
Manoogian
Manucharyan
Manukyan
Marashlian
Marganian
Martirosyan
Matosian, Mataosian
Mazmanian
Mechitar

Megerdichan
Melikian
Melkumyan
Mereshian
Merjanian
Mesrlian
Mikoyan
Minasian
Mkrtychyan — yes, all
   those consonants
Moursalian
Movsesian
Muradyan, Muradian
Mutafian
Najarian
Nalbandian
Narekatsi — of Narek
Narinian
Nazaretyan
Der Nersessian
Nersoyan
Oganesyan — often seen
Ohannesian
Orbelian
Ormanian
Otian
Paloulian
Panosian
Parikian — often seen
Parseghian
Pashyan
Payaslian
Petrosian, Ter-Petrosyan
Pharpetsi — of Pharp
Piranian
Pogosyan
Pogotsian
Racoubian
Ruzgerian
Saakyan, Sakian — com-
   mon
Sahinian
Sanasarian
Sangigian
Sanjian
Sarajian
Sarian — often seen
Sarkawag
Sarkissian, Sarkisyan
Sarukhyan
Semerjian

Seropian, Der Seropian
Shabaghlian
Shahamirian
Shahinian
Shahoian
Shahumian
Shekerjian
Shiragian
Shirvanzadi
Shnorhali — the Gracious
Siradetyan
Siruni
Sisakyan
Siwnetsi — of Siunik
Skirakatsi — of Shirak
Stanboltsyan

Sulahian
Sundukian, Sundookian
Svadjian
Tashjian — often seen
Tathevatsi
Tatoulian
Tehlirian
Tekeyan
Terzian
Thlkurantsi — the fifth
    letter is the first
    vowel
Tigranian
Topalian
Totoventsi
Toulahian

Touryan, Tourian
Urhayetsi
Vardanyan
Vartanian
Voskeritchian
Yanikian
Yardemian
Yeghoian
Yekmalian
Yousoufian
Zadejan
Zakarian, Zakharyan
Zamani
Zamkochian
Zulumanian

ISRAELI

When Israel was formed, it was meant to be a Hebrew nation, and immigrants were strongly encouraged to change their Yiddish, Sephardic, and other foreign names to Israeli ones. Many hark back to the Old Testament; you will not go wrong using the ones out of the Hebrew section.

However, the Israelis often show marks of the Diaspora when the name lists turn up Elisha for girls: a male name in the days of the Kingdoms, but the ending sounds feminine to many modern ears. So don't back-date these to the days before the Second World War, without research.

When it comes to family names, you cannot go wrong by using "Ben-" and a male personal name. This would refer to the original immigrant — or HIS father — but it then becomes an inherited moniker used for females, too. Chavva Ben-Ezra would not be considered improper, any more than Sally Johnson would be in the limited states. You may also use the list of family names under Yiddish.

The numbers following the names refer to poularity in use.

FEMALE NAMES

Abigal
Abira
Abishag
Abital
Ada, Adah —#74
Aderes
Aderet

Adiella
Adina, Adine, Adena,
    Adeana, Adie —#63
Adira
Ahuva, Ahava, Ahouva,
    Ahuda —#42
Aleeza, Alitza, Aliza —#12

Aliya
Alma
Alona
Aluma
Alumice
Alumit
Alvah

Amalyah — #92
Amaris
Amira
Amissa
Anais
Andra
Arella
Ariel, Ariella, Arielle
Ariza
Arna
Arnice
Arnina
Arnit
Arza
Arzice
Arzit
Asisa
Astera, Asteria, Astra
Atara, Ataret
Atida
Atira
Aviva, Avivi, Avivice — #33
Avrit
Ayala, Ayelet, Ayla — #85
Azaria
Basia
Batsheva — #68
Batya, Bathia, Batia — #23
Behira
Belah — #27
Bethia, Bithia
Betula
Bilha — #75
Bina — #94
Bluma — #100
Bona
Bracha — #37
Brurya — #79
Carmela, Carmeli, Carmi, Carmia, Carmiel — #57
Carna
Carnit
Chanah, Chana — #5; Hannah
Chava — #13
Chaya
Chenya — #72
Clara — #35

Dagan, Dagana, Dagania
Dafna — #101
Dalice
Dalilah
Dalit
Dalya — #26
Dani, Dania, Danit, Danya
Denae
Deroit, Derora, Derorice
Devorah — #15
Dickla, Diklice, Diklit
Didi
Dina — #36
Ditzah
Diza
Dodie
Dora — #53
Dorit — #73
Drora — #88
Edna — #43
Elanit
Eleora
Eliana
Elisha
Elisheba, Elisheva — #30
Elza
Ema
Emuna
Ezraella, Ezrela
Fanny — #38
Frieda — #31
Gada
Gafna
Gal, Gali, Galice, Galya
Ganya, Gana, Ganice, Ganit — #70
Gavrilla
Gazit
Geula, Geela — #71
Geva
Gila, Gilah, Gilada — #61
Giora
Gisa, Gissa
Gurice
Gurit
Hadassah — #62
Hagia, Hagice, Hagit
Hania, Haniya
Hannah
Haviva — #89

Haya — #11
Hedia
Helene — #25
Hephsibah, Hephzabah, Hephzibah, Hepzabah, Hepzibah
Huldah
Ida — #64
Ilana, Ilanit — #16
Irit — #82
Ivria, Ivrit
Jaffa, Jaffice, Jafit
Jametta
Jardena
Jezebel
Jona, Jonati, Jonina, Jonit
Jora
Kaija
Kalanit
Karniela, Karniella
Karnis, Karnit
Kenya
Kerenhappuch
Keturah
Ketzi, Ketzia
Kezi, Kezia, Keziah
Kissie
Leah — #8
Levana — #102
Levia
Levona, Livana, Livia, Livona
Liebe, Leeba — #95
Lily — #47
Lirit
Lydia — #97
Mahira
Mahlah
Malka — #14
Mangena
Margalit, Marganit — #39
Marni
Martha — #103
Matana
Mazal — #44
Mehira, Menora
Meira — #104
Merab
Michal — #76
Mina — #51
Miri, Miryam — #2

Moria, Moriel, Morit
Moselle, Mozelle
Nagida
Naomi —#28
Nasya
Nava, Navice, Navit —
   #91
Nechama, Nehama —#40
Nediva
Neta, Netia
Nili —#77
Nira —#65
Nirel
Nitza, Nitzana, Nizana —
   #86
Noga
Nurit, Nuria, Nurice,
   Nuriel, Nurita —#49
Odeda
Odelia
Odera
Ofira, Ophira
Ofra —#98
Olga —#87
Ora —#45
Oralee
Orit
Orli, Orlice
Orna, Ornice, Ornit
Orpah, Orpha, Orphy
Paula —#99
Paza, Pazia, Pazice, Pazit
Peninah, Peninit

Pessia —#105
Pninah, Pnina — yes, PN;
   #24
Ranice, Ranit, Ranita
Razilee, Razel —#3;
   Rachel
Regina —#54
Rimona
Rina —#20
Rita —#96
Rivka —#7; Rebecca
Ronit, Ronia, Ronice —
   #78
Ronli
Rosa —#29
Rut —#10; Ruth
Sabra
Selima
Shamira
Sharai —#1 favorite;
   Sarah
Shifra —#93
Shilo
Shira, Shiri
Shoshanah —#6
Shulamit —#18
Sima —#50
Simcha —#58
Sonia, Sophie —#34
Sylvia —#66
Talia
Tamar —#32
Temira

Thirza
Tikva —#67
Timora
Tivona
Tobit
Tovah —#19
Tzipora, Zipporah —
   #17
Tziyona, Ziona —#80
Tzviy, Zviya —#60
Varda, Vardice, Vardit —
   #52
Victoria — not Hebraic,
   but #55
Yachne
Yael —#46
Yaffa, Yafa —#21
Yardena —#106
Yarkona
Yehudit —#9
Yemina
Yocheved —#59
Yona, Yonina, Yonit,
   Yonita —#48
Yovela
Zahava, Zehava —#23
Zayit
Zera
Zilah, Zillah —#41
Zilpah, Zylpha
Ziva —#81
Zoheret
Zora, Zorah

Male Names

Abia, Abiah
Abiatha, Abiathar, Abi-
   ather
Abiel
Abijah
Abimelech
Absalom
Adir
Adiv
Admon
Adrial. Adriel
Aharon —#13; Aaron
Ahe
Akeem

Akiba, Akiva
Alexander —#28
Almon
Alpheus
Alvan
Amariah
Amiel
Amnon, Amon —#45
Amos
Ardon
Arel, Areli
Ari
Arie
Arieh

Armoni
Arnon
Asa
Asher —#39
Asiel
Assaf
Avi
Avidan
Avidor
Avie
Aviel
Avital
Aviv
Avner

Avniel
Avraham, Avram —#4
Azariah
Azreil
Baram
Barth
Baruch —#32
Benjamin
Benzi
Bethel, Bethell
Binjamin —#19
Carmel
Chaim —#8
Chanoch
Dagon
Dan —#47
Daniel —#40
Dar
David —#5
Deedee
Deror, Derori
Dor
Dotan, Dothan
Dov, Dovev —#23
Dur
Efrayim —#35; Ephraim
Elah
Eli —#33
Eliezar, Eleazar —#21
Elimelech
Eliyahu, Eli, Elihu —#16
Elkan, Elkanah
Eloy
Elrad
Ely
Ezra —#36
Gavriel
Gibor
Gidon
Gilad
Gilam
Ginton
Givon
Giyora —#100
Goel
Gozal
Gur
Ham
Hanan
Harel
Heman

Hilel
Hiram
Hod
Ilan
Ira
Ishmael, Ismael
Japheth
Jaren, Jaron
Jehu
Jephtha
Joab
Joachim
Joah
Jotham
Jubal
Kan, Kaniel, Kanny
Kedem
Kenaz
Kiva, Kivi
Laban
Lavi
Leib, Leibel
Leo —#37
Leor
Leron
Levi
Lot
Mahir
Manasseh
Mark —#38
Marnin
Mehetabel
Meir —#15
Menachem —#20
Mendel
Mered
Michael, Micha —#18
Mordechai —#11
Moshe, Moshel —#1
   favorite
Nadav
Nagid
Namir
Napthali
Natan —#29
Nechemyah —#101
Nili
Nimrod
Nir
Nissan #102
Nissim —#31

Noach
Noy
Nur, Nuri
Obadiah
Oded
Omar
Omri
Oren
Pinchas —#42; Phineas
Rachamim —#43
Ranon
Raphael —#27
Raviv
Raz, Razi, Raziel
Reuven —#24
Rimon
Ronel, Roni
Selah
Seth
Shalom —#22
Shamir
Shaul —#34
Shem
Shimon —#17
Shlomo —#6
Shmuel —#9
Sima
Simpson — the Israeli
   form of Samson
Sivan
Telem
Teman
Teva
Timur
Tivon
Tov, Tovi
Tzadok, Zadok —#104
Tzvi, Zvi —#10
Uri —#41
Uzi —#103
Uzziah
Uzziel
Varda
Vered
Yaakov —#2
Yadid
Yadin
Yair
Yarin
Yativ
Yechezkel —#30

Yehiel, Jehiel —#48
Yehoshua —#25
Yehuda, Yehudi —#14
Yeshayahu, Isaiah —
    #46
Yisrael —#12
Yitzchak —#7

Yochanan
Yonah
Yonatan
Yosef—#3
Yoyi
Zamir
Zared

Zebulon
Zedekiah
Ze'ev —#26
Zephaniah
Zia
Zimri

FAMILY NAMES

Many of these are immigrant names brought from the Old Country, but I have tried to emphasize new Israeli names when I could find them.

Aa'yalon
Afek
Aldubi
Avigal
Avizgar
Bar-Hama
Bar-or
Barak
Ben-Asher
Biton
Cohen
Eckstein
Eldar
Fraenkel
Gelper
Gerstein
Giron
Golani

Halban
Halevi
Hermon
Hertzig
Imbar
Kahn
Kanitz
Katz
Kirsch
Kohen
Kolodny
Levi — most ancient
Mageni
Mann
Morris
Nitzan
Oren
Rak-oz

Rosentzwig
Rothschild
Ruskin
Shamir
Shapirah
Sheinfeld
Shlomo
Shochat
Snir
Steiner
Weizmann
Wingarten
Yaniv
Yehezkel
Zakai
Zimri
Zohar

LEBANESE

In the 19th century, in the area we now call Lebanon, the Turkish Empire created a *millet*, a religious or ethnic enclave, for the Maronite Christians. After the First World War, the French took over the area, so that the names in the area were transliterated for French speakers. Education and Christian choice of personal names became also Gallicized. Later, there was a backlash to English names.

There are always alternative ways to write a Lebanese name. For example:
Joannes Maro/John Maron/Yuhanna Marun (Arabic ver.)
Giuseppe Simon Assemani (Ital.)/Yusuf Sam'an al Sam'ani (Arab)
Beshara al-Khoury (French)/Bisharah al-Khuri (Arab)

Camille Chamoun (French)/Kamil Sham'un (Arab)
Fu'ad Shihab (Arab)/Fouad Chehab (French)

The Moslems and Eastern Orthodox Christians had wanted to be part of Syria, rather than being a permanent under-class to the Maronites, so this country's problems were rooted in its very creation in 1920.

Family names are all recent versions of Turkish-Arabic patronymics or place-names. Moslems have Arabic personal names, Christians French or Anglo ones.

FEMALE NAME

Wadia Sabra

MALE NAMES

Ahmed	Fakhr-al-Din	Pierre
Amin	Fuad	Rachid
Azziz	Ghassan	Rashid
Bashir	Halim	Raymond
Camille	Hassan	Saad
Charles	Henry	Sabry
Cherbel	Iskander	Saeb
Dany	Jean	Suleiman
Dory	Kamal, Kamel	Takieddine
Elias — popular among	Ma'arouf	Tony
Christians	Noureddine	Victor
Emile	Philip	Yacoub

FAMILY NAMES

Abdo	Ghanem	Mansour — Druze
al-Ahdab	Haddad	Nakhle
Arislan — Druze	Harik	Rifai
As'ad	Janblat — Druze	Sa'ad
Barakat	Jumblatt	Saba
Bashir — Druze	Karameh	Salem
Bitar	Kassis	Sarkis
Chehab	al-Khatib	Shihab, Chehab — Druze
Daher	al-Kholy	Solh
Edde, Eddeh	Khuri Hitti	Tueini
Frangieh	Malik	
Gemayel	al-Ma'ni — Druze	

ARABIC

Arabic names are used over a vast stretch of the planet, with many dialectical variations. So what is a proper spelling in Morocco may not be acceptable in Tanzania, Persia, Malaysia, or Chicago. This is like Christians shuffling between John, Sean, Ian, Jean, Jan, Juan, Janos, and other variations on the theme. I have tried to establish some consistency, based on traditional English transliteration and modern American Muslim usage.

Women traditionally did not participate in public life, so they are known by a personal name, and then, if necessary, as "daughter of __," or "wife of __." They obtain a more permanent name as "mother of __." In fact, from the birth of a son forward, a woman may hardly be known as anything but her son's mother, and takes great pride in becoming "Umn Ali" or "Umn Hakim." Two of the wives and one of the daughters of the Prophet (Peace Be Upon Him) are known only as Umn Salma, Umn Habeeba, and Umn Kolthoom.

Male Arabic names are a bit more complicated. To this day, in most countries they do not have "family names." Instead, a man lists up his genealogy, as it were: Sayed, son of Mohammed the Eloquent, son of Ali Mohammed. He may also have a nickname or sobriquet attached to his given name.

Whether at the beginning or in the middle of a name set, "ibn" means "son of." So "Ibn Batuta" is "Batuta's son," just as some people got known as Peterson or Johnson, rather than by their own name. In Arabic names, this may be because the actual personal name is a variant on Mohammed, which is more popular among Arabic men than Mary is among Catholic women: "Blessed is the house where a Mohammed dwells," so every family wants at least one. Some have several. For women, "bint" means "daughter of," put in the same position.

"Abdullah" or "Abdul" are not names, except in places where Islam is the religion but Arabic is not the local language. It means "servant of" and is normally followed by one of the attributes of God: the Merciful, the Triumphant, the Generous, etc. Because of their own naming habits, Europeans, hearing that a man was known as Abd-al-Jalil, mentally classed him as Mr. Jalil, first name Abdul. It can also be a mispronunciation of "abd-al'Allah," since a foreigner may not hear the soft third syllable in there. Karim Abdul Jabbar in Arabic would be Karim abd-al-Jabbar, "Generous, servant of the Repairer."

Many "Jewish" Biblical names are used by Moslems. Islam is considered to be the completion of the religion begun by Abraham, and continued by Jesus. Arabic and Hebrew are closely related Semitic languages, to boot.

There are two titles which are sometimes mistaken for names. Hajji, meaning a pilgrim, is added to the name of any man who has been to Mecca. So Hajji Asad is not Mr. Asad, first name Hajji, but Asad who has fulfilled the pilgrimage, not a common accomplishment. Sharif is a title for any man who is a descendant of the Prophet, even rarer. Again, outside the Arabic-speaking lands,

Moslems may use these as names, indicating a son born while his father was on the Hajj, and Sharif or Sharifa for the concept of nobility. The latter is like Americans naming a son Baron or Duke.

Pronunciation

Transliteration from Arabic to English is not graven in stone, so there are often several possible spellings. Pronunciation is not uniform from one side of the Moslem world to the other, either. Sometimes it will seem a vowel got forgotten, but Q is a back of the throat K-sound, and is not always followed by U. When it is, the U is the vowel, as in tune, not a W sound.

Interchangeable in many cases are S and Z, Y and J, C, Q and K.

FEMALE NAMES

'Aadila — just, honest
Aafreeda, Afrida — created, produced
'Aalia — high, exalted
'Aasima — capitol, protectress
'Aatifa — affection, sympathy
Adeeba — literary woman, authoress
Adjab
'Afa'f — chastity
'Afeefa — modest, chaste
Afroz — illuminating, enlightening
Afzaa — augmenting, increasing
Agda — sweet
Ahlaam — dreams, Utopia
Aisa
A'isha, 'Aai'sha, Ayasha, Ayesha — happy; warrior wife of Mohammed
Akasma — a white climbing rose
Akilah — intelligent, logical
'Aleema, Alima — skilled in music and dance
'Alia — lofty, sublime
Almaas — diamond, adamant
Ameena, Amina, Amineh, Ameenah, Aamina — trustworthy, reliable; secure, protected
'Andaleeb — nightingale
'Aqeela — gifted with reason, wise
Asiyah — rebel
Asma' — beautiful
Atalaya — watchtower
'Atiyya — gift, present
'Atoofa — kind, merciful

Azada
Aziza, 'Azeeza — dear, precious, rare
Badoura
Bahaar — spring
Bahjat — splendor, magnificence
Bakht — luck, lottery
Barakah — blessing
Basheera — happy news, glad tidings
Bilqees — trad. name Queen of Sheba
Cari — flowing like water
Deeba — brocade, cloth-of-gold
Dhabba
Dhabyah — Yemenese
Durdaana — single pearl
Dur-re-Shahwar — pearl worthy of kings
Faachila — meritorious, plentiful
Faa'iza — victor, winner
Faakhira — glorious, magnificent
Faaria — tall, pretty
Fadheelat — virtue, excellence
Fahmeeda — wise, understanding
Fakhriyya — glory, pride
Fareeda, Farida — precious gem, unique
Farhaana — happy, joyful
Farkhanda — happy, blessed
Farzaana — intelligent, wise
Faseeha — literary, eloquent
Fatima, Fatimah, Fatma — daughter of Mohammed; very popular
Fauzia — victorious, triumphant
Gauhar — jewel, pearl

Ghazaala — gazelle
Gulaab, Gulab — rose, flower; Turk?
Gulnaar, Gulnar — pomegranate flower
Gulshan — garden
Gulzaar, Gulzar — garden
Haala — lunar halo, glory
Habeeba, Habibah — beloved
Hafiza, Hafeezah — memory; governess of Mohammed
Hafsa, Hafsah — lioness; wife of the Prophet
Haleema — clement, humane
Hameeda — commendable, praised
Hanaa' — bliss, felicity
Haneefah — true believer
Haseena — pretty, beautiful
Hifni
Hinda — wife of Mohammed
Hinnaa — henna, myrtle
Huda — guidance
Humaa' — lucky bird, phoenix
Humaira — reddish
Huraiva — kitten; occ. male
Husna — beauty, a belle
Ibtehaj — joy, delight
Ibtesam — smile
Ihtizaz
Ilham — inspiration
Iram — heaven
Izora — dawn
Jahash
Jaleela — great, exalted
Jamila, Jameela — beautiful, elegant
Jannat — heaven, garden
Jauhara — jewel, gem
Javairia — wife of Mohammed
Jawaahar — precious stones
Jimena
Kabeera — great
Kalila — sweetheart
Kalim, Kaleema — speaker, mouthpiece
Kamala, Kameelya — perfection
Karida — untouched, virginal
Karli — like snow
Kasbani
Khaalida — immortal, deathless
Khadija; Khadeeja — Mohammed's first wife
Khaleeqa — well-mannered
Khawala — servant, dancer

Khazeema, Khazima — wife of the Prophet
Khwalah
Kubraa — great, senior
Laa'iqa — suitable, deserving
Labeeba — wise, intelligent
La'eeqa — elegant, representative
Lailaa, Layla, Laila, Leila, Leyla, Leilia — born at night; name of heroine of the Persian "Layla and Majnum"; sweetheart
Lala — Berber
Lateefa — witticism, jest
Lubna — mouthful
Lulu, Lo'loo — a jewel; Persian
Lutfiyya — kindness, delicate grace
Maahjabeen — forehead like the moon
Maahpaara — piece of moon
Maajida — glorious, powerful
Maamoona, Maimoone, Maimoune — safe, trustworthy; wife of Mohammed
Maa'sooma — innocent, infallible
Mahbooba — beloved, sweetheart
Mahsa — a little moon; Arab
Mahtaab — the moon
Majeeda — respected, eternal
Malak
Mansourah — Bedu
Maqsooda — intended, objective
Marwaareed — pearl, jewel
Maryam, Meryem, Mariyah, Maryana — Miriam
Mas'ooda — happy, lucky
Mastoora, Mastoura — hidden, chaste
Maysun
Mu-ammara
Mubaarika — blessed, auspicious
Mubeena — evident, clear
Muhsana — well-protected, married
Muhsina — benevolent
Mujeeba — respondent, answering
Munawwara — lighted, illuminated
Muneerah — luminous, brilliant; Egyptian
Muqaddasa — sacred, holy
Mutahhara — purified, chaste
Myrhha, Murrah — myrhh, bitter; Mary
Naadhira — blooming, flourishing
Naadira — rare, scarce thing

Naadiya — caller, announcer
Naaheed — elevated, planet Venus
Naa'ila — winner, catastrophe
Naajia — free, escaped
Naaji'a — beneficial, useful
Naasiha — advisor, sincere
Naazima — poetess, matron
Naazira — onlooker
Naazneen — delicate, a belle
Nabeela — noble, magnanimous
Nadheera — head, foremost
Na'eema — happiness, benefit
Nafeesa — precious, delicate
Nageena — gem, pearl
Naghma — melody, song
Najam — star, celestial body
Najeeba — excellent, intelligent
Najjiyya — beneficial, useful
Najma — star, precious
Naqeeba — soul, group leader
Nargis — narcissus flower
Narriman
Naseeba — luck, share
Naseema — zephyr, gentle breeze
Naseera, Nasira, Naasira — helper, supporter
Nasreen — jonquil
Nathaara — fragments, prose writer
Naufa — excess, surplus
Nawaar — blossom, flower
Nazaakat — delicacy, neatness
Nazli — Egyptian Arabic
Neelam — blue gem, precious stone
Neelofar — lotus, water lily
Nepa — walking backwards
Nighat — sight, glance
Nikhat — small, flavor
Nizaa' — woman, lady
Nooreen — of light, luminous
Noura — light
Numa — pleasant
Oma — commander
Oserrah
Qadira — powerful, potent
Qamra — the moon
Qudsiyya — glorious, holy
Qurra-tul-'ain — delight of eye, darling
Raabia, Rabiah — fourth
Raaheel — Rachel, an ewe
Rabi, Rabi'a — spring, breeze; a Sufi mystic

Racha — hope
Radhia — well satisfied
Ra'eesa — leadress, matron
Rafee'a — exalted, sublime
Rafeeqa — sweetheart, companion
Raheela — departure, exodus
Raheema — merciful, kind
Raihaana — aromatic, sweet basil
Ra'naa — beautiful, graceful
Rasheeda, Rashida, Raashida — conscious, pious
Reshmaan — silky, of silk
Rida — favor
Ridhwaana — pleasure, acceptance
Rihana — sweet basil, a fragrant herb
Ruqayya — enchantment, spell
Saabira — patient, enduring
Saadiqa — truthful, sincere
Saa'iba — straight, pertinent
Saaim — fasting
Saa'iqa — thunderbolt, lightning
Saajida — prostratoress, adoress
Saaleha — right pious
Sabaa — east wind
Sabaa' — Sheba
Sabaah — morning, dawn
Sabeeha — forenoon, beautiful
Sadira — lotus tree, magnolia
Sa'diyya — luck, good fortune
Sa'eeda — happy, lucky
Safi, Safia — lion's share, pure; wife of Mohammed
Sagheera — small, minor
Sahba — red wine, intoxicating
Sakeena — tranquility, devout
Salama, Salma — peace, safety
Saleema — safe, mild
Salwa — quail, consolation
Sameena — plump, attractive
Sameera — jovial, companion
Samsi
Sanobar — pine tree, fir
Sauda — gloomy; wife of Mohammed
Seemaa — mark, sign
Seemeen, Simin — of silver, white
Sehar — enchantment, fascination
Selima — peace
Shaahida — witness, true copy
Shaa'ira — poetess
Shaa'ista — well-bred, polite
Shaakira — thankful, grateful

Shabaana — belonging to the night
Shabnam — dew
Shafeeqa — kind, compassionate
Shagufta — blooming, flourishing
Shahar — the moon
Shahlaa — bluish-black eyes
Shahnaaz — bride, pride of a king
Shahzaadee — princess
Shakeela — well-shaped, beautiful
Shakoora — very thankful
Shama' — candle, wax
Shameema — scent, flavor
Sharaara — spark, lightning
Sharawi
Shareeka — partner, participant
Sharil — running water
Sheereen — sweet, pleasant
Shifa
Shu'la — flame, blaze
Siddeeqa — friend, righteous
Suraab — mirage, phantom
Taahira — pure, chaste
Taaj — crown
Tahiyya — greeting, cheerfulness
Tahseen — praise, beautification
Tahzeeb — culture, education
Tal'at — seen, risen
Talitha, Taletha — gazelle, graceful
Tarub
Taskeen — satisfaction, peace
Tasleem — submission, salutation
Tasneem — Fountain of Paradise
Taymuriyya
Tayyaba — pleasant, well
Thadhellala
Thameena — precious, generous
Tharwat — wealth
Thurayyaa — star, Pleiades
Tohfa — present, gift
'Uzma — greatest
Waajida — finder, excited

Wadha
Waheeda — sole, single
Warda — Syrian
Waseema — graceful, pretty
Yaaqoot — hyacinth, sapphire
Yaasmeen, Yasiman, Yasmine, Yasmina, Jasmine, Jasmina — flower name
Yaziji
Yumn — happiness
Zaahida — hermit, ascetic
Zaahira — outstanding, distinguished
Zaakira — memory, remembrance
Zabibi
Zada — lucky one
Zadah — prosperous
Zaheera
Zahraa' — radiant
Zaib — decoration, beauty
Zaibaa — beautiful, adorned
Zainab — daughter of the Prophet
Zakkiyya — sharp, intellectual, pure, pious
Zamurrad — emerald
Zareena — of gold, golden
Zarifa — graceful
Zarqaa — bluish-green eyes
Zebba
Zeenat — decoration, beauty
Zerdali — wild apricot
Ziyada
Zobeide, Zobeida — flower
Zoebd-el-Khematin — the flower of women
Zohra, Zuhra — blooming, morning/evening star
Zora — dawn; Arab
Zubaida — high hill
Zulafah — Syrian
Zulican

MALE NAMES

Many of these can be compounded to others, with or without hyphen, especially Ali or some form of Mohammed: Mehmet Ali, Fath Ali, Abbas Mirza.

Aaftab — the sun
Aakif — given, attached

'Aalamgeer — conqueror of the world
'Aaqil — intellectual, wise

Aasaf— clear, lined up
'Aasim — protector, guardian
'Aatif— compassionate, affectionate
Abba, Abbas, 'Abbaas — uncle of the Prophet; frowner, gloomy
Abou, Abu
Acar — bright
Acayib — wonderful and strange
Adib, Adeeb — scholar, literateur
Afdhal — excellent, prominent
Afsar — better, explained, officer
Ahmad — the most praised
Aibak — slave, messenger
Aizun
Ajmal — the total, more beautiful
Akar — running water
Akhtar — star, good luck
'Alavi
'Ali — servant; often combined
Alim — wise, learned
Altaaf— kindness, grace; occ. fem.
Altamish — vanguard, commander
Amaanat — security, deposit; occ. fem.
Amjad — most glorious, noble
Anjum — stars
Anwaar — multiple lights, lustre; occ. fem.
Anwar — beautiful, disclosed; occ. fem.
'Aqeeb — following, subsequent
Arqam — writer, the best recorder
Arshad — most honest, better guided
Asad — lion
Asadel — most prosperous
Ashraf— most noble, superior
Aslam — safer, freer
Athar — very pious, pure
'Aun — help, assistance
Ayaz — winter cold
'Azamat — grandeur, pride; occ. fem.
Azim — defender
Baabar — lion
Badr — full moon; occ. fem.
Bahlol — leader of a tribe, jester
Bahram
Bakhtaawar — fortunate, lucky; occ. fem.
Bakhtiaar — lucky, fortunate; occ. fem.
Bakr — young camel, first-born
Barakaat — blessings, abundance

Barakat — blessings, prosperity; occ. fem.
Barmak
Baseerat — insight, perception; occ. fem.
Bashaarat — good omen, prophecy; occ. fem.
Behraam — Mars, planet
Bilal — muazzin, companion of the Prophet
Birjees — Jupiter, planet
Burhaan — proof, evidence
Chiraagh — lamp, light; occ. fem.
Dalair — brave, valiant
Daniyal
Dastgeer — helper, supporter
Dhaamin — responsible, guarantor
Dhameer — heart, conscience
Dhu
Dilaawar — hearty, daring
Duraid
E'jaaz — miracle, astonishment; occ. fem.
Etemaad — faith, trust
Faatir — maker, creator
Fahd — lynx, panther
Faheem — intelligent, judicious
Fakhree — glorious, proud
Faraasat — keen eye, discernment; occ. fem.
Faraaz — elevation
Faraj
Fareed — lonely, unique
Farel — bearer of burdens
Farrukh — young bird, sprout; occ. fem.
Fayyaadh — generous, liberal
Fuad, Fuwaad — heart
Furqaan — evidence, proof
Gaolan
Ghaalib — conqueror, dominator
Ghaazee — war champion, hero
Ghauth — help, succor
Ghiyaath — succor, help
Ghulaam — slave, servant
Ghuzayy
Haafiz, Hafiz — keeper, guardian
Haakim, Hakim — ruler, sovereign
Haaziq — skillful, intelligent
Habib — beloved
Hadi

Haleef— ally, confederate
Halil
Hamal — lamb
Hammad — gracious
Haneef— true believer, orthodox
Hannaan — beautiful, compassionate
Hareef— pungent, hot
Haroun, Harun — for Aaron
Hashmat — decency, dignity; occ. fem.
Hasrat — grief, distress; occ. fem.
Hassan, Hasan — handsome
Hatem
Hayaat — life, existence; occ. fem.
Hayy, Hayyan
Hidaayat — guidance, instruction; occ. fem.
Himaayat — help, support; occ. fem.
Himyar
Hisham
Hubaab — aim, friendship
Humeid
Hunayn — for John
Husain, Hussein — handsome
Ibrahim — Abraham
Idrisi
Iftikhaar — honor, glory; occ. fem.
Ikhlaas — frankness, sincerity
Ikraam — esteem, veneration
Imtiaaz — privilege, distinction; occ. fem.
In'aam — gift, grant; occ. fem.
'Inaayat — concern, attention; occ. fem.
Iqbaal — prosperity, wealth; occ. fem.
Iqtidaar — capability, power; occ. fem.
'Irfaan — knowledge, wisdom
Irshaad — guidance, direction; occ. fem.
Isa
Ishaq — Isaac
'Ishrat — intimacy, companionship; occ. fem.
Iskandar, Iskaner— Alexander
Isma'il — Ishmael; God hears
'Ismat — chastity, purity; occ. fem.
Izhaar — revelation, declaration
Jaabir, Jabir — bonesetter, tyrant
Jabril
Ja'far — rivulet

Jalal, Jalaal — grandeur, glory
Jalees — table companion, associate
Jamil, Jameel — beautiful, graceful
Jaraad — locust, liberal
Jarir
Jauhar — gem, pearl; occ. fem.
Jaysh
Jazari — an engineer
Jubair
Junaid — soldier, warrior
Jurjig, Jurji, Jurj — famous physician
Kaazim — restrainer, controller of anger
Kafur
Kaif— pleasure, high spirits
Karaamat — miracle, nobility; occ. fem.
Karim — generous
Katheer — abundant, copious
Kaukab — star; occ. fem.
Kauthar — ample, abundant; occ. fem.
Khaadim — servant, attendant
Khaawar — East/West, vacant; occ. fem.
Khair — excellent, benevolent
Khairaat — benevolence, charity; occ. fem.
Khaldum, Khaldun
Khalf
Khalil, Khaleel — inner self, heart
Khurdabeh
Khurram — delightful, happy
Khushnood — happy, pleased
Kifaayat — sufficiency, competence; occ. fem.
Kuthayyi
Laa'iq, La'eeq — able, deserving
Labid
Liaaqat —fitness, ability; occ. fem.
Mahboob — beloved, dear; occ. fem.
Makhdoom, Makdoum — master, employer
Malik, Maliki — a king
Mamoun, Mamun
Mansur, Manzur, Manzoor — acceptable, admired
Maqbool — accepted, popular; occ. fem.
Maqsood — intended, proposed
Ma'roof— known, celebrated

Maroun
Marwaan
Masarrat — happiness, delight; occ. fem.
Mashkoor — praiseworth, thankful
Ma'shooq — beloved, sweetheart; occ. fem.
Ma'soom — infallible, innocent; occ. fem.
Mazhar — phenomenon, manifestation
Minhaaj — way, program
Mi'raaj — ladder, ascent; occ. fem.
Misgiah
Mohammed, Mahmud — the Prophet, P.B.U.H.
Mu'aawin — helper, assistant
Mu'awiya —fifth Caliph
Mubarrak, Murbarak, Mubaarak — blessed, auspicious; occ. fem.
Mugheeth — helper, succorer
Muhibb — lover, fancier
Muhsin — benefactor, benevolent
Mukhlis — sincere, frank
Mukhtaar — chosen, authorized; occ. fem.
Munawwar — illuminated, enlightened; occ. fem.
Munim — benefactor, generous
Munsif— justice, righteousness
Muntazier — victorious, triumphant
Muqaddas — sanctified, holy
Muqbil — coming, next
Murshid — spiritual guide
Mursil — envoy, missionary
Mushaqa
Mutawakkil — having faith in Allah
Muti
Muzaffar — victorious, triumphant
Naaji — useful, beneficial
Naasir — protector, granting victory
Naaz, Naz — pride, delicacy; occ. fem.
Naazim — arranger, organizer
Nabeel — noble, magnanimous
Nadeem — companion, confidant
Najib, Najeeb — excellent, noble
Najm — celestial body, star; occ. fem.
Naqeeb — chief, lawyer
Naqqaash — painter, artist
Naseeb — share, participation; occ. fem.

Naseem — fresh air, breeze; occ. fem.
Naseer, Nasir, Nasr — supporter, protector, victor
Nasif
Nathaar — scattered, tiny pieces; occ. fem.
Nawaaz — cherishing, caressing; occ. fem.
Nawwaab — ruler, governor; occ. fem.
Nayyir — luminous, brilliant; occ. fem.
Nazaam — order, discipline
Ni'mat — blessing, grace; occ. fem.
Nishaat — liveliness, energy; occ. fem.
Nishtar — scalpel, surgeon's knife
Niyaaz — desire, offering; occ. fem.
Nudrat — rarity, uniqueness; occ. fem.
Nusrat — victory, help; occ. fem.
Nuzhat — recreation, amusement; occ. fem.
Perviz
Qaabil — acceptor, next, able
Qaa'id — steersman, leader
Qaa'im — upright, stable
Qaaree — reader, reciter
Qamar — moon, satellite; occ. fem.
Qasim
Quadama, Qudama
Qudrat — faculty, power, nature; occ. fem.
Qurbaan — martyr, sacrificed
Qutaybah, Qutaiba, Kutaiba
Quzman
Raahat — rest, repose; occ. fem.
Raashid — conscious, pious
Radhwaan — acceptance, consent
Rafeeq — kind, ally
Rahmat — mercy, clemency; occ. fem.
Raihaan — sweet basil
Ramadhan — for boys born in the ninth Muslim month
Raushan — skylight, bright; occ. fem.
Reyhan — divinely favored
Riaasat — leadership, state; occ. fem.
Ridwan
Rifaaqat — companionship, society; occ. fem.
Rif'at — height, high rank; occ. fem.
Rosteh
Sa'aadat — happiness, bliss; occ. fem.
Saabiq — antecedent, preceeding

Saabir — patient, enduring
Saadaat — master, gentleman
Saalik — follower of a spiritual path
Saalim — secure, free
Sadaaqat — sincerity, truth; occ. fem.
Safdar — piercing lines, fighter
Safeer — mediator, ambassador
Safi
Said, Sayyid
Sajjaad — worshipper (of Allah)
Sakhaawat — suppleness, generosity; occ. fem.
Sakhr
Salaiman, Sulaiman, Saleem, Salim — Solomon; peaceful; by connotation, wisdom, safe, mild; occ. fem.
Sameem, Samim — real, genuine
Sameer — jovial, entertainer
Sanu
Sa'ood — felicities, good fortunes
Saqr — falcon, hawk
Sardaar — commander, head; occ. fem.
Sarfaraaz — respected, blessed; occ. fem.
Sarwar — chief, leader; occ. fem.
Seemaab — quicksilver, mercury; occ. fem.
Sehaam — shares, arrows; occ. fem.
Shaaheen — hawk, falcon; occ. fem.
Shaakir — thankful, grateful
Shafaqat — compassion, kindness; occ. fem.
Shafeeq — kind, compassionate
Shahaab — shooting star, luminous
Shahbaaz — white falcon, King of Falcons
Shaidaa — lover, madly in love
Shakeel — handsome, good looking
Shameem — odor, scent; occ. fem.
Shamshad — tree, pine; occ. fem.
Sharaafat — nobility, good manners; occ. fem.
Shaukat — power, dignity; occ. fem.
Shauq — interest, zeal
Shujaa'at — bravery, courage; occ. fem.
Siddeeq — friend, righteous
Sinan, Sinaan — spearhead, bravery
Subhaan — holy, glorifying
Taajwar — king, crowned

Taalib — candidate, student
Taariq — nightcomer, morning star
Taatheer — effectiveness, impression
Tabaarak — hallowed, magnified
Tabari
Tabassum — smile, happiness; occ. fem.
Taha
Taimur
Tajammul — beauty, dignity; occ. fem.
Talal
Talib
Tammam
Tanweer — enlightening, illuminating; occ. fem.
Taqi, Taqqee — godfearing
Tasadduq — giving alms, donation; occ. fem.
Taufiq, Taufeeq — help; occ. fem.
Thaaqib — piercing, glistening
Thamar — fruit, profit
Tufail — expedient
'Umar, 'Umr, Omar — age, lifetime; uncle of Mohammed
'Umraan — prosperity, populousness
Uqba
Usama — lion
'Uthman, Othman — third Caliph, an 'Ummayad or Ommayad
Uwais — small wolf
Waahib — liberal, donor
Waathiq — confident, strong
Waheed, Wahid — unique, single
Wahhaaj — glowing, sparkling
Wajaahat — esteem, credit; occ. fem.
Waqaar — dignity, sobriety
Waseem — graceful, handsome
Wilaayat — power, state; occ. fem.
Wiraathat — inheritance, legacy
Yaakub — the supplanter; Jacob
Yaameen — towards the right
Yaasir — towards the left, easy
Yazdan — merciful, kind
Yazid
Youssef — for Joseph; he shall add
Zaahir — shining, elevated
Zaid, Zaid — abundance
Zaidan, Zaydan
Zain — beauty, prettiness
Zakkee — intellectual, ingenious
Zareef — elegant, witty

Zauk — taste, perceptivity
Ziryab
Ziyaad — extra, more, increase

Zubair
Zuhair, Zuhayr
Zuhoor — appearing, arising

"-AL-DIN" NAMES

Amongst Turks, Persians, and other eastern Moslems, amongst rulers especially, there is a tendency to use names or titles referring to "al-Din," the Faith (Islam). Saladin, opponent of Richard the Lion-Hearted, was Sal-ed-din, "goodness of the Faith" or "goodness of Islam."

Ala-ad-din	learning of the Faith	Aladdin
Badr-al-din	full moon of the Faith	Bohaddin
Baha-al-din		
Fakhr-al-Din	glory of the Faith	
Farid-ed-din	gem of Islam	Farideddin
Ghiyath-ud-Din	succor of the Faith	Ghiyathuddin
Jalal-ad-din, Jelal-ad-din,		
Jalal-ud-Din	grandeur of the Faith	
Kamal-al-Din	perfection of religion	
Khair-ed-Din	excellence of the Faith	Chaireddin
Majd-al-Din	exaltation of Islam	
Mu'izz-ad-din	magnification of the Faith	
Musaffar-ed-din,		
Muzaffar-ed-Din	triumph of Islam	
Muslin-ud-din		
Nasr-ed-din	protector of the Faith	Nasreddin, Nazruddin
Nizam-ed-Din	discipline of Islam	Nizam Eddin
Nour-al-Din	light of the Faith	Nureddin, Nouredeen
		Nur-ud-din
Rukn-ud-din		
Sal-ad-Din	goodness of the Faith	Saladin, Saladeen
Shams-ud-din	sun of religion	

EKE-NAMES

Often these were place-names like al-Khurasani, someone from Khurasan. Here are some of those, and some which are more personal. You may always make them up from the names which have meanings. Qaa'id means "steersman, leader," so you may make your seafarer Fuad al-Qaa'id. In front of a T-name, you can change the al to at-; in front of R to ar-; in front of an S-name to as-.

PLACE-NAMES

al-Andalusi — the Spaniard, the Andalusian
al-Baghdadi — from Baghdad
al-Bukhari — from Bukhara
al-Firuzabadi — of Firuzabad

al-Hirai — of Hira
al-Khurasani — from Khurasan
al-Ma'arri — from Ma'arrat
al-Samarqandi — of Samarkand

ATTRIBUTE NAMES

al-Aghani — songs, the singer
al-Arnabah — the rabbit
al-Ashra — noble
al-Bayan — the eloquent one
al-Bulbul — the nightingale
al-Caph — kaff, palm of the hand
al-Darazi — the tailor
udh-Dhahab — of gold
al'Em — the knowledgeable
al-Faraj — the pleasure
al-Farid — peerless
al-Ghaib — the mystery
al-Ghazalli, al-Ghazali — the gazelle
al-Ghufran — the forgiven
al-Habib — the beloved
al-Hadi — the guide
al-Hakam — the arbitrator
al-Hamasa — the brave
al-Hamed — the praised
al-Hasan — the handsome
al-Hayawan — the beast
el-Hiri — the wildcat
al-Hizanat — the treasure
al-Isfahani — from Isfahan
al-Jahiz — the goggle-eyed

ul-Jawahir — of precious stones
al-Khafah — assessor
el-Khalidi — the deathless
al-Ma — the learned
al-Mahasin — the beautiful
al-Majnun — the mad
al-M'amun — the trustworthy
al-Mansur — the admired
al-Marid — the rebellious
ul-Mas'udi — the lucky
al-Mer — a prince
al-Mira — the exalted
al-Mujaahid — the holy warrior
al-Mutanabbi — prophecy claimant
al-Nesr, al-Nasr — the vulture
al-Qut — the cat
al-Rahma — divine mercy
al-Reyhan — divinely favored
al-Rumat — the archer
al-Saffaah — the bloodshedder
al-Saffar — the coppersmith
al-Shidda — the painful
at-Tair — the eagle
at-Tih — the perfume, the sweet odor
al-Zarzur — the starling

The following eke-names were used for women, and their structure may betray you if you use them for men.

al-Asilah — the pedigreed mare (a *big* compliment)
al-Bakiyah — the sobbing one
Bedr-el-Budur — moon of moons
al-Gharibah — the peculiar
al-Ja'iah — the hungry one

al-Muta'adhibah — the tortured one
al-Muta'ajibah — the wonderer
al-Mutawahishah — the savage
al-Rajiyah — the implorer
al-Thartharah — the chatterer

THE 99 EXCELLENT NAMES OF GOD

Where I have found them in use, I have given alternate spellings, usually older, and often French-derived, using I for EE. Use these names after "abd-"

al-'Adil — the Just
al-'Afuw — the Forgiver, the Effacer
al-Akhir — the Last
al-Aleem — the All-Knowing; al-Alim
al-Ali — the Most High, the Exalted
al-Awwal — the First
al-'Azeem — the Great, the Mighty; al-'Azim
al-Azeez — the Mighty; al-Aziz
al-Baa'ith — the Resurrector; al-Bais
al-Baaqee — the Everlasting, the Eternal; al-Baki
al-Baaree — the Artificer, the Creator; al-Bari
al-Baasit — the Spreader, He Who Expands; al-Basit
al-Badee — the Wonderful, the Maker; al-Badi
al-Barr — the Righteous
al-Baseer — the All-Seeing; al-Basir
al-Batin — the Hidden
adh-Dhaarr — the Bringer of Adversity
al-Fattah — the Revealer
al-Ghaffaar — the Forgiving; al-Ghaffar
al-Ghafoor — the Pardoner; al-Ghafur
al-Ghanee — the All-Sufficing; al-Ghani
al-Hadee — the Guide; al-Hadi
al-Hafeez — the Guardian, the Preserver; al-Hafiz
al-Hai'yy — the Ever-Living; al-Hayy
al-Hakam — the Judge
al-Hakeem — the Most Wise; al-Hakim
al-Haleem — the Clement, the Most Patient; al-Halim
al-Hameed — the Laudable; al-Hamid
al-Haseeb — the Reckoner, the Noble; al-Hasib
al-Huqq — the Truth; al-Hakk
al-Jaami' — the Collector, the Comprehensive; al-Jami
al-Jabbaar — the Oppressor, the All-Compelling; al-Jabbar

al-Jaleel — the Honorable, the Exhalted; al-Jalil
al-Kabeer — the Great, the Big; al-Kabir
al-Kadir — the Powerful
al-Kaiyum — the Subsisting
al-Kareem — the Generous; al-Karim
al-Khaafidh — the Abaser; al-Khafiz
al-Khaaliq — the Creator; al-Khalik
al-Khabeer — the Aware; al-Khabir
al-Lateef — the Most Gentle; al-Latif
Maalik ul-Mulk — the Ruler of the Kingdom
al-Maani' — the Prohibitor, the Defender; al-Mani
al-Majeed — the Glorious, the Exalted; al-Majid
al-Malik — the King
al-Mateen — the Firm; al-Matin
al-Mu'akhkhir — the Deferrer
al-Muawwir — the Fashioner
al-Mubdee — the Beginner, the Starter; al-Mubdi
al-Mu'eed — the Restorer, the Resurrector; all-Mu'id
al-Mughnee — the Enricher; al-Mughni
al-Muhaimin — the Vigilant
al-Muhsee — the Accountant; al-Muhsi
al-Muhyee — the Bestower, the Life-Giver; al-Muhyi
al-Mu'izz — the Honourer
al-Mujeeb — the Respondent, One Who Answers; al-Mujib
al-Mukkaddim — the Bringer Forward
al-Muktadir — the Prevailing
al-Muqsit — the Equitable; al-Muksit
al-Mumeet — the Bringer of Death; al-Mumit
al-Mu'min — the Faithful
al-Muntaqim — the Avenger; al-Muntakim
al-Muqeet — the Maintainer, the Nourisher

al-Musawwir — the Organizer, the Designer

al-Muta'ali — the Greatly Exalted

al-Mutakabbir — the Majestic, the Haughty

al-Mu'ti — the Giver

al-Muzill — the Degrader, the Subduer; al-Muzil

an-Naafi' — the Beneficial, the Propitious; an-Nafi

an-Noor — the Light; an-Nour, an-Nur

al-Qaabidh — the Restrainer; al-Kabiz

al-Qahhaar — the Dominant; al-Kahhar

al-Qawwee — the Powerful, the Almighty; al-Kawi

al-Quddoos — the Holy; al-Kuddos

ar-Raafi — the Exalter; ar-Rafi

ar-Raheem — the Most Compassionate

ar-Rahmaan — the Most Merciful

ar-Ra'oof — the Ever-Indulgent; ar-Ra'uf

ar-Raqeeb — the Watchful; ar-Rakib

ar-Rasheed — the Concious, the Guide; ar-Rashid

al-Razzaaq — the Provider; al-Razzak

as-Saboor — the Most Patient; as-Sabur

as-Salaam — the Peace; as-Salam

as-Samad — the Eternal

as-Samee — the All-Hearing; as-Sami

ash-Shaheed — the Witness; ash-Shahid

ash-Shakoor — the Grateful; ash-Shakur

at-Tawwaab — the Accepter of Repentance; at-Tawwab

al-Waarith — the Heir, the Inheritor; al-Warith

al-Waasi' — the Enricher, the Omnipresent; al-Wasi

al-Wadood — the Loving; al-Wadud

al-Wahhaab — the Bestower; al-Wahhab

al-Wahid — the One

al-Wajid — the Finder

al-Wakeel — the Guardian, the Trustee; al-Wakil

al-Walee — the Defender, the Master

az-Zahir — the Evident One

az-Zarr — the Distresser

Zul-jalaal Wal Ikraam — the Lord of Splendid Glory and Majesty; Dhu'l-Jalah wa'l-Ikram

AZERBAIJANI

Moslem Central Asia used standard Arabic names. The USSR insisted on Russian-style family names for paperwork in the areas it controlled. They still adhere to the people of the former Soviet republics.

Simply, at name-freezing time a man was asked his father's name, which was turned into a patronymic family name, adding -ev behind I or E, -ov behind all others:

Akhmed = Akhmedov

Ali = Aliev

Izmail = Izmailov

Kerim = Kerimov

Mamed = Mamedov

Mekhdi = Mekhdiev

Salam = Salamov

Zerbali = Zerbaliev

AFGHANI

Among Afghan villagers, women do not tell their names to strangers, so you can get away with referring to your character's hostess as "Ali Hakim's wife [or mother or sister]" if you need to keep the one or two female names for more important Afghan women in the tale. Also, any woman can be named "Noor [man's name]" which means "light of [man's name]." Otherwise, hit the regular Arabic list.

FEMALE NAMES

Hazrat Bibi	Noor Taj	Zarghuna Ghumkhor
Noor Jehan	Simeen Musharaf	

MALE NAMES

Abdul Ali	Dost Mohammed Khan	Nadir Shah
Abdul Wahe	Habibullah Khan	Nasrullah
Akbar Khan	Hafizullah Amin	Shere Ali
al-Farani	Ishaq Gailani	Syed Ishaq Gailani
Amanullah Khan	Jalad Khan	Syed Sher Agha
Babrak Karmal	Khan Mohammed	Ustad Khalilullah Khalili
Bahram Jan	Mohammed Naim	
Bas Gul	Mustafa	

South Asia

HIMALAYAN

The Himalayas are patchworked with many "peoples" who use the same names and language, but who practice different religions; as when one group has not embraced Buddhism, and so can act as a caste of meat-slaughterers for others. For naming, this is as important as the difference between New Jersey farmers and New Jersey factory workers.

Names are usually two-part, but both are personal names. Where Sherpas and other Tibetans have fled to Nepal or Bhutan, they do not use family names. Norbu Tashi can be the son of Chamji Phuti and Ang Sherpa, and the father of Lhakpa Chopka and Mingma Tsering. Many names are unisex, and I suspect any appearance of gendering to be the result of the smallness of the sample.

The Himalayan kingdom of Bhutan is ethnically close to the Tibetans, with similar naming habits. Except for royalty and a few noble families, there are no family names. People use two names normally, but neither is inherited. Of course, in this case women change nothing about their two personal names when they marry. Children's names are normally unrelated to either parents. Some use their village name, or a short form of it as an place-name eke-name; in this case, the eke-name comes first, followed by the personal names. When Bhutanese go abroad, as usual the bureaucracy that cannot stand a lack of family name usually drafts the second of the two personal names to be the family name.

The word for prince is Dasho, for princess Ashi; they are worn at the front of the name. If no one tells you, it is easy to mistake these titles for names. The actual title for the ruler is *druk gyalpo*, "dragon king."

FEMALE NAMES

Ang	Chhoden	Dem
Chamji	Chopka	Dolma
Changi	Dechen	Doma

Dorji	Phuti	Tsomo
Kesang	Sherpa	Wangmo
Lhakpa	Sonam	Yangki
Pema	Tieyung	Yudron
Pemkili	Tshering	Zangmo

MALE NAMES

Abu	Jigme — popular in upper	Rinzing
Adap	classes	Rita
Ang	Kami	Sahrma
Apa	Leki	Sherap
Bajimaya	Lhakpa	Sherpa
Dakpa	Lhendup	Shigpo
Dasho	Lobsang	Singye
Dawa	Mingma	Sonam
Dendu	Namgyal	Srongtsen
Dole	Nawang	Surkhang
Dordrum	Ngawang	Syam
Dorji, Dorje	Nima	Targye
Drugom	Norbor	Tashi
Dugtsho	Norbu	Temba
Gampo, Gompo, Gempo	Norgay	Tenzing
Garma	Palden	Tseri
Gesar	Pasang	Tsering
Gyalu	Pema	Tsewang
Gyalzen, Gyelzen	Phajo	Ugyen
Hari	Phurba	Wangdi
Jangbu	Rampa	Zangmo

FAMILY NAMES

Dorji — noble family of Bhutan; high officials and professionals
Wangchuck — royal family of Bhutan

NEPALESE

Ethnic Nepalese are also found in the southern lowlands of Bhutan, an important point of cultural unrest. Their names are versions of Sanskrit Indian names — Lal combinations, Arjun for Arjuna. Nepal itself is 89.5 percent Hindu, 5.3 percent Buddhist, and 2.7 percent Moslem.

Under long-term British influence, the family name comes last, for men preceded usually by two personal names, or a two-part personal name. The famous Gurkha soldiers of the British and Indian armies are Nepalese; the country was formed by the expansion of the kingdom of Gorkha.

FEMALE NAMES

Aishwarya	Maya	Rana
Devaladevi	Rajendralakshmi — queen	Tripurasundari
Kantavati	of King Rajendra	
Lakshmidevi, Laxmi Devi	Rajya	

MALE NAMES

Abhiman	Gyanendra Bir Bikran	Ram
Akam	Shah	Rama
Amar Singh	Hem Narayan	Rana Bahadur
Amarjang	Hemanta Raj	Rana Jang
Ari	Jagat Jang	Ranajit
Babu Ram	Jang Bahadur	Ranbir Singh
Badri Prasad	Jayajyotir, Jaya Jyotir	Ranoddip Singh
Bal Bahadur	Jayaprakasa, Jaya Prakasa	Ratna
Bala Narasimha	Jayasthiti, Jaya Sthiti	Raymalla
Barta	Juddha	Ripu
Bhim, Bhimsen	Lokendra Bahadur	Rishikesh
Bhuwan Lal	Madan	Roop Singh
Bikram	Mahendra — king	Sahana
Bir	Mahesh Chandra	Shankar Kumar
Bishnu Bahadur	Man Mohan	Sher Bahadur
Bishweshwar Prasad	Mani Lal	Siva Simha, Sivasimha,
Chandra	Marichman Singh,	Shiva Simha
Chandra Shamsher	Marich Man Singh	Sri Lal
Damodar	Mathbar Singh	Subarna
Dev	Matrika Prasad	Surendra Bikram
Devi Prasad	Men Bahadur	Surya Bahadur
Dilli Raman	Mohan	Tej Narasimha
Dravya	Nanda Lal	Thakur Chandan
Fateh Jang	Nanda Ram	Thaman Gurung
Gadul Shumsher Jang	Nar Bhupal — king	Tribhuvan
Gagan	Padma	Trilokya
Ganehman, Ganesh Man	Pradymna	Vidya Bir Singh
Girija Prasad	Pratap Singh	Yadav Prasad
Girvan Yuddha — king	Prithvi Narayan — king	Yaksh Malla
Gyanendra — a prince;	Rajendra Bikram — king	

FAMILY NAMES

Adhikari	Joshi	Rana
Agrawal	Kansakar	Regmi
Bahadur	Karan	Sapkota
Baraith	Koirala	Shah — royal family
Basnyat — old nobility	Kunwar	Shaha
Bhandari	Manandhar	Shamsher
Bhattarai	Mishra	Shresthra
Chand	Pande — old nobility	Singh
Choutariya — old nobility	Pant	Thapa — old nobility
Jha	Pradhan	Upreti

INDIAN

Take India in the complete sense of the subcontinent, and this covers a great many ethnic, linguistic and tribal groups. Even if you cut out Pakistan and Bangladesh as following Arabic nomenclature, there is still no unity in Bharata (the native name for the nation of India).

There are Hindus, Moslems, Christians, Jews, and pagans of tribal religions. The major language-groups include Indo-Aryan and Dravidian, dividing roughly on a north-south basis. Even if two groups are both Hindu and speak Indo-Aryan languages, they may still use names which to an Indian are notably different.

Obviously, this in detail would require volumes. Here is enough for a fiction writer whose characters are Hindu or Moslem, Kashmiri or Tamil, and a sort of generalized Indian, as well as Sikhs, and to help the rest of you recognize and use them.

Think of the name-groups like the draping of the Indian sari. Hindi is like the nivi or National style; it can be worn by a woman from anywhere in India. Normally, only a Maratha woman wears the Maharastrian bifurcate drape, and a Coorg woman their well-wrapped style. Women of Kashmir can wear saris, or their own distinctive gowns. Like this, Kashmiri characters can have generally Indian names, or specifically Kashmiri forms. However, in Moghul days, a Kashmiri belle will only be found in gown and veil, and only in a Kashmiri name.

Equally, in today's India, on the fancy of a parent, a name may be given a child from anywhere in the country, just as the mother may decide to wear the three-pleated Bengali drape for a bit of novelty or exotica. Several baby-name books from India do not even point out that a name like Ahmed is from Islam. Others are so precise as to have separate listings for religious Hindu and general Indian names, while quite omitting Moslem names. Which did your character's parents use?

On top of this, during the Hindu marriage ceremony, the groom has the privilege of re-naming his new wife. Extremely handy if the bride has the same name as his mother, or the girl dislikes her name. This functions to separate her from her old life and allegiances, since Indians often lack family names to change.

HINDI NAMES

Orthodox Hindus read their paurans (Vedic or mythological texts) daily as a religious exercise. Pauranic (mythological) names are quite common, as children are named for the many incarnations of divine beings, who are the heroes of the *Mahabharata* and the *Ramayana*. See the Early Sanskrit chapter in the Ancient section.

There are many compound personal names in use: Ram Das, Govind Lal, Banarasi Prasad, and the like. The first name is usually that of a God or Goddess, or an aspect thereof.

SECOND NAMES

Bakash, Baksh: blessing from ____
Das: slave of ____ (given to boys only)
Datta: provided by ____; may be Dutta or Dutt
Dev/Devi: ____ is God (m/f endings)
Din: provided by ____
Kumar/Kumari: ____
Lal: child in Sanskrit, jewel in Urdu
Mal, Mala: garland (girls only)
Nandan: son of ____
Nandini: daughter of ____
Nath: ____ is master
Pati: wife of ____
Prasad: gift from ____
Raj: ____ is king (given to boys only)
    Rao, Rau, Ray, Roy, Rai, Rae
Sevak: servant ____ (given to boys only)
Singh: ____ is the best (given to boys only); Sinha Sut
Vallabh: wife of ____
Var: husband of ____; sometimes Vir
Vati: female only

Some second names are considered spouse names — Kamala Pati, Gauri Nath, Radha Vallabh, Siya Var — giving the child a close relationship to the Deity. Others indicate that the child is the offspring of the God: Devaki Nandan, Pavan Sut, Janak Nandini.

These secondary elements do not always have God-names in front of them. That place can be taken by pilgrimage towns and holy places, especially if the parents feel that the pilgrimage provided the child: Kashi Nath, Banarasi Das, Gangotri Prasad. Alternately, if you check into Hindu astrology, you can use the names of planets and signs: Swati Dutta, Mekh Chand, Tula Ram, Tisya Dutta, Mithun Singh, Ashwini Prasad, Kumbha Nath, Mool Shankar, Rohini Prasad, Hasti Mal.

Occasionally, boys or girls may be named for a spousal pair of Deities. In that case the names are always Goddess first and spouse God second: Sita Ram; Radha Krishna; Laxmi Narain; Gauri Shankar.

Many modern names can be considered unisex, like Mishri Lal, "candy child," or Hira Lal, "diamond child."

Family names have derived from patronymics, caste and sub-caste names, in imitation of the British during the 19th century. Family names are usually not the same as "gotra" or Brahmin clan names.

FEMALE NAMES

Ambika
Anarkali — pomegranate blossom; Moslem origin
Anu — little
Bhadrakali
Bhageerathi — another name for Ganga
Bhairavi
Bumati
Chambeli — jasmine
Chamunda
Chandika, Chandi
Chhaya — shadow
Chhotimai
Dakini
Damayanti
Draupati
Durga — Goddess
Durgautti, Durgawati
Gauri
Indira — fem. of Indra
Indu — moon
Jindan — Lahore
Jyoti — light
Kali — Goddess
Kalpana — imagination; modern
Kalyani
Kamala — perfection
Kannagi

Kanti
Kanwal — lotus
Karnavati
Karuna — compassion
Kasturbai
Kaumari
Kavuri
Komal — soft
Korravai
Krishnaa, Krishna — black
Kumari
Kunti
Kusum — flower
Lakshmi
Lakshmi Bai
Leela
Madri
Mahamai
Mahishasuramardani
Mamta — affections
Manasa
Mataji
Maya
Minakshi
Nagini
Nutan — new; modern
Padmini
Paraminta
Parvati

Phoolan
Pushpa — bloom
Radha — Krshna's beloved
Raktavati — blood
Rani
Rati
Rekha — line; modern
Rishabha
Sadhana — devotion
Salani
Samarj
Sarama
Sarasvati — Goddess of learning
Sarojini
Saryu
Satya — true, often followed by Devi
Saurandhri
Sena
Shakti

Shakuntala
Shalini
Shitala — the cool one
Sita — a furrow, earth
Snigdha — warm-hearted; yes, SN
Sonamoni
Sukanya
Sulini
Sumati — unity; modern
Surya
Tarabai — starlight; Rajasthani
Ujali
Uma
Urvasi
Usha
Vayu — Goddess of the wind
Vijaya Lakshmi
Vindhyavasini

MALE NAMES

Acarya
Ajatasatru — one who has no enemy
Amara, Amar — immortal
Amitodana
Ananda, Anand — bliss
Anguri — grape; modern
Arjuna — white, clear
Aryabhata, Aryabhatta
Asha — hope
Ashtavakra
Asvalayana
Bana
Benegal
Bhavabhuti
Bhima — the terrible one
Bhrigu
Brahmagupta
Chakravarti
Chand, Chanda, Chandra — moon
Chandrama, Chand Rama — moon +
  Rama
Chandrasekhara, Chandra Sekhara
Chatur — clever
Chettur — Madras
Chhotu — shorty; yes, two H's
Chunder, Chander
Cyavana
Dadabhvai

Daksh — efficient; modern
Daksha
Dasra
Daya — compassion
Dayananda — compassion + bliss
Dhani — wealthy; modern
Dhirtarashtra — Kaurava
Dhule — bridegroom
Dhuleep — Lahore
Din — poor
Dyal — merciful
Ganesh — God
Gopal — go = cow, pal = protector;
  Krishna name
Govind, Govinda — cow-keeper;
  Krishna name
Gunadhya
Hala
Har
Hira — diamond; modern
Ishwar
Jagadis
Jamadagni
Jaswant
Jatayu — king of birds
Jawahar — jewel
Jayadeva
Jhanda — flag; modern

Jwala —flame
Kahoda
Kanada
Kapila
Karam — action, energy
Katyayana
Krishan
Krsna, Krishna
Kusika
Lajpat
Lakshmana
Madhava — Lord of Lakshmi; Krishna name
Madhavacharta
Madhusudana, Madhusudan, Madhu Sudan — slayer of the demon Madhu; Krishna name
Maha — great
Mahadaji
Mahava
Megh — cloud
Meghaduta — cloud messenger
Mishri — candy; modern
Mohun
Motilal
Nain Sukh — eyes' delight
Nakshatra — celestial light, star
Nakula
Narayana — one name of Vishnu; Krishna name
Nasatya
Navin — novel, new; modern
Pandu
Panini
Patanjali
Pramod — rejoicing
Pravarasena
Prem — love
Purshottama — supreme being; Krishna name
Raghu
Raghunath

Ragoba
Rajendra
Rameshwara — Rama as God; Rama + Ishwara
Ranjan
Ranjit
Ravi
Ruldu — wallower in dir"
Rura — dungheap
Sahadeva
Sandracottos
Santosh — satisfaction; modern
Savyaschin — ambidexter, like Arjuna
Sayana
Shankaracharya
Shanti — peace; modern
Sharad — autumn
Shudraka
Sunder — beautiful
Surendranath
Tantia Topi
Teg
Tota — parrot
Vakpati
Varuni
Vasishtha
Venkata
Vijya — victory
Vikas — growth
Vikramaditya — heroic sun
Vinay — politeness
Vinod — amusement
Viswamitra
Viswarupa — all-pervading; Krishna name
Vrikodara — wolf-bellied, insatiable hunger
Yad — memory
Yogarasa — yoga essence
Yudhishthira
Zalim

FAMILY NAMES OR SURNAMES

Acharekar
Achaval
Adhya
Adwani
Ahuja

Ajagavakar
Anagal
Ashtekar, Ashtikar
Ayyangar
Ayyar

Badakar
Bagchi, Bakshi
Bajpeyi, Bajpai
Banahatti
Bandyopadhyay

Barigai
Barvadekar
Bhagat
Bhardvaj
Bhatavadekar
Bhate, Bhatta
Bhattacharya
Bhaumik
Bhavalakar
Bhave
Chadda
Chakarvarti
Chattaraj
Chaudhari
Chetti
Chipalunakar
Chitanis
Chopade
Choraghad
Dalavi
Dattachaudhuri
Dayal
Deshmukh
Devadhikar
Devarukhkar
Devdhar
Dhavale, Dhebar, Dhibar
Divakar, Divekar
Dongerkerry
Dvivedi
Ganapule
Ganguli
Gaur
Gayakvad
Gazdar
Gharapure
Ghoshal
Gulati
Gurnani
Haldar
Haradas
Harish
Havaldar

Hegadi
Heravdakar
Holkar
Jadhav
Jagatap
Jayavant
Jogalekar
Joshi
Kamath
Kanungo
Kapadia, Kapudia
Kapil
Karamchand
Kashyap
Kayal
Khamavant
Kusari
Limbu
Mahalanabis
Mahanta, Mahanti
Malhotra
Mallaya
Malviya
Mandalik
Marwah
Mayadev
Mehrotra
Mirchandani
Misra
Mudaliyar
Mukhtar
Munshi, Munshif
Muzumdar
Naidu
Nambisan
Nambiyar
Nan, Nandi
Navathe
Nayar
Nijasure
Ojha
Padagavakar
Padhi, Padhya

Panda, Pande, Pandey,
   Pandya
Panikkar
Panja, Punja
Parachure
Parekh, Parikh
Patel, Patil
Patvardhan
Pavagi
Phadanis
Phadatare
Poddar
Prabhu
Rajavade
Randhawa
Ranganekary
Roychaudhuri
Sabanis
Sanyal
Sardar
Sarkar
Satavelekar
Shevade
Shiravadakar
Sirasikar
Srivastav
Talavalakar
Tamhanakar
Tavade
Thakre, Thacker, Tha-
   kore
Tipanis
Upadhyay
Upalekar
Upandhye
Upasani
Vad
Vadekar
Vaikar
Vaknis
Valimbe
Viswan
Vyas

• BENGALI •

Family names were being used by the middle of the 19th century, especially under British influence. These family names originally were patronymics, occupational names, and academic honorifics. Only a few hundred exist. This family name follows the two-part personal name.

FEMALE NAME

Toru

MALE NAMES

Akshya Kumar
Aurobindo
Bankim Chandra
Candidas
Chaitanya, Caitanya
Das'iram, Das Iram
Devendranath, Deben-
dra-Nath

Ishwar Chandra
Iswar Chandra Krttivasa
Jagadis Chandra/Chunder
Maladhar Vasu
Mukkundaram
Prosonno Kumar
Rabindranath, Ravin-
dranath; ravi = sun, +

Indra + nath
Ram Gopal
Ram Prasad
Romesh Chunder
Sañjaya
Satyendra Prasanno

FAMILY NAMES

Bose
Chatterji, Chattopa
Dhyaya
Datta
Dutt

Ghose
Ghosh
Guha-thakurta
Gupta
Sastri, Shastri

Sen
Sinha
Telang
Thakur, Tagore

• KASHMIRI •

Here is a mixed and varied area, which in the 14th century underwent forcible conversions to Islam, and later reversions to Hinduism when the Moguls lightened their religious rules. The Gor are Brahmins who continued to study Sanskrit and the religious texts, while their cousins the Karkuns were getting ahead by learning Persian and going into government service. Karkuns who secretly went back to studying Sanskrit under Sikh rule, without taking up priestly duties, are called Pandits. Pandit is a title, a race or caste, and very occasionally used as a name.

Surnames came into use under Moslem and Sikh rule. Many of these are *kram* names. Kram names can be based on occupation, place of residence, particular events, or personal appearance, like most eke-names. The oddity is both their inheritability and instability.

In brief, a kram name is an eke-name a man got, which was passed on to his descendents who use it like a family name. What differentiates it from our concept of the inviolable and important family name is that it can change at any minute.

A Pandit named Jia Lal has been known by the kram name Gooru, because his ancestors collected taxes on milch cows. Then a meal for guests goes awry, and the rice served is watery. Within the week, he will no longer be Jia Lal Gooru, but Jia Lal Ogra (watery rice), and his sons with him, though his brother down the street will still be called Gooru.

More irritating to their betters, many low-caste types are now using more respectable families' kram names. As these are settling into more rigid family names, the first of all Pandit kram names, Koul, is being claimed by more and more people.

Kashmiri do mangle what other Indians would consider the normal Sanskrit pronunciation of many God-name roots:

Sanskrit	Kashmiri
Bhagvandas	Bhog
Bhavani Das	Bhonu
Chidambhara	Chedu
Darshana	Dashu
Deva	Divu
Govinda	Goondu
Hari	Haru
Ishwara	Ishu
Kailasha	Kalas
Kashi	Kaashi
Nila Kantha	Kaantha
Parmananda	Paru
Sarvananda	Sarvu
Shiva	Shevu
Sudhama	Sodhu
Suriya	Siriyu
Tilaka	Teluk
Vasudeva	Vasu
Vishnu	Veshnu

By the 19th century, most Kashmiri male names are compounded with Ram, Dassa, or Chand; Mal was the only thing in fashion for young women. Older men and woman changed to the honoric endings, Kakh and Ded respectively. Through the 1940s and 1950s, Nath, Krishan, and Lal were almost the only compounders used by men.

Girls used Devi, but married women Vati. Then in the 1960s Kumar and the feminine Kumari took over single-handedly as the compounding words. In the 1980s, parents have returned to classic Sanskrit names.

FEMALE NAMES

Kashmiri	*Normal; meaning*
Arni Mal	flower garland
Boni Mal	Chinar garland
Chandravati	
Daya Mal	
Dhanavati	
Durgavati	
Ganga Mal	garland of the Ganges
Himal	flower garland
Kamlavati	
Konga Mal	saffron garland
Krishna Kumari	
Lakshmi Devi	
Leelavati	
Ranim Ded	
Roopa Devi	
Rop Ded	
Padmavati	
Phoola Kumari	
Posh Mal	Pushpa Mala
Prabhavati	
Santhosh Kumari	
Somavati	
Tosha Kumari	
Tulsi Devi	
Vyash Mal	Yasha Mala
Yambar Ded	
Yambar Mal	flower garland
Zacha Mal	shining garland
Zaimal	Jaimal
Zoon Ded	

MALE NAMES

Ajay Kumar	Pawan Kumar	Sunil Kumar
Anil Kumar	Radhakrishen	Vasant Kumar
Ashok Kumar	Raghu Nath	Vinod Kumar
Bansi Lal	Raj Kumar	
Brij Lal	Ramkrishen	
Dayakrishen	Roopkrishen	
Girdhari Lal	Saneh Kumar	
Kiran Kumar	Sanjay Kumar	
Makhan Lal	Sharad Kumar	
Narender Kumar	Shyam Lal	

FEMALE MOSLEM NAMES

Ashu — better class	Janu	Rahmi
Ashumi	Kali	Razia
Begam — better class	Katij — Khadija	Sitaru — better class
Daulati	Mali	Sundri
Farzana, Farzi	Mihri	Taju — better class
Fazli	Mukhti	Zuni — moon maiden
Hazrat	Pristi	

MALE MOSLEM NAMES

"Abd-al-" is sometimes rendered "Abdul" due to British influence.

NAMES BY MONTH OF BIRTH

Rajab	Ramzan	Shaban

Formal	*Daily*	
abd-al-Ahad	Aohud	
abd-al-Allah	Abu	
abd-al-Aziz	Azizu	
abd-al-Gaffar	Gaffur	
abd-al-Gani	Ganu	
abd-al-Majeed	Maju	
abd-al-Qadir	Qadu	
abd-al-Rahaman	Rahman, Ramu	
abd-al-Raheem	Rahimu	
abd-al-Satar	Sataru	
abd-al-Wahab	Wahabu	
Ahmed	Amu	
Akbar	Aku	
Ali	Aliye	
Badul Khaliq	Khallu	
Bashir Ahmad	Bashu	
Ghulam Ahmad	Ammu	
Ghulam Hassan	Hasun	
Ghulam Mohammed	Momma	
Ghulam Nabi	Nabir, Nabu	
Gul Mohammed	Gulla	
Habib-ullah	Habu	
Ibraham	Ibu	
Jabbar	Jabra	
Jamal	Jamalu	
Kamal Ahmed	Kamal	
Khaleel	Khalilu	

Formal	Daily
Maqbool	Magu
Mohammed	Momu
Mohi-ud-Din	Mahda
Mustafa	Musu
Ramzan	Ramuz
Sabir	Sabiru
Sona Ullah	Sonu
Subhan	Subhanu

SURNAMES OF HINDUS AND MOSLEMS

Akhoon	Khoda	Shal
Bhat	Kichloo	Tang
Chakoo	Machama	Vakil
Durrani	Padar	Vani
Kanna	Parimoo	Warikoo
Kaul	Raina	
Khar	Rishi	

EXCLUSIVELY GOR SURNAMES

Bayoo	Kharu	Rogu
Chandar	Khobaru	Sedha
Chintaman	Kumedan	Shal
Gadva	Lotu	Sharma
Handu	Mandal	Thojnu
Jatoo	Nasee	Vachali
Kalla	Panzoo	Zadoo
Kampasee	Picha	Zoru
Khankhoo	Pind	

EXCLUSIVELY MOSLEM SURNAMES

Aetu	Hagroo	Pala
Ahangar	Kara	Parcha
Andrabee, Andraby	Kashani	Puray
Bacha	Khande	Qadiri
Bande	Kirmani	Qurashi
Burza	Lavai	Rafiqi
Daina	Mahraza	Rahtor
Dar	Malik	Rathar
Drangai	Mir	Sofi
Faroqi	Monda	Tantri
Ganai	Naik	
Gandroo	Nengroo	

Kram Names

Badam — almond, almond merchant
Bazaz — cloth merchant
Buju — old woman
Bula — fool
Cheru — apricot
Choor — thief
Darbari — courtier
Gadva — metal tumbler
Guzarwan — customs official
Hazari — employed by Hazari Pathan
Jalla — fish net
Katwa — professional cook
Kaw — crow, black
Kenoo — wet, watery food
Khazanchi — cashier
Kichloo — long bearded
Kotru — pigeon
Labroo — profits
Langoo — lame
Mota — fat

Munshi — a clerk; used throughout India
Nakab — veil; a family that took up Moslem dress for its women
Nehru — canal inspector
Ogra — watery rice
Raghu — thin and frail
Sas — thick dal recipe
Shair — poetry
Shora — gunpowder
Thalchoor — theft of eating plates
Waloo, Wali — chimney
Wantoo, Wachu — hard walnut, miser
Wazir — employed by Wazirs of Kashmir under Pathans or Mughals
Zaraboo — in charge of government Mint
Zradchob — turmeric trader

• MAHARASHTRIAN •

Maharastrians had patrilineal clan names for several centuries before the British came along. However, only under foreign influence did they start being attached to the personal name as a public matter.

Before then, names were like the Hellenic: you were known to be a member of this or that lineage, but while you might mention the fact, it was not part of your name. This is not so much like being Angus MacGregor, as it is like being Angus of the MacGregors. Consider it subsidiary information in the 18th century and before. Use patronymics, "son of," instead.

Female Names

Ahilyabai
Janabai

Male Names

Dandhu
Eknath
Jananesvar

Moropant, Mayura Pandit
Mukteswar

Namdev
Sivaji, Shivaji
Tukaram

• PARSEE •

The Parsees are Zoroastrian refugees from Persia, when it was conquered by Islamic forces.

Most male names end in Ji or Jee, which may be a separate but attached word, or meshed onto the end of the name. The first name is the personal name, the second name is the father's name. However, this may be followed by a third vocational or caste name.

MALE NAMES

Banerji	Jeejeebhoy	Panji
Chatterji	Manikji	Ranoji
Dadabhai	Mukharji	Rostamji
Jamsetjee	Naoroji	

• PUNJABI •

Normally, names are a compound personal name, not a personal name with a patronymic or eke-name.

The Khatri are Hindus of Punjab who do use surnames. Among them:

Bhandari	Kapoor, Kapur	Sethi
Bhatia	Khanna	Tandan
Chopra	Kochhar, Kochar	Uppal
Chowdhri	Mahendru	Vohra
Dhawan	Sahni	
Kakar	Sami	

• SIKH •

Sikhs use pretty much the same names as other Indians, except that they may borrow a bit more from the Moslem names, since their religion was an attempt to find a middle ground between Hinduism and Islam.

An exception are the Nihang Sikhs. This small sub-culture uses a special dialect for speech. In their vocabulary everything is masculinized, i.e., ghori (mare) becomes ghora (horse). Even for Sikhs their turbans are gigantic, and they go bedizened with lots of weapons. They use names which sound transcendent and strange to other Indians, ones meaning "mountain," "star," or the like.

In female names, the Sikhs use any usual name, but append the word or syllable Kaur, simply meaning "woman." She might have such an obviously feminine name as Sita Kaur, or she might be Shiva Kaur.

Sikh men almost always follow the personal name with Singh as the compounding second element. "Sinha" or "Singh" means both a lion, and whatever is the best of its kind. All Sikhs use it, but so do some Jats and Rajputs; it is not exclusively Sikh.

FEMALE NAMES

Balwant Kaur — strong woman   Tara Kaur — star woman

MALE NAMES

Akash — sky; Nihang Sikh
Amar
Angrad
Arjan
Hari
Jahaz — ship
Jarnail — general; Sikhs use as personal name

Karnail — colonel; Sikhs use as personal name
Nanak
Pahar — mountain; Nihang Sikh
Ram, Ramdas
Samundar — ocean; Nihang Sikh
Tara — star; Nihang Sikh

• TAMIL •

Family names are not used, though the names look otherwise to the uninitiate. In these cases, Tajore Madiazhan Prakasam is not Tajore of the Prakasam family. He is Prakasam, son of Madiazhan, from Tajore: village or town place name first; father's name second; personal name last. Often, he will be known as T. M. Prakasam. Tamil never, ever, use Singh or Sinha, nor the names of demons.

Large Tamil communities can be found overseas, as in Singapore and other parts of Malaysia and Indonesia. At last count, they were about 18 percent of the population of Sri Lanka, too. Still, no family names.

Most of the personal names below are from classic Tamil literature. These are shorter than most in common use.

The traditional name order for earlier periods is eke-names followed by personal name. That is, Irayacuyavetta Perunarkilli is not I. of the P. family; he is "Perunarkilli who sacrificed the Rayacuya."

As in Spanish, Ñ is NY.

FEMALE NAMES

Alamelumangatha-
  yaramma
Auvaiyar
Ceyilai

Kannaki
Kausalya
Matavi
Saudamini Bahulikar

Tiru, Tirumakal —
  makal — woman
Yasoda

MALE NAMES

Añci
Antai
Antal
Antuvañcattan
Atanalici
Atiyaman
Atiyarkkunallar
Atti
Ayantiran, Antiran
Azhagiasingar
Badrinatham
Basavanna
Bittaga
Cempiyan
Cenkuttuvan
Ceralatan
Cettiyar
Channa Reddy,
  Channareddy
Chidemberanatha
Cirutiontar
Colan
Elara
Era Sizhiyan
Eyirriyanar
Ilankovatikal

Ilantattan
Iraiyanar
Iravatham
Iyakkan
Jagannatham
Kane'
Kannappar
Killi
Kovalan
Kovurkilar — -kilar indi-
  cates Velalan caste
Gangamma
Gangayya
Ghanapatikal
Guttika
Madhava, Mahadevan
Magizhanan, Madiazhan
Mal — the black one
Manikkavacakar
Manitikilavan — lord of
  great treasure
Mavan
Naccinarkkiniyar
Narayanarao
Nedunchezian
Netunkilli

Padmanabha
Pantulu Garu
Pattabhi
Perunarkilli
Peruñceralatan
Picirantaiyar
Pillay, Pillai
Prakasam
Putanatanar
Putapantiyan, Putappan-
  tiyan
Rajagopalachari
Rajaji
Ramasuramaniam
Sangily
Sena
Tamotaranar
Uraiyur
Valavan
Veerandra Patil
Venkatacami
Venkatasubramania
Viathialingam
Visvanatham

SRI LANKAN

Sri Lanka, formerly known as Sinhala or Ceylon, is three-quarters Sinhalese. Eighteen percent of the population is Tamil, whether those who came to the island centuries ago when the south Indian kingdoms ruled Ceylon, or recent worker-immigrants from Tamil Nadu. Seven percent are Muslims, with 1 percent other: Malay Buddhists, or the Eurasians called Burghers, who may have Portuguese or Dutch family names, like Dias, da Silva, Willems, etc.

Thanks to British rule, not only are names in the familiar order, family name last, but before liberation the educated classes were using English personal names for their sons: Stephen, Richard, Ridgeway, Junius, Solomon, etc.

The Tamil portion of the population uses Tamil names, which are found in the Indian chapter.

FEMALE NAMES

Chandrika	Pattini	Sirimavo
Kuveni	Sanghamitta	Sugala

MALE NAMES

Ananda	Jeyaratnam	Rajasinha
Anura	Kamil	Rohana
Bhuvanekabahu	Kasyapa	Rukman
Chandrabahu	Kentish	Sinnappah
Devanampiya	Mahasena	Tissa
Dhammakitti	Mahinda	Vijaya, Vijay
Dharmapala	Manavamma	Vijayabahu
Dhatusena	Mayadunne	Wijeyananda, Vijaya
Dutthagamani, Duttuge-	Nissankamalla	Nanda
munu	Palipane	
Gajabahu	Parakramabahu	

FAMILY NAMES

Arasaratnam	Jayewardene	Senanayake
Bandaranaike	Kobbekaduwa	Thondaman
Chandananda	Kumaratunge	Wijeweera
Coomaraswamy	Premadasa	Zvelebil
Dahanayake	Ratwatte	

THAI

Like most southeast Asians, Thai put the family name first, followed by the personal name. However, many foreign writers invert this without warning. As a result, name-gathering is fraught with pitfalls, and many an indexer unwittingly lists a Thai by given rather than inherited name: rather like mis-indexing a U.S. President as Woodrow, Wilson.

Again, like its neighboring countries, Thailand has an ethnically mixed population, with minorities of Malays in the southwest, Lao in the east, and hill tribes in the northeast. Even the Thai dialects of the north are recognizably different from those of the Central Thai. It probably won't matter in the case of your U.N. diplomat or Minneapolis restaurateur, but I have marked the non–Central sources where known.

In much of the north and northeast, by the 1960s parents were giving their children Central Thai–type names. Someone from Bangkok might well have hill-country parents. Others are of mixed parentage. So don't be distressed about keeping the differences too sharp in contemporary tales.

Remember, Thai-speakers in Burma and Laos will be using Thai names, too.

Pronunciation

No two authors use the same system of transliteration into English. Several ethnologists use the Haas system, but this requires a number of unusual characters: the upside down C and E; the tailed N; the Greek E; and the undotted question mark. I have tried to follow the system of the one book that used all common ASCII letters, but was so authoritative as to keep Thai names in their proper order.

Additionally, no one includes the tonal markings, so words that are spelled alike may be very different when spoken. Neither do many sources differentiate between long and short duration vowels.

NG should be softened so it sounds more like a French GN than an English NG. I is as in machine, A as in pasta; U in bun, E in bet. All letters are sounded.

Titles of Address

These are listed in relative order, not alphabetically.

Chuj — Grandparent; old person
Pawchuj — grandfather
Maechuj — grandmother
Nawng — younger sibling; unisex
Baw — unmarried young man
Chaj — Older Brother; married mature man, not yet middle-aged
Paw — Father; adult man of middle age or beyond who has children
Paw Luang — Big Father; village headman
Lung — older brother of parent, uncle

Chaw — younger brother of parent, uncle
Saw — unmarried young woman
Pi — Older Sister; woman not yet middle-aged, married, respected
Mae — Mother; married woman with children who is middle-aged or older
Pa — older sister of parent, aunt
Na — younger sister of parent, aunt
Nawj — signifies a former novice
Caw — male connected with the former royal family

FEMALE NAMES

Bejaratana
Bua — Northern hills
Can — Northern hills

Cancum — Northern hills
Cu — Northern hills
Iamamnuaj

In — Northern hills
Indrasakti
Kaew — Northern hills; fairly popular
Kham — Northern hills; popular
Khamnawj — Northern hills
Khankaew — Northern hills
Khaw — Northern hills
La — Northern hills
Laj — Northern hills
Lakshmilavan
Liangphibun
Lumchuan
Mai Taie — mother of death, amazon title
Mali — jasmine flower
Mari
Mun — Northern hills
Na — Northern hills
Ni — Northern hills
Nop — Northern hills
Nophamas
Nuang — Northern hills
Pan — Northern hills
Peng — Northern hills
Rambhai
Sa — Northern hills
Sachi
Saj — Northern hills; fairly popular

Sajthawng — Northern hills
Samanakkha — Surpanakha in Sanskrit
Saowapha
Si — Northern hills
Sida — Sita
Sin — Northern hills
Su — Northern hills
Subha — character in Pali canon
Sucharit
Suda
Sudbhanthad
Suna — Northern hills
Suvadana
Ta — Northern hills
Takham — Northern hills
Ti — Northern hills
Tib — Northern hills
Tirabutana
Toj — Northern hills
Tuj — Northern hills
Tum — Northern hills
Vallabhadevi
Vina
Walai
Wanthong
Wanwadi

MALE NAMES

Aduldet
Aj — Northern hills
Anuman
Aphaiwong
Arromdee
Asavasena
Bongsamara
Boonsanong
Buasuwan
Buranasiri
Can — Northern hills
Cha — Northern hills
Chaimongkhon
Chakrabongse
Charoenaksorn
Charusathiara
Daeng — Northern hills
Dang
Hian — Northern hills

Huntrakun
In-ta — Northern hills
Kaew — Northern hills; fairly popular
Kham — Northern hills
Khemayodhin
Khoom — Northern hills
Kittikachorn
La — Northern hills
Lad — Northern hills
Layraman
Ma — Northern hills
Mahakamon
Mahamontri
Mokarapong
Mun — Northern hills
Nan — Northern hills
Naradhip
Narkswasdi
Nawasawat

Nid — Northern hills
Paeng — Northern hills
Pan — Northern hills; fairly popular
Panitpakdi
Phanomyong
Phanupongse
Phom — Northern hills
Phoosub
Pradid — Northern hills
Ruangvaidya
Saen — Northern hills
Saeng — Northern hills
Samapuddhi
Sanid — Northern hills
Sarasin
Si — Northern hills
Sindusophon
Sing — Northern hills
Siridej
Smaksman
Snidwongse

Songgram
Songkram
Soonthornsima
Srinawk
Sriphayak
Sriyanon
Steeg
Suwanagul
Suwanajata
Svasti
Ta — Northern hills; fairly popular
Tan — Northern hills
Tha — Northern hills
Thanapradit
Thanarat
Thawng
Thisyamondol
Udyanin
Unakul
Ungphakorn

FAMILY NAMES

Chalie
Chinnawoot
Chira
Chootikmanto
Choowit
Chula
Dhamrong
Kasem
Khamsing
Khuang
Khukrit
Kridikara
Krit
Luan
Momluang Dej
Momrachawong
Muni Mahasandona
Netr
Pantum

Phaisan
Phao
Phibun
Phongsri
Phumpiphon
Pia
Pibul
Pote
Prachet
Prajuab
Prapas
Prayad
Pridi
Prot
Puey
Punyodyana
Rajadhon
Raksa
Sanet

Sarit
Seni
Snoh
Sombhund
Sommai
Sucharit
Sumon
Thamrong
Thanom
Thawat
Titaya
Tongkum
Udhis
Virach
Winich
Withan
Yupho

CAMBODIAN

Like many Asian people, Cambodians put the family name first. So Pol Pot (if that were not a pseudonym) would be Pot of the Pol family. The royal family became the Norodams about the 1890s, since then they have included Norodam Sihanouk, Norodam Ranariddh, Norodam Suramarit, etc. To some extent, longer names go with higher status.

Though primarily a country of Buddhists, there is a Muslim minority. They tend to use Arabic names as family names, such as Abdul-Gaffar Syyed. The occasional three-part Cambodian name is almost always a two-word family name with a personal name, like Mey Kom Pot, Pot of the Mey Kom family.

Khmer is virtually four different status languages intermeshed, each with appropriate vocabulary for commoners, the clergy, the upper class, and royalty. The word for sleep in the four: dayk, surng, sahmrahn, ptoom. A married woman of the upper class is addressed as "loksrery," of the middle class, "nayerksrery." So while gender may be questionable — there is a short list of unisex names — status is very hard to mask. The princess may well not know how to speak commoner in order to pass as one.

FEMALE NAMES

Bopha	Phalla	Sray
Kosal	Poew	Theary
Kunthea	Ponnary	Thirith
Maly	Soas	Vuthy
Map	Somally	Yat
Mom	Sophea	
Moum	Sopheap	

MALE NAMES

Ben	Duong	Monivong
Boret	Eng	Ngor
Chakrapong	Hel	Nim
Chan	Heng	Nol
Chay	Kanthoul	Non
Chettha	Khan	Norindeth
Chhoeun	Khoy	Pean
Chhuon	Kunthon	Peangmeth
Chieu	Matak	Phim
Choeun	Minh	Phireak
Dara Khan	Moeuk	Pran
Del	Mok	Ranariddh
Deuch	Monireth	Rith

Saloth
Samouth
Samphan
Samrin
Sann
Sarin
Sarit
Saroeun
Sary
Sattha

Sen
Sileah
Sim
Sisowath
Soeun
Sok
Sophat
Sovan
Suramarit
Sutsakhan

Tam
Thanh
Thomico
Thy
Tioulong
Vet
Vith
Yukanthor
Yuon
Yuthevong

Unisex Personal Names

Chanda
Chandarith
Chhoun
Lai
Lun Ang

Ry
Socheat
Sopea
Sophal
Suon

Tren — usually male
Vanna
Vannak
Vantha
Veng Kim

Family Names

Ang
Buor
Chak
Chan
Chanthou
Chea
Cheng
Chey
Chhea
Chhet
Chhim
Chhom
Dap
Dien
Dith
Haing
Hem
Heng
Hing
Hou
Hu

Hun
Huy
Ieng
In
Ith
Kem
Khieu
Khim
Khin
Kong
Lon
Long
Men
Mit
Nhek
Pach
Pen
Po
Pok
Prom
Prum

Sak
Sam
Samreth
Sar
Saukham
Sieu
Sirik — royal lineage
Sisowath — royal lineage
So
Som
Son
Son Ngoc
Sosthene
Ta
Teap
Tep
Toal
Tou
Vorn
Yun

VIETNAMESE

Family names come first in Vietnamese usage, before the personal name. Of course, once in Europe and America this got pushed around into personal names first, family name last. This means whenever you see a Vietnamese name you must find out whether it is native or Anglicized order before you can tell which part is which. Help out your readers by having the character called Mr./Mrs./Miss/Ms. in the first pages, or introducing more than one member of the family so the family name in common will show up. Then be consistent.

Up until the 17th century, Vietnamese names usually consist of the family name and a single element personal name. Then there is a transition period, through the 19th. During this, some parents are giving children two-element personal names; elsewhere, some families are adding a second element to the family name. This especially is true of Nguyen, the most common family name. Simply, it was getting difficult to tell the lineages apart. So Nguyen Phuc Dao may be Phuc Dao of the Nguyen family, or Dao of the Nguyen Phuc family. You may also have Nguyen Phuc Dao Trac. Emigrants tend to have the family name reduced to one element, the Nguyen.

Because of beliefs about the powers of names, even inside their families people will be called by nicknames and pseudonyms. If Grandfather's name is Dao, which means "peach-blossom pink," by extension "filial piety," in the family if the word "dao" comes up, a synonym will be used. If absolutely necessary, as in the recitation of a poem, it will be purposely mispronounced so as not to use Grandfather's true name.

There are always other opportunities for alternate names. Shopkeepers in town will be known by the names of their stores. Officials will be known by their offices: Mr. Governor, and his wife Mrs. Governor, Mr. and Mrs. Mayor. Bachelor Trinh is a man of the Trinh family who has a bachelor's degree. A second son may be Mr. Two to his family. All ancestors are given new posthumous names, by which they will be called in family ceremonies. Scholars inevitably have pseudonyms under which they communicate, and publish their poems.

Titles

Thay means father, but it may also be used by a man for his teacher.

Title	English equivalent; followed by
Vuong	prince
Cong	duke; name of prefecture
Hau	marquess; name of village
Ba	count; name of village
Tu	viscount

Nam	knight
Nghe	doctor, as in Ph.D

These are not hereditary as we think of them. They were high honors for the mandarin class, and the sons of such men had certain "head-start" privileges in the government, but the Vietnamese kingdoms and empire were very much a meritocracy. Royal blood was the only hereditary determinant. Vuong was only rarely given to some powerful warlord who was not a royal prince, at which time he almost always started eyeing the throne. Cong and Hau would be normally reserved to military commanders and mandarins related to the royal house. Commoners would normally not be found above the level of Ba.

Meanings

Vietnamese is a tonal language, like Chinese. So any single "meanings" for names are half-baked. Depending on tone, Tiep can mean "quick-witted" or "to continue."

Also, for centuries Vietnam had two languages, the ordinary and the scholarly. Thang is commonly a masculine name, meaning "to win." Yet in the scholarly language it is an antique word meaning "hair ornament of paper flowers." Odds are, a girl named Thang has a scholar father.

The depth of connotation in the sophisticated culture of the scholars makes any reference on your part to a name's meaning pretty chancy. You had better research until you have a real feeling for the different nuances of red, cinnabar, and vermilion, or the aura of "pond" in Buddhism, Taoism, and Confucianism. Otherwise, just treat them as monikers.

UNISEX PERSONAL

Diem	Nam	Thuy — gentle
Minh — usually female	Nga	

FEMALE NAMES

The most-often repeated English personal name for Vietnamese-American women listed in the Honolulu phonebook, is Helen.

Am — lunar, feminine	Bui Thi	Chi
Au	Buu	Chuon Chuon — dragon-
Bian — hidden, secretive	Cai — female	fly
Bua — hammer	Che	Dieu Nhan

Giang
Ha — river
Hanh
Hoa —flower, peace
Hong — pink
Huong —flower
Kieu
Kinh
Lan
Le Tunn
Liem
Lien
Loan
Mai
Maimari
Mi Nuong
Minde
Moc — miniature jasmine
My Hanh

Nga
Ngau — sweet yellow flower
Ngu — sleep
Nguyet
Nu Son — vermilion bud
Pham
Phuc
Quyen
Te Que
Thang — hair ornament
Thanh — brilliant
Thao — courtesy, respects parents
Thi — poem
Thi Chinh
Thi Diem
Thi Duyet
Thi Hue

Thi Trinh
Thi Uyen
Thien
Thien Mu — heavenly lady
Tho
Thuoc
Tien Dung
Trac
Trang
Trinh
Trinh Kiet
Truc — wish
Trung
Tuyen — angel
Tuyet — snow
Uyen — graceful, harmonious
Xuan

MALE NAMES

An — peace, security; safety
An Ton
Anh — peace, safety
Ba — often first element for oldest son
Ba Quat
Ba Trac
Bach
Bao
Bay — seven
Binh — piece
Binh Kiem
Bo
Bo Lilnh
Boi Chau
Cadao — folk song
Can — caution
Canh Thac
Cham — hard worker
Chi
Chien
Chieu Thong; Chieu Ton
Chim — bird
Co
Coi
Cong

Cong Tru
Cu Tam
Cuc
Cung
Cuong
Da
Dai
Dan — cinnabar red, loyalty
Dang Doanh
Dang Dung
Dao — peach-blossom pink, filial loyalty
Dat
Diey
Dinh — settle down
Dinh Chi
Dinh Dat
Dinh Diem
Dinh Ho
Dinh Phung
Doanh
Dong — vermilion, love
Du
Duc
Duc Ung
Duc Y

Duoc — moral
Duong
Duy Ninh
Duy Phuong
Duy Tan
Duyet
Gan — to be near
Gia
Giang
Giong
Hai — sea
Hai Tham
Ham Nghi
Hanh
Hau Hop
Hieu — respect
Ho
Hoa Tham
Hoan
Hoang — completed
Hong — red, royal, strong
Huan Trung
Hue
Hung — hero's spirit, brave
Hung Vuong

Huu
Huu Mo
Huy — glorious
Huy On
Huy Thuc
Huyen
Hy Tu
Kha
Khac Khoan
Khac Tuy
Khai
Khanh
Khi
Khoi
Kiem
Kim — gold, golden
Kim Dam — golden
　pond
Kinh Tong
Koang
Lap — independent
Le
Linh
Loc
Loi
Long
Lu
Luan
Ly
Man Giac
Mang
Mat
Min
Muoi
Nghia
Ngoc
Ngon Tong
Nguyen
Nhan An
Phu
Phuc Hai
Phung Than
Phuong
Quang

Quang Bi
Quang Ham
Quang So — place of
　light
Quang Trung
Quat
Quoc
Quoc Tuan
Quy Don
Quyen
Quynh
Sach
Sam
Si Lien
Su Manh
Tac
Tai — talent
Tam — third
Tat
Thai
Thai To
Thai Ton
Thai Tong
Than
Than Nong
Thang — to win
Thanh
Thanh Gian
Thanh Thai
Thanh Ton
Thatch
The Ngu
The Ton
Thi
Thien — smooth
Thieu
Thiha
Thuan — gentleness
Thuan Can
Thuc Phan
Thuong
Tien
Tiep — quick-witted, to
　continue

Tin — to think
To
Toan
Ton Quyen
Tong
Tran
Tran Thieu
Trang
Tri
Tri Phuong
Trieu
Trieu Da
Trinh
Trong Kim
Trong Phu
Truong To
Tu
Tu Duc
Tu Nghi
Tuan — goes smoothly
Tue
Tung — tree, calmness
　and dignity
Tuong
Tuong Duc
Tuyet
Uong
Ut
Uyen
Van
Van Khue
Van Sieu
Van Son
Van Thai
Van Tu
Van Tuyen
Viet
Vinh
Vo
Vu
Vuong
Xuan

FAMILY NAMES

An
Bui
Cao

Chau
Chu
Dam

Dan
Dang, Dang Tran
Dao

Dho	Le [lay]; Le Van	Thang
Diem	Luong	Thanh
Diep	Luu, Lu	Thi
Ding	Ly [lee]	Thich
Dinh [ding]	Mac; Mac Kinh	Thoi
Do	Minh	Thuc
Doan	Ngo	Tin
Du	Nguyen, Nguyen Dinh,	To
Duong	Nguyen Trieu, Nguyen	Tran [trun, chan]
Giap	Phuc	Trieu
Ha	Nhan	Trinh [tring, ching]
Han	Nhieu	Trung
Hien	Nhu	Truong
Ho	Pham	Tu
Hoa	Phan	Tuan
Hoang [hwong]	Phat	Van
Hua	Phung	Vi
Huynh [hwing]	Quang	Vo
Kha	Ta	Vu; Vu Van
Khanh	Tan	Vuong
Ky	Tang	Xuan

LAOTIAN

There are more Laotians in northeast Thailand than in Laos, if you restrict that word to the *Lao Lum*, the valley Lao, who make up from one-third to a half of the Laotian population. Many of the highland Laotians do not speak Lao, and use rather different names. Notably so are the Meo, who have more in common with other Meo on mountaintops in Thailand and Burma than they do with lowland Lao. Like the other *Lao Sun*, or mountaintop Lao, they speak a Miao-Yao language. You will find them listed in the Other Southeast Asian Peoples section on page 246.

So be careful which name you use for whom. Otherwise it is like having your Hispanic-American named Hans Werfelstein — it takes an awful lot of explaining and needs to be central to the plot. About a quarter of the population are from the *Lao Theung* or hill tribes speaking Mon-Khmer languages, and seem to use names pretty much like the Mon-Khmer Lao Lum, as do the Tai, who are about 13 percent of the population. Tai and Lao can partially understand each other's languages.

Since 1943, all Laotians have had "patriarchal surnames" — male-descending family names that come after the personal name. Many people used their village name for this, or else the personal name of the head of house, or something that seemed good at the time. Family names had been developing among the nobility, like the family of Sisouk na Champassak, who were from Champassak. Obviously, "na" was the "from-word" like French "de/du" or Italian "di/da."

Like England in the 14th century, the family names are bureaucratic rather than natural; they are not used in social address among most people.

Spelling is not standardized even in Laotian.

FEMALE NAME

Chantalone	Kongseng	Phouvieng
Daraphon, Dara	Lai	Saysamone
Keo	Mai	Siphong
Khambai	Mek	Sousada
Khamla	Mok	Tai
Khampheng	Moune	Vilayvanh
Khantaly	Ouanna, Oanna	

MALE NAMES

Anou	Phothisarath	Somlith
Borom	Phoui	Somsanith
Boun	Phoumi — popular	Soth
Katy	Phouvong	Souk
Kaysone	Prayasen	Souligna
Khammouane	Savang	Souphanouvong
Khamsouk	Setthathirath	Souvanna
Kou	Siho	Thongdy
Leuam	Singkapo	Vong
Maha Phoumi	Sisavan, Sisavan	Vongsa
Nouhak	Sisouk	
Phetsarath	Sithone — Lao Theung	

FAMILY NAMES

Abhay — old nobility	Lamphouthakoul	Soukbandith
Baravong	Luangpraseut	Souksomboun
Boupha	Luangviset	Sounthone
Champassak — old nobility	Nosavan	Vathanatham
Chittaphong	Oum	Vatthana — royal family
Chounlamany	Pathammavong	Vichit
Chounramany — old nobility	Phetrasy	Vongkhamkeaw
Insisiengmay — old nobility	Phimmasone	Vongprachan
Keola	Phomvihan	Vongsak
Kommadam — Lao Theung	Phouma — old nobility	Vongvichit
	Phoumsovan	Vongsawat
	Sananikone	Voravong — old nobility
	Sasorith	

BURMESE OR MYANMARESE

In traditional Burma, much in life was determined by the day of the week on which you were born, beginning with your name. In this Burmese astrology, each day of the week also had a temperament and a symbolic animal. Yahu is Wednesday, noon to midnight.

Day	Initials	Temperament	Animal
Monday	K, Kh, G, Gh, Ng	jealous	tiger
Tuesday	S, Z, Zh, Ny	honest	lion
Wednesday	L, W	quick to anger or forgiveness	elephant with tusks
Yahu	Y	even more so	same, tuskless
Thursday	P, Hp, B, Hb, M	mild	rat
Friday	Th, H	talkative	guinea pig
Saturday	T, Ht, D, Dh, N	quarrelsome	naga (dragon)
Sunday	all vowels	parsimonious	kalôn (griffon)

Be careful in the names of couples, as the following pairs of days are considered incompatible, unlucky, and likely to result in childlessness and early death of one or both partners:

Monday and Friday
Tuesday and Yahu
Wednesday and Sunday
Thursday and Saturday

Because your very name tells your day of birth, people shy off from possible mates of the wrong days as soon as they meet. Such matches are highly unlikely, and would be a matter of comment.

Men change their name simply by sending a messenger with simple presents like pickled tea, to all their friends to say that in the future invitations to Maung Pyin should be directed to Maung Po Mya. Women almost never change their names, since this would be an implied criticism of their parents, or show themselves dangerously independent of thought.

Men also change their names on entering the Buddhist priesthood, which they do in their early or middle teens as a normal progression to adulthood. These names are also chosen by the day of the week of birth. So Ôn Gyi may become Adesa, but not Pyinya-Zawta.

Maung literally means "brother" and functions like Mr., as Ma does for Ms.— they do not differentiate between Miss and Mrs. Mé might be used for an older woman, as Mi is for young women, and those for whom one has special affection. Mi Mi is the equivalent of "sweetheart." In male titles there is a wealth of meaning and variation. Ko indicates friendship, or is used to honor age or dignity. Nga indicates the superiority of the user. Shwe indicates politeness or affection, but like Po or Ba can be used towards anyone but the loftiest without offense. If you cannot study Burmese palace etiquette, just lay on the obsequiousness in English.

NORMAL FEMALE NAMES

A Si — in a row
A Yi — smiling
Aye
Aye Shwe
E — cold
Eing Saung — house keeper
Ganda — sweet voice
Gyi
Hein — growler
Hin Aye — cool as dew
Hmwe — fragrant
Khaing — sprig
Khin — lovable
Khin Su
Kwe Yo — dog's bone
Le
Lon — round
Mama Gyi

Mami
Mè Nyo — dusky maiden
Mi Meit — affection
Mi Mi — sweetheart
Mya Mya
Mya Shwe — golden emerald
Mya Thin — fragrant emerald
Myat Kyi — noble and clear
Myo
Nat Thami — heavenly damsel
Ne Htun — sunshine
Ngwe Yin
Nu — tender
Ohn
Ohn Kyi

Pan Gaing — spray of flowers
Pusu
Saw Bomi
Sein Ta-Hsok — cluster of diamonds
Shin Gwe Ni
Shin Thuza
Shwe Gôn
Sin Sawbu
So — naughty
Te Gyo — decoy pigeon
Thaw — noisy
Thin — learned
Tin Tin Thuong
Waing Hla — all-around pretty
Yôn — rabbit

NORMAL MALE NAMES (LU NAAMÉ)

An
At Ni — red needle
Aung Zan
Ba Tu — like father
Bo Gale — little officer
Bogyoke Aung San
Chien
Chit Khaing
Chit U
Du Wun — pole star
Gauk — crooked
Gyi — big
Hkyaw Hpe — celebrated father
Hla Aung
Hla Bu
Hno — hate
Ho — yonder
Hpe — satin
Hpo Nya

Htun Aung, Htoon Aung
Kutha Min
Kutha Yaza
Kya-gyi
Kyaung — cat
Kyaw Din
Kyet-hpa — cock
Lu Pe
Lu-gale — little man, boy
Maung — brother
Mu
Mya — emerald
Myaing
Myin — horse
Nge — small, tiny
Ngwe Khaing — silver sprig
Ngwe Yin
Nyein Maung
Ohn, Ôn — cocoanut

Paw Tun
Pè
Po — grandfather
Po Myat
Po Shan
Po Si — grandfather oil
Po Sin — grandfather elephant
Pyant
Pyin — stupid
Sai Long
San Lin
San Nyun — beyond compare
San Ya
Sett Khaing
Shwe — gold, golden
Shwe Thaik
Si — oil
Sin — elephant

Taik Wan
Taik-kyet — game-cock
Te-gyet — decoy cock
Tha Byaw
Tha Htun Aung
Tha O
Tha Zan
Thakin Nu

Than — million
Thet Hnan
Thet She — long life
Thibaw Min
Thiri Raza
Tin Tut
U — old
U O — old pot

U Po Mya — old grand-
   father emerald
U Tin Tut
U Yauk — old individual
Yewun Min
Yo — honesty

MONK'S NAMES (BWÈ)

Adesa
Bamèsoda

Bedaseinda
Koona-lingala

Pyinya-Zawta

A great many names, not in common use, but found in legendry and drama, are transliterations from Indian names, in connection with Buddhist legends.

ELEGANT FEMALE NAMES

Amaya
Barani
Keinnayi
Madi
Mèbadda
Ommadhanti
Pabhawadi

Palèthwè
Papawadi
Pyinasarupa
Selinsupaya
Supayalat
Thanbula
Thubadda

Thudhammasari
Thukethidewi
Thunemadewi
Withaka
Yathawdaya

ELEGANT MALE NAMES

Alompra, Aloung
   P'Houra, Alaungpaya
   (best)
Anatabein
Bimbathara
Buyidat
Bya-ngya-yan
Dhammarit
Mahathamada

Mahawthata
Matali
Menu
Mingadeva
Mintaya Gyee
Nayidda
Nemi
Temi
Tharawaddy

Thawnôtto
Theidat
Thihathu
Thuwunnashan
Wethandaya
Widuya
Yazôtta
Zanekka
Zawtagômma

MALAYSIAN AND INDONESIAN

The area of the East Indies does not follow any neat pattern of ethnicity and borders. Malays have defined themselves as Moslem Malay-speakers, concentrated on, but not limited to, the Malay Peninsula. Hindu Malays form the basis of Indonesia, in what was called the Malay Archipelago.

All in all, there are about six dozen ethnic groups, each with their individual naming systems. Some, like the Batak, have "clan names" that function for all purposes as our family names, in the same position. Chinese have their family names first. European-style family names are common in Christianized eastern Indonesia.

Java is very Hindu, Sumatra very Moslem, Bali pagan with a varnish of Hinduism. Southern Bataks are Moslem, and use Arabic personal names, but Northern Bataks are Christian, with a penchant for British and American names.

Most of the population uses patronymics or eke names. Honorifics abound; many groups will only refer to inferiors by actual personal names. In Borneo, patronymics use the son-word *anak*; elsewhere, the Arabic *bin* or *ibn* is used by Hindus, along with the daughter-word *binti*.

Rightfully it has been claimed that only a native can parse up such names, and even most natives do not know all the systems.

Below, you will find the numerically superior Moslem names for Malaysia and sections of Indonesia, as well as some generalized Hindu and native names. When travelling abroad or emigrating, for a family name either the father's name or a village name will be pressed into service — unless an eke-name or honorific is picked.

Balinese names may include a first word indicating birth order: Wajan or Putu for the first, fifth, or ninth; Made or Nengah for second, sixth, or eleventh; Njoman or Komang for third or seventh child; and Ketut for fourth or eighth.

"Adat titles" are not included, because while I can find lists, I cannot find a description of who outranks whom, or geographic locales for most. Better skip them than use them improperly.

Do not forget that this area also has a large population of Tamil Indians who do not have family names, either. See the Indian section for them.

TEKNONYMIC TITLES

put before the oldest son's name

In Minangkabau

Mamaq si ____	Uncle of ____
Paq si ____	Father of ____

In Tapanuli

Ama ni ____	Father of ____
Nai ____	Mother of ____
Ompu ____	Grandparent of ____

In Bali

Men ____	Mother of ____
Pan ____	Father of ____

NATIVE FEMALE NAMES

May have the first element, in compound, of Endang, Sri, Dwi, or Tri, as in Edang Widyastutui, or Tri Susilowati.

Basariah
Harianti
Harsini
Herawati
Indijah
Lisma

Namora Oloan
Nurhajati Dini
Puteri
Ratu
Setyaningsih
Sulistyorini

Susulowati
Wahjuningsih
Warsijati
Widyastuti

NATIVE MALE NAMES

Adipati
Agus Djaja — good + triumph
Agus Prajitno — good + prudence
Apul
Arya
Bagus Putranto — handsome + son
Bagus Widjojo — safely handsome
Bambang Sugeng — safely handsome
Bambang Sumarno — handsome + patience
Bambangsutarno, Bambang Sutarno
Banjang
Budi Hutomo — first character
Budi Setiawan — faithful character
Djaja — triumphant
Djajengminardo
Djoko Susilo — healthy young man
Djoko Untung — lucky young man
Gatutkaja
Guritno
Gusti
Hadi Utomo — primary excellence
Hadikusumo

Hameng
Heru Purwoko — arrow-like
Hutomo — first
Janting
Kartodirdjo
Kasihan, Kasyian, Kassian
Kertanagara
Kusno
Kusumasumantri
Kusumowidagdo
Manginar
Mangunsarkoro
Mukarto
Noto Prawiro — king and courageous
Notowidigdo
Oejengsoewargana, Oejeng Soewargana
Paidjan
Paku, Pakoe
Pangeran
Panji
Prajitno — prudent
Pramudya Ananta
Prawiro — courage
Purbatjaraka
Purnadi
Rimpeg
Santakartika, Santa Kartika
Sartono
Satra

Selosumardjan, Selo Sumardjan
Setiawan — faithful
Sipi-ih
Slamet
Soejono
Soekaryo
Sri Hutomo — core and the first
Srinarjadi, Sri Narjadi
Sudjatmoko
Sugeng — safe
Sugondo
Suharto
Sukiman
Sumarno — patient
Suparno
Suriadiradja, Suria di Radja
Surjono
Surjountoro, Surjo Untoro
Suryaningrat
Susilo — well-being
Suwandi Pendit
Suwardi
Suwito
Tjabik
Untung — lucky
Utomo — first
Utuytatang Sontani
Wignjawirjanta
Wirjosandjojo
Wishnu

FEMALE HINDU NAMES
IN JAVANESE FORM FROM THE *GITA*

Srikandi	Sumbadra	Surtikanti

MALE HINDU NAMES
IN JAVANESE FORM FROM THE *GITA*

Abimanju, Ardjuna's son	Durta	Petruk, clown
Admenggala	Gagakbengkol	Podangbinorehan
Ardawalika	Gareng, clown	Sadewa — Sahadeva
Ardjuna — Arjuna	Irawan, Ardjuna's son	Salja
Aswatama	Judistira	Samba, Kresna's son
Baladewa	Judistra — Yudishthira	Sandjaja
Bima — Bima	Karna	Sangkuni
Dewa Rutji	Kartamarma	Saraita, clown
Djajarasa	Kendanggumulung	Semar, clown
Djaladara	Kresna — Krsna	Setjaki
Drestaketu	Matswapati	Suwega
Durgandasena	Nakula — Nakula	Tjitraska, Tjitraksi
Durna	Narada — Naruda	

CHRISTIAN BATAK CLAN NAMES

Aritonang	Manullang	Sianipar
Bandjarnahor	Manurung	Sianturi
Bangun	Marbum	Sibarani
Butar-Butar	Marpaung	Siburian
Damanik	Matondang	Sidabutar
Debataradja	Nababan	Sidjabat
Deloksaribu	Nadeak	Sigalingging
Gintings	Naibaho	Sihite
Girsang	Nainggolan	Sihombing
Gultom	Naipospos	Sihotang
Hariandja	Napitupulu	Silaban
Hutabarat	Pandingin	Silalahi
Hutagalung	Pandjaitan	Silitonga
Hutahaean	Pangaribuan	Simandjuntak
Hutapea	Panggabean	Simangunsong
Hutasoit	Parapat	Simatupang
Hutauruk	Pardede	Sinaga
Lingga	Pasaribu	Sinambela
Lumbantobing, Lumban Tobing	Pohan	Sitepu
	Purba	Sitohang
Lumbantoruan, Lumban Toruan	Radjagukguk	Tambunan
	Samosir	Tampubolon
Manalu	Saragi	Udjung
Manik	Sarumpet	

Family Names

often but not always Christian

Sunda Islands

Abineno
Amalo
Cunha-Rompis
Fernandez
FoEh — yes, two capitals
Mbulu
Ndaumanu
Ngefak
Nisnoni
NoEmetto
Parera
Ramosowa
Rays-Nggay
Seda

Moluccas

De Queljoe
Kaimana
Lawalata
Leimena
Lutumeten
Manoehoetoe
Maulessy
Noya
Pattinaina
Pattinama
Pattinasarany
Pattipilohy
Pattynarang
Pelupessy
Putuhena
Sahetapy
Sahulata
Sapulaete
Siwabessy
Tuanakoota
Tupamahu
Tupoly
Wattimena

West Irian

Bonay
Dimara
Jouwe
Rumkorem
Wajoi

North and Central Sulawesi

Frederik
Gerungan
Hamel
Kalalo
Kamah
Kambey
Kandou
Kansil
Katamsi
Kawilarang
Kumontoy
Lantang
Lasut
Lempoy
Lengkong
Linuh
Lumungan
Makaday
Mandolang
Manopo
Manusama
Maramis
Marantek
Massie
Meray
Mokoginta
Moniaga
Mowoka
Pakaya
Palar
Panggey
Panggrapan
Parengkuan
Pondaag
Pontoh
Pusung
Rambing
Rampen
Rangkang

Rantung
Rarumangkay
Ratulangi
Ratumbuysang
Rotty
Rumengan
Runtukahu
Runturambi
Sael
Saerang
Sanger
Sendouw
Sengkay
Sepang
Siwu
Sompotan
Sondakh
Soputan
Sumampouw
Supit
Suwu
Tairas
Tamoe
Tampinongkol
Tarek
Taulu
Tenda
Terroe
Tirajoh
Toloh
Tomalu
Tombokan
Tumbalaka
Tumengkol
Tumilaar
Turangan
Umbas
Umboh
Walean
Waleleng
Walur
Warouw
Waworuntu
Wenas
Wollah
Worotikan
Wuwung

FEMALE MOSLEM NAMES

Aminah   Bibi   Fatimah

MALE MOSLEM NAMES

Any Abdul- names you see are a problem of romanization. Arabic SH becomes SJ.

Abidin
Achmad
Adam
Ali
Almarhum
Amadin
Aman
Asnawi
Badrudin — from
  Badr-ud-Din, full
  moon of faith
Bermawi
Besuki
Djamaloe'ddin
Hamzah

Hasbi
Hasjim
Hassan
Idrus
Iskandar
Kamarsjah, Kamar Sjah
Malik
Mochtar
Muhammad
Muis
Nadjamuddin
Nahar
Nasir
Nasiruddin — from
    Nasir-ud-in

Noor
Nuh
Ramali
Rasjid
Rustam
Sjamsir
Sjamsuddin —
    Shams-ud-din
Sjarif
Syed, Said
Usman
Zaineal
Zainuddin

MOSLEM BATAK CLAN NAMES

Batubara
Harahap
Hasibuan
Hutasuhut

Lubis
Nasution
Pandiangan
Pane

Pulungan
Rangkuti
Siregar
Tandjung

FEMALE BALINESE NAMES

Çurpanakha
Giriputri — wife of Çiva

Kalawenara

Ratna — a great beauty

MALE BALINESE NAMES

Bangkal — wild boar
Çiva — Shiva
Erlangga

Gadjah — elephant
Kalékèk
Lemboe — cow

Matjan — tiger
Singa — lion

OTHER SOUTHEAST ASIAN PEOPLES

Many of these have their own area, or even elevation, which is split between a number of countries, in each of which they are a minority. Since the refugee days, when many were fleeing Laos, Cambodia, and Vietnam, they have settled anywhere they can, including North America and Europe.

• HMONG •

Laotian hill tribe, displaced to Thailand and America.

FEMALE NAMES

Chay	Chou	Yer
Chia	Sheng	

MALE NAMES

Leng	Nao	Vang

FAMILY NAME

actually a clan name, put first before the personal name

Cha	Kha	Thao, Thor
Chang	Khang	Va, Vang
Cheng	Kue	Vang
Chue	Lee, Ly	Vue
Fang	Lo, Lor	Xiong
Ha	Moua	Ya, Yang
Hang	Nao	Yang
Her, Heu	Pha	

• MEO •

The Meo occupy mountaintops in Laos, Thailand, and Burma; and speak a Miao-Yao language.

MALE NAMES

Jua
Kong

Thao
Touby

Vang

FAMILY NAMES

Faydang
Le

Ly
Lyfong

Pao

North Asia

CHINESE

Language determines names. Chinese languages all are based on single-syllable words: Wang, Hu, Min, Lam, Lei, Wu. Each "word," as we would call it, is in fact several words, depending on whether it is spoken with an even, rising, falling, or undulating tone. This causes the "sing-song" quality of Chinese speech.

Also, in each of the languages of the Chinese group, in order to express the same meaning, you will have to use different syllables with different intonations. The traditional Chinese pictogram writing is very important for unity among these people: while all groups agree on the concept represented by a sign, when read out loud the same passage will sound quite different.

With that background, you can see that being dead accurate in Chinese names requires that you decide the language of the character's family, and learn some of it.

Don't panic! Since you are writing in English, and most of your readers do not speak Chinese, this level of accuracy would be a matter of deep dedication more honored in the breach. You can handle it as have hundreds of predecessors: pick any authentic syllable. If you feel it necessary to give the English meaning, either consistently call the character by the translated name — Cloud Lotus, Heron Essence, Big Ears — or else you should find someone who speaks the right Chinese language who can give you the proper combination of Chinese and English for the area. You can look no sillier than by naming a Manchu in Cantonese.

Structuring Names

In Chinese culture, the group is more important than the individual. Therefore, the family name comes first. These were set by law in 2852 B.C., though not fixed in their modern clans until about 400 B.C. It has been estimated that about one-quarter of all Chinese are of families named Chang, Wang, or Li (often

248

Anglicized as Lee). All family names come from the poem, *Po-Chia-Hsing*, or Hundred Clan Names. There are actually 408 single words, which became the legal family names.

About 201 B.C., each family was required to adopt a generational name poem of two dozen or so words. So from that time, each Chinese will have a clan name followed by a personal name, with generational name last.

Please remember: Chinese names have three syllables. Referring to Mao Tse-tung as "Mao" does not mean the rest of the name does not exist.

The generational name is important in a culture where a man may have children by secondary wives or concubines far into old age, so that his younger children may be the age of his eldest grandchildren or great-grandchildren. It is important that it be established who is of the elder generation, because an uncle can take precedence in property or family councils over a nephew fifteen years older.

If your character is Li Gong-hu, he or she will be known as "Gong-hu" only among close family or friends. Formally, "Mr./Miss/Mrs./Dr./etc. Li" will be used. To use the personal name can also indicate the speaker's superiority, the equivalent of the boss calling the office clerk "Freddy" while Frederick Wilson calls his employer "Mr. Reinhardt." So a low-class person, like a street vendor, gofer, or waitress will get "first-named" a lot, while those of a higher echelon do not.

Even though the name you are using is actually nonsense syllables, there is no gender problem. Depending on the family, Cloud Lotus may just as well be male as female. It is a Western writer's habit to give the translated "pretty-sweet" names to female characters.

Also, "Ms." is even less traditional in China than in America. A woman's loyalties, dwelling place, life and death are determined by her marital status. She would go through life as "Miss Mang, Mr. Mang's second daughter," "Mr. Wei's wife" and widow, and "Dr. Wei's mother." Businesswomen from Hong Kong in America for decades can still bristle when called "Ms." when they have earned their "Mrs."

Chinese American, etc.

The Chinese are adaptable. In countries in the West, like England, Australia, and America, they will change the order of their names and often add a Western name, as well. Here in Honolulu, the old line Chinese families will name their children Arthur, Steven, Nadine, Beth, or anything else that sounds good. But Arthur Wei and Nadine Mang will always have *two* middle initials, for Arthur Gong Hu Wei and Nadine Shu Tun Mang.

There are situations which result in a Chinese personal name being split into two parts. Euro immigration officials in many places insisted on forcing newly arrived Chinese into their name-molds, making Li Shong-tsu into Mr. Shong T. Lee on his papers, or Shong Lee. Then, his enculturalization still shaky, Mr. Lee would list his child as Hoon Lee, middle name Chu, in place of the normal (to him) Li Hoon-chu.

Secondly, a person in a book may be referred to by his or her personal names, which, if the author never mentions the family name, may give the illusion of a two-part-only name. Many two-syllable names in legendry amount to nicknames or sobriquets, like Lionheart, Charlemagne, or Barbarossa in Europe. They may also be titles, like "Yu-chou," meaning "lord of Chou."

Transliteration

There is a traditional Wade-Giles system, still used in Taiwan, Singapore, etc. In this, the late dictator of China was Mao Tse-tung. There is the more modern fashion, called *pinyin*, which comes out of Communist China, which spells his name Mao Zedong, and is the one current periodicals use. Note that *pinyin* fuses the personal name into a single unit. Wade-Giles may or may not hyphenate the personal name; I suggest you do in your story.

Pinyin transliteration gives your character a modern, People's Republic feeling. It is often resented, and certainly not used, by those who left China to escape the regime that promulgates it. This is a social and political aspect you cannot ignore. If your characters come out of the 15th century, this may not seem to matter, but writing is a business of connotations more than denotations. Wade-Giles recalls older days, even if it is less accurate. *Pinyin* lists also only transliterate Mandarin or Manchu Chinese place-names and pronunciations, rather than, say, Min or Cantonese or Hakka.

Wade-Giles uses fewer letters, consonants doing double duty by whether or not there is an aspirating apostrophe after them. Thus, *Chin* is pronounced more like "jin," while the sound "chin" in written *Ch'in*; *tan* is sounded like "dan," and *t'an* as "tan." Still, whoever devised *pinyin* was not thinking of your readers, either. "Tsing" is written *cing*, and "chin" as *qin*.

It is very common in literature to drop the apostrophes in the Wade-Giles system and also to render initial I as "Yi" and final I as "ee." Equally, Kwan is a nonsystematic rendering of "Kuan"; and so are the other perfectly Chinese names out there that do not fit either of these systems. This is because adventurers writing home, and immigration officials, frequently spelled names whichever way sounded good to them. This is *common* spelling, and you may use that, too. Just be consistent once you have chosen a system.

Some Names to Treat Cautiously

Man-chu means "pure," but it is also distinctively the name of the last imperial dynasty. Using it will make it seem you are lifting names from anywhere. Names of the provinces or cities should be watched for the same reason; that is, don't let a character wind up with a name like Li Shan-tung.

Infamous debauched emperors, credited with all possible vices, include *Kie* (aka *Kui*, *Ti-kui*, and *Kie-kui*), last of the Hia dynasty; *Chou-sin*, last of the Shang; *Yu-wang* of the Chou.

Heartless, depraved, vicious women include *Mei-hi* (concubine to Kie); *Ta-ki* (concubine to Chou-sin); Yu-wang's *Pau-hsi*; *Nan-tzi* of Wei.

Huang-ti is the legendary Yellow Emperor.

Lau-tzi "the old philosopher," also known as *Lao-tse* and *Li Ir*, the founder of Taoism. *K'ung Fu-tzi*, "the philosopher K'ung," whence the Latin name Confucius, aka *K'ung K'iu* and *K'ung Chung-ni*. *Mong-tzi* or *Mong K'o*, is otherwise Mencius. Other notable philosophers: *Yang Chu* and *Mo Ti*.

Wang Mang was a notorious usurper between the two Han dynasties.

THE CHINESE SYLLABLES

arranged for random selection by drawing a common playing card to determine

Initial Consonant

Wade-Giles	*Pinyin Common*		*Sounds like:*	*Card:*
W-	W-	W	w in wit	2's
Sh-	X-	Sh	sh in short	3's
M-	M-	M	m in mat	4's
Y-	Y-	Y	y in yes	5's
J-	J-	J	French j, as in jeu	red 6's
Hs-/Ss-	S-	S/Hs	sharp, as in mass	black 6's
L-	L-	L	l in lit	red 7's
N-	N-	N	n in nip	black 7's
F-	F-	F	f in fit	red 8's
H-	H-	H	h in hit	black 8's
P-	B-	B	b in bad	red 9's
P'-	P-	P	p in pit	black 9's
Ts-/Tz-	Z-	Ds	dz in adze	red 10's
Ts'-/Tz'-	C-	Ts	ts in hats	black 10's
T-	D-	D	d in dip	red J's
T'-	T-	T	t in tin	black J's
K-	G-	G	g in gun	red Q's
K'-	K-	K	k in kite	black Q's
Ch-	Zh-	J	j in jar	red K's
Ch'-	Q-	Ch	ch in chip	black K's
none	many syllables begin with a vowel			Aces

Wade-Giles: No B, D, G, Q, R, V, X, Z, or stand-alone C or S
Pinyin: No R or V
Common: No R or V, no stand-alone C or, usually, Q.

In Common transliteration, Wade-Giles *ku* followed by a vowel often becomes *kw*, as kuan to kwan, kuai to kwai, kuo to kwo, kuing to kwing, kuei to kway; or it may be spelled *qu* (quan, quai, quo, quing, quei) or *qw* (qwan, etc.). Also, hu followed by a vowel may become *hw*; huang to hwang, huei to hway.

Vowel

Wade-Giles	Pinyin	Sounds like:	Card:
A	A	A in pasta	K's + Q's
Ai	Ai	EI in height	2's + black 3's
Ao	Ao	OU in shout	4's + red 3's
E	E	E in men	5's + black 6's
I	I	I in machine, when ending syllable; I in pin, when followed by any consonant or vowel	J's + red 6's
O	O	O in loco, ending syllable O in love, followed by any consonant or vowel	10's + black 9's
U	U	U in tune, ending syllable U in hut, before N/A/O/ or a diphthong	8's + red 9's
Ou	Ou	as in boo	7's (+ clubs Ace)
Ei		as in eight	red Aces
	Yan, –ian	yen	red Aces
Ir	e/i after c/s/z or ch/sh/zh	ER in deter	spades Ace
Ui	Ui	way; Northern	clubs Ace

In Common transliteration, initial *Ui* may be spelled *way*. *Ai* may be *i* if at the end of a syllable, *Yai* if beginning a word. Final *I* is often *ee*. Terminal *O* or any *Ou* may have been rendered *oo*. *Ao* may be spelled *ow*, especially at the end of a syllable, *oi* as *oy*, and *ei* as *ay* or *ey*. Stand-alone *a* may add an H so it is pronounced "ahh" rather than "uh" or "ay."

Final Consonant

Wade-Giles	Pinyin	Sounds like:	Card:
none	many syllables end with their vowel		black cards
–n	–n		Hearts
–ng	–ng	as in sang	Diamonds

In the south, these also may terminate syllables:

-k-	-k		red Aces
-p	-p		Heart Queen
-t	-t		red Kings

JAPANESE

Japanese-American families will choose a Euro first name for the child, and they are not always content with stick-in-the-mud common ones, either. Half of them sound like the heroes and heroines of high-flying romances in the grand style, like playwright Tremaine Tamayose.

However, an elder of the family will be consulted as to a Japanese middle name. It is not the mother's family name. Instead, a child who seems puny will be given a name that means strength or health; a baby that scowls and screams will be given a sweet-tempered middle name. The name in the now little-used ancestral tongue has taken on an air of magic.

Mainland Japanese

Like the Chinese, traditional Japanese put the family name first. So in Japan, someone introduced as "Yama Daiharu" is Daiharu of the Yama family, or Mr. Yama.

Readers can become confused when names have common roots. Not only may they have difficulty separating Yukio Iida and Iwahide Yoritomo, but pairs like Yoshikawa and Kawamoto, or Matsuhide and Torimatsu may be too close because of the "kawa" or "matsu" connection. Check this as well as initials on your names-in-use list.

Girl's names often end in "-ko" or "-ki": Michiko, Kikuko, Hamiko. Boy's names often end in "-ji" or "-ru." The Japanese can be so superstitious about death that words containing *shin*, death, or even *shi* are avoided in conversations. Yet both Shin and Shinji are not uncommon boys' names!

Beware of borrowing store names. The ending "-ya" means "store." An *okazu-ya* sells *okazu* (noodles). "Mushashiya" means "Mushashi's store." Musashi is a perfectly good last name, but naming a character Musashiya will not do.

Special Cases

Entertainers will often have stage names, and they are not chosen at random. Traditional "families" of actors, dancers, etc., will be given this stage name (*natori*) by their teacher as a sign of competency. The family name will be that of the school, the personal name constructed out of preferred roots. As the, say, dancer advances in skill, he may fall heir to a name (they are used much like titles), vacated by the death of the previous holder a little or a long time ago. The highest level of accomplishment will be marked by being given one of the two or three "legendary" names in the family. This star system goes back centuries, in some cases.

Today's birth certificate to death certificate sameness is so simple compared to naming in the feudal period. The upper classes often were known by a set of titles of obscure mutation. Even commoners would bear several names in a life: childhood name, adult name, acquired titles, clan positions, sobriquets, and religious names taken when retiring from the world into a monastery or nunnery. On top of all this, you could get a posthumous name. If you were important and your ghost seemed very angry, your posthumous name could be changed again when you were deified. Adding to the confusion were people purposely changing their names to avoid the law, vendettas, or in order to spare their families the shame of them having become prostitutes or merchants.

Pronunciation

Japanese does not have sounds exactly like those in English. While *Romaji*, Japanese written in Latin letters, uses R and F, in fact the R represents a sound a little more L than our R, but still closer to R than L, and the F is a kind of "rough H" in which the upper teeth do not quite touch the lower lip; and so forth. Those to note are:

A — a as in pasta
E — e as in pen
I — i as in machine
O — o as in go
U — u as in bun but in a short, clipped way.
G — g as in gun, never as in gin
Z — dz as in adze

All vowels are pronounced, including final E's. Each vowel stands alone, and represents a full syllable count: "shogun" would be more properly rendered "sho-o-gun," it being a three-syllable word. Syllable counts are important in Japanese poetry, remember. "Takai" is also three syllables, but the vowels do run smoothly into one another without pauses.

On a slangier basis, in Tokyo's everyday speech terminal U's tend to vanish, so that Chigamatsu sounds more like "chigamats," among other dialecticisms. Japanese no more sound alike from one area to another than Atlantans and Bostonians do, nor a city kid like a country hick.

Polite Address

Here is a way to sort out the "-san" business connected to names: When you are referring to someone in the third person, you may just use the name. When you speak to, or in the presence of, him or her, you add *-san* to the end. This is something like referring to Jackson, but saying Mr. (or Ms.) when you see them. Thus, you may talk about Sasaki, but when you speak to Sasaki, it's "Sasaki-san." These are titles that follow the name.

This is more constant and pervasive than Mr./Ms., as you use it towards parents, grandparents, and elder siblings. If you are on a chummy basis with Sasaki, you will call him "Sasaki-chan," the ending you might use also for younger siblings, children, and grandchildren. Note that males always rank females; a girl will usually call her younger brother "-san" while he will call her "-chan."

There was the yet more honorific "-sama" which seems to have applied to the lesser and greater nobility. You hear it used when watching *chanbara* films and television shows. Also, women will use it with their friends. It's like "one of the girls" at the bridge luncheon saying, "*Dearest* Peggy, will you pass the mints?" In Japanese, the equivalent is "Miyako-sama," "Lady Miyako."

Whenever you speak to someone directly, if you use the person's name there must be some sort of suffix, most safely "-san."

FEMALE NAMES

Aichi
Aiko
Aiya
Akane
Akiko — autumn child
Akiyo
Aomi
Asako
Ayako
Chidori
Chie, Chieko
Chinami
Chiyo, Chiyome
Cho — butterfly
Eiko
Emi
Emiko — popular
Fujiko
Fumi, Fumiko — popular
Fumiyo — popular
Futame
Gina — silver
Ginko
Giyoko
Hana —flower; also, nose
Haru, Haruko — spring child
Hirako
Hiroyuki
Idzutsu
Ikue, Ikuko
Ima
Imaki
Isa, Isako
Iwako
Jun, Junko — obedient
Juri

Kai
Kame
Kaoyo
Karu
Katsuhiko
Kazuyuki
Keiko — popular
Keiyo
Kesa
Kiku
Kikuno
Kimiyo, Kimyo
Kin — golden
Kinte — gold
Kiriko
Kiuei
Kiyohiko
Kiyoko
Koman
Kooko
Koson
Kuki, Kukiko — snow, snow child
Kumiko
Kuni — country girl, rural
Machie
Makiko
Mariko — popular
Masako
Masayuki — somewhat popular
Matsu, Matsuko — pine tree
Michiko
Miki
Mineo
Mitsuko, Mitsiko — somewhat popular

Mitsuyo
Miyoki, Miyuki
Mutsuko
Nachie
Nami, Namiko —wave
Naoko
Naomi — taken from Europe as an exotic
Natsu, Natsuko — summer
Nijoo
Noboyuki
Nobue
Nobuhiko
Nobuko
Noriko
Ogie
Osame
Otona
Reiko — ceremonious
Rie
Rui
Sachie
Sachihiko
Sachiko — popular
Sachiyo
Sadae
Sakuko
Sawako
Setsuko — Setsu can be masculine
Shidzu
Shidzuki
Shigeko — popular
Shio
Shizu
Shizuko
Shoo, Shooko

Sonoo
Soteme
Sumiko — popular
Sumiye
Tairako
Takako
Takeko
Tama, Tamako
Tami
Tazuko
Teiko
Teruko

Tokiko
Tomo
Tomoko
Tomomi
Tooshi
Tosa
Toshie
Toyohiko — popular
Tsuma
Tsuneo, Tsuneko
Tsuyako
Ukon — can be masculine

Yaeko
Yasuko
Yasuyuki
Yoko
Yorodzuyo
Yoshie, Yoshi
Yoshiko — popular
Yukio — very popular
Yuri, Yuriko — popular
Yuuki

Male Names

Aki — autumn
Akinobu
Akira — popular; intelligent
Akito
Asaichi
Atsumichi
Atsushi
Bunichi
Chihiro
Chikai
Daiharu
Eikichi
Eizo
Fujio
Fujito
Genki
Goichi
Hajime
Haru — spring
Haruo
Hatsuaki
Hatsue
Hide
Hideki
Hideo
Hikogoro
Hikotaro
Hiromu
Hiromune
Hiroshi — popular
Hirotada
Hirotoshi
Hiroyo, Hiroya
Hiroyoshi

Hisami
Hisashige
Hiyoichi
Ichiro
Isao
Ishio
Iwahide
Iwao
Jikai
Jiro
Jitsuji
Jitsuri
Joji
Junichi
Kaku
Kakuzo
Kameichi
Kanichiro
Kaoru
Kazuo — very popular
Kazuto
Kazutoshi
Kazuyoshi
Keiichiro
Keiso
Kenichi
Kenji — very popular
Kentaro
Kenzo
Kichijiro
Kiichi
Kishi
Kitaru
Kiyoshi — popular
Kiyoto

Koichi — popular
Kurushima
Kyozo
Magoichi
Makoto
Mamoru
Mankichi
Masaaki — somewhat popular
Masaharu
Masaichi
Masaji
Masakatsu
Masakazu
Masamu
Masanori
Masao — very popular
Masashi
Masato
Masayoshi
Matsujiro
Minoru — very popular; strong
Mitsugi
Mitsugu
Mitsuo
Mitsuro
Munemasa
Munemitsu
Munetaka
Mutsuo
Nagatoshi
Naoto
Naruo
Noboru

Nobuhiro	Shozo	Tomokatsu
Nobuo — popular	Shuichi	Toshi
Nobuyoshi	Shuji	Toshiharu
Rinichi	Sueo	Toshikazu
Ryoichi	Suetaro	Toshimichi
Ryotaro	Sueto	Toshio
Saburo	Susumu	Toshitada
Sadaji	Tadahiro	Tsunehara
Sadao — popular	Tadanobu	Tsuneharu
Sadashichi	Tadao	Tsuneichi
Saiji	Tadashi	Tsuneo
Satomi	Tadayuki	Tsuruji
Satoru	Takaji	Tsutomu
Satoshi — somewhat pop- ular	Takamasa	Tugio
	Takao	Tsugio
Seiichi	Takashi — very popular	Umekazu
Seiji	Takeshi — very popular	Yasuhide
Seiso	Taketo	Yasuko
Shigenobu	Tamaichi	Yasuyo
Shigeo — popular	Tamayo	Yato
Shigeru — very popular	Taro	Yoshiji
Shin, Shinji — popular	Tataro	Yoshimasa
Shinichi — very popular	Tatsuo	Yoshimitsu
Shinshichi	Teiichi	Yoshio
Shinya	Teikichi	Yoshito
Shinyei	Teruji	Yukichi
Shiro	Teruo	Yutaka — somewhat pop- ular
Shizuo	Tetsu	
Shoichi	Tomio	Zenkichi
Shojiro	Tomoharu	

FAMILY NAMES

Most Japanese family names are compounded of an initial and final root. By giving you a table of 52 roots for each, by pulling 2 cards from a deck you have about 2,700 legitimate names in a very small space. Additionally, we are including some very short and very long family names that do not quite fit the table approach.

Initial Roots

*— can stand alone as a family name

	Spades	*Hearts*	*Clubs*	*Diamonds*
A.	A-	Ai-	Awa-	Chi-
2.	Chiji	Chika-	Dai-	E-
3.	Ebisu- *	Eno- *	Fuji-	Fuku-
4.	Go- *	Hagi-	Hi-	Ishi-
5.	Kami-	Matsu-	Maura-	Mina-

	Spades	Hearts	Clubs	Diamonds
6.	Mitsu-	Miya-	Mori-	Mura-
7.	Naga-, Naka-	Nata-	Nii-	Nishi-
8.	No-	Oka-, Oku- *	Oni-	Saka-
9.	Seki- *	Shimo-	Sugi-	Taka-, Take-
10.	Tama-	Tani-	Tano-	Wata-
J.	Ya-	Yama- *	Yanagi- *	Yasu- *
Q.	Yoko-	Yona-, Yone-	Yori-	Yoshi-
K.	Yu-, Yuku-	Za-	Zeni-	Zuke-

Very rarely do Japanese family names begin with B.

FINAL ROOTS

If the initial root ends in a double vowel, remember you cannot have more than two of the same in a row. So while "Ishi" + "i" = Ishii" is legal, "Nii" + "i" = "Niii" is not.

	Spades	Hearts	Clubs	Diamonds
A	-guchi	-kami	-shiro	-take
1	-tomi	-kuni	-moto	-shashi
2	-ta, -da	-mine	-suji	-tani
3	-mura	-to, -do	-ue	-shige
4	-no	-yama	-mono	-kura
5	-hara	-matsu	-nobu	-yoshi
6	-gawa	-nabe	-maki	-saka
7	-se	-nashi	-tsuka	-saki, -zaki
8	-kawa	-bana	-taka	-wata
9	-naka	-mori	-koku	-muni
10	-sato *	-i	-kuma	-koshi
J	-shita	-gata	-bo	-yasu
Q	-uchi	-nouchi	-mitsu	-tomo
K	-naga	-nagi	-zawa	-zuma

If you are not satisfied with the results, try one of these alternates.

End Root	Initial Root
-zumi	O-
-gusa	Shima-
-ya	Shi-
-miya	
-jima, jime	
-ka	
-oka	
-sugi	
-shi	
-gami	

SOME OTHER FAMILY NAMES

Aburaye	Domai	Yamawaki
Adachi	Domen	Yanai
Awana	Domon	Yasui
Chikasue, Chikasuye	Mezurashi	Yasuma, Yasumi
Chinen	Mogi	Yasunai
Chiyo	Nanbu	Yoichisako
Chujo	Otsuji	Yonaha
Chuman	Yamai	Yoro
Dobashi	Yamane	Yuuki
Dohi	Yamanoha	Zakahi
Doi	Yamaura	Zakimi

RANDOMIZING INITIALS

	Two Dice:	*Cards:*
A	1-1, 4-5	red Twos
E	1-2	black Twos
I	1-3, 4-6	red Threes
O	1-4	black Threes
U	1-5	red Fours
K	1-6, 5-1	Jacks
G	2-1	black Fours
J	2-2, 5-2	red Fives
C	2-3, 5-3	black Fives
S	2-4, 5-4/5	Aces + black Tens
Z	2-5	red Sixes
T	2-6, 5-6	black Sixes
D	3-1	red Sevens
N	3-2, 6-1	black Sevens
H	3-4, 6-2	red Eights
F	3-5, 6-3	black Eights
P	3-6	red Nines
B	4-1	black Nines
M	4-2, 6-4	Queens
Y	4-3, 6-5	red Tens
W	4-4, 6-6	Kings

KOREAN

Korean custom demands that you not marry anyone with the same family name as yours. However, a large chunk of people in the area are now named Park or Kim, with deleterious moral results. In no other language group do one or two family names dominate like this. Smith and Lee are positively rare by comparison.

However, if you name your only Korean character Kim or Park, in your reader's mind it will melt into all the other Kims and Parks, and lack individuality. Put it in the Pyon or Chwe family. If you have several Korean families in your story, by all means use one or both of the Names. It would seem odd if you did not.

Never give a character any combination that comes out Kim Chi or Kim-chi. It will appear to be a cheap joke on the Korean national condiment, kim-chee which, like lutefisk and Limburger, requires a certain acclimatization.

A person may be considered to have either two single-syllable personal names, or a single two-syllable name, sometimes hyphenated. La Migra puts it down all those ways, so that is how you will find Korean-Americans labeled. Scholars now prefer to Anglicize it as a single name, Sungno rather than Sung No or Sung-no or Sung'no. Occasionally, there are single-syllable personal names.

Family names are put first, just like their neighbors, the Chinese and Japanese. Family names are a single syllable, which may be only a single letter, like O.

"Yang-ban" refers to the old nobility, who lived to render civil and military service to the kingdom. There were originally six such families or clans; the Min and Cho were a secondary creation. Old titles of nobility were usually two syllables, like Lord Chongnyong.

Neither Buddhist monks nor kings bothered with family names. Just as monks would often adopt a new name on taking orders, so Prince Suyang became King Sejo on his accession. Royalty and yang-ban could name in a pattern, copying the second syllable of the personal name from one generation to the next: Yejong, Kojong, Kwangjong, Songjong. But this was not even common, let alone invariable.

As for the usual shortage of female names: many of those I found listed as feminine, or attached to actual women, were also used by men, like Cho. As in Chinese, gendering did not matter.

FEMALE NAMES

Chai	In-ye	Sook Hoon
Chang-hwa	Kong-ye	Sue-Chun
Chin-dok	Koon Ling	Sun-gang
Cho	Kwi-gang	Tok-kyo
Eun	Kyong-ae	Ui-son
Ham-bu	Min	Ye
Hye	O	Yom
Im	Sim	Yondok
In	So-so-no	Yong Ae
Inpang	Sook	Yun Sook

MALE NAMES

An
Anin
Bunsuk, Bun-suk, Bun Suk
Cha
Chae
Chaek
Chagyom, Cha-gyom, Cha Gyom
Changson, Chang-son
Che
Chehyon
Chi
Chibaek
Chigyong, Chi-gyong
Chihyo
Chik
Chisang
Chisuk
Cho
Chojung
Chol
Chom
Chong
Chongnyong — settling the peace
Chonhung
Chonhyok
Chonjung
Chul
Chun
Chunbu, Chun-bu
Chungbu, Chung-bu, Chung Bu
Chunggwi, Chung-gwi
Chunghwa
Chungnyol, Chung-nyol
Chungwi
Chungwon, Chung-won
Dai
Gi
Hae
Hanbo
Hang
Hoe
Hon
Hongyun, Hong-yun
Huian, Hui-an
Huichun, Hui-chun

Hwa
Hwal
Hwang
Hyang
Hyon
I
Igum, I-gum
Inchi, In-chi, In Chi
Ingyu, In-gyu
Inim, In-im
Inji
Injo, In-jo
Injong, In-jong
Irom, I-rom
Iryon, Ir-yon
Iso
Ja
Jewu, Je-wu, Je Wu
Kaesin
Kan
Kasin
Ki
Kilpo, Kil-po
Kimun
Ko
Koeng, Ko-eng
Kojong
Kongin, Kong-in, Kong In
Kongmin
Kongsu, Kong-su
Kongui, Kong-ui
Kugui, Ku-gui
Kukkyom, Kuk-kyom
Kun
Kwan
Kwangju, Kwang-ju
Kyebang, Kye-bang
Kyeryang, Kyer-yang
Kyong
Kyongchong
Kyongdok
Kyubo, Kyu-bo
Malli
Mongju, Mong-ju
Munbu, Mun-bu
Nam
Okkun, Ok-kun, Ok Kun

Onjok, On-jok
Paeksun, Paek-sun
Paengnyon, Paeng-nyon
Panggyong, Pang-gyong
Pin
Po
Ponghan, Pong-han, Pong Han
Pusik, Pu-sik, Pu Sik
Pyunghi, Pyun-ghi, Pyun Ghi
Saek
Sammun, Sam-mun, Sam Mun
Sang
Se
Sebung
Sejong, Se-jong, Se Jong
Shihung, Shi-hung, Shi Hung
Shukcho, Shuk-cho, Shuk Cho
Sisup
Sollo
Songgye, Song-gye, Song Gye
Songhui, Song-hui, Song Hui
Songji
Songmyong, Song-myong
Songsin
Songsu
Sookyung, Sook-yung, Sook Yung
Su Yeong
Suhan
Suk
Sukchu
Sukkwon, Suk-kwon
Sumun
Sun
Sung Ho
Sung Hyuk
Sungno
Sungsoo, Sung-soo, Sung Soo
Sunmyung, Sun-myung, Sun Myung
Sunsin, Sun-sin, Sun Sin

Syngman, Syng-man,
   Syng Man
Taesu
Taesung
Taewon, Tae-won, Tae
   Won
Tak
Tojon
Ton
Tongmyong
Uichon
Uijong

Unbo
Ung
Wan
Wi
Wibo
Wije
Wongyok
Wonjun
Wonjung
Yakhae, Yak-hae
Yon
Yong

Yonggyon, Yong-gyon
Yongsil
Yongyu
Yonwon
Yop
Yuet Kuen
Yulgok
Yumon
Yun
Yun Ja
Zachyo

Family Names

Am — yang-ban
An
Cha
Chae
Chai
Chan
Chang
Chi
Cho — yang-ban
Choe
Chong — yang-ban
Chu
Chwe — yang-ban
Ha
Han
Her
Heu
Ho
Hong
Hu

Hui
Hur
Im
In
Ip
Kang
Ki
Kim — yang-ban
Ko
Kum
Kwak
Kwon
Kyong
Li, Lee — yang-ban
Min — yang-ban
Mun
No
O
Pae
Paek

Pak — yang-ban
Park
Pyon
Shin
Sim
Sin
So
Sol
Son
Song
Tam
Tan
Un
Wang
Won
Yang
Yi
Yu
Yun

MONGOLIAN

Lamaism came to Mongolia from Tibet in the 16th century, and strongly affects names since then.

Many names are unisex, but some are specifically female from Lamaistic goddesses, or because of other associations. A few are considered very male because of historical precedence.

Modern names have been Russified with -ov and -ev endings: Ochirov, Badmayev. Russified family names have been devised, like Bimbayev from Bimba,

Basangov from Basang. Nonetheless, family names are only for the sophisticated urbanized Mongol. Most still do well with a personal name and, when necessary, a recitation of near relations.

Few Chinese elements appear in Mongolian names, but many in traditional titles: ong, which means prince; taiji, heir presumptive; jinong.

The traditional, Genghis Khan–period names will come from the gendered lists; avoid the Tibetanized names. Genghis Khan is more appropriately Chinggis, who held the title Qagan.

Pronunciation is simple. Umlauted O and U are as in German. The apostrophes are only there to show you where to break syllables. Chila'un is said (or thought) properly with three syllables, not two and a diphthong of AU.

A baby may be named by the day it is born. The five names, for either boys or girls, associated with the 30-day cycle are:

Name	*Day*
Dorji	1, 6, 11, 16, 21, 26
Rinchen	2, 7, 12, 17, 22, 27
Badma	3, 8, 13, 18, 23, 28
Liji	4, 9, 14, 19, 24, 29
Sanji	5, 10, 15, 20, 25, 30

For the days of the week:

Nyama	Sunday
Dawa	Monday
Myagmar	Tuesday
Lhagva	Wednesday
Pürev	Thursday
Basan	Friday
Bimba	Saturday

FEMALE NAMES

Alakhchit	Dolma	Khulan
Alan	Dugar	Khu'urchin
Altani	Ebegai	Lhamo
Barkhujin	Gurbesu	Orbei
Borte	Ho'elun	Sokhatai
Botokhui-tarkhun	Khada'an	Temulun
Buyan-tegin	Kho'akhchin	Yesugen
Cha'ur-bekı	Khojin	Yesui
Chotan	Khorijin	

MALE NAMES

Achikh-shirin
Alakhush
Alchidai
Alin
Altan
Altun-ashuk
Ambakhai
Arkhai-khasar
A'uchu
Baatar, Bator — hero
Badai
Balakhachi
Barkhudai
Bartan
Batu-khan —firm ruler
Bekter
Belgunutei
Belgutei
Bilge-beki
Bodonchar
Bo'orchu
Borokhul
Boroldai
Bugunutei
Bukha
Bukhatai
Bukhatu-salji
Bukhu-katagi
Buri
Buyirukh
Buyirukh-khan
Chagatai
Chakhurkhan
Charakha
Charkhan
Chigidai
Chila'un
Chila'un-khaiyichi
Chiledu
Chilger
Chimbai
Choibalsan — single-
   named, Premier in
   1950s
Cho'os-chakhan
Daidukhul
Dakhi
Daritai
Dayir-usun

Dei-sechen
Didik-sakhal
Dobun
Dodai-cherbi
Dorbei-dokhshin
Dua
El-khutur
Erke-khara
Guchuluk
Gurin
Gurkhan
Gu'un-u'a
Güyüg
Hulagu, Mongol
Inancha
Inancha-bilge
Iturgen
Jakha-gambu
Jamukha
Jarchi'udai
Jebe
Jebke
Jelme
Jochi
Jochi-darmala
Jurchedei
Khachi'un
Khada'an — unisex, but
   pre–Lamaism
Khada'an-daldurkhan
Khadakh
Khalatai-darmala
Khali'udar
Khargil-shira
Khasar
Khashi
Khorchi
Khori-bukha
Khori-shilemun
Khori-subechi
Khorilartai
Khubilai
Khuchar
Khudu
Khuduka
Khudukha
Khulbari
Khurchakus-buyirukh
Khutula

Khuyildar
Khuyilder
Kiratai
Kishilikh
Kokochu
Kokse'u-sabrakh
Kuchu
Megujin
Megujin-se'ultu
Möngke
Mongler
Monglik
Mukhali
Mutke-totakh
Nakhu
Narin-ke'en
Naya'a
Nekun
Ogodei
Okin-barkhakh
Qubilai — Kublai
Sacha-beki
Sayikhan-tode'en
Sengum
Sengum-bilge
Shigi-khutukhu
Shikiken-Khutukhu
Shiki'ur
Shirgu'etu
Sokhor
Sorkhanshira
Sorkhatu-jurki
Sube'etei
Sugegei
Süke Bator — axe hero
Taichar
Tarkhutai-kiriltukh
Tayang
Telegetu
Temüder
Temuge
Temujin
Temujin-uge
Tochto'a
Todo'en
Todo'en-girte
Togon-temür
Togus-beki
Tokhto'a

Tolui
Tongge
To'oril
Torbi-tash
Tukhu

Tusakha
Ügedei
Umitai
Yedi-tublukh
Yegu

Yeke-cheren
Yeke-chiledu
Yesugei
Yesungge

Unisex Names

Agvan — eloquent
Badma — lotus
Banzaragch — five saints
Bayan — wealthy
Checheg — flower
Damba — holy
Damdin — horse-neck
Damdin-süren — horse-neck–guard
Dondub — Buddha
Dorji — diamond, thunderbolt
Erdeni — jewel
Galdan
Garma — destiny
Gerel — beam, light
Gombo — protector, lord; Gombojab

Ishi — wisdom
Ligdan
Maidar — festival
Mangaljab — blessing-protection
Ochir, Vachir, Bazar — thunderbolt
Pakva — noble, reverend
Sanji — enlightened one, Russianized
   Sanzheyev
Senge — lion
Shirab — wisdom, intelligence
Sodnam — good fortune, happiness
Tsereng — long life
Yeke Nidün — big eyes
Zhamtsarano

Tibetan Roots Used in Mongolian

-bal — glory, splendor
-jab — protection, help
-jaltsan — victory, trophy
-jamtso — sea, ocean
-lodoi — intellect

-luvsan — good sense
-punsug — perfect
-rinchen — valuable, precious
-san — good, fair
-süren — guard, heed

The Pacific

FILIPINO

Many of the names Filipinos commonly use would be considered exotica in most Hispanic places. Filipinos preserve and use the more florid and romantic fund of Hispanic names. You may find you prefer a Spanish hero or heroine to be named Florencio or Cesaria rather than yet another Maria (María) or Miguel.

Conquered by Spain in the Age of Conquest, the Philippines were both Catholicized and Hispanicized. The short American occupation between the Spanish-American War and World War II had little effect, other than to spread English. The very short Japanese occupation had entirely negative results.

There are many Filipino family names that are not found in other Hispanic areas, because they were originally Filipino personal names. There is more than one Filipino language, so check your linguistic map of the islands to find out where the locals talk Tagalog (the official national tongue), Ilocano (the runner-up), or another.

The bizarre and frustrating part is that the sound "F" is absent from all of them; it comes out "P." Periodically, the Philippines try to find a name for itself that the inhabitants can pronounce, but no one's agreed yet on an alternate. But as soon as they can, the name Philippines will go the way of Ceylon and Burma (now Sri Lanka and Myanmar).

Separating family names by area is very difficult, and will hardly be spotted by Filipino readers. This list is cosmopolitan, and lumps them all together.

After several centuries of Spanish rule, the Philippines were pretty thoroughly Christianized. Virtually any Filipino character can be given a semi–European first name followed by either an Hispanic or a more definitely Filipino family name. Between those two usually lie a couple of saints' names if, like most Filipinos, the character is Catholic. However, there is also quite a Protestant community.

While we use "Filipino" generally, this is a masculine term. A woman from the Philippines, or of Philippine descent, is a Filipina.

266

Filipino-Americans seem to have developed a fondness for naming their daughters Melodie or Melody and Desirée. They use many distinguished names for their sons, like Emerson, Jefferson, Napoleon, and Percival. They select Anglo names with the same qualities as the Spanish ones they took for their own.

FEMALE NAMES

Aida	Eva	Luningning
Althea	Fausta	Marianne
Anastacia/Anastasia	Feliza	Mariesa
Aurora — popular	Fernanda	Marita
Beatriz	Florencia	Martina
Carlina	Francisca	Maysana
Cecilia	Genedina	Myrna
Cesaria	Guada, Guadelupe	Norma
Cornelia	Hermina	Nova
Dalisay	Hilaria	Petra
Dionicia	Ida	Sabina
Edita	Irma	Saturnina
Ella	Josefina	Tatiana
Elsie	Leonora	Teodora
Elvie	Leticia	Teodosia
Ermelinda	Ligaya	Valerie
Estrelita, Estrella	Liwayway	Victoria
Eulogia	Luana	Zaida

MALE NAMES

Acasio	Eleuterio	Nestor — popular
Alipio	Eliezer, Eliser	Olegario
Andres/Andrés	Eloidio	Pacifico
Angel, Angeles, Angelito	Elpidio	Paradis
Anselmo	Eusebio	Rocknie
Antero	Faustino	Romeo — popular
Artemio	Fernando — popular	Romualdo
Babylen	Francisco — very popular	Romulo
Bienvenido	Gregorio — popular	Samuel — very popular
Celedonio	Guillermo	Saturnino
Claudio	Heriberto	Sergio
Conrado	Javier — popular	Tranquiliano, Tranquilino
Dakila	Jesus/Jesús	Tripilo
Delphin, Delfin/Delfín	Manuel — very popular	Victoriano
Derico	Mariano — popular	Vincente, Vicente
Dominador — very popu-	Maximo — popular	Zosimo
lar	Nemesio — not uncom-	Zumel
Domingo — popular	mon	

FAMILY NAMES

Abad
Abatayo
Acelador
Acuna
Agbayani
Aglipay
Allado
Battung
Bayang
Ben
Benzon
Bisquera
Blas
Bolosan
Bulawan
Bumanglag
Burgo
Butac
Butay
Caba
Cabaccang
Cabalteja
Cabigaya
Canoneo
Capina
Capinpin
Cazar, Cazares, Cezar
Celebrado
Cenal
Collado
Comilang
Cuaresma
Cubangbang
Curammeng
Dacquel
Dagdag, Dagdagan

Dahilig
Dang
Daoang
Datuin
Delacruz, Dela Cruz, de
    la Cruz, De La Cruz
Delaroza, Dela Roza, de
    la Roza, De La Roza
Digap
Dimaya
Dugay
Dumlao
Edra, Edrada
Elefanta
Embalsado
Escosio
Fajardo
Farinas
Ferido
Gabay
Gagtan
Galang
Galat
Ganir
Gapasin
Garma
Gillia
Golas
Gorospe
Guieb
Gumtang
Haduca
Herme
Hipolito, Ippolito
Honorato
Hugo

Ibarra
Ibason
Ilaban
Imanil
Ines
Ingano
Ipalari
Lacson
Layugan
Macapuguay
Magsaysay
Magwili
Maligaya
Mangabat
Manibog
Mata
Ng
Nipay
Osmeña
Pacpaco
Padilla
Penaranda
Punongbayan
Quezon
Rodriguez
Roxas
Samiento
Singson
Soriano
Sulit
Tabilang
Tagalicod
Tangalin
Uy
Villaflor
Viray

MICRONESIAN

Micronesia is a scatter of island chains, none too heavily inhabited. Your story may take you there, especially if it is set during the Pacific campaigns of the Second World War.

• PALAU •

Republic of Belau
pop. 8845

At present, rather than fixed family names, the people of Belau are using patronymics. The daughter of Yano Otobed is Ukong Yano, and her brother is Sumang Yano. His son is Demei Sumang. However, married women adopt their husband's patronymic as a surname, so that Ukong Y. Ngiraiuelenguul is the wife of Andres Ngiraiuelenguul. Many Anglo personal names are coming into use, and there are signs that some patronymics are setting into family names.

FEMALE NAMES

Barbara	Lillian	Ukong
Berenges	Mitsko	Ulai
Grace	Romana	
Katherine, Katey	Sandra	

MALE NAMES

Anastacio	Klewei	Remeliik
Andres	Ngiraiuelenguul	Sumang
Belas	Ngiraked	Taurengel
Demei	Oderiong	Tellames
Ibedul	Oiterong	Yano
Kesolei	Otobed	Yutaka

• MARSHALL ISLANDS •

Republic of the Marshall Islands

Like most Micronesians, the Marshallese are matrilineal. For the first few days after birth, a child is called Labburo if it is male, Lijjiron if female. This is very much like calling it Girl or Boy. Then the child will be given a name from its (maternal) ancestral line. Sometimes, people later acquire nicknames which become their names.

What you as writers will hate is that male names should begin with La- or Le-, female ones with Li-. If a name should not, a polite Marshallese will add it to the front. This will confuse your English readers, so once the stranger from elsewhere has picked up the language, translation names will be very, very useful to you.

In modern days, novelty names like Love, Tea, Coffee, Sugar, Sweet, Rusty, and Jeep have been given to Marshallese infants.

FEMALE NAMES

Amenta
Carmen
Evelyn
Justina

Lijalurik
Lijiroul
Mari
Marie

Nina
Tanella

MALE NAMES

James
Kijrik — mouse, for a tiny
    child

Lakilmej
Sylvenious
Tion

FAMILY NAMES

Bikafle
Konou
Langidrik

Lanwi
Lokeijak
Maddison

Matthew
Milne

• MARIANAS ISLANDS •

Commonwealth of the Northern Marianas Islands

Marianas culture was so thoroughly uprooted by the Spanish, that most names in use are Spanish, in the Hispanic form of personal name, father's family name, mother's family name. When the islands were under German rule, some German personal names came into use, but very few Japanese names during the Japanese occupation. American personal names increased in use during the American administration.

A few family names which are not of European derivation may be aboriginal names, either male (which would suit the Spanish) or female (as most Micronesians are matrilineal). Then again, they may be clan names, or place-names.

FEMALE NAMES

Bibiana
Consolacion
Elizabeth
Estefania

Felicidad
Lucile
Magdalena
Maria

Maria "Malua"
Rita

MALE NAMES

Benedicto
Cristobal
Daniel

David
Francisco
Kapileo

Lino
Pangelinan
Songao

FAMILY NAMES

Arriola	Ogumoro	Taman
Diaz	Peter	Tenorio
Inos	Rechebei	Uludong
Kaufer	Rogolofoi	

NATIVE CHAMORRO FAMILY NAMES

Aguan	Gumataotao	Quitugua
Agulto	Hokog, Hocog	Songao
Ajuju	Mafnas	Taga
Alig	Manglona	Taimanao
Apatang	Matagolai	Taisacan
Atlaig	Namauleg	Taisague
Attao	Naputi	Taitano
Babauta	Pinauala	Taitingfong
Chargaulaf	Quichuchu	Tatlahe
Chatfaurus	Quinata	
Gogue	Quitano	

• FEDERATED STATES OF MICRONESIA •

Ponape/Pohnpei

During the thirty years of Japanese control, many children, especially girls, were given Japanese personal names. Inherited family names are being used.

Titles

Titles are used by many adults to indicate their status as landowners or in ceremonial. In status order:

Male	Female
Souwel	Eminalau
Soulik	Kadinlik
Oun	Lioun
Kiroun	Liemin
Kaniki	Kan
Lepan	Lampein
Soumadau	Kedinmadau
Soumaka	Kedinmaka
Nahnawa	Nahloio
Sapwen	Lisapwen

With the name of the piece of land, these take the place of personal names.

FEMALE NAMES

Anna
Bahtsipa
Deresihda, Drechita —
  Teresita
Elwihse
Emiko

Enerika
Kairu — frog
Kesia
Kimiko
Marihne — Marina
Nancy

Patsihpa
Renslina
Rosella
SeNellie
Suhle

MALE NAMES

Carles
Ehpel
Ehsa — Asa
Eluel
Eskiel — Ezekial
Etson
Gideon
Henry, Heinrich
Iakopus — Jacob
Ikin, Ikinas — Ignacio

Kapriel — Gabriel
Karat — banana type
Kihng-en-wel — wild
  rooster
Kitik — rat
Konse, Konsep — Con-
  cepcion
Kutohr — egg
Lamwer — gekko
Leminel — Samuel

Likarak — louse
Penito — Benito
Pernando, Perna, Per-
  dong — Fernando
Pitirik — Patrick
Pwurok — chick
Salipa — Salvador
Sarapin — Seraphin
Singeru
Ywao

FAMILY NAMES

Anson
Elanzo
Henry

Joel
Neth
Peterson

Phillip
Santos
Singeo

• YAP •

If there are several persons with the same name in a village, they will add the eke-names Niga, large, Nitoluk, medium, or Ni'ichig, small. If there should be four or five, there is also Nilal, oldest, and Nibitir, youngest. If someone with the same name comes from another village, there is no problem, as he or she merely adds the village name to the personal one.

For the first week after birth, until it is given a real name, an infant is called Sogau if a boy, Ligau if a girl.

The syllables TIN and PIN are considered to make a name feminine, TAM or MOON masculine. On rare occasions, if a man has no sons he may give his father's name to a daughter, but everyone knows the name is masculine, like a girl named Jack or Jerry.

FEMALE NAMES

Anna — European
Bugulpin
Fagaibpin
Fanapin

Gilibpin
Gilimtin
Kabetin
Kamtin

Mangrpin
Matinag
Ruwamtin
Tinag

MALE NAMES

Bamoon
Bazgiz
Defngin
Falemoon
Gilmoon
Giltaman

Googdu
Mangefel
Moonfel
Moonney
Tamag
Tamangidad

Tamdou
Tammou
Tamngin
Yilbasay

FAMILY NAMES

Falgog

• TRUK •

Compared to many other peoples, the Trukese are nearly as informal as we are when it comes to naming their children. A name will be given a few days after the child's birth, without ceremony. This does not mean it is given without thought. A name reflects specialist knowledge, normally from the child's mother's clan (they are matrilineal), and is supposed to reflect what the child will become. One whose clan has specialty warrior knowledge will have a warrior's name like Banana Flower Is Broken (only warriors may wear banana blossoms), while another who will learn navigation will be named Son of a Navigator.

Less formal names can be picked up by a child, and their earlier names forgotten as a name the equivalent of Stinky or Skinny adheres.

Spelling is not standardized. Y, J, and I are interchangeable, as are the pairs N and L, W and U, CH and TR.

In modern times, some parents on Truk have given their children names like Gold, Silver, Cigarette, Carabao, Happy, Inch, Soda, Lucky, Frying, and Weight, but these should be considered unusual.

FEMALE NAMES

Chein — Jane
Enisa — Eliza

Hiroko
Incsoinal — mother of

breadfruit callers
Mata — Martha

Mine   Tonoris — Doloris   Umiko
Shinobu   Tora — Dora   Yomine

MALE NAMES

Anga — dark bird
Chimw — fish head; animal head; stupid
Enis — Hans
Mailo
Meipung — it is right; just, truthful and upright
Mikaen — Michael
Möreta — banana flower is broken
Mwasetapi — shoe stink; recent
Namaneichipw — elements of divination
Nok — mid-rib on palm leaf; thin and weak
Nounötu — child of a navigator
Nuter — Luther

Oururu — happy
Picher — Peter
Posening — dirty smell
Puon — Paul
Ropich — Robert
Sapeneong — popular with women; master of love-magic
Semes — James
Sewi — sorcery of a special type
Son — John or Saul
Sos — George
Upuini — I am your brother; popular man
Uruman — navigation word
Wangko
Wanter

• KOSRAE •

Naming seems to follow the Belauan pattern of patronymics. You can wind up being Benjamin Benjamin, if your parents want to reuse your father's name.

FEMALE NAMES

Adelyn   Elnora   Kenye

MALE NAMES

Benjamin   Justus   Taulung
Jacob   Siba

ABORIGINAL AUSTRALIAN

Depending on your outlook, there are several aboriginal languages or dialects in Australia. On top of this, whenever a band loses a member to death, anyone with a similar name uses the "avoidance name" so as not to call up either the spirit or grief. Any word in the vocabulary that duplicates the name or part of the name must be changed, too, for several years.

So what goes in one band may not fly in another. Nonetheless, I have managed to compile some short lists out of anthropological texts, which will do for a native of unspecified tribe in the city, or studying abroad.

Native names are extremely difficult to find. Anthropologists working with tribal people most often write of them in terms of their functions, rather than according them names. Those who come off the desert are quickly Europeanized, for the convenience of the newcomers.

• NYATUNYATJARA DIALECT •

avoidance name, used for a forbidden one: Kunmanara

FEMALE NAMES

Katapi	Nyurapaya	Tjukapati
Manyi	Tanara	
Nyaputja	Tjanangu	

MALE NAMES

Minmara	Ngampakatju	Tjun
Mitapuyi	Ngayunya	Tjupurula
Mungulu	Nuni	Walanya
Mutinya	Tana	Yuma

HAWAI'IAN

There are Hawai'ian names, and there are Hawaii names, just as there are Hawai'ians, and there are Hawaii people. Hawai'ian names are Polynesian, and transliterations from other languages. Hawaii names are those which are popular or originated in the State of Hawaii. Supposedly well-researched name books list under "Hawaiian" things which contain letters unknown in the Hawai'ian language, like Babara, Cristian, Dorisa, Gladi, Kieley, Pilis, Rahela, Roselani, Silivia, Suke, and Vegenia. "Guaran's ball-bearin's," as we say, some poor writer has gone and given these to premissionary Hawai'ians, on the authority of some great big baby-name book.

Also, I have never heard anyone named any of these things. More common are Nadine, Lisa, Malani, Nohelani, Keola, Kimo, and lots of other names the books never have.

There is no R in Hawai'ian.

There is no S in Hawai'ian.

There are no V's, no G's, no Y's, and no compound consonants, like CR or GL.

All words end in a vowel, never a consonant like N or S.

The Hawai'ians have cross-bred with every ethnic group to come to the Islands. Many Hawai'ians have *haole* (non–Portuguese European) last names. Many have haole first names, too, with an Hawai'ian middle name *this long*, like Kawena-'ula-o-kalani-a-Hi'iaka-i-ka-poli-o-Pele-ka-wahine-'ai-honua, "the rosy glow in the sky made by Hi'iaka, reared in the bosom of Pele, the earth-consuming woman"; Kawena, for short. Nowadays ethnic pride makes many parents give (shorter) Hawai'ian first names, and people are using their middle names instead of their original first names. Still, most continue to use Hawaii names, like Melveen, or good solid Biblical names, as well as the same Ashley and Christopher fashionables that folks do on the Mainland. After all, Hawaii is the fiftieth state, not a foreign country.

Hawai'ian names are not really gendered. They are descriptive phrases, even sentences, in a still-living language. So if you think of your child, male or female, as a blossom from Heaven, you name it Lokilani. However, under European influence some heavily used names have come to be considered male or female, or were used in tradition for notable men and women, which I note below.

Hawai'ian language family names are often the same as given names, because they come from the same source. The Act to Regulate Names of 1860 required that all Hawaii people have Christian personal names followed by patrilineal family names. Most people then made their Hawai'ian name their family name.

Hawai'ian children are never just given a bald God's name — Pele, Lono, Maui. Direct use of a God name would be by *malahini* (new-comer, greenhorn), Hawaii parents acting out of ignorance. I have never actually heard of an occurrence of this in the Islands, so don't do it now that you have alternatives. The Old Gods still get a lot of respect; there are too many stories about what happens to people with pork in their cars who try to drive over the Pali after dark, or about Madame Pele's power.

To remember: Hawai'ians are now a minority in the islands. So are haoles. The single largest ethnic group is Japanese, followed by "Cosmopolitan," better known as "poi dog" or "mixed plate." So in a book set in modern Hawaii, you are going to have some Hawai'ians, but also Japanese, Chinese, *Portagee*, Filipinos, Samoans, and the occasional Tongan, Thai, Fijian, Vietnamese, or Korean, not to mention *popolos* (blacks), and the Native Americans who hold their pow-wow annually in Thomas Square. You name it, we got it.

Traditional Hawai'ian Practices

Children were named by the whole family. The proper name (*inoa*) might be revealed to some relative of the extended family (*ohana*) in a dream (*inoa poo*), by a sign or event (*inoa hoo'ailona*), or spoken by a mystic voice (*inoa 'uulaaleo*). Not to use this name might mean the illness or death of the child. Otherwise, names might be based on special events or persons or places, like Ka-hiki-lani, "the arrival of the chief" on a visit to the valley. Unpleasant names were given to make evil spirits avoid the child, like Palani, "stinky." These would be changed when the danger seemed past, so avoid using these for adults unless they deserve them. A special practice, which otherwise I have found only in African tribes, are "resentment names" commemorating a hurt or an insult.

The *ali'i*, the semi-divine nobility, were privileged far beyond the commoner. Their names were too filled with power for use outside their immediate ohana, so besides the sacred name, they had a public name. The sacred name was often a key to their exact position in rank and lineage. On top of this, they often had honorific names given to show their public image, like Abraham Lincoln being referred to as the Great Emancipator, or Washington as Father of His County. Higher nobles or priests might give them these honorifics to indicate some achievement or service.

The ali'i also had the privilege of naming their dwellings and canoes. Commoners who were caught referring to their canoe by a name other than "our canoe" (all were joint ventures of the ohana) were likely to wind up a choice for the next human sacrifice to Ku, or any other handy form of legalized displeasure.

Names containing the term "lani" are best reserved for the ali'i.

"Nui-a-[fill in the name]" means "son of [fill in the name]." This was used usually only if there was a need to differentiate Kaleikini's son Kimo from others named Kimo, in which case he might be called Kimo-nui-a-Ka-lei-kini. In your story, this allows you to have a character with a fairly short name, say Ilihia, but then add pomp and resonance in a dramatic ceremonial scene where he is announced as Ilihia-nui-a-Ulumaheihei.

Pronunciation

Easy. Accent is always on the next to the last syllable. In words of five syllables or more, another accent falls on the first syllable, as well.

Hyphenated words are accented as separate words. In practice, hyphens are often dropped out of names. Modern family names will not have them.

An apostrophe means that two vowels are part of different syllables. It does not mean a change in stress or pronunciation. It can be the difference between two similar words with very different meanings. An initial apostrophe indicates a vocal stop most people cannot hear; again, its lack can change the meaning.

A — A in pasta
E — E in hey
I — I in machine
O — O in tote
U — U in tune
AI — I in kite
AU — OW in cow, NOT the French "au"

All vowels stand for one *count*. Aaawa is two syllables, four counts [AAA-va]. Aiea is [ai-EY-a]. No vowel is ever silent.

W — W as in win, except before A, when it is V as in vim. So Hawai'i is ha-VAI-i. The other consonants are H, K, L, M, N, and P.

When you are tempted to use "standard Polynesian terms," like *taboo* for something forbidden or *tapa* for bark-cloth, please look up the Hawai'ian word instead. In just these two examples, the Hawai'ian words are *kapu* and *kapa*. It has shifted noticeably away from Tahitian or Maori. The signs say "Entry Kapu" not "Entry Taboo."

Hawai'ian Names

Ahakuelo
Ahana
Ahe, Aheahe — soft breeze
Aikau
Aipoalani
Aka — shadow
Akahi — number one; never before
Akanahe — gentle in speech and behavior
Akeakamai — lover of wisdom
Ala-ula — flaming road; glow of sunrise or sunset
Alama
Alamea — ripe, precious
'Alaneo — clear, serene, unclouded
Alani — scented tree, oahu tree
'Ale-po'i — breaking waves
'Alihikaua — commander in battle
Aloalo — hibiscus; loved and served by many
Aloha-e-kau-nei — love alighting here
'Alohi — brilliant, shining
'Alohilani — shining sky
Ano — sacredness, awe, reverie
'Ano'i — lover, beloved, the one desired
Anuenue — rainbow
Anuhea — cool fragrance, mountain breeze

Aouli — blue sky, firmament
Aowena — pink cloud
'Au-kele — great travelling swimmer
Aumoe — time to sleep; midnight
'Awapuhi — flowering ginger
'E'elekoa — stormy
Ehehene — laughter, giggles
'Ehu — mist; red-tinged hair
'Ele-hiwa — utterly black
'Elemoe — dark and still, as jungle or ocean
'Ena — red-hot, intense
'Ena-aloha — intense affection, longing
'Ena-makani — strong wind
Ha'aheo — proud, haughty
Haali'i-maile — spreading maile vine
Haili
Hakuole
Hali'a — sudden memory, especially of a loved one
Hanini — downpour
Hanohano — glorious, honored, dignified
Hao, Ha'o
Hau-kea — snow, snow white (It snows in Hawai'i!)
Ha'u-lili — trilling chatter
Hau-nani — handsome or splendid ruler

Haumea
Hau'oli, Hau'oli'oli — joy, happiness
Haupuuehuehu — snowflake
He-pua-laha'ole — rare, prized blossom
Heanu
Helekahi
Heleloa
Hewahewa
Hiapo — first-born
Hi'ialo — child who stays close
Hi'i-lani — held in the arms of heaven
Hiinano — male pandanus flower
Hiwahiwa — precious, favorite one
Hoaka — crescent moon, lightning, glory
Hoapili
Hoku-ala — ascending star
Hoku-lele — shooting star, meteor
Holiona
Holokai — seafarer
Holu
Hone, Honehone — sweet as music or perfume
Honi — to touch noses in greeting (the Hawai'ians did not mouth kiss)
Ho'okele — navigator, helmsman
Ho'olai'i — the calm of a bird poised aloft
Hoolapa
Hoomanawanui
Hoopoe-lehua — tall lehua tree in full bloom
Hua-pala — ripe fruit; orange trumpet flower; a handsome boy or pretty girl; sweetie-pie
Huaka — clear as crystal, dazzling
Huna-kai — sea foam; white flowered beach morning; glory; sanderling, a winter bird
Iaukea
Ihe — spear
Ihupani — closed nose; expert, wise person
Ikaika — strong, powerful
'Ili-ahi — sandalwood
'Ilima — a yellow-orange flower
Ilo
'Imi-loa — far-travelling; having great knowledge
Ioelu

Iokepa
'Iolana — soaring hawk
'Iwa — frigate bird, thief

Special note: anywhere that a "Ka-" is translated as "the," you can drop it and use the less definite form of the name, like Hekili, "thunder" instead of Ka-hekili, "the thunder."

Ka-'ahu-manu — bird feather cloak; fem.
Ka-'ahu-paahau — well-tended garment; fem.
Ka-anaana — the healing magic
Ka-'au-moana — the seafarer
Ka-'elele-o-ka-wana'ao — the messenger of the dawn
Ka-ha'i — legendary hero; masc.
Ka-hala-o-maapuana — the pandanus wafted fragrance; fem.
Ka-hanu — the breath
Ka-hau-lani — the dew from heaven
Ka-hau-o-lupea — the dew that weighs down the flowers
Ka-hekili — the thunder, the rage
Ka-hiki-lani — the arrival of the chief
Kaakimaka
Kaalakea
Kaalekahi
Ka'alokuloku — intrepid, fearless
Kaalouahi
Ka'aona — month June 7–July 6; children born then were thought very attractive and lovable
Ka'apeha — cloud of several colors reaching over the; heavens; influential, important
Kaauamo
Kaeo
Kahaialii
Kaha-ka-'io-i-ka-maalie — the hawk poises in calm; said of a handsome person
Kahakalau
Kahakeha — high, inaccessible
Kahaku
Kahale — the house
Kahalekai
Kahalepuna — the house of Puna
Kahao

Kahauku

Kahauolopua

Kahe

Kahele

Kahe-wai — flowing water

Kahiapo

Kahiau — to give lavishly from the heart without thought of return

Kaimi

Kalani — contemporary, popular, usually male

Kalehua — the lehua blossom

Kane — man; modern rather than traditional

Kani — sound, as in music

Kaulana — famous, celebrated, reknowned

Kealii — the noble, the chief

Kiawe — a tree that drops hardwood thorns

Kilakila — majestic, strong; admirable poise

Kina

Kulani

Kea — pale skin

Kekoa

Keola — very popular; big family name, too

Kimo — archetypical male name, like Joe.

Koapaka — valiant and brave in battle

Konane

Kupulau — leaf-sprouting

Kuulei

La-ola — day of life

La'a-kea — sacred light, sunshine, knowledge, happiness

Lae-o'o — mature brow, an expert

La'ela'e — bright, serene, calm, pleasant

Lae'ula — red-brow, well-trained, clever

Lahiki — eastern sun, rising sun

La'iku — great calm, utter quiet, serenity

Lako — rich, prosperous

Lalauahi — grey, stormy, smoke-colored

Lalea — beacon, landmark to steer by

Lamakuu-o-ka-na'auao — torch of wisdom, great thinker

Lanaau — drift with the current, ramble, wander

Lanakila — victory, triumph

Lani-ali'i — heavenly chief, yellow allamanda

Laniloa — vast sky, tall majesty

Lau-lima-kala — leaves of limu-kala, seaweed

Laua'e — fragrant fern, sweetheart, lover

Lawakua — muscular, strong-backed; dear friend

Lehiwa — admirable, attractive

Lei — garland of flowers, shells, or feathers; figure, beloved spouse, child, or younger sibling

Lei-a'i — neck lei, beloved spouse or child

Lei-aloha — love lei, beloved child

Lei-hulu — feather lei, dearly loved one

Leka — slimy

Lele-ua — wind-blown rain

Lelehua — skillful, good thinker

Leo-lani — voice of heaven

Leo-mana — voice of authority

Lihau — gentle, cool rain, lucky for fishing

Li'i — smallest or youngest child

Liko — leaf bud, child of a chief

Lile — bright, shining, dazzling, sparkling

Lilinoe — mists

Lino, Linolino — bright, shining, calm, unruffled

Linohau — perfectly dressed, beautifully done

Loa — long, far, very much, very good

Loea — skillful, clever, esp. women

Lohe-lani — hear heaven's bidding

Lokomaika'i — gracious, generous, benevolent

Lolopua — zenith, highest point

Luala'i, Luana — content, at leisure

Luheihu — beautiful, attractive, festooned

Mahea — hazy, like moonlight

Mahi'ai — farmer

Mahie, Mahiehie — delightful, charming, pleasant

Mahina — moon, moonlight

Mahinahina — pale moonlight

Mahoa — travel together, as canoes

Maiele — eloquent, skilled in speaking

Maika'i — good, good-looking, good health

Maile — sweet-spicy leaf

Maka — beloved, eye, face, sight

Maka-'alohilohi — bright and sparkling eyes, blue or light-colored

Maka-hi'o — mischievously alluring glance

Maka-'imo'imo — twinkling eyes, a constellation

Maka-'io-lani — eye of the royal hawk, a star

Maka-lehua — lehua flower petals

Maka-mua — first end, first child

Maka-nani — beautiful eyes

Makahehi — admiration, desire for, wonder

Maka'ike — to see keenly, esp. second sight

Makakai — sea-washed, spray

Makakoa — bold, fierce, unafraid

Makalapua — to blossom, handsome, beautiful

Makana — gift, reward, prize

Makanahele — wild, untamed, of the forest

Makanoe — mist-laden, a variety of lehua

Makoa — fearless, courageous, aggressive

Mala'e — clear, calm, cloudless sky

Malama — caretaker, fidelity, loyalty

Malana — buoyant, light, to move together

Malia, Malaia — Mary; very popular today

Malina — calming, soothing

Mali'o — dawn light, legendary sorceress

Mali'u — well-salted, seasoned with wisdom

Maluhia — peace, serenity, stillness of awe

Malulani — under heaven's protection

Manaloa — great power, almighty

Mana-piha — absolute power, supreme

Mana'o-akamai — spirit of wisdom

Mano — shark, passionate lover

Manono — persistent, famous warrior chieftainess

Manu — bird

Manu-wai — water bird

Mapuana — sending forth fragrance

Mapuna — bubbling springs, surge of emotion

Mau-loa — everlasting

Mau-'oli'oli — ever joyous

Mauli — life, heart

Mauli-hiwa — choice, precious life

Mea-kalia — one waited for

Mea-kia'i — guard, preserver, protector

Mea-laha-'ole — rare, choice

Mea-lanakila — champion, winner

Mea-nui — beloved, sometimes sarcastic

Mea-wiwo'ole — intrepid, adventurous person

Mea'ono — delicacy

Mehameha — loneliness, hushed silence

Mele — song, chant, poem, to sing

Mele-ho'ala — awakening song

Melemele — yellow, a star name

Melia — plumeria blossom

Mikihilina — most beautiful, of dress and ornaments

Miliani — gentle caress

Mimo — upright, gentle, capable but unassuming

Mino'aka — smiling, to smile

Moani — light breeze, windblown fragrance

Moani-lehua — lehua fragrance on the breeze

Mohala — unfolded blossom, young person

Mo'i — sovereign, ruler

Mo'ike — dream interpreter

Mokihana — tree of fragrant berries

Momi — pearl, Ni'ihau lei shell

Mo'o — lizard

Mopua — melodious, pleasant voice

Nae'ole — never weary

Nahoa, Nehoa — bold, defiant, daring

Nakolo — roaring, as surf or thunder

Nalu — full of waves, surf

Nani, Naninani — beauty, glory, splendor, flower

Nani-ahiahi — everlasting beauty, four-o'clock

Nani-ali'i — chiefly beauty, yellow allamanda
Nani-loa — most beautiful
Nani-mau-loa — everlasting beauty, strawflower
Nani-Wai'ale'ale — Wai'ale'ale beauty, native violet
Na-one — the sands
Na-pua — the flowers
Nene-hiwa — prized, beloved, precious
Niau — flowing or sailing smoothly, swiftly
Ni'o — pinnacle
Niuhi — fierce breed of shark, powerful warrior
Noe-'ula — pink mist, as around a rainbow
Nohea — handsome, lovely, of fine appearance
Nohe'o — rascal, mischief-maker
Nohi — bright-colored, vivid, as a rainbow
Noho-loa — Polaris
Nono — rosy-cheeked, sun-burned
Nonohe — attractive, beautiful
Nonohina — white blossoms of olopua tree
Nui — large, big, important
'Oehu — prancing, leaping, blustery
Ohi — young animal, maiden entering womanhood
'Ohi'a-lehua — lehua
'Ohua-palemo — clever, gets away with mischief
Ola — life, health, recovered, healed
Ola-ka-inoa — the name lives on
Ola-loa — long life
'Olina — to make merry
'Olino — bright, brilliant, dazzling
'Olu, 'Olu'olu — cool, refreshing, kind, courteous
Onaona — soft, sweet fragrance
'Onipa'a — immovable, steadfast
'Opua-lani — heavenly rain clouds
'Oumuamua — warrior in the first rank of battle
Pa'aloha — keepsake, memento
Pa'iniu — native lilies
Pakela — one who excells
Pakeu — to surpass

Pakeupali — excessively great
Palanehe — noiseless, dainty, to move daintily
Pali-loa — distant tall cliff, aristocratic
Pau-mau-no'ono'o — all continuing thoughts, memento
Pawa [PAH-vah] — darkness just before dawn
Pi'i-kea — life ascends, famous chieftainess
Pili-'au-ko'i — trusted friend
Pili-lani — close to heaven
Pilialo — dearest friend, beloved wife
Pilikua — giant, beloved husband
Pohu — calm of the sea after a storm
Po'ina-kai — cresting of the sea
Polani — handsome, beautiful, clean, pure
Polehulehu — twilight, dusk
Polinahe — slim-waisted and broad-shouldered
Polohiwa — dark, glistening black
Pomaika'i — good fortune, prosperity, lucky
Ponia — consecrated
Pono — morally upright, in perfect order
Po'okela — foremost, best, superior, champion
Pua — flower, blossom
Pua-ahi — fire flower, a star name
Pua-'ala — fragrant flower
Pua-lanalana — floating flower
Pua-lei — flower lei, cherished blossom, child
Pua-le'i — flower that attracts many
Pua-nani — beautiful flower
Pua'ehu — to show brightly, as red flowers
Pua'ena — to glow brightly
Puahi — glow like fire
Puakea — pale color, especially palest pink of sunset clouds
Pualalea — clear and bright
Pu'ali — tied, a warrior dressed for battle
Pulelehua — butterfly, blown in the air, spray
Pumehana — warm-hearted, affectionate
Punahele — spring that goes on, favorite child

Punihi — lofty, majestic, dignified
Punohu — rainbow lying close to earth
Pu'o-lani — gathered heavenward
Pu'ukani — sweet-voiced
Ua — rain, which in Hawaii is precious
Ua-kini-maka-lehua — rain of countless lehua blossom faces
Ua-ma-ka-lau-koa — rain amid the koa tree leaves
Uakea — mist-white, as snow or breaking surf
'Uao, 'Uwao — conciliator, peacemaker
U'i-launa-'ole — beautiful beyond compare
Uila, Uwila — lightning

'Ula — red, scarlet, sacred, regal
'Ulili — sandpiper
Uluwehi — growing in beauty, as plants
Wai-'ale'ale — rippling water
Wai-lele — leaping water, waterfall
Wai-puhia — wind-blown spray of a waterfall
Waiakua — godly blood, chiefly aloofness
Wai'olu — cool, pleasant, attractive, pleasing
Wehi-lani — heavenly adornment
Wena'ula — red glow
Wiwo'ole — fearless, brave, bold

HAWAII

These can be used by any ethnic group in the islands.

FEMALE NAMES

Arleen, Arline
Charleen, Sharleen, Sharline, Charline
Cherie — pronounced Cherry
Coreen, Corine
Darlene
Dolores
Doreen, Dorine
Ethelreda
Jordanelle
Kadeen

Kay
Leilani — obsolete among Hawai'ians because of song OD; still used by Portagee and some Filipino parents
Lily, Lillian
Lisa
Marie
Marleen, Marline, Marlina
Melveen

Nadine
Naomi
Nora, Norah
Rolenda
Rosaleen, Rosaline
Taryn
Terry, Teri — very popular, no Theresa involved
Verna
Vernette
Victoria

Anything ending in an "-een" sound will do!

MALE NAMES

Aaron
Albert
Calvin, Kelvin
Daniel
David
Erin

Frank
Galen
Garret, Gareth — pronounced the same, usually, esp. by Japanese

Jack
Joe, Joseph
John — never use Johnny
Melvin — for real!
Samuel, Sam

Simon   Tremaine   Tyrus
Steven   Tyrone   Walter

TAHITIAN

Name is not the concept to Tahitians that it is to us. Rather than a birth-to-death label, Tahitians could be known in a variety of ways, not only according to their time of life, but even in what district they were travelling. As a closed, low-tech society with a leisured nobility, Tahitians could devote enormous amounts of time to tracking who was whom.

Culturally, they lacked both a sense of puns, and of name meanings. As de Bovis says, "If you ask a Tahitian the meaning of a certain name, he will respond that, 'There is no meaning. It is a name.'" This is at least partially due to the fact that syllables used in the name of an *Ari'i rahi* (great noble) cannot be used in ordinary speech, so that new words will be borrowed or invented to take the place of those now forbidden. They are no longer words with meanings; they are monikers.

There is little recorded of the habits of the *manahune* or commoner-serfs. Here one would undoubtedly find simply-meant names, carried out of childhood, though an extraordinary event can result in a permanent nickname taking over. The *Ra'atira* were a landed gentry who were given names, but as early as possible acquired a name-title indicating ownership of a certain property, which is used as a name by the owner.

The *Ari'i* or nobility managed to make this practice even more confusing. At birth, an eldest son would take his father's name-title and honors, so that the father now took something more like a personal name, derived from some characteristic of the *child*. An Ari'i could have name-titles in several districts, according to inheritance, so that he or she would be known by one name-title in one village, and by another elsewhere. Women could inherit titles, and pass them to their children. Chieftainesses were often quite independent of their husbands, especially once he lost his best titles to their first son. Because of this, in Tahitian history you will find both a King Pomare and a Queen Pomare: Pomare is a name-title.

"Te vahine Airorotua i Ahurai i Farepua" translates as Chieftainess (Te vahine, the Woman) Airorotua of Ahurai and of Farepua. If you do not like the Polynesianist's "chieftainess," use Lady or Princess or Queen, depending on her clout.

On top of this, most names begin, not just with T, but with Te-, which is the definite particle. Syllables are few, and variation is hard to find. The average reader is going to get mighty confused by too much authenticity. Do not just drop Te's; sometimes they are integral parts of words, like Teri'i.

Your best bet is to introduce the Ari'i once by their full name-title, then treat them like European nobility and call them by their land. "Teri'itua i Hitia'a" can be "Teri'itua" or changed by stages to "the lord of Hitia'a" and "Hitia'a"; just as you might introduce "William, Lord Colsworth" and call him "Colsworth" and "Lord Colsworth" both.

For manahune, use translation names, or get an English-Tahitian dictionary. So the cheerful fisherman can be Crab, or 'Otu'u; Kingfisher or Ruro.

USED BY FEMALES

Aimata
Airoro
Airoroana'a
Airorotua i Ahurai i Fare-
  pua
Ari'i-manihinihi
Ariioehau
Ariitaimai, Ari'i Taimai
Aroroerua
Auau
Fareahu
Fetefeteui
Hototu
Ino Metua
'Itea
Maheanuu i Farepua
Marae-ura — manahune
Moe
Murihau — manahune
Patea
Pateamai
Peutari
Piharii
Pipiri
Poivai
Purahi
Purea
Taaroa
Taia

Tapuhote
Taura-atua i Amo
Tauraatua
Taurua
Te-aropoanaa, Te-aro-
  poanaa
Te-fete-fete-ui
Teeva
Teeva Pirioi
Tefeau
Tehaapapa
Tehea i Borabora
Teihotu
Temaehuata
Teraha-tetua-i-mataoa
Teraiautia
Teraitua
Teremoemoe
Terero
Teri'i Tapunui
Teriitahi
Teri'itaria, aka Ari'e-paea-
  vahine
Teri'itorai Teremoemoe
Teriitua
Teriivau-iterai Taputapu-
  atea i Faatoai Eimeo
Terite
Terito

Terito i te rai
Tetoroeora i Fareroi
Teroroera i Fareroi
Tetua
Tetau i Ravea i Teahupoo
Tetua-umeritini i Vairao
Tetuaehuri
Tetuahuri
Tetuanui e Marua i te Rai
Tetuanui rea i te Taiatea
Tetuanui-reiaiteatea
Tetuanuireia i te rai
Tetuaraenui
Tetuaraenui of Teva
Tetuaunurau
Tetunania
Tetupaia i Hauiri
Tetupua iura o te rai
Tetupua o terai
Teuira
Tevarua-hoiatua
Tevaruahoratua
Tiipaarii
Tupuetefa i Fareroi
Ura
Vavea i Nuurua
Vavea Tetuanui, ka Tetu-
  anui

USED BY MALES

Ahurei
Aia
Aiani
Aifeuna

Amo
Arii-fataia
Ariipaea
Aru

Auri
Auriro
Enometua
Farerohi

Haamanemane
Hama
Hamau i Maruia
Haneti
Hapai
Haururu
Hiro
Hura
Hurimaavehi
Itiiti
Mahine
Mahui
Mai
Manea
Manua
Maoae
Matafaahira
Mauaihiti
Mauaroa
Moearu
Moemoe
Namiro
Niuhu
Nohoraa
Nuutere
Ohatatama
Omai
Opuhara
Oreo
Ori
Panee
Paofai

Pati'i
Pena
Pihato
Punua-teraitua
Taaroa-manahune
Taauaitatanuurua
Taino
Tamatoa
Tapoa
Taua-i-taata, aka Tau
Taura-atua-i-Patea
Tauraatua
Taute
Tavi
Tavihauroa
Tati
Te-manutunuu
Te-maui-ari'i
Te-mooiapitia, aka
    Temoo
Teaatoro
Teaej
Tefaaora
Tehapai Maheanu'u
Teieie
Teihotu
Teohu
Tepau arii umarea
Tepau i Ahurai
Tepauarii
Terii-maevarua
Teriimana i Moorea

Teruru i Paea
Tetohu
Tetumanua
Teu
Teuira-arii
Teuraiterai
Teva
Tevahitua i Patea
Tiaau
Tiipaarii
Toa — warrior
Tuaroa
Tuhei
Tumoehamia
Tunuieaiteatua i Tarahoi
Tupaia
Tutaha
Tutahau
Tuutini
Uata
Ui
Uruumatata
Vaetua
Vairatoa
Vanaama-i-terai, aka
    Vanaa
Vari-mataauhue
Vavahiiteraa i Mahena
Vehiatua
Veve

TITLES (NEUTER)

Aromaiterai
Terii o Marama i te tauo
    o te rai aka Marama i
    Haapiti
Teri'i Maro-tea — king of
    the yellow loin-cloth

(maro)
Terii-vaetua
Teriinavahoroa
Teriinui o Tahiti
Teriirere i Tooarai
Teriitapunui

Teriitua i Hitiaa
Tevahitua
Tu-nui-ea-i-te-atua —
    great god ... the god
Tuiterai

SAMOAN

Samoans, especially of high lineage, will not infrequently change their name
in use. Certain "titles" or honor-names can be inherited in a family, and when

you have earned such esteem as to be awarded one of these by the clan, assuredly you use it! However, they frequently come with no land, and no power other than prestige.

FEMALE NAMES

Aiono	Lisa	full moon
Arieta	Lua	Sali
Ata	Lusi	Seine
Felesita	Malamaisaua	Suluama
Fetu	Mata	Taligi
Fili	Mere	Tina
Iutita	Pele	Tui'uli
Kolone	Pepe — butterfly	Tupuasa
Lama	Sa'eu	Venis
Lele	Salamasina — perpetual	

MALE NAMES

Ala'i	Losi	Saipele
Apa	Mariota	Tala
Falelauli'i	Mo'e	Tamasese
Falevalu	Niko	Tamotu
Fatu	Nunu	Tapu
Fiti	Nu'u	Tau
Iakopo	Ofo	Tavita
Iosefa	Pati	Ualese
Iosua	Pisa	Ula
Lafi	Pita	Vai
Lalo	Pu'a	
Leasu	Pule	

FAMILY NAMES

Ala'ilima	Leoso	Tele
Enesi	Maiava	Toelau
Faiivae	Malemo	Tonumaipe'a
Fanaafi	Mulitauaopele	Tufele
Fuga	Pulefaasisina	Tuiasosopo
Fuima	Safenu	Tupua
Lea'ai	Savali	
Le'au	Sifu	

MAORI

Most of the Maori personal names written down are those of the chiefly families, the *ariki* or nobility, and the *rangatira* or gentry. While some of these have impressive length, many are only four or five letters. The long names may be shortened, but while fine in modern life, this will not do for chiefs in pre–Contact days.

Unlike some Polynesian societies, the Maori ariki do not use titles instead of their names. Children are given their names by their grandparents, or a gathering of close family members. The child is usually named after some recent notable event, or sometimes an ancestor. Very rarely do parents name their own offspring. It is not uncommon, as in many other Polynesian groups, for the grandparents or another relative to claim a child and take over its raising once it is weaned.

"Te" is the Polynesian definite article —"the"— so do not count it in alphabetization. Many names begin with it. This can be confusing for the readers, so either use just one Te- name, or use four or five so they will look beyond the Te. If you use only two Te- names, your reader may get confused, until you put both names in the same paragraph for comparison. So do that early!

Someone can be referred to as either Aonui or Te Aonui, so you can just drop the Te.

Europeanized Maori may use their Maori names; have a completely unrelated *Paheka* name, like John Green; or use a Christian name before their Maori name. In some cases, a father's or grandfather's Maori name has become a family name, and the descendants may have Christian or Maori personal names before it.

Pronunciation

Final E's are sounded, not silent. Accent is on the next to last syllable.
A — U in nut
AA — A in Chicago
I — I in pit
II — I in machine
E — E in pet
EE — E in hey
O — O in pot
OO — O in pour
U — U in put
UU — U in tune

FEMALE NAMES

Akanui
Te Akau
Te Ao-huruhuru
Te Aokapuarangi
Aotakare
Te Aotaramarae
Apa-kura
Ariari
Ata-i-Rangikaahu, Te
  Ata-i-Rangikaahu
Ataraiti
Te Haerewa
Hape
Hapuriri
Hariata
Herena
Hikitia
Hine-i-kukutirangi
Hine-i-tapaturangi
Hineari
Hinekau
Hinematioro
Hinemoa
Hinerangi
Hinetitama
Hinetore
Horiana
Te Huinga
Hurihia
Ihipera
Iriaka
Irihapeti
Iripu
Kahukore

Kahurangi
Kanea
Karaihe
Kearoa
Te Kirikatokia
Kohurepuku
Koihuru
Te Korupe
Te Kuraimonoa
Mahinarangi
Makereti
Manuariki
Maraea
Maramena
Marara; Marara Maro-
  taua
Te Mata
Mereaira
Merepeka
Mihipeka
Moera
Mokonui
Morehu
Muri; Muri te Kakara
Te Naho
Nari
Ngahina
Ngahuia te Awekotuku
Ngaone
Ngaparuparu, Ngaparu-
  paru
Te Ngaroata
Ngatau
Okeroa

Te Paea
Pareheru
Parewahaika
Pauri
Pekapeka
Pikirama
Pipi
Puhiawe
Puparewhaitaita
Putoko
Rahui
Te Rakautororire
Rakeitahaenui
Rakera
Rangimawhiti
Rangiuru
Rerepeti
Rihi
Roka Ngatupea
Rongo-ue-roa
Takirirangi
Tauri
Tawari
Tipiotawhiti
Tiripa
Tuia
Tuitui
Tupa, Tupawaitiri
Turi-ka-tuku
Turuhira
Waewaekoura
Waiata
Whakaotirangi
Wiripine

MALE NAMES

Akuira
Te Anga-anga-wearo
Te Anumatao
Ao, Te Ao-kapu-rangi
Aonui, Te Aonui
Aoroa
Aowheneke
Te Apiti
Te Awa-i-manukau
Eru

Hako
Te Hara
Hauraki Paora
Hei
Henare
Hinganoa
Hipirini
Hira Irihei
Hoani
Hohepa

Hongi Hika
Houmaitawhiti, Hou-
  mai-tawhiti
Huarere
Te Hunahuna
Ihaia
Kahumaru
Kaikore
Te Kakau
Kaperiere

Te Kapuaiwaho
Kawaarero
Kawiti
Te Kemara
Kupe
Mahuika
Maihi te Kakau Paraoa
Maka
Makiha
Te Manihera
Matangi
Te Moana-nui-a-kiwa
Muturangi
Ngahewa
Ngararanui
Ngatoroirangi
Nopera Panakareao
Nuku, Nuku-tawhiti
Ohomairangi
Te Otene Kikoko
Pahau
Panapate Nihotahi
Paora, Paora te Konui
Paratene, Paratina
Paru
Patuone

Pauro
Perema
Piki-ao
Te Pohue
Poti
Rakapa
Te Rangi Karipiripia
Rangihekere
Te Rangikotua
Rangipouri
Rangiroa
Rangiwhetuma
Raponi
Rawiri Tiro
Rewa
Rihari
Rongokako
Tahuri
Taketate hikuroa
Tama te Kapua
Tamawhakaara
Tangata
Tangimoana
Tarawhai
Tareha
Taunui

Tawake moe Tahanga
Temorenga
Timotu
Toataua
Tonihi
Tuamatua
Tuhourangi
Tukahua
Tumaihi
Tuohonoa
Tupunauia
Tutanekai
Te Ua
Uenuku Mai Rarotonga
Umukaria
Te Waharoa
Wahiao
Waihakari
Waraki
Warerahi
Waru
Te Whareaitu
Te Whatinui
Wiari

MALAGASY

The island of Madagascar was settled by a group of Polynesians who went west across the Indian Ocean instead of east into the Pacific. Over the centuries, they came into contact with both the Africans and the Arabs, but the language remains Polynesian.

Like many Polynesians, the higher your rank the longer your name.

Madagascar became a French protectorate, with the result that any French personal names can be used by men or women. The Polynesian tends to remain in the family names, instead. For these you can use the personal names, as well as place-names on the island.

FEMALE NAMES

Rabodo
Ranavalona, Ranavalo

Rasoherina — chrysalis
Tandra — beauty marks

Valiha — harp

MALE NAMES

Andrianampoinaimerina   Rainilaiarivony   Ratsimilaho
Radama

FAMILY NAMES

Ramanantsoa   Ratsiraka   Tsiranana
Ratsimandrava   Tsiangalara   Vezo

Africa

INTRODUCTION TO AFRICAN NAMING

There are 122 languages in Africa with enough speakers to be worth mentioning, not counting variations on Arabic. Not all these people name their young Tshombe and Ogun, any more than all Europeans name them Tad and Marsha. So use as sources only those books that break things down by language.

A reference that breaks names down by country is only partially useful. The modern nations are formed on the bodies of dead European empires, which paid no attention whatever to ethnic divisions among the native peoples. One nation may contain several different tribes, with their own languages and customs. One tribe may be split between two or three countries. National divisions in name books may be mixed up out of all the languages in that one country; or show only the names of the numerically important tribe; or list from only the politically dominant tribe. In many countries, one tribe abuses the others to the point of rebellion — like the Biafrans' attempt to secede.

Because of the influence of European Christian missionaries, the old empires also determine which brand of Christian names the natives adopted upon conversion, whether English, French, Portuguese, Belgian, or even Spanish. German names did not transfer enough to notice. Many Africans in the western bulge, the north, and the east use Arabic nomenclature, as good Moslems.

On top of this, Africans have experienced mass migrations, invasions, and conquests, just like Europeans, so that at different times in the same area the head honchos will have spoken different languages and had different kinds of names. The south of Africa was all Khoisan country until the Swahili-speakers tromped the autochthons, and the Bulge has seen a succession of native Islamic empires — Ghana, Mali, and Songhai — some of whose names were borrowed by modern countries which are not the same. Check this against your time period. Your Phoenicians will *not* meet Zulus on the Horn.

For some bizarre reason, while writers will give Chinese and Cherokee characters "translation names" like Singing Bird, Many Enemies, or Sleeps Long, I have never seen it done for Africans. Authors seem to prefer making up "Mbooga" names, when they have not picked up some appropriate language. You can take the easy way out with translation names, and start a new trend.

WEST AFRICAN LANGUAGES

Language	*Countries*
Ahanta	Ghana, Côte d'Ivoire
Bambara	French-speaking West Africa
Bassa	Liberia, Cameroon
Dioula	Burkina Faso, Côte d'Ivoire
Efik	Nigeria, 1 million
Ewe/Popo	Ghana, Togo, Benin, 3 million
Fang	Equatorial Guinea, 2 million; Bantu
Fon	Benin, Togo, 1 million
Fulani/Fulfulde	Nigeria, Niger, 10 million
Hausa	Nigeria, Niger, Ghana, 30 million
Ibo/Igbo	Nigeria, 10 million
Kpelle	Liberia, 5 million
Kru	Liberia, Côte d'Ivoire
Malinke/Mandinka	French-speaking West Africa, 10 million
Mende	Sierra Leone, 1 million
Mossi/More	French-speaking West Africa, 3 million
Sarakolle/Soninke	Mali, Burkina Faso, Mauritania
Songhai	Nigeria, 1 million
Twi/Akan	Ghana, Côte d'Ivoire, 4 million
Wolof	Senegal, Gambia, Mauritania, Equatorial Guinea, 2 million
Yoruba	Benin, Togo, Nigeria, 17 million

NORTH AFRICAN LANGUAGES

Language	*Countries*
Bari	Sudan
Berber	North Africa, 10 million
Dinka	Sudan
Nuba	Nile above Aswan

EAST AND CENTRAL AFRICAN LANGUAGES

Language	*Countries*
Afar	Ethiopia, Djibouti, Somalia, 5 million
Amharic	Ethiopia, 12 million
Kamba	Kenya, 1 million

Kibundu	Angola, 2 million
Kikongo	Zaire, 3 million; Bantu
Kikuyu	Kenya, 2.5 million; Bantu
Kiluba	Zaire, 3 million
Kinyarwanda	Rwanda, 5 million; Bantu
Kirundi	Burundi, 4 million; Bantu
Kiswahili	eastern Africa, esp. Kenya, Tanzania, Uganda, 20-60 million; Bantu
Lingala	Zaire, 10 million
Luganda	Uganda, 2 million; Bantu
Oromo	Ethiopia, 10 million
Sango	Central African Republic, 2 million
Somali	Somalia, Kenya, 6 million
Umbundu	Angola, 2 million

SOUTHERN AFRICAN LANGUAGES

Language	Countries
Bemba	Zambia, 1.5 million; Bantu
Herero	Namibia; Bantu
Hottentot	Namibia, South Africa
Malagasy	Madagascar, 8 million
Nyanja-Chichewa	Zambia, Malawi, 4 million
Sesotho	Lesotho, South Africa, Swaziland; Bantu
Setswana	Botswana, 2.5 million; Bantu
Shona	Zimbabwe, 4 million
Siswati	Swaziland, 1 million; Bantu
Xhosa	South Africa, 4 million; Bantu
Zulu	South Africa, 4 million; Bantu

ASSORTED AFRICAN NAMES— IGBO, EWE, OVAMBU, ETC.

• AKAN •

The Akan, or Twi, speakers can be found in Ghana and Côte d'Ivoire. They are a majority in Ghana, and when you see "Ghanese" names in a book, they will usually turn out to be Akan.

Every child has a *akeradini*, given at birth by the midwife, which is based on the day of the week. The second part of its name is the *agyadini*, given by the father on the seventh morning after its birth.

Akeradini

Day	Akan	Male	Female	Meaning
Saturday	Memenda	Kwame	Ama	most ancient
Sunday	Kwasida	Kwesi	Akosua	under the sun
Monday	Dwouda	Kwadwo	Adwoa	peace
Tuesday	Benada	Kwabena	Abena	fire
Wednesday	Wukuda	Kwaku	Akua	fame
Thursday	Yaoda	Yao, Yaw	Yaa	strength
Friday	Frida	Kofi	Afua, Afia	growth

Agyadini

FEMALE NAMES

Ako —first child
Anapa — morning
Anika — goodness
Ano — second child
Asa, Anse — third child

Ede — sweetness
Edo — love
Gyamfua
Juba — born on Monday
Nkruma — ninth child

MALE NAMES

Abena — manly
Adofo — one who loves
Adom — help from God
Adwin — artist, thinker
Afram — river name
Ahonya — prosperity
Ahoto — peace
Ako —first child
Ano — second child
Antobam — sufferer
Asa, Anse — third child
Badu — tenth-born
Danso — reliable
Fodjor — fourth-born boy
Gyamfi

Kofi Karikari
Kojo — born on Monday
Kumi — forceful
Kwamin — born on Saturday
Manu — second child
Mensa
Nkruma — ninth child
Offin — river name
Ohini, Ohene — chief
Okera — likeness to God
Osei — maker of the great
Owusu — clearer of the way
Pra — river name
Prempeh
Tawia — born after twins

FAMILY NAMES

Afram — river name
Aidoo

Dibango
Nkrumah

• BENIN •

French personal names can be used.

FEMALE NAMES

Enomwoyi — grace, charm
Erinmwinde — E-rin-mwi-nde
Ode — one born along the road

Omolara — born at the right time
Oseye — the happy one
Zinsa — for female twin

MALE NAMES

Christophe
Emile-Derlin
Enobakhare — what the chief says
Evian
Hubert
Justin
Mathieu
Nicéphore
Obaseki — the Oba surpasses the market
Ode — one born along the road
Odion — first of twins

Omolara — born at the right time
Omwokha — second of twins
Orammiyan, Oranmiyan — prince of Ife who ruled Benin
Osahar — God hears
Osakwe — God agrees
Osayaba — God forgives
Osayande — God owns the world
Osayimwese — God created me all right
Osaze — Whom God likes
Sourou-Migan

FAMILY NAMES

Ahomadegbe
Apithy
Kerekou

Maga
Soglo
Trudo

Zinsou

• DINKA (SOUTH SUDAN) •

FEMALE NAMES

Achan — female child in first pair of twins

MALE NAMES

Mading
Manute

Monyyak — man of the drought

FAMILY NAMES

Alier   Bol   Deng

• EFE (SUDANIC SPEAKING ITURI PYGMIES) •

FEMALE NAMES

Aluta	Maratsi	To'kuta
Atosa	Melika	Undetobo
Ediobo	Okalese	Zatu
Keniteefo	Safarani	
Mapiembi	Teema	

MALE NAMES

Abamu	Chabo	Ondikomvu
Abusa	Dingono	Pekele
Apumbai	Eembi	Temu
Arungele	Kosiani	Zetina
Baranga	Mokomoko	
Batinanza	N'dolu	

• EWE •

Day	*Female*	*Male*
Saturday		Kwame, Kwami
Sunday	Esi	
Thursday		Yao

FEMALE NAMES

Afafa — first-born child of a second husband
Agbenyaga — life is precious
Akpenamawu — thanks to God
Atsukpi [ah-CHOO-pee] — name for female twin
Esinam — God heard me

Gzifa — one is at peace
Hola — savior
Mawunyaga — God is great
Xetsa — name for one of two female twins

MALE NAMES

Atsu — name for male twin
Domevlo — don't take others at face value

Dzigbode — patience
Mensah — third-born
Yesuto — belongs to Jesus

UNISEX

Dela Edem — savior   Sela — savior

• GHANESE, NOT AKAN OR HAUSA •

FEMALE NAMES

Abba — born on Thursday
Abmaba — born on Tuesday
Ajua — born on Monday
Akosua — born on Sunday
Ama — born on Saturday
Asantewa — Ashanti
Efia — born on Friday; Fante
Efua — born on Friday
Ekua — born on Wednesday
Kaya — stay and don't go back; from Ga

Kesse, Kessie — born fat; Fante and Ashanti
Koko — second-born female; Adangbe
Kwesi, Sesi — born on Sunday; Fante
Naki — first girl in family; Adngbe
Sroda — respect
Tawia — first child after twins; Ga

MALE NAMES

Abrefa
Abrofo — warrior, executioner
Ata — male twin
Bobo — born on Tues.; Fante
Claudius
Essien — Ochi and Ga; sixth-born
Frederick
Fynn — River Offin
Ignatius
Jerry
John
Joseph
Kabaka — name of kings of Buganda

Kesse — born fat
Kofi
Kojo, Kwadjo — born on Monday; Fante and Ashante
Kontar — only child
Kwesi, Sesi — born on Sunday; Fante
Manu — second son
Oko — male twin; Adangbe
Ottoba
Sekou
Tano — river name
Tawia — first child after twins; Ga

FAMILY NAMES

Acheampong
Afrani
Aklamagpe [ah-klah-MAH-gpeh]
Akrobettoe
Akuffo

Ankrah
Armah
Awoonor
Busia
Cogoano
Hamidou

Kwei — Ga
Limann
Offei
Offrata
Sembene
Toure

• HAUSA (WEST AFRICA, NIGERIA) •

The Hausa are Moslems, so you may use the Arabic chapter to name them. See also the Moslem names under Swahili. The patronymic "son of" word is "dan." The "daughter word" is "yar."

FEMALE NAMES

Amina — Moslem name
Aminatu — Hausa, queen of Songhai
Annakiya — sweet face
Ayeshetu, Ashetu, Shetu, Shatu, Ayesha
Daura
Gumbo — daughter born after two sons

Hasana — first-born of twins
Tanisha — born on a Monday
Tarana — born during the day
Turunku — Hausa, queen of Songhai
Yar-Jekada — daughter of the tax collector
Zaire — Hausa of Songhai

MALE NAMES

Ajuji — if several before have died
Auta
Bayajida
BiSalla — day after a feast
Daren — born at night
Fodio
Hassan — first-born of twins

Kura — hyena
Lahidi — born on Sunday
Laraba — born on Wednesday
Othman
Shaba
Tanko — son after two daughters
Yohance — John the Baptist

FAMILY NAMES

Burja
Habe — royal family

Rumfa

• IBO •

The Ibo are a tribe primarily located in Nigeria, whose language is called Igbo. In the little I have found on their naming customs, Matabere Iwundu always refers to "a child," so that I suspect much of the gender split in names is an artificiality of "Name Your African-American Baby" books.

FEMALE NAMES

Ada — for first-born females
Adama — beautiful child, queenly

Adanna — father's daughter
Amadi — rejoice, the name of the sun God

Chinaka — God decides
Chinara — may God receive
Ifeoma — a good thing, beautiful
Kambiri — allow me to join this family

Ola — precious, worth
Onaedo — gold
Uchenna — God's will
Ulu — second-born female
Urenna — father's pride

MALE NAMES

Amadi — rejoice, the name of the sun God
Amazu — no one knows everything
Beluchi — provided God approves
Chinua — may God hear
Diji — farmer
Eziji — the king of yams
Jaja — honored, God's gift
Kamalu — lightning God

Matabere
Ndulu — dove
Obasi — in honor of the supreme God
Obi — heart, common
Obike — a strong household
Oji — bearer of gifts
Tobechukwu — praise God
Uchechi, Uchi — God's will
Zebenjo — avoid sins

FAMILY NAMES

Achebe

Iwundu

NON-GENDERED NAMES

Akubueze — wealth makes one equal to a king
Anyakaoha — eye that surpasses the community
Azueze — after the king
Azunna — behind the father (posthumous child)
Eberechukwu — mercy of God
Iwueze — law of the king
Iwundu — law of life

Maduabuchi — man is not God
Ndueze — life of the king
Ndukaaku — life surpasses riches
Obijiaku — home has wealth
Osonduagwike — the race of life is not tiring
Uchendu — thought of life
Ucheze — thought of the king

• KENYAN (NOT KIKUYU) •

FEMALE NAMES

Chanya — Taita
Kanika — black cloth
Khatiti — tiny, little; Luhya
Naliaka — wedding; Luya of W. Kenya
Nangla — born while parents are trav-

elling; Luya
Nazi — coconut; Giriami on coast
Ndila — goat; Kamba
Nigesa — born during harvest season; Lumasada

MALE NAMES

Ali
Amos
Edward
Gede — precious; Galla
Henry
Jimiyu — born in the dry season; Luhya
Jomo — farmer; Gikuyu
Kaaria — speaks softly but with wisdom
Kalume — Giriami
Khatiti — tiny, little; Luhya
Kipchoge — Kalenjin
Lusala — whip; Luhya
Matunde — fruits; Luhya

Meja — from the English "major"
Muenda — cares for others; Meru
Nangla — born while parents are travelling; Luya
Ndila — goat; Kamba
Nyasore — thin one
Odero — granary; for one born at harvest; Lua
Othieno — born at night; Luo
Wambua — born during rainy season; Kamba
Wamocha — never satisfied; Luhya
Wanjala — famine; Luhya
Wekesa — born during harvest; Luhya

FAMILY NAMES

Akii-Bua
Bitok
Biwott
Dunde — Luo
Kaigwa
Keino — Kalenjin
Kibaki
Kibet
Kilonzo — Akamba
Kimanthi
Kiongo
Kiprotich
Kitur

Korir
Kosgei — Nandi
Lusalah
Lusweti
Matiba
Matiku
Mazrui
Mboya
Muhavi
Mukabi — Luya
Mwachofi
Mwale
Mwangi

Ngala
Nzibo
Odinga — Luo
Omolo
Osewe
Owiti
Rono
Shikuku
Tanui
Thuku
Wandabwa

• KIKUYU NAMES (KENYA) •

Traditionally, Kikuyu alternate names between first-born males. That is, Njau Kimane is Njau the first-born son of Kimane. Njau will name his first-born son Kimane, who will often be known as Kimane Njau, who will name his eldest son Njau, so alternating down the generations.

FEMALE NAMES

Makena — the happy one
Mumbi, Moombi
Muthoni — [TH as in then, not as in thin]

Noni
Wambui — singer
Wangari
Wanjiru

MALE NAMES

Chege
Kago
Kimane — large bean
Kimathi — earnest provider
Mathani — commandments
Mogo
Mwangi

Njau — young bull
Wachiru
Wang'ombe [wah-NGOH-mbeh] —
  owns many cattle
Wanjohi — brewer

FAMILY NAMES

Kariuki
Kebiro
Kenyatta

Kimathi
Maathai
Maina

Mika
Mwangi

• MALAWI •

A former British colony, Malawians can be given any British Christian name. Additionally, boys are sometimes given British place-names as personal names. I have too few examples to tell if this is also be applied to girls, but it is not impossible. You can also give English "meaning" names, like Golden or Danger. There are six tribes, including the Chichewa and Ngani.

FEMALE NAMES

Chrissie
Doreen
Feric

Njemile — upstanding; Ngani tribe
Norah

MALE NAMES

Ben
Blair
Brighton
Danger
Frank
Golden

Hastings
Hetherwick
James
Kamuzu
Kenan
Marton

Matthias
Pambuka
Patrick
Sam
William
Wyse

FAMILY NAMES

Banda
Bvumbwe
Charula

Chikanga
Deary
Kacheche

Kadzola
Kakhobwe
Kamwana

Kaunjika	Malinki	or "clever"
Khonje	Mambo	Ntaba
Kunje	Mwafulirwa	Nyerere
Makata	Mzungu — Chichewa,	Nzumwa
Makeba	meaning "white man"	Phiri

• MASAI •

FEMALE NAMES

Esiankiki — young maiden
Loiyan

Nyokabi — of mixed Kikuyu and
Masai blood

MALE NAMES

Batian   Lenana   Nelion

FAMILY NAMES

Saitoti | Sindato

• NAMIBIAN •

MALE NAMES

Andreas — Ovambo
Frans — Ovambo
Josia — Ovambo
Mandanda — Ovambo
Peter — Ovambo

Sam — Ovambo
Shafilshuna — Ovambo
Shikongo — Ovambo
Solomon — Ovambo

FAMILY NAMES

Kalangula — Ovambo
Kutake
Manjer — Ovambo
Marengo

Mifima — Ovambo
Nujoma — Ovambo
Shipanga — Ovambo
Taapopi — Ovambo

• SOMALI •

FEMALE NAMES

Amina — Moslem
Ashia — from Aisha
Ayan — bright
Aziza — gorgeous
Deka — one who pleases
Dolie
Fowsia
Habiba — beloved, sweetheart; Moslem
Iman — faith; Moslem
Jwahir — golden woman

Kadija — Moslem
Kamaria — like the moon
Khalifa — holy woman; Moslem
Nadifa — born between two seasons
Naja — success; Moslem
Obax — flower
Rhaxma — sweet
Sharufa — distinguished; Moslem
Yasmin — jasmine flower; Arab
Zeinab — good

MALE NAMES

Abdelahi
Abdi — my servant
Abdikarim — slave of God
Abdiraxman — abd-al-Rahman
Aberashid
Ali
Dalmar — versatile
Ghedi — traveller
Issa — Jesus
Kalif — holy man; Moslem
Korfa
Labaan

Nadif — born between two seasons
Nureddin
Omar — most high; Moslem
Roble [ROH-blay] — born during the rainy season
Sharif, Sherif — noble, descended from the Prophet
Shermarke [sher-MAR-keh] — brings good fortune
Taban
Yussef, Yusef

FAMILY NAMES

Barre
Bile
Farah — personal for

"happy"
Garane
Issa

Liyong
Shermarke

• UGANDAN •

In the north are the Muslim Kakwa (Idi Amin's minority tribe), speaking a Nilotic language, as do the Karamojong and Iteso in the east; Central Sudanic speakers, the Lugbara and Madi; the Western Nilotic Acholi, Alur, and Lango. The south is filled with Bantu speakers, including the single largest tribe, the Christian Baganda; the Banyoro, Bakonjo, Batoro, Bakiga, Banyarwanda, Banyankole, Basoga, and Bagwere. If you had not already guessed, Bantu tribal names begin with BA, meaning "people."

Being a former British colony, any fairly Anglo-Christian name can be used for personal names, or some of the Puritan Biblical names found under Renaissance English Names.

Bantu:

Taata = Father, or paternal uncle

Maama = Mother, or maternal aunt

FEMALE NAMES

Agatha — Christian Baganda

Alice — Christian Baganda

Esther — Christian Baganda

Florence — Christian Baganda

Kezia — Christian Baganda

Kibibi [chee-BEE-bee] — beautiful fat girl; Runyankore

Kissa — born after twins; Baganda

Mwaka — born New Year's Eve; Baganda

Najja — second-born; Baganda

Nalongo — taken by a woman who has borne twins; Baganda

Nantale — Baganda; lion clan

Negesa — born during harvest; Lugisu

Nnambi — first woman; Baganda

Okello — child following twins; Ateso

Penina — Christian Baganda

Sarah — Christian Baganda

Solome — Christian Baganda

Taban

MALE NAMES

Adam

Akello — I have brought forth; Alur

Ayub — Moslem

Balinda — patience, endurance, fortitude; Rutooro

Christopher — Baganda

Edward

Frederick

Godfrey — Baganda

Kaguta

Kato — second-born male twin; Runyankore

Kavuma — Baganda; Ngo (leopard) clan

Kintu — Baganda; Ngo (leopard) clan

Kissa — born after twins; Baganda

Magimbi — Baganda

Milton

Mori — son born before mother's dowry has been paid off

Musa — Baganda

Mwaka — born New Year's Eve; Baganda

Najja — second-born

Okello — child following twins; Ateso

Okot

Okoth — born during rainy season

Patrick

Salongo — taken by father of twins; Baganda

Theodoros — Baganda; Greek Orthodox

Tiko

Tito

Semakokiro — old Baganda

Usefu

Yoweri

Yusufe — Baganda

Zesiro — first-born twin; Baganada

FAMILY NAMES

Akii-Bua
Binaisa — Baganda
Bulagulwa
Gwasaze
Kalule
Kimala
Lule — Baganda
Lutwa
Musevini

Mutesa — old royal family
Nankyama — Baganda
Obote — Lango tribe
Okino
Okoth
P'Bitek
Ssemwanga

• WOLOF •

A Muslim tribe, they use many Islamic names — Aisa, Yusuf, etc.

FEMALE NAMES

Aminata
Binata

Jaineba
Ramatula

Safara — fire

MALE NAMES

Babukar
Lat Dior

Malik
Musa

Youssou

FAMILY NAMES

Dior

N'Dour

Sow-Fall

• XHOSA (SOUTH AFRICA) •

FEMALE NAMES

Linda [LEE-ndah] — wait
Lindiwe — have waited

Mandisa — sweet
Noni — from Kikuyu, Muthoni

MALE NAMES

Paki — witness
Xola — stay in peace

Zola — quietness

FAMILY NAMES

Jabavu

• ZIMBABWE •

FEMALE NAMES

Amadika — wishing to be beloved; self-naming by a neglected wife
Chenzira — born on the road; Shona
China [CHEE-nah] — born on Thursday; Shona
Chioneso — guiding light; Shona
Chipo — gift; Shona
Chuma — bead, wealth; Shona
Dorleta
Japera — offer thanks; Shona
Kamali — spirit that protects newborns from disease
Katura — I feel relieved
Magara — sit, stay; Shona
Maideyi — What did you want? Shona

Mashama — you are surprised; Shona
Massassi — mythic first woman; Makoni
Muchaneta — you will get tired; Shona
Mudiwa — the loved; Shona
Nehanda — hardiness; Zezuru or Shona
Nyagasikan — Shona
Rudo — love; Shona
Rufaro — happiness; Shona
Runako — beauty; Shona
Sekai — laughter
Sekayi — to laugh; Shona
Spiwe — we were given; Shona
Teurai Ropa — blood-spiller

MALE NAMES

Banga — knife; Shona
Betserai — to help; Shona
Canaan — Biblical
Gabriel
Gamba — warrior; Shona
Goredema — black cloud; Shona
Hondo — warrior; Shona
Jiri — forest of wild fruits; Zezuru
Kaseko — mockery, ridicule, revenge name given son by mother thought barren
Katura — I feel relieved
Kokayi — summon the people; Shona

Lobengula — Matabele in South Rhodesia
Marar — var. Marara; dirt
Matope — last child
Mosilikatse — Matabele
Moyo — heart, common; Zezuru
Mundan — garden
Pepukayi — Wake up! Shona
Robert
Simba — strength; Zezuru
Sodindo
Sondai — to push; Shona
Tichawona — we shall see; Shona

FAMILY NAMES

Banana
Mugabe
Nhongo

Nkomo — Matabele
Nyoni
Saruchera

Sibanda

• OTHER IDENTIFIED •

FEMALE NAMES

Abena — pure; West Africa
Abi — to guard; West Africa
Adadimo — Dahomey
Adama — majestic; West Africa
Adero — life-giver; Central Africa
Adjua — noble; West Africa
Adong — posthumous daughter; Acoli,
Central Africa
Afi— spiritual; West Africa
Ahurole — loving; West Africa
Akua — sweet messenger; West Africa
Alice — Zambia
Ama — happy; West Africa
Aminata — good character; West
Africa
Amma — famous; West Africa
Andaiye — daughter comes home;
East Africa
Andito — great one; Central Africa
Ashaki — beautiful; West Africa
Assata — warlike; West Africa
Assitou — careful; West Africa
Ayanna — beautiful flower; East Africa
Ayeola — rainbow; West Africa
Azinza — mermaid; Mina of Togo
Banny — West Africa
Bazao — Nigeria, tribe south of Zaria
Binta — West Africa
Bintou — royal; West Africa
Bisa — greatly loved; West Africa
Bupe — hospitality; Nyakyusa of
Tanzania
Damali — beautiful vision; East Africa
Dimi — Mauritania
Djenaba — affectionate; West Africa
Efra — Egypt
Efuru — daughter of heaven; West
Africa
Eintou — pearl; West Africa
Ewunike — fragrant; East Africa
Fanta — Guinea and Côte d'Ivoire
Fatimata — Muslim popular w/Diawara
of Mali
Fatoumata — beloved by all; West
Africa
Fembar — Liberia
Fitima — evening, dusk; West Africa

Hadiya, Hadiyah — guide to righteous-
ness; Muslim
Hassiba — Algeria
Hawanya — a tear; West Africa
Huda — proper guidance; Muslim Egypt
Iyangura — Nyanja of Zambia
Kafi— quiet; Central Africa
Kai — lovable; West Africa
Kaipkire — Herero
Kamra — moon; Arab
Kemba — faithful; Central Africa
Kifuniji — Ngola
Kilolo — youthful; Central Africa
Kimbaveta — Congo
Koko — Cameroon
Koumba — helper; West Africa
Laraba — Wednesday; West Africa
Llinga — Congo
Lubangi — born in water; East Africa
Lueji [loo-AY-jee] see Rweej; Lunda
of Central Africa
Lumengo —flower; Central Africa
Macouda — Dahomey
Makemba — Central Africa, Congo
Malene — tower; West Africa
Manana — lustrous; West Africa
Mantatisi — queen of baTlokwa, dis-
placed by Zulus
Mariama — gift of God; West Africa,
Senegal esp.
Marka — steady rain; West Africa
Mawakana — yielding; Central Africa
Mayimuna — expressive; West Africa
Mbandi — Congo
Migozo — earnest; Central Africa
Mijiza — works with hands; East Africa
Mint — Mauritania
Moena Monenga — Central Africa
legend chief; Zaire and Angola
Muga — mother of all; East Africa
Mujaji — South Africa rain queen
Mukaya — Luba queen
Mukumbu — Ngola
Mussasa — Congo queen
Nadia — full of dew; Sudan
Najuma — abounding in joy; East
Africa

Nakpangi — star; Central Africa
Nalo — much loved; West Africa
Nalungo — beautiful; Central Africa
Nana — mother of the earth; West Africa
Nataki — of high birth; Central Africa
Nausica — Dahomey
Nazapa — of sacrifice; Central Africa
Ndunba — happy; Central Africa
Ndunga — famous; Central Africa
Ngina — one who serves; East Africa
Ngozi — blessing; West Africa
Niambi — melody; Central Africa
Nini — stone, or industrious; West Africa
Njeri — anointed, West Africa; belonging to a warrior, East Africa
Nkechi — loyal; West Africa
Nkenge — brilliant; Central Africa
Nneka — tender; West Africa
Noni — gift of God; West Africa
Nsenga — womanly delight; Central Africa
Nsombi — abounding joy; Central Africa
Ntombi — Swaziland
Nzinga — from the river; Congo
Nzingha — beautiful; Ngola
Ofrah — moon; Mandinka, West Africa
Okolo — friendly; West Africa
Ona — fire; Iggara of West Africa

Oni — desired; West Africa
Onyema — sorrow; West Africa
Oure — saintly; West Africa
Poni — second-born female; Bari of South Sudan
Raisa — leader; Arab
Rweej [rou-EHDJ] — queen, Lunda of Central Africa
Sadio — pure; Fr. West Africa
Safia — Sudan
Sala — gentle; East Africa
Sama — noble, lofty; Arab
Sana — look upon, gaze; Arab
Sarah — popular in Sudan
Saran — joy; Guinea and Côte d'Ivoire
Seh-Dong-Hong-Beh — Dahomey
Serwaa — jewel; West Africa
Sia Jatta — legendary beauty; Soninke
Sibongile — Zulu
Sittina — queens of Shendi in Sudan
Soyini — richly endowed; West Africa
Tafui — glory to God; Mina of Togo
Tembandumba — Congo queen
Tene — love; West Africa
Thwala — Swaziland
Tiombe — shy; West Africa
Tuere — sacred; West Africa
Wambui — singer of songs; East Africa
Yoko — Sierra Leone
Zola — productive; Congo

Male Names

Abayomi — friend; West Africa
Abdou — Senegal
Abeid — leader; East Africa
Afiba — by the sea; West Africa
Ahmadou — Côte d'Ivoire
Ajene — true; West Africa
Akelo — son born after twins; Acoli, Central Africa
Albert — Sierra Leone
Alexandre — Cameroon
Alimayu — in honor of God
Amadu — Sierra Leone
Aneerood — Mauritius
Apiy and Acen — names for twins; Acoli, Central Africa

Asinia — stern; West Africa
Atiba — understanding; West Africa
Atiim — violent; West Africa
Ato — brilliant; East Africa
Ayize — let it come; South Africa
Azikiwe — healthy; West Africa
Babatu — peacemaker, West Africa
Babu — willing, West Africa; man of medicine, East Africa
Balewa — happiness; West Africa
Basel — brave; Muslim Sudan
Baye — straight-forward; West Africa
Bayete — between God and man; South Africa
Bhoke — wanderer; East Africa

Birago — red earth; West Africa
Biyogo — Equatorial Guinea
Blaise — Burkina Faso
Bloke [BLOH-keh] — proud chief;
   West Africa
Bomani — warrior; East Africa
Boutros — Peter; Muslim
Butu — weary; West Africa
Camara — teacher; West Africa
Cancanja — medicine man; East Africa
Cazembe — wise man; Central Africa
Changa — strong as iron; Monomo-
   topa, now Mozambique and Zim-
   babwe
Changamire — like the sun; Mono-
   motopa
Chicha — beloved; West Africa
Chinyelu — invincible; West Africa
Chukwuemeka — God has done
   well; Igbo
Dabir — teacher, secretary; Egypt
   and Algeria
Damani — thoughtful; West Africa
Dedan — town dweller
Dia — champion; West Africa
Diaba — cliff-dweller; West Africa
Diallo — bold; West Africa
Diallobe — heroic; Central Africa
Diara, Diarra — gift; Fr. West Africa
Din — great; Congo
Dingane — person in need; South
   Africa
Diop — ruler; Central Africa
Dombo — from another village;
   Central Africa
Duguma — spear
Dunduza — man of adventure; Cen-
   tral Africa
Enaharo — like the sun; West Africa
Erasto — man of peace; East Africa
Fati — robust; West Africa
Fela — warlike; West Africa
Fodeba — Guinea
Frank — Tanzani
Gabarone Matlapin — Botswana chief
Gaika — wood carver; South Africa
Gnassingbe' — Togo
Gogo — like grandfather; Nguni of
   South Africa
Goukhouni — Chad
Guila — dark stranger; West Africa

Hamadou — Guinea
Hiji — West Africa
Hosea — Herero of NE Namibia
Idowu — famous; West Africa
Idris — Muslim Libya, Nigeria
Idrissa — immortal; West Africa,
   esp. Senegal
Ifoma — lasting friend; West Africa
Italo — full of valor; West Africa
Jabulani — happiness; Zulu
Jaja — God's gift; West Africa
Jakobi — star; Mandinka of West
   Africa
Jamal — popular in Sudan; Muslim
Jaramogi — traveller; East Africa
Jawanza — dependable; Central Africa
Jawara — peace-loving; Senegal and
   West Africa
Jean-Baptiste — Burkina Faso
Jojo — storyteller; East Africa
Julius — Tanzania
Kagale — trouble; East Africa
Kahero — conceived at home; East
   Africa
Kakuyon — maker of weapons; Cen-
   tral Africa
Kala — tall; West Africa
Kalambo — Luba
Kalomo — the unexpected; Central
   Africa
Kalonji — man of victory; Central
   Africa
Kamau — quiet warrior; East Africa
Kambarage — Tanzania
Kambon — of the people; West Africa
Kambui — fearless; East Africa
Kandia — fortress; West Africa
Kanyama — guard; Central Africa
Karamoko — studious; West Africa
Karanja — guide; East Africa
Kareem — generous; Muslim Sudan
Karume — forest keeper; East Africa
Kashka — friendly; West Africa
Kasimu — keeper of the forest; West
   Africa
Kasongo — Luba
Keita — worshipper; West Africa
Ketema — from the valley; East Africa
Ketumile — Botswana
Khari — kingly; West Africa
Kiambu — rich; East Africa

Kibwe — blessed; Central Africa

Kimani — sailor; East Africa

Kitaka — good farmer; Central Africa

Kobie — warrior; West Africa

Kodjo — humorous; West Africa

Kojo — unconquerable; West Africa

Komunyaka — passionate; Central Africa

Konata — man of high station; West Africa

Koro — golden; West Africa

Kwesi — conquering strength; West Africa

Lansana — Guinea

Larbi — Morocco

Lasana — poet; Central Africa

Léopold — Senegal

Lucala — Ndongo of Angola

Luki — West Africa for Luqman

Lumumba — gifted; Zambia

Luqman — West and North African Muslim

Mabula — born during rainy season; Bajita, East Africa

Macharia — lasting friend; East Africa

Machumu — spears, warrior, blacksmith; Bajita, East Africa

Magoti — born during tax collection; Bajita, East Africa

Mahweshwe — Zulu

Maijo — herd of cattle; Bajita, East Africa

Mainza — rich; Central Africa

Manas — South Africa

Mani — from the mountain; Congo

Maputo — Mozambique

Maragesi — born at the time of a wedding; Bajita

Masilo — Setswana of Botswana

Matsimela — the roots; South Africa

Maurice — Burkina Faso

Mbiyu — fast runner; East Africa

Mganga — herbalist, healer; Bajita, East Africa

Michael — Sierra Leone

Milton — Sierra Leone

Misana — born in the morning; Nyamwezi

Modeira — teacher; West Africa

Modiba — Mali

Modibo — helper; West Africa

Moktar, Mukhtar — Muslim

Momar — philosopher; South Africa

Mombera — man of adventure; East Africa

Mona — jealous; Swaziland

Mongo — famous; West Africa, Cameroon

Moriba — curious; West Africa

Mory — Mandingo of Cameroon

Moussa — Mali

Mswati — Swaziland

Muata — searcher; South Africa

Mugabe — athlete; Central Africa

Muganda — bundle of grass; Bajita, East Africa

Mugeta — born at night; Bajita, East Africa

Mugo — wise man; East Africa

Mukama — born during chief's taking office; Bajita

Muriu — unknown; East Africa

Mutope — protector; Central Africa

Mwambutsa — Burundi

Mwando — good worker; East Africa

Mwangi — father of many children; East Africa

Mwanza — wise protector; Central Africa

Mwata — sensible; Central Africa

Nabate — little; West Africa

Nadir — precious, rare; Muslim Sudan

Nantambu — man of destiny; West Africa

Natare — Burundi

Negue — Equatorial Guinea

Ngarta — Chad

Nguema — Equatorial Guinea

Nico — Cameroon, Nigeria

Njonjo — holy man; East Africa

Nkosi — ruler; South Africa

Nldamak — world ruler; West Africa

N'namdi — worthy; West Africa

Nogomo — prosperous; Central Africa

Nuagobe — Mozambique

NwaOkoerie — born on market day Okoerie; Igbo

Nyahuma — helper of men; Central Africa

Nzinga — from the river; Central Africa

Obafemi — tall; West Africa
Obiang — Equatorial Guinea
Oboi — second son; Acoli, Central
 Africa
Odai — third son; Acoli, Central Africa
Oding — wood carver; East Africa
Oginga — drummer; East Africa
Oji — gift bearer; West Africa
Okang — first son; Acoli, Central
 Africa
Okpara — shelter; West Africa
Onwubiko — may death forgive; Igbo
Opio — liberated; Central Africa
Oraefo — affectionate; West Africa
Oronde — appointed; Central Africa
Piankhi — Nubian Pharaoh
Quett — Botswana
Rakanja — Muarusha of Tanzania
Rami — love, Muslim Sudan; popu-
 lar w/Christian Arabs
Rolihlahla — South Africa
Ruhinda — Karagwe and Nkore
 kingdom, Tanzania and Uganda
Salif — Mali
Samori — Mandinke
Sanga — from the valley
Sangoule' — Burkina Faso
Saye' — Burkina Faso
Sédar — Senegal
Seewoosagur — Mauritius
Segundo — large bird; East Africa
Seitu — artist; East Africa
Sekou — fighter; West Africa
Senghor — descendant of the gods;
 Senegal

Seretse — Botswana
Shafilshuna — Namibia
Shamba — Bakongo of Zaire
Sigidi — a thousand; South Africa
Silko — Nubian Aethiop
Simon — Zaire
Sinawothi — fox; Central Africa
Sobhuza — Swaziland
Sokoni — from the sea; Central Africa
Soyica — thin; West Africa
Sulaiman — North Africa, Songhai
Sule — adventurous; West Africa
Sundiata — hungry lion; Malinke of
 Mali; also Sundyata, Soundiata,
 Sunjata
Tabu — Zaire
Tacuma — alert; Central Africa
Tashfin — Arab-Berber Almoravid
Toola — workman; West Africa
Tutu — cliff-dweller; West Africa
Wali — moon, West Africa; governs
 all, Arab
Xolo — peace; Zulu
Yameogo — wealthy; West Africa
Yamro — courteous; Central Africa
Yannick — Cameroon
Yavu — Lunda of Zaire
Yera — warrior; southern Africa
Yero — warrior; Central Africa
Yerodin — studious; Congolese
Yeta — Lozi of South Africa
Yulisa — Sierra Leone
Yusufu — enchanter; East Africa
Zawdie — chosen leader; East Africa
Zili — Thanga

UNISEX

Djidade — Fulani
Guedado — wanted by no one; Fulani
 of Mali

FAMILY NAMES

Abba — Mauritania
Abbas — Tanzania
Abelo — Zaire
Adhoum — Tunisia
Ahanda — Cameroon

Ahidjo — Cameroon
Akintunde — West Africa
Atebe — Cameroon
Ba — Senegal, West Africa
Babito — royal Bunyoro of Uganda

Bagaza — Burundi
Bahinda — royal; East Africa
Bakita — Sudan (Josefina)
Bankole — West Africa
Barek — Morocco
Barry — Guinea; Peul, Fulani, or Foulbe tribes
Bayi — Tanzania (Filbert)
Beavogui — Guinea
Beti — Cameroon
Biko — South Africa (Steven)
Biya — Cameroon
Biyidi — Cameroon
Boesak — South Africa (Allan Aubrey)
Bokassa — Central African Republic
Bongo — Gabon
Boshosho — Tutsi of Rwanda and Burundi
Boulmerka — Algeria
Bourguiba — Tunisia
Bundu — Sierra Leone
Busia — West and East Africa
Buthelezi — South Africa
Buyoya — Burundi
Cabral — Guinea-Bissau
Camara — Guinea; Mandinka or Sousa tribes
Chileshe — Zambia
Compaore — Burkina Faso
Cylima — Tutsi royal family
Dacko — Central African Republic
Dadie — Côte d'Ivoire
Dafalla — Sudan
Dali — Tunisia
Deby — Chad
Dia — West Africa
Diaka — Zaire
Diallo — West Africa
Dibango — Cameroon
Diop — Senegal
Diori — Niger
Diouf — Senegal
Eyadema — Togo
Fung [FUHNJ] — former Sudanese royal family
Habre — Chad
Habyarimana — Rwanda
Hakki — Egypt
Jugnauth — Mauritius
Kabwe — Zaire

Kane [KAH-ney] — Guinea; also Senegal
Kante — Mandingo of Guinea; also Senegal
Kasavubu — Central Africa
Kashamura — Zaire
Kaunda — Zambia
Kawawe — Tanzania
Kayibanda — Rwanda
Kayra — royal; eastern Sudan
Keira — royal; Fur of Sudan
Keita — Guinea and Mali, Malinke/ Mandingo tribe
Kenga — royal; Chad
Kera — Senegal
Khama — Botswana
Kimbangu — Zaire
Kisimba — Zaire
Kolingba — Central African Republic
Konare — Mali
Kountche' — Niger
Kourouma — Côte d'Ivoire
Kulibali — Bambara, West Africa
Kunene — South Africa
Kunta — West Africa Muslim royal
Kutako — Herero of NE Namibia
Lamizana — Burkina Faso
Laye — Guinea
Lenshina — Zambia
Longo-longo — Zaire
Lumumba — Central Africa
Lutambo — Caprivi
Luthuli — Zulu, South Africa
Maddy — Sierra Leone
Maire — Botswana
Makanda — Zaire
Makeba — South Africa
Makiadi — Zaire
Makoni — Zaire
Malloum — Chad
Margai — Sierra Leone
Masekela — South Africa
Masire — Botswana
Massamba — Congo
Matete — Zambia
Matlapin — Botswana
Mbarga — Cameroon, Nigeria
Mbasogo — Equatorial Guinea
Micombero — Burundi
Milongo — Congo
Minah — Sierra Leone

Momoh — Sierra Leone
Monenga — Central Africa
Morceli — Morocco
el-Moutawakel — Morocco
Mubarak — Egypt
Mutara — royal Tutsi
Mutolo — Mozambique
Mwinsheshe — Tanzania
Mwinyi — Tanzania
Myongo — Caprivi
Mzali — Tunisia
Ndong — Equatorial Guinea
Ngouabi — Congo
Nguesso — Congo
Nkosi — South Africa
Noah — Cameroon
Ntesa — Caprivi
Nujoma — Namibia
Nyerere — Tanzania
Opango — Congo
Oueddei — Chad
Ouedraogo — Burkina Faso
Ousmane — West Africa

Oyono — Cameroon
Ramaphosa — South Africa
Ramgoolam — Mauritius
Rochereau — Zaire
Rusere — Mozambique
al-Sa'Dawi — Egypt
Sankara — Burkina Faso (Thomas)
Sassi — Tunisia
Sassou — Congo
Sebangeni — Tutsi
Senghor — descendant of the gods;
   Senegal
Silkiluwasha — Tanzania
Tambo — South Africa
Tombalbaye — Chad
Toure — Guinea, Maninke or Sous-
   son tribes
Traore — Mali
Yame'ogo — Burkina Faso
Yhombi — Congo
Youlou — Congo
Yuhi — royal Tutsi
Zerbo — Burkina Faso

SWAHILI

In many African languages, meaning is altered by changing the front of the word, not the back, and Swahili is one of these. The language is actually referred to as Kiswahili, the speakers as the Waswahili. Swahili is widespread through East Africa as a second language, being an amalgam of Bantu and Arabic.

A name (*jina*) may be waiting for a child when it is born, or it may have a temporary *jina la utotoni*. Depending on the parents, by either the seventh or fortieth day (not any time between) the child will be given the permanent *jina la ukubwani*. However, just as you or your friends may be called Sissy, Bubba, Scooter, Skip, or Feeny throughout your life, the *jina la utotoni* nickname can persist alongside the formal *jina la ukubwani*. Even if the *jina la ukubwani* is given immediately after birth, someone is still likely to pick up a nickname if it suits them. People are people the world over.

The Waswahili are mostly Moslem, so there is a dominance of Arabic-derived names. They will also have Moslem prejudices: a nickname like Mbwa, "dog," is always highly derogatory, as an unclean animal. But among good Moslems, insulting nicknames are very rare, usually reserved for outsiders.

It is here in Africa that you will find Abdulla used as a name, a contraction of the formal Arabic abd-al-Allah.

The Moslem names have been separated in case your characters are from a pagan tribe, or are Christians, or your novel is set before Islam reached Africa.

Patterns of passing down names in the family are:

> first boy gets the name of his mother's father
>
> first girl gets the name of her father's mother

After this, children may be named for other relatives, dead or alive. They may be named to commemorate the family's situation at their birth, recent events, a holiday, or their own appearance. They may be named for the day of the week, or birth order, which results in the same number names.

Terms of Courteous Address

Many of these are based on kinship, but as in many village cultures, one can extend these to complete strangers as a matter of respect. Especially when you are a young adult walking up to an older stranger, it is more polite to open a request for information with, "Good day, Uncle," or "Excuse me, Grandmother," rather than making a bald demand.

MALE NAMES

Baba, Ba — Father	Kaka — Brother
Baba mdogo — Uncle	Mjomba — Uncle
Babu — Grandfather	Mzee — Elder
Bwana, Mbwana — Mr.	Sheikh, Shekhe, She — Chief

FEMALE NAMES

Bibi, Bi — Ms., Grandmother	Mwana — Lady
Dada, Da — Sister	Nana — Lady
Mama, Ma — Mother	Shangazi — Aunt
Mama mdogo — Aunt	

Pronunciation

All letters are sounded. Accent is always on the next to last syllable.

Cutting words into syllables often confuses English speakers. Kujuwakwangu is not parsed Ku-ju-wak-wang-u; it is Ku-ju-wa-kwa-ngu. Mtakwishayenu is Mta-kwi-sha-ye-nu. Just remember that every syllable should end in a vowel when possible.

Compound consonents — NG, MT, MB, etc. — are not pronounced as if there were a missing unaccented "nothing vowel," any more than you would for STR, KW, BR, or the others you use every day. For NG, put your tongue and lips in the position for N, but say G in your throat as you voice the sound. If your brain, let alone your mouth, cannot handle this, let the first of the consonants be silent and only sound the second.

In Kiswahili names beginning with C, E, O, P, U, V, or X are absent or extremely rare. This is like our rarity of initial Q's, U's, X's, and Z's. You can find some, but often you cannot get initial pins or pre-monogrammed silverware in them.

Equally, some "Mbooga" names like those listed by Zawawi as horrible examples in *What's in a Name? Unaitwaje?*— Mthinklulu, Mapfumo, Tapfuma, and Ikechukwu — would never be used by the Waswahili, to whom they would sound ugly and bizarre.

EE should be pronounced like AY in "say," not our EE in "see." U is always as in "put," not "hut."

• JINA LA UTOTONI •

Chaki — chocolate, dark brown, after 1800
Cheche — mongoose, little part
Chiku — chatterer
Dodo — beloved, large, round mango
Doli — doll
Hobo — gift
Kidagaa — sardine
Kifimbo — twig
Kigongo — stick

Kijana — kid, youth
Kuku — chicken
Mashavu — cheeks
Mtoto — child, kid
Paka — cat
Panya — mouse
Sanura — civet cat
Tatuni — little one
Tumbo — stomach, tummy

DAY NAMES

These include some of the few unisex names.

Day	Kiswahili	Male	Female	Meaning
Saturday	Jumamosi	Mosi	Mosi	first
Sunday	Jumapili	Pili	Pili	second
Monday	Jumatatu	Tatu	Tatu	third
Tuesday	Jumaane	Jumaane	Maane	fourth
Wednesday	Jumatano	Machano	Tano	fifth
Thursday	Jumakhamisi	Khamisi, Hanisi	Khamisuu, Mwanakhamisi	sixth
Friday	Juma	Juma, Jimoh	Mwanajuma	seventh

• ISLAMIC •

Use any from Arabic; these are samples.

FEMALE NAMES

'Aisha — life
Amira — princess
Ashura — born in first ten days of Islamic new year

Asura — born in the month of Ashur
Badriya — moonlike
Baraka — blessings
Barke — blessings

Bilqisi — Queen of Sheba
Farida — unique
Fatuma, Tuma, Fatma — Fatima
Hawa — longing; Eve
Horera — kitten
Kadija, Khadija, Dida
Kamilya — perfection
Latifa — gentle
Mahbuba — beloved
Mariamu, Maryam — Mary, Miriam;
  also used by Christian Waswahili;
  Mae, Mera, Mai, Meyye, Meyya
Mastura — protected from blemish,
  well-covered
Maulidi — born on the Prophet's
  birthday

Nadra — rare, scarce
Radhiya — agreeable
Rasheeda — righteous; Rashida,
  Rachida, Raashida
Salima, Salma — safe; Salme, Sala-
  muu
Sara — Sarah; joyful
Sharifa — noble
Sultana — queen
Ummkulthum — daughter of the
  Prophet
Umsa'ad — happy mother
Yathriba — Medina
Zainab, Zianabu — daughter of the
  Prophet

MALE NAMES

Abdalla, Abdulla, Abdullah, Abdula;
  Abdu, Dala, Dula
Ali — noble, exalted
Boraafya — better health
Farjalla — Allah's consolation
Haidar — strong, stout
Haji — pilgrim, born while father was
  on pilgrimage
Hamza — strong, Prophet's uncle
Haruun — Aaron
Hasani — good
Hashil — emigrant
Humud — gracious
Huseni — dim. of Hasan
Idi — festivity, born on Idd, the end
  of Ramadan
Ilyaas — Elijah
Isa — Jesus
Islam — submission to God
Jamaadar — army general
Jamshid — Persian king, Solomon,
  Jonas

Khalafu, Khalfan — succeed, succes-
  sor
Khayralla — Allah's best
Mahmud — praised; Muhammad,
  Mohammed, Muhammed,
  Mohamet; Muh'd, Modi, Madi,
  Edi
Maliik, Maliki — king, owner
Maulidi — born in the month of the
  Prophet's birthday
Mbaarak — blessed
Mkadam — ahead, leader
Rejalla — Allah's wish
Salaahuddin — improves religion
Salim, Saleem — safe; Saalim, Saliim
Sefu — sword, bravery
Sulaymaan, Soloman; Selemani, Sle-
  mani, Suli, Sulaiman, Selemani
Sultaan — ruler
Umar — longevity
Yusuf — Joseph

• JINA LA UKUBWANI •

UNISEX

Hindi — Indian, sharp armor
Maarifa, Ma'rifa — experience; Arabic

Majaliwa
Maulidi

Mgeni
Msiba
Mwaka

Nuru — light, born during the day;
  Arabic
Ubwa

FEMALE NAMES

Abla — wild rose
Adhra — apology
Adilia — just, fair
Adla — justice
Afua — forgiveness
Ajla — quick, fast
Alama — sign
Amali — hope
Amne — secure
Amra — lasting power
Arusi — born at the time of a wedding
Asatira — legend, saga
Asiya — console
Asma — higher, more exalted
Asmahani — exalted
Asumini — jasmine
Awena — gentle
Aza — powerful
Bahati — luck, fortune
Bahiya — beautiful
Basha — act of God
Basma — a smile
Batini — innermost thoughts
Baya — ugly
Bebi — baby
Bia — home, environment
Bimbaya — ugly lady
Bimdogo — young lady
Bimkubwa — older lady
Bimnono — fat lady
Bishara — good news
Bitisururu — daughter of happiness
Bititi — strong lady
Biubwa — baby-like, soft and smooth
Chausiku — born at night
Chinjo — slaughter, cut
Chipe — sprout
Chuki — dislike, resentment
Dalali — broker
Dalila, Dalia — gentle, sign, proof
Dawa — medicine
Dhambizao — the sins are theirs
Dhuriya — descendant
Doto — one of the twins

Ducha — little
Duni — small
Eshe — life
Fahima — learned, understands
Faida — benefit
Fakhta — pierce
Farashuu — butterfly
Fathiya — triumph
Fidala — faithful
Fila — badness
Furaha — happiness
Fursiya — heroism
Ghalye, Ghalya — expensive, precious
Ghaniya — rich
Gharibuu — stranger, visitor
Hadiya, Hadiyah — gift
Hafidha — mindful
Haifa — slim
Hanuni — cheerful
Haoniyao — self-righteous
Harbuu — warrior
Hartha — arable, fertile
Hasanati — merits
Hasnaa — beauty
Hayati, Hayaat — life
Hiba — gift
Hudham — astute
Hujayja — evidence
Ibtisam — smile
Iffat, 'Iffat — virtue
Inaya — providence
Intisar — victory
Itidal — symmetry
Jaha, Jahi, Jahia — dignity, promi-
  nence
Jana — yesterday
Jifunza — teach oneself
Jiona — be vain
Jioni — evening
Johari — jewel
Jokha — embroidered brocade
Judhar — uproot
Juwayria — damask rose
Juza — notify

Kalolii — feeble
Kanisa — church
Kashore — smiles
Kaukab — star
Kauthar — abundant
Kazija — plenty of work
Kesi — exemplar
Khanfura — snort
Khola, Khawla — deer
Kibibi — young lady
Kidawa — medicine
Kijakazi — young maid
Kijicho — envious
Kujuwakwangu — my knowing
Kurwa — repetition, second of twins
Leta — bring
Lubaya — young lioness
Lubna — storax
Lyuntha — the wealthy
Machui — leopard-like
Mafunda — instruction, training
Mahfudha — protected
Maliha — pleasant
Marini — fresh, healthy, pretty
Marjani — red coral
Masara — happiness
Masika — born during the rainy season
Maskini — poor, humble
Mathna — extol, praise, appreciation
Matima — full moon
Maua — flowers
Mayasa — walks proudly
Mboza — sulky, a type of tree
Menkaliya — you are against me
Meyyaan — not a real friend
Mgeni — visitor
Mkali — fierce
Mkiyoni — you don't see it
Mmanga — journey, emigrant
Moza — distinguished
Mpenzi, Mapenzi — beloved
Mrashi — rose water sprinkler
Mshinda — successful
Msiba — grief
Mtakuja — you will come
Mtakwishayenu — you will exhaust your tricks
Mtama — millet
Mtumwa — messenger, servant
Muhima — important

Mvita — full of life
Mwaka — born in new year
Mwamini — believer
Mwammoja — only one, first one
Mwana — lady
Mwanabaraka — brings blessings
Mwanadongo — earthy
Mwanakheri — brings goodness
Mwanakweli — brings truth
Mwanamize — distinguished
Mwasaa — timely
Mwasham — unlucky
Mwatabu — person of difficulty
Mwema — good
Nafla — gift
Najaat — safety
Natasa — skillful
Natasha, Natalia — foreign, but currently popular in East Africa
Nayfa — benefit
Naysun — dangling seedless grapes
Neema — born amidst prosperity, bounty
Nina — mother
Nisriin — wild rose
Nuha — consoled
Nunuu — extol
Nuzha — pleasure
Nyimbo — song
Penda — loved one
Rabuwa — grow
Ramla — teller of fortunes, divination
Randa — show off, dance
Rayha — small comfort
Rayyan — luxuriant, lush
Razina — strong and patient
Reem, Rim — white antelope
Riziki — sustenance, fortune
Rozi — rose
Ruzuna — calm, composed
Saada — happiness, help
Salha — good
Samiha — magnanimous
Sauti — voice
Sebtuu — born on Saturday
Semeni — speak
Shamba — plantation, branches
Shangwe — celebration
Shani — unusual, marvelous, circumstance
Shawana — grace

Shemsa — sunlight
Shiba — satiated
Shukuru — grateful
Shuruku, Shuruuq — dawn
Sibadili — I will not change
Sihaba — not a little
Siham — sharing, participation
Sijaona — I have not seen
Sikitu — it's all right, it's nothing
Sikudhani — I never thought
Siwatu — they are not people
Siwazuri — they are not good people
Siyasa — politics
Somo — instruction, godmother
Somoe — her godmother
Staajabu — surprised
Stara — well-covered, protected
Sumaiyya — of good reputation
Surayya — noble
Taabu — difficulty
Taanisa — sociable
Tabana — make incantations
Tabasamu — smile, happiness
Tabia — talents, habit
Tafida — benefit
Tafle — infancy, beginning
Talha — easy life
Tamaa — desire, ambition, greed
Tanabahi — be cautious
Taraja — hope

Tausi — peacock
Tawilu — tall
Tisa — ninth-born
Tufaha — apple
Tuni — tune
Tunu — novelty
Turkiya — beautiful
Umayma — young mother
Umi — my mother
Unguja — Zanzibar; born while father was working there
Wafaa — long life, accomplishment
Wahiba — gift
Wanyika — of the bush
Winda — hunt
Yusra — ease
Yuuthar — wealthy, plentiful
Zaararani — saffron
Zahina — popular in Tanzania
Zaina — beautiful
Zaituni — olive, guava
Zamzam — holy spring
Zawadi — gift
Zera — blooms, dawn
Zeyana — ornament
Zina — beauty
Zuri — beautiful
Zuwena — small and beautiful
Zwena — good

MALE NAMES

Asani — rebellious
Asante — you have been good, thank you
Azazi — a treasure
Baba — father
Babechi — father echi
Babu — grandfather
Badilini — change
Bakari — first-born
Barghash — gnat; Zanzibar sultan
Bausi — knife-sharpener
Bavuai — fishermane
Bilali — stood a test
Boma — fortress, enclosure
Chacha — strong
Chaga, Chega, Cheja — holiday
Chandu — octopus

Chimaisi — young and proud
Chum — black
Chuma — iron, strength
Dahoma — long life
Daraja — bridge, stage
Dogo — small
Faki — hollow, simple
Fauzi — successful
Fehed — lynx, panther
Fikirini — reflect
Fogo — high
Fumu, Fumo — majesty
Fundikira — learned
Funga — tie, bind
Furaha — happiness
Ghali — expensive, scarce, precious
Gharib — stranger, visitor

Gheilani — type of tree
Hami — defend
Harub, Haarub — warrior
Hasnuu — handsome
Hauli — power, strength
Himidi — grateful
Hurani — restive
Husni — goodness
Jaha — dignified
Jahi — dignity
Jecha — sunrise
Jela — father was suffering during birth
Jelani — great
Jenebi — affectionate
Jengo — building, strength
Kame — desolate
Kandoro — yam
Karume — master
Kesi — judging, rational
Keto — depth
Kheri — goodness
Khiari — preference
Kiango — lampstand, light
Kibasila, Kibasira — insight
Kibwana — young gentleman
Kibwe — blessed
Kigoma — small drum, joy
Kimameta   cloth
Kimweri — ruler, chief
Kinjeketile — he killed himself, commemorates a suicide
Kipanga — falcon
Kisasi — revenge
Kito — jewel
Kitunda — small fruit
Kitunzi — reward
Kofi — handful
Kombo — impoverished, bent
Kondo — warrior
Kongoresi — old contest
Lali — flexible
Liyongo — talks nonsense
Majaliwa — destined
Machungwa — orange season
Machupa — enjoys drinking
Magoma — celebration
Majuto — regret
Makame — high rank, ruler
Makungu — initiation
Makwetu — our place

Mandara — leader
Maneno — words
Manzi — residence
Mapute — empty, taken away
Makini — poor
Matari, Matar — rainy season
Matata — troublemaker
Matogo, Matojo — markings on the face
Matwa — sensible
Mbamba — branch of a tree, thin
Mbaya — bad, ugly
Mbita — quiet
Mbogo — buffalo, spokesman
Mdahoma — long life
Mdogo — young
Mfaki — exalted
Mfaume — king
Mgeni — visitor
Mhina — comfort
Miujiza — miracle
Mkamba — rope maker
Mkubwa — senior
Moshi — smoke
Mrehe, Mrekhe — easy life
Msamaki — fisherman
Msellem — flawless
Mshabaha — resemblance
Mshangama — rising
Mtavila — you'll eat it
Mtoro — runaway
Mudrik — intelligence, reasonable
Mufid — beneficial
Muhashmy — weak
Muhashsham — respected
Muombwa — beseeched
Muyaka — good and truthful
Mwalimu — teacher
Mwapacha — twin
Mwendapole — walks slowly, cautious
Mwinyi — ruler
Mwinyimadi — just ruler
Mwinyimkuu — great ruler
Mwita — caller
Mzale — native
Mzee — elderly
Nabhani — sensible, judicious
Nadila — honey
Nanji — safe
Nguvumali   power is wealth
Nyuni — bird

Pandu — artistic
Pongwa — cured
Popo — bat, day-sleeper
Rubama — possibility
Rubani — pilot
Rubanza — courageous
Rumaliza — deliverance
Saburi — patience
Sadaka — a religious offering
Sadiki — trustworthy
Safwani — sincere
Saghiri — young
Sahalani — ease
Shaafi — healer
Shakwe — sprout, growth
Shamakani — leader of the place
Shambe — leader
Shazidi — growth
Shilingi — shilling, money
Shinuni — attack
Shomari — long, thin mango
Shujaa — brave
Sikujua — I didn't know
Songoro — smith
Stima — engine, ship, steam
Sudi — good luck, success

Sulubu — tough
Sululu — consolation
Sumai, Simai — high
Sumait — reputable
Suwedi — young master
Suwesi — to govern
Thani — second one
Tharwat — power
Thayru, Thairu — rebellious, furious
Thuweni — diminutive of Thani
Tindo — active
Turki — handsome, beloved, one of
   the planets
Ubwa — delicate, young
Uki — sadness, impediment
Uledi — young man
Usi — hard
Vuai — fisherman
Waduud — companion
Waiyaki — unto you
Wakili — trustee, attorney
Zakwani — thriving
Zamoyoni — of the heart
Zende — forearm, strong and firm
Zuri, Zuhri — good-looking

SESOTHO

In English, we might say that Sothians in Sothia speak Sothoese. But as Sesotho is a Bantu language, a Mosotho is a member of the Basotho tribe in Lesotho.

Most infants are named for events near the day of their birth. There are "journey" names for children born while their parents are travelling, others to commemorate appearances in court, fights in the village, or other social situations. A prolonged labor will earn the child a name meaning delay, or haste for a premature baby.

The second most common source of names is their relatives. Especially, first sons are named after their paternal grandfathers.

If preceding infants have died, a new one may be given an unpleasant name like "skunk" or "dog" to keep demons at bay.

The custom of "in-law avoidance" results in people referring to brides by new names, and the use of *mna*· "mother of" and *ra-* "father of" names. Yet not all Mna- and Ra- names come from this. Rantsho, Ra-ntsho, is not "father of black," but "the black one." Rantwa is "one of war," not "father of war"; Mnantwa has the same meaning for females, as Mnantsho does.

Twins are a sign of ancestral pleasure, but need special care and naming. The Basotho long ago noticed that multiple-birth children are often smaller than singles, and see not only to their pampering, but to making sure that their mother eats especially well so that she can feed both children properly. The following special sets of names are used for twins:

Identical Boys, First/Second

Masilo/Masilonyane
Molefi/Molefinyane, payer
Ntai/Ntainyane
Tefo, payment/Tefelo, payment on behalf of someone
Thabo, joy/Teboho, gratitude

Identical Girls, First/Second

Dipuo/Dipuonyane, talks, rumors
Masimong, at the fields/Maingwaneng, at small fields
Mesi/Mesinyane, smokes
Mosemodi/Mosemotsane

Boy/Girl

Moromodi/Moromotsane
Mosiuwa/Ntshiuwa, forsaken one
Neo, present/Mpho, gift
Thabiso, that which gratifies/Nthabiseng, make me happy!
Thabo, joy/Thabang, be happy!
Tshepo, trust, hope/Tshepiso, promise

Families ideally are half boys, half girls. Sons are inheritors of the family line, but daughters bring in bride-price which is used to get wives for their brothers. A family all of one or the other is a problem. A daughter born after several brothers will probably be called Ntswaki, the mixer. A boy after several sisters will be Modise, herdsman, or Mojalefa, inheritor, also used for first sons.

NEUTER NAMES

Mamello — perserverence
Nyakallo — merriment

Tebello — expectation

FEMALE NAMES

Dibuseng — return them! marriage or bride-wealth name
Difelile — they are finished, bride-price finally paid
Dikeledi — tears
Dilahlwane — forsaken one
Dimakatso — wonders
Disebo — gossips
'Felleng — in the wilderness
Fumane — one who is found
Kgauhelo — mercy
Lerato — love
Makgokolotso — collected things, questionable fatherhood
Matlakala — garbage/litter, questionable fatherhood
Matshediso — consolations
Modiehi — delayer
Mohanuwa — disclaimed one, questionable fatherhood
Moitheri — one who planned his own marriage
Molelekeng — expel her! (the bride)

Monono — prosperity
Mookgo — tear
Moselantja — dog's tail
Mosele — tail
Motshehwa — ridiculed one
Nkamoheleng — accept or welcome me!
Nthuseng — help me!
Ntjantja — dog-dog
Ntshediseng — console me!
Ntshiuwa — forsaken
Palesa — flower
Pulane — rain, dim.
Puleng — in rain
Puseletso — recompense
Sellwane — dim. crying
Seponono — pretty one
Tlalane — famine, hunger
Tlaleng — famine, hunger
Tsebo — knowledge
Tselane — small road
Tseleng — road, path
Tshepiso — promise

MALE NAMES

Bohlale — wisdom
Kamohelo — acceptance
Keisara — Kaiser, from German
Kganyapa — thunderstorm
Kgotso — peace, popular
Kotsi — danger, accident
Leeto — journey
Lefu — death
Lefufa — jealousy
Lefuma — poverty
Lekgotla — court of law
Mahlomola — grief
Makalo — wondering
Masopha — one of the few king's names in use
Moeshoeshoe [moh-SHWAY-shway]
Mohanwe — disclaimed one, questionable fatherhood
Mohlalefi — wise one
Mohloki — one who needs
Mohlouwa — hated one

Moiketsi — one who lets himself down, marriage name
Monyatsi — despiser
Mopotlaki — one who hurries
Mosiuwa — forsaken
Motsamai — traveller, walker
Motseki — one who disputes
Nakedi — skunk
Nthofeela — just a thing
Ntja — dog
Phehello — persistence
Polo — alligator
Potlako — a hurry
Pule — rain
Sefako — hail
Sehloho — disaster
Sello — crying
Serame — cold
Setene — Steyn, a Boer leader
Tahleho — state of being neglected
Tatello — insistence

Tefo — payment
Teko — temptation
Thota — plain, veldt
Tieho — delay
Tiisetso — endurance
Tjutje — (King) George
Tladi — lightning
Tlale — famine, hunger

Tseko — a dispute
Tshediso — consolation
Tshepo — hope
Tsie — locust
Tsietsi — accident
Tumelo — belief
Tumo — fame

FAMILY NAMES

Mofolo

Any male personal name can be used for a family name.

YORUBA

Yoruba personal names are of two sorts: those which are given at the naming ceremony a week or so after the birth, and those which circumstance dictate right at the time of birth. If you are given an immediate "name brought from heaven," you will still get one or more names at the ceremony, and as time goes on one of the secondary names may stick instead.

Among the special names are those which reflect an unusual birth, those which indicate that a family member is reincarnated in the child, and those often called "born to die names." These reflect a series of infant deaths which have convinced the parents that the child is a forest spirit who wants to be human, but keeps getting called back every time it incarnates. These are names admonishing Death, or calling the child something vile so that Death passes it by in disgust.

There are also ordinal names: the first-born twin has a name from heaven, as does the second, and the third if it is triplets. A baby who cries incessantly at birth, or does not cry at all, determines the instant name for the next six children of the mother. Akinnaso does not give gender for these names, while being careful of this elsewhere, so these are unisex names. The names below are listed in the order they are used.

MULTIPLE BIRTH NAMES

Taiwo — first of twins or triplets
Kehinde — second of twins or triplets
Oko — third triplet

Idowu — born next to (after) twins or triplets
Alaba — born next to (after) Idowu

CRYING NAMES

Oni — cried excessively at birth, or not at all

Ola — born after Oni

Otunla — born after Ola

Ireni — fourth (day or birth-order name); third born after Oni

Orunni —fifth (also day/birth-order name); fourth born after Oni

Ifani — sixth (also day/birth-order name); fifth born after Oni

Ijeni — seventh (also day/birth-order name); sixth born after Oni

FEMALE NAMES

Abebi — we asked and received her

Adeleke — the crown gets on top

Adeola — the crown has honor

Aderimi

Aduke — much loved

Aina — born with umbilicus around neck

Alake — one to be petted and looked after

Asabi — one of select birth

Ato — head and face completely covered by caul

Ayo — joy

Ayodele — joy comes home

Ayoka — one who brings joy to all

Bosede — born on Sunday

Fayola — luck walks with honor

Fola — honor

Iyabode — a mother-reincarnation name

Iyayemisi — mother-reincarnation name

Monifa — lucky

Olabisi — joy is multiplied

Olaniyi — glory in wealth

Olufemi — God loves me

Olufunke — God gives me to love

Olufunmilayo — God gives me joy

Oluremi — God consoles me

Oni — born in a sacred place

Talabi — born with umbilical cord hanging over shoulder

Temitope — thanks to God

Yejide — mother is reincarnated

Yekemi — mother-reincarnation name

Yeside — mother-reincarnation name

Yetunde — mother has returned

Yewande — mother came back to find me

MALE NAMES

Abiola — born at New Year

Adan — big bat

Adelaja — the crown settles the quarrel

Aja — dog

Ajagbe — one who carries off after a contest

Ajamu — one who seizes after a fight

Akin — warrior, hero, brave man

Akinlabi — we have a boy

Akinlawon — one who comes after several daughters

Akinsanya — bravery gets revenge

Akinsunmade — valor is next to rank to the crown

Akintunde — a boy has come again, bravery returns

Akinwale — Akin (a relative) returned home

Akinwole — bravery enters this home

Akinwunmi — like a hero

Akinyemi — fated to be a hero

Alafin — king (an old title)

Amusan — head and face completely covered by caul

Apata — rock

Babajide — father is reincarnated
Babarinde — father returned voluntarily
Babatunde — father has returned
Babatunji — father wakes again
Babawale — father returned home
Babawaye — father returned to earth
Bandele — born away from home
Bolaji
Ekolo — earthworm
Kayin — long-awaited child
Kayode — he brought joy
Mongo — famous
Ogunseye — Ogun (war God) has done the becoming thing
Ojo — born with umbilicus around neck

Okanlawon — one who comes after several daughters
Ola — precious, worth
Olatunde — joy comes again, honor or wealth returns
Olorun — owner, creator-God
Olujimi — God gave me this
Olutosin — God deserves to be praised
Omotunde — a child returns
Oni — born in a sacred place
Owodunni — it is nice to have money
Salako — born with umbilical cord hanging over shoulder
Shangobunmi — Shango (thunder God) gave this child
Tunde — he returns

UNISEX

Aiyetoro — peace on earth
Ajasa — born with membrane uncovering only head and feet
Ajayi — born face down
Ambe — we begged God for it
Banjoko — born-to-die name
Bankole — born-to-die name
Beyioku — born-to-die name
Biobaku — born-to-die name
Dada — born with unusually curly hair
Durojay — born-to-die name
Durosimi — born-to-die name
Durosomo — born-to-die name
Ekinne — born with unusually soft and curly hair
Erinle Abatan — umbilicus around left hand
Erinle Ibu Igberi — umbilicus around right leg
Erinle Ibu Oso — umbilicus around waist
Erinle Ojutu — umbilicus around right hand
Erinle Ondu — umbilicus around left leg
Foluke — placed in God's hands
Gbekude — born-to-die name
Igbekoyi — born-to-die name
Ige — breach birth
Igisanrin — curled umbilicus

Ilori — conceived without prior menstruation
Jumoke — everyone loves the child
Kalejaye — born-to-die name
Kokumo — born-to-die name
Kosoko — born-to-die name
Kuforiji — born-to-die name
Kujoore — born-to-die name
Kukoyi — born-to-die name
Kumapayi — born-to-die name
Kurunmi — born-to-die name
Kusaanu — born-to-die name
Kusika — born-to-die name
Kusoro — born-to-die name
Kuyinnu — born-to-die name
Maboogunje — born-to-die name
Majekodunmi — born-to-die name
Malomo — born-to-die name
Masominu — born-to-die name
Matanmi — born-to-die name
Odu — six fingers on each hand
Oke — believed allergic to hot water and medication
Oke — born inside unbroken membrane
Olorunrotemiwo — God took my problems into consideration
Olugbodi — six toes on each foot
Oluseyi — God did this
Rotimi — born-to-die name

FAMILY NAMES

Agbebi | Akinnaso

NIGERIAN

If tribal affiliation is immaterial to your Nigerian character, this is a nice, fat list. Some few names I have found with tribe attached, to bail you out when it matters:

FEMALE NAMES

Abeni
Abiona
Adamma
Adesina
Akanke
Akim — Ibibio
Akisatan
Alake
Alike
Amoke
Aniweta
Apara
Aret — born on market day, Edet; Ibibio
Asabi
Ayoka
Banjoko — sit down and stay with me
Bassey — Efik
Buchi
Dela o Kande — female born after many males

Durosimi — wait and bury me
Durosomo — stay and play with the child
Ebiere — Ijaw
Effiwat
Ega
Fayola
Femi
Hasana
Iniko — given to children born during civil wars; Efik and Ibibio
Iverem — blessing, favor; Tiv
Kosoko — no hoe to dig a grave
Malomo — don't return to the spirit world
Matanmi — do not deceive me
Nkechi — loyal
Oba
Oni
Sarauniya
Titi — flower

MALE NAMES

Agu
Akin
Anikulapo
Aren — eagle
Atuanya
Azi — youth

Bassey — Efik
Bem — peace
Chi
Chimela, Chimel
Cyprian — European
Edet — market day; Efik or Ibibio

Effiom — crocodile; Efik
Essien — a child belongs to everyone;
  Efik or Ibibio
Fela
Gowon
Ibrahim
Ilom
Iniko — for children born during civil
  wars; Efik and Ibibio
Kalechi
Kashka — friendly
Kayin
Koofrey — don't forget me; Ibibio and
  Efik
Kwako
Morenike — good luck
Muhammadu — Mohammed
Murtala
Nnamdi
Nwa
Nwake
Odion — first born of twins

Ogun
Ogunkeye
Ogunsanwo
Ogunsheye
Oko
Olorun
Olufemi
Olujimi
Olukayode
Olusegun, Olushegun
Olushola
Orji
Orunjan
Ottah
Sunday, Sunny
Tomi — the people; Kalarbari
Tonye — Ijaw
Tor
Uzoma — born during a journey
Wole
Yakubu
Zifa — Ijaw

FAMILY NAMES

Abiolo
Achebe
Ade
Adenyi
Adesanya
Aguiyi
Aluko
Amadi
Anaba

Azikiwe
Babangida
Biobaku
Buhari
Ekwensi
Emecheta
Gowon
Ironsi
Jimoh

Kukah
Kuti
Obasanjo
Okara
Shagari
Solaja
Soyinka

ETHIOPIAN

Most Ethiopians do not yet use family names. Instead, if the personal name is not identification enough, the father's name is added, without any special "child of" word.

Two name prefixes used by Coptic Christians are Haile-, "by the power of," and Gebre-, "an offering unto." This should be followed by the name of an archangel, saint, or other holy figure, resulting in names like Haile-Mariam and Gebre-Mika'el. The name prefix Zere- means "descendant of—" and should be followed by the name of a notable ancestor.

TITLES

Dejazmatch — general, commander
Lij — lord, prince

Ras — nobleman (honorary title)

FEMALE NAMES

Abeba —flower
Abrihet — light; Tigrinya
Adanech — rescuer; Amharic and
    Tigrinya
Adina — she has saved; Amharic
Alitash — may I not lose you;
    Amharic
Ayana — beautiful flower
Azmera — harvest; Amharic and Tig-
    rina
Belkis
Berhane — my light; Amharic and
    Tigrinya
Dengel — virgin
Desta — joy, happiness; Amharic
Esther
Fana — light; Amharic and Tigrinya
Kifle — my class
Lishan — award, medal; Amharic
Makda — Magdalen
Makeda — beautiful armrest; Amharic
Nishan — awar, medal; Amharic
Ozora
Seble Wengel — harvest of the New

Testament; Amharic and Tigrinya
Selam — peace; Amharic and Tig-
    rinya
Selamawit — she is peaceful; Amharic
    & Tigrinya
Selassie — Holy Trinity; Amharic and
    Tigrinya
Sisay — blessing; Amharic
Taitu
Tavavich
Teru — good; Amharic
Teruworq — good gold; Amharic
Totit — female monkey, a nickname;
    Amharic
Wagaye — value, price; Amharic
Worq — gold; Amharic
Wub — gorgeous, beautiful; Amharic
Yehudit — Judith
Yeshi — for a thousand; Amharic
Yeshi-emebet — mistress of a thou-
    sand people; Amharic
Zauditu, Zawditu — she is the crown;
    Amharic
Zena — news, fame

MALE NAMES

Abai — River Nile; Amharic
Abebe —flourishing; Amharic
Afework — speaks of pleasant things;
    Amharic
Afeworki — ditto; Tigrina
Aman — peace; Welo; often a nick-
    name
Amare — handsome; Amharic and
    Tigrinya
Assefa — increase; Amharic
Azmera — harvest; Amharic and
    Tigrina
Bekele — he has grown; Amharic
Berhane — my light; Amharic and
    Tigrinya

Berhanu — his light; Amharic
Berihun — let him be our gate/guide;
    Amharic and Tigrinya
Berta — be strong and vigilant;
    Amharic
Daniachew — be their judge, arbi-
    trate; Amharic
Dawit — David
Demissie — destroyer; Amharic
Desta — joy, happiness; Amharic
Elesbaan — Axumite emperor and
    Catholic saint
Ermias — Jeremiah
Ezana — Axumite
Fasilidas

Gabra, Gebre — an offering; Amharic and Tigrinya
Getachew — their master; Amharic
Geteye — my master; Amharic
Hagos — joy; Tigrinya
Haimanout
Hakim — doctor, healer; Muslim, Amharic and Tigrinya
Iacob — Jacob
Iskinder — Alexander
Ismail — Muslim
Iyasu, Yasu — Amharic and Tigrinya
Kaldi —
Kaleb — Cain; Amharic and Tigrinya
Kassa — compensation; Amharic
Kedaref
Kelile — my protector; Amharic
Kifle — my share; Amharic
Lalibela
Lebna — soul
Lema — cultivated; Amharic
Makonnen, Mekonnen — respected, elite; Amharic and Tigrinya
Mamo — used for any small boy, like "Sonny"
Markos — Mark
Maskal
Melaku — angel; Amharic
Melesse, Meles — he has returned it; Amharic and Tigrinya
Melicoth, Melekot
Menelik — son of the wise man, or What will he send? Amharic
Mengistu — government

Mercha
Mika'el — Michael
Miruts — chosen; Tigrinya
Negash — bound to be king; Amharic and Tigrinya
Negasi — sure to be crowned; Amharic and Tigrinya
Negus — king, emperor; northern
Retta — triumph; Amharic
Sarsa
Selam — peace; Amharic and Tigrinya
Selassie — Holy Trinity; Amharic and Tigrinya
Sisay — blessing; Amharic
Tamirat — miracle; Amharic
Tariku — story; Amharic
Taye — seen; Amharic
Teferi, Taffari — ferocious; Amharic and Tigrinya
Tegene — my protector; Amharic
Teka — he has replaced; Amharic
Tekle, Tecla — my seed; Amharic and Tigrinya
Tesfaye — my hope; Amharic and Tigrinya
Tessema — people will listen; Amharic
Tewodros — Theodore
Yacob — Jacob
Yekuno Amlak — let him be good to God; Amharic
Yohannes — John
Yonas — Jonas
Zere — descendant of; Amharic

FAMILY NAMES

Afewerk
Bayesa
Bikila — Oromo
Debtera — priest in training
Demessie
Dula

Kassai
Kess — priest
Lalibela
Nazaret
Siyon
Suhul
Tulu

Walasma
Wolde
Worku
Yifter
Zagwe
Zenawi

TUAREG

The Tuaregs — to themselves, the Kel Tagelmoust — speak a Berber language, besides Arabic since Islamicization. As a result, they have their own versions of Islamic names as well as older, non–Islamic names in use. A fast way to tell an Arab from a Tuareg: the Arabic son-word in the area is *ben*, as in Ibrahim ben Mohammed; the Tuareg son-word is *ag*: Ibrahim ag Mohammed. Even today, patronymics rather than family names are used.

Tuareg women use the daughter-word, *ult*, followed by the father's name. So Ibrahim ag Mohammed might have a son, Ourzig ag Ibrahim, and a daughter, Malla ult Ibrahim. There is a predominance of T- names for women; it's a feminine sound.

A man who has made the difficult pilgrimage to Mecca is thereafter known as El Hadj; either El Hadj Alemhok, or Alemhok El Hadj. The supreme chief of the Tuaregs is the Amenukal. Always, he is of the Ihaggaren (old warrior nobility). Most Tuareg are Imrad or Kel Ulli, the productive, gardening and goat-herding commoners.

FEMALE NAMES

Aisha — somewhat popular
Amena
Baya
Bella
Dasha
Dassine
Demu
Dhabba
Eljamit, El Jamit
Elkubra, El Kubra
Elmamoum, El Mamoum
Essebet
Fadimata — very popular; dim., Tata
Fatma — popular
Feduda
Hadada
Hadeja
Hariza
Hashisha
Kahina
Kana
Katouh
Kella
Khaouila

Khatti
Kodda
Lalla
Lella
Lemtuna
Malla
Meriama
Mimi
Raeraou
Rahma
Rahmadu
Raisha
Ratma
Raysha
Rayshabu — somewhat popular
Regida
Sada
Sekata
Shemama
Sherifa
Sheyma
Tabehaout
Taber'ourt
Tagouzamt
Tahat

Tahe
Tahenkot — gazelle
Tahyart
Takama
Tamagit
Tamat
Tamerouelt — doe rabbit
Tamu — somewhat popular
Tandarine
Tanelhir
Tanermat
Tanloubouh
Tar'aoussit
Tebeshit
Tebubirt
Tekawilt
Tiguent
Tihit
Tinhert — antelope
Tinhinan
Tioueyin
Umeyda — somewhat popular
Wertenezzu
Zahra

MALE NAMES

Abahag
Abidine
Aboura
Adebir
Aflan
Agag
Ahag
Ahmed, Ahmedu — fairly
  popular
Ahu
Aitarel
Akhemouk
Akhiou
Akorebi
Akrud
Alemhok
Allgoui
Amanrassa
Amar'l
Amastame
Amayas
Amder
Amellal
Amer
Amjer
Amma
Amoud
Anaba
Ansar
Aqqasen
Askiou
Attici
Aziouel
Baba
Badjhoud
Bay
Beh
Beketa

Bekkai
Biska
Bouhen
Bubekir
Buzin
Chekkadh
Chikat
Danguchi
Echerif
Ehenkouen
Ehenu
El Boghari
El Hamous
El Hosseyni, Hosseyni
El Khir
El Kounti
El Menir
El Mokhtar
El Mostafa
El Mouden
Elwafil
Goma
Hama
Heguir
Howedi
Ibrahim, Brahim
Ihemma
Ihemod — somewhat pop-
  ular
Iherhe
Ikemma
Ikhenoukhen
Iklan
Ilaman
Ilbak
Ilou
Kenan
Keneiss

Keradji
Khabte
Khebbi
Khelba
Khemidou
Khyar
Lamine
Louen
Louki
Makhia
Mama
Marli
Mellou
Meslar
Mohammed — popular
Musa, Moussa — very
  popular
Okha
Othman
Ou-Fenait
Ould
Ourzig
Rali
Rezkou
Salla, Salah
Ser'ada
Sid Ahmed
Sidi
Sidi Mohammed
Souri
Tamaklast
Tinekerbas
Tissi
Uksem — somewhat pop-
  ular
Uray
Yakhia
Younes

North America

INTRODUCTION TO
NATIVE AMERICAN NAMING

Some people say "North American Indian," but the only connection between the native peoples of North America and India is Columbus' ignorance in believing he was sailing to India.

Most "name the baby" books, if they list Native American names at all, lump them all together, as if they were all one culture and one language. The same authors would never dream of lumping Latinate and Celtic and Slavic names together as "European," but they have far more in common than, say, Tonkowan, Siouan, Athabascan, and Zuni.

Native American languages are so foreign in structure to English that it is a rarely dedicated author who troubles to learn them well enough to create names in them.

The names are understandable to speakers of the language, not meaningless traditional or invented sound-chunks. So it is often easiest to use "translation" names. That is, you don't call a Native American character Satanta or Not-o-way; you refer to him as White Bear or Thinker.

Names are often translated two-part — Speckled Snake, Red Leaf, Black Shawl, Sitting Bear — but while adjective-noun may be a common pattern, more baroque names are equally authentic — Particular Time of Day, Chased by Bears, There He Goes, Drinks the Juice of the Stone, and (my favorite) Runs Against Something When Crawling. Names may also be singular, like Gall, Thighs, or Bull.

The two-part commonness may be a prejudice on the part of translators for the form. "Breaking Up" could just as well have been rendered as "Shatter" or "Breaker" or "Destroyer." The translation suits ancient structures of Frankish and Anglo-Saxon two-element naming.

Especially when you are using translation names, try to avoid the boredom of only two-part names. Remember how many patterns are available to you even in that form: 2-2, 1-2, 2-1, 1-1, 1-3, 3-1, 2-3, etc. For example, Summer Rabbit, Day Thunder, Iron Wolf, Black Fox, Fat Buffalo, Untangled Rope, Spotted Antelope, and so forth.

Do avoid making all the names color-animal or color-object, an easy hole to fall into. Keep a character list. This is separate from the one with the descriptions and background. This is just the names in a column, with a column for the pattern number and the type. The pattern number is 2-1, 3-1-1-1, etc. The type would be "season-object," "color-animal," "verb-object," "condition-animal," etc. Not all the names should contain animals, though they are most common.

A family containing the brothers Crazy Horse, Yellow Horse, and Running Horse may be authentic, but so is one with Donald Pike, Daniel Pike, and Darrel Pike. In either case, fiction readers will not appreciate the confusion. As innumerable writing teachers have dinned, "Mere facts are no excuse" — at least not in art.

Instead, you would be better off naming the brothers Yellow Horse, Running Horses, and Horse Falls Down. They retain the horse theme, which may be important for some reason in your scheme, but in singular, plural, and a non-two-parter.

As a final note of subtlety in separating characters, avoid end alliteration, internal assonance, etc., when possible. That is, Brown Deer and Dawn Bear may seem very different to you because you've lived months with their story, and know their personalities, but to the reader the B-D/D-B, -own/-awn, -eer/-ear, patterns may be confusingly alike.

Sexism?

Some tribes have particular prefixes, suffixes, or infixes which indicate that a name is female. Most often, this is indicated in translation by adding "Woman" as part of the name. The horse brothers above might have sisters named Many Horses Woman and Spotted Horse Woman, sometimes just Horse Woman.

Some authors drop this because they think this is repetitive, and as confusing as calling everyone *something*-Bear. Others seem to feel it is somehow "not right" to keep rubbing the fact of gender in the reader's face constantly, just as they skip over high infant mortality, seasonal food shortages, and polygyny in some tribes. This is an intrusion of unisex-clothed, non-gender-named, monogamous thought patterns, by people who are romanticizing Native American cultures into something they were not.

In these cultures, not just names, but work, dress, skills, entertainment, *everything*, was often gender-dependent. Adding "Woman" is no more sexist than using "Ms.," or calling a female character "Roberta" instead of "Robert."

ASSORTED — IROQUOIS, HOPI, APACHE, ETC.

• ARAPAHO •

MALE NAMES

All Around Chief	Little Raven	Shakes the Spear
Black Horse	Little Shield	Sharp Nose
Bull	Runs Behind	Yellow Calf
Charcoal, Black Coal	Sage	
Ghost Man	Scar Face — Washakie	

• BLACKFEET — ALGONKIAN •

MALE NAMES

Clears Up | Weasel Tail

FEMALE NAMES

Double Steel Woman	Grizzly Woman	award-name
Two Cutter Woman	Hate Woman	Sinopa
Bearskin Woman	Running Eagle — a	
Brown Weasel Woman	supremely heroic	

CHILDREN NAMES

Snow Bird | Spopeia

FAMILY NAME, MODERN
Hungry Wolf

• CHOCTAW •

Whenever possible, a Choctaw avoids using his or her own name, and women will avoid using their husband's name by referring to him as "Father of So-and-so." Also, they never refer to dead family members by name.

The word for red, Humma or Homma, may be added to a name as a mark of distinction. Abi means killer, and indicates a war-name. Similarly, tub-bee means "to kill," and has become a Choctaw family name as Tubbe, Tubbie, or Tubby.

Most names are animal-related, or based on events surrounding birth, like Full Moon. An adult, usually male, will often change his name after striking events. For example, Careless got so busy killing enemy warriors that he did not see their reinforcements coming up, and his friends had to shout at him to get a move on. His name thereafter was *Chikk-Bulilih-Chia.*

MALE NAMES

Achukma-hoyoh — Successful Hunt
Ahaikahno — Careless
Alota-hushi-ninak-aya — Full Moon
Chata
Chikasah — Chickasaw
Chikk-Bulilih-Chia — "Quick, Run!"
Chula — Fox
Ha-tchoq-tuck-nee — Snapping Turtle

Hilih-ah-tasah-umba-ok-pulo —
   Thunderstorm
Mo-sho-la-tub-bee — He Who Reaches
   Out and Kills
Neshoba — Howling Wolf
Tullock-chish-ko — Drinks the Juice
   of the Stone

FEMALE NAMES

Oklewona

Owanah

• COMANCHE •

Women retain their birth name; boys usually change their name to indicate manhood.

MALE NAMES

Big Eagle
Ee-shah-ko-nee — Bow and Quiver
Hah-nee — Beaver
Ish-a-ro-yeh — He Who Carries a Wolf
Kots-o-ko-ro-ko — Hair of the Bull's

Neck
Otter Belt
Post Oak Jim
Ta-wah-que-nah — Mountain of Rocks

FEMALE NAMES

Sanapia

• CREEK •

MALE NAMES

Hol-te-mal-te-tez-te-neekh-ee
Hot Gun
Oputhleyaholo, or Hupuehelth
   Yaho'lo

Red Eagle
Speckled Snake
Stee-cha-co-me-co, Great King
Wolf Warrior

FEMALE NAMES

Cousaponakeesa

• ESKIMO (INUIT) •

Most Eskimo (more correctly known as Inuit) are using Christian personal names, and possibly European family names. As common with newly bureaucratized peoples, they often use a Christian name with their native name after it, which can develop into family names.

FEMALE NAMES

Anauta
Avdla
Katsoo Eevic
Koodloo Pitsualak

Pitseolak
Slwooko
Ticasuk

• HOPI •

FEMALE NAMES

Duvangyamsi
He'-e'-e'
Polingaysi — Butterfly Sitting Among

Flowers in the Breeze
Sevenka

MALE NAMES

Apha
Lololoma
Matcito
Qoyawayma

Sinoyva — Running After Flowers
Tawaquaptewa
Yeokeoma

FAMILY NAMES

Sekaquaptewa

Qoyawayma

• IROQUOIS •

The Iroquois use the same set of birth-order names for infants as you will find in the Sioux chapter.

Ho-de-no-sau-ne — "long house dwellers," self-name

Irinakhoiw — "real adders," corrupted into Iroquois

FEMALE NAMES

Watch-e-kee

MALE NAMES

Cornplanter
Dekanawida
Erie — Wild Cat
Gallichwio — A Good Message

Ganiodaiyo — Handsome Lake — a person, not a place
Hiawatha — He Makes Rivers — use only the translation

Not-o-way — Thinker
Red Jacket

Tonawanda — Swift Running Water

• KICKAPOO •

MALE NAMES

Ah-ton-we-tuck — Cock Turkey
Ke-chim-qua — Big Bear

Kee-an-ne-kuk — Foremost Man
Ma-shee-na — Elk's Horn

FEMALE NAMES

Ah-tee-wot-o-mee
Crying Wind

She-nah-wee

• KIOWA •

MALE NAMES

Bon-son-gee — New Fire
Buffalo Coming Out
Eagle Feather
Guipago — Lone Wolf
Kicking Bird
Kots-a-to-ah — Smoked Shield
Little Mountain

Quay-ham-kay — Stone Shell
Red Tipi
Sitting Bear
Teh-tto-sah
Tunk-aht-oh-ty — Thunderer
Two Hatchet
White Bear — Satanta

FEMALE NAMES

Eagle Plume
Spear Woman

Wun-pan-to-mee — White Weasel

• MENOMINI •

MALE NAMES

Au-nak-quet-o-hau-pay-o — Sitting
  in the Clouds
Auh-ka-na-paw-wah — Earth Standing
Chee-me-na-na-quet — Great Cloud
Chesh-ko-tong — Sings the War Song
Coo-coo-coo — Owl
Ko-man-i-kin-o-shaw — Little Whale

Ko-man-ni-kin — Big Wave
Mah-kee-me-teuv — Grizzly Bear
Mash-kee-wet — Thought
O-ho-pa-sha — Small Whoop
Pah-shee-nau-shaw
Sha-wa-no — South
Tcha-kauks-o-ko-maugh — Great Chief

FEMALE NAMES

Au-wah-shew-kew — Bear Woman

Me-cheet-e-neuh — Wounded Bear's
  Shoulder

• MESKWAKI/MESQUAKI •
AKA SAUK AND FOX, SAC AND FOX

The Meskwaki word for a *berdache* is *i-coo-coo-a*, and they were definitely rare (one per village, maximum) and homosexual; however, *berdaches* are sometimes transvestite but not homosexual.

MALE NAMES

Ah-mou-a — Whale
Black Sparrow Hawk — Ma-ka-tae-mish-kia-kiak; in Catlin, Muk-a-tah-mish-o-kah-kaik — Black Hawk
I-o-way — the Ioway
Kee-o-kuck — Running Fox
Nah-pope
Nah-se-us-kuk — Whirling Thunder

No-kuk-qua — Bear's Fat
Pah-ee-pa-ho — Little Stabbing Chief
Pam-a-ho — Swimmer
Wa-saw-me-saw — Roaring Thunder
Wah-pa-ko-las-kuk — Bear's Track
Wah-pe-kee-suck — White Cloud
Watchful Fox
Wee-sheet — Sturgeon's Head

FEMALE NAMES

Dalottiwa
Poweshiek

Wa-quo-tha-qua — Buck's Wife, Female Deer — Buck Woman?

FAMILY NAMES, MODERN

Wanatee

Waseskuk

• MOHAWK •

MALE NAMES

Thayendanegea — Joseph Brant
Hiawatha

Thunder Cloud

FEMALE NAMES

Anahareo
Kateri

Tekahionwake
Kahn Tineta

FAMILY NAMES, MODERN

Horn

Lone Dog

• OJIBWA/CHIPPEWA •

MALE NAMES

Gaw-zaw-que-dung — He Who Hallows
Gitch-ee-gaw-ga-osh — The Point That Remains for Ever

Ka-be-mub-be, Sits Everywhere
Ka-bes-kunk, Travels Everywhere
Kay-ee-qua-da-kum-ee-gish-kum — Tries the Ground with His Foot

I-an-be-wa-dick — Bull Caribou
Manabozho — He Makes Rivers
Na-pow-sa — Bear Travelling in the
Night, Potowatomie
On-saw-kie the Sac — Potowatomie
Ot-ta-wa — the Ottowah

FEMALE NAMES

Earth Woman
Ge Chi Maung Won
Gesis
Ju-ah-kis-gaw
Nokomis
Shawan
Thanadelthur

• OMAHA •

MALE NAMES

Inshtamaza
Ki-ho-ga-waw-shu-shee — Brave Chief
Man-sha qui-ta — Little Soldier
Nom-ba-mon-nee — Double Walker
Om-pa-ton-ga — Big Elk
Shaw-da mon-nee — There He Goes
Standing Bear

FEMALE NAMES

Inshtatheamba — Bright Eyes

• OTTOE •

MALE NAMES

No-way-ke-sug-ga — He Strikes Two
at Once
Non-je-ning-a — No Heart
Raw-no-way-woh-krah — Loose Pipe Stem
Wah-ro-nee-sah — The Surrounder
We-ke-ru-law — He Who Exchanges

• OUTSIDERS •

Broken Hand — Thomas Fitzpatrick,
  pro–Indian agent
Nose with Wart
Red Hairy Neck
Slow with Gas — a careful motorist
Yellow Fat Boy

• PAWNEE •

MALE NAMES

Ah-sha-la-coots-a — Mole on Forehead
Ah-shw-wah-rooks-te — Medicine Horse
Haw-che-ke-sug-ga — He Who Kills
  Osages
La-doo-ke-a — Buffalo Bull
La-kee-too-wi-ra-sha — Little Chief
La-shaw-le-staw-hix — Man Chief
La-wah-ee-coots-la-shaw-no — Brave
  Chief
Le-shaw-loo-lah-le-hoo — Big Elk
L'har-e-tar-rushe — Ill-Natured Man
Lo-loch-to-hoo-la — Big Chief

Loo-ra-we-re-coo — Bird That Goes
  to War
Particular Time of Day
Shon-da-ki-he-ga — Horse Thief

Sky-se-ro-ka
Te-ah-ke-ra-le-re-coo — The Cheyenne
We-tah-ra-sha-ro

FEMALE NAMES

Kah-kee-tsee — Thighs
Old-Lady-Grieves-the-Enemy,

  awarded at age 50
She-de-a — Wild Sage

Skidi Band

MALE NAMES

Big Eagle
Eagle Chief

Petalesharo

Quohada Band (A.K.A. Kwahadis)

MALE NAMES

Nokoni
Pecos

Peta Nocona
Quanah — Fragrant

FEMALE NAMES

Topasannah

• SEMINOLE •

MALE NAMES

As-se-he-ho-lar — Osceola,   Black
  Drink
Co-a-had-jo
Ee-mat-la

La-shee — Licker
Mick-e-no-pah
Nick-a-no-chee
Ye-how-lo-gee — Cloud

• SENECA •

MALE NAMES

Deerfoot
Eghobund
Good Hunter

Hard Hickory
Red Jacket

FEMALE NAMES

Sah-Gan-De-Oh

• SHAWNEE •

The Shawnee do not reuse names if they can help it, and certainly do not "honor" anyone by using a dead person's name. Two name-givers will ponder an infant's name in an all-night vigil. In the morning, each will offer the parents a name, so they have two choices.

MALE NAMES

Cornstalk
Elskwatawa
Hee-doh'ge-ats — Chinook, for someone come from another tribe
Lalawethika
Lay-law-she-kaw — Goes Up the River
Lay-loo-ah-pe-ai-shee-kaw — Grassbush and Blossom

Pah-te-coo-saw — Straight Man
Stone Eater
Ten-squa-ta-way — Open Door
Tenskwatawa
Tikamthi, Tecumtha, Tecumthe — Tecumseh
White Loon
Winnemac

FEMALE NAMES

Ka-te-qua — Eagle Woman

• WINNEBAGO •

FEMALE NAMES

Mountain Wolf Woman

Neenah — rapids; running water

MALE NAMES

Crashing Thunder
Hoo-wan-ee-kaw — Little Elk
Nau-naw-pay-ee — Soldier
Naugh-haigh-ke-kaw — Moistens the Wood
Naw-kaw — Wood
No-ah-choo-she-kaw — Breaks the

Bushes
Wa-kon-chash-kaw — Comes on the Thunder
Wa-kon-zee-kaw — Snake
Wah-chee-hahs-ka — Puts All Out of Doors
Won-de-tow-a — The Wonder

• OTHER IDENTIFIED •

FEMALE NAMES

Awashonks — Wampanoag
Bad Old Woman
Bo-i-naiv — Grass Maiden, Shoshoni
Cherry — Crow
Cogewea — Okanogan
Geieish — Cree
Her Eyes Grey — Apache

Hum-ishu-ma Mourning Dove; Okanogan
Lozen — Apache
Madas Spiel — Penobscot-Passamoquoddy
Magpie — Crow
Matoaka — aka Pocahontas

Maxi'diwiac, Buffalo-bird Woman —
   Hidatsa; aka Waheenee
Mi-neek-e-sunk-te-ka — Mink;
   Mandan
Mini-aku — in Wyoming
Moon Rainbow — Pueblo
Nalin — Apache
Other Magpie
Pohaha — Tewa
Pretty Shield — Crow
Slow Woman
Stetsa-kata — Arikawa
Thoc-me-to-ny — Paiute
Throwing Down
Tsa-ka-ka-wias — Bird Woman,
   Minnetarre; Sacajawea
Tsaka'kasakic — Hidatsa
Tuhbenahneeguay — Missisauga,
   close to Chippewa
Wah-pe-seh-see — Kaskaskia
Waiyautitsa — Zuni
Walenquela — Yaqui
Watches All — Gros Ventre
Weetamoo — Wampanoag
White Butterfly
Winema, Wi-ne-ma — Modoc
   woman chief
Woman Chief — Crow
Yoimut — Chunut of North Califor-
   nia

MALE NAMES

Bloody Knife — Arikawa; Long Hair's
   scout
Bread — Oneida
Cameahwait — Shoshoni
Canonicus — Narragansett
Cu-sick — Tuscarora
Ee-tow-o-kaum — Both Sides of the
   River; Mohican
Foolish Woman — an old man
Garakonthie — Onondaga
Go-to-kow-pah-a — Stands by Him-
   self; Wee-ah
Goyathlay — One Who Yawns;
   Apache; "Geronimo" is Spanish
H'co-a-h'co-a-h'cotes-min — No
   Horns on His Head; Nez Percé
Hee-oh'ks-te-kin — Rabbit Skin Leg-
   gings; Nez Percé
Hinmaton-Yalakit — Chief Joseph;
   Nez Percé
Humaweepi — Laguna
Iron Eye — in Wyoming
Iroquet — Algonquian
Kahkewaquonaby — Missisauga, close
   to Chippewa
Kee-mo-ra-ni-a — Peoria
Kee-mon-saw — Little Chief; Kas-
   kaskia
Kiwe'gapawa — "he stands here and
   there," wanderer; Algonquian
Little Turtle — Miami
Mah-to-toh-pa — Four Bears; Mandan
Mahican — Wolf; Mohican
Massasoit — Wampanoag
Men-son-se-ah — Left Hand; Pianke-
   Shaw
Metacom, Pometacom, Metacomet —
   King Philip; Wampanoag
Miatonomo — Narragansett
Ni-a-co-mo — Fix with the Foot;
   Pianke-Shaw
Notch-ee-ning-a — White Cloud;
   Ioway
Opechancano — Powhatan
Opitchapan — Powhatan
Pah-me-cow-e-tah — Man Who
   Tracks; Peoria
Pah-ta-coo-che — Shooting Cedar; Ioway
Rotten Belly — Crow
Sassacus — Mohican, Pequot
Shikellamy — Cayuga
Shmoqula — Preacher; Nez Percé
Spotted Tail — in Wyoming
Tah-gah-jute — Logan; Cayuga
Tayo — Laguna
Tod-hah-dohs — Cayuga
Uncas — Mohican, Peqot
Ush-ee-kitz — Fights with a Feather;
   Wico
Wa-pon-je-a — Swan; Wee-ah
Wahunsacook — Powhatan
Was-com-mun — Busy Man; Ioway
Washakie — Shoshoni
Waun-naw-con — Dish; Mohican
Wi-jun-jon — Pigeon's Egg Head;
   Assiniboin
Winnemuca — Paiute
Wy-ee-yogh — Man of Sense; Ioway

PROBABLY MALE

Cherry Eye	Handsome Elk	Looks and Kills
Cloud Chief	Hard Heart	Respects Nothing
Crooked Leg	Laughing Water	Scabby Face
Fast Horse	Little Moon	Swift Bird
Fire Thunder	Lone Dog	West Wind
Full Stomach	Lone Hill	

FAMILY NAMES

Outside — Crow

DELAWARE (LENNI LENAPE)

Names of deceased members are almost never used. A name is so much the person that it dies with him or her. After someone's death, their actual name is never mentioned.

A person receives his or her true, permanent name when they are between the ages of nine and twelve. Until then, they are known by temporary nicknames. Perhaps the same one all the time, but these are not *true* names. True names are only given by visionary name-givers. Without this sacred gift, a parent could not choose a permanent name for their own children.

Some refuse to disclose real names. Parents might refer to children by birth order: "my middle son," "my first born," "my last born," "my second from oldest daughter." Speaking a polysynthetic language makes this easy.

True names are so powerful that the real one is rarely mentioned outside the family house or sacred ceremonies. The full-length names are usually shortened, a couple of syllables becoming the "calling name." Adults will also often acquire other names according to their personalities or accomplishments. Peanto sounds little like Enequeto, yet in records these are the same man. Ditto Sassoonan is the same as Olumapies.

A frail child will not be given a strong, aggressive name, nor a husky boy an effeminate name. The Delaware do not try to change people with names.

Also, there is no pattern of names in families. Three brothers might be named Tamaque, beaver; Shingas, marshy ground; and Pisquetomen, he that moves in the dark.

Family names were imposed on the reservation. Many are just "American names": English, Scottish, Irish, some French or German. Some are translations of Lenape names: Elkhair, Buffalo. Yet some, like Sohappy, that sound like translations, are transliterations of a name like Sohappe.

Pronunciation

In the scholarly items — the ones with all the hyphens — X represents a guttural like German CH. The out-of-place captial H represents a definite but not harsh aspiration.

In the common, historical items, figure they were written by an Englishman early in the 18th century, trying to get the sounds right.

FEMALE NAMES

eXkway — woman, sometimes written ochqueu

Ah-luh-mah-tah-eX-kway — flower beginning to bloom woman; Allummatta-ekway

Awp-pah-tah-eh — white flower; Delaware would recognize as female name

Ay-hell-lee-nowX-kway — woman who looks like someone else

Don-tees — my little daughter, a nickname

Lay-huh-law-kwun-ah-tah-eX-kway — the flower that blooms in the evening woman

Mah-mah-lee-loong-gaw-neX-kway — striped wing woman

Pingtis

Sah-kah-tah-eX-kway — flower which has just come up woman; Sahkataequay

Sawm-Xkway — great lady; calling name

Way-en-dah-naH-kwee-now — she appears like boughs that touch each other

Way-en-gee-paH-kee-huh-leX-kway — Touching Leaves, tips of leaves rustling as they touch each other

Way-lay-luh-mah — the esteemed one; Waylaylumah

Weh-mah-tah-eX-kway — woman who blooms everywhere like the flowers

Wool-lee-nowX-kway — woman who looks good

MALE NAMES

Allemewi

Aw-Xay-ahp-pah-nooX-way — he who walks before daylight

Coquetakeghton — called Grey Eyes

Ee-laht-tut — little warrior, a nickname

Em-mah — calling name

Gelelemend

Gum-uh-wing

Honkarkus

Hopocan

Idquahon

Iduqueywon

Janottowe

Katenacku Esippens

Kee-shay-lum-moo-kawng

Konieschquanohill

Kwul-pee — calling name

Lyckewys

Maghingua Keeshoch — great moon

Mameckus

Matapagisckan

Meas

Memmagmomeck

Menanse

Meoppitas

Merkekowen

Mettomemeckas

Mocktowekon

Moo-Xoom-sah — grandpa

Moosh-hah-kwee-nund — he who appears like a clear sky

Nahoosey
Nannacussey
Neckosmus
Nee-kah-nahp-paH-kee-kum-
mun — he who causes leaves to
turn up with each step
Nee-kah-nahp-pah-nooXway —
called Na-pan
Nee-ko-man — the answer
Nekatcit — tame little fellow
Non-on-da-gon
Oh-huh-lum-mee-tahk-see — one
who can be heard from afar, called
Lahkw-see
Okonickon
Olumapies
Oreckton
Oshemahamon
Papunhank
Pem-pay-huh-lock — Running Water
Pisquetomen — he that moves in the
dark
Popotakan — he who blows with
puffed cheeks
Quenameckquid
Sachimak
Sah-sah-kee-paH-kee-kum-mun
Sahoppe
Sawappone
Secane

Secatereus
Shaurwaughon
Shingas — wet, marshy ground
Swanpisse
Tachgokanhelle
Tamanend
Tamaque — beaver
Tay-men-end, Taimenend — one to
whom luck is given
Teedyuskung, Tedyuskung, Tadeu-
skund
Teotacken
Tepakoaset
Teshakomen
Tishekunk
Tohawsiz
Tomackhickon
Wahem-hic-amund, Wem-hik-
kum-mun — he who is in contact
with everything.
Week-peh-kee-Xeeng — he who is
like receding water
Weet-tahp-pah-nooX-way — he who
walks by daylight, called Ta-pan
Wee-Xuh-weengw — hairy face
Weheeland
Weheequeckhon
Westdeditt
Yaqueenkhon

Family Names (Modern)

Buffalo
Crow
Elkhair

Falleaf
Killbuck
Longbone

Secondine
Witcher

CHEROKEE

Imagine: Sign Steel and his brother, Horn Steel, with their cousins Seacat Silk, Mistress Killwoman, and Rider Silk, take out on the trail of Stealer Sevenstarr. The plots almost write themselves with names this gorgeous. Each of those names showed up exactly as combined in the 1880 rolls of the Cherokee Nation.

You will immediately spot the native Cherokee names, because they look nothing like English. Having only the *concept* of writing explained to him, Sequoyah went home and devised the Cherokee syllabary in the 18th century. Many of the spelling variations below are a matter of transliterating from Cherokee to Latin letters.

Many Cherokee adopted European ideas, including family names, fairly early. Those who became Christians used their new baptismal names of George, Henry, Isaac, etc. In some cases they assumed, or married, European family names like McCarthy and Adair. Others used their Cherokee name as a surname, that later became a family name. In 1880, you still will find an older man with a single name, Cherokee or its English translation, then that name used as a surname by two younger generations. So any of the male personal names can be used as a family name.

The Trail of Tears has had its effect: young parents named Ned and Nellie name their infant son something like Kenletah, throwing aside European alliance. Still, the great majority use Victorian American nomenclature: Henry, George, Mattie, Lizzie, Anne, Elizabeth, Lucy, Susan, Clem, etc. Peculiarly Cherokee habits include a taste for naming boys Loony or Looney, Columbus, Stealer, Naked, Alleck, and Blueford or Bluford; and girls Wuttie, Darkey, Jinny or Jinnie, Minerva or Menerva, and any version of Araminta: Minta, Areminta, Arminta, Armenta, etc. Tennessee is fairly popular for girls, and a certain number were called Cherokee, as were a few males. The use of tribes' names as personal names appears to have begun in native tribes, later passing to the American community at large.

What you have to mix and match: English personal and family names; native Cherokee personal and family names; and English translations of the meaning of Cherokee names. I believe that in many cases someone named Blackfox never was called Oo-ya-la-he, but that English words were being used in a Cherokee manner. Mix all three kinds among your characters. Overall, when not given English personal names women are more likely to have Cherokee names, men are more likely to have translation names.

Almost no parents name by pattern. Two young sisters, Cunaha and Sunaha, show up, and the brothers, Huckleberry, Whortleberry, and Mulberry Downing. But these were the only two cases I spotted in the census rolls.

Dollar Red-Bird, White-Girl Rabbit, Red Cloud Scruggs, Detaskaski Rooster, Lord Murphy, Getmoney Locus, Three Jacks Chucalate — can you resist putting their like in your contemporary or historical story? Part Cherokee will do. Most of those wonderfully clear, and therefore dramatic, family names like Night, Sunshine, and Steel come out of the innumerable Cherokee who moved easily into the dominant society of the South. There never seems to have been the red color bar that operated against the natives in the West.

Pronunciation is as feels good to you. The many recorders spelled the names as sounded, which is why some names are broken by hyphens and others are not.

FEMALE NAMES

Acqualla
Ahkelake
Ahleki
Ahnaler
Ahneeyoh
Ahnuwaker
Ahtinny
Ahuewega
Ahyahne
Ahynque
Ahyokah
Aki — fairly popular
Akire
Alla
Aniwaki
Anoga
Araminta — very popular
Arnarookee
Arnuwake
Aryahmula
Ayokay
Black Hawk
Cahawk
Cahitah
Cahtahna
Callet
Canohie
Cantake
Cariarah
Casawyarki
Catayah
Cawhena
Cayahe, Cayahye
Che-kah-nae
Checonald
Checoowa, Checoowee, Checoower
Checoyu
Chegosa
Chenasgaw
Cherkarne
Chewone
Cheyahnonth
Cheyalnernoo
Cheyoka
Cheyose
Chicayu
Chicohi
Chicunala

Chinie
Chinlaga
Chinusa
Chokohe
Choweyuka — fairly popular
Chucanil
Chunasah
Chunyuku
Clarherher
Clokohe
Cohenah
Cootiya, Cotiye
Cunaha
Daka
Darkey — popular
Detaskaski
Echar-cah, Echarcah
Echee-coo
Echuca
Elhunon
Ezana
Gayacha
Hianie
Huctiyah
Huetiyah
Jenney, Jinny — fairly popular
Jinanna
Kah-no-lie, Kahnolie
Kahhetah
Kahhogah
Kahlelahhi
Kahlelole
Kahlohe
Kahloncrskc
Kahluhela
Kahneyohe
Kahokah
Kahuga
Kalstiye
Kartchar
Kartryoie
Kayhohe
Kayohe, Kahyohe — popular
Kayrukah
Kayugah
Kazaher

Koheno
Koo-estah
Koyokah
Kunnerwele
Lahtiye
Minta — popular
Mistress
Mohewee
Nakay, Nake
Nakee, Naki
Nawana
Necootie
Neecootahye
Neyutaie
Nickati
Onahlezoonker
Oniwaki
Ookerwe
Ookiley
Ooluchu
Oonie
Ootahye, Ootiye
Ooyoste
Paralle
Pinelipi
Quah-le-yu-kah, Qual-la-yu-kah, Quar-leyukah, Quarligukah
Qualeka
Quaty — somewhat popular
Raniyahah
Runied
Sakinay
Sarlkinney
Sewarstah
Silvery
Sittuna
Somesta
Squarnegole
Sthaga
Sulah
Sunaha
Tahki, Takey, Taki
Tahyoneh
Te-tar-ke-yar-skee
Tenah
Tennessee — fairly popular

Tookah — very popular
Toonaya, Tooney
Usurga
Wah-ne-nah

Wakie, Waki, Waky —
   fairly popular
Wanona
Warlesa, Warlese

Watiyah, Wattiyah
White Girl
White Woman
Wuttie — popular

Male Names

Ah-le-chah
Ah-mah-su-ie
Ah-ne-you-ske
Ahnalesky
Ahtletohe
Ahtola
Ahyunki
Alexandrew — Cherokee
   blending of Alexander
   and Andrew; popular
Atolahe
Badger
Bear
Beaver
Bender
Bigfeather
Bird — fairly popular
Birdchopper
Blackbird
Bloom
Blue — somewhat popular
Blueford, Bluford — very
   popular
Boot
Bushyhead
Cahinahe
Candy
Caneyah
Catcha, Catcher, Ketcher
Catugum
Cawloomar
Che-te-qui
Chee-la-na-hee
Chiamorge
Chicalely
Cholukee
Chooneyomer
Chooworluky
Chow-u-ka
Chu-wa-lokee, Chu-wa-
   loo-kee
Chucernerter
Chukelele

Chuktute
Chuleoh
Chulera
Chulersuttah
Chulixie
Chunetie
Chunstute
Chusalete, Chuserlerter
Chutogaste
Chuwanoske
Cla — somewhat popular
Clarstarmar
Cloud
Constitution
Creek
Crying Bear
Culstiye
Dark
Deer
Dirt
Diyahlana
Dollar
Dull Hoe
Eagle
Easter
Echucu
Etagerstah
Fall
Firekiller
Fish
Flute
Fog
Fox — somewhat popular
Frost
Getmoney
Getup
Gima
Going Sleep
Goose
Goround
Green
Ground Hog
Ground Squirrel

Gugaytu
Gutts
Hawk — fairly popular
Henerlookee
High
Hogshooter
Horn
Humming Bird
Hunter — popular
Ice
Ieyuste
Jealous
Kahnerche
Kanugee
Karcummah
Karloyate
Kartuher
Kenletah — fairly popular
Kenleuche
Ketlechule
Ki
Kunertetah
Kusunne
Lamo
Layingby
Leaf
Little
Little Deer — with any
   other animal, too
Longarm
Lord
Lulertane
Mankiller
Meducenial
Mink
Mironia
Moose
Nah-hool
Naked — fairly popular!
Ne-coo-tie
Nertah-we-yah
Nietidahni
North

Nula
Nunktetahne
Okohimunt
Ookonale
Oolanahsteske
Oolawhuli
Oonatagee
Oonokartah
Ooteya
Ootulutane
Oowastarna
Ooyotuck
Osi
Otter
Overtaker
Owalorka
Pathkiller
Peace
Pleasant
Polecat
Rain
Ready
Red Bird, Redbird
Rider
Runabout — fairly popu-
   lar
Saluke
Sawam
Sawwatchie
Scale

Seacat
Sellout
September, etc.
Sequayah, Sequoyah
Shadow
Shake-in-the-bush
Sign
Sinagooyah
Six
Skontahhe
Sonna
Spade
Sparrowhawk
Spirit
Spring
Squirrel — fairly popular
Staggerabout
Standabout
Stay
Stealer — very popular
Sultiski
Suttewakie, Sut
Suyoter
Swimmer
Tagotah
Tahlaterk
Tarksehagee
Tehuyah
Tekahtunas
Tick-er-lo-gee-skee

Tickerneegoneske
Tickernochilly
Tieska
To-she-wa
Tobacco
Tochelane
Tockernohela
Tooleist
Tundi
Tyarka
Ummarteskee
Wa-la-na-tah
Walanketan
Walkabout
Wasala
Wasting
Waterfalling
Welanhite
White
Whitepath
Wildcat
Writer
Yartunnah
Yonah
Young Bird
Young Butcher
Youngbeaver
Zonawene

FAMILY NAMES

Acorn
Ahkilanigi
Ahleach
Arquatoke
Backbone
Bark
Bat
Bean
Beanstick
Bearpaw, Bear-paw,
   Barepaw
Beaver, Beavertail
Beehunter
Bendabout
Bigfeather
Bigfoot
Bigheaven

Blossom
Bow
Bread
Brown
Buffalow — with W
Bull
Buzzard
Canoe, Canoo
Chewachucker
Chewalooga
Chicken
Chickenroost
Choctaw
Chowenah
Chucalate, Chukelate,
   Chukeloke
Chulio

Chunequah
Chusalete
Clo-yah-cah
Coldweather
Coming
Comingdear
Cooweeskoowee
Cornsilk
Creeper
Cricket
Cristie
Czamakon
Daylight
Deerinwater
Degotnohe
Dew
Dirteater

Doublehead
Downing
Dreadfulwater
Drum
Dry
Drywater
Duck
Eagle
Empty
Feather
Feeling
Fields
Fivekiller
Flowers
Flute
Foreman
French
Frog
Glad
Glass
Goback
Grass
Green
Gritts
Guess
Gugaytu
Hailstack
Hair
Horn
Hornet
Hothouse
Irons
Judge
Jumper
Kahleskawe
Kanugee
Karcummah
Karnuche
Killer
Killwoman
Leach
Lie — could be Norwegian
Liver
Locus
Lone
Love
Middlestriker
Mixwater
Mole
Mush

Muskrat
Nakedhead
Neyahittah
Night
Nofire
North
Oatrun
Onelasa
Oo-yu-tah
Oolanahsteske
Oonatagee
Oowastarna
Overtaker
Pan
Pathkiller
Peace-maker
Pheasant
Pickup
Pigeon
Polecat
Poorbear
Poorboy
Poorwolf
Pumpkin
Rabbit
Rainwater
Rat
Raven
Red-bird
Redman
Rider
Rooster
Runabout
Runningbear
Sakinay
Sallateskee
Sam
Sanders
Scraper
Scruggs
September
Sequoyah
Sevenstarr, Sevenstars
Shade
Shadow
Shake-in-the-bush
Shell
Silk
Sixkiller
Sittingdown
Skitt

Smoker
Soap
Sort
Sparrowhawk
Speaker
Spears
Springfrog
Springwater
Squirrel
Stand
Starr
Stealer
Steel
Still
Stop, Stops
Summerhill
Sunday
Sunshine
Suwake
Tadpole
Tagotah
Tahlaher
Take
Takeup
Tarksehagee
Tarlosa
Tarripin
Teehee
Tesarkee
Teyarneskee
Thorn
Tobacco
Trap
Triplet
Tyeska
Walker
Walkingstick
Walnut
Warmosse
Watatooka
Water
Waterdown
Whitecatcher
Wolf
Wowastana
Yellow Bird, Yellowbird
Young Pig
Youngblood
Youngpuppy

SIOUX (LAKOTA)

Young children will have a name based on birth order until they get a more appropriate one in a few months or years. These names are also used by the Iroquois.

	Male	*Female*
First	Chaske'	Wenonah
Second	Haparm	Harpen
Third	Ha-pe-dah	Harpstenah
Fourth	Chatun	Waska
Fifth	Harka	We-harka

If a boy is born first, the next child, if a girl, will be Harpen, not Wenonah. Wenonah, or Winona, is a name a woman may re-adopt when she is grown, if she has proved worthy of it. The others are strictly baby names.

FEMALE NAMES

Appearing Day
Beautiful Dwelling,
   Tateyohnakewastewin

Black Shawl
Warcaziwin
Wih-munke Wakan

Zitkala-sa

MALE NAMES

Bad Face
Big Eagle — Wa-nah-de-tunck-a
Big Head
Black Hawk
Blue Medicine — Toh-to-wah-kon-da-pee
Breaking Up
Brown Wing
Bull Eagle
Chased by Bears
Conquering Bear
Fast Thunder
Fire Coal
He-Dog
High Eagle
Iron Cutter — Muzzabucksa
Jumping Badger
Killing Ghost
Little Bear — Mah-to-chee-ga

Little Crow
Lone Bear
Medicine Bottle
No Flesh
O-kup-pee
Old Man Afraid of His Horses — may be mistranslation of Man Whose Very Horses are Feared
One Horn — Ha-wan-ghee-ta
Painter — We-chash-a-wa-kon
Red Leaf
Red Man — We-chush-ta-doo-ta
Red Pipe Stone — Tchan-dee-pah-sha-kah-free
Red War Bonnet
Red Wing
Rotten Pumpkin
Runs Against Something When Crawling

Scraper
Shakopee
Sitting Bull — Tatanka Yotanka
Spotted Eagle
Stands on Both Sides — Ah-no-je-
nahge
Tangle Hair
Three Bears
Toh-ki-e-to
Torn Belly — Tah-zee-kee-da-cha

Two Lance
Wa-be-sha
Wa-pa-sha
Water All Gone
White Bear — Matoska
White Cloud
Wooden Leg
Yellow Weasel
Woman's Dress

Osage

Big Crow — Ko-ha-tunk-a
Big Track
Black Dog — Tchong-tas-sab-bee
Constant Walker — Moi-een-e-she
Handsome Bird — Shin-ga-wos-sa
He Who Is Not Afraid — Mun-ne-
pus-kee
He Who Takes Away — Wa-mash-ee-
sheek
Little Chief— Cah-he-ga-shin-ga
Little White Bear — Meach-o-shin-
gaw
Mad Buffalo — Tcha-to-ga

Mad Man — Wash-im-pe-shee
Man of Good Sense — Chesh-oo-
hong-ha
Man of the Bed — Nah-com-e-shee
Mink-chesk
No Fool — Wa-hon-ga-shee
Tal-lee
Wa-saw-see
Waho-beck-ee
War — Wa-chesh-uk
White Hair
Wolf— Sho-me-cos-se

Oglala

Black Elk
Crazy Horse — Tashunca-Uitco

Curly
Red Cloud — Makhpiyaluta

Brule'

Spotted Tail

Hunkpapa/Onc-pa-pa

Black Moon
Dog — Shonka
Gall — aka Pizi'

Iron Hawk
Steep Wing — Tah-teck-a-da-hair

FAMILY NAMES (20TH CENTURY)

Eastman
Goodhouse
Higheagle

Kills-the-Enemy
Medicine
Pumpian

Standing Bear

VOCABULARY
(from Catlin)

Antelope — Tah-to-ka-no
Arrow — Won-hee
Bad — Shee-cha

Bear — Matto
Beaver — Chapa
Bow — Eta-zee-pah

Boy — Okee-chin-cha
Buffalo — Pe-tay
Child — Chin-cha
Cold — Sinee
Dark — Ee-ohk-pa-zee
Day — On-pah
Deer — Teh-cha
Dog — Shon-ka
Drum — Chon-ohe-a-ha
Elk — Opon
Face — Ee-tay
Fire — Pah-ta
Fish — Oh-hong
Foot — See
Girl — Wee-chin-cha
Good — Wash-tay
Gun — Mon-za-wakon
Hair — Pay-kee
Hand — Non-pay
Heavy — Te-kay
Horse — Shon-ka-wakon
Hot — Mush-ta
Lance — Wow-oo-ke-za
Leggings — Hons-ka
Light — O-jan-jee

Long — Honska
Medicine/Magic — Wa-kon
Moccasins — Hong-pa
Moon — On-wee
Night — On-ha-pee
Not heavy — Ka-po-jel-la
Quiver — O-ju-ah
Rain — Ma-how-jea
Rattle — Waga-moo
Raven — Kong-hee
River — Wah-ta-pah
Robe — Shee-na
Shield — Woh-ha-chonk
Shirt — O-ken-dee
Short — Pe-tah-cha
Snow — Wah
Spirits, ghosts — Wa-nough-hgee
Stars — We-chash-pe
Sun — Wee
Tobacco — Tchondee
War Eagle — Wa-me-day-wah-kee
White Buffalo — Ta-his-ka
Wife — We-noh-cha
Woman — Wee-on

CHEYENNE

An older relative of the child's father — grandparent, uncle or aunt — gives the newborn a name. Boys often get an animal or physical attribute name, with an added descriptive word or phrase (Tall Bull, Spotted Wolf, Little Hawk). Not uncommonly they are called Young-something. It is not unknown for Hog's son to be called Young Hog until he earns something more distinctive.

Girl-names included "woman"; that is, they used a female infix (Owl Woman, Buffalo Calf Road Woman, Little Creek Woman). Young Hog's sister might be called Hog's Daughter.

Nicknames are used until age five or six for both sexes. A favorite endearment for children is "Potbelly" (boys, Moksois; girls, Moksiis).

When grown, especially after his first battle, a man's parents might change his name. After their son's sterling courage at the battle of the Rosebud, Spotted Wolf and his wife sent a crier through the village to announce, "The name of Young Black Bird is thrown upon the ground! Hereafter, he shall be called White Shield!"

Name changes continue throughout life. Maple, Maple Tree, Dog on the

Range, Dog on the Ridge, Dog Standing, Old Brave Wolf— all of these were legit-imate names for the famous medicine man best known as Box Elder. Any name that sticks for a while can count.

Since most Cheyenne names are given in translation, the following is arranged by concept. For example, under Animal Names there will be Wolf Names, Bear Names, Deer Names (including elk). Under Appearance Names will be things like Stub Foot and Tangle Hair.

These sorts of names would be used by any of the Plains tribes. Despite lan-guage differences and specific tribal magic, the Cheyenne, Sioux, Arapaho, and others closely allied swapped members in marriage, the men often going to their wives' tribe.

All family names are modern, adopted on the reservation. They are almost always the translation name of the last free-ranging ancestor, whose children then were straitjacketed into the Christian name–family name pattern. Most still receive individual names in Cheyenne. Those with a white-eyes family name can trace it to one who married into the tribe.

The names below are as I found them, so sometimes the female ones are translated with Woman, sometimes without. Note that Woman is most often added when leaving it off would result in a single-word adjective name (Flying, Buffalo, Lame); and most often omitted when the name already has at least two elements (Big Body, White Necklace, Without Weapon), or the name has a fem-inine edge (Pretty Walker, Buffalo Cow).

Some names almost defy classification. What lies behind the name of the famous warrior, Mouse's Road, or North Left Hand? These you will find under Miscellaneous Names, and they will loosen your stereotypes.

FEMALE NAMES

Untranslated, Unclassified

Ehyophsta
Hoistah
Ho'ko

Me-o-tzi aka Monasetah
Mochi

Activity Names

Bathes Her Knees — Tis-see-woo-na-
    tis
Fingers Woman

Glad Traveller
Pretty Walker
Stands by the Fire

Living Things Names

Animal Names

Bear Woman
Bird Bear
Buffalo Calf Road Woman

Buffalo Cow
Buffalo Girl (so translated because of
    her extreme youth)
Buffalo Woman
Frog Woman

Hog's Daughter
Tail Woman
Weasel Woman
White Buffalo Calf Woman
White Buffalo Cow

Bird Names

Crane Woman
Owl Woman

Plant Names

Leaf
Old Bark

Appearance Names

Personal Appearance Names

Belly Woman
Big Body
Crooked Nose Woman
Lame Woman
Little Woman
Red Hair
Ribbed Woman
Shell Woman — Minia; means an
  extremely pretty woman
Short Woman

White Woman
Yellow Hair Woman — Plains tribes
  sometimes had golden-brown hair
Yellow Woman

Clothing Names

Plume Feather Ornament
Porcupine Dress
Red Feather
Red Head or Red Hood
White Necklace

Foreigner Names

The Enemy
Pawnee Woman

Plains Woman
Sioux Woman

Incident Names

Brave One
Comes Together
Sweet Taste Woman

Twin Woman
Walks in the Middle
Without Weapon

Mystic Names

Flying Woman
Ghost Woman
Medicine Rock

Medicine Woman — who got her new
  name when she became clairaudient
Singing Cloud

MALE NAMES

Untranslated, Unclassified

Hotoanamos

Minimic

Activity Names

Angry
Blacksmith
Comes in Sight
Kills at Night

Mower, or Cut Grass
Pushing Ahead
Sitting Man

Standing Names

Standing on the Ground
Standing on the Hill
Standing Twenty
Stands Different
Stands in Timber

Walking Names

Highwalking, Highwalker
Noisy Walking
Walks Last
Walks with the Wind

Animal Names

Bear Names

Bear Shield
Black Bear
Bull Bear
Coal Bear
Foolish Bear
Half Bear
Iron Bear
Lean Bear
Leaving Bear
Little Bear
Living Bear
Lone Bear
Old Bear
Porcupine Bear
Roan Bear
Sitting Bear
Sun Bear
Walking Bear
White Bear

Beaver Names

Beaver Heart
Black Beaver
Many Beaver Dams

Bird Names

Bird
Black Bird
Black Turkey
Chicken Hawk
Crow Necklace
Crow or Old Crow
Crow White
Eagle Feather Horse
Eagle Head
Egg
Flying Hawk
Head Swift
Heap of Birds
Hollering Eagle

Little Hawk
Little Swift Hawk
Magpie
Magpie Eagle
Medicine Bird
Old Crow
Red Bird
Sand Crane
Screeching Bald Eagle
Spotted Blackbird
Turkey Legs
White Bird
Yellow Eagle

Buffalo Names

Buffalo Medicine
Buffalo Wallow
Bull
Bull Bear
Bull Coming
Bull Hump
Bull Thigh
Bull Wallowing
Erect Horns
Last Bull
Medicine Bull
One Horn
Stone Calf
Stump Horn
Tall Bull
White Buffalo
White Bull

Deer Names

Elk River
Lame Deer
Lone Elk
Medicine Elk
Standing Elk
Starving Elk
Whistling Elk

White Antelope
White Tail

Horse Names

American Horse
Big Horse
Black Horse
Bob Tail Horse
Crazy Mule
Eagle Feather Horse
Gentle Horse
Horse Roads
White Horse

Pig Names

Spotted Hog
Wild Hog
Young Hog

Wolf Names

Big Wolf
Black Wolf
Blind Wolf
Brave Wolf
Fire Wolf
High Wolf
High-backed Wolf
Howling Wolf
Little Wolf
Medicine Wolf
Old Little Wolf

Spotted Wolf
Starving Wolf or Hungry Wolf
Wolf
Wolf Chief
Wolf Feathers
Wolf Necklace
Wolf on the Hill, Nee-hee-o-ee-woo-tis
Wolf Tooth
Wolf Satchel
Wolf Voice

Other Animals

Bat
Dragging Otter
Little Fish
Medicine Snake
Porcupine
Sleepy Jack Rabbit
Spider — Veho, Wihio, trickster
White Frog

Other Canine Names

Black Coyote
Black Dog
Black Hairy Dog
Dog
Little Coyote
Little Kit FoxStarving Coyote
Low Dog
Walking Coyote

Appearance Names

Clothing Names

Big Leggings
Big Moccasin
Black Moccasin, Dirty Moccasin
Black War Bonnet
Calfskin Shirt
Fan Man
Feather Hair Ornament
Hard Robe
Little Robe
Red Hat
Red Hood
Red Robe
Small Blanket
Yellow Calfskin Shirt

Hand Names

Closed Hand, or Fist
Limber Hand a.k.a. Limber Bones
North Left Hand
Strong Left Hand
Yellow Hand

Peculiarity Names

Big Foot
Black Bodied Man
Crooked Neck
Cut Foot
Deaf Man
Limpy
Long Back

Scabby
Stub Foot
Three Fingers

Personal Appearance Names

Big Head
Braided Hair
Braided Locks
Crooked Nose
Crow Split Nose
Curly Hair
Cut Nose
Fringe
Great Eyes

Grey Beard
Grey Hair
High Forehead
Little Face
Long Jaw
Pug Nose
Roached Hair
Roman Nose
Slim Face, Lean Face
Squint Eyes
Tangle Hair
White Mustache
Wooden Leg — for leg strength
Wrapped Hair
Yellow Nose

Geography Names

Black Stone
Bridge
Sand Hill

Water Names

Dirty Water
Little Creek
Little Spring
Red Water

Mystic Names

Medicine Names

Buffalo Medicine
FlyingSweet Medicine
Ice
Little Finger Nail
Medicine Bird

Medicine Bull
Medicine Elk
Medicine Snake
Medicine Top
Medicine Water
Medicine Wolf

Plant Names

Corn Names

Corn Planted on Good Level Ground
Red Tassel
Rustling Corn Leaf
Sweet Root Standing

Tree Names

Box Elder
Maple, Maple Tree

Oak
Pine

Other Plant Names

Hollow Wood
Plum Man
Pumpkin Seed
Red Cherries

Sky Names

Celestial Names

Alights on the Cloud
Black Moon

Little Sun
Morning Star
Red Moon
Rising Sun

Stands on the Cloud
Star
Sun Bear
Thunder Cloud
Two Moon
White Moon

Gray Thunder
Hail
Little Whirlwind
Walks with the Wind
Whirlwind
White Thunder

Weather Names

Blown Away
Dark

Tool Names

Black Kettle
Black Whetstone

Broken Dish
Whetstone

War Names

Weapon Names

Bear Shield
Broken Bow
Dull Knife
Iron Shirt
Left Hand Shooter
White Shield

Injury Names

Cut Belly
Shot in the Head
Wounded Eye
Wounded in the Head

Miscellaneous Names

Around — nothing more, just "Around"
Important Man
Little White Man
Mouse's Road
One Eyed White Man
Red Woman — not Red (feminine),

but a man named "Red Woman"
Short Sioux
Stone Forehead, Hohonai'viuhk'-
  Tanuhk
Twins
Two Twists

Old Names

BRETON

Long ago, when Julius Caesar was storming through Gaul, this was called Armorica. In the 5th and 6th centuries, when the English and the Danes were making Britain too exciting, tribes of Britons from Wales and Cornwall crossed the Channel for good. As a result, Armorica became known as "little Britain," Brittany — Bretagne, in French.

Breton names are neither fish nor fowl. Never English, their Celtic was somewhat influenced by Norman and French, but there are some "French" names that just do not look really French. Nine times out of ten, they belong to Bretons (the tenth is Provençal).

Notably, Breton names use the letter K (French will always use C), and use Z where French puts J, or to end a name instead of an accented E.

Since the coming of modern communications, the last barriers between Brittany and the rest of France are fading out. So, too, are the preponderance of Breton names as the French move in, and Breton parents give their children fashionably French names. Indeed, by the beginning of the 20th century most Bretons had French personal names, even though they spoke Breton. But women still kept their natal family names, rather than changing to that of their husband.

However, in the heyday of Channel smuggling between Brittany and southern Britain, your anti–Napoleonic spy is as likely to take refuge at the farmhouse of someone named Jakez as Jacques.

UU is pronounced W, and is the equivalent of the Welsh or Cornish GW. It appears only in very old names, suitable before 1400 or so. Instead of a Welsh double L, the Bretons use LH.

Titles

aotrou — lord

itron — lady

dimezell — young lady

Female Names

Azilicz
Barbaik, Barbe, Barba
Bazilize
Bellah
Claire

Corentine
Del
Katrina
Lise, Lisette
Maï [mah-EE]

Marianne
Rozennik
Téphany
Varia — Marie

Male Names

Alain, Alan
Anatole
Armand
Auguste
Austol
Barnabé
Bernèz
Bertrand
Bryak, Brieuc
Budok
Canao
Carantcar
Carantoer
Caranton
Caratnou
Clet — very popular
Conan — popular
Conbrit
Congar
Corentin — popular
Daniel
Dei
Denis
Edern
Édouard
Gauan
Gourgons — very popular
Guezennec
Gui
Guigner
Guillaume
Haerveu
Hedr
Hedroc

Herbot
Hersart
Hoel
Houarn
Illoc
Iudcant — splendid lord
Iudhael — generous lord
Ives
Kenan
Kerentin, Kerenin
Jakemon
Jakez
Jakig
Jalm
Jégu
Jodoc
Joz
Judicael
Kel
Kenguethen
Kodelig
Lan
Louis
Maban
Maioc
Malscuet — princely
    shield
Maodez
Marzinne
Melor
Meren
Meriadek
Merion
Meven

Perig
Peronnik
Piron
Prosper
Rangof, Goff
René
Rogéar
Roparz
Roperzh
Samson
Sezni
Simon
Sulenn
Talan
Tangi, Tangy, Tanguy —
    fire dog
Uualatr — leader
Uuethenoc
Uuethien
Uuin — fair, splendid
Uuinhaeloc — splendid
    generosity
Uuinou — splendor
Uuinuuoloe
Uuoletic
Uuorien
Uuorloies — very
    pure/holy
Xavier
Yann — very popular
Youenn
Yves

FAMILY NAMES

Aballain, Aballan
Abarnou
Abasq
Allen, Allené, Alleno,
  Allenou
L'Aot
Appéré, Apéré, Apperry,
  Appéry
d'Argentre, Argenton
Arhantec
Audeyer
Auzou, Auzoux
Azenor
Bacon, Le Baccon
Le Bail
Balc'hou
Baoudour
Barguil, Barguillet
Bégo, Bégoc, Bégos
Berc'houc
Beyo, Beyou
Bidolec
Bihan, Le Bihan, Bihanic,
  Bihannic
Bizouarn
Bléjean, Bléjan
Blougorn
Bobiec, Boninec, Bobin-
  nec
Bolez
Bonderf, Bonderff
Bono, Bonou, Boniou
Bosser
Botrel
Bouet-Willaumez
Bourhis
Le Braz
de Brehan de Galinee
Brehier
Breton
Brizeux
Broc'h
Broustal
Budes de Guebriant
Cabellec, Le Cabellec,
  Cabellic, Cabellou
Calloch
Calvez
Cariou

Chuiton, Chuitton, Le
  Chuitton
Cloarec, Clorec, Le
  Clouérec
Clugéry, Clujéry
Coatanoan
de Coetnempren
Corentin
Le Corres
Le Coze
Créoff
Croc, Crocq
Cucurru
Cussec
Dagorn
Danguy
Daouadal
Le Dévédec, Le Déventec
Diffendal
Dissillour
Doll, Dolliou, Dollo,
  Dollou, Dolo, Dolou
Doucen, Doucin,
  Doussen
Draoulec
Drezen
Duault
Duguay-Trouin
Le Dylio
Ealet
Efflan
Enizan, Enisan
Espern, Esperne
Euzenat
Evanno, Evano
Ezan, Ezanno, Ezvan
Failler, Faillier
Fanic
Le Fay, Le Fé, Le Fée
Le Fèbvre
Feulvarch
Fleuter
Fouasnon
Foulgoc
Fraval, Fravalo, Fravallo
Furic
Gabellec, Gabellic
Le Gall
Geffray, Geffroy

Gentil
Gestalen, Gestalin
Gigaden
Gingomard
Glanndour
Gléran, Gléren, Glérin,
  Glérand
Le Glouahec, Le Glouan-
  nic
Goardet
Le Goffe, Le Goffic
Le Gonidec
Granic, Grannec
Guéhenneuc, Le
  Gue'hennec, Gue'hen-
  neux
du Guesclin
Guinoda
Guivarch
Habasq
Harzic
Hélias
Hémon
Hénaff
Hili, Hily
Hilliou, Hiliau, Hiliou
L'Horget
Houel
Huellou, Hulo
Huon
Hyvinec
Iaouanc, Iaouancq
Inquel, Inquiel
Ithoré
Izel
Jaffray, Jaffré, Jaffrés,
  Jaffret, Jaffrez, Jaffry,
  Jeffret
Jallu, Jalu
Jéhan, Jéhanno
Jentric
Jicquel
Le Jincq
Le Joa
Jollu, Jolou, Jolu
Jugeau
Justum
Kaigre
Keralum

de Keratry
Kergroas
Kerhir
Kerhornou
Kericuff
Keriou
Kerodron
Kerveillant
de Kobor
Kongar
Labado
Laennec
Lagadeuc
de Langlais
Lekain
Lesconnec
Lesguern
Lestideau
Letty, Lety
Le Leuxhe
Le Lévearec
Lharidon
Lhelchat
Lhénaff
Lherrou
Lhostis
Lhuriec
Lhyver
Luzel
Malmanche
er Mason
Mathiez
Maunoir
Meilhac
Mensonge
Merlin de Douai
Mondragon
Mordiern
Moreau de Maupertuis
Morvan
Le Nabour
Le Namour
Le Nancelot
Navennec, Navénee, Naviner
Neiz

Le Neriec
Nigeou
Nijou
Nivannic
Le Noc, Le Noch
Le Noën
Notret
Le Noxaïc
Le Ny, Le Nys
Ochou
Ollu, Olu, Ollo
Orio, Oriou
Ourvouai, Ourvouay
Le Pabic
Palamour
Pankoucke
Pelleteur, Pelleter
Piqueller
Plouhinec
Pogamm
Le Portz, Le Porz, Le Porzo
Postik
Proux
Puloch, Puloche, Le Pulloch
Quaran, Quaren
Queffelec
Quier
Quiniquidec
Quistrebert
Quv'emard
Radenac
Redon
Resonet
Le Rest
Restif de la Bretonne
Riou
Roho, Rohou, Rohu
Le Roze, Le Ruz
Le Ru
Rumain, Rumen, Rumin
Rungoat
Ruquellou
Saizour
Sakesep

Savina
Sclotur
Scraign, Scraigne
Scuiller
Le Sinq
Sioc'han, Sioc'hen
Souêtre
Squividan, Squividen
Strill
Suün
Tabarec, Tabaric
Tallarmin
Tellec, Le Teillec
Thersiguel
Thiritel
Timen
Toulgoat
Tréguier
Troboa, Troboas, Trobois
Truscat
Tuauden
Tuffigo
Turuban
Le Tyran, Le Tyrand, Le Tyrant
Uhel
Ulliac
Ulvoa, Ulvoas
Urvoy
Le Vaccon, Le Vacon
Varclaye, Varcleye
Le Véo, Veu
Verven
Vidamant, Vidament
de la Villemarqué
ar Vinell
Le Vot
Vuillou
Le Yar
Yhuel
Ylliac
Yoncour
Yquel
Zaouter, Zaoutter
ar Zaut

YIDDISH

When the Romans began the work of scattering the Hebrews of Judea, the Hebrew language was already, like Latin for the Roman Catholic Church, or Sumerian for the Babylonians, a fossilized language reserved for holy ritual. That is why the New Testament was written in Aramaic, the everyday language of Judea, as well as in Greek. During the Diaspora, this became more exaggerated, to the point that women and children in Jewish communities often had little or no knowledge of Hebrew.

In Iberia, the common Jewish language of these Jews was Ladino, carried to the coasts of Africa and into the Mideast, as well as to England, after their expulsion from Spain by Ferdinand and Isabella. The Ashkenazim of Eastern Europe, spoke the several dialects of Yiddish—Lithuanian, Polish, and Ukrainian Yiddish, which are used in Romania, Austria, and Hungary, too. Yiddish is based on the German of a thousand years ago. The earliest Jews in America were Sephardim from England and the Lowlands, but after the middle of the 1700s the Ashkenazim begin to dominate.

The Ashkenazim, the Yiddish-speaking Jews, do not name children after living relatives. They worry even if a selected spouse has the name of an older relative: the newcomer will usually adopt a second name or use a nickname. They fear that the Angel of Death, coming for the elder, will be confused and carry off the younger. However, children were usually safely named for relatives that had already died.

Because of this, and because many parents gave double names, it was common for Yiddish people to be known by two names: Hinde Esther, Yizroel Yeshua, Shlomo-Zvi, Dovid-Aharon. Both Yiddish and Hebrew names were used. The Ashkenazim were very much aware of their past, and every boy over six was at least marginally literate in Hebrew.

Family names were both imposed and forbidden by European authorities; the Jews got along fine on Abraham son of David for millennia, Avram ben-Dovid by the Yiddish period. Many names are place-names, or father-names, like Mendelsson (Mendel's son). The "daughter-word" was *bas*: Avram's sister would be Rivke bas-Dovid.

The ordinary word for "Mister" was *Reb*. *Rebbe* was a mark of respect for rabbis, Hasidic masters, and other influential men. The wife of a Rebbe is a *Rebbetzin*.

Diminutives are made by adding "-l," "-el," "-le" or "-ele" to the end of a name or its root—sometimes repeatedly.

Americanization

In order to avoid anti–Semitic discrimination in business and education, immigrant Jews and their descendants often began the process of Americanization by giving their children "American" names, or by legally changing their own. Thus, in the Jewish neighborhood in which I grew up, the couple that ran the fruit store, despite their heavy accents, and the blue numbers tatooed inside their forearms at the Nazi extermination camps, were officially named Black.

Hebrew or Yiddish names were "translated" to something similar. In place of Itzik would be used Isadore, Irwin, or the common Irving; Allan, Albert, Alvin or Arnold for Avrum; Hyman, Herman, Herbert, or Charles for Chaim or Haim.

The tendency to name children after a deceased relative is still strong, but fashion has made the link tenuous. In honor of Moshe, a boy may be named Merwyn, Marvin, or any M-name. Likewise, Beryl or Bambi is considered to perpetuate Bathsheba or Brocha.

In the lists, assume the version is Yiddish. In some cases, the Hebrew version is marked, if notably different. The English version of the name, for everyone who does not know that Joshua is a *goyisher* corruption of Yeshua, is in parentheses.

FEMALE NAMES

Alte
Baile
Bathsheba
Batya
Blum, Bluma
Brocha, Broche
Channah, Chana (Hannah)
Chave
Chizha
Dvora, Dwora (Deborah)
Esther
Feigel, Feigele
Frieda, Freda, Freyde
Fruma
Genendele

Gisela
Gita
Golde, Golda, Goldie
Hendele
Hinda, Hinde
Hodel
Ita, Itele, Ittele, Itta
Kayle
Kelula
Kine — rare
Kyla
Leye, Leyele, Leyenyu,
  Leyinke, Leyinkele,
  Lyke, Leykele,
  Leykenyu, Leyche,
  Leychel, Leychenyu,

Lea (Leah)
Mindl
Mirele
Raizel (Rose)
Rifka, Rivke, Rivkele
  (Rebecca)
Rochele, Ruchel (Rachel)
Sarah
Sheine, Shaina
Taube, Taubele
Temerl
Udil
Yachne
Yenta, Yentl
Yosele

MALE NAMES

Abba
Adi
Aharon (Aaron)
Alein
Alter
Ansel
Arele
Arye
Asher
Avrum, Avram, Avraham,

Avromele
Azriel
Baruch, Boruch, Barukh
Benjamin
Berish, Berele
Brezel
Bunam
Chayim, Chaim, Cham
Dovid (David); Dawid,
  Dowid, where W = V

Dussa
Elhanan
Eliezar, Elie, Eli
Elimelekh
Eliyahu
Ephraim
Ezikiel
Fischel, Fishel
Gedaliah
Gershom, Gershon

Haim, Hayim
Hanina
Haskele
Henia
Hillel
Hoshaiah
Icek
Immanuel
Isaiah
Ishmael, Ish
Isidor
Itamar
Itche, Itzhak, Itzik (Yid-
    dish), Yitzak, Yitshok,
    Yitshak (Hebrew)
    (Isaac), Aizik; Itzikl
Koppel, Kopel
Kuper
Label
Leben
Leib (Levi), Löb, Loeb
Leizer
Mayer (Meir), Mayerl,
    Meirl
Meitel
Menachem
Mendel, Mendeley
Micah
Michel, Mikhel (Michael)

Moises, Moshe, Mozes,
    Moshele (Moses)
Mordecai
Mottel, Mottele
Nahman, Nachman
Nahum
Naphtali
Natan (Nathan)
Notte
Pakuda
Pinhas, Pinhos
Raphael
Ruben
Samson
Saul
Schmuel, Shemuel,
    Shmuel (Samuel)
Shammai
Shelomoh
Shepsel
Shimon (Simon)
Shlomo, Schlomele
Shmelke
Shneur
Sholem, Shalom, Sholom
    (Solomon)
Shur
Simcha
Tobias

Todros
Traitl
Uri
Velvel
Welfel
Welvel
Wolfe
Yacob, Yankel (Jacob)
Yehezkel
Yehiel
Yekele
Yeshua (Joshua)
Yisroel (Israel)
Yochanan, Yohanan
Yoel
Yousef, Yosef, Yosel,
    Yussel, Yosseleh,
    Yoshke, Yozifl, Yosheh,
    Yosenyu, Yoshenuy,
    Yosinkeh, Yoshkenyu,
    Yosinkleh, Yosinkeleh
    (Josef)
Yudl, Yudel (Judah)
Zakkai (Zacharias)
Zalman
Zeide
Zeira
Zusia
Zvi, Ziv, Zeev, Zevi

FAMILY NAMES
(Polish or unidentified)

Notice how place-of-origin names become family names: Gorshkover, from Gorshkov; Premishlaner, of Premishlan. Simply add -er to the Yiddish name of a town or village.

Abramowitz
Agnon
Asch — Polish
Ben-Zion
Berdichevski
Berenfeld
Berkowitz
Besser
Blecher
Bloom
Bloomgarden
Brandes

Brenner
Cohen, Cohn, Kohen,
    Kohan — very common
Druyanow
Dubnow
Edels
Efros
Epstein
Feierberg
Flederbaum
Frishman
Gorshkover — of Gorshkov

Hadas
Hakohen
Hanft
Herzl — Hungarian Zion-
    ist
Herzog — Polish rabbi
Horowtz
Hurwitz
Imper — Polish
Isaacs
Kliger
Kosower

Krochmal
Kuzmer, Kuzmirer
Leibele
Levi, Levy — common
Levinski
Liachower
Lilienblum
Lisitzski
Lubin — Polish
Maimon
Mapu
Mattes
Melamed

Musiker
Natanson
Persky
Pietrushka
Premishlaner — of Prem-
   ishlan
Przepiorko
Rachover — of Rachev
Ribalow
Rosenzweig
Rubenstein
Rubinlicht
Scharfstein

Schechter — Rumanian
Shoffman
Shverdsharf
Silkiner
Sokolow
Steinberg
Warshawiaks
Waxman
Wise — Hungarian and
   Bohemian
Zangwill

FAMILY NAMES
(German)

Notice the patronymic transformed into the family name, as Mendel's son Avram becomes Avram Mendelssohn. Any male name can be so transformed: Avramssohn, Isaakssohn, Meyerssohn.

Baruch
Blumgart
Carlbach
Einhorn
Frankel
Gompertz
Gottheil
Hirsch

Kalisch
Kohler
Kohn
Krauskopf
Lazarus
Leeser
Mendelssohn
Salomon

Schindler
Singer
Sulzberger
Wasserman
Weingut
Weizmann

(Russian)

Bialik
Fichman
Kahn
Schulman

Shimonwitz
Shneour
Shoar
Smolenskin

Sokolow
Tchernichovski
Wiener

VICTORIAN AMERICAN

PERSONAL NAMES

When your story falls from about 1830 to 1920 — or at least the characters are born in that span — using these names will give a better period flavor. British personal names at this time tend more to French influence, while the Americans went off their own way. There is a strong revival of Germanic and Biblical names, also Classic ones.

Of course most boys still get named William, Henry, Charles, etc., and most girls Mary, Elizabeth, and so forth, but here are the other popular names, the temporal equivalents of Christopher and Jason, Jennifer and Nicole.

These Victorian names did not drop out of existence, any more than the Renaissance English names of Hope, Faith, and Charity, but they became very uncommon. Some girls born in the 1940s or 1950s wound up with them by being named for grandmothers born in the 1880s or 1890s, and hated their names. Who wants to be something "old-fashioned and ugly" like Harriet when you could have been Carol, Linda, or Denise?

Modern baby-name books try to avoid the names of conquerors and other war-mongers, but those "win-all" names were considered a boost in life for a 19th century son; Cyrus, Darius, Caesar, or Hannibal.

A peculiarity most American is using titles of British nobility for boys' personal names: Marquis, Baron, Duke, etc.

FEMALE NAMES

Abigail
Adah — not unusual; sometimes Ada
Adelaide, Adela, Adelle, Adele, Adel, Della, Addie, Addy, Adeline, Adelina — very popular
Agnes
Aimee
Alice
Aljarine
Alma
Amelia, Amy
Angelina
Ann (notice lack of final E), Anna, Annie — long-term favorite
Augusta — fading; a leftover from the 18th c.
Barnabetta
Belle, Bella
Belva
Bertha
Bethenia — rare
Beulah
Blanche

Carrie, Carey, Carry
Cassie
Catharine — long-term favorite
Cecilia
Celeste
Charlotte — especially before 1820, after the Princess Royal
Christabel
Cladonia
Clara
Cora
Cordelia, Delia
Cornelia — popular
Daisy — distinctively American in the 19th c.; for Marguerite
Desdemona — any of Shakespeare's heroines are used
Dinah
Donna — usually a middle name
Dora
Dorothy, Dorothea
Edna
Edyth, Edith

Elaine
Eleanor, Ellen
Eliza
Elizabeth — long-term favorite; Lizzie
Ella — somewhat popular
Ellis — as in Ellis Knight
Elsa, Elsie
Emma
Emiline, Emmeline
Emily
Estelle
Esther
Ethel, Ethelwyn
Eunice
Evangeline, Eva
Flora — very Edwardian
Florence, Florrie, Flossie, Flo — popular
Florinda
Frances
Freda
Geraldine
Gertrude — popular
Gladys
Gypsy
Hallie
Hannah

Harriet — very popular;
  rarely Harriot
Helene, Helen
Henrietta
Hester, Hessie
Hilda
Honora
Ida — popular
Ina
Isabel, Isabelle, Isabella,
  Isobel
Isadora
Jane — fairly popular
Jemima — Anglo, too
Jennie
Jessie
Julia — fairly popular
Kate, Katie, Katy — with
  or without the Kather-
  ine
Laura
Lavinia
Lilian, Lillian, Lillie,
  Lily
Louisa, Lossie
Lucretia
Lucy — fairly popular
Luisa
Lydia — popular

Mabel
Mag, Magdalene
Maldorene
Malvene
Margaret
Marietta
Martha
Mary, Maria — long-term
  favorite
Matilda, Mattie — fairly
  popular
Maude
May, Maybelle
Millicent, Millie, Milly
Minerva, Minnie
Miriam
Molly
Myra
Myrtle, Myrt
Nancy, Nance
Nellie, Nelly, Nell
Netty, Nettie — for any
  "-ette" name, or free-
  standing
Oma
Oveta
Pamela
Pauline
Pearl, Perle, Perla — pop-

ular
Phillis (British), Phyllis
Phoebe
Portia — big Shakespeare
  revival; any of the
  heroines
Primula
Prudence, Prue
Rachel
Rebecca, Reba
Rheta
Rhoda
Rose — popular; Rosalie,
  Rosina
Rowena
Sarah — very popular
Selina
Serena
Sophia
Susan
Tamza
Tessie
Victoria
Vinnie
Zelia
Zoe, Zoë

MALE NAMES

Adna — popular
Albion
Alexander
Alonzo
Alphonso
Alvan
Anson
Anthony
Artemas
Asaph
Azariah
Beau, Beauregard
Beriah
Bing, Binge, Bingo
Bion
Bliss
Bonamy
Branch

Bushrod
Cecil
Charles — long-term
  favorite
Chester
Cosmo — popular
Cutcliffe
Cyrus
Dana — popular
Delos
Dwight — from family
  name
Eden
Edward — long-term
  favorite
Edwin
Elbert
Elizur

Elkanah
Ely
Ethan
Evelyn — since 18th c.
Frank — long-term
  favorite; Francke
Gale, Gayle — up through
  1930s
Galliard
Galusha
Gamaliel, Gamalial
Gano
Garet
Garnet — since at least
  1833
George
Gilbert
Godlove

Hablot
Hannis
Henry — long-term
    favorite
Hiram
Horace — fairly popular
Humphrey
Ignatius
Ira
Isaac
Ivy
Jaret
Jem — 18th–19th c.
Joaquin
Joel — very popular
John
Jonas — popular
Josiah
Linus
Loammi
Lorado
Lorenzo — since at least
    1837

Luther
Lynn
Meredith
Merle — since at least
    1897
Nathaniel
Olinthus
Orello
Orpheus — and anything
    else you want to steal
    from the Greek myths
    in Latin form
Oscar
Othniel
Otis
Page, Paige
Pegram
Peleg
Persifor
Pharcellus
Porter
Ralph
Rezin

Roeliff
Royal
Rufus
Salomon, Salmon
Selah
Sereno
Seymour
Shade
Shirley — for boys in the
    late 19th and early
    20th c.
Silas
Starr
Thaddeus
Thomas — long-term
    favorite
Titus
Ulysses
Vance
Vernon
Waddy
William — long-term
    favorite

Renaissance and Reformation (1400–1700)

RENAISSANCE ENGLISH

While the British largely stuck to their immemorial list of three dozen names, at this time there is an influx not only of Classical names, but also Old Testament names and brand new ones, thanks to the various Protestant movements, especially Puritanism.

The main differences from modern Anglo-American naming you must remember are to avoid using family names as first names; ditch the glamor spellings of first names, and all Americanisms; and remember the Spanish and Italian Protestant families are very new in town, and will not have Anglicized their names yet. For example, Ferdinando Gorges was born in 1566 in Somersetshire.

French personal names have not yet become acceptable: it is always Margaret, never Marguerite. Avoid Irish names for any but the Irish. There is a negative cachet to naming your child Sean or Eileen.

Family names are, early in the period, not cast in stone. In the 1400s a man may still be William le Aunseremaker, indicating that he manufactures scales. Spelling is a long way from regularized, in names as well as other words. You often have your choice of a familiar spelling like Eleanor, Hannah, Susan, or Frances, or you may add to the period flavor by calling the woman Ellinor, Hanah, Susand, or Frauncis. There are nicknames and diminutives, like Beaten for Beatrice, that we no longer use. Family names are sometimes spelled two or three different ways in the same paragraph. Use "the funny spellings" rather than the familiar forms to give that "olde tyme ayre" to characters.

Puritan and Bible Names

This started with English Protestants, but it spread widely across the colonies at an early date — remember who landed at Plymouth Rock. By the 19th century, one way British writers made a character instantly American was to give him an Old Testament name.

You can name your character the same way its parents might have: open the Bible at random, put your finger down, and run down the column to the first name you hit — not always of the proper gender, or even a person's name. Ebenezar is a place-name. One suspects that their literacy was often limited and the first proper noun was used. You can use the Hebrew chapter if you don't have a Bible.

The common thread in these religious movements, whether you consider them reactionary or revolutionary, is anti–Catholicism. Some purposely avoided the common names associated with any sorts of saints — Paul, Peter, John, Mary, Margaret, etc. So they gave their children non-saint names like Oliver or sat down and invented names out of everyday English.

Puritan "virtue names" are fun. Male and female names were not often that different. The girls did get some shorter names, nice enough that Hope and Chastity have survived their origins. Boys usually got short admonitions, which are long names. These can be used for their sisters equally well in most cases.

The light-foot Puritans would give their children names indicating their preciousness, or flower names to the girls. I have not found either Topaz or Opal in use; while the first is possible, the latter is often considered an ill-luck gem.

Some virtue names crossed over into common use. Others survived the demise of Puritanism in the strict Southern Baptists, especially black Baptists, which is why some of them may sound "Negro" to your ear.

Texas produced the longest of these slogan or virtue names:
Daniel's-wisdom-may-I-know,-Stephen's-faith-and-spirit
-choose,-John's-divine-communion-seal,-Moses'-meekness,
-Joshua's-zeal Murphy.
Notice how it scans; I suspect it is from a hymn. The victim's middle names were Win-the-day and Conquer-All, and he was born in 1883.

PURITAN FEMALE NAMES

Abigaiol
Amity
Aphra, Afra, Aphara, Ayfara
Beryl
Charity
Chastity
Constance
Coral
Deborah
Faith
Felicity

Fortitude
Fortune
Grace
Handmaid
Hester — not Esther
Honour
Hope
Ithamar — though male in the Bible
Keepsilent
Lament
Lia — Douai version of Leah

Listenwell
Mahala — not Mahalia, which is 20th c.
Mercy
Misericordia-adulte-rina — "Give me mercy for my adultery"
Modesty
Patience
Primrose
Prudence — Prudie or Pru for short

Rachel
Rebecke, Rebeckah,
    Rebecca
Ruby
Sapphira, Sapphire
Sarah
Silence

Submit
Susannah, Susanna
Tabitha
Temperance
Thanks
Trial
True

Unite
Verity
Violet
Virtue
Wait-still

Puritan Male Names

Aaron
Abel
Abraham
Ananias
Capability
Conquer-All
Constant
Cotton
Daniel
Eben, Ebenezer
Elijah, Elias
Eliphalet
Elisha
Elkanah
Esdras, Ezra
Experience
Faint-not — popular, in
    this group!
Fear-not — popular
Feargod
Fight-the-good-fight-of-

faith
Finis
Fly-debate
Fly-fornication
Freeborn
Freedom
Glory
Hallelujah
Hosea, Osee
Hoshea
Hosius, Osius
Humble, Humbleness
Increase
Isack, Izaak, Isaac
Jeremiah
Jerome
Jewel, Jewele
Josiah
Kill-sin
Makepeace, Make-peace
Nehemiah

Pearl, Pearle
Pelatiah
Phineas
Praisegod, Praise-God
Preserved
Prosperity, Prosper
Return
Sojourner
Tolerance
Treasure
Truth
Whom-the-Lord-pre-
    served
Win-the-day
Zabdiel
Zachary
Zeal-of-the-land —
    invented by Ben Jon-
    son, but it's right!
Zephaniah

Unsexed

Abstinence
Accepted
Arise
Ashes
Be-courteous
Be-faithful
Be-thankful
Believe
Comfort
Confidence
Consider
Deliverance, Delivery
Desire
Diligence
Discipline

Donation
Dust
Earth
Elected
Experience
Faith-my-joy
Fathergone — a posthu-
    mous child
Fear
Forsaken
Freegift, Free-gift
Freewill
From-above
Given
God-reward

Godly
Gracious
Hate-evil
Help-on-high — more
    than once used
Helpless
Hew-Agag-in-pieces-
    before-the-Lord
Hope-for
Hope-still
Hoped-for
Hopeful
Humble
Humiliation, Humility
Job-raked-out-of-the-ashes

Joy, Joy-again
Just
Lamentation
Learn-wisdom
Love
Meek
More-fruit
More-mercy
More-trial
Much-mercy
No-merit
Obedience
Peace
Peaceable
Perseverance
Purify
Redeemed
Reform, Reformation

Rejoice
Remember
Renewed
Repentance
Resolved
Restore
Safe-deliverance
Safe-on-high
Salvation
Search-the-scriptures —
    more than once used
Seek-wisdom
Silence
Sin-deny
Small-hope
Sorry-for-sin — more
    than once used
Stand-fast

Stand-fast-on-high
Steadfast
Thankful
The-Lord-is-near
The-peace-of-God
Through-much-tribula-
    tion-we-enter-into-
    the-kingdom-of-
    heaven — often
    nicknamed Tribby
    when female
Tremble
Tribulation
Truegrace
Truth
Weep-not
Wrestling

COMMON PERSONAL NAMES
OF THE
TUDOR AND STUART PERIOD

Four out of five people will have one of these names, nothing more distinctive. The British had not yet been bitten by the French yen for novelty and individuality. The upper classes are therefore most commonly known by their titles or family names, because there are scores of "Lady Elizabeths" or "Lord Edwards."

FEMALE

Upper and Middle Class
Anne, Anna, Ann
Eleanor
Elizabeth
Jane
Joanna, Johanna
Katharine, Catharine
Margaret

Mary

Lower Class, Nickname
Hannah, Hanah
Nell
Bess, Betty
Janet
Joan

Margery
Martha
Mary
Sarah

Male

Upper and Middle Class	Lower Class, Nickname
Ambrose	Ambrose
Anthony	
Arthur	Art
Benjamin	Ben
Charles	
Christopher	Kitt
Edmund	Ned
Edward	Ned
Francis	
George	
Gilbert	Gil, Gib
Henry	Harry
James	Jim — rare
John	Jack
	Joseph
Matthew	Matty
Peter (less popular)	Peter
Richard	Dick, Dickon
Robert	Robin
Roger	Roger, Hodge
Samuel	Sam
Thomas	Tom
Walter	Wat
William	Will

Uncommon Female Names

Adeline
Agatha
Agnes — not that uncommon
Alethia
Alice
Amabel, Amabella, Arrabella, Arabella
Amicia
Amy
Anastasia
Anchoret
Audrey
Audrian
Aureole
Avice, Avis
Barbara, often Barbery
Bassilly
Bawden

Beatrice, Beaten
Benedicta, Bennet
Benigna
Bertha
Blanche
Bridget, Briget — Scandinavian saint, not Irish Brigit
Bona
Bonyface — for Boniface
Brilliana
Cassandra
Catherine
Cecilia
Christian, no A or E at end
Cicely
Clara
Denise

Diana
Dido
Doras
Dorcas
Dorothy — not that rare
Douglas — if Scots
Dousable
Douze
Dulcia
Eglantine
Ellinor, Ellen, Elen
Emma, Emmet, Emmote
Eva
Felice
Florence
Frances, Francesca, Frauncis
Frediswid
Gertrude

Gillian
Gladuse
Goodeth
Griselda, Grissel, Gresell
Helline, Helene, Hellen, Helena
Ida
Isabel, Isabell
Isott, Izott, Ezotta, Isolt, Isolde, Isolda
Jacquetta
Jana
Jenet
Joyce
Judith
Julianne, Juliana
Kingburgh
Laura
Laurentia
Lettice
Loara, Lora
Lucia
Lucretia
Lucy
Lydia

Mabel
Magdalen
Margaret
Margery
Matilda
Maude, Maud
Meraud
Mildred
Millicent
Muriel
Nest
Nicia
Nicola
Olympias
Orabilis
Penelope
Pernel
Petronilla
Phebe — no O
Philadelphia
Philippa
Phyllis
Polyxena
Prisca, Priscilla
Radegunde

Rosamund
Rose
Sabina
Sanchia
Scholastica
Selina
Sidonia
Sophia
Sophronia
Susan, Susand
Sybyl
Tace
Theodora
Theodosia
Thomasin, Tamsin
Ulalia
Ursula
Venus — rare
Warburg
Wilmetta
Winifred — not that uncommon among middle and lower classes

Uncommon Male Names

Abre
Adam
Adelard
Adolph
Adrian
Aelward
Alban
Albert
Aldred
Alexander
Algernon
Alphonse
Alwin
Amery
Amias, Amyas
Andrew
Archibald
Arnold
Augustine, Augustin
Avery
Baldwin
Banastre

Baptist
Bardulph
Barnabas
Bartholomew, Bart, Tolly
Barton
Basil
Bede
Benet
Bernard
Bertrand
Blase
Bodwine
Bonaventure
Boniface, Boneface
Botolph
Brian
Brian, Bryan — from Scotland, not Ireland
Brutus
Caesar
Caius
Calasthenes, Calisthenes

Caleb
Caradoc — Welsh
Chrysostom
Clemens
Connop
Conrad
Constantine
Cornelius
Crescens
Cuthbert, Cuddy, Bert
Cyprian
Cyriac
David
Demetrius
Denis
Denzil
Devon
Drogo
Dunstan
Eadulph
Ealdred, Ealred, Ethelred
Edgar

Edwin
Egbert
Ellis
Elmer
Emanuel
Engelbert
Enion
Erasmus
Ernest
Ethelbert
Ethelstan
Ethelwolph
Eusebius
Eustache
Eutropius
Evan
Everard
Ezechias
Ezechiel
Fabian
Felix
Ferdinand
Florence
Frederic
Fremund
Fulbert
Fulcher
Fulke
Gabriel
Gamaliel
Garret
Gawen, Gawain
Geoffrey, Jeffrey
German
Germase, Gervase, Jervis
Gideon
Giles
Godard
Godfrey
Godwin
Gregory
Griffith
Grimbald
Grivell
Gurdon
Guy
Hamon
Hannibal
Hanserd
Harhold
Hector

Hengest
Herbert
Hercules
Herman
Herwin
Hierome
Hilary
Hildebert
Horatio
Howel
Hubert
Hugh
Humphrey
Israel
Jackamyn
Jacob
Jasper
Jeremy
Joab
Joachim
Jocelin
Jonathan
Jordan
Josceline
Joseph
Joshuah
Josias
Julius
Kenard
Kenelm, Kenhelm
Lambert
Lancelot
Laurence — not that
    uncommon
Leger
Leofstan
Leofwin
Leonard
Leopold
Lewis
Lewlin
Lion
Lionel
Ludovic
Luke
Madoc
Malachias
Manasses
Marcel
Mark
Marmaduke

Martin
Maugre
Maurice
Maximilian
Mercury
Meredith
Michael
Miles
Morgan
Nathaniel
Neal
Nicholas
Noel
Norman
Odo
Oliver
Original
Orlando
Osbern
Osbert
Osmund
Oswald
Owen — from the Welsh
Parse
Pascal
Patrick
Paul
Payn
Percival
Peregrine
Perkin
Philbert
Philip
Posthumus
Quintin
Raffe
Ralph
Randle
Raphael
Raymond
Reginald
Reinfred
Reinhold
Reuben
Roland, Rowland
Romane
Samson
Saul
Scipio
Sebastian
Sigismund

Silvester
Simonds, Simon
Solomon
Stephen
Swithin
Sylvanus
Theobald
Theodore
Theodoric
Theophilus

Timothy, Tim
Titus
Tobias
Tristram
Turstan
Uchtred
Urban
Urian
Valens
Valentine

Vincent
Vivian
Waldwin
Wilfred
Wimend
Wischard
Wolstan
Wulpher

FAMILY NAMES

Compare them to the regular English listing. This may show you how to adapt a modern family name to make it look period. These names come from the period 1400 to 1700, and many of their bearers were notable in one reign or another. Do check your history to see if there is a conflict in your period. The original bearer might have been prime minister at the time.

Abby, Abbey, Abbys
Aburne
Addison
Ainsworth
Alabaster, Arblastier
Alden
Alleine
Allerton
Alsop
Ambrose
Amis
Andrew
Andros
Archdale
Argall
Armstrong
Arydon
Applebee, Appelbee
Apps
Ascham
Ashburnham
Ashmole
Askew, Ascue, Aske
Atkyns
Atterbury
Aubrey
Audley
Aylmer
Badcooke
Baldwyn, Bauldwyn

Ballerde
Ballisster
Barbet
Barclay
Bardell
Barebones, Barbones
Barefoote
Bareleggs, Bearleggs
Bargeman
Barnes
Barrowe
Bartholomew
Basill
Basnett
Bastard
Bastwick, Bostwicke
Bath
Battman
Battye
Bawdwyn
Baynard, Baynerd
Beake
Beane, Beanne
Beare
Bearewoode
Beaufort
Beaver
Bedcocke
Bedell
Bell

Bellamont, Bellomont
Bellingham, Belingam
Bellyster, Bellystre
Benbow
Berners, Bernes, Barnes
Bever
Bibye
Bicke
Biddle
Bigland
Bilney
Bilson
Bingham
Birdseye
Blackmore
Blackstone
Blake
Blanchflower
Blaxestone
Blithman
Blondelle, Blondell, Blundell
Blount, Blunt
Blow
Bodley
Body, Bodye
Boleyn, Bullen, Bouleyne, Bollan, Bollen
Bollinge
Bonamee

Boner, Bonner
Bonyfelowe
Boorde, Borde
Borlase
Borough, Borrough
Bowring
Boyle, Boyleston
Bracegirdle
Bradford
Bradley
Bradshaw
Bradstreet
Brathwaite, Brathwait,
    Brathwayte
Brayne
Brent, Brenton
Breton, Britton, Brittaine
Bridgeman
Bright
Brome
Brooke
Broughton
Browne
Bubb
Bulkeley
Bull
Burgess
Burnet
Busby
Button
Byk
Byllynge, Byllinge
Byng
Byrom
Calamy
Caliborne
Callowhill
Camden
Campion
Capel
Cardwelle
Carleton, Carlton, Charl-
    ton
Carnabee
Carrol
Carteret
Carver
Caslon
Cat
Catesby
Cave

Cavyll
Caxton
Centlivre
Chacellor
Chaderdon
Chalkhill
Chalkley
Chaloner, Challoner
Chapman
Chauncy
Cheke
Cheselden
Chettle
Child
Chudleigh
Churchyarde
Claiborne
Claypole
Cleaves
Cleiveland, Cleveland
Clokmaker
Coddington
Cole, Colet
Conant
Constable
Conybeare
Cooke
Cookworthy
Cooper
Coram
Coryate, Coryat
Cotgrave
Cotton
Courtenay
Coverdale
Cowley
Cowper, Cooper
Crashaw
Croft, Crofts
Crossley
Cudworth
Culpeper, Colepeper
Cushman
Cuthbert
Cutts
Daggot
Darcy
Dare
Davenant
Davenport
Day, Daye

Deane, Dean
Dee
Dekker, Decker
Deloney, Delone
Desborough, Desborow,
    Disbrowe
Device
Dimblebee
Ditton
Dixwell
Doddridge
Dodington
Dollond
Dolman
Downing
Draper
Drayton
Drury
Dummer
Dwight
Dyer
Earle
Eaton
Echard, Eachard
Eden
Edwards, Edwardes
Egerton
Eliot, Elyot
Ellwood
Endecott, Endicott
Endicott
Etherege
Eusden
Evelyn
d'Ewess
Fabyan
Fairfax
Faithorne
Fanshaw
Farnaby
Farrabee
Fastolf
Fenwick
Farramt
de Feckenham
Feild — yes, ei
Felltham, Feltham
Felton
Fendall
Fenwick
Ferrers

Fetherston
Fiene
Filmer
Finch
Firth
Fish
Fishwick
Fitch
Fitzalan
Fitzherbert
Fleetwood
Fletcher
Foe, Defoe, De Foe
Foote
Forster
Fortescue
Forwood
Foster
Flatman
Foxe, Fox
Fraunce
Freeman
Freind, Frend
Frith
Furnival
Gardiner
Garret
Gascoigne
Gauden
Gerard
Gibbes, Gibbons
Gilpin
Gist
Glasse
Goffe
Golding
Gooch
Gooderidge
Gookin
Gower
Graun
Greene
Grenville, Granville,
   Greynvile, Greville
Gresham
Grew
Grey, de Grey
Grierson
Grimald, Grimalde, Gri-
   moald — from Italian,
   Grimaldi

Grindal
Grinset
Grocyn
Gumble
Hacker
Hadley
Hake
Hales, Hale
Hallowell
Harcourt
Harington, Harrington
Harley
Harrington
Harshorne
Hartlib
Hatteclyffe
Hatton
Haughton
Hauksbee, Hawksbee
Havers
Hawarde
Hawke
Heath
Heathcote
Heneage
Henslowe
Herbert
Herrick
Hesilrige, Haselrig
Heywood
Higgins, Higginson
Hildersham
Hoadley
Hobbes, Hobson
Hoccleve, Occleve
Holles
Horrocks
Howard
Howe
Howmam
Hungerford
Hutchison
Hyde
Ingle
Ingoldsby
Ireton
Jaggard
James
Jasper
Jeffrey
Jenner

Jentleman
Jerome
Jewel
Johnson
Jolebody
Kees, Keys, Kay, Key
Kelderley
King
Kneller
Knollys
Kyteler
Lambert
Langdale
Lawes
Leade, Lead
Lee
Leete
Lenthall
L'Estrange — French ori-
   gin [leh-STRAYNJ]
Leverett
Leyland
Lightfoot
Lilburne
Lillo — from the Dutch
Lilly, Lily, Lilye
Linacre
Locke, Lok
Lodge
Lodlow
Loe
Louth, Lowth
Love
Lovelace
Lowin, Lowine, Lowen,
   Lowyn
Lownes
Lucy
Ludlow
Lydgate
Lyly
Lyttleton, Littleton
Malory
Malynes, Malines, de
   Malines
Manley
Marbury
Le Marchant
Markham
Marshall
Martyn

Marvell

Mason

Massinger

May

Mayhew

Mayle

Mayow, Mayouwe, Mayo

Mead

Meorys

Milot

Minot

Minshull

Monk, Monck

Montagu

More

Morland

Morris

Morton

Moyle

Mullens

Mun, Mundy

Myddleton, Middleton

Nashe

Naunton

Nearchus

Neoton

Neville

Newman

Newport

Newton

Niccols

Norden

Norris

North

Nowell, Nowel, Noel

Oates

Occleve, Hoccleve

Old

Oldcastle

Oldham

Oldys

Otway

Overton

Oxenbridge

Palmer

Parris

Partridge

Paston

Patyn, Patten, Patton

Pearson

Pecock

Peel

Pelham

Pell

Pepperell

Pepys

Perrot

Persons

Pettie, Petty

Phaer, Phayer

Phipps

Powell

Pride

Prince

Prynne

Purvey

Pym

Pynder

Radclyffe

Rich

Ridley

Roach

Robynson

Rood

Rowe

Rygge

Rymer

Sacheverall

Sackville

Sadleir, Sadler

Saint John

Sale

Saltonstall

Sampson

Sancroft

Sandys

Savage

Savile, Saville

Segar

Simmons

Simnel

Skeares

Skinner

Sloughter

Somers, Sommers, Sum-
mers

Somerville

South

Speed

Spelman

Spenser

Springett

Steele

Steevens

Sterne

Steward

Stille

Stillingfleet

Stock

Stoddert

Stokes

Stone

Stoughton

Stoutlock

Strachey

Strode

Strype

Stucley, Stukely

Style

Suckling

Sumner

Swete

Swift

Sylvester

Tallis, Tallys, Talys

Tarleton

Taylor

Teach

Temple

Thatch

Thirlwall

Tickell

Tillotson

Tindal

Tomkins

Tonson

Torporley

Tottel

Trahern

Tuffley

d'Urfey, Durfey

Vane

Vere, de Vere

Vertue

Villiers

Vines

Wagstaffe

Wakeling

Walsh

Walter, Walters

Walwyn

Warburton

Warde

de la Ware, Delaware
Warham
Waterland
Wheelwright
Whitelocke
Whitgift
Whittington
Wiclif, Wycliffe, Wyclif,
   Wicliffe, Wickliffe
Wigglesworth

Wilcocks
Willoughby
Wingley
With
Wither — notice, no final
   S
de Wiveleslie
a' Wood
Woodcock
Wotton

Wright
Wriothesley
Wycherley
Wysdom
Yale
Yeardley
York
Young
Zouche

RENAISSANCE GERMAN

Place-names and titles finally become inheritable family names, but these are confused by the Renaissance. A lot of scholars thought their new family names uncouth, and Latinized them, literally. These often persisted side-by-side with their cousins who did not worship Mediterranean culture, and kept the Germanic.

To make up the shortage of women mentioned, borrow from the Medieval German list. It is better to reach back, and name her for her great-grandmother, than to accidently use something Victorian.

FEMALE NAMES

Agnes
Elena

Jacoba
Katharina

Sidea
Veronica

MALE NAMES

Abraham
Albrecht
Andreas
Barthel, Bartholomäus
Bernhard
Burkard
Christoffel
Christoph
Cosmas
Damian
David
Dietrich
Egid
Eitel-Friedrich
Ernest

Ernst
Georg, Jörg
Gerold
Gothardt
Gottfried, Götz
Gunther
Hans
Heinrich
Hieronymus
Hlob
Jakob
Joachim
Johann
Johannes
Konrad

Kunz
Leonhard
Ludolph
Lukas, Lucas
Matthias
Maurice
Melchior
Michel
Nikolaus
Otto
Peter
Philipp
Quirin
Roelof
Rudolf

Sebald
Sebastian
Seth

Ulrich
Valentine
Veit

Wenzel
Wilhelm
Wolfgang

FAMILY NAMES

Abelin
Agrippa von Nettesheim
Alsted
Altdorfer
von Amsdorf
von Andernach
von Andlau
Andreä
Aquila
Arnd, Arndt
Asam
Aurifaber
Balde
Baldung
Bauer
Behaim, Beham, Beheim
Bengel
von Berlichingen
Bernauer
Bock, Bockh
Bodenstein
Boheim
Boner
von Bora
Brant, Brandt
Breitkopf
Brenz
Bruyn
Bugenhagen
Burckhardt
Burgkmair
Busembaum, Busen-
  baum
Buxtorf
Callisen
Calov, Calovius
Camerarius
von Canitz

Capito
Chemnitz, Kemnitz
Cranach, Kranach, Kro-
  nach
Dillen, aka Dillenius
Eccard
Eck
Elsheimer
Emser
Eslibach
Faber, von Faber
Fabricius
Fagius
Froben
Frosperger
von Frundsberg, Fronds-
  berg, Fronsperg
Fugger
Fust, Faust
Gerhardt
Goldschmidt
Greif
von Grimmelshausen
von Guericke
Heussgen, Hussgen
Hevelius aka Hewel,
  Hewelke, Hewelcke,
  Höwelke, Höwelcke
Hosemann, aka Osian-
  der
Huysmann
Jamnitzer, Jamitzer
Junius of Bamberg
Kallwitz
Kämmerer
von Kauffungen
Kilian
Köpfel

Krapp
Kuhhorn, aka Bucer,
  Butzer
Leibhard
von Leibniz
Lotter
Ludolf
Lufft
Murner
von Niem, Nieheim,
  Nyem
Nithardt
Olevianus
zu Pappenheim
Pencz, Penz
Peutinger
Pickel aka Celtis, Celtes
Reyher
Rottenhammer
Schöffer
Schwarzerd
Sneider, Schnitter
Sohre, Sore
Spalatin — from Spalt
Spener
Stoss
Tauler
Vischer
Waldis
Waldseemuller,
  Waltzemuller
von Wallenstein
Wohlegemuth, Wohlge-
  mut, Wolgemut
Zähringen

RENAISSANCE FRENCH

The better class of people have family names. Those who want to associate with them, adopt one. The common peasant is still Jacques, Jean's boy — or Marie's boy, if she is the more notable parent.

This is a sampling, though a healthy one. You can use it as a guide to adapting modern French names, or creating family names on your own. The taste of Huguenot names is from history. Alas, no women showed up with their religious affiliations attached. They used Biblical rather than Catholic saints' names about a quarter of the time. You cannot possibly name as many characters "Jean" as they actually did, so I have added in some Protestant-sounding personal names.

FEMALE NAMES

Adelaide
Adrienne
Agnes
Améliane
Angélique
Anne — popular; Ninon (dim.)
Antoinette
Athénaïs
Aubigny
Barbara
Breniguc
Catharine, Catherine — popular
Charlotte
Claire
Clarisse
Esmeraude
Francine
Françoise
Gabrielle
Geneviève
Germanine
Grésinde
Griseldis
Henriette, Henrietta
Hortense
Jacqueline
Jeanne
Laure
Leonora
Louise
Madeleine
Marguerite — very popular
Marie
Marie Madeleine
Marion — with an O
Olympe
Pernette
Perrette
Pierronne
Renée
Thérèse

MALE NAMES

Abraham
Adelaide — as a male name
Aimé-Marie — female would be Aimée
Albret
Aldonce
Amédée
André
Anne — as masculine primary personal name
Antoine, Antonin (dim.)
Antoine-Michel
Armande
Auguste
Aymar
Balthasar
Barnabé
Bartélemy
Bénigne
Bernard
Blaise
Bonaventure
Bretagne
Celse
César
Charles — popular
Claude, Claudin (dim.)
David
Denys, Denis
Edmé
Ennemond
Esprit
Étienne
Eustache
François
Gabriel
Gauthier
Geoffroy

Georges
Gérard
Godin
Guillaume
Guy
Henri
Herault
Hercule
Hermann
Hermès
Huault
Hugues
Ier
Jacques — popular
Jean — very popular

Joachim
Louis
Malo
Mathieu
Mathurin
Maurice
Michel
Nicolas, Nicholas
Noel
Olivier
Paul
Philibert
Philippe
Pierre
Pontus — somewhat pop-

ular
Remi
Rivière
Sandras
Sébastien
Stanislas
Sylvestre-Antoine
Symphorien — rare saint
  name
Théodore
Thomas
Valentin
Xavier
Zenobius

FAMILY NAMES

Abbadie
d'Aguillon
d'Amboise
d'Amerval
Amiot, Amyot
Amyraut, Anjou
Armagnac — comtes
  descended from the
  Merovingian kings
Arnauld
d'Aubray
Audiffret
d'Aumont
de la Baume Le Blanc
Bejart
Belleau
Besme
de Bethencourt
de Beze
Billaut
Blanchet
Blondel
Bodin
de La Boétie
de Bolland
Bolsec
Bosse, Bossuet
de Boulainvilliers
de Bourdeilles
Bourignon
Boursalt
Bouvet

Le Bovier de Fontenelle
de Brebeuf
Brisson
Brulé
Le Brun
Bruyas
Buache
de Buade
Bude
Buridan
de Bus
de Callieres Bonnevue
Campra
Le Caron
de Castelnau
de Catinat
Cauchon
Cauvin
de Cervolle, de Cervole
Chabanel
de Chabannes
de Chabot
de Chambonnières
Champier
de Champlain
Chapelain
Le Chapelier
Chardin
de Charlevoix
Charron
Chartier
Chateaurenault, Chateau-

renaut, Chateaureg-
  naud
Châtillon, Châteillon
de Chauliac
Chaumonot
du Chesne
de Choiseul
de Chomedy
Claude
Le Clercq
de Clermont
Clermont-Tonnerre
Clouet
Coiffier de Ruzé
Colombe, Colomb,
  Columb
de Cosse
de Costes de la Cal-
  prenede
de Courcelles
Cousin
Crozat
Cujas
Cusson
Danican
Delaye
Deschamps
Desfontaines
Deshoulières [day-ZOO-
  lyahr]
Desmarets de Saint-
  Sorlin

Desportes
Dolet
Domat, Daumat
Dorat/Daurat
Dorigny
Drouais
Dufresny
Dunois
Dupleix
de Durfort
d'Entragues
d'Estrées
Farel
Felbien
De Flacourt
Flamel
Fléchier
de Forbin
Fouquet, Foucquet
Fourré de Poix
Le Franc
De Franqueville, De
    Francheville
Freminel
Frémiot
Froment
Frontenac
Furetière
Galland
Garamond, Garamont
de Gassion
Gérard
De Glandèves
Godefroy
de Gomberville
de Gontaut
de Gourville
de Grafigny, Graffigny
Gringore, Gringoire
du Guast
du Guillet
d'Harcourt
Hardouin
Hardy
Hédelin

Hennepin
d'Herbelot de Molainville
L'Hermite
Heroet
L'Hôpital, Lhôpital,
    L'Hospital
d'Issembourg d'Happon-
    court
Le Jeune
Justel
Labé
Laisné
Lalement
de Laval-Montmorency
Lecouvreur
Lefevre d'Étaples
Lemaire de Belges
Lemercier
Lemery
Lenclos, de Lenclos
Liance
du Ligier de la Garde
de Lorme or Delorme
Lorrain, Le Lorrain
Mabillon
de Magny
de Malebranche
Mansart, Mansard
Marin
Mariotte
Maurevel
Membre
Le Métel de Boisrobert
Mignard
Milet
Molinet, Moulinet
Monsart, Monsard
de Montchrétien
Montmagny
de Montmorency
La Mothe
Le Moyne
Le Nain
Nanteuil
Nompar de Caumont

Olier
Padeloup
Papin
de Pardaillan de Gondrin
Paré
Pécour
Peletier or Pelletier
Des Periers
Perrault
Perrin
Perrot
Pétau
Du Pin
Du Puget
de Rabutin
de Rabutin-Chantal
de Retz
Rochechouart
Le Roy
Sagard-Theodat
de Saint-Balmont
de Saint-Nectaire
de Sainte-Croix
de Salignac de la Mothe
    Fenelon
de Saumaise
de Saxe
Scaliger — from Italy
Scève
Le Sueur
Tavernier
Le Tellier
de Thiard or Tyard
de Thou
Tory
de La Tour
de La Trémoille
Le Valois de Villette de
    Murçay
Le Vau
du Vergier de Hauranne
Viete/Vieta
de Voyer d'Argenson
Wateau

• PROTESTANT, HUGUENOT •

FEMALE

Anne	Judithe	Naomi, Naomie
Barbe	Lia	Rachelle
Débora	Mariamne	Rebeque
Elizabeth	Marie	Sara
Jeanne	Marthe	Simione

MALE

Abraham	Isaac	Moise, Moïse
Absalon	Jacques	Odet
Adam	Jean	René
Davide	Jonas	Simion
Esdras	Josephe	Thadée
Gaspard	Luc	

FAMILY

Allaire	Drelincourt	Martineau
Ancillon	Faueuil	Ribaut
Bayard	Fonblanque	de Rohan
de Beausobre	Fontane	Saurin
de Coligny	Goulaine de Laudonnière	
Daille	Marion	

RENAISSANCE ITALIAN

These differ from modern ones only in the frequency or popularity of certain names. Real solid family names were common only in the noble classes, after about 1000, beginning in Venice. They become general for all but the lowest by 1300 or so, much earlier than in the rest of Europe.

Many people became known to history as "So-and-so of Someplace"; the "da" and "di" names are usually "of" names. Sometimes "di" before a recognizable personal name means that it is a patronymic: Giulio di Pietro is Jules son of Peter.

Until 1600 or so, surnames and family names remain fairly fluid. So someone called Baldasarre di Fabio in his hometown of Verona becomes Baldasarre da Verona when he moves to Pisa, without anyone batting an eye.

Many people are known to history only or primarily by their nicknames:

Gatamelata, Masaccio, Colleoni. You must either borrow one from the list at the end, or learn enough Italian to be able to create them.

If you think only English historians are irritating enough to always "translate" names — calling Filippo "Philip" and Juana "Joanna" — note that a famous mercenary captain of the period, Giovanni Aguto, was in fact an Englishman, John Sharpe.

Diminutives and augmentatives are endings to names that give variation, while slightly changing meaning. They are covered in detail in the contemporary Italian chapter. However, here we will recap:

Italian diminutives reference gender: -ino/-ina, -etto/-etta, -ello/-ella; "-uccio/-uccia" can indicate reproach, "-accio/-accia," real disgust. The augmentative ending is "-one."

Pronunciation

There are no silent letters — those final E's are pronounced.
A = A in pasta
C = hard as in cat, except before E and I
CC = TCH as in Dutch
E = E as in pen; before R, as in person
G = G in gun; before E or I, as in gin
I = I in machine
CH = K in kin
O = O in hope
SCH = SH in shin
U = U in tune

FEMALE NAMES

Addolorata	Beatrice	Clarice
Adria	Bianca	Clarisa
Alberta	Biancinetta	Concetta
Albina	Bice	Consolata
Alessandra	Brunela	Cornelia
Angela	Camilla	Corsetta
Anna	Carmela	Costanza
Anna Maria	Cassandra	Credentia
Annunziata	Catarina, Caterina —	Elena
Antea	popular	Eleonora
Antonia	Cecilia	Elisabetta
Aquilana	Celestina	Elvira
Ardelia	Christierna, Christina	Faustina
Artemisia	Cia	Fiametta
Assunta	Claire	Filiberta
Barbara	Clara	Fiora

Francesca — fairly popu-
 lar; Checa
Franceschina — popular
Gaspara
Gianna
Giovanna, Vannozza
Hippolyta
Honora
Hortensia
Ieronima
Immacolata
Imperia
Innocenza
Iovenetta
Irene
Isabella
Gemma
Ginevra
Giovanna
Giulia
Giulietta
Laura
Lavinia

Leonora
Lisa
Lorenzina
Lozana
Lucida
Lucrezia — fairly popular
Luigia
Maddalena
Margherita, Margarita
Margheritona
Maria — popular
Marietta
Marzia
Masina
Michelina
Monica
Nanna, Nannina
Nicolosa
Oliveta
Olympia
Onorata
Orsolina
Ortensia

Pacifica
Parisina
Perina
Pietra, Pippa
Porzia
Rosalia
Rosaria
Schiavona
Simonetta
Susanna
Teresa
Tiberia
Tina — for any "-tina"
 name
Tirrhenia
Tullia
Valentina
Veronica
Viena
Violante
Vitruvia
Vittoria

Male Names

Adriano
Agnolo
Agostino
Alberico
Alberigo
Alberto
Aldo
Aldobrandino
Alessandro, Alessio
Alfonso
Allori
Alvise
Ambrogio
Andrea — popular
Aniello
Annibale
Anselmo
Antonio
Aonio
Astorre
Attendolo
Aurelio
Azzo, Azzolino
Baccio

Baldassare
Barnabo
Bartolommeo, Bar-
 tolomea
Bastiani
Benedetto
Benozzo
Benvenuto
Berengario
Bergonzio
Bernadino
Bernarbo
Bernardo
Bertoldo, Bertolazzo,
 Bertin, Bertuzzo,
 Bertolino, Bertoldino
Bonifazio
Borso
Braccio
Brunetto
Camillo
Carlo
Castruccio
Caterino

Cencio, Cenzio
Cesare
Ciriaco
Cola
Concino
Cornelio
Cosimo
Costanzo
Cristofano, Tofano
Cristoforo
Daniele
Daniello
Davide
Desiderio
Diomede
Domenico, Demencio
Donato, Donatello (dim.)
Dovizio, Dovizi
Duccio
Emilio
Enea
Enrico
Ercole
Ermolao

Evangelista
Ezzolino
Fabio
Fabrizio
Fausto
Federigo
Fermo
Ferrante
Filippo, Lippo
Flavio
Floriano
Folco
Francesco
Gabriel, Gabriello
Gaddo
Galeazzo
Galileo
Gasparo
Gastone
Gaudenzio
Gentile
Giacinto
Giacomuzzo, Muzio
Giambattista
Giammaria
Giampaolo
Gianciotto
Giangaleazzo
Giorgio
Giotto
Giovanni, Gian, Giovan,
    Giano, Giovian, Gio-
    viano
Girolamo
Giuliano
Giulio
Gofredo
Gregorio
Guarino
Guibert
Guido
Guittoncino
Idi
Innocenzo
Ippolito

Jacopo
Lamberto
Lazzaro
Lelio
Leone
Lionardo, Nardo
Lionello
Lodovico
Lorenzino
Lorenzo
Lotario, Lothario
Luca
Lucchino
Luigi
Luzzasco
Maffeo
Marcantonio
Marcello
Marco
Mariono
Mariotto
Marsilio
Martire
Matteo
Melozzo
Michele
Michelozzo
Mino
Nanni
Neri
Nicolo, Niccoló
Obizzo
Odoardo
Oliverotto
Onofrio
Orazio
Ostasio
Ostilio
Ottaviano
Ottavio
Ottone
Palo — rare
Pamfilo
Pandolfo
Paolo

Paris
Pasquin
Pellegrino — rare
Petrus
Pier, Piero
Pierfrancesco
Pierluigi
Pietro, Pietro Santi
Polidoro
Pompeo
Pomponio
Prospero
Raffaelle, Raffaello
Ranuccio
Ridolfo
Rinaldo
Rodrigo
Romolo
Rosso
Ruberto
Ruggiero
Salinguerra
Salvator
Sciarra
Scipione
Sebastiano
Senibaldi
Sigismodo
Silvio
Simone
Taddeo
Teobaldo
Teodoro
Teofilo
Tiziano
Tommaso, Maso
Torquato
Ugolino
Ulisse
Vincenzo
Virgilio
Virginio — rare
Vittore
Zorzo

FAMILY NAMES

Accolti — of Arezzo and
   Tuscany
Accorso, Accursio
Aconzio, Aconcio
Adriani, Adriana
d'Agnolo
Albani — of Rome
Alberti
Alciati
Aldobrandini — of Flor-
   ence
Aldrovandi
Algardi
Allori
Alpini
Alunno
Amalteo
Amati
Ambrosini
Ammanati
Andreani
Andreini
Anerio
d'Angelo
d'Anghiera
Animuccia
d'Antonio
d'Arborea
Aretino — from Arezzo
Ariosto
Armeno
d'Ascoli
Aselli, Asellio
Attendolo
Aurispa
de Avalos
Avanzo
Badile
Bagio
Baglioni — of Perurgia
Baglivi
Bagnacavallo
Baldi
Baldovinetti, Balduinetti
Balestra
Banchieri
di Banco
Bandello, Bandinelli
Barberini — of Florence

and Rome
da Barbiano
Bardi, de'Bardi
Barocchio
Barocci, Baroccio
Baroni, Baronio
Barozzi
Bartoli
di Bartolommeo
Bartolozzi
Bassano
Beccafumi
Begarelli
Bellarmino, Bellarmin
Beltraffio, Boltraffio
Bembo
Benincasa
Bentivogli, Bentivoglio
Berettini
da Bergamo
Berni, Bernini
de Biagio
Bianchini
Bianco
Bibbiena — of Tuscany
Bigordi
Blandrate, Biandrata
Boccaccio, Boccaccino
Boccadipecora
Boccanera, Boccanegra —
   of Venice
Boccasini
Bocchini
da Bologna — from
   Bologna
Bonasone
di Bondone
Bonfigli
Bonvicino, Buonvicino
Bordone
Borelli
di Borgo
Borromeo — of Milan
Borromini
Boscoli
di Botta
Bracceschi
Braccio da Montone
Bramante

Brandolini
Bregno
Bressano — from Brescia
Briosco
Broccardo
Bugiardini
di Buoninsegnia
Burchiello
Bussone
Buti
Cagliari, Caliari
Caldara
Calvi
Camiaso, Camiasi
Campeggio
Campi — of Cremona
Canani
di Candia — from Crete
Canneschi — of Bologna
Capelletti — of Verona,
   aka Capulet
Capelo, Capello
Capisucchi, Capisucco
Caraccioli — of Naples
Carafa, Caraffa — of
   Naples; since 12th c.:
   Carafa dell Spina,
   Carafa della Stadera
Cardano
Cardi da Cigoli
Carlone, Carloni
Carmagnola
Caro, Caroto
Carpaccio
Carracci — of Bologna
Carrucci
della Casa
del Castagno — of Flor-
   ence
Castaldi
de Castelfranco
Castellesi — of Tuscany
Castelli, Castello
Castiglione
Castracani degli
   Antelminelli
Cataldi
Catena
dei Cattanei — of Rome

Cavalcanti — of Florence
del Cavaliere
Cavedoni
Cecchi — of Florence
Cenni di Pepo
Cerchi — of Florence,
  leader of Bianchi
  (Whites)
Cervini
Cesari, Cesarini
di Chellino
Chiabrera
Chiaramonti
Chigi — of Siena
Cibo
Cini
Ciocchi del Monte
de Cione, di Cione de Ser
  Buonaccorso
Civitali
Colonna — of Rome
delle Colonne, da Col-
  lonna —13th c.
Columbo
da Como
Concini
Condolmieri
Conti
di Corneto
Corsi
Corsini — of Florence
Cosmati — of Rome
Cossa
Costa
di Credi
Crescenzi
Crescimbeni
Dalmata
Dandolo
Dati
Davila
Diodati
de Dominis
Donati — of Florence,
  leader of Neri
  (Blacks)
Dori
Doria — of Genoa,
  Ghibelline; since
  12th c.
d'Este — adopted 996

Eustachio
da Fabriano
Fabrizio
Facchinetti
Falcone, Falconetto
Falieri, Faliero — of
  Venice
Fallopia, Fallopio
Feliciano
Feramola
da Fermo
Festa
Ficino
di Fieschi — of Genoa
da Fiesole
dei Filipepi
Finiguerra
Fiorentino
Fogliani
Folengo
da Foligno
da Forli — from Forli
Forteguerri
Foscari — Venice
Francucci
Frangipane
Frescobaldi
de Furli
Gabrieli
Gaddi
da Gagliano
Galigai
Galli da Bibiena
Gambarelli
Garofalo
Gatti
Gaulli
Gelli
Geminiani
Genga
Gentileschi, Gentili
Geraldini
Gesualdo
della Gherardesca
Ghiberti
Ghirlandajo, Ghirlan-
  daio, Grilandajo
Gianibelli, Giambelli
Gioja
di Giovanni Massi
Giunta, Giunti — of

Venice
Giustiniani — of Venice
Gonzaga — of Mantua
de Gourges
Gozzoli
Grassi
Grimani — of Venice
Gualandi
Guarini, Guarnieri
Guicciardini
Guiccioli
Guidiccioni
Guidobaldo
Guiducci
Guigni
Guinizelli, Guinicelli
da Imola — from Imola
Landino
da Laurana
Leoni
Leopardi
Lippi
Lombardo
Loredano — of Venice
Luini, Luvinini
della Luna
Lusitano
di Lutero
Luzzaschi
Malvezzi
Manso
Mantegna
Manuzio — of Venice
de'Marignolli
Marino, di Mariano
Marsuppini — of Arezzo
  and Florence
Mazzuoli
Merisi
Michieli
de'Migliorati
di Milano — from Milano
Mocenigo
Mola, Mola di Roma
Montecchi — of Verona,
  aka Montague
Montemezzano
de Montorsoli
Morando — of Verona
Morone, Moroni
di Murrone

MALE EKE-NAMES

Aguto — sharp
il Bagnacavallo — from Bagnacavallo
il Bamboccio — large child
il Bergamasco — from Bergamo
Botticelli — little barrel
il Braghettone — the breeches maker
il Bronzino — sculptor
il Buranello — from Burano, island
   near Venice
Gatamelata — honeyed cat
il Giovane — the younger
il Giuseppino — the little Joseph
il Gobbo — the hunchback

il Gottoso — the gouty
il Magnifico — the magnificent
il Moretto — the little Moor
il Parmicianino — the little Parmese
il Parmigiano — from Parma
il Pesarese — from Pesaro
Pinturicchio — good little painter
il Romanino — the little Roman
lo Spagna — the Spanish (man)
lo Spagnoletto — the little Spaniard
il Tintore — dyer
il Tintoretto — little dyer
il Vecchio — the elder
lo Zingaro — the gypsy

FEMALE EKE-NAMES

Bel-Fronte — beautiful visage
la Bellina Hebrea — the beautiful
   Jewess
la Brunetta — the brunette
la Checa — our Franny
la Diana Romana — the Diana of
   Rome
la Farfalla
la Faustina — our Faustina
la Grechetta — our Gretchen
la Hebrea — the Jewess
la Laura — our Laura
la Livia — our Livia
la Lozana — our Lozana

Matrema-non-vol — "Mother doesn't
   want me to"
la Padoana — the Paduan
la Romana — the Roman
la Romanina — the little Roman
la Spagnola — the Spaniard
la Tinetta — our little Tina
la Todeschina — the German
la Tortora
la Zaffetta — the policeman's daughter
la Zingara — the Gypsy
la Zufolina

RENAISSANCE SPANISH

Spanish naming habits have not changed so much that they warrant a separate listing. This is the period when family names take over from patronymics,
but all you need do is use them for your better class of people and keep the peasants down in the Medieval fashions.

Don't worry that there is no Medieval Spanish to reference. It is necessarily
divided into Catalan and Aragonese, Basque, and Frankish. Pay least attention
to the last of those.

NAHUATL

Nahuatl is the language spoken by Nahuas. The Aztecs were only one of several peoples who spoke Nahuatl, from the upper valley of Mexico down into Yucatán. It had been spoken in the region of Teotihuacán since at least the 4th century, and the Aztecs did not even arrive in the Valley of Mexico until the middle of the 13th century, founding Tenochtitlán about a century later. They did not begin to become real conquerors until the early 1400s.

Nahuatl is still spoken, and written, and there is a preservation movement much like that of Catalonian and Basque, to prevent permanent submersion in the Spanish monolith.

Latin-written Nahuatl is pronounced much like Spanish, except that X stands for the sound of SH in shush. Accent is almost always on the next to last syllable. If you are writing of pre–Contact Nahuas, and wish their names to look less immediately Aztec to the English eye, use SH in place of the X, so that Oxomoc becomes Oshomoc, and Axayaca becomes Ashayaca. You can also put an E between the common end-letters TL, so that Xochitl is transformed into Shochitel.

These are the classic names you will find at the time of European contact. Remember, the Spanish only provided a spearhead for native armies of Nahuatl speakers to overthrow the Aztecs. Many noble families of the Tlaxcaltecs and other allies retained the personal name of their then family head as a Nahuatl family name under the Spanish.

Look out for the ending "-tzin." Only the highest nobility will use it. Never use it for a commoner nor, oddly, a king or prince. In many cases, you can simply drop it, and use the name bare.

Most Nahuatl names look like impossible alphabet soup to Anglo eyes, and they are easily confused, especially when they run past fifteen letters. So be very careful to spread initials across the alphabet; within an initial, use different second letters; and vary length. Call tertiary characters "the wizened farmer," "the boatman," "the sacred weaver," and don't waste names on them. Endings can also have an anesthetic sameness, with the "-tzin" and "-tl" repeating.

Actual female names are so difficult to find, that I am including a number of words that *might* be used as names. You can spot them by their lack of capitalization. Cacomistl can become the lady Cacomistzin, if not used plain for the apparently doomed village maiden. If you are in a big saga, bail yourself out with some names in translation: Sacred Jewel, Knife-of-the-Sun, Spring Corn, etc.

God-names are included because they can be used as a base for theophoric personal names. Tlaloc gives Tlalocan, so Cintli can give Cintlican. The references to God and Goddess without further description indicate titles of the henotheistic Deity who was both and neither male nor female, in the developed

Toltec-descended religion that was short-circuited by the dominance of the crude, bloody, polytheistic Aztecs. A preceding asterisk (*) indicates the name of a Deity. If you are writing a Prehistoric, these may be the names of your characters who will later be deified.

FEMALE NAMES

anecuyotl — feathered belt
cacomistl — ring-tailed cat, related to raccoon
chalchihuite — precious green stone; jade
*Cihuacoatl — earth Goddess
*Cintli — corn Goddess
*Ciuacoatl — woman snake
*Coatlicue — serpent skirt
comale — wide, flat dish type
Erendira — the one who smiles
etl — bean
huipile — long-sleeved woman's blouse
*Huixtocihuatl — Goddess of salt

ichtilmatli — cloak
icnocuicatl — songs of sorrow
mamalhuaztli — three stars of sacred import
*Mictecacihuatl — Lady of the Region of Death
*Omecihuatl — Lady of Duality
otli — road
Oxomoc
Papantzin
petate — rush mat
quetzal — brilliant green bird
xochitl — flower
Yacotzin

MALE NAMES

Acacitl
Acamapichtli
Acxoxecatl
Ahuelitoc
Ahuitzol
Amantlan
Atlixcatzin — title for capturing 4 prisoners
Axayaca
Axayacatl, Axayacatzin
Axoquentzin
Azcapotzalco
Aztautzin
Cacama
Cahuecahua
Caltzontzin
Cenyautl
Chimalpain
Chimalpopoca
Cicpatzin Tecuecuenotzin
Coanacoch
Cocomitecuhtli
Cohualpopocatzin
Cohuamacotzin

Cohuayhuitl
Coyohuehuetzin
Coyotl — coyote
Cuacuauhpitzahuac
Cuapan
Cuappiatzin
Cuatlazol
Cuauhcoatl
Cuauhnochtli
Cuauhtemoc
Cuauhtlehuanitzin
Cuexacaltzin
Cuitlahuac, Cuitlahuatzin
Cuitlalpitoc
Culhuacan
*Ehecatl — air
Hecateupatiltzin
*Huehueteotl — fire God
Huehuetzin
Huemac — big hands
Huitzilihuitl
*Huitzilopochtli — humming bird; Aztec war God

Iaztachimal
Ilhuicamina — archer of heaven
*Ipalnemohuani — Giver of Life; God
Itzcoatl, Izcohuatl
Itzcohuatzin
Itzcuauhtzin
Itzpalanqui
Itzpotonqui
Ixtlilxochitl — ... flower
Macuilxochitl — five flower
*Mictlantecuhtli — Lord of the Region of Death; God
Mixcoatl — cloud serpent
Moquiuix
Motecuhzoma — the sad one; Montezuma, Moctezuma
Motelchiuhtzin
Motelhuihtzin

*Moyocoyatzin — He Who creates Himself; God

Nezahualcoyotl

Nezahualpilli

Nezahualquentzin

Ocuitecatl

*Ometecuhtli — Lord of Duality; God

*Ometeotl — Deity of Duality; God and Goddess

Opochtzin

Oquitzin

Panitzin

Patlahuatzin

petlacalcatl — head steward

Piltecuhtli

Pinotl

Pizotzin

Quauhtotohua

Quetzalaztatzin

*Quetzalcoatl — feathered serpent; culture God

Tecocoltzin

Tecohuentzin

Tecpanecatl

Tehuehuelli — shield with 4 eagle feather clusters

Temilotzin

Temoctzin

Tepantemoctizin

Tepeoatzin

Teputztitloloc

Tetlanmecatl

Tetlepanquetzaltizin

Textlipitl

*Tezcatlipoca — sun God

Tezozomoc

Tizoc

Tlacaelel

Tlacahuepantzin

Tlacantzolli — men squeezed together, 2-headed man

Tlacateotl

Tlacochcalcatl — chief of the house of arrows;

title

Tlacotzin

Tlalchiac — lord of what is below; title

Tlaloc — rain God

Tlalocan

Tlaltecatzin

Tlaquiach — lord of what is above; title

Tlilpotonque

*Tloque-Nahuaque — Lord of the Close Vicinity; God

Tohil — rumbler

Topantemoc

Tzihuacpopocatzin

Tzilacatzin

Tzoyectzin

*Xiuhtecuhtli — fire God

Xochitl — flower

Xocoyotzin

Xoxopehualoc

Yolcuatl — rattlesnake

Names Used in Sacred Calendar

Alligator — Cipactli

House

Wind — Eecatl

Lizard — Itz

Serpent — Coatl

Death

Deer

Rabbit — Tochtli

Water — Atl

Dog — Itzcuintli

(spider) Monkey — Ozomatli

Grass

Reed — Acatl

Ocelot, Jaguar — Ocelotl

Eagle

Vulture

Earthquake — Ollin

(flint) Knife — Tecpatl

Rain — Quiauitl

Flower — Xochitl

Mayan

Mayan Classic (200 B.C. to C.E. 900) glyphs have been deciphered, and histories of the city-states written. The names of rulers and some nobles are available.

There does not appear to be any gendering, other than some prefixes that would not necessarily show in English. "Na" is the prefix for a noblewoman, so that they are often referred to as "Lady" So-and-so. Other than this, they may have names identical with men.

Names are built out of a repertoire of elements, so that following the historical pick-list is a table for build-it-yourself Mayan names. The English equivalent is complete with a randomization table, since to the Anglo mind the name combinations look pulled out of a hat.

Commoners were irrelevant to the inscription carvers, so your educated guess is as good as any. Odds are that, like most people in most cultures, children were given names that reflected hopes or events, and adults were often called by names that reflected their appearance, behavior, or occupation. Translation names will save you here, but do check what sort of animals and plants were found in your time period.

Mayan names of the simpler variety continue in use to this day as family names in the area.

Pronunciation

The accent is almost always on the last syllable.
A = A in pasta
C = hard C as in cat, always, no matter the following vowel
E = E in prey
I = I in machine
J = H; transliteration done by Spaniards, remember
K = glottal K
O = O in open
U = U in tune; at the end of a word, or with another vowel, W
X = SH in shush

At the risk of some loss of accuracy, I am omitting aspirations because most English speakers cannot hear the difference, and many sources are inconsistent.

FEMALE NAMES

Rather than feminine suffixes like "-ette" and "-ina," the Maya used a feminine prefix, "Ix" or "X-." This would be insupportable in fiction, so you should reserve it for noblewomen and Goddesses, making it the formal term Lady. Ix-Ahau, "female lord" is a common term. Ix-Hun-Ahau, Sole Lady, is a Goddess name.

Ah-Kin — He the Sun
Ahau-Xoc — Noble-Shark
Ahpo-Hel —

Ahpo-Katun — Blowgun-Hunter-Katun
Balam — Jaguar

Balam-Ix — Jaguar [day-name]
Chac-Xib-Chac — Eveningstar
Colel-Cab — Mistress of the Earth
Hun-Colel — Only Mistress
Itzam — Iguana
Ix Kaknab, Kuknab — Lady of the Sea
Kan-Le-Ox — Yellow Breadnut Leaf
Kanal-Ikal
Kayam-Kuk
Kitza
Matactin
Pacal — Shield
Tactani
Tahal-Tun —
Te-Xoc — Tree-Shark
Ton-Ahau —
Ton-Multun-Kul-Na — (Tun) Stone-

Mound Holy Edifice
Tu-Kul-Tok —
Wac-Chan-Ahau — Six Sky Lord, or
Upraised Sky Lord
Wac-Chanil-Ahau — Six Celestial
Lord, or Upraised Celestial Lord
Wac-Tun — Six Tun, Upraised Stone
Xibalba — region of death
Xob — Maize
Xoc — Shark
XTacunbilxunan — Hidden Lady,
Guarded Lady
Zacal-Noh — Weaving Cloth
Zac-Kuk — Resplendent Quetzal

Great-Skull-Zero
Jaguar-Throne

MALE NAMES

The "Ah-" can be treated as a masculine prefix, and dropped, if you like. In one household, there might be father Can-Xoc, his son, Ah-Can-Xoc, and a daughter Ix-Can-Xoc. It was not unheard of for a girl to have the same name as her father or older brother, with the feminine prefix.

Ac-Kan — Turtle Yellow
Ah-Ahuaal
Ah Cacaw
Ah-Kan-Xoc — He of the Yellow Shark
Ah-Mac-Ik — He Covers Up the
Winds
Ah-Muluc-Tok
Ah-Nab-Pacal — He of the Waterlily
Shield
Ah Tz'ib — He the Scribe
Ah Yax-Ac — He, Green Turtle
Ah Zacal — He the Resplendent
Ahau-Kin — Lord Sun
Ahau-Uinic — Lord Human
Ahpo-Balam — Blowgun-Hunter-
Jaguar
Balam-Kuk — Jaguar-Quetzal
Balam-Te-Chac — Jaguar-Tree-Red
Butz-Chan
Can-Ek — Serpent-Star
Cauac-Sky
Chaacal
Chaacal-Ah-Nab
Chaan-Muan

Chac-Hubil-Ahau — Great Lord of
the Couch
Chac-Zutz
Chan — Sky
Chan-Balam — Sky Jaguar
Chan-Kawil — Sky-God Kawil
Chan-K'in — Sky Sun
Chan-Yat — Sky Penis
Cit-Chac-Coh — Father Red/Great
Puma
Co-Te-Ahau
Colop-u-Uich-Kin — Tears Out the
Sun's Face
Cu-Ix — Owl-[day-name]
Ha, Ahau-Ha — Water, Lord Water
Hub-Tun-Ahau — Lord Stone Couch
Hun-Ahau — Unique Lord; morn-
ing/evening star
Hun-Hunahpu — Sole Unique
Blowgun-Hunter
Hun-Kak — Unique Fire
Hun-Pik-Tok — Eight Thousand Flints
Hunahpu — Unique Blowgun-Hunter
Ik-Balam — Moon-Jaguar

Kai-Yum — Singing Lord
Kak-Ne-Xoc — Fire Tail Shark
Kakupacal-Kawil — Fire-Eyed–Kawil
Kakupacat — Fiery Glance
Kan — Precious, or Yellow
Kan-Balam-Mo — Precious-Jaguar-
  Macaw
Kan-Hok-Xul
Kan-Xul — Yellow [day-name]
Kin-Cimi — Sun Dead
Kinichil-Cab — Sun-face Towards
  Earth
Kuk-Kawil — Quetzal-Kawil
Manik
Muan-Balam — Bird-Jaguar
Muan-Chaan
Na-Yaxhal
Nab-Balam — Waterlily-Jaguar
Naum-Pat
Ox-Ha-Te
Pacal — Shield
Pacal-Balam — Shield-Jaguar
Pacal-Kawil — Shield-Kawil
Pacal-Tzek — Shield-Skull
Pacam
Pauah-Tun
Sastun-Chan — Jade-Sky
Sastun-Tzek — Jewelled-Skull
Ta-Tzek — Ta-Skull
Tactani
Tah-Mo — Torch-Macaw
Ti-Kan-Toc — shell-winged-dragon
Tok-Caan-Kawil — Flint-Sky-Kawil
U-Cit-Tok — Father of the Flint
U-Xix-Chan
Vucub-Hunahpu
Wa-ca-wa
Wac-Tun-Xtz'unun-Balam — 6-tun-
  Bird-Jaguar
Xbalanque

Xbaquiyalo
Xix-Chan
Xtz'unun-Balam — Bird-Jaguar
Xulu
Yahau-Chan-Ah-Bac
Yat-Balam — Progenitor, Jaguar
Yax-Balam — First Jaguar; sun per-
  sonification
Yax-K'amlay — First Steward
Yax-Kuk-Mo — Green Quetzal Macaw
Yax-Moch-Xoc
Yax-Pac
Yax-Pac-Chan-Yat
Yax-T'ul
Yax-Uk-Kawil
Yich'ak-Balam
Zac-Balam — Resplendent Jaguar,
  White Jaguar

Curl-Head
Curl-Snout
Double-Bird
Double-Comb
Double-Jawbone
Eighteen-Rabbit
Eighteen-Rabbit-Kawil
Great-Jaguar-Paw
Jaguar-Paw
Jawbone-Fan
Kan-Boar
Knot-eye-Jaguar
Moon-Zero-Bird
Scroll-Ahau-Jaguar
Smoke-Imix-Kawil
Smoke-Monkey
Smoke-Shell
Smoking-Frog
Smoking-Squirrel
Split-Earth
Stormy Sky

RANKS OF NOBILITY

mah kina — high king
kina — king, royalty
ch'ul ahau — holy lord, early king
ahau — noble, chief, patriarch

na ahau — noble lady
ah nab — waterlily people" the
  nobility; all of the above
cahal — gentry

English Vocabulary for Translation Names

This is set for randomization by drawing playing cards from a deck. "Smoking-Smoke" should be Double-Smoke, which would be perfectly authentic. Two close words, like Waterfall-Waterlily, would be clunky. Draw a new card to replace one element, or add a number. Waterfall-Eight-Waterlily is much better. Remember, names contain from one to four elements. To randomize that, first draw a card and read it:

one element — twos and threes
two elements — fours through tens
three elements — face cards
four elements — Aces

Diamonds

A — bird
2 — blue or green, or first
3 — boar
4 — cloud
5 — comb
6 — earth
7 — eveningstar, morningstar
8 — fan
9 — frog or iguana
10 — great, large
J — holy, holiness
Q — jade, greenstone
K — jaguar

Clubs

A — jawbone
2 — lightning
3 — macaw
4 — monkey or squirrel
5 — moon
6 — mountain
7 — noble
8 — ocelot or margay
9 — owl
10 — precious, jewel
J — prophecy
Q — quetzal
K — rabbit

Hearts

A — rain
2 — rainbow
3 — red
4 — resplendent
5 — scroll
6 — serpent, snake
7 — shell
8 — skull
9 — sky
10 — shield
J — smoke, smoking
Q — star
K — stone or flint

Spades

A — storm, stormy
2 — sun
3 — torch
4 — throne
5 — thunder
6 — tree
7 — upraised
8 — water
9 — waterfall
10 — waterlily
J — white
Q — yellow
K — a number from zero to twenty

Alternates

A — alligator, crocodile
2 — ant
3 — ax
4 — bat
5 — bones
6 — cloud, clouds
7 — cord
8 — deer
9 — dog
10 — ebony
J — forest
Q — growth
K — heron
A — huge, great
2 — kindly
3 — lighting
4 — mead
5 — noise, noisy
6 — puma
7 — rain cloud
8 — reed
9 — shark
10 — song, singing
J — star
Q — sun-face
K — tarantula
A — thunder
J — tobacco
Q — turtle or dwarf
K — unique, sole, only
Even — wasp
Odd — wild beast

MAYAN VOCABULARY FOR MIX AND MATCH

Pull a first card to determine whether you use the red or black range, then a second for meaning.

Range Card: Red

Second Card:
Diamonds

A, 2	ahau	noble
3–5	balam	jaguar
6	cab	earth
7	can	snake, four, sky
8	cauac	anything of stone
9	chac	red, great
10	chan	sky
J	chel	rainbow
Q	chikin	west
K	cu	owl

Clubs

A	ek	star
2	ha, haha	water, much water
3	hapay	sucking
4	hom	conquest, to knock down buildings
5	ik	wind, soul, spirit
6	kak	fire
7	kan	yellow, precious (Classic Maya did not use gold)
8	katun	time measurement
9	Kawil	any of the four Gods of direction; sometimes read "bountiful harvest"
10	kin, ke	sun
J–Q	kuk	quetzal bird, precious green feathers
K	kul	holy

Hearts

A	lac mam	lightning bolt
2	lakin	east
3	mo	macaw
4	muan	bird
5	na	edifice
6	nab	swamp, shallow lake; also waterlily
7	nohol	south
8	otot	house
9–10	pacal	shield, a flexible mat
J	pitzil	ballcourt
Q	sac	clear
K	suhuy	pure; virgin

Spades

A	tah	torch
2	te	tree
3	tun	stone; also a time measurement
4	wac, uac	six; upraised, lifted up

5	waxac	eight
6	way	sleep, dream, transform, sorcery, shaman, animal familiar
7	xaman	north
8	xtz'unun	bird
9–J	yax, yaxal	blue-green, first, new
Q, K	zac	white, resplendent

Range Card: Black

Second Card:
Diamonds

A	ac	turtle or dwarf
2	baat	ax
3	bac	
4	bacha	heron
5	balche	mead, flavored w/balche-tree bark
6	batz	howler monkey
7	bil	growth
8	bolon	most, many, myriads; nine
9	ceh	deer
10	chauc	thunder and lightning
J	chob	squint eye
Q	chuen	spider monkey
K	chuy	kite (bird)

Clubs

A	cit	father
2	citsil	
3	coh	puma
4	couoh	tarantula; common Yucatec family name
5	hadz	lightning strike
6	hopop	sets alight
7	hub, hubil	couch, of the couch
8	hun	unique, only
9	itzam	iguana
10	kaax	forest
J	kai	singing, song
Q	kakche	ebony tree
K	kakna, kaknab	sea, of the sea

Hearts

A	kinich	sun's face
2	kun	kindly, kindness
3	lelem	lightning
4	mac	covers up
5	mai	20; powdered tobacco
6	mayel	fragrant
7	muialha	rain cloud
8	mul	mound
	witz	mountain, hill; only for places
9	multun	stone mound
10	muyal	clouds
J	ne	tail

Q	nucuch	huge
K	pec	thunder
Spades		
A	pek	dog
2	rayo	thunderbolt
3	sastun	jade or crystal
4	tab	u tab kin = sunbeams, sun cords
5	tok	flint
6	tox	death
7	tzek	skull
8	ul	wild beast, or snake
9	uo	orange-striped black frog
10	yat	penis; bowdlerized to progenitor
J	xob	maize
Q	xoc	shark, to count or read, recite
K	zotz	bat

Alternates

A	ahpu	blowgun hunter
2	ain	crocodile, alligator
3	akab	night
4	amai, amaite	corner, cornered
5	batab	axe-wielder
6	chicbul	groove-tailed *ani* bird
7	chilan	prophet, seer
8	colop	tears out
9	habin	a kind of tree
10	ik	black, or moon
J	imix	abundance
Q	kabul	producer with his hands
K	kolop	wounder
A	ku	God; XKU, Goddess
2	le	ramon or breadnut tree
3	maben	chest
4	mizcit	mesquite bush
5	mumul	mire
6	noh	great, cloth
7	ocote	pitch pine
8	ox	leaf
9	tacunbilxunan	hidden or guarded
10	tecutli	master or
	ciuatl	woman, mistress
J	tul	rabbit
Q	uich	face, eyes
K	xoctun	keeping count
A–2	xux	wasp
3–4	yaxche	ceiba tree
5–6	yol	heart
7–9	yum	ruler or
	colel	mistress

| 10–J | xulab | a kind of ant |
| Q–K | zay | ant, in general |

Numbers

1	hunab	8	waxac, uaxac
2	ome	9	bolon
4	can	10	lahun
6	wac, uac	11	buluc
7	uuc	13	oxlahun

(Note: There are no numbers 3, 5 or 12.)

When in doubt for a name for a commoner *in the highlands*, consider him or her to be named for the day or month of birth, and use one of those below. This was never done in Yucatán.

MONTHS OF THE YEAR
from the Haab year of 365 days

Pop	Mol	Muan — bird
Uo	Che'en	Pax
Zip — a kind of godlet	Yax — first	Kayab
Zotz' — bat	Zac — white	Dumku
Zec	Ceh — deer	Uayeb
Xul	Mac — covering	
Yaxkin — green sun	Kankin — yellow sun	

DAYS OF THE MONTH
from the Tzolkin year of 260 days

Imix	Lamat	Men
Ik — wind, soul, spirit	Muluc	Cib
Akbal	Oc — ocelot	Caban
Kan — yellow, precious	Chuen	Etz'nab
Chicchan	Eb — jaguar skull	Cauac — stone
Cimi — Death	Ben	Ahau — nobility
Manik — grasping hand	Ix	

QUECHUA

The current inhabitants of Tahuantinsuyu, the Four Quarters of the World under Inca rule, now use entirely Hispanic names. You will use the ones below before the Conquista, or in the early colonial days, when many people, who had been born under the pagan regime, simply prefaced their native name with their new, Hispanic, Christian name.

The same names can be used more than once in a dynastic list, so certainly don't worry about using them for your characters. However, using the names of the well-known rulers does make it look as if you have only done superficial research.

Titles are often mixed in with names, but can be recognized by being optional. "Coya" means princess, and is borne by women of royal blood, usually at the end of their name. "Mama" is added to the name of any married woman as a term of respect. It may start the name, end it (rarely), or wind up in the middle, as in Cuci Chimbo Mama Micay Coya.

"Capac" means powerful and can be a title or part of a name. "Capac Apo," powerful lord, is definitely a title, one of high rank. Yet "Apo" is often part of a name. The Incap Rantin is the second most powerful man in the empire, like a vizier, but only accidently related to the King. An hereditary office, the Incap Rantin is descended from a line of kings put aside by the Incas.

"Inca" does not mean king or emperor by itself, so states Felipe Huaman Poma de Ayala, of the royal blood. Nonetheless, most sons of the King had it attached to their names, as if it meant prince. Its position is variable; Inca Roca, Tupac Inca Yupanqui, Bilcac Inca, are all authentic.

As a fiction writer, you would do well to drop it, as it is a hook for confusing the reader. Of all Quechua words, it is one of the most familiar in English, and will blaze out as part of a name. The reader may then fail to notice that one character is Tupac INCA and the other is INCA Illapa; they are both "Inca-something" to the careless. Save it for historical characters where you cannot make it optional with a clear conscience.

Great ones might sometimes bear the same name as a God, not because they were being deified, but to signal their particular devotion to that God, as in the case of Viracocha Inca.

FEMALE NAMES

Anahuarqu
Azca
Capac Huarmi Poma
   Huallca
Capacome Tallama

Cari
Cari Topa
Cava
Caya Cuzco
Chachapoya

Chimbo Occlo
Chimbo Urma
Chimpu Ocllo
Chuquillanto
Ciccla — a flower

Cicllallay
Cora Ocllo
Cuci Chimbo
Cuci Huarcay
Curi Ocllo
Huaco
Huanacauri

Inquilcuna — a blue
    flower
Inquillay
Ipahuaco
Machi
Mallco Huarmi Timtama
Manco Carua

Micay
Ocllo
Pillco Ziza
Rava Ocllo
Yachi
Yunto Cayan

MALE NAMES
* = God-name

Ancaullo
Apo — lord
Apo Alanya
Apo Camac
Apo Maytac
Apo Pinto
Atahuallpa
Atapillo
Atauchi
Atoc Rumi Soncco
Auqui Tupac
Bilcac
Cacya Marca
Capac Yupanqui
Capcha
Challcuchima
Chilche
Chuquillanti
Colla Quispe
Cuci Huanan Chire
Cullic Chava
Curi Paucar
Curi Paucar Manacutana
Hilaquita
Huaman — falcon
Huaman Capac
Huaman Chava
Huaman Mallqui
Huaman Poma
*Huanacauri
Huari Callo

Huari Titu
Huascar
Huayna — young
Huayna Alanya
Huayna Capac, Huaina
    Capac
*Illapa
Illapa Tupac
Illescas
Inti Auqui
Lloqui Yupanqui
Mallco — condor
Manacutuna
Manco
Manco Capac
Mata Callo
Mayta Capac
Mullo — colored shell
Naccha Huarcaya
Ninan Cuyochi
Ninancuro
Ninarua
*Pachacamac
Pachacutec
Pachacuti — cataclysm,
    disaster
Paullu Tupac
Pinau Capac
Poma — puma
Puca Llama — red llama,
    a peasant name

Puyca Caxa
Quille
Quiso Yupanqui
Quispe Huarcaya
Quizo Yupanqui
Quizquiz
Roca
Rumiñahui, Ruminyahui
Rumiñavi, Ruminyavi
Sayri Tupac
Sinchi Roca
Suna
Suyca
Tanpulla Apo Hualpaca
Taypimarca
Tingo
Titu Atauchi
Tocay Capac
Tocay Capac Pinahua
    Capac
Tupac Amaru
Tupac Cucihualpa Huas-
    car
Tupac Yupanqui
Urco
Uturuncu — jaguar
Uturuncu Achachi
*Viracocha
Yahuar Huacac
Yupanqui
Zatuni

NAMES IN TRANSLATION
the rulers of an early dynasty
listed in dynastic order

| Great Cruel Unyielding Sacred | First King |
| Falcon | White Puma |

Yellow Puma
Noble Primitive People
Shining White Falcon
Puma as Agile as Lightning
Origin of the Primitive People
Origin of the Condor
Origin of Fire
Origin of the Playful Puma
Origin of the White Conqueror
Great Lord Battling Puma
Puma Darting Tongues of Fire
Shining Puma
Golden Puma
Cruel Unyielding Condor
Godlike Puma
Crimson Puma — Puca Poma
Blue Puma
Prince of Pumas
Cunning Falcon

Captain of the Pumas
Powerful Puma — Capac Poma
Old Puma
Puma of the Fortress
Cruel Unyielding Puma
Roaring Puma
Falcon with the Burning Beak
Swift Puma
First Twin Falcon and Lesser Twin
  Falcon, twin brothers
Cruel Unyielding Falcon
Rapacious as the Sparrow-Hawk
Powerful Condor — Capac Mallco
Powerful with Teeth of Fire
Powerful Sparrow
Flashing Puma
Powerful Earthquake — Capac Pacha-
  cuti
Old Puma Serpent

Middle Ages
(1100–1450)

MEDIEVAL FRENCH

While ruled by the Franks, French names emerged from that Germanic influence with a Celtic buoyancy, just as they had from Latin. Ludwig became Louis and Karl, Charles, and ancient Gaulish favorites like Alice surfaced, spelled a bit differently, perhaps with an ending change, but directly traceable. Note that the later favorites of Marie and Anne were not so fashionable. You can use any Frankish -hild or -berg name by adding a final A. Men's names are more varied. In either case, remember that there are Bretons out of Brittany, troubadours out of Provençe, and Basques out of Gascony to add spice to the mix.

During this period, family names begin to come into use, beginning mostly as place-names. The list below is a guide to ones actually used. You may well want to invent, working off an historical atlas of France.

FEMALE NAMES

Agnes — very popular
Alianore — until 1350,
  when Eleanor takes
  over
Alice
Anne — occasional
Basina
Bertrade
Blanche — popular
Blanchefleur — rare
Catharine — rare
Charlotte

Christine
Clotilde
Diane
Ennasuitte
Ermengarde
Gabrielle
Gerberga
Hawise
Héloïse
Hermentrudis
Isabeau — popular
Isabelle, Isabella — very

  popular
Jambicque
Jeanne — very popular
Longarine
Marguerite — popular
Marie — rare
Matilda — very popular
Nomerfide — rare
Oisille — rare
Parlamente — the talker
Sybilla

MALE NAMES

Abbon
Abélard, Abeilard, Abae-
   lard, Abeilard
Adhemar
Aimeri, Aymeri
Alain
Alizandre, Alixandre =
   Alexandre
Anselm
Archambaud
Arnaud
Astrolabe
Aubert
Aubry
Baldwin
Benoît
Bernard
Bertrand
Bouciquaut
Bovon
Caesarius
Chrétien, Chrestien
Constantin
Emmanuel

Erard
Eustace
Evre
Frédéric
Fulbert
Fulk
Galans, Galant, Galland
   = Weiland, Voelund,
   Weland
Garin
Gaston
Gaudri
Geoffroi
Gerbert
Girard
Girars
Godefroi
Guibert
Guillaume — very popular
Helias
Henri
Hernaut
Hildebert
Hugues

Ingeleram
Jean
Jehan
Mathieu
Maurice
Olivier
Prosper
Raimond
Rainouart
Ramonalt
Rannulf, Ralph
Renart — 13th and 14th c.
   for Reynard
Renauld
Richard
Robert
Roger
Roscelin
Saire
Théodose
Tybald
Waldo, Valdo
Vivien

SURNAMES

d'Ailly
Aubriot
Bachelin
Basselin
de Beaujeu
de Bologne
de Born — troubadour
Bouguer
Braos
de Brienne
de Champaux
de Chartres
Clopinel, Chopinel, de
   Meung, 1240
Coeur
de Compiègne

de Durfort
de Fayel
Foix
de Laon
de Lille
de Lorris
de Macaire
de Maine
de Manny, de Mauny
del La Marck
Le Meingre
de Montdidier
de Montfort
de Montreuil
de Nangis
de Nogent

d'Orange — governor of
   Toulouse, hero of cycle
d'Orleans
de Palerne — hero of
   Romance
de Quincey
Rubruquois = of Ruys-
   broeck, Flanders
de Sorbon = from Sorbon
de la Tour D'Auvergne
de Troyes
de Vergy
de Viane — hero of epic
de Villehardouin

NORMAN

Don't be fooled by the historians' fondness for "regularizing" names much too early. Many of those false family names are place-names, whether of origin, or of title. All the "Fitz" names are patronymics; that is, Gilbert Fitz Gilbert may have a son known as Richard Fitz Gilbert, but *his* son will be Fulk Fitz Richard. "Fitz" is just the Norman "son of" word.

You may read claims that "surnames" became common in England by 1150, but do not confuse "inheritable family name" with mere "after-names." In 1245, famous men in England are still known as Someone of Thisplace, like Alexander of Hales. When people live in the same place for generations, this can well imitate a family name, but it is shot as soon as somebody else takes over the name with the fief, or younger sons becoming lords elsewhere. That same authority says that "surnames did not descend regularly" until 1350. Until they "descend regularly" they are only eke-names.

Norman ceased to be a spoken language by 1400, as English and French take over in England and Normandy. So your Normans will be adding some of the surviving Saxon personal names to the family by then.

Also, the form of a name well may depend on when and by whom your source, or your source's source, was writing. William de la Pole and William atte Pool are the same 14th century gentleman.

Be careful of racking up too many things in one name, as you would need a few paragraphs to straighten it out for the reader. Is Gilbert Fitz Gilbert de Clare Strongbow

1) Gilbert Strongbow, the son of Gilbert of Clare;
2) Gilbert, the son of Gilbert of Clare called Strongbow;
3) Gilbert of Clare called Strongbow, son of Gilbert?

You will also have to choose between modernization — calling people William, John, etc. — or authenticity, which makes them Guillaume and Jean. Modernizing, or Anglicizing, will make your story seem ageless men-in-tights stuff, which many readers expect. The names will also be easier for many to remember. Using the actual old names makes the reader stop and say, "Hey, this isn't the king just before Queen Victoria. This is a real different culture."

As well they ought.

FEMALE NAMES

Adela	Agnes, Anyas	Arletta
Adelaide	Alice — popular	Avis
Adelasia	Amice	Berengaria
Adeline	Anne	Bertha

Constance
Devorguila
Eleanor, Elenor,
  Eleonor — very popular
Emma
Emmeline
Isabel, Isabella
Jocelyn
Joyce
Laura

Lauretta
Leonor
Margery, Marjorie
Marie
Matilda, Maud,
  Maude — extremely
  popular
Melisande
Melisine
Millicent

Muriel
Olive
Oriel
Philippa
Rosamund, Rosamond
Rose
Sibylla, Sibyl
Yolande
Yvonne

Male Names

Alexander
Alfred
Alured
Amalric, Amaury, Amauri
Amaury
Ambrose, Ambroise
Baldwin, Baudoin
Berengar
Bernard
Bertrand
Blondel
Bohemond, Bohemund
Dolfin
Enguerrand
Ernulf, Arnulf
Eustace
Fulk
Galfrid, Geoffrey
Gerbert
Gervase

Gilbert
Giraud
Godfrey
Gui, Guy
Guillaume = William
Henri = Henry
Hubert
Hugh
Humphrey
Ivo
Jocelin, Jocelyn
John, Jean
Lanfranc
Layamon
Leopold
Matthew
Nicholas
Nigel
Odo, Ottobonus
Orderic

Osbern
Otho, Otto
Philip
Raimund, Raymond
Ralph
Ranulf
Richard
Robert
Roger
Rolle
Simon
Stephen
Taillefer
Tancred
Thomas
Wace
Waleran
Walter

Surnames

de Beauchamp
Beaumont, Belmont, Bel-
  lomont
a' Becket
de Belesme
Bigod
de Bohun
Bokenam, Bokenham
de Born
de Borneil
de Bracton, Bratton,
  Bretton
Bradwardine

de Braklonde, de
  Brakelond
Breakspear
de Breteuil
Burgh, de Burgh
de Chandos
de Clare
de Clifford
le Despenser — inherited
  title
de Fiennes
Flambard
de Glanville, or Glanvil

Gower
Grosseteste
de Guader
Guiscard
de Hampole
de Harcourt
Haward
de Hawkwood
Higden, Higdon —
  English, 1299–1363
Hood
de Hoveden, de Howden
de Lacy

de Marigny	Mortimer, de Mortimer	Paris
Marshal — inherited title;	Neckam, Necham	de Quincey
Mareschal	de Newburgh	de Roet
de Merton	de Newmarch	Simmons, Symeonis
de Montfort	Niger	Walworth

MEDIEVAL ENGLISH

One major effect of the Norman invasion was the drastic removal of most Saxon names from use. The Normans had a positive aversion to name variety, and two dozen for each sex did fine for most of the upper class.

These names come from actual people, often the rolls of the populace of London. Saxon names like Ragenilda lived on into the 1300s, but grew increasingly rare. The Renaissance finished them off. Do not expect to see Kingburh replace Jennifer in today's popularity charts. The Norman names, like Alice and Eleanor, are the ones that prospered.

Women often bore male names, especially in the earlier parts of the period when Anglo-Saxon unsexed naming still had strong effect. In Latin, Philippa was a grammatical necessity, but in all–English texts, and therefore around the village, she was called Philip!

Some names had simply not reached England. For example, never use the personal name Aaron until the 1500s. The one in a million occurrence before then will always be Jewish.

At this period, many variants, often called nicks or nicknames, were created by the English shortening, changing sounds, and adding to, the Norman/French names: Robert gave Bob, Robyn, Hob, Hobelot, Dob, Nob, Nop, Hop; Isabel, Nibby, probably via Ibby; and Matilda turned into Maude, as well as Tillot. The Saxon commoners would use these as baptismal names, the upper classes more often as nicknames.

Spelling was irregular: the same place-name can be spelled six ways in one paragraph. Nonetheless, some spellings were preferred. Those in parentheses are the modern versions of a name or nick that were not used in this period. For example, in the 1300s, John may be Jakke or Jankyn, but never Jack or Jenkin. Of course, you may use the later version for your readers' familiarity, but you are losing a chance to make them realize that your story did not occur just in their grandparents' day.

If you are working so early in the period that the Normans and Saxons are still hassling, simply compare this list to the Medieval French and Norman chapters to see what is likely Norman, and to the Saxon section to find your English names. Do not use Welsh names for either. The Britons are still fighting both sets of invaders.

Surnames

By the 1300s, surnames are used in official records, but hardly ever in conversation, or when addressing a person. For the upper classes these are becoming inherited family names, starting about 1270, but for a long time to come (1379 and later) the same person may be known by his or her personal name plus: a patronymic, a place-name, an occupational name, or a personal trait; all with equal legality. This is sometimes referred to by older authors as "the surname period," indicating that while record-keeping, travel, and population are requiring a second name, it has not yet frozen into an invariable family name.

This shows up in Normanized surnames using the French equivalent of "the." For men it will always be "le," for women *sometimes* "la." Not that Anglo-Saxon does not contribute its own gendering. A man will be "Back*er*" but a woman in the same trade will be "Back*ster*." "De" indicates a place-name, the Norman equivalent of the Saxon "atte."

Also, there are far more matronymics than the male supremacists would like to admit. You were surnamed for the more memorable parent, not just the male one, who may have been gone or dead while your mother became a village notable.

Your French — and English! — may prove false in devising eke-names, so I have included a list. You may want to say your knight is bold, but Hardred de la Bold is "Hardred from the small farm." He should be Hardred le Bold.

FEMALE NAMES

Adela
Adeline
Agnes, Aggy, Taggy — somewhat popular
Albon
Alditha
Aldwina
Alisoun, Alison, Alice — very popular; rarely Alicia
Alveva
Amabel, Amabilla, Annable
Amice
Angelet
Anne, Annot
Armynel, Armine — fem. Armand
Ascelina — unusual
Avis, Avice
Barbara — var.: Barb, Bab, Barbot, Babelot, Bar-

bata, Barbota
Basilia
Bersaba = Bathsheba
Bertha
Betrix, Beatrix, Beaten
Bontyng
Camilla — very rare
Cassandra — very rare
Christen, Chesten
Clarice
Custance, Custelot — popular; rarely Constance
Dionise
Donat, Donnet
Dyota
Ede, Edelot
Edild
Edith
Ediva
Eleanor — most popular; var.: Nel, Elena, Elen

Emma, Emelot, Emmet, Emmot
Emmeline, Emblyn
Estrilda
Ethelreda
Eve, Evelot
Extranea — very rare
Frethesantha, Frethesence — Saxon!
Giliana, Gillian, Gillett
Goda
Goditha
Godiva
Godleva
Godrun
Golda
Goldburga
Goldcorna
Goldhen
Grecia — very rare
Grisilde
Hawisia

Holdyva
Isabel — extremely popular; var.: Nibb, Bibby
Ismenia — very rare
Isota, Isause, Isotte — extremely popular; less common: Isolt, Isolda, Isolde; from Cornish
Italia — very rare
Jaquet — rare
Jocelyn
Johanna, Johannes — popular; var.: Jowett
Joyce
Juliana — very popular
Kingburh
Laura, Lauretta
Lavina — very rare
Leda — very rare
Leofrun
Leveva

Livilda
Loveday, Lowdy
Magota
Margaret, Margareta — extremely popular
Margery, Marjorie
Mary, Mariot, Malekyn — extremely popular
Matilda, Maud, Maude — extremely popular; var.: Tillot
May
Megge, Magg, Moggy, Mog — for Margaret or Marjorie
Melodia — very rare
Milda
Millicent
Muriel
Norma — very rare
Olive

Oriel
Pavia — very rare
Ragenilda
Rosamond, Rosamund
Rose
Sabyn (Sabine)
Sara
Sisselie, Sisselot, Sissot, Cecilia
Sophie
Sybyl, Sibyl
Theobalda, more often Tibbot, Tibet — var.: Ibb, Ibbot
Theofania — var.: Teffan, Tiffan, Tiffanie
Thomasine, Tamsyn
Wakerilda
Yvonne
Zenoby, Siney

MALE NAMES

Aalard — popular
Abel, Nab
Absalon (Absalom) — very popular
Adam
Ailmar
Ailred
Ailsi
Alan — popular
Albold
Aldred
Alexander — unusual
Alfred
Alfric
Algar
Alnod
Alsi
Alward
Alwin
Alwold
Amery
Archibald
Arnold
Aymon — popular
Barduf, Bardolf

Barnard, Bernard
Bartholomew, Bartelot
Basil
Bateman
Bermund
Berold, Berraud, Berard
Beton
Bevis
Bike
Blithe
Brian
Bruning
Brunloc
But
Coleman
Conan
Damyan
David
Denis
Derman
Dodo
Drew
Durand
Edgar
Edmer

Edmund
Edric
Edstan
Edulf
Edward
Egidius
Elias
Ernald
Estmar
Estmund
Eudes
Eustace
Everard
Fromund
Fulbert
Fulk
Geoffrey
Gerald
Gerard
Gervase — popular
Gilbert — popular; var.: Gibb, Gibelot
Gillemin, Gilmyn — popular
Gladwin

Godman
Godric
Godwin
Goldwin
Goscelin
Guichard — popular
Gyles
Hamlet
Hamo
Harding
Hardred
Harvey
Henry, Harry — popular
Herbert, Herbelet
Hereward
Huberd — popular
Hugh
Hugo — unusual
Humfrey, Humphrey
Huwe (Hugh) — popular
Ingram
Ingulf
Ivo
Jermyn
Joel
John — popular; var.:
    Jakke (Jack), Janckyn
    (Jankin), Jannet
Layamon, Lawman,
    Lazamon — man of
    law, or son of Leove-
    nath
Leofric
Leofstan
Leonard
Lewis, Louis

Martin
Maurice, Morris
Mervin
Michael
Nicholas, Nicholay —
    popular; var.: Nick,
    Colle
Norman — somewhat
    popular
Odo
Oliver, var.: Noll, Nol
Ordric
Ormar
Osbert
Osmund
Oswald — popular
Otto
Payn
Philip
Piers (Peter) — popular;
    var.: Perkyn
Rauf (Ralph) — popular
Raymond
Rayner
Reginald
Renaud — popular
Reynold
Richard, Richart, Rik-
    ard — popular; var.:
    Richelot, Rikelot,
    Hick, Dick
Robert, Robyn — popu-
    lar; var.: Hobelot,
    Hob, Dob, Nob, Nop,
    Hop, Rob
Roger — popular; var.:

Hodge, Hogge, Dodge
Roland
Rolf
Sagar, Saer
Saward
Seman
Sperling
Stefan
Swetman
Symond, Symkyn
    (Simon, Simkin) —
    popular
Theodgar
Theodric
Theodulf
Thomas, Tom, Tomkin —
    popular
Thurstan
Turbert
Viel
Walter — popular; var.:
    Wat, Watekyn; never
    Walt
Warren
Watman
Willelmus
William — popular; var.:
    Will, Wilekyn; never
    Bill
Wulfred
Wulfric
Wulmar
Wymar
Wymond

Some Period Surnames
x/y indicates male/female form

Arkwright — maker of meal bins
Atte Elme — at the elm
Attenalre — at the alder
Atteneshe, Ate Nasse — at the ash
Attenoke, Atte Noke — at the oak
atte Place, de la Place — a place or
    stead, or courtyard
le Backer/le Backster — the baker
Baker/Baxter — baker
cum-Barba — with beard; in 1273, a

rare thing
la Barbaresse — the woman barber
Barbot
Barduf
Barfot — later, Barefoot
le Bat — the bat
Batayle, de la Batayle — of the battle
    (army unit)
de Batisford
Batte

Batty
de Beauver
la Beke, le Beke
Bendbow — archer
Bene
de Berelay
le Bereward — the bear-keeper
le Blakesmith — iron smith
Bland
Blaxter, Blakester — woman bleacher
Blundel, le Blount, le Blound, le
  Blund, le Blunt — the blond(e)
de la Bold — from the small farm;
  watch this!
Bold, le Bold — the bold
de Bolebek
Bordwrygt — carpenter
Botewright — boat-wright
Breakspear
le Bredemonger/le Bredemongster —
  the bread seller
Brewer/Brewster — brewer
Brounsmyth, Bronsmyth — copper-
  smith
le Brune — the brown
le Candlemakere — the candlemaker
le Cartwright — the cart-maker
Chesewright — cheese-maker
Clavynger — the mace-bearer
le Cornmonger — the *grain* seller;
  maize has not yet come from the
  Americas
le Crask
Crease — squeamish
Curteis — courteous
Danyll
Deemster/Dempster
le Dun — the brown
le Fatte — the fat
le Fleshmongere — the meat seller
Flesschewer, Fleshewer — butcher
Freebody
le Garlykmonger — the garlic seller
Gay — gladsome, merry
Gentle — noble, refined
Gerrish — showy
Gladcheer
Glaser/Glaister — glazier
le Glaswrighte — the glassmaker
Good
Govi

Grensmythe — lead smith
Hendy, Henty — refined
le Heymonger — the hay seller
le Hore — the white
Humble
Kempste, Kembester, Kemster —
  woman wool-comber
le Kissere — the maker of thigh-
  armour (cuishes, cuisses)
ye Ladimayden — the lady's maid
le Lene — the lean
le Lettle, Le Litle — the smaller
le Limwryte — the lime burner
Litter/Litster
Littleproud
Longfellow
Makejoy
Makepeace
Mathewman/Mathewoman — ser-
  vants of Mathew
Meek
le Melmongere — the meal seller
Merry, Merriman
Merywedyr — Meriwether
Monemaker
Moody, Moodiman, Musard — muser
Orped — brave, daring
le Otemonger — the oat seller
de Otteley
le Ould — the old
Paliser/Palister
Parchmentmaker
le Pennager — the ensign bearer
Piper/Pipester — the piper
Pollit — polite
le Potager — the maker of pottage
Pouchemaker
Proud, Prout
Proudfellow
Quick
Reyngud
Righteous
Rodesmithe — red smith, gold smith
Rokster — female occupation
de Ryseford
Saper
le Schipwryte — the shipwright
Sclater/Sclaster — slater
Shakelance
Shakespear
Sharparrow — archer

Sillyman
Simister — seamstress
Slater/Slaster — slater
Slaywright — maker of looms
Slyman
Slynge — the slanger, the insulter
Smart
Snell — alert
la Sore, le Sor — with the sore
Sprynge — springing
Stonehewer
Strongbow — archer
Sweet
Tellwright — tile maker

Thacker/Thackster, Thaxter — thatcher
le Thikke — the thick, the bulky
le Tukere — the fuller
le Wainwright — the wagon-maker
Wagstaff
le Walkere/Walkester — fuller, cloth finisher
de Wathe
Webster — weaver, a female occupation
Welwryghte — wheelwright
de Westcot
le Wodehyewere — the wood hewer
Wryght — maker, often wheelwright

MEDIEVAL GERMAN

Noble sorts have place-names or land-titles appended to their personal names. However, Walter von Nuremberg may not be of the family that rules Nuremberg; he may just be a former resident of Nuremberg. By the end of the period, some are becoming true family names. As usual, names rarely make hard, sharp changes, but shade over into the next set of practices.

Almost all of the Minnesingers, the Germanic minstrels equivalent to troubadours and trouveres, have place-names because most of them are from noble families. These are not penniless vagabonds, but courtiers travelling among distant relatives and friends of friends. In the Germanies, a younger son with a talent for music and poetry did have an alternative to being either a mercenary or a cleric. The upper-level commoner who does have the talent and mien to become a Minnesinger, like Heinrich von Meissen, has risen a long way in the world.

If there are insufficient women's names, lots of the Frankish ones would continue in use.

FEMALE NAMES

Adelheidis, Adelaide, Adelheid
Agnes
Bertha
Fredegunde
Gertrude
Hermangarde

Hilde
Hildeburg
Hildegard
Judith
Kondwiramur
Kunigunde
Mechtilde

Orgeluse
Sabina
Sidea
Sophie
Zimburgis

MALE NAMES

Adalbert
Adolf
Albert
Albrecht
Anno, Hanno
Benno
Bernward
Berthold
Berward
Bruno/Brun
Caesarius
Cunibert
Danhuser, aka Tannhau-
    ser
Eike
Eneit = Aeneas

Engelbert
Erwin
Freidrich
Gebhard
Gottfried
Hartmann
Hatto
Heinrich
Hildebert
Johannes
Konrad, Conrad
Lambert
Leudegast
Liudger
Ludolf, Lliudolf
Manfred

Neidhart
Oswald
Otto, Odo
Ottokar
Peter
Reinmann
Reinmar
Rudolf
Runcifal
Siegfried
Walram
Walther
Welf
Werner
Wirnt
Wolfram

EKE-NAMES

Frauenlob — praise of
    women

Fuchs — the Fox
der Pfaffe — the Priest

der Stolze — the Proud

PLACE-NAMES

von Aue
of Bohemia
von Brennenburg
von Eschenbach
von Gravenberg
von Hagenau
von Hausen
von Hersfeld

von Hochstaden
von Kühn
von Marburg
von MegenBurg
von Meissen
von Ofterdingen
von Regensburg
von Repgau

von Reuenthal
von Steinbach
von Strassburg
von Veldeke
von der Vogelweide
von Wolkenstein
von Wurzburg

FAMILY NAMES

Eckhart, Eckart
Eilenburg

Parler or Arler, 1333-97,
    aka von Gmünd

Wielin
Zähringen

MEDIEVAL ITALIAN

The Middle Ages ends sooner in Italy than the rest of Europe. At least the transition period to the Renaissance starts earlier. Consider this sample to apply from about 1000 to 1300.

Many of the names to be used are Italian versions of Germanic names: Folco for Fulke, Welf for Wulph, Arnolfo for Arnolph, Liutprand for Ludbrand. Others, like Enzio and Marozia, look simply Italian. Family names are still over the horizon, though the d'Este family claims to go back to the 900s. As this is a place-name, they may well have been using it that long, but I doubt that anyone who moved elsewhere continued to use it. Place-names like da Brescia, di Cambio, de la Riva, and d'Arezzo; and eke-names like Latini, Caccianemici, Da Todi, and Allucingoli, separate one Welf from another. For your readers, it is more meaningful to say it in English.

FEMALE NAMES

Adelaide	Cuniza	Matilda
Alrude	Marozia	

MALE NAMES

Alberic	Folco	Obizzo
Anselmo	Gerard, Gherardo	Olderic
Arnolda	Guibert	Pandulf, Pandolfo
Arnolfo	Guittone	Rainerius
Azzo, Azzolino	Hugo	Sordello
Berengar	Irnerius, Warnerius,	Thom, Tunc, Tum,
Bonvesin	Guarnerius	Tenque
Brunetto	Jacopone	Ubaldo
Enzio, Enzo	Liutprand, Liudprand,	Ulfilas
Ezzelin, Ezzelino	Liuzo	Welf

PROVENÇAL

Once upon a time, Provençe was a kingdom unto itself, where romantic love was high art, carried on in that version of French called langue d'oc, or Provençal. Here the troubadours came into being, and even the lord of Blaye became one of the musical wanderers. The lords of Languedoc might more often stay in their domains, but many became famed for their music and poetry.

"Family names" are strictly illusory. Even the lords of the land have only place-names, and a commoners will only have a nickname to differentiate this Guillem from all other Guillems. Often you will see two-part names — Isarn Bernart, Bernart Oth — but the second is not a family name, any more than in Billy Bob or Mary Jane.

As unusual as some of these names might seem, especially women's, they are not fictions taken from chivalric fantasy. The records of the Inquisition and genealogists provide these actual names. Remember that the final E is often sounded, rather than silent, and they will sound prettier to you.

FEMALE NAMES

Agnes [AH-nyes]
Algaia
Aliénor [AH-lee-ay-NOHR]
Berengaria
Blanche
Blandina
Cassanea
Cavilia
Constance
Dolça [DOHL-sah]
Ermengarde [ER-min-GARD-ah], Ermen-
garda
Ermessinde, Ermessinda
Esclarmonde, Esclar-monda
Eugénie
Faydide, Faydida
Flamença, Flamensa
Florine, Florina
Geralda
Griselde, Grisilde, Griselda
Guirande, Guiranda
Imperia
Mabilia
Mamille [mah-MEEL-lah]
Margherita
Marquesia
Misse [MEES, MIHS-sah], Missa
Nova
Sybelle, Sybella
Torqueri [tor-keh-REE]
Willelma
Yolande [yo-LAHND-ah], Yolanda

MALE NAMES

Abit
Aimery
Alaman
Arnault
Arnaut
Azemar
Barral
Berengar
Bernart, Bernard
Bertran
Boé
Bonnet
Boson
Cercamon
Claud — note, no final E
Clément
Daniel
Darius
David
Emeric
Estolt
Étienne
Fabre
Folquet
Foulquois
François
Gaspard
Gaston
Gaucelm
Girart
Girault, Gerald
Guido
Guilabert
Guillem
Huc, Hugues
Irénée
Isaag
Isarn
Jasmin
Jaufré
Jean
Jogues, Jacques
Josephe
Kyot
Louis
Marcabrun
Martin
Marty
Maurice
Olivier
Oth
Paul
Peire
Pey, Peyrot
Pierol
Pierre
Pons
Pothin
Raimbaut
Raimon
Raynouard
René
Savario
Seguin
Sicard
Toussaint
Tristan
Uzalger
Vidal
Walter

CATALAN AND ARAGONESE

The two are close dialects, name the same way, and were politically joined.

The contribution of the Catalonians is often lost when their names are transliterated into the equivalent in Spanish or French. You may know Raimond Lully, Arnaud de Villeneuve, Pedro Torrellas, or Salvador Dalí. Until you start Catalan research, you will not find their original names: Ramon Lull, Arnau de Vilanova, Pere Torroella, or Salvat Dalí.

In the Medieval heyday of Catalan (12th to 15th centuries), the custom of using patronymics progressed to only the nobility having family names, a frozen patronymic or based on their holdings, to most people having them by the end of the period. Indeed, for artists they are in use by the early 1300s. This is much earlier than in most of Europe; right up there with Renaissance Italian names.

The patronymic is the father's name, little changed, with an "-ez" suffix. So Ramiro Díaz will have a son called Pere Ramírez, and his son will be Jaume Perez. It is very common to alternate names with first-born sons: Alfons Ferrandez names his son Ferrando; Ferrando Alfonsez names his son Alfons, so that the two names leapfrog generations.

A writer should probably avoid the other noble customs, like giving every eldest son the same name, such as the string of Counts of Barcelona and Urgell named Ermengol I through VIII. The exception would be if the others of the name had died and were only referred to in passing. Also confusing: naming one son Ramon Berenguer, and the younger brother Berenguer Ramon, unless you absolutely need mistaken identities for your plot.

In more modern times, Catalan speakers follow Spanish custom in compiling family names. That is, following a child's personal names will be put the father's family name, a lower-case "i," and the mother's family name; as in Jaume Bofill i Mates.

Apostrophes can be used to indicate that the letter preceding the apostrophe would have an accent over it. This is a pronunciation guide, telling you that the syllable of that vowel is stressed. It does not change the sound of the vowel, so you could omit it. Ç indicates an S-sounding soft C, which can be written C-dollar sign (c$) or "apiece" (@) if you lack international characters. In desperation, it can be written S.

When you are making up churches and place-names, note that in Catalan, a masculine saint is not the Spanish "San," but "Sant"; "Santa" is still used for the female ones.

Female Names

Agata	Basque	Antonia
Almodis	Anna — not common in	Aurembiaix
Andregoto — from the	upper classes	Beatriu

Berengueria   Eulàlia   Mata
Blanca   Güelfa   Petronilla
Catalina   Isabel   Rois
Caterina   Joana   Sança
Constança   Leonor   Sibilla
Elicsenda   Magdalene — unusual   Teresa
Elionor   Margarida   Violant
Eugeni   María — very popular

MALE NAMES

Name	Patronym	Notes
Aguiló	Aguiloz	
Alfons	Alfonsez	= Alfonso
Alvar	Alvarez	
Andreu	Andreuez	= Andrew
Angel	Angelez	
Anselm	Anselmez	
Arnau	Arnez	
Ato	Atoz	
Ausies	Ausiez	
Aznar	Aznarez	
Bello	Belloz	
Berenguer	Berenguerrez	
Bernat	Bernatez	= Bernardo
Bertran	Bertranez	
Borell	Borellez	
Cabreta	Cabretez	
Centulle	Centullez	
Cervari	Cervarez	
Enrique	Enriquez	= Henry
Ermengol	Ermengolez	
Fadrique	Fadriquez	= Frederick
Felip	Felipez	= Felippe, Philip
Feliu	Feliez	= Felix
Ferando, Ferrando	Ferandoz	
Ferran	Ferranez	
Ferrante	Ferrantez	
Ferrer	Ferrerez	
Folc	Folcez	= Fulk
Francesch	Franceschez	= Francisco, Frances
Galindo	Galindoz	
Garcia	Garciez	
Genís	Genísez	
Geribert	Geribertez	
Gil	Gilez	
Gilabert	Gilabertez	= Gilberto, Gilbert
Guerau	Guerez	
Guifré	Guifréz	
Guillem	Guillemez	= William; very popular

Hug	Huguez	= Hugo, Hugh
Iñigo	Iñiguez	
Jacinto	Jacintoz	
Jacobo	Jacoboz	
Jaume	Jaumez	= James
Joan	Joanez	popular; dim. Joanot
Joaquím	Joaquimez	
Johanot	Johanez	
Jordi, Jordá	Jordez	
Josep	Josepez	= Joseph
Just	Justez	
Karles	Karlez	= Carlos, Charles
Llorenç	Llorençez	= Lorenzo, Laurence
Lluis	Lluisez	= Luis
Marcúç	Marcúçez	
Mariano	Marianoz	
Martí	Martiez	= Martín
Miquel	Miquelez	= Miguel, Michael; popular
Mir	Mirez	
Miró	Miróz	
Narcís	Narcísez	= Narcissio
Nunyo	Nunyez, Nuñez	
Oleguer	Oleguerez	
Oliba	Olibez	
Pau	Pauez	= Paul; unusual
Pere	Perez	= Pedro, Peter
Poc	Pocez	
Ponç	Ponçez	= Ponce, Pons
Quirze	Quirzez	rare
Ramiro	Ramírez	
Ramon	Ramonez	popular
Roderigo	Roderiguez	
Salvat	Salvatez	= Salvador
Sanç	Sançez	= Sancho
Sebastiá	Sebatiez	= Sebastiano, Sebastien
Sunifré, Sunifred	Sunifrez	
Sunyer	Sunyerez	
Tomás	Tomasez	
Vicent	Vicentez	= Vincente
Víctor	Victorez	

PLACE/FAMILY NAMES

Albert	Bofill	Callico
Alcover	Borassà	Callis
Arbó	Boscan Almogaver	de Cardona
Aribau	Botet	Carner
Bassa	Buil, Boil	de Castellet
Belluga	de Cabestanh	Catalá
de Berguedan	de Caldes	de Cervera, de Cerverí

de Corella	de Lluçà	Puyol
Costa	López	Reglà
Dalmau	Lull	Riba
Desclot	de Malla	Riber
Eiximenis	Manent	de Rocabertí
de Empúri	Maragall	Roig
Espriu	March	Rosell
Febrer	Martorell	Ruyra
Ferrando	Mates	Sabaris
Ferrer	Metge	Sagarra
Foix	Mieres	Salvá
Garcés	de Montcada	Sanchez
de la Guardia	de Montgri	de Sant Jordi
Guerrero	Muntaner	Serra
Guimerá	de Odena	Sobrequés
de Gurb	Oller	Soldevila
Huguet	d'Ors	Solé
Johan	de Palol	de Torodela, Torrodella
Juan	Papasseit	Turmeda
de Liost	Paradís	Verdaguer
Llobera	Picó	de Vilanova
Llor	de Plegamans	Vives
Llorente	de Próxita	

BASQUE

Basque — Euskeria to its speakers — is one of the few languages of Europe that is not Indo-European, and can be traced to pre–Roman roots in Iberia. The Basques have not always occupied their current strongholds of Vizcaya and Guipúzcoa; they date back farther in Alava (Alaba), and at one time spread far into France, creating Gascony. Note how many early Gascon dukes are named Sancho. The Basque Medieval centers were Pamplona (Pamplune) and Navarre.

Most modern Basque use Hispanic personal names — Juan, Joaquin, José, Pablo — just like my cousins in Santander. Others do use Eukeni, Iñaki, and the like. Many of the extremely Basque personal names are modern artificial creations in Euskeria, not traditional.

Family names date from the Middle Ages, often being carry-overs from earlier patronymics. Some names that you think are very Spanish — Sanchez, Mendoza, Salazar — are in fact Basque in origin, but in the New World especially this has become immaterial. Basque is simply one of the sources of Renaissance and modern Spanish names, just as the Saxons and the British are for modern English names.

Up through the 11th century, they still show strongly matrilineal, unlike the Indo-Europeans, with every man identified in a legal document as the son of a woman, rather than by a father's name. They were not even nominally Christianized until the 760s, though caught between the Visigothic kingdoms of Spain and the Franks. Much later, Basque witch-cults — survivals of the Old Religion — were notorious.

An interesting point in fashion: in the Middle Ages every third male Basque would be named Sancio.

Remember, as in Spanish, final E's are pronounced; all E's as in "hey," I is as in machine.

FEMALE NAMES

Acibella
Adulina
Ana — one N
Andregoto — not unpopular
Assona
Bella
Blanche
Blasquita
Brisca
Dadildis
Egeria
Elvira
Estefania
Faquilo
Fausta
Galga
Gayla
Guldreguth
Iñiga
Jimena
Magrelina
María — only after 1200
Matrona
Munia
Nina
Onecha
Onneca, Oneca — very popular
Quisilo
Rebelle
Sancha — very popular
Sanza
Teresa
Tota — popular
Urraca — very popular

MALE NAMES

Name	Patronym	Notes
Atila	Atilez	
Ato	Atez	
Azenar	Azenariz	= Aznar in Catalan
	Aznari, Asnari	
Belazo	Belazoiz	
Braulio	Brauliez	
Centolle	Centollez	
Centullo	Centulliz	
Chorso	Chorsoiz	
Didaco	Didacoiz	
Diego	Diégez	
Eukeni	Eukeniz	
Ezterio	Ezteriz	
Fernan	Fernanez	= Fernando
Fortún	Fortunez	popular
Galindo	Galíndiz	extremely popular
Garzéa	Garzéiz	= Garcé
Gazo	Gazoiz	
Gidavoz	Gidavoziz	

Giderio	Gideriz	
Gonzalo	González	
Herri	Herriz	
Iñaki	Iñakiz	
Iñigo	Iñiguez	extremely popular
Jimeno	Jiménez	
Lope	Lópiz	popular
Mome	Momiz	
Monio, Monnio	Monioz, Monnioz	
Munnico	Munnicoiz	
Nunas	Nunasoz	
Oriollus, Oriolus	Oriollez	
Ortio	Ortiz	
Otso	Otsoiz	
Pére	Pérez	
Raimundus	Raimúndez	
Ramiro	Ramírez	
Sancio	Sanccoiz	= Sancho; most popular
Sidoc	Sidoccez	
Taio	Taiez	
Velazquo	Velázquez	
Vigala	Vigilaz	
Vincomal	Vincomalez	

Family Names

Aizpurua	Gamboino	Onaindia
Alzate	de Garibay	Onis
Apalategui	Gaztambide	Opilano
de Azkuë	Goñi	Reguera
Baroja	Goyhenetxe	Salazar
Batasuna	Jauregui	de Sarriegui
Caro	de Larramendi	Valda
Cillán	Laztago	Vasurta
Echegaray	Lescano	Zaenáriz
Elío	Letamendia	Zamudiano
Espeleta, Ezpeleta	Ligizamon	Zumalcarregui
Fertungonio	Manto	Zurbarán
Fortuniones	Mendoza	
Fusi	Oihenart	

BYZANTINE

"Byzantine" is a designation invented by 17th century French historians. "Eastern Empire" is used only by those of the Western Empire. To themselves, these people were *the* Roman Empire. They lived under Roman law, with a few adjustments because of their Christianity, including reduced male privilege. Latin was the official language until the early 600s, when Greek replaced it. Even then, they called themselves Romans — "Romaioi."

The editing by historians make Byzantines appear to early on have changed their naming practices from those of the Romans. However, "Constantine" was actually Flavius Valerius Aurelius Constantinus.

The official Early Byzantine Period is 641 to 867. Names are structured much the same as in the chapter "Late Latin, a Note," pages 465–466. Use the list below for choices, as well as the Hellenic chapter.

By the Middle Byzantine period of naming, 867–1204, the upper classes use a pattern familiar to us, of personal name first, followed by a family name. Do note that family names have male and female versions that have to be matched to the bearer. Once again, there will be no accidental cross-gendering unless someone just hears the name wrong.

The use of eke-name surnames continues for those who do not have family names, including emperors. Sometimes the surnames are honorifics, like Mono-machus for an emperor who has actually fought hand-to-hand, rather than only as a general in the back ranks.

The Late Byzantine runs from 1204 until Constantinople falls to the Turks in 1453, the last Emperor dying in battle in the streets.

If you use a list of saints' names, be certain you are using Greek or Eastern Orthodox saints of the early period, not Roman saints. In the early period, many of these have a pagan flavor, because the people did not have a real concept of "Christian" names yet. Thus, you wind up with saints named Bacchus and Demetrius and Apollinaire. You can often take them from the Hellenic names. The use of their names fades off in the later eras.

Still, the vast majority of the people in the Empire are still known by one name with perhaps a place-name, as is even more common in western Europe.

FEMALE NAMES

You can use the feminine of any Latin praenomen, nomen, or cognomen, as well as the "-illa" versions.

Anastasia	Callinia	Epiphania
Anna	Casiane, Casia	Eudocia
Anthemia	Constantia	Eudoxia
Aretha	Constantina	Eulalia
Athenais, Athenaïs	Delmatia	Fausta
Aurelia	Demetria	Helena
Calixta	Eirene, Irene	Justina

Leontia
Libania
Lucia
Lucilla
Marcellina
Marcia
Martina
Nonna
Olympia
Olympiodora

Popilia
Prisca
Priscilla
Prudentia
Pulcheria
Rhoda
Serena
Sophie, Sophia
Synesia
Theodora

Theodosia
Theophania
Theophilia
Theosebeia
Therosia
Verina
Vincentia
Zena
Zoë

Male Names

Alexius
Alypius
Ambrosius
Anastasius
Ancius
Andronicus
Annibalianus
Anthemius
Apollinare
Apollonius
Arethas
Athanasius
Aurelius
Auxentius
Bacchus
Bardas
Basil, Basilides, Basilius,
   Basiliscus
Belisarius
Caesar
Calixtus
Callinicus
Cephalas
Cerinthus
Chrysaphius
Clemens
Constantius, Constantine
Critobulus
Cyril
David
Delmatius
Demetrius
Dioscorus
Epiphanius

Eulalius
Eunomius
Eusebius
Eustachius
Eustathius
Euthymius
Eutropius
Evaristus
Evgrius
Faustus
Gemistos
Georgius, Georgios
Gregorius
Harmatius
Heracleonas
Heraclius
Hilarius, Hilarianus
Hippolytus
Iamblichus
Isaac
Isidorus
Joannes, John
Justinianus, Justinian
Laonicus
Leo
Leontius
Libanius
Liberius
Lucas, Lukas
Manuel
Marcian
Mauricius, Maurice
Maximus
Michael

Narses
Nestorius
Nicephorus
Nicetas
Nonnus
Olympiodorus
Petrus
Philippicus
Photius
Priscianus, Priscian
Priscillian
Proclus
Procopius
Prudentius
Psellus
Quintus
Romanus
Sabbatius
Satyrus
Sergius
Simplicius
Suda
Synesius
Theodoretos
Theodosius
Theophanes
Theophilus
Trascalisseus
Valens
Vincentius
Vitalius
Zeno
Zephyrinus

FAMILY NAMES

Masculine	Feminine	Status
Acominatus	Acominata	1204
Acropolita/Akropolites	Acropolite	1217
Angelus	Angela	imperial, 1185
Attaliates	Attaliate	11th c.
Bardanes	Bardane	
Bardas	Barda	
Botaniates	Botaniate	
Caerularius	Caerularia	1043–49
Cantacuzene	Cantacuzene	
Chalcocondyles	Chalcocondyle	1400s
Comnenus	Comnena	imperial, 1081
Constantinus	Constantina	
Diogenes	Diogene	
Ducas	Duca	
Glycas	Glyca	12th c.
Gregoras	Gregora	14th c.
Ingerinus	Ingerina	9th c.
Kerularios	Kerularia	
Kurkuas	Kurkua	
Lascaris	Lascari	1259
Lecapenas	Lecapena	920–44
Lucapenus	Lucapena	
Macrembolitissus	Macrembolitissa	1021
Maniakes	Maniake	1050
Melodus	Meloda	6th c.
Ooryphas	Oorypha	880
Palaeologus	Palaeologa	imperial, 1259
Palamas	Palama	
Philoponus	Philopona	6th c.
Phocus	Phoca	imperial, 867
Phrantzes	Phrantze	
Sphrantzes	Sphrantze	15th c.
Planudes	Planuda	1310
Prodromus	Prodroma	12th c.
Psellus	Psella	1018–78
Ptochoprodromus	Ptochoprodroma	12th c.
Rhangabe	Rhangabe	
Rhagabe		845
Staurakios	Staurakia	
Stauricius		811
Stratioticus	Stratiotica	
Vatatzes	Vatatze	1222–54
Ypsilanti	Ypsilantis	
Zimisces	Zimisce	
Tzimiskes	Tzimiske	969–76
Zonaras	Zonara	12th c.

Surnames

	Meaning	*Status*
Balbus	stammerer	829
Bulgaroctonus	slayer of Bulgars	
Caesariensis	of the Caesars	500 C.E.
Calaphrates	the calker	1041
Chrysostom	golden mouthed	345–407
Copronymus	dung-named	Emperor, 719–75
Monomachus	single combat	1000–1055
Pogonatus	bearded	
Porphyogenitus	born in the purple	
Scholasticus	lawyer	Grk, 536–600
Smyrnaeus	of Smyrna	4th c.

Dark Ages
(300–1100)

NORSE

The term Viking actually refers to an activity — "going a-viking" — which was raiding, robbing, and pillaging people of other areas. The Saxons and Irish once considered this an excellent endeavor too. Christianization seems to have had a dampening effect.

The Norse were great settlers as well as reavers. They colonized Greenland (which froze out in global cooling), Iceland, parts of Ireland, England, and Scotland, and became both the Normans (used by some for older Norse, not just the later half–French of Normandy) and the Rus, the non–Slavic ruling class that gave their name to Russia. As the Varangians, they serve the Byzantine Emperor as mercenaries in the Varangian Guard.

Artistic Decisions

A decision to make in transliteration of Norse names: to end in R or drop it? The R is often (but not always!) a grammatical ending, and not immutably part of the name.

You may be influenced by how you see the name translated, but common usage is not always accurate. All those female "-hild" names are usually found as "-hildr," but Latin and Latinate writers drop the R, which is okay. But then they add an A or E to feminize it to their taste, winding up with Brunhilda. On the other hand, you always read of the dragon Fafnir, but it could be rendered Fafni. In this case, translators may have thought the I-ending diminutive and too weak. So common usage is commonly inconsistent.

Thorgrim or Thorgrimr, or even Thorgrimur? Use Thorgrim if you already have selected a Gripir, Thorgrimur if you have a Steingrim.

You may also have to decide about the diminutive "-kl." Thorkl may look better to you as Thorkel, or Thorkil.

Gender

Many names are virtually unisex, like Nereid. Endings like -leif, -heid, and -laug are found equally in both lists.

Still, other endings are definitely female: -dis or -disi, which means woman; -hild, which means battle; -ör or -oer; -berg, which is a first element only for men. Only masculine names use -ulf or -olf as a second element; ditto -kel and -ald. For men, -gerd/gard is rare but not unknown, as are -gunn and -frid. You can consider these feminine, as in a thousand different male names they only appeared once or twice. It is like the modern boys' names Shirley, Pearl, or Marion.

FEMALE NAMES

Aase, Åse	Asdis	Biarlaug
Alaibu, Alof, Olof	Asfid	Biarnhild
Aldis	Asgerd	Birgingu
Alfdis	Asgunn	Bödhvi
Alfgerd	Ashild	Bödvild
Alfheid, Alfiva	Ashilf	Borghild
Alfhild	Askatla	Borgny
Alfny	Aslaug, Aslog	Botey
Alfrun	Asleif	Bothild
Alfvör	Asmod	Brum
Algun	Asny	Bryndis, Brynhild
Allaug	Astrid, Esdrid, Esdret,	Dagbjört
Alvoer	Hestrith	Dageid
Anddisi	Asvi	Dagny
Anoana	Asvör	Dagrun
Arnbjörg	Audbiörg	Domhild
Arneid	Audgerd	Dyrfinna
Arngerd, Armgard	Audhild	Dyrhild
Arngunn	Bankfrid	Eburinu
Arnis	Baudvilde	Einfrid
Arnivi, Arnny, Oerny,	Baugeid	Eldrid
Eyrny, Erny	Baugerd	Ellensborgh, Jellensborig
Arnkatla	Beda	Engilborg
Arnlaug, Arlaug, Arlög	Bekkhild	Ermegerth
Arnleif	Bera	Erna
Arnljot	Bergdis	Eydis, Jodis
Arnrid	Bergey, Biargey	Eyfasta, Jofasta
Arnthrud	Berghild	Eygerd
Arnvi	Bergljot	Eyhild
Asbjörg	Bergthora	Eylaug, Eyvör
Asbod	Bestla	Falda

Fastheidi
Fastlaug
Fastny
Fastvi
Fenja, Fimila, Fyorgyn
Fjörleif
Folkwi
Freydis
Freygerd
Freyleif
Fridgerd
Fulla
Gala
Gefjon, Gefn
Geirahoo
Geiravor
Geirlaug
Geironul
Geirskogul
Gerda
Glaunvör
Gleda
Gna
Gnor
Goll
Gondul
Gressa
Grimhild
Groa
Gudr, Gudur
Gudrid
Gudrun
Gullveig
Gunn, Gunna, Gunner
Gunnlod
Gunnvor
Gunvara
Guth
Gytha
Hafthora
Hagny
Hallbera
Hallbjörg
Halldis
Hallfred
Hallgrima
Hallkatla
Hallthora
Hallveig
Hallvi
Hallvör

Hardhthrud
Harthgrepa
Heilvi
Heimlaug
Helfred, Hellefred, Hul-
  lefred
Herborg
Herdis, Hjördis
Hergerd
Hergunn
Herlaug
Herniu
Herthrud
Herrid
Hervör
Hildigunn
Hildisif
Hithintis
Hjalmdis
Hjalmgerd
Holmdis
Holmfrid
Holmgerd
Holmlaug
Hrafnhild
Hrafnung
Hrodhlöd
Hrodhny
Hrodhvi
Hrodlaug
Hungerd
Hunvör
Ikulfrid, Inge, Igulfrid,
  Julfrid
Inggerd, Ingegend
Ingibjörg
Ingilaug
Ingileif
Ingirun
Ingithora
Ingrid
Ingunn
Ingvild, Irpa
Isgard
Islaug
Isrid
Jadhthrudr, Jorthrud
Jarngerd
Jofrid
Jofurfrid
Joreid

Jorfrid, Jord
Joris
Jórunn
Ketilbjörg
Ketilelf
Ketiley
Ketilfrid, Ketilrid
Ketillaug, Ketilloegh
Ketilvi
Kinlaug
Kiolvoer
Kolfinna
Kolgrima
Kristrun
Kunigund
Langlif
Likny
Liufvina
Ljotunn
Magnild
Malhild
Mardoll
Menglöd
Moeid
Oddbjörg
Oddfrid
Oddlaug
Oddleif
Oddny
Oddrun
Oddver
Odindisa, Odindis
Olrum
Ormhild
Otta, Ota
Ottkatla
Ragnfrid, Ragnrid
Ragnhild
Ragnvi
Ran
Randalin
Randeid
Randgrith
Randvi
Ranlaug
Rannveig
Reginleif
Regnburg
Regnhilf
Regnthrud
Rikauka

Rikhild
Rind
Ringeid
Rota
Roth
Runa
Runfrid
Runhild
Rusla, Rusila
Ruta
Saeunn, Saeud
Salbjörg
Saldis
Salgerd
Salvör
Sela
Selkolla
Sigbjorg, Seburgh
Siglaug
Signy
Sigrdrifa
Sigrid
Sigrlinn
Sigrun
Sigthrud
Siguna
Sigvör
Silkisif
Sin
Skadi
Skeggjold
Skialdgerd
Skialdis
Skialdvör
Skialf

Skogul
Snaefrid
Snaelaug
Steinburg
Steinfrid
Steingerd
Steinhild
Steinlaug
Steinunn
Steinvör
Stikla
Sula
Sunnifa, Sunngifa
Sunnlöd
Svafrlöd
Svanhild
Svanlaug
Svava
Thjodbjörg
Thjodfrid
Thjodgerd
Thjodhild
Thjodunn
Thjodvör
Thodburg
Thora
Thorarna
Thorbjörg, Thornbjörg
Thordis
Thorelf
Thorey
Thorgerd
Thorgunn, Thurgun
Thorhall
Thorhild

Thorlaug
Thorljot
Thorny
Thorrid
Thorunn
Thorveig
Thorvi
Thorvild
Thorvör
Thraslaug
Thruth
Thyre, Thyri, Thyra,
  Thorvi
Tola
Torborg
Tove
Valbjörg
Valdis
Valgerd
Vebjörg, Vibrog
Vedis
Vefreyja
Vefrid
Vegerd
Velaug
Veny
Vigdis
Viglaug
Vilborg
Vilgerd
Ulfeid
Ulfhild
Ulfrun

MALE NAMES

Adhisl
Agnar, Einar, Eynir
Agvald, Aghwald
Alfar, Alfarinn
Alfeid
Alfleik
Alfljot
Alfvard
Almveig
Alstygg
Altulf
Alvaldi

Analaf, Olaf
Andfinn, Andvin
Angilaskalk
Ansugisal
Arnfast, Arfast
Arnfrid, Arnrid
Arngeir, Arger
Arngrim
Arniaut
Arnkell, Arkel
Arnmod, Armod
Arnmund, Armund

Arnsteinn
Arnthór, Arnthóri
Asbjörn, Abiurn
Asegeir
Asgaut, Agaut
Askunnr, Askud
Aslaug, Alaug
Asleif, Aleif, Aleib
Asmund, Amunt
Astiarf, Atiarf
Astulf, Asulf
Athalkind

Audhgrim
Audhleik
Audhvald
Audhveli
Aurgeir
Authun
Baldrek
Barthakn
Bengeir
Berglijot
Bergulf, Biörgolf, Biörolf
Biarnhaufdhi
Bjarmar
Bjartmar
Blotsveinn
Bödauk
Bödfrid
Bödhvar, Bödhver
Brandulf
Brunketill
Brynjar
Dagar
Dagfinn
Dolgfinn
Domar
Dragvandill
Egesvold, Egisuold
Eifastr, Ifast
Eithorn, Ithorn
Enerth
Enwald, Eenvold, Jen-
    uold, Ainvit
Erik, Jerik
Erilar
Eyfröd, Eyfred, Eyfreyd
Eylaug
Eylifr, Eileifr, Eilafr, Elef,
    Jelluf
Eythjof
Faraukir
Farvald
Fastgeir
Fiallar
Findor
Finngeir
Finnvard, Finnvid
Foldeid
Folkmar
Folkvard
Forgeir, Furkair, Fairgeir
Frawaradhar

Freygeir
Fridleif
Froewin
Funnulf
Geitfinn
Hadhulaikar
Hafrbjörn
Hafthi
Hagbard
Hagustaldar
Hallfinn
Hallgrim
Hallvard, Halwarth, Hal-
    worth, Haldword
Halmbjörn
Hanef
Hardhskafi
Harek
Hauknef
Haukothur
Heimar
Heimrek
Herbard, Herbjart
Herbrand
Herfrid
Hergeir
Herlaug
Herleifr, Hjörleif, Herliuf
Herthjof
Herulf, Herjolf, Hjörolf,
    Hairuwulafir
Hiallkar
Hiarthwar, Hiartwar
Hildar
Hildigrim
Hithinbiarn
Hjalmar
Hjalmgeir
Hjörmund
Hladhgud
Hlewagastir
Holmgaut
Hördhakari
Höskuld
Hreidhar, Hreidhmar
Hrodhalf
Hrodhbiarn, Hrodhbiörn
Hrodhgaut
Hrodhsteinn
Hrollaif
Hrossbjörn

Hugleik
Hunding
Hunolf, Unulf
Hunthjof
Hvatmod
Hvithaufdhi
Idulleif
Inggeir
Ingiald
Ingleif
Ingvild
Isar
Isger
Isleif
Isröd, Israud
Jarthar
Jofursteinn
Jorgeir, Jogeir
Jörunt, Jörund, Jörunn,
    Jaerund
Ketilbjörn
Ketilhaufdhi
Kinnad, Kinad
Kolbjörn
Kolgrim
Lambkar
Leifdag
Lifsteinn
Likkair
Lodhhött
Malmfrid
Motrek
Mundgerd
Nattulf, Nottolf, Notulf
Nefsteinn
Oddleif
Oegot, Ugot
Ormgeir
Ottmar
Ottver
Radhorm
Radhstaf
Ragnfast, Ranfast
Rainmot
Raskvid
Raudhsveinn
Rikithir
Rikrid
Rögnvald
Rugval
Saligastir

Selthorir
Sigbjörn, Sebiorn
Sigfast
Sigfröd
Siggeir
Sighialm
Siging
Sigleik
Sigmund
Sigref
Sigtiarf
Sigtrygg
Sigulf
Sigvald
Skagvard, Skavard
Skamkell
Skervald
Skinthalaubar
Skirlaug
Skogdrif
Smidhkell
Snaebjörn
Snaevald
Sneribiörn
Snjallsteinn
Steinfinn
Steingrim
Steinmod
Steinolf
Steinthor, Steinthorir
Storverk
Stufialt
Sturlaug
Styrkar
Sunnleif
Sunnolf
Svarthaufdhi
Sveinalt
Sveinbjörn

Svipdag
Swartbani
Swidhbalki
Thjodar
Thjodkell
Thjodmund
Thjodrek
Thjostar
Thjostolf
Thoraren, Thorarin
Thord, Thordar
Thorehund
Thorgil, Thorgild, Thor-
    gils
Thorgot
Thorir
Thorkel, Thorkil
Thormód, Thormóður,
    Thormodur
Thorod, Thorodd
Thorstein, Thorsteinn,
    Torsten
Thorvaldur, Thorvald,
    Thorwold
Thrandr, Thrand, Thro-
    and, Thrond
Thrydrek
Tindulf
Toke
Torgöt
Toste
Tove
Trandil
Tryn
Ulfar
Ulffast
Ulfgest
Ulfketill, Ulfkell
Ulfnad

Valbjörn
Valdar
Valgard
Valraffn
Valthjof
Vatiarf
Vealfi
Vefari
Vefot
Vegaut
Vehjalm
Vekunn
Vemund
Verald
Veseti
Vestar
Vestmar
Vethorm, Vethorn, Veörn
Vidhar
Vidhgrip
Vidhkunnr, Vitkunr,
    Vidhkud
Vidhridhi
Vigbiörn
Vigfuss
Vigleik
Vigmar
Vigniaut
Vigtiarf
Vilhjalm
Vilrad
Vingaut
Vitgeir
Vjefröd, Vjefred, Vje-
    freyd
Wodhuride
Wulthuthewar
Ygrim, Jogrim

EKE-NAMES

Aifor — Ever Fierce
Alwys — the Allwise
Athalsteinfostri — Athelstan's fosterling
Blódøx — Blood-ax
Brynjubitr — Armor-Biter; sword-
    name
Fafnisbana — Fafnir's Bane; substitute
    your choice

Frode — the Wise
Frodi — the Learned
inn Gamli — the Old
Ganger — the Walker; too big for horse
Grafeld — Grayskin
Grafell — Gray-Cloak
Gullinhjalti — Golden-Hilt; sword-
    name

enn Haardrada — the Stern
enn Hardradi — the Ruthless; Hard Ruler
Harfagr — Fairhair
Harpstreng — Strong Harper
Hen — Gentle
Hundingsbana — Hunding's Bane; sub. name of choice
Hundr — the Hound
enn Hviti — the White
Klapa — the Clumsy
Knaresmed — Crooked Knee

Kraki — the Raven
Kyrre — the Quiet
Lagebøter — Law-Mender
Landeythan — Landwaster
Langbrand — Longsword
Lodbrok — Hairy Breeches
Ormstungu — Serpent Tongue
Skaldmaer — Skald-Maiden, used for rare female skalds
Starki — the Stout
Svanhvita — the Swanwhite

SAXON

The old Celtic inhabitants of Britain called themselves Britons. The invaders from Frisia called themselves and their language English (Anglish). The term "Anglo-Saxon" is fairly modern. These names can also be used for the "old" Saxons left in Germany, who gave Charlemagne a lot of trouble.

Families would settle on a root word and work variations on it, so that Aethelstan's sons would be Aethelbald, Aethelwulf, and Aethelraed, while his daughters would be Aethelbeorht and Aethelflaed. It is like the families where the parents are Daniel and Denise, so they name their kids Dana, Dennis, Della, and Dain. Instead of having family names, descendants of a notable ancestor would be known as "-ings," like Alfred the Great's descendants were the Aethelings, since he was of the Aethel-lineage (even though his name was Aelfric — you start running out of variations sooner or later).

Names had no obvious gender. The equivalent of Bliss or Blithe would be given to a child of either gender, as would something fancier like Beorhtraed, "shining counsel." Only some endings are grammatically male or female, though -mund is feminine, but exclusive to men.

Because of this, there is no name list. Instead, you get to build your own out of common and uncommon roots. Don't take the "place-name" category too strictly: one queen was Osburh, "divine fortress."

Your common churl is likely to be known as Slim, Whitey, Lark, Rabbit, or Blossom — in Anglo-Saxon, of course, not modern English. But you can get away with a certain number of these "meaning not sound" translation names for the peasantry.

A great many people had an all-too-common personal birth name, to which was added a place-name by which they were actually distinguished from all the other villagers named Dikke or Pere. Think of all the Johns you know who are known by their last names. These "place-names" were descriptions of farms and dwelling places, because towns were so few. So a man would be known from his home as Deorwode, "deer wood," Blacstan, "white stone," Blaecwielle, "black spring"; these became the modern Derward, Blakeston, and Blackwell.

The common root "aelf" is commonly rendered "elf," but don't think Tolkien. Think nature spirits, like those of the Norse Aelfheim, ruled by Frey and Freya. Actually, it is best translated as "wise" or "wisdom."

As a quick history, the traditional date for the arrival of the English is 449. The first Christian missionary reached those shores in 596, and according to good Christian historians "during the 7th century all the English accepted the new religion." In uncomfortable reality, for centuries thereafter paganism flourished, with many village rites led by the village priest, and kings writing letters of complaint to their bishops. Paganism still continued in a strong underground until it could reemerge in the 20th century. So don't expect anyone in the upper classes, or half of the lower, to have Christian names.

Pronunciation

Final E's are pronounced, as a soft, unaccented short sound.
A = A as in take
AE = A as in tack
C = hard C, always, as in cat, even before I or E
CC = TCH as in itch
E = E as in tunnel
G = hard G as in gun, never soft
HL = HL, L with air coming out the sides of your tongue.
HR = HR, a soft R
HT = KT, as in act
HW = WH as in when, NOT wen
I = I as in machine
K = rare, late period
SC = SH in shush
TH = hard TH in then
U = U as in tune
X = KS as in oxen
Y = I in bit
no Q; sound written CW
Otherwise, as in normal English.

Building Names

People knew what these names meant, just as you would understand if someone were named "Accountant" or "Media-star" or "Restaurant-Row." Yet, they did not pay them any more or any less attention than those of other names.

Names about oxen, rabbits, and beans are commoners' farm-type names. Reserve "noble" and "royal" for those of the better class.

If you are building the clan of the Garings you may select or randomize the names for the brothers Garbeorht, Garwulf, and Garhere, making the endings as different as possible. This culture forces alliteration. Their sister is Garsige, or maybe Garhilde. If you decide on Garhilde, you had better change Garhere to Garmund or something else more distinct. Their mother can be Sigemaere, because she's from outside the line.

However, if all the endings anyone can think of have been used with Gar- in the family, they may start calling the younger children Gythwulf or Glaedhilde, keeping the G. Remember, their poetry is based on alliteration, not rhyme!

As you write, you may find you need to refer to the Garings' grandfather in passing. Randomize the ending to save thinking. Just exert control if it comes up Gargar, or something too similar to the working characters.

During your planning period, random up a hundred names or so, so that you have an original pick-list ready.

Beginning Roots	Meaning
Aelf-	elfin, wise
Aenes-, Ains-	awe-inspiring
Aethel-	noble
Aew-	law
Ald-	old
Alh-	sacred
Ard-	hearth
Arm-	arm
Baerh-	bare
Bald-	bold
Barda-	axe
Bay-	reddish
Bel-	beautiful
Beo-	
Beorht-	bright, shining
Beorn-	warrior
Bitan-	persevering
Blac-	fair, pale
Blaec-	black, dark
Blaed-	prosperity, glory
Bland-	grey-haired
Bote-	herald
Cadda-	war, warlike
Caed-	
Cene-	enthusiastic, keen
Cromb-	crooked
Cyne-	royal; cyning = king
Daeg-	daylight, brightness
Daegel-	day
Daegga-	bright one; God?

Beginning Roots	*Meaning*
Deal-	proud
Deora-	dear
Derne-	hidden
Dun-	hill, downs
Ead-	prosperous
Eald-	old
Ealh-	sacred
Ear-	sea, ocean
Ecg-, Secg-	sword
Freo-	free
Fridu-	peaceful
Gar-	spear
Gifu-	[GEE-fu, hard G] gift
Gisel-	[GEE-sehl, hard G] pledge, hostage
Glaed-	kind, cheerful
God-	God
Gold-	gold
Graeg-	gray
Grand-	great, grand
Guth-	
Gyth-	gift
Haetho-	war
Halig-	holy
Hard-	courageous
Hari-	army
Herle-	army
Hilde-	warrior woman
Hrof-	sky
Hroth-	reknown
Hwit-	white
Isen-	iron
Lang-	tall
Leod-	prince
Leof-	preferred
Maccus-	capable, influential
Mael-	sword or speech
Maht-	might
Ondes-	zealous
Ord-	pointed, spear
Orme-	ship
Os-	divine
Rand-	shield
Read-	red
Regen-	[REH-gehn, hard G] mighty
Ruh-	rough
Sae-	sea
Sige-	[SEE-geh, hard G] victorious
Strang-	strong
Tila-	liberal, good
Treuwe-	faithful

Beginning Roots	*Meaning*
Trum-	sturdy
Ric-	ruling
Run-	secret
Waer-	true
Walt-, Wald-	mighty
Wig-	battle, warrior

Ending Roots	*Meaning*
-arm	arm
-bald	bold
-beorht	brightness, light
-beorn	warrior
-bote, -boda	messenger, herald
-cromb	crooked
-cyne	royalty
-deal	proud
-ecg	sword
-flaed	
-frith	peaceful
-gar	spear; war, warrior
-gifu	[g'fu, hard G] gift (f.)
-gold	gold
-gyth	gift
-hard	brave, courage
-heard	herder
-here	army
-hild	battle
-in	diminutive ending for any root
-lac	
-leod	prince
-maere	fame
-maht	might
-mon	
-mund	protector (m.)
-nyd	compulsion
-rand	shield
-red, -raed	counsel, advice (m.)
-ric	ruler
-sele	hall
-sige	[SEEG] victory (m.)
-son	son of the beginning root
-strang	strong
-thryth	puissant (f.)
-uald	ruler
-waer	true
-walt, -wald	mighty
-ward	warden, guard
-weald	powerful
-weard	guardian, warden
-weorth	worth

Ending Roots	*Meaning*
-wig	warrior
-wine	friend, patron (m.)
-wold	forest, power

Nature Names	*Meaning*
	Can be beginning or ending roots, or stand-alones
ac	oak tree
aeldra	elder tree
aesc	ash tree
aler	alder tree
assa	donkey, from the Celtic
barh	boar
beorc, beecere	beech tree
bene	bean, legume
beran, bero-	bear
berc	birch
bere	barley
boc	buck deer
braem	bramble-bush
bran	raven
brocc	badger, from the Celtic
brom	broom-plant
byrd	bird
caerse	watercress
claefer	clover
clacg	clay
colfre	dove bird
cran	crane bird
crawe	crow bird
deor	deer
ear	sea
earn	eagle; war-bird, as scavenger of battlefields
efer, eofer	boar
el	elm tree
gyr	fir tree
haesel	hazel tree
haeth	heath
haga	hedge
hara	hare
heort	hart deer, stag
holen	holly tree; considered a symbol of masculinity
hramm, hraefn	raven; war-bird, as scavenger of battlefields
hreade	reed
hroc	rook bird
hwaete	wheat
iw	yew
laefer	rushes
lin	flax
lind	linden
minte	mint

Nature Names	*Meaning*
oxna	oxen
pise	peas
rae	roe deer
ramm	ram sheep
roc	rock
ryge	rye
rysc	rush plant
sceap	sheep
snaw	snow
staerling	starling bird
sterre	star
thorne	thorn tree; adj. thornig
wethr	wether sheep
wire	alder forest
wulf	wolf (m.)
wylig	willow
wythe	willow tree

Place Beginnings	*Meaning*
Aecer-	[AHK-er] acre
Aethre-	spring of water
Ban-	white water
Beonet-	bent grass
Brad-	broad
Caer-	castle, fortress
Cald-	cold, usually, not always, with a water-ending
Circe-	[KIRK-eh] church
Clif-	cliff
Dael-	dale
Dene-	valley
Dryge-	dry
Ea-	river
Est-	east
Gara-	triangular
Graf-	grove
Heal-	hill slope
Hean-	high
Hol-	hollow
Hris-	brush wood
Hrycg	[HRIKG] ridge
Huntan-	hunting
Lad-	[LAYD] canal
Lang-	[LAYNG] long
Lindes-	pool
Maed-	meadow
Mere-	lake, mere
Mersc-	marsh
Myln-	mill
Niew-	new
North-	north

Place Beginnings	*Meaning*
Penn-	enclosure, pen
Pic-	peak
Rot-, Rote-	root, stump
Sand-	sandy
Scelf-	[SHELF] ledge
Schad-	[SHAYD] arbor, shed
Smethe-	smooth, flat
Stoc-	tree stub, stock
Suth-	south
Up-	upper
West-	west

Place Endings	*Meaning*
-aethre	spring of water
-brigge	bridge
-broc	brook
-burh	fortress (f.)
-caster, -ceaster	Roman army camp
-colne	colony
-cott	cottage
-croft	cultivated field
-cumb	valley, combe
-barre	gate, barrier
-burne, bourne	brook
-clif	cliff
-dacl	dale
-dene	glen
-dun, -doune	hill, downs
-ea	river
-ere	trees
-feld	field
-fen	fen, marsh
-ford	fording-place in river
-graef	ditch
-graf, -grav	grove
-haefen	haven
-ham	home
-heafod	headland
-heal	hill slope
-healh	nook
-healle	hall, manor
-hid	hide, land to support one family
-hlinc	bank, ridge
-hloew	hill
-hrycg	ridge
-hus	house
-hyll	hill
-ig	island
-lache, -laec	lake
-land	place, area, land

Place Endings	*Meaning*
-leah	meadow
-lin	pool
-luel	tower
-maed	meadow
-mere	lake, mere
-mersc	march
-mor	moor
-ofer	edge
-stan	stone, fortress (m.)
-stigols	stiles
-straet	straight track, street
-tun	estate, holding, town
-weald	heath
-weg	paved road
-welle	well
-wic	village, estate
-wiella	spring, well
-wode	wood
-worth	enclosure
-yate	gate

Stand-Alones — can be used as roots

Aeldra — of superior rank
Aelfa — elfin
Averil — April
Blacey — diminutive of fair-colored
Bletsung — blessing, consecration
Blithe — joyful, cheerful
Bliths — bliss, gladness, joy
Blostm — blossom, fresh, lovely
Bondig — freeman
Brand — fire-brand
Brant — proud
Denu — from the valley
Dice — [DIHK-eh] Richard; some-
    times Dikke
Dunn — brown
Eostre — Goddess of spring and growth;
    Easter
Fearn — fern
Filmen — veil; mist
Fleotig — swift, fleet
Freca — bold man
Gal — gay, lively
Geol — [GOHL] Yule, for someone
    born at
Gibbe — Gilbert
Goda — good

Haele, Hale — hero
Hretha — Goddess
Hring — ring, a rare piece of jewelry
Hugi — spirit, intelligence
Ing — chief God, of youth, renewal,
    strength
More — dark-skinned
Nata — Nathan
Pere, Peers — Peter
Reod — ruddy
Sped — success, prosperity
Stille — quiet, still
Sumer — summer
Symon — Simon
Thawian — ice-thaw
Thearle — stern, severe
Tripp — traveler
Wace — feudal tenant
Waed — foot-ford, river shallow
Waer — prudent, wary
Waerlogga — oath-breaker
Wille — William
Winter — winter
Witta — witsome, wise; feminine
    Witte

Occupations

Aecce — sword-wielder	Grayve — reeve, bailiff
Archere — archer	Hearpere — harp-player
Bacere — bread-baker; masculine	Huntere — hunter
Bacstere — bread-baker	Hwistlere — piper, whistler
Backstere — feminine bread-baker	Mylnweard — mill-keeper
Bemeere — trumpeter	Preost — priest, or his servant
Beomann — beekeeper, bee-man	Raefa — bailiff
Bicca — hewer	Rapere — rope-maker
Biscop — bishop; often used for his	Ridere — horseman, knight
servants	Runa — magician, feminine Rune
Bocere — scribe	Sceaphierde — sheep-herder
Boernet — leader	Sceranman — shearer
Brewere — brewer; masculine	Stiward — bailiff, steward
Brewstere — brewer; feminine	Stodhierde — horse-keeper, stud-herd
Byrle — cup-bearer	Tannere — leather-maker, tanner
Calfhierde — calf-herder	Thacere — thatcher; Thackere
Carla — farmer	Thegn — warrior attendant, thane
Cartere — carter	Tuppere — ram-raiser
Ceapmann — merchant, chapman	Tylere — tile roofer, tile-maker
Colier — charcoal merchant	Waenmann — wagoner
Coltere — colt-herder	Weallere — mason, wall-builder
Cupere — barrel-maker, cooper	Webbestre — weaver; feminine
Demastere — judge	Wicca — sorcerer; feminine Wicce
Dry — magician, from the Celtic	Wrihta — carpenter
Duruward — gate-keeper	Wysard — wise one; wizard
Garmann — spearman	Yoman — retainer, member of staff,
	yeoman

RANDOMIZING MATRICES

First pick a card. Black means the first table, red the second. Put the card back, and pick another for the actual syllable.

Do exert a little editing by back-checking meanings.

BEGINNING ROOTS
Range Card: Black

Second Card:

	Spades	*Hearts*	*Clubs*	*Diamonds*
A	Aelf-	Aethel-	Aenes-, Ains-	Aew-
2	Ald-	Alh-	Ard-	Arm-
3	Baerh-	Bald-	Barda-	Bay-
4	Bel-	Beo-	Beorht-	Beorn-
5	Bitan-	Blac-	Blaec-	Blaed-
6	Bland-	Bote-	Cadda-	Caed-
7	Cene-	Cromb-	Cyne-	Daeg-
8	Daegga-	Daegel-	Deal-	Deora-
9	Derne-	Dun-	Ead-	Eald-
10	Ealh-	Ear-	Ecg-	Freo-

	Spades	Hearts	Clubs	Diamonds
J	Fridu-	Gar-	Gifu-	Gisel-
Q	Glaed-	God-	Gold-	Graeg-
K	Grand-	Guth-	Gyth-	Haetho-

Range Card: Red

Second Card:

	Spades	Hearts	Clubs	Diamonds
A	Halig-	Hard-	Hari-	Herle-
2	Hilde-	Hrof-	Hroth-	Hwit-
3	Isen-	Lang-	Leod-	Leof-
4	Maccus-	Mael-	Maht-	Ondes-
5	Ord-	Orme-	Os-	Rand-
6	Read-	Regen-	Ruh-	Sae-
7	Secg-	Sige-	Strang-	Tila-
8	Treuwe-	Trum-	Ric-	Run-
9	Waer-	Walt-, Wald-	Wig-	Ac-
10	Aeldra-	Aesc-	Aler-	Barh-
J	Beorc-	Berc-	Boc-	Bran-
Q	Broc-	Deor-	Earn-	El-
K	Gyr-	Iw-	Thornig-	Wulf-

ENDING ROOTS
Range Card: Black

Second Card:

	Spades	Hearts	Clubs	Diamonds
A	-arm	-bald	-beorht	-beorn
2	-bote, -boda	-cromb	-cyne	-deal
3	-ccg	-flaed	-frith	-gar
4	-gifu (f.)	-gold	-gyth	-hard
5	heard	-here	-hilde	-in
6	-lac	-leod	-maere	-maht
7	-mon	-mund (m.)	-nyd	-rand
8	-red, -raed (m.)	-ric	-sele	-sige (m.)
9	-son	-strang	-thryth (f.)	-uald
10	-waer	-walt, -wald	-ward	-weald
J	-weard	-weorth	-wig	-wine (m.)
Q	-ac	-aeldra	-aesc	-aler
K	-barh	-beorc, beecere -bene	-beran, bero-	

Range Card: Red

Second Card:

	Spades	Hearts	Clubs	Diamonds
A	-berc	-bere	-boc	-braem
2	-bran	-brocc	-brom	-byrd
3	-caerse	-claeg	-cran	-crawe
4	-colfre	-deor	-ear	-earn
5	-efer, eofer	-el	-gyr	-haesel
6	-haeth	-haga	-hara	-heort

7	-holen	-hramm, hraefn	-hreade	-hroc
8	-hwaete	-iw	-laefer	-lin
	Spades	*Hearts*	*Clubs*	*Diamonds*
9	-lind	-minte	-oxna	-rae
10	-ramm	-roc	-ryge	-rysc
J	-snaw	-sterre	-thorne	-wire
Q	-wulf	-wylig	-wythe	-brand
K	-filmen	-haele, -hale	-hring	-hugi

BRITISH

Be careful not to use these for English or Vikings in the Isles. It would be like giving Companions of the Conqueror Saxon names. The Britons were invaded by the Saxons and the Danes, slowly retreating into Wales and Cornwall, and migrating to Armorica, giving it its new name, Brittany. The relationship is rarely cordial, and they did not borrow the invaders' names.

The Britons were P-Celts, so you can't interchange their names with the Q-Celt Irish, which are about as alike as Spanish and French. Welsh, Cornish, Manx, and Breton are all P-Celtic languages as a result. We will concentrate here on Old Welsh forms, which are the most ancestral.

People, as in most times and places, have a personal name, and if necessary a sobriquet or eke-name, or else they mention who their father was. The Britons, though Christianized during the Roman occupation, seem to have used relatively few "Christian" names, and only a couple of Roman ones.

Names are given with meanings because they can be used as eke-names, as well. Guaur Sulwyn is Guaur Fair-as-the-sun, but Sulwyn Wyry is Sulwyn the Virgin. The few eke-names for which I found meanings are so marked; you may name your heroine Galava Dec, but not Dec Galava; nor Wyry Sulwyn. Many eke-names were used; many had two-part names as a result; but they are not family names. Bleddyn Mawr may well be the son of Geraint Vychan.

Pronunciation

The Welsh LL is nothing like the Hispanic double-L. The Welsh use it for a sound like an unvoiced L: tongue in that position, breathe out hard to make a sound.

W as a vowel sounds the double-O in "typhoon." Y is pronounced long E, as in "keen"; I is short I, as in "pin."

DD may be treated as DH, which is a little softer than the TH in "then." RH is a breathy R, if you want to be precise; a plain, soft R will do.

FEMALE NAMES

The daughter-word is "merc," as in Tancostel merc Ouein.

Adsiltia — she who is gazed at
Adwyn
Agandica — snow-faced
Angharad, Angarad — much loved;
  Hagharat, Agharat
Angwen — very beautiful
Anor, Aanor, Aenor, Adenor — also
  Azenor, Azenoria
Anwyl [ahn-WEEL] — dear
Arianwen — silver-white
Badellfawr
Belisama — most warlike
Blodeyn — flower-like
Blodwen — white flower
Bosmina — soft palm
Brangwaine, Brangwen — white
  bosom
Brangwirin — little raven
Cain — beautiful
Canda — brightness
Ceinwen — beautiful jewels
Coalaulin, Coolaulin — beautiful hair
Coalmin — soft-haired
Cordula
Coulava — soft-handed
Creiddylad — jewel of the sea
Darerca
Dec — the Beautiful; eke-name
Ebrdil
Eira — snow
Eiralys, Eirlys — snow-drop
Eirian — silver
Eirwen, Eirwyn — golden fair
Elin — angel, nymph
Eluned — idol, eidolon
Elwy — benefit
Elwyn — white-browed
Enit — woodlark, purity
Ennogen, Innogen, Ennoguent
Eryl — watcher
Eurgain
Eurwen — golden fair
Euyrdyl
Ewaedah
Eysllt — fair, beautiful
Flamina — softly mild; not from

Latin
Galava — milk white
Gaolnandona — the love of men
Goleudid
Guardid, Wawrddydd, Gawrddyd
Guaur
Guendoloena — originates in Geof-
  frey of Monmouth
Gurycon
Gwefr — amber
Gwen — white
Gwendolyn — white-browed; wife
  of Merlyn; see Guendoloena
Gwendydd — star of morning
Gweneal — white angel
Gwenhifar, Gweniver — fair and
  smooth
Gwenhwyvar — white wave/white
  phantom
Gwenhywach
Gwenllian — white flax; Gwenlian,
  Gwenlliant
Gwennol — swallow (bird)
Gwenog — smiling
Gwladys — from Claudius or gladius
Gwlithyn — dew drop
Gwylfai — May festival
Hafwen — beauty of summer
Heulwen — sunshine
Kambreda, Kembreith — Kein Breit
Kein
Kicva
Lanshuil — full-eyed
Llewi
Llinos — linnet (bird)
Luned
Lupida
Mabyn — youthful
Malvina — smooth brow
Mederei — skillful
Medhuil
Medlan
Meinwen — slender
Meleri
Methahel, Methlael, Atathahel,
  Methael

Modwen — maiden, queen
Morgant — shore of the sea
Morved, Morfydd, Morfudd
Morwenna — maiden
Nest — common; used for Agnes
Oichova — tender maid
Olwen — white foot
Regau, Ragau
Rhian — maiden
Rhiannon — Goddess-name
Rhonwen — slender and fair

Rorei
Strinadona — contention
Suigorum — blue eyes
Suilaliun — beautiful eyes
Suilmalda — meek-eyed
Sulwyn — fair as the sun
Tangustel, Tancostel, Taghwystyl
Tegan — beautiful
Valmai — mayflower
Wyry — the Virgin, an eke-name
Yseult

MALE NAMES

The "son of" word is ap or Ap, attached to the front of the father's name by a hyphen, as in Ganfael ap-Owein. An asterisk (*) indicates one of the knights of King Arthur from the old legends, not the Frenchified romances. Later it will be Map or ab-.

Aedd
Aelhaearn — iron brow
Aer
Aeron
Affallach
Affech
Ambreu
Amhar
*Amren
Anant — from the
  stream
Anarawd — eloquent
Aneurin — of true gold
Angwyn — very hand-
  some
Anlawd
Anwyl — dear one
Arelivri
Arryfuerys
Arthien — bear born
*Arthwr — noble one
Auryn — gold
Auwyn
Avaon
Bedrawd
Bedwin — birch-like
Bedwor
*Bedwyr
Beli — bright
Bendigeid

Bleddyn — little wolf
Bran
Brychan — speckled
Brys — quick
Cadan
Cadawg — battle-keen
Cadel — battle spirit
Cadeyrn — battle king
Cadfael — battle metal
Cadnou — battle-
  known
Cadoc
Cadreith
*Cadwr — shield
Cadyrnerth
*Cai — rejoicer; Kai
Cain — clear, bright
  water
Calporn
Cant — white, bright
Capoir
*Caradoc — abounding
  in love
Carannawc
Carannog
Carantauc
Carantoc — loving
Caswallawn
Caw
Celynen — holly

Cenau — cub
Cenwyn — splendid
  chief
Cerenhir
Ceri — loved one
Cherenir
Cledwyn — blessed
  sword
Clodoc — famous
Clud
Clydno
Clywd — warm
Coed — forest
Coel — trust
Conan
Conguethen — lofty bat-
  tle
Conhibrit
Cunedda
Custennin
Cynan — chief; = Conan
Cynbel — warrior chief
Cynbryd
Cyndeyrn — chief lord
Cynfarch
Cynfor — great chief
Cynhael — generous
  chief
Cynhaern — iron chief
Cynidr — bold chief

Cynwal — powerful chief
Dedwydd — happy
Dewi — beloved
Dillus
Doged
Dremhidydd
*Drydvas
Dryw — wise
Du — black
Dufrhealh — riverbank
Dungarth
Dyfan — tribal ruler
Dyfnog
Dyfrig — princely hero
Dylan — God of the ocean
Dynand — gift
*Edeyrn
Eidoel
Einion — anvil
Eiros — bright
Elfed — autumn
Elian
Elidir
Eliwlod
Elphin
Emyr — honor
Erbin
Euroswydd
Evnissyen
Evrawk
Flewddur
*Gadwy
Gaerwen — white fort
Gandwy
Ganfael
Garanhir
Garanwyn
Garselit
*Gawain
Gawedd
Gawl
*Geraint — old; common
Gildas
Glanmor — seashore
Glewlwyd
Glivi
Glyn — high valley, glen
Glyndwr
Goch

Gofannon
Goreu
Greidiol
Gruffin — ruddy
Gruffudd — fierce chief
Gruffydd — strong warrior
Grugwyn — white heather
Guital — from Vitalis
Guorhitir — very bold
*Gurhyr
Gwalchmei — Gawain
Gwern — alder tree
Gwernach — alder river
Gwiffert
*Gwilim = William
Gwion — elf
Gwyar
Gwyddno
Gwyedd
Gwynedd — fair and blessed
Gwynfor — a fair place, fair lord
*Gwynn — fair
*Gwyr — pure
Gwythyr
Haco
Hael — generous
Haerngen
Heilyn — cup-bearer
Heveyd, Heveydd
*Hywel — eminent; Howel
Iddic
Idwallawn, Idwal
Illtyd — ruler of town or district
Iolo
*Iona
Ionwyn — fair lord
Iorwen — beautiful lord
Iorweth — worth a lord
Irfon — the anointed
Ithel — generous lord
Kadyriath
Karantoc
Kelyddon

Kilwed
*Kilwich
Kilydd
Kyner
*Kynon
Kynvelyn
Laodegan
Letewic
Law Ereint — of the Silver Hand; eke-name
Llenleawg
Lleu — guide, ruler
Lleuddad
Lleufer — splendid
Lliver
Lloyd
Lludd
Llwyd — grey-haired
Llyn — pool/waterfall
Llyr — God of the sea
Llywarch
Llyweilun — like a ruler
Llyweith — ruler
Luman
Lynfa — place of the lake
Mabon — youth
Madag
Madawc — benefactor
Madern
Madoc
Mael
Maelgan
Maelgwyn — metal chief
Mabon
Manawyddan
Math — treasure
Matholch
Mawr — great; often an eke-name
Meilyr — common
*Meneu
Meredud — mortal day
Meredydd — guardian from the sea
Merfyn
Meriawn
Meric
Merin
Mewan
Modron
Moelwyn — fair-haired

Morcan — white sea
Mordeyrn — great
 monarch
Morfyn
Myfanwy
Myrddin
Nennog — heavenly one
Nerys — lord
Newyddllyn — new pool
Nissyen
Nudd
Odyar
*Odyaw
Ol
Olwyd
Onllwyn — ash grove
*Owein — well-born;
 Owain
Padarn — fatherly
Penkawr
Perceval — Peredur
Pwyll — prudence

Pyderi
Regen
Ren — chief/ruler
Rhain — a lance
Rhinfrew — still river
Rhodri
Rhun — grand
Rhys — burning, glory
*Riogoned
Rumenea — curving river
Saer — carpenter
Sedwei
*Sel
Selgen
Selgi
Succat — clever in war
Sulgen — sun-born
Taliesin — radiant brow
Taran — thunder
Teirgwed
Teirtu
Tewdwr

Trahayarn — powerful
 iron
Treman — house at the
 rock
Trevelian — from Elian's
 homestead
Tringad
Tryphin
*Trystan — noisy/bold
Tudwal — wall of the tribe
Turgadarn
Urbgen — town-born
Usber
Uther
Varwawc
Vychan — small
Ynyr — honor
Ynywl
Yspadaden
Ywain — young warrior

GOTHIC AND FRANKISH

These are the sackers of Rome, and also the creators of the Holy Roman Empire. You will need their names for Germanic people on the frontiers of the Roman Empire from the time of Caesar. By 450, they have overrun the Celtic Continent, and moved into northern Italy. You will continue using the names through about 900 or 1100. Then you should begin using the slightly modernized and nationalized forms called Medieval French, Medieval German, and Norman.

Please read the note in the chapter for Celtic names, beginning on page 498, on who was really Germanic in the Classical world. Triboci, Nemetes, Vangiones, Sugambri, Ubii, Mattiaci, Cimbri, and even the Teutones *use Celtic names*, not Germanic.

Alemanni, Goths (Ostrogoths and Visigoths), Gepidae, Franks, Vandals, Bajuwari, Burgundii, Suebic Quadi, Chauci, Chatti, Cherusci use the names below. Remember that Latin-speakers will twist them all out of shape, turning Herman into Arminius.

Gothic and Frankish "family names" are really tribes or lineages, whose root name can often but not unfailingly be found as part of the name of the individual, like Amalaric and his mother Amalswint of the Amal family. Her father, however, was Theodoric the Great, so it is not iron-clad. The family connection may be done by the end root, as in Hadubrand and his son Hildebrand, or the Visigoths, Athanagild, Leovigild, and Hermenegild, or Alboin, son of Audoin.

You will find some name roots familiar, if you know Anglo-Saxon names, and yet others quite strange. You will find the start of all the "-ric" amd "-bert" names, and something as common as Charles — though it began life as Kerl. However, unless you are trying to pull the reader out of the rut of stereotype, you had better call the greatest Frankish king Charlemagne rather than Great Kerl, just as you had better be wary calling Arthur, Artwr.

Because of modernizations down the centuries, you often have your choice of versions of a name. Hlodhild, the saint-wife of Clovis I is Clotilda in English, Clotilde in French, and Chlothilde in German. In general, the German is closest to the original.

Besides a short selection of names of historical personages, you will find a section of roots, out of which you can build the more original names you will need for a decent-sized historical saga. Simply take one from the "Fore Roots" Table, and one from "End Roots." If you like, use a root for several characters related in the male line.

GERMANIC TRIBES TRUE AND FALSE

Alemanni
Bajuwari
Bastarnae — on the lower Danube; from Vistula
Batavi — at the mouth of the Rhine
Burgundii
Catti, Chatti — incl. Batavi and Bastarnae
Chamavi — Netherlands in 100 C.E.; absorbed by Franks
Chauci
Cherusci
Cimbri — Celtic
Franconii — Franks
Gepidae — mouth of Vistula
Goths
Harudes — between Danube and upper Rhine

Hermunduri — Suebic tribe
Heruli — 3rd c. move into Danube basin
Langobardi — Suebic tribe
Marcomanni — Suebic tribe
Nemetes — W. of Rhine; Celtic
Norici — S. of Danube
Ostrogoths — Goths
Quadi — Suebic tribe
Sedusii — German
Semnones — Suebic tribe
Teutones — powerful tribe; Celtic
Triboces — near the Rhine; Celtic
Tulingi — Germans N. of the Helvetii
Ubii — in Germany; Celtic
Vandals — Goths
Vangiones — Germans; Celtic
Visigoths — Goths

GOTHIC NAMES C.E. 1–700 FEMALE NAMES

Amalasuntha, Amalasuentha, Amala-swintha
Argotta

Athildis
Aurinia — war–Goddess
Basina

Chrodielde
Friia — Freya
Gambara — Lombard
Gudrun, Kudrun
Gundreguth
Holda, Hulda — Goddess
Hrosamund, Rosamund — daughter
  of Cunimond
Ildico
Leodegunda
Leubevere

Nehallenia — Goddess
Nerthus — Goddess in the Baltic
Sichelgaita — Lombard, wife of Rob-
  ert Guiscard
Sinthgunt
Sunna
Tefana — Goddess of the Marsi
Thusnild, Thusnelda
Veleda
Volla

Male Names

Aadagast
Aistulf
Alaric
Alberic
Alboin
Alugod
Amalaric
Anselm
Atawulf, Ataulf — Lat.
  Ataulphus
Athalaric
Athanagild
Athanaric
Audoin
Balderes — Balder
Edecon, Edicon
Euric, Evaric
Eutharic
Fafila
Fairhomund, Pharamond
Fairhonath
Fortun
Fritigern, Fridigern
Fruela
Gelimer, Geilamir,
  Gilimer
Genseric, Gaiseric
Godigisel
Gottewald — Lat. Catu-
  alda, of Cherusci

Gundemar
Gunderic
Gunthamund
Haduwulafiz, Haduwulf
Haeruwulafiz, Haerawulf
Harjaz
Helmichis — probably
  actually Helmric
Hermen
Hermenegild, Hermeni-
  gild
Hildebad
Hilderic
Hlewagastiz — C.E. 400,
  Ludagast
Holtagastiz
Holtijaz
Hunneric, Huneric
Kunimond — king of
  Gepidae, C.E. 572;
  Cunimund
Leovigild
Liutprand/Liudprand
Liuva
Marcomir
Merobaud
Nepotian
Odoacer, Odovacer
Oppila
Ordonyo

Pelagius
Pelayo
Phol
Raunij, Raunijaz —
  3rd–4th c. Norway
Recared, Rechiarius
Rhadagast
Roderic, Roderick
Sisebut
Sisenand
Stilicho — Roman general
Suinthila
Teias
Theodemir
Theudisclus
Theudohad
Theudomar
Theudoric
Thorismund
Thrasamund
Totila
Uuodan — Wodan, Odin
Wallia
Wamba
Weldelphus — Woldulf
Widuhad, Widuhudaz —
  3rd–4th c. Norway
Wiliesind
Witigis

FRANKISH NAMES
700–1000
FEMALE NAMES

Adelheidis, Adelaide,
 Adelheid
Aude
Bercthildis, Berthild
Brunihild, Brunhilde,
 Brunehilde, Brune-
 childis, Brunehaut
Chlodhild
Emma
Ermengarde
Fredegund
Galswintha

Gerberge, Gerberg, Ger-
 berga
Gisela, Gisel, Gisele
Gudrun
Guerlinta
Gunnefair — Genevie've
Hermintrudis
Hilde
Hildeburg
Hildegard
Hrotvitha, Hrotswitha,
 Roswitha

Ingunthis
Kriemhild
Kunigunde
Mathild
Mechtild
Per-ahta/Bertha, Bertrade
Radegunda, Radegonde
Richilde, Rikhild
Rimenhild
Velda

MALE NAMES

Adeleric, Athalaric
Aeblus, Aebla
Aighyna
Angilbert
Anshelm
Arbogast
Arnebert
Arno/Arn — Latinized as
 Aquila
Arnulf
Ausgar
Austrovald
Bandonin
Bauto
Bernart
Berthar
Biterolf
Bladast
Burgundio
Childebert
Childeric
Chilperic
Chilping
Chlodwig, Clovis — later
 Ludwig, Lewis
Chlotar, Lothair
Chrodegang — Gode-
 grand (Gallicized)
Chugobert, Hugbert
Chunibert

Chunoald
Clodion
Clodoald
Clodomir
Clotaire
Dagobert
Ebroin
Eggihard
Eginhard, Einhard
Ekkehard
Elipando
Erkinoald
Fredegar
Galactorius
Genial
Gerbert
Godescalc — Gottskalk
Gondovald
Gottfried
Guenonis = Ganelon
Gundebald, Gumbald
Gunther
Guntram, Gontran
Guntran
Hadubrand
Hartmut
Hatto
Heimric
Herwig
Hettel

Hildebrand
Hincmar
Hludovic
Hrabanus, Hramnbann
Hrodland = Roland
Hucbald/Hubald/Hug-
 baldus/Ubaldus/Ugu-
 baldus
Hugues/Huc/Hughes
Hunald
Karibert/Caribert/Chari-
 bert
Karloman
Kerl — not Karl
Kuonraet
Leidrad
Leodegar
Luidger
Luitard
Mantio
Merovech
Merowig-Mèrovèe (Fr.),
 Merovaeus (Lat.)
Nithard
Oderic
Odo, Oddo, Eudes
Ortwin
Otfreid
Otho
Peppi

Radbert	Sigebert, Seigbert	Theudoric
Ridieger	Sigiwin	Waiofar, Waifer, Gaifier
Roderic	Tassilo	Weilant
Rupprecht	Theudebert	Willibrord
Siegfried	Theuderich	Wulfoald

OLD GERMAN ROOTS

You can exert immediate artistic control by going down these lists, picking one from Table A and one from B, so that you have names that please you. There are no separate male and female tables. The names are fairly unisex, except that there is a tendency to use the end roots "-hild," "-gund" and "-swith" for women. Since the first means "battle," it must be put down to the authentic mindlessness of real-world naming habits.

Better is to randomize up a list of names, so you can choose the ones that have the right ambiance or aura by sound. A century ago, Waldo would have been fine for your heroic army-slaying warrior. Now? It doesn't matter if Waldo means "mighty," if the reader thinks of some skinny cartoon figure in a striped shirt and glasses. So once again, the meaning of a name is minor compared to its irrational connotations.

Swapping Pairs

D for T, but not in TH; walt/wald, munt/mund, hlut/hlud; newer
T for D; wald/walt, mund/munt; older form
W for V; woll for voll; older
V for W; vald for wald; older
CH for initial H; chlod- for hlod-, childe- for hilde-; newer
O for U; hlod for hlud, wolf for wulf; much newer

FORE ROOTS

Adal–	noble
Adlar–	eagle
Aist–	
Ald–	old
Alh–	all; divine, sacred, holy
Amal–	industrious
Angil–	angel; obviously only for the Christianized
Ans–	divine
Ap–	father

Arbo-	
Arn-/arni-	eagle
Athan-/Athana-	
Aus-	
Bald-/balde-	bold, princely
Bann-	commander
Berht-	bright, shining, brilliant
Berin-	bear
Bero-	bear
Bogo	bow
Brand-	sword
Bruun-	brown
Bryn-	hauberk
Childe-	
Chrode-	
Chugo-	
Dag-	day
Diet-	
Ebor-	wild boar
Ede-	
Egin-, Ein-	
Ehren-	honor
Ekke-	
Engel-	angel; for children of Christians
Ermin-	partner
Fair-	world, life
Fri-	free
Fridu-	peaceful
Gaise-	
Geb-	
Geili-/Geli-	
Ger-	spear
Gode-/gott-	god, divine
Gris-	grey
Guer-	
Hadu-	strife
Hard-	brave, stern
Hari-	army; also Heri-
Haim-	supporting, supporter
Heim-	home
Helm-	helm, protection
Her-	
Hermene-	
Hildi-	battle
Hinc-	
Hlut-	famous
Hoh-	high, eminent
Hramn-	raven
Hrodo-	renowned; also Hroud-, Hroed-
Huc-/Hug-	
Hugi-	mind

Huldi-	graceful
Hunne-	also Hune-
Ing-	young; God-name
Isen-	iron
Kerl-	farmer
Kriem-	
Lant-	land, country
Lei-	
Leode-	
Linde-	linden tree
Luit-	
Madel-	counsel
Mecht-	large, great
Mero-	
Neit	also Nit, Neid
Nor-	hero
Odo-	wealthy
Ort-	
Otho-/Ot-	prosperous
Peraht-	bright, brilliant, shining
Rade-/Rad-	
Ragin-/Regin-	counsel
Rand-	shield
Rhada-	
Ric-	ruling
Rimen-	
Ros-/Hros-	horse
Ruod-	renowned
Rup-	
Sel-	
Sigi-	victorious
Theudo-/de-	the people; often Latinized Theo-
Thoris-	
Thrasa-	
Voll-	tribe
Warin-	guardian, watchman
Wei-	
Willi-	resolute, will
Wulf-	wolf

END ROOTS

-ar	
-bad	
-bald, -balde	bold, prince
-bann	commander
-baud	
-behrt	brightness, light
-berg	hill
-bern	bear

-brand	sword
-brord	
-con	
-frid	peace
-funs	ready
-gang	walk, advance
-gast	guest
-ger/-gar	spear
-gern	
-gild	
-grim	fury
-gund, -gun	(feminine ending)
-had	
-hard	brave
-hardt	strong, hardy
-helm	helm, protection
-heri	army
-hild	battle (feminine)
-hold	gracious
-honath	
-hramn	raven
-huld	graceful
-hwas	keen, sharp
-lant	land, country
-lint/-linte	latter female
-mar	fame
-mey	spirit
-mod	spirit or mind
-munt	protector, protection; also -mund
-mut	
-oin	
-prand	
-reth	counselor
-ric	ruler
-run, -rum	
-sel	
-som	fame
-swint	(feminine)
-vech	
-wald	forest; mighty
-walt	mighty
-wig	fight, warrior
-win	friend
-wulf	wolf, hero

Stand-Alones

Adler	eagle
Behrt	brightness
Harti	hard, bold, daring

Hatto	
Hettel	
Hilde	battle; probably female
Huc	Hugh
Hoh	high, tall
Kerl	farmer
Odo	wealthy
Otho	prosperous
Peppi	perseverer, petitioner; Pepin
Regin	wise, cunning
Saelec	blessed, happy
Saerle	armor, armored one
Velde	female
Waldo	ruler
Wendel	wanderer
Wido	warrior

RANDOMIZING

Using a regular deck of cards, you will choose one card for the fore root, another for the end root. You can mess with the junction a bit — sigi + berht = Sigisberht, for example — or swap some spellings. Spelling was not utterly standardized in Old German, any more than it was in English until the 19th century.

Actually, there are so many fore roots that you will choose first a "range" card. If it is a red card (hearts or diamonds) then your fore root card should be decoded using the first table. If the range card is a spade or club, use the second fore root table.

FORE ROOTS
Range Card: Red

Second Card:

	Spades	Hearts	Clubs	Diamonds
A	Adal-	Ald-	Alh-	Amal-
2	Berht-/Peraht	Berin-	Bero-	Biter-
3	Bogo-	Brand-	Bruun-	Dag-
4	Ebor-	Ehren-	Engel-	Ermin-
5	Eva-	Eutha-	Fair-	Fri-
6	Fridu-	Gal-	Geili-/Geili-	Ger-
7	Gode-/Gott-	Gris-	Gud-/Gude-	Wido-
8	Hadu-	Hard-/Hart-	Hari-/Heri-	Haim-
9	Heim-	Helm-	Hildi-	Hlut-/Chlod-
10	Hoh-	Hrodo-	Hugi-	Huldi-
J	Hunn-/Hunne-	Isen-	Karl-	Kuon-
Q	Kuni-	Lant-	Linde-	Madel-
K	Mat-	Mecht-	Nor-	Odo-

Range Card: Black

Second Card:

	Spades	Hearts	Clubs	Diamonds
A	Otho-/Ot-	Rand-	Athana-	Hermene-
2	Sigi-/Sigis-	Theudo-/de-	Chrode-	Egin-
3	Voll-	Warin-	Leode-	Kriem-
4	Ragin-/Regin-	Ede-	Muni-	Harti-
5	Ros-/Hros-	Ruod-	Ekke-	Rhada-/Hrada-
6	Thrasa-	Thoris-	Athana-	Wai-, Geb-
7	Willi-	Wulf-	Wei-	Lei-
8	Karl-	Gaise-	Erkin-	Her-
9	Ort-	Guer-	Aist-	Rade-/Rad-
10	Huc-	Chugo-	Hramn-	Luit-
J	Neit-/Nit-	Rup-	Sel-	Ap-
Q	Leovi-	Saerle-	Grim-	Berg-/Burg-
K	Diet-	Bryn-	Hinc-	Gunda-/Guntha-/Gunde-/Gunthe-/Gunte-

END ROOTS

	Spades	Hearts	Clubs	Diamonds
A	-bald, -balde	-bern	-berg/-burg	-brand(m)/-hild(f)
2	-frid/fried	-funs	-gang	-ger(m)/-swint(f)
3	-gast	-grim	-gern	-gisel
4	-hard	-hardt	-heri	-helm
5	-hold	-honath	-huld	-hwas
6	-con/-kuon	-lant	-mar/-mir	-mey
7	-mod	-munt	-raet	-reth
8	-som	-wald	-walt	-ric(m)/-gund(f)
9	-wid	-wig	-win	-wulf/-ulf
10	-run/-rum	-had	-gild	-oald
J	-baud	-vech	-brord	-lint
Q	-oin	-mut	-ar	-sel
K	-bann	-hramn	-prand	-acer

LATE LATIN (300–1000)

Standard Latin naming practices continue, with mutation, throughout the late Imperial period. The Empire goes Christian, and Constantine the Great moves the capitol to Constantinople, newly built near the old port of Byzantium, in the 4th century.

Editing by Medieval historians makes the Romans *appear* to have violently changed their naming practices from those of Augustan Rome. However "Constantine" was actually Flavius Valerius Aurelius Constantinus. His father, "Constantius Chlorus," was born in 250 as Flavius Valerius Constantius surnamed Chloris (the pale), while Constantine's sons were Flavius Claudius Constantinius (Constantine II), Flavius Julius Constantius (Constantius II), and Flavius Julius (called Constans). Remember, historians are from later cultures, and often try to force things to the mold of their own times to make their readers comfortable.

So in this late–Latin period, the praenomen has been dropped; then comes the nomen family name, followed by one or more cognomina used as personal names. Note that the "Valerius" was not carried down to any of Constantine the Great's sons, who use an intersort of Claudius, Julius, and Constantius. You can dummy these up out of the Latin names.

While there were still Latins who kept up the old names, like Constantine's opponent, Marcus Maxentius, for the most part the old family names, even of the aristocracy, have been made meaningless because of their use by people not actually in the family: freed slaves, clients, and plain old phonies.

Aristocrats will cling to their nomen, but the names added thereafter are at will, and number from one to four. Women do still gender their names, like Constantine's sister, Flavia Constantia. Because of the new liberality in naming, peculiar Greek names like Helena first appear for women in the late 3rd century. Borrow these from Byzantine.

NEO-PUNIC/ROMAN CARTHAGINIAN

After the Roman destruction of Carthage, the Romans reorganized the area under their control. This had its effect on the local population. Up until Christianization, Neo-Punic speakers in this area used a Punic name followed by a Latin name (take it from the list of cognomens, Table Five or Eight in the Latin chapter). This was not a family name; Himilcho Tapapius had a son listed in inscriptions as Annobal Rufus.

FEMALE NAMES

Abdilia	Anniboni	Bebia
Amotmicar	Arisuth	Elissa

Male Names

Abdalonimus
Abdilius
Abdismunis
Abdusmyn
Abeddonis, Abedonis
Abolim
Admicaris
Agbor
Amicaris, Ammicar, Ammicaris
Annibal
Anniboni
Anno
Annobal
Annonis
Aris
Aristo
Aristonem
Arisus
Asmunis
Avolim
Baisillecis, Balsilechis, Balsillec — Baal nourishes
Baldir
Baliaho
Baliahon
Baliatho
Baliaton
Baliddir
Balithonis
Balsamo — Baal hears
Banno
Baric, Baricha, Barichio
Baricbal, Barecbal, Barig-

bal, Berecbal, Biricbal, Birictbal, Burucbal
Bartha
Bebius
Berect, Berict, Berregt, Birich, Byrycth
Birihtina
Bochor
Bodmilkar
Bomilcar, Bomilcaris
Boncar, Bonchor
Boncarth
Bosiharis
Bostar, Bostaris
Bubalus, Bubbal
Chiniti
Chubud
Gadia
Giddeneme
Giddinis
Gidius
Gisaco, Giscone
Gisgonis
Hamilcar, Hamilcare
Hannibal, Hannibale
Hanno
Hannone, Hannonis
Himilco, Himilconi, Himilconis, Imilcho, Imilco, Imilcone
Himilis
Iadir
Iarban
Iddibal, Iddibalis, Idnibalis

Itibalis
Mago
Magonem
Magonus
Maharbal, Maharbale
Masopis
Methun, Metun, Mitun, Motthun, Muthun, Mutthun, Muttines, Muttun, Mutum, Mytthum
Methunilim, Muthunilim, Mutthunilim
Miggin
Milcatonis, Milchatonis
Mitthunbal, Muthunbal, Mutthumbalis, Mutunbalis, Mytthymbaal
Mochus
Mughunilim
Mutgo
Otmilc
Pupinus
Sachonis
Samunio
Sanchuniathon
Sapho — keep watch
Secchun
Sicharbas
Sidiathones
Suniatus
Sychaeus, Sicarbas
Tironis
Zecenor

ASIA, A NOTE

During this time, China continues blithely on, unaware of any cultural darkness, and Asia reads by her light.

Use the contemporary chapters for Chinese, Korean, Mongolian, Burmese, Vietnamese, and most other Asian countries. The only change in Southeast Asia might be omitting family names, as not yet adopted in Thailand, Sri Lanka, India.

If your Frankish adventurer somehow winds up in the Philippines, either use translation names, or use the family names which have no Spanish basis.

Polynesia and Micronesia are business as usual, in the pre–Christian mode.

Ancient Europe
(3000 B.C.–C.E. 300)

GERMANIC NAMES, A NOTE

The opening of the Celtic chapter explains the business about who was Germanic, and who was Celtic. The Germanic names we have from the earliest recorded period are Latinizations of names you will find in the Gothic and Frankish chapter. That chapter will provide names for characters back to the age in which the Germanic tribes start fading into their ancestral, undifferentiated, Indo-European forebearers.

GAELIC, OR IRISH CELTIC

Long after Christianization, both the Irish and the Dal Riada colonists who became the Scots are single-namers, of the usual pattern: Myname, son of Hisname, of Thatplace. Women used "daughter of" and "wife of." The character might also be known as So-and-so the Whatsis: Deirdre of the Sorrows, Diarmit the Handsome, Setanta the Hound of Chulainn, etc.

In Irish history one sometimes runs into the secondary character known by a two-part compound name, but neither of these is an hereditary family name. Being Enna Fionn is like being Mary Jane, when there are Marys and Janes as well.

Names are taken from history and legend, so do check a good history to see if you might have a conflict with your fictional folk. Note that the Celts did not have many distinctively male and female name endings, and frequently used -a for men.

Pronunciation

Modern Irish words and names are simplified from the ancient ones. Many written letters are considered to be silent in modern Irish or Scottish. However, you can be sure each was needed to sound right in the ancient days when they first were committed to writing.

In Ireland, the native Ogham alphabet was used in pagan days, or perhaps Greek writing. During the Dark Ages, anyone north of the Alps who knew Greek was assumed to be Irish, or Irish-educated.

Due to modernization of the living folklore, many old Irish names have several spellings, so that Finn MacCool of the Fenians may by Fion mac Cumhaill of the Fianna, or Fin Mac Cumaill of the Fena, and his son Oisin is also Ossian.

MH is much like V; DB something like the TH in "then"; CH is the back-of-the-throat K, the uvular fricative, GH a little forward of that, but still in the throat. C is always hard, like K. Note that there is no J. In foreign words SH or I is always substituted.

FEMALE NAMES

The wife-word was ban, so that "Manissa ban Fionn" is Fionn's wife, Manissa. The daughter prefix is Ni-, Nic- if her father's name begins with H or a vowel.

Aeife, Aife	Ciannait	Evir
Aifric	Ciarnit	Evirchomi
Ailbhe	Coinchend	Fainche
Ailech	Cred, Creide	Faoiltighcarna
Aine	Creidne	Fea
Aislinn	Dairine	Fedelm
Aodnait	Damhnait	Feithlinn
Aoibheann	Dara	Fiacc
Athracht	Dearbhail	Fiadhnait
Baine	Deardriu	Fiala
Banba	Dectaire, Dechtire	Findmor
Beara	Deirdre	Fionna
Bebhinn, Bebhionn	Devorgilla	Fionnghuala
Befind	Doireann	Fithir
Blath, Blathnaid (dim.)	Eabha	Fodla
Blinne	Edain	Gobnait
Blunse	Eibhlin	Gormfhlaith, Gormlaith
Breathigrend	Eideann	Grainne
Brighid	Eire'	Irnan
Buanann	Emer	Itu, Ita
Cailin	Eodon	Lasairfhiona
Cailleach	Ercnat	Lendabair
Canair	Erni	Lot
Caoimhe	Etain	Luighseach
Carthann	Ethne, Ethni — popular	Macha

Madhbh, Maeve — popu-
  lar
Manissa
Maolmhin
Mealla
Moina, Moyna
Moira, Moyra, Moir
Mong-Fionn
Moninne
Mor
Morrigan, Morrigane
Muadhnait
Muireann, Muirinn,
  Murainn
Muirgel
Muirgheal

Muirne
Nemain
Nessa, Ness
Niamh
Odharnait
Oonagh
Orfhlait
Rathnait
Richeal
Rioghnac
Ronait
Rosgrana
Sabia
Samair
Saraid
Scathach

Scenmed
Scota
Sgeimsolas — light of
  beauty
Sheelagh
Siobhan, Siubhan
Siobhrach
Sionon
Slaine
Sorcha
Taillte
Tea [TEE-ah]
Tlachtga
Treasa, Treise
Uallath
Uathach

MALE NAMES

The son-word was mac ("mak" if you want to look more primitive), the grandson-word was ua or ui. An ending of -an or -en is often a diminutive, like calling someone Johnny instead of John.

Adna
Aed, Aedh
Aengus, Aongus
Ailbe
Ailill
Ainmire
Airleas
Airt
Aitharne
Amalgaid
Amergin
Amlaid
Andli
Aod, Aodhan
Ardan
Athairne
Baiceade
Baithen
Benin
Blathmac
Brandbh
Brann
Breandan
Breasal
Breccan

Brian
Bricriu
Brogan
Buaigne
Cailte
Cairbre'
Caman
Caoilte
Caplait
Cathair
Cathal
Cathan
Ceann
Ceannfaelad
Ceara
Cellach
Ceolan
Cet
Ciaran
Cillian
Cimbaoth
Cobtach
Colga
Colm
Comgall

Comin
Conaire
Conal
Conari
Conchobar
Conlaeth
Conn
Connachar
Connla
Cormac
Crimthann
Crionna
Cronan
Cruagh
Cuain
Cullanan
Cumhail
Curan
Curoi
Daire
Dallan
Daman
Dari
Dathi
Deagad

Declan
Derga
Diarmuid
Dichu
Dicuil
Dimian
Dithorba
Domhnull
Donal
Donn
Duach
Duan
Dubhain
Dubtach, Dubthach
Dunlaing
Eber
Elatha
Elim
Eochaid
Eogan
Erc, Erca
Eremon
Ernan
Etaine
Etchan
Fachtna
Fallomain
Faollan
Feidlimid
Feirceirtne
Felim
Feradach
Fercertni
Ferchar
Ferdiad
Fergus
Fiacaid
Fiacc
Fiacha
Fiachra
Fiallan
Finbar
Fingar
Finghin
Finian
Finneadh

Fionn
Firdomnach
Fithal, Fithil
Flannan
Fiolla
Forgaill
Frigrind
Gabran
Garad
Geide
Gelban
Gobhan
Goll
Iarlath
Ibar
Indech
Innatmar, Iondadmar,
   Iondatmar
Ir
Irial
Ith
Labraid
Laeg
Laegaire, Laoghaire,
   Laogare
Lasrian, Lassaran
Lochain
Luchru
Lugad
Lugair
Lughaid
Luignech
Macaille
Maein, Maen
Maeldubh
Magach
Maidoc
Maine
Mal
Mani
Maoltuile
Miliue
Mochua
Mochuma
Mogcorf
Mogh

Moluan
Morann
Morna
Muirdeach
Naoisi
Nathi
Neide
Niad
Niall, Niull, Niallan
Niedi
Ninnid
O'c, Oc
Odhran
Oilill
Pogan
Ro
Ronan
Roзза
Seadhal
Sechnall
Senan
Senchan
Sesgne
Sgeulaiche
Sharvan
Siadal
Sorcer
Sreng
Sruthair
Sruthan
Sualtim
Tadhg
Taithleach
Teimhnean
Tighearnach
Tighearnmas
Tiobraide
Tirchin
Torna
Treabhar
Treun
Tuathal
Ugani
Uisnech
Ultann
Usnech

EKE-NAMES

Airgead Lam = of the Silver Hand	Rechtmar = the Lawgiver
Balc-beimnech = of the Evil Eye	Ruadh = the Red
Ollgotach = of the Beautiful Voice	Taidlech = the Splendid

LATIN

If you are planning a novel set in ancient Rome, you need to research the structure of the Roman family. But your novel may be set in Celtic Britain, where the Romans are just irritating visitors, or you only need the Roman ambassador to the Sassanid court. Maybe you just need a phony Roman historian.

You can read a lot of histories, and "everyday life" books and articles, and they will never explain the procedure for naming. They are geared for the historian who memorizes dead people, not the writer who needs to create new ones. You can take many years of Latin and not know how names are formed.

Ancient Names, Modern Readers

Roman history is filtered through Medieval Latin and French into English. No one was called Aurelian, Catiline, Pompey, or Anthony by either friends or enemies. The classic Romans did not have the letters J or W, and other letters changed usage; especially check V's pronunciation. You will have to choose between being authentic or being familiar to your readers. Most sword-and-sandal epics opt for familiarity.

Also, many readers know English but not Latin. To them, Fabius will be shaded with teen-idol Fabian and model Fabio and "fabulous"; they will not think "bean farmer." "Crassus" will bring "crass" to mind, not "fat"; "Nigeria" will summon up the African country; and "Manlia" will seem "manly." Consider this, so that it works for and not against you. Give names that may cause difficulty from outside connotations to characters that appear later in the book. When the reader is well out of the here-and-now and deep in Rome of the Caesars, the name is more likely to be accepted on its own.

Parts of the Name

All Romans were originally single named, like most people in most places. This is the legendary time of the *Aeneid*, the early kingdoms, and the Greek colonies.

By the time of the historical kingdom, most free Romans were divided into *gentes*, singular *gens*: clans or tribes. You could be a tailor with the same gens as a praetor. The name of the gens provides a person's *nomen*.

In front of the nomen is put the *praenomen*. There were only twenty-three praenomens, much as in those times when all the men in an English village would be named Will, Jack, and Tom. Many come from Etruscan.

The few praenomens were so heavily used that, just as J. stands for John, Jo. for Joseph, and Wm. for William, so C. stood for Gaius and Q. for Quintus, among others. By the 4th century, praenomens were rarely if ever used anymore. Even in the 3rd century, their use was failing, and they can be considered optional.

Please note: Gaius was never pronounced Caius. The C is left from using the Greek *gamma*, which looked like < or C. The praenomen Caeso is abbreviated K. for *kappa*, which remained in Latin in only two other places: Kartago (Carthage) and kalendae (calendar). The Romans invented the G so they could use the C for the k-sound.

By 100 B.C., the praenomen and nomen were commonly followed by the *cognomen*, then an eke-name. For example, the last of the kings of Rome was Lucius Tarquinius, surnamed Superbus, whose son was Lucius Tarquinius surnamed Priscus.

As the gentes grew, they were divided into families, and the cognomen became the secondary family name for a person. Sometimes an *agnomen*, an honorific, would be added after the other three, like "Africanus" for a general who won battles in Africa. This agnomen could be inherited, or not, but then only by males of the family.

This is not as cumbersome as it may seem, since a man would often be referred to by two of his names only. In order of commonness, using Marcus Iulius Proculus:

1) nomen + cognomen = Iulius Proculus
2) praenomen + nomen = Marcus Iulius
3) praenomen + cognomen = Marcus Proculus
4) single name = Proculus

Tiberius was known by his praenomen, "Horace" (Horatius) by his nomen, Brutus by his cognomen, and Augustus by his agnomen. You had to be very famous to get by with just one, normally. Of course, in any piece of writing, once you establish a character, you can begin referring to it by a distinctive single or double name, just as "Terry Lee Gilford" becomes "Terry" or "Gilford" or "Terry Lee" in a contemporary story.

In the later Republic, more so in the Empire, adoption of a male heir was common. Because of this, some men would have a fourth name, in the same place as the agnomen, or sometimes between the nomen and the cognomen, that indicated the gens from which they originally came.

For example, Gaius Iulius Caesar adopted his grandnephew, Gaius Octavius, who became Gaius Iulius Caesar *Octavianus*, better known to you as Octavian. The tables that follow include male and female possessive, for this and other situations.

"Pliny the Elder" and "Pliny the Younger" were, in Latin, Plinius Major and

Plinius Minor. The same words sorted out women in the same family, like Antonia Major and Antonia Minor.

Female Names

Latin has built-in gender. All the names must have their endings changed to agree with the bearer's sex. In Latin, it is linguistically impossible for a girl to have a "boy's name," unless the family for some bizarre reason considers her a boy and refers to "him" in the masculine form. Accidental cross-gendering of name is not possible.

Once the Romans came out of the single-name stage, women originally had a feminine praenomen, followed by the feminine of their father's nomen and the possessive of his cognomen — Tiberia Flavia Tertiana would be a daughter of Gaius Flavius Tertius. Upon marrying, they would change this to their husbands' nomen and cognomen. Later, the words *filia* (daughter) or *uxor* (wife) were added like Miss and Mrs. So Tiberia Flavia Tertiana *filia* would become Tiberia Horatia Pauliana *uxor* if she married Gnaeus Horatius Paulus.

By the end of the Republic, the female praenomen vanishes from inscriptions; it had begun fading out of use in the middle of the Republic. After this point, any daughter is known by the feminine of her father's nomen. Officially, all women of a gens had the same name. Practically, they added the feminine of the cognomen, so only all the women in one family shared a single name.

So the daughters of Marcus Iulius Proculus all would be Iulia Procula. To keep your readers straight, you should give them nicknames off the lists of cognomens, Tables Five and Eight, or see the information on "-illa" below.

By the Empire, women are also staying with their birth names, as divorce and remarriage become common. Sound familiar?

Why Drusus always becomes Drusilla and not Drusia; and why there are Claudillas and Terentillas as well as Claudias and Terentias; is not explicated anywhere. In some cases it seems idiomatic to certain cognomens, as it occurs after the S or SK sound: Drusus/Drusilla, Priscus/Priscilla, Naso/Nasilla.

In other cases, the "-illa" form of a nomen is a case of using "maiden names" as cognomens for younger daughters. That is, if Terentia Procula marries M. Claudius Drusus, their first daughter will be called Claudia Drusilla, the second Claudia Terentilla, the third possibly Claudia Sempronilla after her paternal grandmother, Sempronia Rutilia. Thus, some level of individuality was returned to women by about C.E. 100.

In general, in feminizing Latin names, "-us" becomes "-ia," "-o" becomes "-a," and masculine names ending in "-a" become "-ina."

Well-Washed Masses

After the Lex Canuleia of 445 B.C. that permitted intermarriage of plebians and patricians, and the Lex Hortensia of 286 B.C., the differences between patrician and plebian gentes were relatively minor.

Many people of Rome were not of the gentes at all. Your line lost its generic membership if it were reduced in status, or if you were enslaved, even if your descendants were later freed. Low commoners hardly kept track of their family names (cognomen), and often went by a name and a nickname, if not just the nickname: "Albius the Short," "Felicia from the island," etc. You can take these names from the praenomens, or the list of cognomens.

Common, non-gentes birth was never a bar to power. "Pompey the Great" who nearly ruled Rome instead of Caesar, was Gnaeus Pompeius later surnamed Magnus. His son was Sextus Pompeius who added Pius because he was avenging his father and brother. Pompeius was the the family name/cognomen; they had no nomen. Three names always looks classiest to a Roman.

Foreign slaves, especially Greeks, kept their foreign names. Enslaved or slave-born Latin men added *-por* to their praenomen, so that Quintus became Quintipor and Publius, Publipor — remember, they had no nomen. In the Kingdom and early Republic they added the possessive of their master's nomen (cognomen, if he were non-gentes), and by the late Republic the master's praenomen in possessive. To this they appended *servus* once the Empire was well established. Rufipor Aurelianus Publianus *servus* was the slave Rufipor who belonged to Aurelius Publius. If Rufipor were sold to the non-gentes Lucius Scribonius, he would be Rufipor Lucianus Scribonianus *servus*. There is no direct mention of the names of slave women, who were probably usually called by nicknames like Ignavia or Musa (see Table Eight), but otherwise might follow a similar handling — Aureliana Publiana *serva*, since they had no praenomens.

Upon being freed, a slave was expected to show his or her gratitude for new life by treating the former owner thereafter as a kind of parent/patron. This included keeping the possessive form of his nomen or cognomen. The increase in slavery, and freedmen and their descendants, required the introduction of *servus* to keep straight who was property and who was not.

Using the Tables

Remember that related characters must have some names in common depending on their particular place in a gens or family. Use the parts which are different in your most common references. Other than that, as in any name you will choose by artistic or plot criteria.

To sum it all up and put it in one place:

FREE CHARACTERS

Male Character

1. Go to Table One, first column, and get a nomen for the character, if it has a gens;
2. Get a praenomen from Table Two, first column, in any case;
3. Get a cognomen from Tables Three through Six;
4. If the character has earned or inherited an agnomen, they are in Table Seven;
5. If he is adopted, his "origin name" is in Table One, third column.

Female Character

Early Period
1. Take a praenomen from Table Two, second column;
2. Build the rest off a known father or husband:
    i. find his nomen in Table One, first column; her version will be in the second column;
    ii. find his cognomen in the first column Tables Three through Six; her version will be in the fourth column;
3. or, if she is the more important character, choose her nomen from Table One, second column, and her cognomen from the fourth column of Tables Three through Six, then back-track to him.

Later Period
1. Her nomen will be in the second column of Table One;
2. Her cognomen may come from the second column of tables three through six, or from the fifth column of Table One.

SLAVE CHARACTERS

Male Characters

1. Change his praenomen to "-por" form, Table Two, fifth column;
2. Base on his master, if known:
    i. Possessive of his nomen, Table One, third column;
    ii. Possessive of his master's praenomen, Table Two, third column;
3. If his master has no nomen, then use the third column form of his cognomen.

Female Characters

1. Base on her master, if known:
    i. possessive of his nomen, Table One, fourth column;
    ii. possessive of his praenomen, Table Two, fourth column;
2. If her master has no nomen, then use the fourth column form of his cognomen.

Pronunciation

A = A in father (long) or idea (short)
AE = AI as in aisle (diphthong)
AU = OW as in cow (diphthong)
BS = PS as in naps
BT = PT as in apt
C = C as in car
CH = CH as in chorus; K
E = E in they (long) or net (short)
EI = EI as in rein (diphthong)
EU = EU as in feud (diphthong)
G = G as in get
GU = GU in sanguine; GW
I = I in machine (long) or pit (short), Y in yet (initial)
O = O in open (long) or obey (short)
OE = OI as in oil (diphthong)
PH = PH as in alpha; F
S = S as in set
TH = TH as in thin
U = U in rude (long) or sub (short)
UI = UI as in cuisine; WEE (diphthong)
V = W as in wet
X = X as in vex
Z = DZ as in adze

Two-syllable words are accented on the first syllable. Longer words accent on the next to the last if that is a long syllable; otherwise, accent is on the third from the end. A long syllable has a long vowel or a diphthong, or if the vowel of the syllable is followed by two or more consonants, or by X or Z.

Now you only have to develop the gut instinct for when E, I, O, or U are long or short. When you consider how much Latin vocabulary was carried into English, you will probably guess right.

Try to remember that Titus Valerius Victor is [TEE-tus wa-LEY-ree-us WIHK-tor] *not* [TY-tus va-LAR-yus VIHK-tor], and do not worry about rhyming your Roman poetry. Rhymed verse was not exported from Ireland to the rest of Europe until the Dark Ages.

TABLE ONE: NOMENS

= seem very common

Masculine	Feminine	Possessive Masculine	Possessive Feminine	Feminine Cognomen
Acerronius	Acerronia	Acerronianus	Acerroniana	Acerronilla
Acilius	Acilia	Acilianus	Acilliana	Acilla
Actorius	Actoria	Actorianus	Actoriana	Actorilla
Aelius	Aelia	Aelianus	Aeliana	Aella
Aemilius	Aemilia	Aemilianus	Aemiliana	Aemilla #
Annaeus	Annaeia	Annaeianus	Annaeiana	Annaella
Annius	Annia	Annianus	Anniana	Annilla
Antistius	Antistia	Antistianus	Antistiana	Antistilla
Antonius	Antonia	Antoninus	Antonina	Antonilla
Aquilius	Aquilia	Aquilianus	Aquiliana	Aquilla
Arrecinus	Arrecina	Arrecinianus	Arreciniana	Arrecinilla
Arrius	Arria	Arrianus	Arriana	Arrilla
Asinius	Asinia	Asinianus	Asiniana	Asinilla
Atius	Atia	Atianus	Atiana	Atilla
Atticus	Attica	Atticanus	Atticana	Atticilla
Aurelius	Aurelia	Aurelianus	Aureliana	Aurella #
Aurunculeius	Aurunculeia	Aurunculeianus	Aurunculeiana	Aurunculeilla
Caecilius	Caecilia	Caecilianus	Caeciliana	Caecililla
Caesetius	Caesetia	Caesetianus	Caesetiana	Caesetilla
Caesonius	Caesonia	Caesonianus	Caesoniana	Caesonilla
Calpurnius	Calpurnia	Calpurnianus	Calpurniana	Calpurnilla
Caninus	Canina	Caninianus	Caniniana	Canilla
Cassius	Cassia	Cassianus	Cassina	Cassilla
Catulus	Catula	Catulanus	Catulana	Catulilla
Cerrinius	Cerrinia	Cerrinianus	Cerriniana	Cerrinilla
Cestius	Cestia	Cestianus	Cestiana	Cestilla
Claudius	Claudia	Claudianus	Claudiana	Claudilla

(Never, ever use the praenomen Lucius.)

Clodius	Clodiana	Clodianus	Clodiana	Clodilla

(Plebeian portion of Claudius gens.)

Cornelius	Cornelia	Cornelianus	Corneliana	Cornelilla #
Cornutus	Cornuta	Cornutian	Cornutiana	Cornutilla
Cossutus	Cossuta	Cossutanus	Cossutana	Cossutilla
Cremutius	Cremutia	Cremutianus	Cremutiana	Cremutilla
Curiatius	Curiatia	Curiatianus	Curiatiana	Curiatilla
Domitius	Domitia	Domitianus	Domitiana	Domitilla #
Ennius	Ennia	Ennianus	Enniana	Ennilla
Fabius	Fabia	Fabianus	Fabiana	Fabilla #
Fabricius	Fabricia	Fabricianus	Fabriciana	Fabricilla
Flaccus	Flacca	Flaccianus	Flacciana	Flaccilla
Flavius	Flavia	Flavianus	Flaviana	Flavilla #
Fonteius	Fonteia	Fonteianus	Fonteiana	Fonteilla
Fulvius	Fulvia	Fulvianus	Fulviana	Fulvilla
Furius	Furia	Furianus	Furiana	Furilla
Gabinius	Gabinia	Gabinianus	Gabiniana	Gabinilla

Masculine	Feminine	Possessive Masculine	Possessive Feminine	Feminine Cognomen
Gallius	Gallia	Gallianus	Galliana	Gallilla
Helvidius	Helvidia	Helvidianus	Helvidiana	Helvidilla
Helvius	Helvia	Helvianus	Helviana	Helvilla
Horatius	Horatia	Hortianus	Horatiana	Horatilla #
Hostilius	Hostilia	Hostilianus	Hostiliana	Hostililla
Julius/Iulius	Iulia	Iulianus	Iuliana	Iulilla #
Junius/Iunius	Iunia	Iunianus	Iuniana	Iunilla
Laberius	Laberia	Laberianus	Laberiana	Laberilla
Laetorius	Laetoria	Laetorianus	Laetoriana	Laetorilla
Licinius	Licinia	Licinianus	Liciniana	Licinilla
Livius	Livia	Livianus	Liviana	Livilla #
Lutatius	Lutatia	Lutatianus	Lutatiana	Lutatilla
Manlius	Manlia	Manlianus	Manliana	Manlilla
Marcius	Marcia	Marcianus	Marciana	Marcilla
Memmius	Memmia	Memmianus	Memmiana	Memmilla
Mestrius	Mestria	Mestrianus	Mestriana	Mestrilla
Mettius	Mettia	Mettianus	Mettiana	Mettilla
Minucius	Minucia	Minucianus	Minuciana	Minucilla
Munatius	Munatia	Munatianus	Munatiana	Munatilla
Nigidius	Nigidia	Nigidianus	Nigidiana	Nigidilla
Nonius	Nonia	Nonianus	Noniana	Nonilla
Nymphidius	Nymphidia	Nymphidianus	Nymphidiana	Nymphidilla
Octavius	Octavia	Octavianus	Octaviana	Octavilla
Oculatus	Oculata	Oculatanus	Oculatana	Oculatilla
Oppius	Oppia	Oppianus	Oppiana	Oppilla
Palfurius	Palfuria	Palfurianus	Palfuriana	Palfurilla
Pappacus	Pappaca	Pappacanus	Pappacana	Pappaella
Plautius	Plautia	Plautianus	Plautiana	Plautilla
Plinius	Plinia	Plinianus	Pliniana	Plinilla
Pontius	Pontia	Pontianus	Pontiana	Pontilla
Poppaeus	Poppaea	Poppaeanus	Poppaeana	Poppaella
Porcius	Porcia	Porcianus	Porciana	Porcilla
Publilius	Publilia	Publilianus	Publiliana	Publilila
Pupius	Pupia	Pupianus	Pupiana	Pupilla
Quinctilius	Quinctilia	Quinctilianus	Quinctiliana	Quinctililla
Quinctius	Quinctia	Quinctianus	Quinctiana	Quinctilla
Rabirius	Rabiria	Rabirianus	Rabiriana	Rabirilla
Rufrius	Rufria	Rufrianus	Rufriana	Rufrilla
Rustius	Rustia	Rustianus	Rustiana	Rustilla
Sallustius	Sallustia	Sallustianus	Sallustiana	Sallustilla
Salvidienus	Salvidienanus	Salvidiena	Salvidienana	Salvidilla
Salvius	Salvia	Salvianus	Salviana	Salvilla
Scribonius	Scribonia	Scribonianus	Scriboniana	Scribonilla
Sempronius	Sempronia	Sempronianus	Semproniana	Sempronilla
Septicius	Septicia	Septicianus	Septiciana	Septicilla
Septimius	Septimia	Septimianus	Septimiana	Septimilla
Sergius	Sergia	Sergianus	Sergiana	Sergilla
Servilius	Servilia	Servilianus	Serviliana	Servililla
Statilius	Statilia	Statilianus	Statiliana	Statililla

Masculine	Feminine	Possessive Masculine	Possessive Feminine	Feminine Cognomen
Sulpicius	Sulpicia	Sulpicianus	Sulpiciana	Sulpicilla
Terentius	Terentia	Terentianus	Terentiana	Terentilla
Tertullius	Tertullia	Tertullianus	Tertulliana	Tertullilla
Tullius	Tullia	Tullianus	Tulliana	Tullilla
Valerius	Valeria	Valerianus	Valeriana	Valerilla
Vergilius	Vergilia	Vergilianus	Vergiliana	Vergililla
Vibius	Vibia	Vibianus	Vibiana	Vibilla
Vinicius	Vinicia	Vinicianus	Viniciana	Vinicilla
Vinius	Vinia	Vinianus	Viniana	Vinilla
Vipsanius	Vipsania	Vipsanianus	Vipsaniana	Vipsanilla
Vitellius	Vitellia	Vitellianus	Vitelliana	Vitellilla
Volusenus	Volusena	Volusenianus	Voluseniana	Volusenilla

TABLE TWO: PRAENOMENS

Masculine	Feminine	Possessive Masculine	Possessive Feminine	Slave -por	Abbrev.
Aulus	Aulia	Aulianus	Auliana	Aulipor	A.
Caeso	Caesa	Caesonus	Caesona	Caesipor	K.
Decimus	Decima	Decimianus	Decimiana	Decimipor	D.
Decius	Decia	Decianus	Deciana	Decipor	D'./Dec.
Gaius	Gaia (	Gaianus	Gaiana	Gaipor	C.
Gnaeus	Gnaeia	Gnaeianus	Gnaeiana	Gnaepor	Cn.
Lucius	Lucia	Lucianus	Luciana	Lucipor	L.
Manius	Mania	Manianus	Maniana	Manipor	M.'/Man.
Marcus	Marcia	Marcianus	Marciana	Marcipor	M.
Publius	Publia	Publianus	Publiana	Publipor	P.
Quintus	Quintia	Quintianus	Quintiana	Quintipor	Q.
Sergius	Sergia	Sergianus	Sergiana	Sergipor	none
Servius	Servia	Servianus	Serviana	Servipor	Ser.
Sextus	Sextia	Sextianus	Sextiana	Sextipor	Sex.
Spurius	Spuria	Spurianus	Spuriana	Spuripor	Sp.
Tiberius	Tiberia	Tiberianus	Tiberiana	Tiberipor	Ti.
Titus	Titia	Titianus	Titiana	Titipor	T.

Certain patrician families used:

Masculine	Feminine	Possessive Masculine	Possessive Feminine	Slave -por	Abbrev.
Appius	Appia	Appianus	Appiana	Appipor	Ap.

(Only the Claudians and Junians [Iunians] use Appius.)

Masculine	Feminine	Possessive Masculine	Possessive Feminine	Slave -por	Abbrev.
Mamercus	Mamercia	Mamercianus	Mamerciana	Mamercipor	none

(Aemilians only.)

Masculine	Feminine	Possessive Masculine	Possessive Feminine	Slave -por	Abbrev.
Numerius	Numeria	Numerianus	Numeriana	Numeripor	N.

TABLE THREE: THE ORDINAL COGNOMENS

Masculine	Feminine	Possessive Masculine	Possessive Feminine	Meaning
Primus	Primia	Primianus	Primiana	the first
Secundus	Secundia	Secundianus	Secundiana	the second

Masculine	Feminine	Possessive Masculine	Possessive Feminine	Meaning
Tertius	Tertius	Tertianus	Tertiana	the third
Quartus	Quartia	Quartianus	Quartiana	the fourth
Quintus	Quintia	Quintianus	Quintiana	the fifth
Sextus	Sextia	Sextianus	Sextiana	the sixth
Septimus	Septimia	Septimianus	Septimiana	the seventh
Octavius	Octavia	Octavianus	Octaviana	the eighth
Nonus	Nonia	Nonianus	Noniana	the ninth
Decius	Decia	Decianus	Deciana	the tenth

TABLE FOUR:
MOST COMMON COGNOMENS IN THE LEGIONS
FROM MOST COMMON TO LESS COMMON

Masculine	Feminine	Possessive Masculine	Possessive Feminine	Meaning
Felix	Felicia	Felicianus	Feliciana	happy
Secundus	Secundia	Secundianus	Secundiana	second
Saturninus	Saturnia	Saturninianus	Saturniniana	of Saturn; Antonine
Fortunatus	Fortunatia	Fortunatianus	Fortunatiana	lucky
Primus	Prima	Primianus	Primiana	first; Antonine
Maximus	Maxima	Maximianus	Maximiana	great
Ianuarius	Ianuaria	Ianuarianus	Ianuariana	of January or the God Janus
Rufus	Rufia	Rufianus	Rufiana	red
Severus	Severia	Severianus	Severiana	
Victor	Victoria	Victorianus	Victoriana	winner
Sabinus	Sabina	Sabinianus	Sabiniana	of the Sabines
Proculus	Procula	Proculianus	Proculiana	
Faustus	Fausta	Faustianus	Faustiana	
Priscus	Priscilla	Priscianus	Prisciana	ancient, early
Hilarus	Hilaria	Hilarianus	Hilariana	laughter
Crescens	Crescensa	Crescenianus	Cresceniana	
Tertius	Tertia	Tertianus	Tertiana	third
Vitalus	Vitalia	Vitalianus	Vitaliana	life, lively

TABLE FIVE: OTHER COGNOMENS
used for general naming, too
when known, a gens for the family is listed
* = there is a gens name the same as this

Masculine	Feminine	Possessive Masculine	Possessive Feminine	Gentes Meaning
Aelianus	Aeliana	Aelianus	Aeliana	Aemilian
Afer	Afera	Aferanus	Aferana	Tedian
Agricola	Agricolina	Agricolanus	Agricolana	farmer
Agrippa	Agrippina	Agrippanus	Agrippania	Vipsanian

Masculine	Feminine	Possessive Masculine	Possessive Feminine	Gentes Meaning
Ahenobarbus	Ahenobarba	Ahenobarbianus	Ahenobarbiana	Domitian
Albinus	Albinia	Albinianus	Albiniana	
Albius	Albia	Albianus	Albiana	white; * pale; blonde
Ambustus	Ambusta	Ambustianua	Ambustiana	Fabian
Asina	Asinina	Asininianus	Asininiana	Cornelian
Aurelius	Aurelia	Aurelianus	Aureliana	golden *
Ausonius	Ausonia	Ausonianus	Ausoniana	
Aviola	Aviolina	Aviolanus	Aviolana	Acilian
Avitus	Avita	Avitianus	Avitiana	
Baculus	Bacula	Baculanus	Baculanian	staff
Balbus	Balba	Balbanus	Balbana	stammering; Atian
Balventius	Balventia	Balventianus	Balventiana	
Basilus	Basilia	Basilianus	Basiliana	king, Minucian
Bestia	Bestina	Bestinanus	Bestinana	Calpurnian
Bibulus	Bibula	Bibulanus	Bibulana	drinking Calpurnian
Brutus	Bruta	Brutanus	Brutana	brutal; Iun- ian
Burrus	Burra	Burranus	Burrana	
Caecilius	Caecilia	Caecilianus	Caeciliana	*
Caecus	Caecia	Caecianus	Caeciana	Claudian
Caesar	Caesaria	Caesarianus	Caesariana	

(Note: after Gaius Iulius Caesar and Iulius Caesar Octavianus created the Empire, Caesar becomes a title.)

Calvus	Calva	Calvanus	Calvana	bald; Licinian
Camillus	Camilla	Camillianus	Camilliana	Furian
Caninius	Caninia	Caninianus	Caniniana	dog-like *
Capito	Capita	Capitanus	Capitana	big head;* Fonteian
Catilina	Catilinina	Catilinianus	Catiliniana	Sergian
Cato	Catilla	Catianus	Catiana	shrewd; Porcian
Catullus	Catulla	Catullianus	Catulliana	Valerian
Catulus	Catula	Catulanus	Catulana	Lutatian
Censorinus	Censorina	Censorinianus	Censoriniana	Marcian
Cicero	Cicera	Ciceranus	Cicerana	pea farmer; Tullian
Cimber	Cimberia	Cimberianus	Cimberiana	Annian
Cincinnatus	Cincinnatia	Cincinnatanus	Cincinnatana	curly
Cinna	Cinnina	Cinninianus	Cinniniana	Cornelian
Claudius	Claudia	Claudianus	Claudiana	lame
Clemens	Clemensia	Clemensianus	Clemensiana	Arrecinni
Clodius	Clodia	Clodianus	Clodiana	*
Cocles	Coclita	Coclitanus	Coclitana	one-eyed; Horatian
Coesius	Coesia	Coesianus	Coesiana	cat's eyes

Masculine	Feminine	Possessive Masculine	Possessive Feminine	Gentes Meaning
Collatinus	Collatina	Collatinianus	Collatiniana	
Considius	Considia	Considianus	Considiania	non-gentes
Constantius	Constania	Constantianus	Constaniania	brave, steady
Corbulo	Corbula	Corbulanus	Corbulania	Domitian
Corvinus	Corvina	Corvinanus	Corvinania	of a raven
Cotta	Cottina	Cottinanus	Cottinana	Aurelian and Aurunculeian
Crassus	Crassia	Crassianus	Crassiana	thick; Licinian
Crastinus	Crastina	Crastinianus	Crastiniana	
Donatus	Donatia	Donatianus	Donatiana	
Drusus	Drusilla	Drusianus	Drusiana	Claudian and Livian
Durus	Dura	Durianus	Duriana	Laberian
Epicadus	Epicada	Epicadanus	Epicadana	Asinian
Fabius	Fabia	Fabianus	Fabiana	beangrower*
Flaccus	Flaccia	Flaccianus	Flacciana	flap-eared Horatian
Flamininus	Flaminina	Flamininianus	Flamininiana	Quinctian
Furius	Furia	Furianus	Furiana	raging *
Gabinius	Gabinia	Gabinianus	Gabiniana	*
Gallus	Galla	Gallanus	Gallana	Asinian
Gemellus	Gemella	Gemellianus	Gemelliana	Memmian
Glabrio	Glabria	Glabrianus	Glabriana	Acilian
Iucundus	Iucunda	Iucundianus	Iucundiana	Caecilian
Labeo	Labea	Labeanus	Labeana	Antistian
Labienus	Labiena	Labienianus	Labieniana	
Laelius	Laelia	Laelianus	Laeliana	non-gentes
Laevinus	Laevina	Laevinianus	Laeviniana	Valerian
Lamia	Lamina	Laminanus	Laminana	Aelian
Larentius	Larentia	Larentianus	Larentiana	
Lentulus	Lentula	Lentulianus	Lentuliana	Cornelian
Lepidus	Lepida	Lepidianus	Lepidiana	Aemilian
Longinus	Longina	Longinanus	Longinana	Cassian
Longus	Longia	Longianus	Longiana	tall; Sempronian
Lucanius	Lucania	Lucanianus	Lucaniana	
Lucius	Lucia	Lucianus	Luciana	light
Luparius	Luparia	Luparianus	Lupariana	wolf-hunter
Luscinus	Luscina	Luscinianus	Lusciniana	Fabrician
Mancinus	Mancina	Mancinianus	Manciniana	Hostilian
Marcellus	Marcella	Marcellianus	Marcelliana	Claudian; * Asinian
Maro	Marilla	Marianus	Mariana	
Martius	Martia	Martianus	Martiana	of Mars
Messala	Messalina	Messalanus	Messalana	Valeria
Metellus	Metella	Metellianus	Metelliana	Caecilian
Milo	Mila	Milanus	Milana	Annian
Molo	Mola	Molanus	Molana	
Musa	Musina	Musinanus	Musinana	Antonin

Masculine	Feminine	Possessive Masculine	Possessive Feminine	Gentes Meaning
Naso	Nasilla	Nason	Nasona	big nose; Actorian
Neptunius	Neptunia	Neptunianus	Neptuniana	of the sea-God
Nero	Nerilla	Neron	Nerona	

(Often used by the Claudians since 3rd c. B.C.)

Masculine	Feminine	Possessive Masculine	Possessive Feminine	Gentes Meaning
Nerva	Nervina	Nervinianus	Nerviniana	
Niger	Nigeria	Nigerianus	Nigeriana	black
Papus	Papilla	Papianus	Papiana	Aemilia
Paulus	Paula	Paulianus	Pauliana	little; Aemilian
Petrosidius	Petrosidianus	Petrosidia	Petrosidiana	non-gentes
Phillipus	Phillipa	Phillipianus	Phillipiana	loves horses
Philo	Phila	Philanus	Philana	Publilian
Pictor	Pictoria	Pictorianus	Pictoriana	painter of pictures
Piso	Pisa	Pisianus	Pisiana	Calpurnan
Plancus	Planca	Plancanus	Plancana	Munatian
Pollio	Pollia	Pollianus	Polliana	Asinian; Clodian
Pompeius	Pompeia	Pompeianus	Pompeiana	non-gentes
Pomponius	Pomponia	Pomponianus	Pomponiana	non-gentes
Porcius	Porcia	Porcianus	Porciana	swineherd
Postumius	Postumia	Postumianus	Postumiana	non-gentes
Probus	Probia	Probianus	Probiana	Aurelian, Valerian
Procillus	Procilla	Procillianus	Procilliana	Valerian
Proculus	Procula	Proculanus	Proculana	Acerronian
Propertius	Propertia	Propertianus	Propertiana	non-gentes
Publicola	Publicolina	Publicolanus	Publicolana	Valerian
Pullo	Pulla	Pullianus	Pulliana	non-gentes
Pulvillus	Pulvilla	Pulvillianus	Pulvilliana	Horatian
Quadratus	Quadrata	Quadratianus	Quadratiana	Voluseian
Reblius	Reblia	Reblianus	Rebliana	
Reginus	Regina	Reginianus	Reginiana	Antistian
Regulus	Regula	Regulianus	Reguliana	little king
Rullianus	Rulliana	Rullianianus	Rullianiana	Fabian
Rutilus	Rutila	Rutilianus	Rutiliana	Sempronian
Salinator	Salinatoria	Salinatoria	Salinatoriana	
Scaevola	Scaevolina	Scaevolianus	Scaevoliana	left-handed
Scipio	Scipia	Scipianus	Scipiana	Cornelian
Scribonius	Scribonia	Scribonianus	Scriboniana	non-gentes
Secundus	Secunda	Secundanus	Secundana	Plinian
Sejanus	Seiania	Seianianus	Seianiana	(Seianus) Aelian
Seneca	Senecina	Senecanus	Senecana	Annaean
Silvius	Silvia	Silvianus	Silviana	of woods
Strabo	Strabilla	Strabianus	Strabiana	squinting
Sulla	Sullina	Sullinianus	Sulliniana	Cornelian

Masculine	Feminine	Possessive Masculine	Possessive Feminine	Gentes Meaning
Sulpicius	Sulpicia	Sulpicianus	Sulpiciana	non-gentes
Tacitus	Tacita	Tacitianus	Tacitiana	silent
Tertullus	Tertulla	Tertullanus	Tertullana	Cornutian
Torquatus	Torquata	Torquatianus	Torquatiana	Manlian
Triarius	Triaria	Triarianus	Triariana	non-gentes
Varro	Varra	Varrianus	Varriana	Terentian
Varus	Varilla	Varianus	Variana	bow-legged
Vatinius	Vatinia	Vatinianus	Vatiniana	non-gentes
Verginius	Verginia	Verginianus	Verginiana	
Vestinus	Vestina	Vestinanus	Vestinana	Attican
Veturius	Veturia	Veturianus	Veturiana	non-gentes
Vibulanus	Vibulania	Vibulanianus	Vibulaniana	Fabian
Volero	Volera	Voleranus	Volerania	Publilian
Volso	Volsilla	Volsianus	Volsiana	Manlian
Vorenus	Vorena	Vorenianus	Voreniana	non-gentes
Vorvinus	Vorvina	Vorvinianus	Vorviniana	

TABLE SIX: PLACE-NAME COGNOMENS

Albanus/Albana: from Alba
Alpinus/Alpina: from the Alps
Antiatinus/Antiatina: from Antium
Aquitanus/Aquitana: from Aquitaine
Ardeanus/Ardeana: from Ardea, 20 miles south of Rome
Atheniensus/Atheniensa: from Athens
Babylonus/Babylona: from Babylon; *Babylonius* is a Babylonian
Coriolanus/Coriolana: from Corioli, a town SE of Rome

Dyrrachinus/Dyrrachina: from Dyrrachium, an Illyrian port
Gallicanus/Gallicana: from Gallicia
Germanianus/Germaniana: from the Germans
Massilanus/Massilana: from Massilia (Marseilles)
Norbanus/Norbana: from Norba
Pompeianus/Pompeiana: from Pompeii
Spartianus/Spartiana: from Sparta

TABLE SEVEN: AGNOMENS
only given to males

Achaicus: of Achaia (Greece)
Africanus: of Africa
Allobrogicus: of the Allobroges
Aquitanicus: of Aquitaine
Aremoricus: of Aremorica, now Brittany
Asiaticus: of Asia, now Asia Minor or the Near East
Augustus: for emperors
Britannicus: of Britain
Creticus: of Crete

Gallicus: of Gaul
Germanicus: of Germany
Ibericus: of Spain
Illiricus: of Illyria
Macedonicus: of Macedon
Mauretanicus: of Mauretania
Numantinus: of Numantia
Numidicus: of Numidia
Scythicus: of Scythia
Siricus: of Syria

DIMINUTIVES

Even Romans used pet names. Tullius might call his daughter Tulliola, "little Tullia," and her suitors, husbands, lovers, mother, aunts, and friends might do the same. "Little" had our connotation of affection, so that *cordulum* means either "dear heart" or "little heart."

The diminutive endings are -olus for masculine, -ola for feminine, -lum for neuter.

TABLE EIGHT: POSSIBLE COGNOMENS

These are structured correctly enough to pass, but only a few have been found attached to an ancient Roman. They will suit your commoners, and fictitious families.

Masculine	*Feminine*	*Meaning*
Aequorius	Aequoria	of the sea
Aerisius	Aerisia	of bronze
Aestatius	Aestatia	of summer
Aestuarius	Aestuaria	from the tidal marsh
Aeturnius	Aeturnia	eternal
Alacrius	Alacria	eager, spirited
Amabilius	Amabilia	worthy to be loved
Amenta	Amentina	mad
Amicius	Amicia	friendly
Amplius	Amplia	large, great
Aprilius	Aprilia	April
Arator	Aratoria	plowman
Arbiter	Arbiteria	judge
Argentarius	Argentaria	of the bank
Argentius	Argentia	of silver
Asperius	Asperia	harsh, rough
Auctor	Auctoria	instigator, authority
Audaca	Audacina	reckless, bold
Aurius	Auria	of gold
Avarius	Avaria	greedy
Avidius	Avidia	eager, avid
Barbatius	Barbatia	bearded
Bellicosus	Bellicosa	warlike
Blandus	Blanda	flattering
Bruma	Brumina	mid-winter
Caecius	Caecia	blind
Caelestus	Caelesta	heavenly
Calamius	Calamia	reed pen
Calidius	Calidia	hot
Callidius	Callidia	sly, crafty
Candidus	Candida	shining white

Masculine	Feminine	Meaning
Cantius	Cantia	singing
Cantor	Cantoria	singer
Canus	Cana	frosted, hoary
Caprus	Capra	goat
Celeber	Celebria	famous
Celer	Celeria	swift
Certus	Certa	trustworthy
Cervus	Cerva	deer
Chlorus	Chlora	greenish pale
Citharoedus	Citharoeda	sings with cithara
Citus	Cita	quick
Clarius	Claria	bright, loud, famous
Columba	Columbina	pigeon/dove
Commodus	Commoda	advantageous, desired
Concitorus	Concitora	instigator
Copiosus	Copiosa	well-supplied
Corvus	Corva	raven
Croceius	Croceia	saffron yellow
Cruentatius	Cruentatia	blood-stained
Cruentius	Cruentia	gory
Cultius	Cultia	refined
Cupidus	Cupida	desirous, loving
Cursus	Cursa	running
Defessius	Defessia	exhausted
Delectus	Delecta	select, chosen
Desertus	Deserta	deserted, lonely
Desidius	Desidia	indolent, lazy
Dignius	Dignia	worthy, deserving
Dimidius	Dimidia	half
Dirus	Dira	frightful, dire
Discipulus	Discipula	the scholar
Divinius	Divinia	of a Diety
Dolorus	Dolora	sorrowful
Dominus	Domina	master, mistress
Dubius	Dubia	dubious
Dulcius	Dulcia	sweet
Durus	Dura	hard, harsh
Ebrius	Ebria	drunken
Eburneius	Eburneia	of ivory
Electus	Electa	picked out
Equius	Equia	of horses
Essedarius	Essedaria	charioteer
Fagius	Fagia	of the beech tree
Falsus	Falsa	false
Ferius	Feria	wild, savage
Ferreus	Ferrea	made of iron
Fidius	Fidia	faithful
Firmus	Firma	strong, firm
Flavius	Flavia	golden yellow
Fluvius	Fluvia	of the river

Masculine	Feminine	Meaning
Formosus	Formosa	beautiful
Fremius	Fremia	roaring
Fulvus	Fulva	tawny yellow
Funestus	Funesta	deadly
Gloriosus	Gloriosa	glorious
Gratius	Gratia	pleasing, grateful
Honestus	Honesta	honorable, honest
Ignarius	Ignaria	ignorant
Ignavius	Ignavia	slothful, lazy
Ignotus	Ignota	stranger, unfamiliar
Invisius	Invisia	hated
Iovius	Iovia	of Jove
Iratus	Irata	irate, enraged
Iunonius	Iunonia	sacred to Juno
Iuppiterius	Iuppiteria	of Jupiter
Laetus	Laeta	joyful, happy
Laevius	Laevia	unpropitious
Lassus	Lassa	tired
Latius	Latia	wide
Lentius	Lentia	slow
Magnus	Magna	great, noble
Marinus	Marina	of the sea
Medicus	Medica	doctor, healer
Mercurius	Mercuria	of Mercury
Mirius	Miria	miraculous
Mus	Musa	mouse
Neptunius	Neptunia	of Neptune
Nummus	Numma	coin
Obscurus	Obscura	dark, obscure
Odoratus	Odorata	perfumed, fragrant
Optimus	Optima	best, most favorable
Palius	Palia	of the swamp
Pallidus	Pallida	pale
Parcius	Parcia	frugal
Parvus	Parva	small, trifling
Pelagius	Pelagia	of the sea
Peritus	Perita	skillful, experienced
Plagosius	Plagosia	fond of flogging
Pluvius	Pluvia	of the rain
Portitorius	Portitoria	ferryman
Praeclarius	Praeclaria	glorious, dazzling
Praedo	Praeda	robber
Pristinus	Pristina	ancient, original
Procus	Proca	suitor
Pronus	Prona	bent forward
Prosperius	Prosperia	fortunate, prosperous
Publicius	Publicia	of the people
Purpurius	Purpuria	purple, dark red
Quaestius	Quaestia	gain, treasure, profit
Ramius	Ramia	of the bough or branch

Masculine	Feminine	Meaning
Rapidius	Rapidia	rapid
Rectius	Rectia	straight
Refugius	Refugia	ever-fleeing
Regius	Regia	of a king
Repentinus	Repentina	hasty, unexpected
Rivius	Rivia	of the stream
Roburius	Roburia	of the oak; vigor
Rubius	Rubia	of the briar
Rusticus	Rustica	rural
Saevius	Saevia	raving, fierce
Sagittarius	Sagittaria	archer
Sanus	Sana	healthy, whole, sound
Saucius	Saucia	wounded, sick, ill
Sceleratus	Scelerata	wicked; descecrated
Scelius	Scelia	wicked, sinful
Securus	Secura	careless, heedless
Sentius	Sentia	thorny
Solius	Solia	of the sun
Solus	Sola	alone, solitary
Splendidus	Splendida	splendid, glittering
Stellatius	Stellatia	starry
Stridulus	Stridula	hissing, whizzing
Stultius	Stultia	foolish
Superbus	Superba	haughty, arrogant
Tardius	Tardia	sluggish, late, tardy
Taurius	Tauria	of the bull
Temerarius	Temeraria	rash, heedless, reckless
Temperatus	Temperata	mild, controlled
Tonsor	Tonsoria	barber
Tremebundus	Tremebunda	trembling
Tremulus	Tremula	trembling
Trepidus	Trepida	frightened
Vagius	Vagia	wandering
Vastius	Vastia	huge, vast
Verberus	Verbera	flogging, striking
Verus	Vera	truthful
Villosus	Villosa	shaggy
Vulcanius	Vulcania	of Vulcan

ETRUSCAN

They did not call themselves Etruscans, but *Rasna* or *Rasnea*. While they did conceive of themselves as a cultural unit, the city-states never could work together against outside aggression. Even more than the Hellenes, the individual thought of himself or herself as a citizen of the city, not of a national unit. Yet often, they were not averse to changing their city if another offered greater opportunity. The first, historical kings of Rome, who found a group of villages and left a planned city with drains and stone streets, were Etruscan adventurers.

The Etruscans had people who used only one name — artisans and the like — and a better class who had family names. You'll be glad to hear that they put personal name first, family name second. Occasionally there is a third name at the end, and that often seems a place-of-origin-name. Some experts, like Helmut Rix, say that the third name is a sub-family name, like the Latin cognomen.

While the family names do gender (and shift their endings as parts of speech) there is not the symmetry of Latin where every male fore-name has a female equivalent. Larth and Larthi, Vel and Velia, Arnth and Arnthia, do match, but the vastly popular women's names Thana/Thania and Fasti/Fastia have no male equivalent of Than or Fast. Nor do we find the many feminine equivalents for male names we would expect in a Latin-like system.

So think of Etruscan names in the same league as you would Russian or Czech names, not Latin: praenomen or personal name, nomen (clan name), cognomen (sub-family name); or personal name with a two-part family name.

Popular praenomens are extremely common, probably accounting for two-thirds of the population. Rix lists them as popular or rare, according to his sources; the numbers are from their frequency in the *Corpus Inscriptionum Etruscarum Wisconsinense*, the first such compilation done with computer aid.

For a writer, praenomens are confusing if you have more than a half-dozen characters. Get past it by referring to people by their nomens or cognomens — far more varied — rather than the praenomens. Etruscan cities were home to many western Hellenes, especially craftsmen, so some of your characters might have non–Etruscan names.

Etruscans of the *Aeneid* period should be given single names based on the cognomens and nomens. After the absorbtion of Etruria by Rome, Etruscans become part and parcel of the Empire, their source hidden by Latinization. Both Virgil and Sejanus were Etruscan. To help you with this, Latin equivalents are given where known.

Pronunciation

X is the throat-clearing sound at the end of a Scottish loch, and was written with the Greek chi. SC and SH sound alike. TH is the Greek theta. C could stand for C, K, Q, and G. F was used for F, PH, B, and BH. P was sometimes itself, sometime B; as T was sometimes D. In the vowels, E was sometimes I, and U sometimes O. Now you know why Etruscologists mutter as they read. There is room for a certain amount of misunderstanding in notes your Etruscans send each other.

It is less messy below. Remember the chi-X, and otherwise, pronounce all the letters, with the I from machine and the A from pasta.

FEMALE PRAENOMENS (FIRST NAMES)

	Frequency	*Latin*
Arnthia, Arnthi	2 + 1	
Aula, Aulia	2 + 2	Aulia
Caia	19	
Fasti, Fastia	popular; 96 + 11	
Hasti, Hastia	popular; 38 + 35	
Larthi, Larthia	popular; 269 + 77	
Ramtha, Ramthia	38	
Ravnthu	7	
Sethra, Sethria	9 + 3	
Thana, Thania	popular; 335 + 141	
Thanicu	4 + 1	
Thanxvil, Thancvil	14 + 1	Tanaquilia
Velia, Veilia	popular; 62 + 21	

MALE PRAENOMENS

	Frequency	*Latin*
Arnth	popular; 171	
Arnthur	rare; 1	
Arnza	18	
Aule	popular; 107	Aulus
Aulza	rare; 1	
Cae	70	
Cuinte	rare; 1	Quintus
Cure	3	
Larce	24	
Laris	popular; 54	
Larth	popular; 232	
Larza	15	
Laxu	2	
Luci	4	
Pesna	3	
Pup, Pupli	rare; 3 + 7	Publius
Sethre	popular; 18	
Shertur	rare; not in *CIEW*	
Sure	4	
Tarxi	4	
Thefri	1	
Tite	rare	Titus
Vel	popular; 249	Velus
Velthur	17	
Velxe	7	
Venza	6	

NOMENS
(CLAN NAMES)

Masculine	Feminine	Latin Masculine
Acilu	Acilunn	
Aclni	Aclinia, Alcni	
Acsi	Acsi	
Alfni	Alfnia	
Alpiu	Alpui	
Alvni	Aluni	
Amthne	Amthni, Amthnia	
Anani	Ananla	
Anei	Aneinei, Aneinia	
Ani	Ani	
Aprthe	Aprthia	
Arnt(i)le	Arntilia	
Arntni	Arntnei	Arrius
Ate	Atia	
Athnu	Athnui	
Aulni	Aulnia	
Avaini	Avainia	
Avle, Aule	Aulia	Aulus
Axu	Axuni, Axui	
Axuni	Axunei	
Cacni	Cacni	
Cae, Cai in Perusia	Cainei, sometimes Cai	
Calisna	Calisnei	
Calisni	Calisnia	
Carcu	Carcui	
Cnevna	Cnevnei	
Cumere	Cumeria	
Cvenle	Cvenlia	
Frentinate	Freninatia	
Haltu	Haltuni	
Hamphna	Hamphnei	
Hanusa	Hanusnei	
Hele	Helia	
Herini	Hirinia	Hirrius
Larce	Larcia	
Larci	Larci	
Larthru	Larthruni	
Latini	Latini	Latinus
Latithe	Latithia	
Lecne	Lecnia	
Marcni		
Minate	Minatia	
Nemsu	Nemdui	
Numsi	Numsinei	Numerius, Niumsis
Paci	Pacinei	Pacius
Pethna	Pethnei	

Masculine	Feminine	Latin Masculine
Petru	Petrui	
Precu	Precuni	
Pulfna	Pulfnei	
Pumpu	Pumpuni	Pompeii
Purni	Purninei	
Remzna	Remznei	
Rusina	Rusinei	
Sale	Salla	
Sentinate, Seiante	Sentinati, Seianti	Seianus, numerous
Serice	Sericia	
Sethre	Sethria	
Sethrni	Sethrnei	
Shali, Shalie	Shalia	
Shalvi	Shalvia, occ. Shalvi	Salvius
Shelvashl	Shelvashlia	
Shemna	Shemnei	
Sherturi	Sherturi	
Teti	Teti	
Tetina	Tetinei	
Thansi	Thansinei	
Theprini	Thepainia	
Thuceri	Thuceria	
Tite	Titi	Titus, numerous
Tlesna	Tlesnei	
Tutna	Tutnei	Tutillius
Uthle	Uthli(a)	
Uxumzna	Uxumznei	
Valashna	Valashnei	
Velcialu	Velcialui	
Veli	Velia, sometimes Veli	
Velsi	Velsia, sometimes Velsi	
Versni	Versnia	
Veti	Veti	Vettius
Vetu	Vetui	
Vipi	Vipia, sometimes Vipi	Vibius; huge membership
Vipi Alfa	Vipia Alfania	
Vipi Ancari	Vipia Ancaria	

COGNOMENS
(SUB-FAMILY NAMES)

Masculine	Feminine
Acilu	Acilunia
Alfa	Alfania
Alu	Alunia
Amre	Amria
Apice	Apicnei

Masculine	Feminine	
Aris	Arigia	
Ashia	Ashiania	
Ataris	Atarissia	
Athnu	Athnu	
Aulni	Aulni	
Canath	Canetha	
Cancu	Cancunia	
Canthusa	Canthusania	
Carcu	Carcunia	
Casni	Casnia	
Cazrtu	Cazrtunia	
Cencu	Cencunia	
Cestna	Cestnei	
Cesu	Censunia	
Cicu	Cicunia	
Clan	Clana	
Clan Nurziu	Clan Nurziunia	
Claniu	Claniunia	
Clanti	Clanti	
Clauce	Claucia	
Cnare	Cnaria	
Crapilu	Crapilunia	
Craufa, Craupa	Craufania, Craupania	
Creice	Creicia	
Crespe	Crespia	Crespinius
Cretlu	Cretlu	
Cucu	Cucunia	
Cuishla	Cuishlania	
Culpiu	Culpiunia	
Cumere	Cumurunia	
Cutlis	Cutlisnei	
Cutu	Cutunia, Cutui	
Eple	Eplia	
Etrnis	Etanigia	
Faltusa	Faltusania	
Faru	Farui	
Fastntru	Fastntrunia	
Ferme	Fermia	
Feru	Ferui, Ferunia	
Fetiu	Fetiunia	
Fulu	Fuluni, Fului	
Halistre	Halistrea	
Hanu	Hanunia	
Helzu	Helzunia	
Hercle	Herclenia	Hercules
Herme	Hermia	
Hisu	Hisunia	
Hulu	Huluni	
Hurace	Huracia	
Huzlu	Huzlunia	

Masculine	Feminine	
Ianzu	Ianzunia	
Latuni	Latuni	
Leixu	Leixunia	
Lentis	Lentisnei	
Lethiu	Lethiunia	
Letis	Letisa	
Leusa	Leusei	
Lule	Lulia	
Lupu	Lupunia	
Lusce	Luscenia	
Luscesa	Luscesei	
Macre	Macri	
Macute	Macutia	
Marale	Maralia	
Marcna	Marcnei	
Masu	Masui	
Meluta	Melutnei	
Metus	Metusnei	
Mlnane	Mlnania	
Mute	Mutenia, Muteni	
Namult	Namulta	
Natis	Natienei	
Nufre	Nufria	
Nufrzna	Nufrznei	
Numna	Numnei	
Nurziu	Nurziunia	
Nushte	Nushtenia, Nushtia	
Pacre	Pacrenia	
Papa	Papania	
Patu	Patunia	
Pece	Pecania	
Penthe	Penthia	
Peris	Perisnei	
Pestiu	Pestui, Pestiunia	
Phauxane, Phauxa	Phauxania	
Phesu	Phesu	
Piste	Pistia	
Plancure	Plancuria	
Plaute	Plauti	Plautius
Precu	Precunia	
Prexu	Prexunia	
Prute	Prutia	
Pulpae	Pulpainei	
Pultus	Pultunia	
Pumpna	Pumpnei	
Rafe	Rafia	
Ranazu	Ranazunia	
Raufe	Raufia	
Razis	Razisnei	
Resciu	Resciunia	

Masculine	Feminine	
Rufe	Rufia	Rufius
Rutane	Rutania	
Sameru	Sameruni, Samerunia	
Satna	Satnei	
Sceva	Scevania	Scaevius
Scire	Sciria	
Secu	Secunia	
Sepre	Sepria	
Shene	Shenevia	
Shepu	Shepunia	
Shinu	Shinunia	
Shuza	Shuzania	
Spaspu	Spaspunia	Spaspo
Strume	Strumiana	
Sulu	Sulunia	
Svea	Svenia	
Svetu	Svetunia	
Talce	Talcei	
Taphu	Taphunia	
Teltiu	Teltiunia	
Thare	Tharia	
Theresh	Theresha	
Thethure	Thethuria	
Thurmna	Thurmnei	
Tiazu	Tiazunia	
Tlapu	Tlapunia	
Tlapuni	Tlapuni	Tlabonius
Trepa	Trepei	
Trepu	Trepunia	Trebius
Tumu	Tumunia	
Tushnu	Tushni	
Ucar	Ucara	
Ulthe	Ulthia	
Umithe	Umithea	
Umpre	Umprea	
Urfa	Urfania	
Uvilane	Uvilania	
Vari	Vari	Varius
Varna	Varnei	
Varni	Varni	
Velimna	Velimnei	
Venetesh	Venetesha	
Vente	Ventia	
Venu	Venunia	
Vepu	Vepunia	
Verpe	Verpia	
Vercna	Vercnei	
Veru	Verunia	
Vescu	Vescunia	
Vezra	Vezrania	

Masculine	Feminine
Vilia	Viliania
Visce	Viscenea
Visce	Viscenei, Viscia
Zixu	Zixunia
Zuxu	Zuxunia

TITLES

lauxme — monarch
zilax — supreme magistrate; tyrant; occ. zilath

ORIGIN NAMES

Clevsinax — from Clusium
Curtunax — from Cortona
Phlevax — from Blera
Puplunax — from Populonia
Rumax — from Rome
Suthrix — from Sutrium

Sveamax — from Suana
Tarxunax — from Tarquinii
Urinax — from Aurinia
Velathrix — from Volaterrae
Velznax — from Velcha
Vetlunax — from Vetulonia

ETRUSCAN CITIES WITH LATIN NAMES AND MODERN LOCATIONS

Latin	Etruscan	Modern
Arretium	unknown	Arezzo
Aurinia	Urina	Saturnia
Blera	Phleva	near Norcha and Castel d'Asso
Caere	Xaire, Xaisr	Cerveteri
Clusium	Clevsina	Chiusi
Cortona	Curtun	Cortona
Cosa	unknown	
Faesulae	unknown	Fiesole near Florence
Perusia	unknown	Perugia
Populonia	Pupluna	near Piombino
Rusellae	unknown	Roselle
Suana	Sveama	Sovana
Sutrium	Suthri	Sutri
Tarquinii	Tarxuna	Corneta or Tarquinia
Telamon	unknown	
Veii	unknown	near Isola Farnese
Vetulonia	Vetluna	
Volaterrae	Velathri	Volterra
Volci or Vulci	Velxa	
Volsinii	Velzna	Bolsena

Founded by Romans in Etruscan Territory:

Latin	Etruscan	Modern
Florentia	none	Florence
Pisae	none	Pisa
Saena Julia	none	Siena

CELTIC

Many tribes called Germanic by Romans were in fact Celts, by the ethnological standards you must use as a writer. It shows in the names, and in the archaeological remains. This is because the Romans defined Celts and Germans differently than we do.

To modern scholars, a Celt is someone who speaks a Celtic language, and leaves Celtic cultural remains. A Germanic tribe is one that uses a Germanic language and culture.

To the Romans, a Celt was anyone living west of the Rhine at the time Caesar entered Gaul. A Germanic tribe was any that lived east of the Rhine. Their definition was geographic, ours is linguistic. This is similar to the ancient Greek definition: any barbarians that live in Western Europe are Celts; any that live in Asia Minor or Central Asia are Scythians; anyone in between is a Celto-Scythian. So they would call Scythian any Celtic-speakers that were, say, living south of the Black Sea.

Among the "Germanic tribes" of the Romans that were Celtic speakers: the Cimbri, the Ubii, the Mattiaci, the Sugambri, the Vangiones, the Nemetes, the Triboci, and the Teutones. The last gave us the word Teutonic, only because 19th century scholars trusted politicians like Caesar, instead of looking at the evidence for themselves.

Gender

The reading of Gaulish is still problematical in many cases. In many inscriptions, a certain string of letters will be said by one authority to represent a couple of Celtic names, while another will agree about the first name, but say the second is other words. A third will say the second name is correct, but the first is inscriptionary. "What about Latin manuscripts like Livy or Caesar?" Those came down to the Age of Print through hand-copied manuscripts, and they do not all agree on spelling.

Famous men were Vercingetorix and Orgetorix. Yet some -ix endings are definitely female, as inscriptions refer to the bearer being wife, mother, daughter, or sister of someone. All U-endings with attested gender are female. But as scholarly sources have the miserable sexist habit that anyone not specifically identified as female is lumped in with the definitely male — rather than keeping three sets, known male, known female, and unspecified — all -IA, -ILLA, -INA, -ENA, -EA, in fact all -A endings not specifically male, are below listed as female.

This is not arbitrary: as in the case of -U, almost all those that have gender information are female. Especially when one finds the same root with a male ending, one can be safe in declaring the other feminine. A few of the matching gendered pairs:

Cambaria, Cambarius
Eburia, Eburius
Iccia, Iccius
Leuca, Leucas; Leuconia, Leuconius
Macaria, Macarius
Meddila, Meddillus
Perra, Perrus; Pera, Perus
Regina, Regenos; Reginia, Reginius
Riceina, Ricenus
Sennicia, Senecius
Trita, Tritus; Tritia, Tritius

As most usual, most people went by a single name. A patronymic would not be used except in Imperial paperwork, or the occasional inscription. There are no family names. However, daughters very often, if not always, would have a feminine version of their fathers' names. Sons' names rarely connected directly to their fathers'.

Latinization

As "allied" (conquered) Gaul was pulled more securely into the Roman orbit, many Celts realized that the way to power was to cozy up to the southerners with the clout. In some cases, those enfranchised (made full Roman citizens) by a certain Emperor would take his *nomen* as their own. Thus there were clans of Julii and Claudii, who were individually listed as Julius Togirix, or Julius Gedomo: Latin family name followed by Celtic personal name. Their children or grandchildren were given Latin-language personal names, so that by C.E. 69 these families have Julius Classicus, Julius Civilis, Julius Tutor, or Julius Auspex.

However, as soon as the Julian name became a political disadvantage, it was dropped in favor of the single personal name, as monuments prove. Consider this a foreign affectation. In some cases, the Celtic name of a famous member of the family became the family name, like Iccius among the Remii.

FEMALE NAMES
* = gender definite

Abrexta	Adbugiouna	Adiania, Adianta
Acca	Adbugissa	Admata
Acisillia	Adginna, Adgonna	Adnama

Adnamatia, Adnamata
Adnamita
*Adnamu
Adreticia
*Aduorix, *Advorix
Aesica
Aesiua
*Agedia
Agisiaca
Agisilia, Agisilla
Aisa
Albina
Albisia
Albucia
Aleasiumara
Alla, Allia
Alleicea
Alleticia
Allouira
Allusa
Alpina, Alpinia, Alpinula
Alteurita
Ambada
Andaitia
Andarta
*Andebrocirix
Andeca, Anderca
*Anderica
*Anderina
Anderitia
Andilia
Andoca
Andueia, Anduenna
Annama
Ariola
Arrotala
Arsulana
Atebodua
Atectorigiana
Ategenta, Atigenta
Ategnissa
Atepa, Atepu
Atessatia, Atestatia, Atestia
Ateurita
Atioxta
Atismaria
Atreba, Atrebia
Attisaga
Atturita
Auamacimaria

Audata, Audenta
Auentina, Aventina
Aulricmara
Avitianomara
Balatonaua
Ballatulla
Banona, Banna, Bannua
Betudaca, Bitudaga
*Bileseton
Bilisa
*Billia
Bimottia
Bora, Borissa
Boudilla
Boudinna, Boudenna
Brocchia
Brogimara
*Buscilla
Bussia
Bussugnata
Cabrilla
Cabura, Caburena, Caburia
Caccosa, Cacossa
Cacudia
Cambaria
Cambosa
Camelognata
Camula, Camulia, Camullia
Camulata, Camolatia, Camulatia, Camoulatia
Camuledu
Camulilia
Cantexta
Caraddouna
Caranta, Carantia, Carenta
Carantana, Carantiana
Carantilla, Carantila
Carantina
Carantodia
Carantusa
Carata
Caratilla, Caratila, Caratulla
Careia, Kareia
*Caretosa
Caria
Carina, Karina
Carisia, Carissa

Carosa, Carosia
Carrotala
Cartulla
Caruca
Caruiliena
Caruonia
Cassa, Cassia
Cassibodua
Cassicia
Cassimara
Cassiola
Casticia
Castina
Cata, Catia
Catalia
Catica
Catilia, Catilla
Catiola
Catnea
*Catronia
Catta, Cattea, Cattia
Cattara, Cattura
Cattulla, Catulla, Catullia
Cattuviqqa
Catuallauna
Catucia
Caturica
Caturigia
Caturisa
Caura, Cauru
Cavaria, Cauaria
Ceniuria
Cenna, Cennia
*Cenos
Censonia
Centa
*Centogenea
Centusmia
Cigemma
Cincia
Cincissa
Cingetissa
Cinia, Cenia
Cintucra
Cintugena
Cintusma
Cintusmina
Cintussa, Cintussia
Cloutina
Clutamilla

Cobiatia
*Coblanuo
Coblucia
Cobnerta
Cobromara
Cobronia, Cobruna
Comacia
Comatia
*Comatimara
Comatulla
Combara
Comerta
Comiumara
Condexua
Congenetia, Congenncia
Consuadullia
Contessia
Corasia
Corobilla
Corrodu
Cotina, Cottina
Cotira, Cottira
Cotta, Cottia
Cottulla, Cotulia
*Cotu
*Cotuconi
Counerta
Cricconia
Cunacena
Dagania
Dania, Dannia
Danissa
Dannumara
Danotala
Danu
Deiotariana
Derceia
Deuila, Deuillia, Diuilla
Devignata, Deuognata
Diona
Diorata
Diuuogna, Diuvogna
Diveca
Divogenia, Diuogenia
Donilla
Donisia
Dubna, Dubnia, Dumnana, Dumnia
Eburia
Eburila
Eliomara

Elovissa, Elvissa
Emogenia
Epa, Epia, Eppa, Eppia
Epetina
Epilla, Epillia
Epiu
Eppaxta, Eppaxtia
Epponina
Etiona
Etolugnia
Exapia
Excinga
Excingilla
Exobna, Exomna, Exouna
Fimmilene
Friagabi
Gabra
Genaca, Genucia
Genetodia
Genna
Genobia
Gnata, Gnatia
Gnatilla
Iantulla
Iantumara
Iantura
Iatta
Iattossa
Ibliomaria
Iccia
Ilateuta
Inderca
Indercilea
Isosae
Itta
Lanipendia
Larma
Leuca
Leucena
Leucimara
Leucona, Leuconia
Litania
Litogena, Litugena
Littiossa
Litu, Litua
Litucca, Lituccia
Litullina
*Loucita, *Loucitta
Lugiola
Macaria
Maccira, Maccirra

Magunia, Magunna
Magusatia
Mandelana
Manduilla
Manduissa
Martidia
Martilia, Marilla
Martiria
Martna
Mata, Matia, Matta, Mattia
Mataura
Materiona
Maticia, Matucia
Matidia
Matina, Matona, Matonia, Matuna
Mattosa
Mattua, Matua
Matucenia, Matugena, Matugenia
Matullina
Medilotamica
Medlotama
Meducena
Melicia
Meliginna
Messilia, Messilla
Metela
*Metilia
Moria, Moriena
*Mottu
Motuca
Motuidiaca
*Nama, Namma, Namia, Nammia, Namu
Namidia
Namiola
Nammota, Namuta
Namusa
Nantia
*Nantiorix
Nemetogena, Nemetocena
Nerta, Nertilla
Nertomaria
Netelia
Nitiogenna
Ollia
Olliadu
Olluna

Olugnia
Orbia, Orbiana
Orbissa
Origena
Oxidubna
Pera, Perra
Peruia
Perula
Rega, Regallia
Regina, Reginia
Regula
Rematia
Resia
*Ressatu
Ressilla
Ressona
Resta, Restia
Reticiana
Rexstugeniana
Riceina, Ricina
Ricua, Rikua
Riguiru
Ritomara, Ritumara
Ritulla
Rituscia
Rotama
Rotania
Sagila, Sagillia
Sama, Samma, Samia,
    Sammia
Samacia, Samicia
Samaxa
Samianta
Samicantu
Saminia
Sammiola, Sammola,
    Sammulla
Samuda
Sattomata
Sedata, Sedatia
*Sedecennis
Sedida, Sedia
Segla
Segolia
Segusiaua
Senila, Senilla
Sennaucia

Senocenna
Senodona, Senodonna
Sila
Solimara
Suadugena
Suaduilla, Suadulla
Suagria
Suausia
Sucaria
Sueta
Sumaria
Sumela*, Sumeliu
Sumenu
Talauia
Talavica
Taliounia
Talisia, Talissa, Talussa
Taluppa, Luppa
Tancina
*Tancorix
Tauria
Taurica
Taurilla
Taurina
Tascilla, Tasgilla, Tasgilia
Teolugnia
Teuta
Teutalu
Teutana
Trita, Tritia
Trocina
Troucetissa
Troucissa, Troucisa
Valagenta
Valeia, Vallia
Valicinia
Vebronara, Vebromara
Vebrumna
Veca
Vecticia
Vectinia
Velacena
Velacosta
Veleda
Velitia
Vellibia
Vena, Venia, Venna

Venaesia
Veniala
Venica, Venicia
Veniena
Venimara
Veninia
Venisama
Veniuallia, Venivallia
Venixama, Venixema,
    Venixiema
Vennonia
Venulanta
Venuleia
Verbronara
Verica
Verodumna
Vertia
Verucia
Vicana
*Viccu, Viccus
*Victisirana
Victulliena
Vindaina, Vindania
Vindama
Vindauscia
Vindilla
Vindoinissa
Vindu
Viniuallia
Viralira
Viratia
Viriana
Viriata
Viriciu, Viricia
Viriola
Viriondaga
Virodu
Virotouta
*Visurix
Vlattia, Vlattu
Vlatuna
Vocara
Vocontia
Volatia
Vritea, Vrittia
Vrogenia

MALE NAMES

Acedillus, Acedilu
Adbitus
Adcanaunos
Adcomaros
Adebugi, Adebugius
Adginnius, Adgennus,
  Adgenus
Adiatorix
Adiatumarus, Adietuma-
  rus
Adietuanus
Admatius
Adnamati, Adnamatius,
  Adnamatus
Adretilis
Adrotus
Advorix
Aesarius
Agedilios, Agedilli,
  Gedilli, Agedilicus,
  Agedilio, Agedillus
Agedovirus
Agisilius, Agisillus
Aicovindo
Aisus
Albic
Albius, Albus
Alebece
Allecnus
Allinus
Allobroxus
Allovico
Alluci, Allucius
Alpius, Alpus
Ambadus
Ambaxius
Ambilli, Ambilo, Ambi-
  los, Ambillus
Ambimogidus
Ambisauus, Ambisavus
Ambudsuilus
Andagelli
Andangi
Andecarius, Andecarus
Andegasi, Andegasus
Andereseni
Andergos, Andergi
Andolatius
Andosten, Andosteni,

Andosteno, Andoston,
  Andosion
Andreine
Anducor
Annamatus
Annamoris, Annamus,
  Annamatus
Antedrigus
Anteremius
Areobindus
Arimanus
Ateano
Atecilus
Atecurus
Ategnutis
Atepatus, Atepiccus
Ateponius, Atcponirus,
  Ateponus
Ateratos
Atesios, Atesos, Atesso
Atesmertus
Atessatis, Atestas
Ateuritus
Atgite
Atolisus
Atporix
Atrectus, Atrectius,
  Atregtius
Atrexstus, Atrixtos
Attectius
Atuirus
Atusonius
Audatus
Audeti
Audoenus
Audoti
Aventinius, Aventinus
Balaesus
Balatonus
Balorix
Banni, Bannio
Banu, Banui, Banuo,
  Banuillus, Banuus
Bellognatus
Bilicedo, Billicedo
Biliureto
Billiccissioni
Birucatus
Bocontius

Bodeni
Bodocenos, Bodocenus
Boduogenus
Bogionius
Borili, Borillus
Boritus
Borso, Borsus
Boruonicus, Borvonicus
Boudillus
Bravecci
Brigomaglos
Britomartus, Britomartis
Brocchus, Broccius, Broc-
  cus
Bussumarius, Bussumarus
Butiro, Buturo, Busturo
Cabriabantos
Cabrus
Caccuso
Cacurio, Cacurius
Cambo, Cambus
Cambulus
Camerianus, Camerinus
Camulatucus
Camulixus
Camulorigi
Caracco, Caracus
Caraddounus, Carad-
  dounius, Carathounus
Caramantius
Carantacus
Carantillo
Caranto
Carantorius
Carasius
Caratillus
Caratodius
Cariaus
Carigo, Carigus
Carino
Carisianus
Caritosus
Carix
Caromarus
Carominius
Carucenus, Carugenus
Carulirus
Cassicius, Cassicus
Cassitalus

Cassutus
Castonius
Catabar
Catacius, Catacus
Catamanus
Catavignus
Caterto
Cathirix
Caticorix
Catinius
Catlus, Cattulus
Catonianus
Catotigirni
Catoualos
Cattabbott, Cattabus,
 Cattabuttas
Cattaus
Cattedius
Cattuvir, Cattuvvir
Catuenus, Catuen
Catumanus, Catumandus
Caturicus
Caturo
Catusius, Catusus
Catuviqqa
Catvvirr
Cauarius, Caurius, Cau-
 rus
Cenalus
Cenicus
Cenno, Ceno
Cenocantus
Centugeni
Centus
Cicedu
Cimarus, Cimarius
Cinge, Cinges
Cingessus
Cingetoutus
Cingius
Cintio, Cinto, Cintu
Cintugenus
Cintumarus
Cintusminius
Coaeddus, Coneddus
Cobledulitauus,
 Cobledulitavus
Cobnertius, Cobnertus
Coimagni
Colomagni
Comanus

Comatullus
Combaromarus
Comnertus
Conconnetodumnus
Condarillus
Condercus
Congenno
Congonetiacus, Congon-
 netiacus
Conteddius
Contesilo, Contessilo
Contoutos, Cotutus
Convictolitavis
Corbagni
Corio, Coro
Cornutos
Corobus
Coteus, Cottio, Cottius,
 Cotto, Cotius, Cottus,
 Cotus, Cotis
Cotillus, Cotilius, Coti-
 lus, Cottalus, Cottilus
Cottro
Couertomotul, Coverto-
 motul
Covirius, Covirus
Criciro, Criciru, Crigiru,
 Cricirus
Cunegni, Cunigni
Cunovicodu
Curcagni, Curcagnus
Dacotoutus
Dagillus
Dagobius
Dagomarus
Dalagni
Dannonus
Dano
Dattovir
Deoratus
Dercillus, Dercillos
Deuus, Devus, Divos
Diddignatus
Diocaitus
Diorix
Divicatus, Diuicatus
Dobagni, Dovagni
Doninas
Donnadu, Donnedo
Donnius, Donnus
Donnotaurus

Drutalus
Dubnotalus
Dubnovellaunos, Dum-
 novellaunos, Dubno-
 vellaun, Dumnobel-
 launus
Ebicatos
Ebredus
Eburianus
Eburio, Eburius, Eburo
Elusco, Elusconos
Endouellicus, Endovelli-
 cus
Epacus
Epasius
*Epatus
Epetinus
Epo, Epos, Eppo
Epomeduos
Epotsorouidus, Epot-
 siorouidus
Eqqegni
Ercaviccas
Escengolatis
Escincos
Esumagius
Excingillius, Excingillus
Excingomarus
Exscincius
Exsomnus
Gabrius, Gabrus
Genetlus, Genillus, Gen-
 nalo
Giragni
Gnatusius
Grimiggni
Haesus
Iantasio
Iantinus, Iatinius, Ienti-
 nus
Iantumalius
Iantumar, Iantumarus
Iccalus
Iccinus, Iccnus
Icomius
Ientius
Iliatus
Illiomarus
Indercillus
Iotobito
Isarnouallanos

Itavus
Itosius
Itotagi
Lanianus
Laniogaisus
Leucamulo
Licnos, Licnus, Licno
Litauus, Litauis, Litavis
Litugenus, Litogenes,
    Litugenius
Litugius
Lituriri
Losagni
Lucterius
Lugetus
Lugius
Lugurix
Macareus, Macarius,
    Maccarus
Maccis
Magiacos
Maglagni
Magurio, Magurius
Mailagni
Malucnus
Mando
Maritalus, Martalos
Martilinus
Martoualus, Mertoualus
Meddignatius, Meddug-
    natus
Megaravico
Melmandus
Mesillus, Messillus
Metilius, Metillius
Miletumarus
Moddagni
Nantonos
Nertomaros
Netacari
Nisigni
Oclicno, Oclicnos
Ollocnus, Ollognus
Onalisus
Oppianicnos
Perrius, Perrus, Perus
Peruincus
Qasigni
Qenilocgni
Regenos, Reginus, Regi-
    nius, Rigenus, Rigeninus

Remico, Remicus
Reovalis
Reticius, Reticus
Retomarus
Rextugenos
Rigalis
Ripcicnus
Ritogenus
Rittuvvecc, Rituvvecas
Rovicus
Sacrovir, Sacrovirus
Sagillius, Sagillus
Samaconius
Samalus
Samis, Samius, Sammus,
    Samus, Sammus, Sam-
    mio, Samio, Sammo,
    Samo
Samoccnus, Samogenus,
    Samocinus
Samognatius
Sancotalus
Scilagni
Segolatius
Segomaros
Senicios, Senecio,
    Senecius
Senocarus, Senucaris
Scnovir
Silanus
Smertulitanus
Sollovico, Sollouico
Suadinus
Suadugenus
Suadutto
Suratus
Talagni
Talavus
Talius, Talis, Tallius, Tal-
    lus
Tallutius, Talotius, Talu-
    tius
Talussanus
Tanco
Tanotalos
Tarbunus
Taruiacus
Tarusius
Tascius, Tascus
Tasgetius, Tasgetios
Tauratis

Tauri, Taurio, Taurou
Taurocutius
Teutagonus
Teutomalius
Teutomus
Totavali
Toutio, Touto, Toutos,
    Toutus, Teuto
Toutobocios, Toutobocio
Trenaccatlo, Trenacatus
Tritos, Trito, Tritus, Triti
Trogimarus
Trouceteius
Tuticanius, Tuticanus
Ulcagni, Ulccagni
Urogenonertus
Valatonius
Valis, Vallius, Vallus
Vallio, Vallo, Vallus
Vebro, Vebru
Vecatus
Vecconius
Vecius
Vectimarius, Vectimarus
Vecto
Velagenus, Velagenius
Velenius
Velitas, Velitius
Vello
Velorius
Velugni, Velugnius,
    Veugnus
Vendogni, Vendagni
Venedius
Venextos
Venicarus, Venecarus,
    Vinicarus
Venixamus, Venixxamus
Vennonius, Vennenus
Venucius
Vepotalus
Veqreq
Vercatus
Vercombogius, Vercom-
    bogio, Vercombogus
Versicnos, Versignos
Verter
Verto, Vertos, Vertros
Veruecco, Veruico
Vicatus
Vicixtillus

Victi, Viction
Vindedo
Vindicatus
Vinovaleius
Viranus
Virato, Viratus
Viriacius, Viriaicus
Virianto
Viriatius, Viriatis
Virico, Virici, Viri
Viriodacus

Virisimi
Virlus
Virocantus
Vironianus
Virotalus
Virotutus
Vitousurix
Vlatcani
Vlatos
Vlatucnos, Vlatugni,
     Vlatucni

Vocagni
Vocarantus
Vocorix
Vogitoutus
Voltodaga
Vopiscus
Voretoviros, Voretouirius
Vosegus
Vridolanos
Vrittakos

IRANIAN

This includes Medes, Persians, and the Mitanni, with the occasional Sagartian, all of whom are speakers of Iranian dialects. Many names fall on a borderline between the three groups.

You are probably used to these in Hellenized forms. Yet between the records in the Persian cities and cuneiform documents, we can recover quite a bit of the original. As usual, there is a terrible dearth of female names in the record. In a pinch, you can carefully steal some of the male names.

You will notice the dominance and repetition of the roots "arta" (servant of) and "kshat" or "xshat" (kshatria = warrior). It is simply Iranian fashion. All you can do is spread them as thinly as possible. Take extra time introducing confusable characters, and give your readers both names together so they can see the difference.

Pronunciation

X marks the KS sound, though sometimes it is re-rendered K or KH. Č is TS. Vowels are as in Italian: A as in pasta, I as in machine, U as in tune, O as in pole, E as in prey. Nothing else is tricky.

FEMALE NAMES

Persian	*Greek*	*Biblical/Notes*
Amestri	Amestris	wife of Xerxes
Amytish	Amytis	
Apame		
Artakame	Artakama	daughter of Artabazus
Artazostra		
Artiante, Artaynte		

Persian	Greek	Biblical/Notes
Artystone		
Astartanikku		
Astera, Istera, Istar		Esther, Ester
Atossa		
Az		
Gashshuliyawie		
Iuni		
Kassadane		
Mandane		
Parasati, Parisatish	Parysatis	
Parmi	Parmys	
Raokshna	Roxana, Roxanna	
Sheherazade		
Shirin		
Spako		
Statira		
Vashti		

MALE NAMES

Persian	Greek; notes	Persian	Greek; notes
Agabshe		Artashshumara	remembering the Law
Agabtakha			
Akhli-Teshup, Akhlia		Artasirari	
Akhlibabu		Artatama	
Akhlibshara		Artavardiya	
Aki-Teshup		Artaxshahr	
Akikit-Teshup		Artaxshara	
Akkuya		Artaxshathra	Artaxerxes
Akparu		Arzaviya	
Aniri		Asali	
Ar-Teshshupa	Teshshup has given	Ashpabara	
		Ashpashtatauk	
Arashtu, Arashtua		Astivaegha	Astyages
Arastya		Athrina	
Arbaku		Bag-Teshup	
Ardara		Bagabuxsha	
Ardumanish		Bagadushta	
Argistu, Argistis		Bagavira	
Arioparna	Arioparnus	Bagdatti	
Ariyaramna		Bageshu	
Arpis		Baghush	
Arsames		Bahram	also Vahram, Varahran, Varanes
Arshaka, Arshakus	Arsacid		
Artaia, Artaya		Bara	
Artakhepa		Bardiya	Smerdis
Artakhshara		Bartacus	
Artamanya		Barziya	
Artamenia	Artamenus	Berezata	lofty one
Artaraeva		Berezaxwathra	lofty splendor
Artasari		Biridashva	

Persian	Greek; notes	Persian	Greek; notes
Čarshena		Khattushil	
Činshixrish		Khismia	
Čishpaish, Čishpais		Khosrau/Khusrau/	
Dadarshish		Khosru	
Dadarshu	bold	Khosru Nashirvan	
Dadii		Khshathraeshu	
Daduhya		Khshathrapavan	
Dalta		Khshathrita,	
Darayavaush,		Khasatritti	
Darayavahush	Darius	Khshayarsha	Xerxes
Data		Khu-Teshup	
Datana		Khubidi	
Dekharda		Kikia	
Dirnakush		Kobad	
Dudkhaliya		Kurush	Cyrus
Dugdammei		Mamanish	
Duioku		Mamitarshu	
Dushratta		Manushtana	
Erimina	Erimenas	Marduniya	Mardonius
Frada		Martia, Mariya	
Frahata		Martu	
Fravartish		Matra	
Gagu		Mattiuza	
Gal-Teshup		Mattivaza	
Gaubaruwa		Mavarzana	
Gaubruva		Mazdak, Mazdaka	
Gaumata		Mikki	
Gieshkhaaya		Mitaaki	
Gil-Teshup, Gilia		Mitatti	
Gushtasp		Mizdaeshu	
Habaki		Munsuartu	
Hakhamanish		Naditabira	
Haxamanish		Namyawaza	
Huvaxshatara		Nanyavaza	
Ik-Teshup		Narbattum	
Ikhli-Teshup		Nibe	
Imanish		Nubanani	
Iranzu, Iranzi		Ormizd, Hormizd	
Irruwabi		Parikhia	
Irtizati		Parmashta	
Ishpabara		Parshandatha	
Ishpaka	Aspakos	Parthama	
Ishteliku		Parukku	
Ishtesuku		Parumartish	Phraortes
Kambuzia,		Parushta	
Kambujhiya	Cambyses	Pauku	
Kashtariti		Perizadeh	
Kavadh		Pirishati	
Khanasiruka		Prada	
Khardukka		Ramatiya	

Persian	Greek; notes	Persian	Greek; notes
Ratta	chariot	Upu	
Rusas		Urik	
Ruzmanya		Urkhi-Teshup, Urkhiia	
Satiria		Ushpia, Aushpia	
Saushshatar		Utana	
Shabilish		Uvakhshatara	
Shapur		Uvarkhshatra	Cyaxares
Sharati		Uzumanda	
Sharuti		Vahauka	
Shatiya	faithful one	Vahyasdata	
Shaushshatar		Vaumisa	
Shishpish		Vayaspara	
Shubandi		Vidarna	
Shurkitilla		Vindaspa	
Shuta		Vishtaspa	
Shutarna, Shuttarna		Vivana	
Shutatna		Warezana	protection
Shuvardata		Wayaspara	
Sishshantakma,		Wifarna	
Citrantakhmam		Xoshak	
Spitama		Xshathra-aesha	
Tadua		Xshathrapavan	
Taishenni		Xshathravarzana	
Takuwa		Xshathrita	
Tayau		Xshayarsha	
Tekhibtilla		Xwathra	splendor
Tendi		Yashdata	
Teuvatti, Teuwatti		Yautarsh(i)	
Timtilla		Yazdegerd	
Titamashka		Zarishu	
Tugdamme		Zinzakrish, Sinsakrish	
Tuishratta		Zirdamyashda	
Tulubbi		Zishpish, Cishpish,	
Tunip-iwri		Cishpaish	
Tushratta			

SURNAMES, EKE-NAMES

Anushirvan — having an immortal soul

Gor — the wild ass

Parvez — the victorious

HELLENIC (ANCIENT GREEK)

As the translations of Linear B have shown, Hellenic names are pretty much the same from the Mycenaean period (1600 B.C.) through the Christian period.

Once the Eastern Empire is well established, "Christian" names and derivations from Latin are added to the Hellenic base, but this is the Hellenic base! It is only after the fall of the Empire to the Franks and Turks that many of the old names begin disappearing from common use.

The many important Greeks and Greek freedmen in the Roman Empire will use these. If they are slaves, they will put their Hellenic name after the possessive form of their owner's.

Hellenic names are also used throughout the Mideast during the Hellenistic period, when many people were adopting Hellenic culture and philosophy. This ranges from Hellenized Jews to the royal houses descended from the generals of Alexander.

Transliteration

You can transliterate Greek with or without K's. The K is more authentic for the letter *kappa*, but when the Romans transliterated from the Greek alphabet to their own, they changed all the kappas to cees. Since most Hellenic names were filtered through Latin texts, "Polynices" is the common form, but "Polynikes" looks more Hellenic, and will be pronounced correctly. The same applies to using CH instead of KH. You can use F instead of PH, but this substitution looks far more bizarre.

This change will throw the reader off visual stride if your story is set in Classical times, an effect you may desire, or that you prefer to avoid. It makes tales of Mycenaean times look rougher and more ancient.

However, if your Greeks are living in the Roman Empire, especially in Rome itself, you should use the Latinized, "common" versions with the C and "-us" intact.

Very Male World, Very Small Families

Everyone has a single, personal name. If there is some cause for confusion, a man will add a patronymic: "Timon Agathoklou" (Timon son of Agathokles); a place-name, "Timon Syrakusus" (Timon of Syracuse); or an eke-name: "Timon Poliorketes" (Timon Taker of Cities). Sometimes a person is better known by an eke-name or a nickname than their birth-name. As in our culture, a man formally named Edward may be known as Sonny, Buck, or Red.

Hellenes often consider themselves members of certain tribes or lineages, but *these do NOT appear as family names*. Only collectively might a group be referred to as Heracleidae, sons of Heracles, but no one would be called, say, "Polynikes Heraklidou" *unless* Polynikes' father were actually named Herakles. Note, direct God-names, like Heracles and Dionysos, were rare before the Roman period. There are many myths warning mortals against assuming the dignity of Gods. Perikles and Alkibiades were both Alkmaenidae, but these things are rarely mentioned and difficult for most people to discover. For your characters, it doesn't matter at all. Almost always, it is So-and-so, son of Hisname.

By Classical times (700 B.C.), the Hellenes have fallen into the custom of naming the first son after his father's father. So if these eldest sons live to grow up, there is a constant alternation of two names between the generations.

Women are so unimportant by this point of Athenian-Ionian culture — they are considered to be only warm decanters, the child being entirely the father's — that her family does not come into naming. So the second son would have a more original name, or a variation on his father's or grandfather's. The daughter often but not always would be given a name which was based on the first element of her father's: Hipponocus' daughter Hipparete, as example.

So Timaeus second son of Timarkhus could name his sons Timarkhus and Timon, and his daughter Timaea. It was apparently considered bad form to name a child after its parents. Readers tired of mixing their mail and calls with same-name parents will see the wisdom of this.

The baby is named by the tenth day after birth, in a solemn ritual becoming a member of the family. Any time before that, the father can decide to abandon it: in early periods on the hills outside the city, or later in a large pot at the temple. Customs of inheritance divide an estate equally between all surviving sons, so there was a strong tendency to only keep one or two, maximum three for a rich man. So only if one dies will a father allow a later boy-child a place in the family. Daughters are a drain of dowries by the Classic period (in the Mycenaean period they brought in bride-price), so that only a wealthy man or king can afford the luxury of two or more. It is exceedingly rare for a woman to have a sister. A later child does not use the name of a dead sibling.

Sons are necessary to offer sacrifice to the ancestors, so if a man finds himself aging without one, he will adopt, often a relative's second son. An expensive alternative to breeding, the son must usually be literally bought from his father's family. A poor man, or one without near relatives, often will adopt one of the anonymous infants abandoned by its own family — as in the legend of Oedipus. Otherwise, the children did perish.

Adoption involves no special naming procedures, unlike the Latins.

Re-gendering Names

The Classic Athenocentric Hellenes would approve of the old New England dictum that "a Lady" only appears in a newspaper three times in her life: birth, marriage, and death. Outside of myth, it is difficult to find women's names, though not as impossible as in some language groups. Fortunately there were hetairas and amazons.

Male names that end in "-os" can be made feminine by changing to "-is," and vice versa (Nereos, Nereis). Ditto "-on" to "-a" (Medeon, Medea); or "-us" to "-a" (Timaeus, Timaea).

Strange as it may seem to our Latin-trained ears, plain "-o" is a *feminine* ending (Callisto, Alecto). When sometimes it seems masculine, as in Plato, remember that common Greek names have come down through Latin and the Middle Ages, and that the philosopher was actually named Aristocles, and nicknamed Platon, "the broad one." Masculine "-o" names are corruptions of "-os" or "-on," sometimes even "-og." Many "-us" endings are Latin corruptions of "-os" names, like Agesilaus for Agesilaos, though on rare occasions it designates a "from this place" name, like Amphissus for someone from Amphissa. Equally, male names ending in "-e" should usually be "-es."

Masculine Endings	*Feminine Endings*	*Unisex Endings*
-on	-a	
-os	-is	-is
-es	-e	
-us	-a	
-as	-as	-as
-o		
-enes	-ene	
-anthus/thes	-anthe/this	
-andros	-andra	

A Warning Note

As always, check your period so that you do not have your fictional Athenian sculptor or Spartan warrior get confused with an actual one of the same name, with which your Graecophile reader is familiar. The index in Durant's *The Life of Greece* is very misleading because, being incomplete, it only refers to some of the names, not all, in the book. More thorough indices can be scanned quickly for this sort of unintentional conflict.

Greek Alphabet and Pronunciation

final E's are sounded, not silent
Alpha = A as in pasta
Beta = B as in bit
Gamma = G as in gun, never as in gin
Delta = D as in dot
Epsilon = E as in hey
Zeta = Z as in zero
Eta = E as in get
Theta = TH as in thin
Iota = I as in machine
Kappa = K as in keep
Lambda = L as in let

Mu = M as in met
Nu = N as in net
Ksi = X as in box, sounding ks at word beginning, not Z
Omicron = O as in hot
Pi = P as in pot
Rho = R as in rot
Sigma = S as in sun
Tau = T as in top
Upsilon = U as in up
Phi = PH as in phone; sometimes F
Chi = CH as in loch, not church or machine; KH better
Psi = PS; both sounds run together, not a silent P
Omega = O as in potato
asper = H as in hot

The common feminine ending "-oë" is pronounced [OH-eh].

Below are listed the proper spelling of names, followed by their common spelling and notes.

FEMALE NAMES

If many of these seem excessively warlike for damsels of Periclean Athens, they are traditional for Amazons, and Hellenic warrior-queens. They are also variations on their fathers' names.

Admete — Admeta; untamed
Adrastea — inescapable
Aegesta — pleasing goat
Aëllo — whirlwind
Aërope — sky face
Aethra — bright sky
Agaue — Agave; illustrious, noble, high born
Aglaia — brilliance; a Grace
Ainia — swiftness
Ainippe — swift mare
Akakia — acacia
Akanthe — acanthus
Alekto — Alecto; she who rests not; Fury
Aleris — from a city near the sea
Aletheia, Alethia — to be trusted
Alisia — possessive
Alkaia — mighty one
Alkandra — Alcandra; mighty man
Alkestis — Alcestis; might of the home
Alkibie — Alcibie
Alkinoë — Alcinoë; mighty wisdom

Alkippe — Alcippe; powerful mare
Alkithoë — Alcithoe; impetuous activity
Alkmene — Alcmene; mighty wrath
Alkyone — Alcyone; queen wards off storms
Althaea — boar
Althaia — healer
Alyssa — cure for madness
Amaranthe — unfading
Amaltheia — tender
Ambrosia — immortality
Amethystis — not intoxicated
Aminta — protected
Amymone — blameless
Amynomene — blameless defender
Anaea
Anaxarete — king's valor
Anaxilea
Anaxo — royal woman
Androdameia — subduer of men
Andromakhe — Andromache; man fighter
Andromeda — ruler of men

Annikeris — Anniceris
Antandra — preceding men
Antea
Anteia — precedence
Anthia — of the flowers
Antianara
Antianeira
Antibrote
Antigone — in place of a mother
Antiklea — Anticlea; false key
Antimakhe — Antimache; confronting warrior
Antiope — confronting face
Antiopeia — of the confronting face
Aoide — early Muse
Aphaea — the vanisher
Arakhidamia — Arachidamia
Arakhne — Arachne; spider; weaver
Areia — warlike
Arene — like a male warrior
Arete — excellence, virtue, valor
Arethusa — the waterer
Areto — unspeakable
Areximacha
Argea — bright one
Argeia — whitened
Ariadne — most pure
Arisbe — she travels best
Aristippe — best mare
Aristo — the best
Aristoklea — Aristoclea; best fame
Aristomakhe — Aristomache; best warrior
Arkhe — Arche; early Muse, ancient
Arkheanassa — Archeanassa
Arkhippe — Archippe; ancient horse
Arrhippe — best of mares
Arsinoë — male minded
Arsippe — she who raises her foot
Artemisia — of Artemis
Aspasia — welcome
Asteria — of the sun
Astraea — starry
Astydameia — tamer of cities
Atalante — Atalanta; unswaying
Athaliah
Atthis [AT-this]
Augea — bright ray
Autonoë — her own mind
Barkida
Baukis — Baucis

Berenike — Berenice; harbinger of victory
Beroë — bringing eggs
Beryllis — beryl, gem
Bilistikhe — Bilistiche
Bremusa — raging female
Briseis — she prevails
Britomartis — good maiden
Damalis — fair conqueror
Damaris — gentle as a lamb
Danae — she judges
Daphne — laurel
Deianira — Dejanira; strings together spoils
Deidameia — taker of spoils
Deinomakhe — Deinomache; terrible warrior
Delia — from Delos; title of Artemis
Demetria — of Demeter
Deone — queen of spoils
Derimakheia — Derimacheia
Derinoë
Desmis — a vow
Dia — bright
Dike — justice
Dione — divine queen
Dionysia — of Dionysus
Diosanthe — flower of Zeus
Diotima — honor of Zeus
Dirke — Dirce; double
Dolope — snare
Dorikha — Doricha
Dorinda — bountiful gift
Doris — bountiful
Dorkas — Dorcas; dark eyes, a gazelle
Dropis
Dryope — woodpecker
Dysdaimonia — unlucky
Earanthe — spring blossom
Eirene — peace
Ekhenais — Echenais; reinsholder
Ekhephyle — Echephyle; chief defender
Ekhidne — Echidna; she viper
Elais — of the olive
Elakate — distaff
Elektra — Electra; amber
Elodi — fragile flower
Elpinike — Elpinice
Enarete — virtuous
Ennea — ninth

Eos — dawn
Erato — Muse of erotic poetry; passionate
Erigone — child of strife
Erinna — angry
Eriobea — rich in cattle
Eriphyle — tribal strife
Erythra — crimson
Euadne — Evadne; little nymph
Euandra — Evandra; well-doing
Euandre — Evandre; good for men
Euania — child of peace
Euanthe — Evanthe; flowering
Eudaimonia — lucky, fortunate
Eudokia — Eudocia; of a brave father
Eudora — generous
Eukleia — good glory
Eukrateia — Eucrateia; good strength
Eulalia — speaking well
Eumakhe — Eumache; good warrior
Eunike — happy and victorious
Eunoë— good intelligence
Eunomia — good government
Euphemia — auspicious speech
Euphrosyne — Grace; good cheer
Eurybe — grand strength
Eurydike — Eurydice; great justice
Euryleia — woman wanderer
Euryleonis — of the great lion
Eurymede — wide cunning
Eurymone
Eurynome — wide wandering, wide ruling
Eurypyle — wide gate
Eurytia — widely honored
Euterpe — muse of lyric poetry; rejoicing well
Galanthis — weasel
Galateia — Galatea; milk-white
Glauke — Glauce; owl
Glykera — Glycera
Gnathaena
Hagne — pure one
Halimedes — thinking of the sea
Halkyone — Halcyone; sea-conceived; kingfisher
Harmonia — unifying
Harmothoë — sharp nail
Harpalyke — Harpalyce; ravening she-wolf
Hedea — sweet

Hekuba — Hecuba; moving far off
Helike — willow
Helle — bright
Heraklea — Heraclea; glory of Hera
Hermione — of the world
Hero — of Hera
Herpyllis
Hesione — queen of the East
Hesperia — evening star
Hesperidis — of the West
Hipparkhia — Hipparchia
Hippo — mare
Hippodameia — horse trainer
Hippodamia — horse tamer
Hippolyte — stampeding horse
Hippomache — mare warrior
Hipponoë— horse wisdom
Hippothoë— imperious mare
Hyagnis
Hyale — woodswoman
Hygeia — health
Hypate — Hypatia
Hypermnestra — excessive wooing
Hypsikratea — Hypsicratea; high strength
Hypsipyle — high gate
Ianthinis — violet-colored
Iaso — healer
Idole — lovely vision
Idyia
Ino — makes sinewy
Iolanthe — violet flower
Iole — Iola; dawn cloud; violet color
Iphemedia — of mighty mind
Iphianassa — mighty queen
Iphigenia — mother of might
Iphinoë— mighty intelligence
Iphito — mighty shield
Iris — Goddess of the rainbow
Ismene — knowledgeable
Kabira — Cabira
Kaenis — Caenis; renewed
Kaeria — Caeria
Kalandra — Calandra; like the lark
Kalanthe — Calanthe; beautiful blossom
Kalliope — Calliope; Muse of epic poetry; fair face
Kallipateira
Kallirhoë— Callirhoe; fair flowing
Kallisto — Callisto; most lovely

Kalypso — Calypso; concealer
Kanake — Canace
Kassandra — Cassandra; entangling men
Kassiopeia — Cassiopeia
Kastalia — Castalia
Kelaeno — Celaeno; swarthy
Keto — Ceto; whale
Khariklea — Chariclea; graceful fame
Kharis — Charis; grace
Kharope — Charope; brilliant confrontation
Khelidonis — Chelidonis
Khibonis — Chibonis
Khilonis — Chilonis
Khione — Chione; snowqueen
Khlidanope — Chlidanope; delicate face
Khloe — Chloe; young, verdant; Goddess of green grain
Khloris — Chloris; pale, greenish
Khryseis — Chryseis; golden
Kinara — Cynara; daughter of the moon, thistle, artichoke
Kleianthe — Cleianthe; glory-blossom
Kleio — Cleio; proclaimer; Muse of history
Kleis — Cleis; famous
Klematis — Clematis; vine, brush-wood
Kleobuline — Cleobuline; famous counsel
Kleodike — Cleodice; famous justice
Kleonike — Cleonica; famous victory
Kleopatra — Cleopatra; a famous father
Kleoptoleme — famous war
Klete, Kleite — Clete, Cleite; re-knowned
Klio — Clio; Muse of history
Klonie — Clonie
Klymene — Clymene; famous might
Klyte — Clyte; famous
Klytemnestra — Clytemnestra, Clytaemnestra; famed wooing
Klytia — Clytia; splendid
Korinna — Corinna; maiden
Koronis — Coronis; crown; crow
Kreousa — sovereign being
Kresida/Hrisoula — Cressida; golden
Kreusa — Creusa; sovereign being

Krokale — Crocale
Kupriania — Cupriania; of Cyprus; title of Aphrodite
Kydippe — Cydippe; glorious horse
Kydoime
Kymothoë — Cymothoë
Kynane — Cynane
Kynisca — Cynisca; she-pup
Kynosura — Cynosura; dog's tail
Kynthia — Cynthia; of Mt. Kynthos; title of Artemis
Kyrene — Cyrene; mistress of the bride
Kytheris — Cytheris; of the harp
Laena
Lais — adored
Lalage — cheerful speaker
Lalita — candid
Lampedo — burning torch
Lampetia — brightness of the year
Laodamia — tamer of people
Laodike — Laodice; people's justice
Laodoke
Leontis
Leukippe — Leucippe; white mare
Leukothea — Leucothea; white goddess
Lotis — lotus
Lotosanthe — lotus blossom
Lykopis — she-wolf
Lysandra — liberating men
Lysippe — loosing the horses
Marpe — to snatch
Marpesia — one who snatches
Matanira — lives among maidens
Medea — ruling one
Megaera — Fury; grudge
Megalostrata — great army
Megara — oracular cave
Meilikhis — Meilichis; gentle
Melanippe — black mare
Melanis — dark or black; title of Demeter
Melanthis — dark flower
Melete — early Muse
Meliboëa — sweet cattle
Melissa — honey; a bee
Melita — attention
Melousa — sweet being
Melpomene — Muse of tragedy
Merope — eloquent

Messene
Metaneira — skill for stringing together
Metis — skill
Milto
Mimnousa
Mintha — mint plant
Mirias — abundance
Mneme — early Muse; mindful
Molione — queen of warriors
Molpadia — death song
Myrrhine — myrrh
Myrtis — myrtle
Nakaria — Nacaria
Nanno
Nausikaa — Nausicaa — burner of ships
Neaera
Neis — youthful
Neomenia — light of the new moon
Nephele — cloud
Nereis — swimmer; sea nymph
Neysa — pure
Nikaea — Nicaea; victorious
Nikarete — Nicarete; triumphant valor
Nikia — Nicia; triumphant
Nikostrate — Nicostrate; conquering army
Niobe — snowy
Nipha — snowflake
Nyssa — starting point
Nyx — night
Oenone — queen of wine
Okyale
Okypete — Ocypete; Erinye; swift wing
Olympias — from Olympia
Omphale — navel
Onyx — onyx
Ophis — serpent
Orea — of the mountain
Orithia, Orithya, Oreithyia — raging in the mountains
Otrera — nimble
Ourania — heavenly, of Uranus
Palaemona — wrestler
Pallas — maiden or youth; title of Athena
Panakea — Panacea; heals all
Pantariste — best of all

Panthea — all Gods
Parthenea — sweet virgin
Parthenope — virgin face
Pega — joined together
Pelopia — muddy face
Penelope — worker of the web
Penthea — fifth child
Penthesilea — compelling men to mourn
Periboea — surrounded by cattle
Persis — of peace; Persian
Phaedra — bright one
Phaethusa — shining being
Phaidra — brightness
Phersephone — Persephone; bringing destruction
Phersephonia — of Persephone
Philandra — loving mankind
Philanthis — loving flowers
Philida — loving
Philippis — loving horses
Philomela — nightingale
Philomene — loving the moon
Philyra
Phoebe — radiant
Phosphora — light bearer
Phosphoria — of the morning star
Phryne
Phyla
Phyllis — green branch
Physkoa — Physcoa
Pisto
Plakia — Placia
Plusia
Polemusa
Polydamna
Polymnia — Muse of hymns
Polyxena — many guests
Polyxo — itchy
Praxagora
Praxithea — active goddess
Prokne — Procne
Prokris — Procris; preference
Pronoë — thinking ahead
Prothoë — first in might
Psappha — poet Sappho
Pyrgomakhe — Pyrgomache; fiery warrior
Pyrrha — fiery red
Pythia — of the Python
Pythodoris — gift of the Python

Rhodanthe — rose blossom
Rhoeo — pomegranate
Rhu — rue-herb
Selene — Moon Goddess; moon
Semele — mother of Dionysios; moon
Sida — water-lily
Simaetha
Siphis — sword
Skyleia — Scyleia; of the Render
Skylla — Scylla; she who rends
Smaragdis — emerald
Sterope — lightning
Sthenaboea — strength of cattle
Stratonike — Stratonice; army victory
Strymo — harsh
Symaethis
Synoppe
Tecmessa — ordainer
Teisipyle
Telepyleia — far-sailing
Telesilla — far-jeering
Terpandra — delighting men
Terpsichore — Muse of choral music
    and dance; rejoicing in dance
Thais — giving joy
Thalassa — from the sea
Thalestris
Thalia, Thaleia — blooming; Muse
    of idyllic poetry
Thargelia
Thea — divine
Theano — Goddess
Theia — divine
Thekla — Thecla; divine fame
Thele — a nursling
Thelxinoe — early Muse
Themis — Goddess of justice and
    order

Themisto — oracular
Theone — of the Gods
Theonoe — divine intelligence
Theora — watcher
Theoris
Thera — hunter
Therisa — reaper
Thessalonika — Thessalonica
Thetis — determined, destroyer
Thisbe
Thoösa — impetuous being
Thraso — confidence
Thymele — raging
Timaea — honor
Timandra — honored by men
Timoklea — Timoclea; famous honor
Tisiphone — vengeful destruction
Toxaris — archer
Toxis — arrow
Toxophile — loving archery
Trypheena — luxurious
Tryphosa
Urania — Muse of astronomy; heav-
    enly
Ursa — she-bear
Xanthe — yellow
Xanthippe — yellow mare
Xantho — yellow
Xenia — hospitable
Xylia
Xylina
Zarina
Zephrytis — of Zephyr
Zerynthia
Zetha — seeker
Zeuxo — yoke
Zoë — life
Zosima — woman of wealth

MALE NAMES

Admetos — Admetus; untamed
Adrastos — Adrastus; stands his ground
Aegeos — Aegeus; goatish
Aeskhrion — Aeschrion
Aeson — pos. ruler
Agamedes — very cunning
Agathon

Agenor — very manly
Agrios — Agrius — wild
Aias — Ajax; eagle
Aketes — Acetes
Akhates — Achates; agate
Akrisios — Acrisius; ill judgement
Alexandros — Alexander; helping men

Alkmaeon — Alcmaeon; mighty endeavor

Alphenor — white man

Ambrotos — Ambrose; divine, immortal

Amphion [am-FEE-on] — of two lands

Ampyx

Amyntas — popular in Macedonia; defender

Anakreon — Anacreon

Anaximenes — kingly strength

Andriskos [an-DRIS-kus] — Andriscus; little man

Androtion

Ankaeus — Ancaeus; mighty one

Antenor — instead of a man

Antilokhos — Antilochus; ambush against

Antisthenes — against strength

Apelles

Aphareos — Aphareus; without clothes

Apollonios — of Apollo

Aratos — Aratus

Arion — lofty one

Aristeas — the best

Aristippos — Aristippus; best horse

Aristogiton

Aristomenes — best strength

Aristophon — best sound

Arkhidamos — Archidamus; ancient tamer

Artemas — from Artemis

Athamas — reaper on high

Athenaeos — Athenaeus; from Athena

Athenodoros — Athenodorus; gift of Athena

Autolykos — Autolycus; his own wolf

Bakkhylides — Bacchylides

Baltasaros — protect the king

Bathykles — Bathycles; deep fame

Battos — Battus; tongue-tied

Belos — Belus; lord

Bion — forceful one

Biton — bison, wild ox

Boethus — herdsman

Briareos — Briareus; strong

Briseos — Briseus; he prevails

Bryaxis

Bupalos — Bupalus

Damon — subduer

Damophon — subduing noise

Danaos — Danaus; judge

Deinarkhos — Dinarchus, Deinarchus; ancient terror

Deinokrates — Deinocrates; terrible power

Deioneus — son of the queen of spoils

Deiphobos — Deiphobus; scaring the despoiler

Delphis — of Delphi

Demaratos — Demaratus

Demas — popular

Demetrios — Demetrius; of Demeter

Demodokos — Demodocus

Demokritos — Democritus; people

Demophilos — Demophilus; loved by people

Demos — of the people

Demosthenes — people strong

Didymos — Didymus

Diktys — Dictys; net

Diodoros — Diodorus; gift of Zeus

Diomedes — god-like cunning

Dionysios — Dionysius; of Dionysos

Diphilos — Diphilus

Dorios — from the sea

Doron — gift

Doros — Dorus; gift

Drakon — Dracon

Dropos — Dropus

Enkelados — Enceladus

Ephialtes — leaps upon

Ephoros — Ephorus

Epikharmas — Epicharmas

Epopeos — Epopeus

Erasmios — worthy of love

Eteokles — Eteocles; true glory

Euagoras — Evagoras; good of the marketplace

Euandros — Evander; well-doing

Eubulos — Eubulus; good counsel

Eudamidas

Eudoxos — Eudoxus; of good repute

Euhemeros — Euhemerus; good day

Eukrates — Eucrates; good power

Eulalos — well-spoken

Eumenes — good might

Eumolpos — Eumolpus; good song

Eunomos — Eunomus; of good name

Eupolis — good of the city

Euryalos — Euryalus; wide wanderer

Eurylokhos — Eurylochus; wide ambush

Eurymakhos — Eurymachus; wide battle
Eurymedon — wide ruler
Eurystheos — Eurystheus; widely forcing back
Eurytion; widely honored
Eutykhedes — Eutychedes
Gelastikos — prone to laughter
Gelon — laughter
Geminos — Geminus
Geranion — crane
Glaukos — Glaucus; grey-green
Glykon — Glycon
Gorgias — grim
Gylippos — Gylippus
Haemon — making bloody
Halimedes — thinking of the sea
Hamon — faithful
Hegesinos — Hegesinus
Hegias — master
Heliodoros — Heliodorus; gift of Helios
Hephaestion — one of Hephaestos
Heraklitos, Herakleitos — Heraclitus, Heracleitus; Hera's fame
Hermeias, Hermias — of Hermes
Hermogenes — born of Hermes
Herondas, Herodas
Herostratos — Herostratus
Hesperos — evening star
Hieron — sacred
Hikesias — Hicesias
Hipparkhos — Hipparchus; horse ancient
Hippolytes — Hippolytus; dragged by horses
Hippomedon — horse ruler
Hipponax — horse king
Hipponikos — Hipponicus; horse victory
Hipponoös — Hipponous; horse wisdom
Hylaeos — Hylaeus; of the wood
Hymaenaeos — Hymaenaeus
Hyperides
Hyrieos — Hyrieus; of the bee hives
Hyrtakos — Hyrtacus
Iadmon
Ianthinos — violet-colored flower
Iasios — Iasius; healer
Iason — Jason; healer
Ibykos — Ibycus

Idaeos — Idaeus; of the wooded mountain
Idas — of Mt. Ida
Ikaros — Icarus; Icarian
Ikelos — Icelos
Ilioneos — Ilioneus; son of queen of Ilium
Ilos — Ilus; troop
Iobates — goes with the moon
Iolaos — violet gem
Ion — native
Iphikrates — Iphicrates; mighty strength
Iphis — mighty
Iphitis — shield might
Isaeos — Isaeus
Isagoras
Iseas
Iskhys — Ischys; strength
Isokrates — Isocrates; equal strength
Ister
Itys — willow
Ixion — strong native
Kaekulos — Caeculos
Kalkhas — Calchas
Kallias — Callias; excellent
Kallikrates — Callicrates; excellent power
Kallimedon — Callimedon; the crab
Kallipos — Callipus; beautiful feet
Kallistratos — Callistratus; beautiful army
Kalos — beautiful
Kapaneos — Capaneus
Kebes — Cebes
Kedalion — takes charge of sailors
Keleos — Celeus; flaming, burning
Keyx — Ceyx; sea-mew
Khabrias — Chabrias
Khaeremon — Chaeremon
Kharaxos — Charaxus
Khariton — Chariton
Kharondas — Charondas
Kheladon — Cheladon; the swallow
Khersiphron — Chersiphron
Kimon — Cimon
Kineas — Cineas
Klearkhos — Clearchus; famous ancient
Kleidemos — Cleidemus; fame of the people
Kleisthenes, Klisthenes — Cleisthenes, Clisthenes; famous strength
Kleobis — Cleobis; famous life

Kleombrotos — Cleombrotus
Kleomenes — Cleomenes; famous might
Kleon — Cleon; glory, fame
Korax — Corax
Korydon — Corydon; helmented; with a crest
Krantor — Crantor
Kratippos — Cratippus; strong horse
Kratylos — Cratylus
Kritios — Critius
Ktesias — Ctesias, Ctesibius, Ctesiphon; possessor
Ktesiphon — Ctesiphon
Kylon — Cylon
Labdakos — Labdacus; help of torches
Lampros — Lamprus
Laomedon — people ruler
Lapithes
Leandros — Leander
Learkhos — Learchus; ruler of the people
Leokhares — Leochares; lion grace
Leokrates — Leocrates; lion power
Leonidas
Leonnatos — Leonnatus
Leotykhides — Leotychides
Leukippos — Leucippus; white horse
Likhas — Lichas; sheer cliff
Linos — Linus; flaxen thread
Lydiadas
Lykidas — Lycidas
Lykomedes — Lycomedes; wolf thought
Lykophron — Lycophron
Lykos — Lycus; wolf
Lykurgos — Lycurgus; wolf work
Lynkeos — Lynceus; lynx
Lysandros — Lysander; liberator of men
Lysanias
Lysias — liberty
Lysikles — Lysicles; loosing fame
Lysikrates — Lysicrates; liberating power
Lysippos — Lysippus; looses the horses
Makhanidas — Machanidas
Makhaon — Machaon; lancet
Megakles — Megacles; great fame
Megas — great, mighty
Meilanion
Melampos — Melampus; black foot
Melanthes — Melanthus; dark blossom
Melas — black
Meleagor — Meleager; guinea hen

Meleanthios — Meleanthius
Melikertes — Melicertes; sweet power
Melisseos — Melisseus; honey-man
Melissos — Melissus; honey; a bee
Menedemos — Menedemus; mighty people
Menippos — Menippus; might horse
Menoekeos — Menoeceus; strength of the house
Menos — force, purpose
Mesomedes — in the midst of thought
Milon — Milo
Miltiades
Mimnermos — Mimnermus
Mnesikles — Mnesicles
Mnesitheos — Mnesitheus; thinking of God
Moskhos   Moschus
Musaeos — Musaeus; of the Muses
Myron — fragrant oil
Myrtilos — Myrtilus
Nabis
Naucydes
Nauplios — Nauplius
Nausithoös — Nausithous
Nearkhos — Nearchus
Nemos — from the glade
Neseas
Nesiotes
Nestor — traveller; one who leaves
Nikandros — Nicander; victory over men
Nikanor — Nicanor; victorious man
Nikias — Nicias; victorious
Nikolaos — Nicolaus; victorious people
Nikomakhos — Nicomachus; victory in battle
Nikomedes — Nicomedes; victorious cunning
Nikostratos — Nicostratus; victorious army
Nikoteles — perfect victory
Nisos — Nisus; brightness
Obelos — pointed pillar
Oeneaos — Oeneaus; wine man
Oeneos — Oeneus; wine man
Oenomaos — Oenomaus; whim of wine
Oenopides
Oenopion — wine in plenty
Oinopides
Onomakritos — Onomacritus

Onosandros — Onosander
Ophelimos — useful
Ophelos — help
Opheltes
Ophion — native snake
Oreias — Orestes; mountaineer
Orion — son of fire or light
Otos — Otus; keen ear
Pammon — full moon
Pamphilos — Pamphilus
Panthes — Panthus
Parmenides
Pausias
Peleos — Peleus; muddy
Pentheos — Pentheus; grief
Perdiccas — popular in Macedonia;
   partridge
Periandros — Periander; surrounded
   by men
Persaeos — Persaeus; destroyer
Phaedon — Phaedo; shining one
Phanodemos — Phanodemus; peo-
   ple's torch
Phaon
Phegeos — Phegeus
Pheidon — merciful
Philemon — loving one
Philippos — loving horses; popular in
   Macedonia
Philolaos — Philolaus; loving people
Philomelos — loving music
Philon — loving
Phokion — Phocion; of the seals
Phorbas — fearful
Phrixos, Phryxos — Phrixus, Phryxus
Phthisis
Pleisthenes — sailing strength
Pleuron
Plexippos — Plexippus; braided horse-
   hair
Polemon
Polydoros — Polydorus; many gifts
Polyeuktes — Polyeuctes
Polymnestor — thinking of many
Posidonios — Posidonius; of Posidon
Pratinas
Prokles — Procles; challenger
Protogenes — born ahead
Proxenos — Proxenus
Pylades — gate of Hades
Pyrrhon — Pyrrho; fiery red

Pytheas
Rhadamanthes — Rhadamanthus;
   divines with rods
Rhoekos — Rhoecus
Salmoneos — Salmoneus
Sarpedon — rejoicing in a wooden chest
Seleukos — Seleucus
Simonides
Sinon — plunderer
Skopas — Scopas
Solon — egg-shaped weight
Speusippos — Speusippus
Spintharos — Spintharus
Sthenelos — Sthenelus; forcing back
   strongly
Stilpon — Stilpo
Strepsiades
Strophios — Strophius; twisted head-
   band
Talaos — Talaus; suffering
Telegonos — Telegonus; last-born
Temenos — Temenus; of the sacred
   enclosure
Tereos — Tereus; guardian
Tessares — fourth child
Thaddaios — Thaddeus; courageous
Theognis
Theokritos — Theocritus
Theoron — watcher
Theramenes — animal strength
Therison — reaper
Theron — hunter
Theskelos — Thescelus
Thestios — Thestius; devotee of the
   Goddess
Thrasyllos — Thrasyllus
Thyestes — pestle
Thyreos — shield-bearer
Timanthes — blossoming honor
Timarkhos — Timarchus; ancient honor
Timoleon — honorable lion
Timotheos — Timotheus; honored by
   God
Timun, Timon — honor
Tisias — vengeance
Troilos — Troilus
Trophonios — Trophonius; increaser
   of sales
Tydeos — Tydeus
Tyrtaeos — Tyrtaeus
Urian — greatest star

Xanthippos — Xanthippus; yellow horse
Xanthos — yellow
Xenokles — Xenocles; famous guest
Xenokrates — Xenocrates; stranger's power
Xenophanes — stranger appearing
Xenophon — guest's noise
Xenos — stranger; guest
Xuthos — Xuthus; sparrow
Xylon — from the forest
Zaleukos — Zaleucos

Zelotes — zealous
Zenas — of Zeus, living
Zenbios — life from Zeus
Zenon — Zeno; life from Zeus
Zetes — searcher
Zethos — Zethus; seeker
Zeuxidamus — chariot master
Zeuxippos — Zeuxippus; yokes horses
Zeuxis — of the yoke
Zoilos — Zoilus

A FEW EKE-NAMES

Alastor — Avenger
Dyskkolus — Dysccolus; the Crabbed
Euergetes — Well-Doer
Euphranor — Joyous
Kobalos — impudent rogue
Nikator — Nicator; Victor

Pedanius — the teacher
Philadelphus — Loving His Brothers
Philopater — Loving His Father
Physicus — the physicist
Soter — Savior
Theos — God

HEBREW

In your Biblical epic, you have to make a decision: to use the modernized form with which most people are familiar — John, Abel, Elizabeth — or to use the actual ones of the period — Yehokhanan, Heb-hel, Elisheba. Of course, the first is the modernized English form. If you get foreign-language sales in translation, John becomes Johan or Giovanni or Juan. But if you use the originals, they at least stay put.

No matter which way you decide, the listings below are in original form alphabetical order, with the English equivalents to the right, if there is any difference. Note that many call on pagan Gods and Goddesses. The prophets *were* always complaining about pagan Israelites.

There are no family names. A man is "Someone son of Somebody," or "Someone the Merchant" or "Someone of Thatplace." The son-word is *bin* — Yehonathan bin-Uzziyel. "Benjamin" was Binyamin, meaning "son of my right hand"; but *ben* as the son-word gives a distinctly post–Diaspora, Christian Empire/Medieval feel to the name. *Bar* as the son-word is Aramaic and Greek. In Islamic lands, the Jews came to use *ibn*, same as their Moslem neighbors. The only daughter-word is *bat*. So "Judith daughter of Job" is properly Yuhudith bat-Iyyohb.

The Hebrew "of" word is *ha-*, used both for place-of-origin names and for tribal names, like Adham ha-Lewi, Adam the Levite. Also, ha- introduces eke-names, like ha-Kadosh, "the holy one" or ha-Nasi, "the prince."

Names are not gendered. A small number have been used for both men and women in the Bible, but once it becomes attached to a famous person, their gender may determine the name's use thereafter.

Yet everything else in the language is gendered, so there should be no gender slips, unless the speaker is a foreigner having difficulty with the language, in which case you should write the dialogue as stumbling and spotty. For example, the masculine plural ends in "-im" (as in seraphim, cherubim), the feminine plural in "-ot."

In Old Testament times, check the Mesopotamian listings to find out what Nebuchadnezzar and Shalmanaser were really called — those are Hebraicizations of the Babylonian or Assyrian, like James is an Anglicization of Ya'aqob. Also, some characters should have Phoenician/Canaanitic names: Jezebel is probably Hebraicized from Yahaz-Ba'al, "May Ba'al gaze upon the child."

Don't assume you can carry all the names in the New Testament back to older times. The Jews had abandoned Hebrew except for liturgical purposes, and had as everyday language either Aramaic or Greek. The name of Dorcas, the woman raised from the dead by St. Peter, is Greek, for example. You cannot use it for Jews before the time of Alexander the Great, if that early. Ditto for "Timothy" from Timotheos. "Martha" is specifically Aramaic, but can be used after the return from exile, say 400 B.C.

Especially be careful not to use Greek-derived names for resistance fighters against the forcible Hellinization laws, just because their neighbors are using them.

The names below are first listed by Hebrew, then English translations followed by notes or meanings.

FEMALE NAMES

Aberah — Avera
Abi — my father; short for something
Abigayil, Abigal — Abigail; my father rejoices
Abihail — unisex
Abishag — my father is a wanderer
Abital — my father is dew
Adah — ornament
Agiah
Ahinoam — my brother is comfort
Ahlai — unisex; protected
Akhsah — Achsah
Amaryah — Amaris; promised by Yahu
Asenath
Atarah — crown
Athaleyah — Athalia, Athaliah; Yahu is exalted
Azubah — unknown
Baara
Basemath
Bat-sheba — daughter of the oath
Bat-shua — daughter of Shua
Beulah — married
Bilhah
Bithia
Deborah — bee

Delilah — languishing; gentle
Dinah — judged
'Ednah — Edna; rejuvenation
Eglah
Elisheba — Elizabeth: my Lord is my word
Eprathah — Ephrathah
Gomer
Hadassah — myrtle
Hagar, Haghar — forsaken
Haggith — festive; Punic
Hammolecheth
Hamutal
Hazzelelponi
Helah
Hephzibah — my delight is in her
Hodesh — new moon; Punic
Hoglah
Huldah — mole
Hushim
Iskah
Keren-happuch
Keziah
Khannah — Hannah; favor; Aramaic: Anna
Khavva, Hawwa — Eve

Kozbi
Leah — wild cow
Lebhanah — Lewanna, Luanna; beaming, white; the moon
Maacah
Mahalah — Mahalia; tenderness
Mahalath — tenderness
Mahlah — tender
Marah
Martha — Aramaic; lady; mistress
Matred
Meheytabel — Mehitabel, Mehetabel; benefited by El
Merab — increase
Meshullemeth — preserved; Assyrian
Michal — who is like El?
Milkah — from Milk (Phoenician God)
Miryam — Miriam, Mary; beloved of Amun
Naamah
Naarah
Nehushta
Noadiah
Noah — you might spell it Noa; rest
Noomi — Naomi; pleasantness
Oholibamah
Orpah — a fawn
Peninnah — coral
Qeturah — Ketura, Keturah; incense
Rahablah — Rahab, Yahu name
Rakhel — Rachel; ewe
Reumah
Rhoda — Aramaic; rose
Ribqah — Rebecca, Rebekah; noose
Rizpah — hot stone
Ruth — companion; compassionate
Salome — late period; peace
Sapphira — Aramaic; good, beautiful
Sarai — Sara; quarrelsome
Serah, Sarah — princess

Seruyah — Zeruiah
Sharai — of the king; Babylonian
Sheerah
Shelomith — peaceful; Punic
Shemariyah — Samara
Shimeath
Shimrith — of hearing; Punic
Shiphrah — judgement; Punic
Shoshannah — Susannah; lily
Shua
Shulammite — peaceful; Punic
Tabitha — Aramaic; gazelle
Tamar — Tamar, Tamara; date palm
Taphath
Tema — Tammy
Timna
Tirzah — Thirza; pleasantness
Uzziye — Ozora; my strength is Yahu
Yael — Jael; live in El; Punic
Yedidah — Jedidah; friendly
Yehoaddin — Jehoaddin
Yehoshabeath — Jehoshabeath
Yehosheba — Jehosheba
Yehudith — Judith; praised
Yekoliah — Jecoliah
Yemimah — Jemimah; a dove
Yerioth — Jerioth
Yerusha — Jerusha; possessed
Yokhebed — Jochebed
Zarah — Zara; blossom
Zebidah
Zemiah
Zera'im — Zera; seeds
Zeresh — seed is planted; Ass. Bab.
Zeruah — seed of Yahu
Zeruiah — my seed is Yahu
Zibiah
Zillah — shadow
Zilpah — dignity
Zipporah — sparrow, swallow

The following female names are not Biblical, but from later Kabbalistic sources.

Adinah — voluptuous
Agrath — beating
Batna
Eisheth
Hurmiz
Iggereth
Ita
Kea

Lilidtha — little Lilith
Lilith
Makhlath, Mahalath, Mahlet
Masket
Meshullahel — messenger of God
Meyalleleth — the howling one
Nega
Obizuth

Ornias
Partasah

Satrina
Zenumim

MALE NAMES

Abdon — Abdon; father is master
Abhner — Abner: father is light
Abiathar — my father is Atar
Abihu — my father is my brother
Abimelekh — Abimelech; my father is counsel
Abinadab — my father is noble; Punic
Abishai — my father is my deliverance; Punic
Abiyah — Abijah, Abijam; my father is Yahu
Abiyel — Abiel; my father is El
Abraham — father of multitudes
Abram — father is lofty
Abshalom — Absalom, Absolam; father is peace
Adham — Adam; red earth
Adlai — my ornament
Adonaiyah, Adoniyah — Adonaijah, Adonijah; my Lord is Yahu
Adoni-zedek — Adonizedek; Adonis vindicates; Punic
Adoniram — Adoniram, Adoram, Hadoram; Adonis is lofty
Adriyel — Adriel; one of El's
Ahab — brother is father
Aharon — Aaron; lofty, exalted
Ahiram — Hiram, Phoenician; my brother is lofty
Akhan — Achan, Achar; troubler
Akhaz — Ahaz; brother is help
Akhazya — Ahaziah; brother helping is Yahu
Akhikam — Ahikam
Akhimaaz — Ahimaaz: my brothers are help
Akhimelekh — Ahimelech; my brother is counsel
Akhish
Akhitopel — Ahithophel [hith], Achitophel (khit); my brother is El's goodness
Akhitub — Ahitub; my brother is good
Akhiyah — Ahijah; my brother is Yahu
Akiba

Alvah — exalted
Amariyah — Amariah; my promise is Yahu
Amasa — bearer of burdens
Amasyahu — Amaziah; Yahu bears my burdens
Aminadab — my Mother is noble
Amittai — my Mother brings joy
Amnon
Amon — from Egyptian God
Amos, Amoz — Ahmose; Egyptian
Amram — Mother is lofty
Amrapel — Amraphel, Babylonian; a bull calf is the heir
Anaq — Anak, Canaanite; necklace
Arba — Canaanite; ?dim. Arbela name
Arika — ?forecast, judgement
Ariyel — Ariel; lion of El
Armoni
Arvad
Asa — given
Asael — Asahel; given by El
Asap — Asaph
Aser — Asher; from the God Ashur or Goddess Asherah
Ashi
Azariyah — Ezra; our help is Yahu
Azaziyah — Azaziah; my helper is Yahu
Aziyel — Aziel; helped by El
Baanah
Balaq — Balak; destroyer
Baraq — Barak; lightning
Bartalmai — Bartholemew; Greek/ Aramaic; farmer
Barukh — Baruch; blessing
Basha — Baasha; Baal hears
Bealiah
Benaya, Benayahu — Benaiah; son from Yahu
Benoni — son of my sorrow
Berechiah — blessed by Yahu
Besalel, Bezalel — Bezaleel; in the shadow of El
Betuel — Bethuel; our house is El
Bichri

Bilam — Balaam; Baal protects; Punic
Bildad — Baal-Adad; see Punic
Bin-ammi — Ben-ammi; son of my
  Mother
Binyamin — Benjamin; son of the
  right hand
Boaz — strength
Carmi
Chesed
Chileab
Chilion
Dan — judge
Daniyel — Daniel; my judge is El
Dathan
David — beloved
Ebed
Eber — Hebrew eponym.
Efraim — Ephraim; fruitful
Eglon — young bull
Ehud — united
Elah — El is brother
El'azar — Eleazar, Lazarus, Eliezer;
  El is help
Eldad — El has loved
Eli — belonging to El
Eliakim — El owns the brothers
Eliam — I saw El
Eliashib — El is my judge; Punic
Elihu — our brother belongs to El
Elimelek — Elimelech; El is counselor
Elipaz — Elifaz, Eliphaz; El is victo-
  rious
Eliphalet — ?El is my escape; Punic
Elishah — Elisha, Eliseus; El is salva-
  tion
Eliyahu, Eliyah — Elijah, Elias; El
  and Yahu; see Punic
Elon — oak
Elyaqim — Alcimus; Eliakim
Elymas
Enosh — consecrated
Epron — Ephron; gazelle
Esaw — Esau; hairy
Eshbaal — Eshbal; Baal has heard
Eythan — Ethan; firmness, strength
Gaal
Gabhriel — Gabriel; man of El
Gad — luck; also Punic
Gaham
Gamalyel — Gamaliel; recompense
  of El

Gedalyah, Gedalyahu — Gedaliah
Gehazi — Gehazi; dwell in my sight
Gersom — Gershom; sojourner
Gerson — Gershon; sojourner
Geshem, Gashmu — Geshem;
  important man
Gidon — Gideon; hewer
Gilead
Golyat
Habbakkuk — embrace
Hadad-ezer — Hadadezer, Syrian;
  Hadad's seed
Haggay — Haggai; festival
Ham — hot
Hanania, Hanani — grace is mine
Hanun — favored
Haran
Hazayel — Hazael; seen by El; Syrian
  king
Hazo — gaze; Punic
Heb-hel — Abel; breath, vapor
Heber — Heber; associate
Heman
Hiel — my brother is El
Hillel — new moon
Hilqiyahu — Hilkiah
Hiram, Huram, Huramabi — Phoe-
  nician; my brother is lofty
Hizqiyahu, Hizkiyah — Hezekiah; my
  strength is Yahu
Hobab
Hopni — Hophni; tadpole
Hosea — Hosea, Hoshea; salvation
Hoshaiah — my salvation is Yahu
Hur — sanctuary, mountain; Punic
Hushay — Hushai; my brother's gift
Hyrkanos
Ibzan — swift
Iddo — dim. Iddin "an heir" Ass. Bab.
Ikhabod — Ichabod; glory has departed
Imlah
Ira — watchful
Ishbak
Ishmael — El will hear
Ithamar — ith + promise
Ithream
Ithro
Ittay — Ittai; know joy; a Philistine
Iyob, Iyyobh — Job; persecuted
Kaleb — Caleb; dog
Kemuel

Kenaan — Canaan; eponym.
Khanok, Hanokh, Henokh, Hanok —
  Enoch; dedicated, consecrated
Khayim — Hyman; life
Kish
Korah
Laban — Laban; white
Lapidot — Lappidoth
Lemek — Lamech; vigorous youth
Lemu'el — Lemuel; consecrated to El
Lewi — Levi; united
Lot — covering
Maacah
Mahlon
Makir — Machir; bought; hireling
Malaki — Malachi; counselor
Malkisedeq — Melchizedek; Milk vin-
  dicates; Punic
Manoah — Manoah; resting place
Mari — beloved; fr. Egyptian Meri
Mattaniah — gift from Yahu
Mattathias — Mattathias
Mattithyah — Matthew; given by Yahu
Medad
Medan
Meir
Menahem — Manaen, Menachem;
  comforter
Menasseh — Manasses, Manasseh; has
  made forget
Mesha — salvation, savior
Methuselah — servant of the moon-
  God, Selah
Midyan — Midian; eponym
Mika — Micah; who is like?
Mikayahu — Micaiah; who is like
  Yahu?
Mikhael, Mikael — Michael; who is
  like El?
Mishael
Mizraim
Mosheh — Moses; child of; probably
  short for the Egyptian Ahmose
Naaman — pleasantness
Nabal — fool; story name
Naboth — pos. sprouts
Nadab — noble
Nahem — Nahum; comfort
Nahor
Naphtali — wrestler
Nathan — gift

Neboth
Nehemeyah — Nehemiah; Yahu has
  comforted
Ner — light
Neriyah — Neriah; my light is Yahu
Nethan'el — Nathaniel; gift of El
Nimrod
Nimshi
Nun
Obadyahu — Obadiah; worshipper of
  Yahu
Obed-edom — Obed-edom; wor-
  shipper of Edom
Oholiab
Oman
Omri
Oreb — raven
Othniel
Pahathmoab
Palti — my escape
Paltiel — Phaltiel; my escape is El; Punic
Parosh
Pashur — Pashhur; loosens; Ass. Bab.
Pedahzur
Peleg — to divide
Peqah — Pekah; opened
Peqahyah — Pekahiah; opened by Yahu
Peres — Perez, Pharez; bursting forth
Pildash
Pinehas — Phinehas
Putiel
Qayin — Cain; smith
Qehat — Kohath; pos. obedience
Qis — Kish; bestow
Qorah — Korah; bald
Raguel or Reuel
Rehabam — Rehoboam
Rekab — Rechab
Resin — Rezin
R'fael — Raphael; healed by El
Ruakh — breath, wind
R'ubhen — Reuben, Ruben; behold a
  son
Sabbas
Selopehad — Zelophehad
Sepanya, Sepanyahu — Zephaniah
Serayah — Seraiah
Shallum — Shallum; dim. Ass.
  Mushallum, saved
Shamgar — Shamgar
Shapan — Shaphan

Sha'ul — Saul; asked for
Shealtiel
Shear-yashub — Shear-jashub
Sheba — an oath
Shebnah, Shebaniyah — Shebna
Shekem — Shechem
Shelah — one of Selah, the Moon God
Shelomon, Shalom — Soloman; peace, peaceful
Shem — hearing
Shemayahu — Shemaiah; hearing is Yahu
Shemuel — Samuel; heard by El
Shephatiah
Sheshbazzar — Shamasb-ab-user, Babylonia
Sheth   Seth; appointed
Shimei — Shimei; pos. I was heard
Shim'on — Simon, Simeon; one who hears
Shimshon, Shemesh — Samson; one of Shamash the sun–God
Shuah — Shuah
Siba — Ziba; delight
Sira — Sirach
Sopar — Zophar
Tabeel
Tahash
Tebah — goodness
Terah
Tibni — Tibni — my good
Tobiyah — Tobiah, Tobias; my good is Yahu
Tola
Tsadhoq, Sadoq — Zadok; just, righteous
Tsiddhqiyah, Sidqiyahu — Zedekiah; justice of Yahu
Tubal-qayin — Tubal-Cain; Tu-Baal, Punic
Uri — my light
Uriya, Uriyahu — Uriah; my light is Yahu
Uriyel — Uriel; my light is El
Uz — strong
Uzzah — strength
Uzziyah — Uzziah; my strength is Yahu
Uzziyel — Uzziel; my strength is El
Ya'aqob — Jacob; supplanter
Yabal — Jabal
Yabin — Jabin; Yahu, a son!

Yaddua — Jaddua; known
Yair — Jair; may God shine/enlighten
Yaosh — Yahu helped
Yarobam — Jeroboam; may the people be great
Yeberakhiyah — Jeberachiah
Yedidiyah — Jedidiah; friend of Yahu
Yehoahaz — Jehoahaz; Yahu the Brother is help
Yehoaiakim — Joachim; Yahu owns the brothers
Yehoash — Jehoash; Yahu hears
Yehoiakhim — Jehoiachim; Yahu owns the brothers
Yehokhanan — Jehohanan; John; Yahu is gracious
Yehonathan, Yonatan — Jonathan; Yahu's gift
Yehoram — Jehoram or Joram; Yahu is lofty
Yehoshaphat — Jehoshaphat
Yehoshua — Joshua; Yahu is salvation
Yehoyada — Jehoiada
Yehoyakin — Jehoiachin
Yehoyaqim — Jehoiakim; Yahu owns the brothers
Yehozabad — Jehozabad
Yehu — Jehu; of Yahu or praise
Yehuda — Judah, Judas, Jude; praised
Yekhezqel, Yehezqel — Ezekiel; may El strengthen
Yeshayahu — Isaiah; salvation is Yahu
Yepet — Japheth; may God enlarge
Yeshua — Jeshua
Yether — Jether
Yidlap — Jidlaph
Yiptah — Jephthah
Yirmeyahu, Yirm'yah — Jeremiah; appointed by Yahu
Yishay — Jesse; wealthy
Yismael — Ishmael; El will hear
Yissakar — Issachar
Yitro — Jethro; pre-eminence
Yitshaq — Isaac; laughter
Yizreyel — Jezreel; sown by El
Yoab — Joab; he is Father
Yoash — Joash; He is Ashur
Yoel — Joel; He is El
Yohanan — Johanan; John; He is gracious
Yokhai — Jochai; He is life

Yokshan — Jokshan
Yonadab — Jonadab; He is noble
Yonah — Jonah; dove
Yoseph — Joseph; He will add
Yosiyah — Josiah
Yotam — Jotham
Yoyada — Joiada
Yozacar — Jozacar
Yubal — Jubal; given life by Baal; Punic
Zakkai, Zakkay — Zacchaeus; proclaimed; Assyro-Bab
Zarah — blossom

Zared
Zebulun — Zebulon; dwelling place
Zedek — justice
Zekharyah, Zekaryah — Zachariah, Zachary; remembered by Yahu
Zerah — seed, offspring
Zerubbabel — seed-gate is El; Assyrian
Zimran
Zimri — dim. pos. for Babylonian Zimri-lin
Zoar
Zuriyel — Zuriel; my rock is El

MALE EKE-NAMES OR TITLES

ha-Binyamini — the Benjaminite
ha-Gaddi — the Gaddite
ha-Kadosh — the holy one
ha-Levi — the Levite
ha-Nasi — the prince; figurative,

noble, brave
ha-Nesher — the eagle
ha-Yehudi — the Judite
ha-Zaken — the elder

EARLY SANSKRIT

Many of these names are still in use, as a glance at the Indian chapter will show, just as children are still getting named for the patriarch Abraham or Helen of Troy. The base patterns of names is the same, and if you compare the two chapters you will find correspondences, just as you do if you compare the Frankish and German chapters.

Vedic India is a tremendously under-exploited area for adventure of the sword-and-sandal variety. As Jacob van Velze says, "the oldest material [collected names] ... lacks the spirit of the negative philosophy and view of life so typical of the later brahman, buddhist and jainistic world of thought. Hardly anything about karma, samsara, moksa. The Indian names may be put on a par with the Hellenic and Germanic, they breathe an animated, combative, many-sided inspiration...."

Rigvedic Aryans differ on other points from the timeless Hindus in your mind. They practice polyandry, and not always of the "brothers take a wife" variety. One queen was married to three kings in different areas, at once. Polygyny flourished alongside it, so that husband and wife might have other spouses as well, who were not married to each other. Many people had matronymics, alongside those with patronymics. There was no suttee, or widow suicide: that was a concept brought up much later from the Tamil south.

So if you feel Mycenaean warlords and hordes crossing the Rhine have lost their sparkle, try the descent of the Indo-Aryans on the native Dravidians. Names for the latter can be adapted from Tamil.

Like the Hellenes and the Germanic tribes, the names below were normally used one to a customer. Some are two-element names, some are single element. I found only the most general and categorical meanings for them, so they are omitted on most.

Despite appearances, the look-alike male and female names are distinguishable in speech and writing to their users. Female names end in a different kind of A, one of greater duration using a different letter in Sanskrit, than male ones.

Rigging the Plot

According to the "Laws of Manu," parents should avoid giving a girl the name of "a constellation, a tree, a river, a mountain, a bird, a servant and a terror." Manu positively forbids a proper Aryan man from marrying a girl with such a name, as she would probably be either one of the autochthonous people, or from a family that was going native.

In the much later *Kama Sutra* (not nearly as racy as a modern romance), there is reference to names which "some [Classical Indian] authors" feel are a bad influence on women. That is, a man should avoid marrying "a girl who is called by the name of one of the twenty-seven stars, or by the name of a tree, or of a river … [or] whose name ends in 'r' or 'l.'"

These names were used, and by not a few queens. When all else fails to make the hero cavil at marrying your superlative heroine, name her after a tree!

Varna in Names

The four castes originated by the Sanskrit Aryans were the Brahmins, the priests and scholars; the Kshatriyas, the warrior and government class; the Vaisya, artisans and merchants; and the Shudra peasants and serfs.

Four suffixes, or secondary compound names distinguish them: sarman, varman, gupta, and dasa. All calling on Visnu, a Brahmin would be names Visnusarman, a Kshatriya Visnuvarman, a Vaisya Visnugupta, and Visnudasa for a Shudra. These could also be written Visnu Sarman, Visnu Gupta, etc. If you must have several characters named for Visnu, this would separate them better. If you have two or more Varmans, however, running it all together in one name soft-pedals the endings.

Chandra Varman, Visnu Varman
Chandravarman, Visnuvarman

It is too easy for the English-speaking reader to decide the first two guys are both in the Varman family. You don't want to have to sit down and spend paragraphs explaining names; you want to get on with the story.

Pronunciation

Scholarly texts are full of under-dotted and over-marked letters, which your readers and publisher would not appreciate. Names in those works containing the under-dotted R are given with the implied vowel: Amrta, Amrita. The over-marked, aspirated S is given as SH: Kesava, Keshava. Cases of an N with the tilde you may have seen in Spanish have been given as straight N, then NY spellings.

For all other letters, I have ignored marks, and treated them as their English equivalents. Soft and hard H's, long and short vowels, all go undifferentiated.

Some names have come into English with aspirations that were not there in the originals: Visnu = Vishnu; Krsna = Krishna; Candra = Chandra. Unless the names referring to God are vital to the plot, and you have no time or space to say "Visnu the preserving God" or "Candra, Lord of night's silvery orb," stick to the unfamiliar original. This keeps your story's ambiance ancient, rather than contemporary.

FEMALE NAMES

Abandhaka
Abja — lotus name
Adrishyanti
Ahalya
Aksamala
Alambusa
Amalaja
Amba, Ambika —
   mother
Amrita
Ananta
Anibha
Apala
Arcismati
Arundhati — star name
Arusi
Asmaki — sling stone
Asti
Asvapali
Atiki
Badhiraka
Bahula — star name
Bala
Balada — ox
Balandhara
Bandhaki — unfaithful in
   marriage
Bhadra

Bhagala
Bhanugupta
Bhanumati
Bindumati
Brihatsena
Canda
Caruhasini
Carumati — star name
Citra — star name
Citralekha
Citrangada
Cuda
Cudala
Damayanti
Dasi
Datta
Dattadevi
Devaki
Devayani
Devika
Dharmavati
Dharmini
Dhenuka
Dhritadeva
Dhruvadevi — star name
Dhruvaka — star name
Dhumini — smoke
Dhusala — a kind of lance

Drisadvati — river name
Durga
Durmitra
Dvarapali
Eraka — grass
Ganda
Gandhapingala
Gauri
Ghosa
Ghritaci
Ghurnika
Giribhadra
Girika
Gocapala
Gopajala
Gopika — shepherd
Gupta
Haimini — golden orna-
   ment
Hamsi — bird name
Harsigupta
Havismati
Ilini
Indrasena
Jangha
Jatila
Jayasvamini
Jitavati

Kadamba — tree name
Kakudmati
Kalavati
Kalindi — river name
Kalyani
Kama
Kamadyu
Kamsa
Kamsavati
Kanistha
Kapila, Kapilika — monkey
Karambha
Karenumati
Karmavati
Kaveri — river name
Keshiki
Keshini
Khadonmatta
Khala
Khalya
Khalyaka
Kisorika — colt
Krata — intellectual power
Krimi, Karmi — insect, worm
Kripi
Kritvi
Kuksi
Kulata — unfaithful in marriage
Kumaradevi
Kumari
Kumarika
Kumudvati
Kundala — earring
Kundini
Kusherika
Kutharika — war ax
Kuverika — tree name
Laksmana
Laksmivati
Lapita
Lilavati
Madalasa
Madayanti — Arabian jasmine
Madira
Madra
Mahi
Maitreyi

Malini — a kind of garland, a borderline forbidden name
Malti — a garland, a borderline forbidden name
Mamata — selfish
Manasvini
Manini — haughty
Manipali — a jewel
Manthara
Marisa
Maryada — boundary stone
Mayadevi
Mena, Menaka — woman
Menaka
Mitravinda
Mudavati
Mura — tree name
Musika — mouse
Nalini — lotus name
Nanda
Nandini
Narmada — river name
Nava — baby
Nili — dark blue
Nilini — indigo tree name
Nriga
Oghavati
Padmini — plant name
Pila — perfume
Pindi
Pingala
Pivari
Prabhavati
Pradvesi
Prajavati
Pramadvara
Pramatha — tree name
Prapti
Praticya
Pritha
Priti
Puramdhi
Purohitika
Pskaradharini, Puskarini — lotus name
Putakrata
Radha — star name
Rajadhidevi
Rajivalocana

Rajni, Rajnyi
Ramadevi
Rangavati
Rastrapali
Rathamtari
Renuka — pollen
Revati — star name
Riksa, Raksa — bear
Rocana
Rohini — star name
Ruci
Rudra
Rudramati
Rukmini — golden ornament
Sahadeva
Sampriya
Sarasvati — river name
Sarparajni
Satya
Satyabhama
Satyaratha
Satyavati
Savarna
Savitri
Shabari
Shalaka
Shalakabhru
Shalavati
Shanta
Sharmistha
Shikha
Shiksita
Shiva
Shrideva
Shrutadeva
Shrutavati
Shubha
Shudra
Shuvhangi
Sita — a furrow
Subhadra
Subhaga
Subhima
Sudarshana
Sudesna
Sudeva
Sudevala
Sudharma
Sugandhi — tree name
Sujata

Sukanya — girl
Sukeshi
Sukumari
Sulabha
Sumana
Sumitra
Sunamni
Sunanda
Sundari
Sunitha
Suniti
Suprabha
Surasa
Surohika
Surohitika
Suruci
Sushila
Sushobhana
Sushrava
Sutanu
Sutara
Suvarna
Suyajna

Suyashas
Svayamprabha
Tala
Tamrapaksa
Tamrarasa
Ugraseni — a kind of
    lance
Upadeva
Upadevi
Upagupta
Upama
Urjasvati
Urmila
Urvasi — Ganges river
    name
Usa
Utpalavati — lotus name
Uttara
Vadava — mare
Vadhrimati
Vahini
Vahyaka
Vajrajvala, Vajrajivala

Vanaraji — tree name
Vapusmati
Vapustama
Vara
Varangi
Vasavadatta
Vedavati
Vidula — species of reed
Vijaya
Vimala
Vipatha — a kind of arrow
Vira
Vishala
Vriddhakanya
Vrkadeva, Varkadeva —
    wolf + Goddess
Vrkala, Varkala
Yashoda
Yashodevi
Yashodhara
Yaudheyi

Non-Theophoric Male Names

Abhiru
Acyut
Ahovirya
Ajitashatru
Akopa
Alikayu
Amitaujas
Anadhristi
Anuharant
Anuvaktar
Apratipin
Aradhin
Arijit
Ashmaratha
Aupajihvi
Ayobahu
Ayutajit
Bahu
Bahvashin
Bhadrabahu
Bhajya
Bhayankara
Bhoja
Bhuritejas

Brihanmanas
Candabhargava
Caru
Cirakari
Cirakarin
Dabhiti
Dambhodbhava
Dandasharman
Dhimant
Dhrisnu
Dhriti
Dhritimant
Dhritimitra
Dhuni
Dhvasan
Dhvasanti
Dirghalocana
Dridhacyut
Duli
Durgama
Durmukha
Duryodhana
Dustaritu
Ekadyu

Ekayavan
Gauragriva
Gauramukha
Ghosavasu
Ghujyu
Harishmashru
Hiranyaroman
Hrasvaroman
Hridya
Hritsvashaya
Itant
Jaimini
Janghabandhu
Janu
Jayaka
Jihvavan
Jisnu
Jyayan
Kalmasanghri
Kapatu
Karnashravas
Katujit
Khandapani
Kohada

Kratumant
Kratuvid
Ksanabhojin
Ksanti
Ksemadarshin
Ksemadhurti
Ksemari
Ksemavriddhi
Kuruvasha
Laugaksi
Lohitaksa
Lomaharsana
Mahabhauma
Mahakarni
Mahamati
Mahanandin
Mahasvant
Manas
Mandhatri
Margamarsi
Mayuraksaka
Mitrayu
Mridu
Nabhi
Naikadrish
Naimishri
Nami
Natha
Nirvriti
Nivaku
Nrisad
Palin
Parahan
Parakrathin
Paravrit
Pathin
Pattanadhipati
Prabahu
Prakaramardin
Prakshringavant
Prasanneyu
Pratibahu
Pratiksatra
Pravasu
Prenin
Pulasti
Purujanu

Putakratu
Rajastambha
Ranavanya
Raudrakarman
Riju
Ripu
Ritavac
Ritayus
Ruciparvan
Sabhapati
Sadahsuvak
Sahisnu
Samnateyu
Samraj
Saptapala
Satrajit
Satyadharman
Satyajit
Satyaketu
Satyashri
Satyavan
Satyavant
Senajit
Shamtanu
Shankhapada
Shanti
Shashaloman
Shatapati
Shatrughatin
Shatrujit
Shatursaha
Shiras
Shirsin
Shrusti
Shrutavid
Shvetakarna
Sthaulasthivi
Sucetas
Sudaman
Sudhaman
Sudhriti
Sukriti
Sulabhin
Sumanas
Sumnayu
Suparshva
Surari

Susamchi
Sushanti
Suvarnashiras
Svarupa
Tamas
Tandi
Tandin
Tarasvin
Trasadayu
Tuji
Tustimant
Uccairmanyu
Udhajit
Ugrayayin
Upamashravas
Upaveshi
Upavi
Ushant
Utathya
Vadanya
Vajabandhu
Valgujangha
Varayu
Varcas
Varcin
Varpeyu
Vatavant
Vatsahanu
Vibhuti
Vicarin
Vidabhrit
Vidanvant
Vikriti
Vikuksi
Vinitatman
Virabahu
Virajas
Viryacandra
Vishrutavant
Visri
Vitarka
Vrijinavant
Vrijinivant
Vyudhoru
Yudhamanyu
Yuyudhana

MALE THEOPHORIC NAMES

Abhijit — star name
Acalavarman
Agnitejas
Agnivay
Ahina, Ahinas
Ajatashatru
Anangi
Angarasetu — star name
Apratimaujas
Aristakarman
Asadha, Asadhi — star name
Atibhanu
Aviksit
Balin, Balina
Barhin
Bhadracaru — star name
Bhagavaddosa
Bhanumant
Bhaskara
Bhavasvamin
Bhrigu
Bhrigubhumi — star name
Bhutasharman
Brahmabali
Brahmavriddhi
Brihadbhanu
Brihaspati — star name
Brihatkarman
Camasin
Candraketu
Caru — star name
Carugupta — star name
Chandogi
Dandapani
Darbhi, Darbhin
Devabhuti
Devadarsha
Devaki
Devamidhusa
Devapi
Devashravas
Devasvamin
Devavant
Devavisnu
Dharmaketu
Dharmanetra
Dharmasarathi
Dharmeyu

Dhruvasharman — star name
Divakarasvamin
Dridharuci
Dyutimant, Dyumant
Ganapati
Garavant
Gopali
Gopati
Govindagupta
Govindasvamin
Harimedhas
Harishcandra
Havirdhaman
Havismant
Hotrapaci
Ilin
Indrahu
Indrapramati
Indrota
Jamadagni
Ketu — star name
Krisnadhriti
Kritagni
Kumarashanti
Madhu
Madhushcut
Mahant
Mahanta
Matarishvan
Meghayati
Mitrabhanu
Mitravarcas
Nagadatta
Nandin — Shiva's bull
Naradin
Niramaya
Paramesthin
Parthin
Pashupati
Pavitrapani
Pitrivartin
Prabhanu
Pracinabarhis
Pradyumna
Pramshu
Pratibhanu
Prithukarman
Purusaprabhu

Ravikirtti
Rudrabhuti
Rudradaman
Sahasrapad
Sakrajit
Samkriti
Sarpamalin
Sasthidatta
Shakandhi
Shambhu
Sharvavarman
Shayu
Shivagupta
Shivashri
Shribhanu
Shrimant
Shucanti
Sikhavant
Sindhuksit
Somakirti
Somashravas
Sthandileyu
Subhanu
Subhraj
Sudarsha
Suditi
Suhavis
Sunvant
Suprabha
Surakrit
Surupa
Sutvan
Suyastavya
Svarjit
Svaryati
Svati — star name
Tanu
Tapasvin
Tapodhriti
Tapomurti
Trisoka
Urjayoni
Usangu
Uttanabarhis
Vama
Vamadeva
Vasati
Vasu
Vasudharman

Vataki	Virupa	Vrisaparvan
Vayuretas	Visnudeva	Yajnabahu, Yajnyabahu
Vibhavasu	Visnusimha	Yajnapati, Yajnyapati
Vidyutprabhu	Visnuyashas	Yamaduta
Vipulasvant	Vrateyu	

PUNIC AND PHOENICIAN

The Punic version of a name is not something you can actually put in front of your readers, but there is a body of transliteration in Latin, Greek, and Assyrian. Semitic scholars rarely provide vowels and other luxuries, so I have looked for analogs in Akkadian, Assyrian, Hebrew, etc., besides its close predecessor, Canaanite.

This section will cover all Phoenician, Punic, and Neo-Punic names, whether in Phoenicia, Carthage, Sardinia, or any of the other colonies. The difficulty is that the Punic inscriptions do not include vowels, so only the occasional bi-lingual inscription lets us know that '*h.mlkt* is the equivalent of Himilco, or that '*dnb'l* is usually rendered Idnibalis. Yes, the direction of the apostrophe matters.

The Holy Trinity of Carthage was Tennit, the Goddess, and the Gods Melqart, also known as El, and Baal Hammon. They will show up most often in Carthaginian names. In Phoenicia, Ashtart, El, and Aduna are the names used, but Baal-names still appear in lesser numbers.

Wide-ranging travellers, not only did Phoenicians adopt nearby Assyrian Deities into Punic names, but many Egyptian ones, notably Isis, Bastet, Osiris (as Osar), and Horus (as Horon). In the pick list, the God names will be integrated into the name. In the list of theophoric name formulas — add the Deity of your choice — you can see the breakdown. You may choose either version, Binan or Bin-An. A hyphen may make a very long theophoric more manageable, like Shapat-Melqart instead of Shapatmelqart.

If you want to give a character a formal long name, like, "Yahazibaal, son of Saponisedeq," the "son word" is *bin*: Yahazibaal bin Saponisedeq. His sister would be Hinnibaal *bat* Saponisedeq; unless she were married, in which case she might be Hinnibaal *asht* Bodeshmun, "wife of Bodeshmun."

Pronunciation

If you refer to the great Carthaginian general as Khannibal or Channibaal, your readers may freak. Nonetheless, those are possible transliterations. Virtually all the H's in Punic are hard H's, coming out of the back of the throat, like a soft KH. So don't just slide them by silently at the ends of words. Yaptih-Addu sounds more like Yaptik-Addu than like Yapti-Addu.

FEMALE NAMES

Ab — father; short for any Ab- name
Abbaal — father is Baal; unisex
Akbarit — mouse
Ashtnamit — woman of pleasantness
Bannit — to build
Batbaal — daughter of Baal
Batnam — daughter of pleasantness
Batnamit — pleasant daughter
Berrekt — blessed, blessing
Besho
Eldeshi, Aldeshi
Gaddnam, Giddnamit — good fortune is pleasure
Girgishi, Girgishit
Hagnit, Hegnit
Hanno, Hanni — grace, favor
Hesheqemit — desired one
Hinnibaal, Hannibaal — unisex

Huld, Heled, Huldel — mole
Kabidit — honor
Kineshit
Mattan, Matten, Mitton — gift
Mattenitel — female gift of El
Namgidda, Namitgadda — pleasure is good fortune
Phamea
Saponibaal — Lat. Sophoniba, Sophonisba
Shamohit — gladness, be glad
Shema, Shuma — unisex
Shumazabaal
Tamemit — perfect
Tennit — glory, radiance
Tirisht — wine
Toara — vision
Yatunit — given; gift

MALE NAMES

Ab-kal-li-pi
Abbaal — father is Baal
Abbir — strong
Abdi
Abdili'ti
Abdmelqart — popular
Abdsihar
Abimilk — my father is the King
Abinadab — my Father is noble
Abiqom — my Father stands
Ada, Adi
Adbaal, Adbaali
Addir, Addira — mighty, glorious
Addirbaal
Addirmilk
Aduna = Adonis, Lord
Adunaiz
Aduniba'al — Idnibalis, Iddibal
Aduniiha — Adonis is alive
Adunisha — Adonis delivers/saves
Ahimeti, Ahimiti
Ahimilk — my brother is King
Ahimilkat — my brother is the Queen
Ahinadab — my brother is noble
Akbar — mouse
Anzor — wild pig; fierce and wily
Aris

Ashaddir, Ashaddira — man of glory
Ashader — man of the Mighty One
Awibaal, Aoibaal — unexplained
Azor — help
Azorbaal — Hasdrubal, Azdrubal; popular
Azuri
Ba'al, Baali — diminutive
Baaladdir — Baliddir, Baldir
Baalishapat — Baal judges
Baalshillem
Ba'lu
Barik, Bariho — bless
Barqan — lightning
Berekbaal, Birikbaal — blessed by Baal
Binhodesh — son of the new moon
Binur — son of light
Bodashtart — the most common name
Bodi
Bodmelqart — 2nd or 3rd most common name
Budibaal
Dabar — bee
Deshi — green growth
Eshmunadun, Eshmunaduni — Eshmun is lord

Gadda, Gidda — lucky
Gallab, Gallabu — barber
Gamar — to avenge
Gan — pride
Gashur — strong
Girahal — dweller in tents
Girhekal — dweller in the temple
Gisco
Haggay — festal
Halam, Halem
Hamay
Hamelqart — somewhat popular; Hamilcar
Hanesh
Hanmelqart — Ammicar
Hanno; Hannon, Hanni — favor; popular
Har — mountain
Hesheq, Hesheqem — desired one
Hiempsal
Himelqart — Himelkart; popular
Himilk —15th most common name
Hirrom
Hiwwiyo — preserved; to live
Hodesh — new moon
Hurbaal — mountain is Baal
Iluyatanu
Isitkin — Isis establishes
Kabid
Kalb — dog
Kalbeli — dog of the Mighty One
Kalbelim — dog of the Gods
Kinesh
Luli
Magon — benefactor; Mago
Magonbaal — bestowed by Baal
Mattan, Matten, Mitton, Muthun — gift; also Mutthun, Mytthum, Motthum, Mutum, ad infinitum
Milkiashapa
Milkilu
Milkyasop — the King adds
Milkyaton — the King gives
Mitinti, Mytint
Mittoni — gift
Namar — leopard
Niqmael, Niqmiel — El has taken vengeance

Palibastet — ____is Bastet
Paltibaal — my escape is Baal
Panesimlot — face of the image
Parosh —flea
Pumihiwwiyo — Pumi has preserved him
Rukiptu
Sa-mu-nu-ya-tu-ni
Sapatibaal, Sibitibiil
Saponisedeq — Sapon vindicates
Sasa — moth
Sedeq — vindication
Shabaal — delivered by Baal
Shamashshillek — Shamash nourishes
Shamosid — heard by Sid
Shapan — badger
Shapatibaal — a judge is Baal
Sharludari
Shillembaal — recompensed by Baal
Shipitibili — my judge is Baal
Shiptiadad — Adad has judged
Shemago — swift
Sheqoa — lowlife
Shumir — to keep
Shumirbaal — keep (this one), Baal
Silukidi
Tagi
Takilanabel
Taom — twin
Tirsh — wine
Tubal, Tubaal
Tuhaw — may She preserve
Urbaal — light of Baal
Yahimilk — may the king live
Yahonbaal — be gracious, Baal
Yakonshilam — establish (this child), Shilam
Yala — mountain goat
Yaptihadad
Yatanael
Yatanu
Yedamilk — known to the King
Yuhaw — may He preserve
Zabul — prince
Zamir — strong, protection
Zikar — to remember
Zizy — leader-boar

SURNAMES

Barqan = lightning; as in Hamilcar Barca

Harish = craftsman

DEITIES

Addu, Adad — Adad, storm God of the Middle East

Aduna — Adonis, consort to Ashtoreth; means "Lord"

Api — Apis, adopted Egyptian God

Ashtart — Ashtoreth, Goddess; equivalent of Ishtar

Baal — God; means "Master"

Bastet — Bast, adopted Egyptian Goddess

Dagan — God of grain, popular in Philistia

Edom — Goddess

El — storm God, just as in Hebrew

Eshmun — storm God of Tyre

Hadad — ancient Semitic storm God, chief God Arameans

Hammon — Baal Hammon, "master of the incense altar"

Hodesh — new moon; either moon God or moon Goddess

Hor — Horus, adopted Egyptian God

Horon — NW Semetic God

Ilat — the Goddess

Isit, Auset — Isis, adopted Egyptian Goddess

Melqart — "king of the city," God of Tyre

Milk — "King" for a God, or "king" for a ruler

Milkat — "Queen" or "queen"

Osar, Ausar — Osiris, adopted Egyptian God

Pumi — God

Sapon — God

Shamash — sun God

Shihar — God of sunrise

Shilam, Shulmani — God of dusk, "peace"

Sid, Zid — God

Tennit — Goddess in Carthage

THEOPHORICS

Abd____; male servant of ____

Aduni____; my lord is ____ (may be the Goddess)

Ah____; brother of ____

Ahal____; protection is ____

Ahi____; my brother is ____

Ahot____; sister of ____

Amot____; female servant of ____

Ash____; man of ____

Asht____; woman of ____

Azi____; my help is ____

Azor____; helped by ____

Bat____; daughter of ____

Berek____; blessed by ____

Bin____; son of ____

Bod____; from the hand of ____

Budi____

Gidd____, Gadd____; fortune is ____

Giri____, Gir____; dweller in ____, masculine

Girit____; dweller in ____, feminine

Ha____; the one of ____

Ham____; protected by ____

Hanni____,   Hannon____; favor/grace of ____; ungendered

Hasdru____

Hepsi____; pleasure of ____

Hur____; sanctuary/mountain is ____

Ibin____; our father is ____

Idni____

Im____; mother is ____

Kabid____; honor is ____

Magon____; bestowed by ____

Mattan____; gift of ____; unisex

Miggen____; given by ____

Niqma____, Niqmi____; take vengeance, ____
Palti____; my escape is ____
Rom____; exalted is ____
Sha____; rescued by ____
Shamo____; heard by ____
Shapati____; judge is ____
Shillem____; recompense of ____
Shipitti____; my judge is ____
Shipti____; ____ has judged
Shumir____; keep (this one), ____
Sikar____; remember, ____

Taman____; perfection from ____
Ur____; light is ____, light of ____
Yahazi____; gaze (on this child), ____
Yahi____; my life, ____
Yahon____; be gracious, ____
Yakon____; establish, ____
Yaptih____
Yaton____; give, ____
Yeda____; known by ____
Yit____; unisex
Yuhaww____; preserve, ____

____alahy
____azor; ____ helps
____ba'li;   is my Lord
____berek; ____ blesses
____gadd, ____gidd; ____ is fortune
____gon; ____ protects
____han; ____ shows favor
____harum; ____ is holy
____hilq; ____ (gives this) portion
____hiwwiyo; ____ has given life
____iashapa
____iha; ____ is alive
____ilu; ____ is my God
____ishapat; ____ judges
____kin, ____koon; ____ establishes
____maluk, ____malok; ____ has reigned
____rom; ____ is exalted
____saloh; ____ has prospered
____sedeq; ____ vindicates

____sha; ____ rescues
____shalep; ____ is ancestor
____shamo; ____ has heard
____shillek; ____ has nourished
____shillem; ____ has completed/recompensed
____shipit; ____ has judged
____shumir; ____ keeps
____shyt; ____ establishes
____sikar; ____ remembers
____turi; ____ is my rock
____yahon; ____ is gracious
____yashupu
____yaton; ____ gives
____yit
____yuhaww; ____ preserves, gives life
____zabul; ____ is prince; both examples feminine

GENTILICS

These are names you get according to where you have been or where you have come from. They are always given to outsiders. No one in Sardinia is called the Sardinian.

Origin	Male	Female
Akkoite	Akkoi	Akkoit
Arabian	Arabi	Arabit
Aramean	Arami	Aramit
Cushite	Kushi	Kushit
Libyan	Libi	Libit
Egyptian	Mishri	Mishrit
Persian	Perisi	Perisit
Sardinian	Shardani	Shardanit
Tyrian	Ziri	Zirit

ANCIENT EGYPTIAN

You do *not* want in your book to have the four-hundredth Egyptian heroine who is named Nefertiti.

Modern Egyptians are culturally Arabic, and name their sons Ramses as often as British parents name their daughters Aethelflaed. In the later periods of paganism, the Hellenized pharaohs used Greek names like Ptolemaios and Kleopatra, later Medievalized as Ptolemy and Cleopatra. Many place-names and personal names that you know from Egypt are not Egyptian; they are Hellenizations, like Thebes for the native city-name, Uast.

This section covers the Egypt of the native rulers, the Black Land, Land of the Two Kingdoms; and for commoners under the Ptolemies and later rulers.

Basics

Family names were unknown. You had a personal name and some sort of eke-name — Enen the Round, Ukha the Northerner, Thohem the Gilder — though of course you would know the names of any immediate or illustrious ancestors. You might be Thehen son of Amakh — or Thehen *daughter* of Amakh: the names don't seem to gender. Just when I thought I had found a real masculine ending in "-hotpe," it turned up on someone's wife. When "nefer" looked like a girl-root, here's a guy named Seshemnefer.

Before you go wild on gender-mistake plots: most of the grammar is so gendered, you can hardly go wrong. Second and third person singular pronominal suffixes are gendered. This means that you not only must say "his field" or "her field" (*sekhet-f, sekhet-s*) but in speaking to someone "your field" (really, "thy field"; "you" is second person plural) is clearly "thy-male field" (*sekhet-k*) or "thy-female field" (*sekhet-th*). There is almost no way a person could be discussed in advance, or even be spoken to and overheard, without gender slipping out. Of course, if it's just a name on a list, or groaned by a dying victim…

The meanings of names were known, but they were often reused to honor relatives or patrons, or simply because most parents are not terribly imaginative or poetic. So they do function as simply monikers rather than constantly being treated as descriptive phrases.

In the Middle Kingdom, an eldest son might be named for his father's father. This became moderately common in the New Kingdom, and later even more de rigueur, since it was an Hellenic practice.

Theophorics and Titles Long as Your Arm

Like all early Semitic speakers, Egyptians are fond of God-names, especially in the upper classes. You can take any such Egyptian God-name, take out the name of one God, and substitute another. So Amenhotep can give you Anqet-hotep, Heruhotep, etc. However, to do this you must know the Egyptian names for their Gods. The ones you thought you knew — Isis, Osiris, Horus — are the later Greek transliterations. They still get used for familiarity's sake.

Commoners will do nicely with animal, object, and flora names. For this reason, you will find a short glossary at the end. Remember, the adjective comes after the noun, not ahead of it as in English. "Golden Swallow" is not Nub-ur, but Ur-nub (Swallow, Golden).

Rulers have whole lists of different names and titles, so that part of the challenge of Egyptology is not just finding an inscription, but then figuring to whom exactly the inscription belongs.

In transliterating ancient Egyptian the kind and location of vowels can be pretty optional. Combined with the Hellenizations, one name can be rendered four or five ways, maybe more. These are used by different authorities in different books:

Aahmes, Ahmes, Ahmose, Amasis;

Amonhotep, Amenhotep, Amenhotpe;

Thothmes, Tutmose, Tuthmose, Tutmoses;

Ramses, Rameses, Ramisis, Ramsis, Ri'amsese.

Beyond This

You can always do as many writers with Chinese or Native American settings do: don't use the sounds, use the meanings in English. In this case, your characters can be Heron, Wings-of-Neith (or Wings-of-the-Sky), Beloved-of-Ra (or Beloved-of-the-Sun), Dragonfly, Papyrus-Blossom, and that sort of thing.

In that case, you had better know what Egyptians thought was attractive, which can be very different from our Euro-derived symbolism. Red is not beautiful, but often evil or misfortunate. Green is not unlucky, but the color of life. Dung beetles are well thought of.

Pronunciation

Egyptian is related in sound to Hebrew, Arabic, and of course Coptic. This means there are some sound differentiations not common in English. The properly used letters follow, but please note that in most popular texts, the scholarly over- and under-dots and such are omitted, sometimes with great harm to pronouncing things right. When possible, I've gone back to the scholars so that you will name your hero Shenar ("a storm"), not Senar.

P followed by H in Egyptian indicates one syllable that ends in P followed by one beginning with H. It is *not* the same as F, unless it is a Greek word like "pharaoh," which should be Pa-ra-oh (the title for the ruler commonly used by Egyptians was "nisut"). Be merciful and hyphenate, so your readers will see that Hat-hor is not "Hath-or"(actually, it was H'at-H'eru, but how far to push accuracy beyond familiarity is your call).

A = A in pasta

Å = A with an overdot; can be plain A

AA = prolonged A; often shown as A with a long line over it; like doubled vowels in Japanese or Hawaiian, duration, not sound, changes

E = E in pen

I = I as in machine; sometimes written Y

U = U as in hum

R = half-way between R and L; Japanese R as in Reiko

H = H as in hum

H` = underdotted H; soft KH

KH = hard KH, like the CH in loch

SH = SH as in shush

K = K as in kick

Q = like K

K` = underdotted K; can be KH

T = regular T as in ton

T` = underdotted T; hard TH as in then; can be TH

TH = soft TH, as in thin

TCH = as in hatch

Some use Y to force the EE sound, so that "siyt" is not pronounced like the English "sit," etc.

THEOPHORICS (GOD-NAMES)

Small underlines (__) can be filled in not only with the names of Deities, but abstract terms like soul, truth, etc.

Akh-en-____; spirit of ____
Ankh-es-en-pa-____
Ankhen-____; eternal life in ____
Beket-____
Har-____
Harsi-____
Men-kheper-____; to come into
 being-____
Meri-____; beloved of ____
Meryt-____
Nefer-ka-____; good soul of____
Nefer-nefer-u-____
Nefer-nefru-____
Nefer-u-____
Nefru-____
Sit-____
Tashent-____

____'ah'a
____-em-h'et
____-em-opet
____-emone
____-emwia
____-her-khepesh-ef
____-h'etpe; ____ pleases
____-hirkhopshef
____-hotpe — very common ending
 for both men and women
____-irdis
____-maaat-ka; ____-truth-soul
____-mose
____-sheri — little (person's name)
____-tifi
____-tuya

FEMALE NAMES

A'h-h'etpe
'Ahmose-Nofretari
Amen-irdis
Anhai
Ankh-es-en-pa-Aten
'Ashayt
Beket-Mut
Bent-anta
Ese-nofre
Hat-sup-heres
Hathor-hotpe, H'et-
  h'eru-hotpe
Hen-he-net
Hetep-her
H'etep-h'eres
Ibi
Idut
Iput
Iti
Itiwert
Iy-nefer-ti
Ka-wit
Kem-siyt
Kha-merer-nubti

Khenmet
Khent-kaus
Khnem-hotpe
Khnemt
Khuit
Kiya
Ment
Meryt-amun, Merit-
  Amun
Miy
Mut-emwia
Mut-tuya
Myt
Nakht-____
Neb ____
Nebettawy
Nebkau
Nefer-nefer-u-Re
Nefer-tari
Neferu-Re
Nefret-ity — this is the
  proper form of Nefer-
  titi
Nefru-Re

Nefru-Sobk
Nofret
Nofretari
Ra'maat-ka
Seneb-tisy
Senne-djem
Sent-seneb-tisi
Sentyotes
Sesh-seshet
Set-merhut
Shepenwepet
Sit-H'et-H'eru
Smenkh-kare'
Tahesyt
Tashent Min, Tashent
  Amsu
Teti-sheri
Teye
Ti'a
Twosre
Zadeh

MALE NAMES

A'h-mose
Akh-en-Aten — Akh-en-
  _____; "Spirit of ____"
Akhti-hotpe
Amen-em-h'et; ____-em-h'et
Amen-emone; ____-emone
Amen-em-opet; ____-em-opet
Amen-hirkhopshef; ____-hirkhop-
  shef
Amen-hotpe
Amun-her-khepesh-ef; ____-her-
  khepesh-ef
Anebni
'Ankh-tifi; ____-tifi
Ankhen-____; "Eternal Life in ____"
Aperia
Aspelta
Aya
Djeho
Djehuti
Djehuti-emhab
Djehuti-hotpe

Espamai
Hapu
Har-hotpe
Har-khuuf— Har-____
Har-Min — Har-A'msu; Har-____
Harma'kheru
Harsi-ese — Harsi-____
Hemy-unu
Hep-ren-pu
Hetepka
H'or
Horus'ah'a — s/b H'eru'ah'a;
  ____'ah'a
Ib-pemeny
Ibu
Inyotefoqer
Ipeq
Itefibi
Ka-mose
Ka'aper
Key-nebu
Kha'em-h'et; ____-em-h'et

Kha'sekhem
Khesuwer
Khety
Khnum-hotpe
Ma're'
Me-tje-tjy
Men-kheper-____; "to come into being-____"
Mereruka
Meri-____; Beloved of ____; almost every ruler had this in their list with one Deity or another.
Nakht
Nakht-Min — Nakht-A'msu; Nakht-____
Ne-woser-Re' — Ne-woser-____
Neb-amun — Neb-____
Neb'ankh
Nefer-hotpe
Nefer-ka-Re' — Nefer-ka-____
Nekht-harhebi
Nekht-ti, Nekhti
Ni'ankh-khnum — Ni'ankh-____
Nufer
Pa-neh`esi
Pa-sebkha'nu
Pa-ser
Pakhelkons
Peh-su-kher
Pemehyt
Pet-amenope — Pet-____, God-name begins with vowel
Pete-ese
Pete-mihos — Pete-____, God-name begins with consonant Pet-osiris
Pinu-djem

Psammetik-seneb
Ptah-hotpe
Ra'mose
Re'hotpe
Rehuer-djersen
Re'nofre; ____-nofre
Sahu-Re' — Sahu-____
Sebek-emsauf; ____-ensauf
Sehetepibre'-'ankh
Sekhemkhet
Semenkh-ka-Re' — Semenkh-ka-____
Sen-wosret
Senen-Mut — Senen-____
Senwosret'ankh
Seshem-nefer
Sethy
Shepen-Min — Shepen-A'msu; Shepen-____
Shepses-kaf
Shoshenq
Sit-Hathor-Yuunet — s/b Sit-H'et-H'eru-Yuunet; Sit-____-Yuunet
Ta'o
Teshnufe
Tetu
Th'ut-mose
Thuty-hotpe
Tje-kerti
Tje-nenu
Tje-nuna
Tut'ank-____
Usr-Re' — Usr-____; "Strength of ____ (will sustain)"
Wekhe-hotpe, Uekhe-hotpe

GODS' NAMES

Name	Deity of; (m)/(f)	Greek	AKA
Åaah`	moon; (m)		
Aanqet	(f)		
Aapep	destruction; (m)	Apophis	
Åmen	(m)	Menu	Åmsu
Amenemhet			
Åmsu	(m)	Min	
Amun	(m)		
Ån-h`eru	(m)		
Ånpu	protecting the dead; (m)	Anubis	
Anukis			

Name	Deity of; (m)/(f)	Greek	AKA
Aten	everything; ltd. duration		
Åusår	eternal life	Osiris	Åsår
Åuset	life, magic, love; (f)	Isis	Åst
Bast	music, family, cats; (f)	Bastet	
Beb	first son of Osiris		
Bes	wealth; (m)		
Buto	cobra Goddess of Lower Egypt		
Geb	earth; (m)		
H`aapi	the Nile; (m)		
Hap, Hapi	elder Horus	Haroeris	
H`eqt	(f)		
H`eru	sun, pharaoh, vengeance	Horus	
H`eru-khuti	(m)	Harmachis	
H`et-H`eru	childbirth; (f)	Hathor	
Khensu	(m)		
Khepera	(m)		
Khnemu	(m)		
Khnum			
Khons	son of Amun	Khonsu	Måat, Maat
Maaat	truth personified; (f)		
Meh`ent	(f)		
Meh`it	(f)		
Mi-hos	lion–God, son of Bast		
Mon-tu	war–God		
Mut	(f)		
Nebt-h`et	(f)	Nephthys	
Nefer-Temu	(m)		
Nekhebet	vulture Goddess of Upper Egypt		
Net	(f)	Neith	
Nut	sky, mother of the Gods; (f)		
Panebtawy	lord of the 2 lands; (m)		
Ptah`	learning; a late God; (m)		
Ptah`-Tanen	learning; a joint God, (m)		
Raa	solar-sky; (m)		Ra, Re
Raa-usr-Maaat	Raa, mighty one of Maat		
Renenutet	serpent–Goddess		
Satis			
Seb	husband of Nut		
Sebek	(m)		
Seh`er	fear, driving away; (m)		
Sekhet	marshes, pleasure; (f)		
Sesheta	(f)		
Seth	evil; (m)	Set	
Shesmu	wine; (m)	Seshmu	
Sheta			
Shu	the sun; (m)		
Sobk	(m)	Sobek	
Ta-tunen	(m)		
Tanen	(m)		
Tasenetnofret	the good sister; (f)		

Name	Deity of; (m)/(f)	Greek	AKA
Teh`uti	learning; (m)	Thoth	
Tem	setting sun; the dead; (m)	Temu	
Un	hare; (m)		
usr-Maaat	strength of truth; (f)		
Uadjit Wen-nofre	title of Osiris		
Wadjit	cobra–Goddess; childbirth, protection		

Vocabulary

åaah` — the moon, a month
åaah` — a necklace
aab — a tooth; mistress, lady; wide
aaf — a fly
aankh — life; ankh, 'ankh
aaq — a duck
aar — an oryx
aaraa — a serpent; a Goddess (in general)
aarp — grape arbor; wine
aash — a lizard; abundance
aat`et — rain
åau — old, aged
åaut — cattle
ab — an elephant
åb — to dance
åbt` — the moon, a month
åbu — a panther
åh` — an ox
åhait — stable
åh`t — a cow
akeru — the Lions of Yesterday and Today (or Tomorrow)
akh — lotus and papyrus growing; a field
akhet — season of inundation
am — to eat
a'makh — eye of a hawk; pious, sacred
åmen — to conceal, hidden
åment — the West; the right side
åmhet — an ape
åneb — a fort or wall
åner — a stone; stone
ankh — a flower
åpt — a hippopotamus
åpt-renpet — opening of the year, New Year's
asfet — wickedness
åshet` — an acacia tree
at — a crocodile; to gather together
åthi — prince, king

åu — a calf
ba — a ram
bå — a calf
båa — metal, ore
båt — a bee
bener — a palm tree; sweet, pleasant
bennu — phoenix-like bird
beti — barley
betu — a fish
enen — submission, inactivity, stillness
fent — a worm
hai — rain
h`ef — a worm
h`efen — a young frog; 100,000
hememu — mankind
h`emt — metal, ore
hen — to praise
h`en — to love
henkset — hair
h`ent — mistress, lady; wide
h`enti — a prince
heqer — hunger
h`erit — fear, awe
h`es — to sing, to praise, to be favored; to play music
h`esp — nome; dukedom
h`et — silver
h`etch — white; shining; light
h`etem — to destroy
h`eter — friendship
hru — day
ka — an ox
kaut — a cow
k`erh` — night
khabes — the beard
khaut — a knife
kheb — a rhinoceros
khekh — a winged jackal
kheper — to roll; to come into being
khepersh — a helmet

khepesh — a sickle-sword

kherefu — the Lions of Yesterday and Today (or Tomorrow); kherp — to direct, to govern

khesef — to turn back

khet — fire

khetem — a ring, a circle

khut — the horizon

khuti — the two horizons

ma — a lion

maaau — a lion

maar — a pomegranate

maashaa — a bowman

måu — a cat

mefket — a turquoise

meh`t — the North, the Delta country, Land of the Lotus

menaa — to nurse, to breast-feed

menf — a soldier

mer — to love; a ditch, a waterway

merhu — unguent

merti — two eyes; to see

mestchem — eye paint

meter — to give evidence, to be in the center

mu — water

mut — a vulture

neb — man-headed lion; Sphinx (Greek); lord; all; bowl

nefer — a horse; a lute; that which is good

nehebet — a neck

neh`em — a flower bud

nekht — strength, to be strong

nem — a Pygmy or dwarf

nemmehu — poor folk

ner — a vulture

net — a bee

netchem — sweet, pleasant

neter — god, divine being, king

nini — act of homage

nub — gold

nui — a dagger

peh` — a swamp or marsh

peh`ti — two-fold strength, doubly strong

pennu — a rat

pet — a bow

qam — black; a crocodile skin

qebh` — coolness, cold water

qeh` — an axe

qem — to find

qet — dagger

rekhit — intelligent person, mankind; a griffon

renpit — a flowering plant

rer — a pig

res — the South, the Land of the Papyrus

ruha — evening

sab — a jackal; a wise person

saneh`em — a grasshopper

sati — purity

sba — star, morning star, hour, to pray

seb — a door or gate

sebti — a wall or fort

seh`er — to drive away

sekhem — to gain mastery, to be strong

sekhen — to embrace

sekhet — crops, plants in a field; a fowler's net

semehi — the left side

sent` — fear, terror

sepa — a centipede

Sept` — the star Sothis; to be provided with

seqa — a crocodile; to gather together

seqer — captive

ser — great, great man, prince, chief; a giraffe

serq — a scorpion

sesem — a horse

seshesh — a sistrum

set — purity; an arrow

set` — to tremble

set`eb — what is hostile

setep — to select

sfent — a knife

shaa — lotus and papyrus growing; a field

shaaa — a cord; 100

shaat — a book, a papyrus roll

shefit — strength

shemaa — South; a class of priestess

shemaatu — southern

shemu — harvest season

shen — a circle, a ring

shenar — a storm

sheråu — a sparrow; little

shersheru — wind

shesa — to be wise
shet — a turtle; evil, that which is bad
sma — to slay
smu — copper
stimu — green herbs
sun — an arrow
tchebaa — a finger, or 10,000
tchefa — bread, cake, food
t`eben — to go round about
tebt — a sandal
teha — to invade, to attack
teh`uti — an ibis
tekhen — an obelisk
temt — to collect, to join together
t`emtu — sharp
ten — old, aged
t`enh` — to fly, a wing
t`es — a knife
t`esher — red
theh`en — lightning
theh`ent — crystal

thet — a buckle or knot or tassle
thohem — to rejoice
ti — eagle
t`u — a mountain; wickedness
t`ua — star, morning star, hour, to
    pray
uaa — a boat
uasm — copper
uatch — green
uben — splendor
uher — a dog
ukha — a pillar
un — a hare
un-h`râ — a mirror
ur — great, great man, prince, chief;
    a swallow
urit — a chariot
ursh — a neck-support
usekh — a pectoral, armor or orna-
    ment; mistress, lady; wide
ut`en — to write; offerings

NUMBERS

uaa — one
sen — two
khemet — three
ft`u, åft`u — four
t`uau — five
sås — six
sefekh — seven

khemennu — eight
pest` — nine
met — ten
tchaut — twenty
maab — thirty
h`ement — forty
sefekh — seventy

khemennui — eighty
shaaa — 100
kha — 1,000
tchebaa — 10,000
h`efennu — 100,000
h`eh` — 1,000,000
shennu — 10,000,000

PLACE-NAMES
Classical Name — Egyptian Name

Abydos — Abedju
Alexandria — Iskanderia; from Alex-
    ander the Great
Ankyronon Polis — Teudjoi
Antaeopolis — Djew-qa, Tjebu
Apollinopolis Magna — Djeba or
    Mesen
Apollinopolis Parva — Gesa/Gesy
Aswan — Swenet
Athribis — Hut-Repyt
Bubastis — Bast
Busiris — T`et`et
Cairo — modern
Canopus — Per-Gwati

Cusae — Qis
Diosopolis Parva — Hut-sekhem, Hut
Egypt — Kam; Tamer
Eileithyiaspolis — Nekheb
Gebel el Silsila — Kheny, Khenu;
    "place of rowing"
Heirakonopolis — Nekhen
Heliopolis — Iunuio
Herakleopolis — Henen-nesut
Hermonthis — Iuny
Hermopolis — Khmun
Karnak — Ipet-isut; most select of
    places
Khemmis Panopolis — Pu Kent-min

Koptos — Gebtu
Latopolis — Iunyt, or ta Senet
Leontopolis — Nay-ta-hut
Letopolis — Khem
Lykopolis — Zawty
Memphis — Åneb-h`etchet, Mennu-
fer
Ombos — Nubt

Oxyrhynchus — Per-Medjed
Pathyris/Aphroditopolis — Per-Hathor
Sais — Sa
San el Hagar — Tanis
Tehinis — Tjeny
Tentyris — Iunet Tantere
Thebes — Uast, Wasat
Tuphium — Djerty

INTRODUCTION TO MESOPOTAMIAN NAMING

From Sumer and Akkad, through the empires of Babylon and Assyria, the system of making names was very conservative for a couple of millennia. While Sumerian is a language unrelated to any other, the other tongues of Mesopotamia are Semitic, like Egyptian, Arabic, or Hebrew.

In all of them, most names are formulaic: you fill in the blanks. Others are more original expressions of parental concerns or wishes. The formulas allow any one name to be multiplied by a couple of dozen alternatives. So these chapters each contain the potential for thousands of names for your characters.

The formulas are largely *theophoric*. That is, they call on a Deity to protect the child, give thanks for recent divine favors, or praise or promote the Deity. Theophoric names are common not only to this area, and Semitic languages, but show up strongly in early Sanskrit and early Celtic naming.

The Akkadians invented, and passed on to the Assyrians and Babylonians, a class of formula names for which I use the term "courtier names," though there are cruder alternatives.

In a "courtier name," a child's name is praise to or prayer for the ruler. If the ruler is Puzursutukulti (Akkadian for "His protection I trust"), then one of his courtiers will name a hapless baby Puzursutukultililabirhatam — "May Puzursutukulti keep the scepter for a long time." In the same class are "Mighty is the king," "Precious is the king," "The king is light to the land," and "O [fill in the God], protect the king!" These are rare in Akkadian, but become much more common in Assyrian. If these are used outside court circles, it indicates a parent with a fanatical devotion to the throne.

Writing is only invented about 3000 B.C., the earliest Sumerian cuneiform. Names have provided the keys to unlocking many of these languages, but many readings are still questionable. Not every name has a meaning given because often none has been figured out.

For a long time, Sumerian and Akkadian names flourish side-by-side, with Sumerian dominating the deltas, Akkadian the north. There is a broad transition zone of peaceful comingling. After the period of Akkadian empire-building under Sargon, there is a reactionary revival of Sumerian.

About 1850 B.C. Sumerian names finally fade out, as Semitic takes over in the area. About this time, Babylon promotes its city–God, Marduk, to Supreme God, but how much anyone in other cities really agreed is open to question, even under the Babylonian empire.

This is the transition time between Akkadian and Assyrian-Babylonian naming. Courtier names proliferate, and the Gods called upon in theophorics change.

Throughout Mesopotamia, often the only difference between the names of two groups is the choice of Deity. Hittites go for Teshup, Elamites for Umman, while all royal Assyrians are named for their king–God Ashur: Ashurbanipal, Ashurnasirpal, Ashur-etil-shame-u-irsiti-uballitsu.

Mesopotamians didn't choke at long names. There is a status to it, especially during militaristic periods. The more population you control, the longer it takes to announce you. So if your hero and heroine have short little names, they're going to sound like slaves and peasants — which they may be. But no one named Bani is going to be an ensi of a city-state, let alone a prince of an empire.

The Sumerians, who would rather rebuild a temple than conquer another city, had more manageable names, but Enshakush-Innana isn't out of place.

ASSYRIAN AND BABYLONIAN

Many names reveal gender. To begin with, no female names refer to the macho royal Gods like Marduk and Ashur. A great many female theophorics call on the Goddess, under Her title of Belit, translated as Lady or Mistress. When divine protection is invoked, male names use *usur*, female names may use *usri* instead. When someone is called after their city of origin (because they are in a different one), men are "-aya," women "-itu" after the city name. But there are quite a few names found in both camps, like Belli (Bel-li), "The Lord is mighty," or Danni-ilu, "mighty is Deity."

Like most very foreign languages, you will have to get used to the fact that the arbitrary boy-girl traits of Romance naming are violated. Frequently, men's names end in A, and "-itu" is a standard feminine ending. You can either edit to suit preconceptions, thereby losing a lot of the female names, or shrug and name the heroine Bu'itu ("the desired one," the equivalent of Desiree). But does Bu'itu look as pretty-sweet as Talia or Marqikhita?

Once again, do not let meanings foul you up. Unless it is connected to the plot, or the meaning will be discussed, put a card over the meanings and choose by looks. Meanings are included only so you do not give one of the a-boy-at-last! names to a character with older brothers on the scene. Also, "[fill in the blank] establishes my reign" and other lordly names should be reserved for kings and princes.

Names that seem extremely long to us are normal and part of the atmosphere of Assyria. Ashur-etil-shame-u-irsiti-uballitsu, brother of Ashurbanipal, had his name abbreviated in inscriptions all the way down to Sharshameuirsitiuballitsu. To Assyrians, short names were suitable for peasant soldiers, oxen, field slaves, and other domesticated animals. Expect most characters to have at least three, often four syllables to their names; do not cavil at five or six for a few.

God-Names

A long Mesopotamian tradition allows people to think of their personal deity as their older brother or parent, so sometimes names meaning "my father protects me" and the like are theophorics. Temples, in general or by name, can also fill this blank, as may kings, queens, or even the local landlord as *bel*, "master."

The plethora of Gods, and fewness of Goddesses should not be interpreted to mean that Goddesses were minor-league. Rather, Gods proliferated like saints, one or more per city or nation, while Ishtar/Inanna/Nana remained the pan-riverine Deity with many epithets, like Belit, Urkittu, or Arbela.

Spelling and Pronunciation

You don't want to know, and your readers don't want to see, all the diacriticals used by specialists to write this in Latin letters. Any Y can be written with an I. The KH's can be dropped in favor of H's. Otherwise, pronounce each vowel separately. Gone are the thousands of hyphens used to separate each and every syllable in scholarly texts. If you are an Assyriologist, you can probably figure out even the ones that have been mangled by cutting "Ta-a-a-ar" down to "Taar."

In general, you can get away with the usual:

A = A in pasta
E = E in bet
I = I in machine
KH = rough H, a little throat-clearing but not much
Q = K in kill
U = U in tune
QU = KU as in cool, not KW

Not used: C, F, J, O, V, W. Even using Y is non-standard, but clears pronunciation for English-speakers and gives a bit more variety.

In this chapter, an asterik (*) preceding a name-formula means that it can be reversed. That is, ____dan can also be Dan____; Ashurdan and Danshur are equally authentic.

FILL IN THE BLANKS WITH THESE

Unless otherwise noted, they are the names of male Deities. Follow a name with "-ma-" to say "truly" as in Anumali, "truly Anu is mighty."

abi — my father; sometimes My Father
Adad — Amorite-Assyrian storm God
Adgi — a rare name for Adad
Adunu — aka Adonis
Ae — God
akhi, akhua — my brother
Aku — God
Alla, Al — God
Amurru — Amorite God
Anu, Anum — Babylonian chief deity
Aplu — God
Arbail — Arbela; sacred city of Ishtar
Ashir, Ashur — chief God of Assyria
Atar, Attar — Aramaic Deity
Aya — Goddess, consort of Shamash
ba-ashma — the serpent
Baal — Canaanite God
Banitu — "The Beaming Goddess" of childbirth
Ba'u — Sumerian and Old Babylonian Goddess
Bel — Lord; also Enlil or Marduk
Bel-Kharran — lord of Kharran (Harran); Sin
Bel-sarbe — Nergal
Belit — Lady; the Goddess
bit-mashtari — the writing-house
Bunene — wagon-ladder of the sun-God
Dadi — God
Daguna, Dagan — aka Dagon
Dammu — Damu; God of healing
Damqu — Mitanni God
Dayan, Dayanu — the Judge
Ea — chief God of Eridu; Babylonian
Eamkurkurra — temple of Enlil at Asshur
Eanna — temple of Ishtar and Anu at Uruk
Ekarra — temple
ekur — temple; ekursha, her temple; ekurshu, his temple
Ekur — temple of Enlil at Nippur
Enlil — chief Sumerian God, and everyone later

Esaggil — a temple
Esagila — temple of Marduk at Babylon
Eshar, Esharra — temple of Ashur in Asshur
Esheriga — temple at Dur-Sharrukin
Eshitlam — temple of Nergal at Kutha
Eshu — the Goddess Isis
Eulmash — temple of Ishtar at Agade; Babylonian names
Ezida — temple of Nabu at Calah
Gamlat — "The Merciful One," the Goddess
Gula — "The Great One," Sumerian Goddess of Healing
il-biti — household God
ilani — the Gods
ili — his God
ilu — Deity, in general
iluka — thy Deity
Ishtar, Ishara — the Goddess; Her name is used in constructions that literally mean "Ishtar is lord" or "Ishtar is father"
Ishum — Sumerian fire and pest God
Khaldi — chief God of Urartu or Khaldia (Chaldea)
Khar — God
Lamashshu — personal Deities, like a lars or genius
Lamshit — temple of Nergal at Tarbisi
Makhir — God of dreams, big with Ashurnazirpal
mar — Aramaic for lord
Mar-sharri — royal prince
Marduk — chief God of Babylon
Nabu — chief God of Borsippa, very popular w/Assyrians
Nana — early name of the Goddess
Nashkhu — West Semitic God, still sometimes Assyrian Nergal — chief God of Kutha; consort of Laas
neshe — lions
Nikkal — aka Ningal, "The Great Mistress"

nishu — lion
Nusku — God
Ramman — God
sabe — warriors
Salmu, Zalmu — a God
Samu — Eshmun
Shada — a God
Shamash — sun God, consort of Aya
Sharrat — the queen; may mean Ningal or Ishtar
sharri — my king
Sharru — the king; may mean Ea or Enlil
Sher — Sherua, dawn–God
Sherua — a name of Ishtar
Shibarra — Cassite deity, possibly Shiimaliia
Shiimaliia — Cassite "Lady of the Shining Mountains"
Shipak — Cassite God, identified with Marduk
Shugab — Cassite God, identified with Nergal

Shulman, Sulman — West Semitic Deity
Shum-ili — name of the God
Shuqamuna — Cassite God of war, identified with Nergal-Nusku
Shuriash — Cassite God identified with Shamash
Si — God
Sibitti — "those seven," a cluster of Gods
Sin — moon God, very important
Sir/Zir — God
Sumu — God
Tashmetum — aka Tashmet, Goddess, consort of Nabu
Tekmet — Goddess
Tutu
Ummi
Urash, Ura — God
Urkittu — "the Goddess of Uruk"; Ishtar
Zaba, Zaban — river God of Zab
Zamama — God

FEMALE NAMES

Abi-lirim
Abi-rami
Abida
Abikha'li
Abili-ikhia
Adadidaalli
Adataa
Addati, Adatum, Addatim
Adirtu, Adirtum — mourning
Adrakhii
Agbaraa
Akhat-abisha — sister of her father
Akhat-immaa
Akhat-lamur — may I see the sister
Akhati-tabat — my sister is good
Akhi-dalli, Akhi-talli
Akhi-shame
Amat-____; maid of ____

Amti-____; handmaid of ____
Anaattalabalatu — I behold life
Arba'il-khamat — Arbela is the nation
Arba'il-sharrat — the city of Arbela is queen
Arbashi
Arrabati
Asaa
Ashshur-sharrat — the city of Asshur is queen
Atar-malausur
Baaassi
Baal-teyaabate — riches
Babaa
Bada
Badia
Baiaa
Bailu
Bakishadishaummi

Baltasi
Banitum-dannat — Banitu is mighty
Basii
Batusu
Bauyaa
Belidi
Belitneshe — Lady of the lions, epithet of Ishtar
Belitsunu — their Mistress
Bi'a
Bidadi
Biea
Biittuu
Bikhii
Bilatsunu — their produce
Bilikutu
Biniti
Bisaa
Bitaa
Bu'itu — the desired one
Daammate

Daanqii
Daliyaa
Daltaa
Damqaa
Damqaati
Danni____; mighty is
    ____
Dieru
Diimtu — tear, or pillar
Ekursha-lamur — may I
    see Her temple
Ekursha-namir — Her
    temple is shining
Erishtu
Etillit-Arba'il — Mistress
    of Arbela; epithet of
    Ishtar
Eziptum, Eziptu
Gabia
Gagaa, Gaga — necklace
Giizir
Gulate, Gulati
Ilusaa
Immaa
Indibii
Inqaa
Irkullu
Ishtar-Arba'il — Ishtar is
    Arbela
Iuni
Kabili
Kabtaa
Kabtiya
Kali
Kalkhaa
Karrite
Khaandi
Khanabushaa
Khaninaa
Kharimate
Kharra
Khate'
Khatezaa
Khazalaa
Khinnibel
Khipaa
Khiptaa
Khitubarra
Khuda
Khudieshalibbi
Khulaliti

Khulutti
Khumbushtu
Khuunnubat____
Khuzalatum
Kidiniti
Kiidi
Kullaa
Kurlamur — may I see
Kuunzuubtum
Laamashshi
Lakha
Lakhal
Lalaaltu
Lariindu — grape
Late'
Likkiimmaa
Lubaltaat — may she live;
    masculine would be
    Lubalat
Ludakie
Luunti
Makhlara
Mannuki____; who is
    like ____
Maqartu
Marqikhita — perfumed
Marti-rapie — my lady is
    a healer
Martii — my daughter,
    or, my lady
Mesaa
Muballitat-Sherua
Murabataash
Naannia
Naaptera
Naditu
Naki'a
Namirti
Nanaa
Naqia
Niika
Ninqaa
Ninuakha
Nur-ekalli — light of my
    palace
Pakhii
Papaa
Parsuu
Pa'u — bird-name
Qunabatu
Ramti

Ramtu
Rimute — graceful
Rimutu — grace
Rubuutum
Saammuramat = Semi-
    ramis
Sa'an
Saarpalli
Saggaa, Saggiya
Sagibie
Sakhdie
Sakhiish
Salientu
Samiltu
Saraa
Sarpi
Sha____aaninni; to ____
    we belong
Shaalmisha
Shaditu
Shakintu
Shamma
Shapiikaari
Shapiraakh
Sharraa
Sheguu
Shiidannati
Sihati
Siinqishaamur — see her
    need
Sikhaa
Sil____
Siliinni
Sinqi____
Sudalaa
Sukkiitu
Sumuitu
Suuhkhru
Tabuua
Talia
Teie
Teitu
Tuati
Tuliikha
Tuqu
Uari
Uma
Ummakhnu
Ummatkha
Ummiabia
Ummii

Ummishede
Unsharti
Uqubutu
Uyaa
Waduukki

Yabibie
Yapa — the beautiful lady
Yaqarakhi
Yaqiratu
Zabibie

Zakutu — the clean one
Zarpi
Zazaa

____abausur; ____, protect the father
____abusri; ____, protect the father
____ada
____agausri, ____agausur; ____, protect the crown
____akhatusri; ____, protect the sister
____amat; ____ is the word (after vowel) ____ramat
____beldaini
____belitusri; ____, protect the mistress
____belusri; ____, protect the master
____dan; ____ has judged
____dari
____dinini; ____, judge me
____duri; ____ is my wall
____durusri, ____durusur; ____, protect the wall
____elit; ____ is shining
____etirat
____khashina
____ilaa; ____ is God
____ishme
____ittiya; ____ is with me
____kashdu

____khaam
____khuundu
____killiinni; ____, support me
____li; ____ is mighty
____li'at
____mayali
____mudammiqsarbe
____na'id; ____ is exalted
____napshir; ____, be kind again
____rimeinni; ____, have mercy on her
____rimeni; ____ is merciful
____rishat
____sabtini; ____, succor me
____sallatti; ____ shadows
____sharau; ____ is strong towards them
____sharrat; ____ is queen
____sharusur; ____ protect the king
____sillit; ____ shades
____taklak; In ____ I trust
____umme; ____ is mother
____ummisharrani; ____ is mother of our king; Ishtar
____ushabshi; ____ has called into existence

Female Native of:

Arba'ilitu — Arbela
Ashshuritu — Asshur
Balikhitu — the city of Balikh
Barsipitu — Barsip (Bor-

sippa)
Bazitu — Bazi (Bazu)
Dursharrukinaitu — Dur-sharrukin
Kalkhitu — Kalkhi

(Calah)
Ninuaitu — Ninua (Nin-eveh)

MALE NAMES

Amel-____; man of ____
Amel-al-Gubbu — man of (city) Gubbu
Amel-Gula — man of Gula
Arba'ilaya — Arbela
Ashshuraya — (city) Asshur
Babilaya — the Babylonian
Barkhalsaya — Barkhalsu
Eridaya — Eridu

Gargameshaya — Gargamesh (Car-chemish)
Isanaaya — Isana
Kalkhaya — city of Kalkha (Calah)
Khalsuaya — Khalsu
Khamataya — Khamath (Hamath)
Kharranaya — Kharran (Harran)
Kumaaya — city of Kuma (Kume)
Kutaaya — Kuta (Cutah)

Native of:

Mar-Ishnunak — man of the city of Ishnunak
Ninuaya — Nineveh
Qumanaya — Comana
Rasapaya — Rezeph

Sidunuaya/Zidunaya — Sidon
Sulaaya — city of Sulu
Tabalaya — Tabal
Tamdimua — native of the Sealand, delta region

A-bil-kish-shu — bringing power
A-khi — my brother is ____ (can be a Goddess)
A-khu-lu
A-li-li — the strong one
A-mar-____; Fullness of ____
A-me-qi
Abdi____; servant of ____
Abi-____; father is ____
Abi-ina-ekalli-lilbur — my father may grow old in the palace
Abi-lishir — may father succeed
Abi-ulisi — I did not know my father; posthumous child name
Abi-ya-qar — the father is dear
Abi-zer-utir — father has reestablished offspring
Abitsharriushur — keep the decision of the king
Abkharudi
Abunu
Abu-shalim — father is safe
Adalal, Adallali
Adasi
Addar-aya, Addaya — born in the month of Adar
Agala — foal
Agru — hired laborer
Akhali
Akhallili
Akhanaarshi — we got a brother
Akhe-shullim
Akhi-lamur — may I see my brother!
Akhi-lishir — may my brother succeed
Akhi-qa-bi — my brother commands
Akhi-qamu — my brother has arisen
Akh-lurshi — may I get a brother
Akh-tab-shi, Akh-it-tab-shi — A brother is brought into existence
Akhua-eriba — my brother has rewarded
Akhunu, Akuni — little brother
Aki-su, Ak-ki

Am-me-ni-____; why, o ____?
Amsini
Amur-____; I saw ____
Amur-ilutu-____; I saw the divinity of ____
Anaakh-____; I sigh, ____
Ana-____-qaalla
Ana-____-taklak; in ____ I trust
Apil-____; son of ____
Aqar-____-lumur — may I see the glory of ____
Aqru — precious
Arad-____; servant of ____
Arad-akheshu — servant of his brothers
Arad-nu-bat-ti — born on the nubattu day
Arba'il-bel-iddin — Arbela is lord of an heir
Ardi, Ardu, Arduti
Arik-den-____; long is the judgement of ____
Arikhu, Arikhi
Arkat-____-damqa — the forecast of ____ is auspicious
Arrizu
Ashapi
Asharidu
Ashshi-idi — I lifted up my hands (prayed)
Ashupiwa____
Atamardumuq — I saw the favor of the God
Atanaakh — I sigh
Atanakh-____; I sigh, ____
Atequ
Atrie, Atru
Attailuma — Thou art truly God!
Azii
Baal-tu-____; ____ is wealth
Baaltunu — our riches
Babanu
Bakilya
Balatsu, Balatu

Baltiyau

Bamuu

Banakhe, Banakhua

Bani, Banini, Banunu

Baraakhu, Barruqu

Bashutrie

Batulu — youth

Belaakh____, Bilaakh____; Fear ____!

Belbiti____; ____ is lord of the
family/house

Beldallil-iliaa — the lord of the
needy is my God

Belmati____; ____ is lord of the
country

Belmati-ilu — the lord of the country is the God

Bilaaa

Bir____, Bur____; son of ____

Birakhi

Bishu — the bad one

Bit____lumur — house of ____ may
I see

Bitmashtariibnu — the writing house
has created

Buna____; child of ____

Buridri

Dabibi

Dadusu

Dagililu

Dakhaa

Dakuru

Damqa-amate____; the commands
of ____ are friendly

Damqi

Damqi-ilishu — graciously received
by his God

*Dan____, Dani____, Dayan____;
____ is judge

Dananu

Daniyati-ilu — my judge is the God

Danni____, Dannu____; mighty is

____

Darusharru

Dikhaya

Dilil____, Dalil____; devotee of

____

Dinanu

Dishii — my growth

Diti____taba — decision of ____ is
good

Dugul____; obey ____

Dugulpan____; obey the will of

____

Dumqi____; graciousness of

Dumuya

Dur____; a stronghold is ____;
popular

*Durmaki____; a stronghold for the
frail is ____

Durna'id — the stronghold is exalted

Du'uzaya — born in the month of
Tammuz

Ebisi, Ebishum

Edasi

Egibi

Ekulu

Ellu — brightness

Ellubabkhinni — bright is the gate
of khinni

Emidana____; I relied on ____

Ena____; be merciful, ____

Eni____; eye of ____

Ennam____; be merciful, ____

Ennushi

Eresh____; planted has ____

Eriba — rewarded

Eriba____; rewarded by ____

Eshraya — born on the twentieth day
(of month)

Eteru

Etilli — lordly

Etilpii____; ____ is lord of the word

Etilqabi

Etir____; spared by ____

Ezipata

Gabatim

Gabbi____eresh — everything ____
planted

Gabbiyaana____; everything belonging to ____

Gabbuamur — everything sees

Gabbuana____; all belongs to ____

Gabbuinaqata____; everything is in
the hand of ____

Gakhal

Galulu, Galul

Gimil____; gift of ____

Gimil-dumqi-lumur — may I see the
gracious gift

Gimillu — gift

Giri____, Giru____; client of ____

Giritu, Girtu, Girte

Gungunuum
Gurn, Guruna
Ibaqame
Ibashshi-ilani — there exist gods
Ibi____, Ibbi____; ____ has called;
  popular
Ibni____; created by ____
Idaate____alaka — at the side of
  ____ I walk
*Idanni____; ____ has looked upon
  me
Iddina____; given by ____
*Idi____; ____ knows
Ikkaru — peasant
Illuu, Illuuknu
Ilqisu
Ilu____; the Deity is ____
Imashshi
Imbiyati — he called me
Imbupaniya
Immani____
Ina____yaallak — with ____ I walk
Inaeshietir — from destruction he has
  delivered
Inaqibi____; by order of ____
Inasharri____alak — in the breath of
  ____ I walk
Inibi____; fruit of ____
*Iqbi____; announced by ____
*Iqisha____; ____ has presented
Iqisu
Irashshi____
Irbi____; great is ____
Irishum — of the earth
Irsietu
Ishdi____
Ishma____; ____ has heard
Ishmanni____; ____ has heard me
Itti____aninu — from/with ____ are we
Itti____balatu — with ____ is life
Itti____banu — with ____ is joy
Izba____; sprout of ____
Izbu — sprout
Izbulishir — the sprout may succeed
Izkur____; ____ has called by name
Kabti
Kadamu
Kallitu
Kandal, Kandalani, Kandalanu
Kaparu — shepherd
Kapdu — bird catcher

Karashtu
Karsiaku
Kasutu
Khaakhkhuru
Khabaki
Khabanamru, Khabani
Khabasu, Khabasi
Khabatali
Khalsitu
Khanasi, Khanu
Khapini
Kharakhu
Khasabu
Khatianu
Khazanu, Khazianu
Khazugu
Khidatani — Thou hast renewed me
Khimagu
Khunii
Khushanu
Khuutni____; my protection is ____
Kibarim
Kilakuu
Kilsi
Kimunu
Kin____; true is ____
*Kinanni____; establish me, ____
Kiraakhe
Kiribitu____; blessed of ____
Kiribtii, Kiribtu — blessed
Kiru____
Kishitu — property
Kisir____; property of ____
Kitri____; my ally is ____
Kitti____; righteous is ____
Kudurana — the cock/rooster
Kulu____
Kurii, Kurie
Kurzabu
Kuzub____; splendid is ____
Ladagil____; ____ does not deal
  falsely
La'iti____
Lakie — the weak one
Laliim
Laqipu
Latadar____; don't be angry, ____
Lategi____; don't sin against ____
Lidan____; child of ____
Lidanbelmatatti — child of the lord of
  the lands

Limraaslibbi____; may the heart of ____ have compassion

Limur____; heart of ____

Lipit____; work of ____; popular

Lubalat, Liblut — may he live

Ludari

Ludimu, Ludime

Lukhail

Lulabbir-sharrussu — may his royalty grow old

Lushakin

Lushulmu

Lusiananur____; may it come forth into the light, ____

Makhdie

Manki____

Mannipite

Mannuishassi — who cries?

Mannuka____; who is like ____?

Mannuki____li' — who is mighty like ____?

Mannukima____khatin — who is like ____ protecting?

Manzarne, Mazarne

Mar____; son of ____

Mar-shelibi — fox-cub

Mashmashani — our charmer

Miinulaanshi — how should I forget?

*Milki____; my counsel is ____

Minuakhtiana____; how have I sinned against ____?

Minulaqbe — what shall I say?

*Mudammiq____; ____ makes favorable

Mukin____; ____ establishes

Mumar____

Munamme

Munepush____, Munipish____

Muqalilmitu — comforting for the dead

Muranu, Murana — young lion

*Mushabshi____; brought into being by ____

*Mushallim____; saved by ____

Mushtali

Mutakkil____; strength of ____

Mutarris____

Muzuraa

*Nadin____; a giver is ____; God-first, very

Nadinbel____; given the lord by ____ popular

Nadinshum — given progeny

Nadnu

*Na'id____; exalted is ____; both very popular

Namru — shining

Naram____; beloved of ____

Nasib____

Neshu — the lion

Nigazi

Niiskhur____

Nishpatiutli

Nuniya, Nunu, Nunua

Nur____; light of ____

Nuur, Nuri, Nuriya — light

Paliikhkaliblut — May the worshipper of Thee live!

Palkhushezib — He saved the god-fearing

Pan____lamur — May I see the face of ____

Panilikamish — Before the God he is prostrate

Pappu

Parutu

Pasii, Pashii

Pilaqu, Pilaqa — the axe

Pir____; offspring of ____

Pulu — the stone

Pushulu

Puuglu — the radish

Puzuur____; security is ____

Qabasuilu

Qali — lamenting

Qama____

Qaqqadanu — the grasshopper

Qassuni

Qatar — rock

Qibit____

Qishti____; present of ____

Qishtiya

Quqii — the pelican

Qurbuunasir

Qurdi____; my strength is ____

Qurritu

Raamushailanishu — grace of his Gods

*Rabi____; great is ____

Raksali

Ram____

Renshu____; his favor is ____

Ribat____
Ribaya — born on the fourth day
Riish____; servant of ____
Rikhanu — remainder
Rikhate
Rim____, Rimut____; servant of ____
Rimanni____; be merciful to me,
____
Rimush
Ritti____; my hand (help) is ____
Riupikhati
Riziinni
Ruradidi
Saambuukbel
Saansuru/Zaanzuru — locust, insect
Saasi, Sasi, Sasiya
Sabri/Zabri, Sapri/Zapri
Sabuum/Zabuum
Saeru, Sairu
Sakuku — the deaf one
Salama____; peace is ____
Salamu/Zalamu
Sallaya/Zallaya, Salaa/Zalaa
Samakhi
Sanini
Sapiku, Sapiki
Sarsaru/Zarzaru — locust
Sayadu/Zayadu — hunter
Sha____ninu — to ____ we belong
Shaddinnu
Shadu____; a mountain of refuge is
____
Shaibua
Shakhamilrama
Shakinshum
Shakiru, Shakizu — drunkard
Shalamashaiqbe — He has announced
  her prosperity
Shalimdu
Shalmuetir
Shamardi
Shamshi____; my sun is ____
Shaqalautirshu
Sharbi____
Sharilaniiliya — the king of the Gods
  is my god
Sharishtar — the king is Ishtar
Sharkalesharri — the king of the uni-
  verse is my king
Sharru____; king is ____
Sharru-iqbi — the king has commanded

Sharruludari — may the king live for-
  ever!
Shashii
Shei____
Sheimka
Shelibi, Shelipi — the fox
Shepa____, Shepa____asbat — I
  took hold of the feet of ____ (I
  supplicated ____)
Sherabusur
Sheriq
Shezibanni — save me!
Shiguua
Shilaani
Shimanni____
Shiqilaa
Shiriqtu — present
Shitariba — She has increased
Shukubi, Shukubiim
Shullumu
Shumaat____
Shumiliashipush — the name of the
  god is his diviner
Shumlibshi — may it be a son/the
  name may subsist
Shurdi
Shusisii, Shusisai
Shuzubu
Setinu
Sidalabiri
Sihir____
Sikilti____
Silbel/Zilbel
Silim____; grace of ____
Simanaya — born in the month of
  Siwan
Siparanu
Sitenu
Sualii
Sukaari
Sulili
Sutie
Tabali
Tabashab____; good is the dwelling
  of ____
Tabeter____; good is the protection
  of ____
Tabi
Tabni____; preserve,____
Tabrigimili — Good is the cry to the
  God

Tabsagal
Tabsil____; good is the shadow/
  protection of ____
Tagalii
Takiel____; trusting in ____
Takisham____
Taklakana____; I trust in ____
Taklakana-beliya — I trust in my lord
Tameraniti
Tammeshenshu
Tappubelilani — a companion is the
  lord of the gods
Taqisa____
Taqisu, Taqish
Tarasi
Taribi — reward
Taribi____; reward of ____
*Taris____; directed by ____
Tashpuru
Tebetaya — born in the month of
  Tebet
Tikaamurri
Tubusalu, Tubusu
Tukulti____; my help is ____
Turi
Uazaru
*Uballitsu, Uballitsu____; ____ has
  called him into life; very popular
Ubbuku, Ubbuki, Ubuukki
Ubru
Ubuku
Udammiq____
Uddanu

Uginie
Ukhati
Ululaya — born in the month of Elul
Unzarkhu____, Unzirkhu____
Upakhkhir____; strength from
  ____
Upaqaana____, Upaq____; I wait
  for ____
Upaqu
Uqur____
Urruda
Uru____
Usatu
*Ushaanni____
Usurmamaate — keep the oaths
Uznanu
Yaali — a steenbok
Yabar
Yaburu
Yalamaa
Zaanduru
Zaarkhi____
Zabanu, Zabbaanu
Zakhaar
Zaruti, Zarutu
Zer____; seed of ____
Zeri — seed
Zerkhaaatu
Zibari
Zinili
Zirritsu
Zukhattim

____abua; ____ is my father
____akheidden; ____ has given
  brothers
____akhelumur; ____, may I see
  brothers
____akheriba; ____ has given a
  brother as a reward
____akhiddina, ____akhiddin; ____
  has given a brother; very popular
____alikidenshi; ____ goes beside
  the weak one
____alikidiya; ____ goes by my side
____alikpani; ____ is leader
____apaliddina, ____apaliddin;
  ____ has given a son/an heir; very
  popular

____apallishir; ____, may the son
  prosper
____apalusur; ____, protect the son
____asharidu, ____asharid; ____ is
  first in place
____asu; ____ is a healer
____balat; ____ is life
____balatani, ____ballitani
____balateresh; ____ has planted life
____ballit; ____, keep him alive;
  popular
____baltunishe; ____ is abundance
  for the people
____banaplu; ____ is begetter of
  the son
____bani; ____ is creator

____baniya, ____bunaya; ____ is
my creator
____bel; ____ is lord
____belani; ____ is our lord
____beldan, ____beldani; ____ is
lord of judgement
____beli; ____ is my lord
____belka'in, ____belkin; ____,
establish the lord
____belmati; ____ is lord of the
country
____belnisheshu; ____ is lord of
the people
____belshumati; ____ is lord of the sons
____belukin; ____ has established
the lord
____belusur, ____-bulusur; ____,
protect the lord/master
____binaukin; ____ has established
a son
____bushuqusur; ____, preserve
the property
____dabibnir; ____, destroy the
slanderer
____damiq, ____udammiq; ____ is
friendly
____dananni, ____dainanni; ____
is our judge
____danani, ____daninanni
____daninani; ____, strengthen me
____dari; ____ remains forever
____diniamur; ____, regard my
lawsuit
____dumeqaanni
____dumuqilani; ____ is the most
friendly of the Gods
____durenshi; ____ is a stronghold
for the weak
____duri; ____ is my wall; very
popular
____durkusur, ____durusur; ____,
preserve the wall; popular
____durqali; ____ is a refuge for
lamenting
____emuqi, ____emukie; ____ is
my strength
____emurinni, ____emuranni;
____ has looked at me
____epishilu; ____ is the making
God
____eriba; ____ has rewarded; pop-

ular
____eshtaqel; ____ has paid
____etilkinaplu; ____, lord, estab-
lish the son
____etillu; ____ is lord him alive!
____etiranni; ____ spared me
____etiraple; ____ spares the sons
____gabbiiqbi; ____ has announced
all
____gamelat; ____ spares
____garuaniri; ____, destroy my
adversary
____ginieeresh
____ibashi; ____ exists
____ibni; ____ has created; popular
____iddin; ____ has given; very
popular
____idri; ____ is my helper
____ili; ____ is God
____imetti
____iqishanni; ____ has given me a
present
____ishmeani, ____shimani; ____
has heard me
____ishtagal; ____ has paid
____ittiya; ____ is with me
____kabi; ____ is mighty
____kallimanni; ____, let me see a
child
____karsibubaash; ____ has put the
slander to shame
____kashidayabi; ____ defeats the
enemy
____kashir; ____ brings good luck
____kasir; ____ preserves
____khamannu
____khamatua; ____ is my refuge
____khasis
____khudin
____khusanni; ____, spare me
____kibsiusur; ____, protect my path
____kinaplu; ____, establish the son
____kindugul; ____, look upon the
faithful one
____kinuser; ____, protect the
faithful one
____kinzer; ____, establish the seed
____kusuranni; ____, save me
____kusurshu; ____, save him
____kuzubilani; ____ is the splen-
dor of the gods

____lamur; may I see ____

____li; ____ is mighty/wise

____li'kullati; ____ is almighty

____malik; ____ is counselor; popular

____marsharriusur; ____, protect the king's son

____mattaqqin; ____, order the country

____matusur; ____, protect the country

____mituballit; ____ has returned the dead to life

____mukinpaliya; ____ establishes my reign

____mushammir; ____ guards

____mushezibnapshate; ____ saves the living beings

____mutabe-el; ____ is guardian

____mutaqqin; ____ orders

____nada; ____ is lofty

____nadinakhu; ____ gives a brother

____nadinaplu; ____ gives a son; popular

____nadinshum, ____nadinshumu; ____ gives a name/posterity

____napishti; ____ gave me life

____narari, ____nirari; ____ is helper

____nasiraplu; ____ protects the son

____nasirubarshu; ____ protects his friends

____nirdabibi; ____ destroys the slanderer

____nishu; ____ is a lion

____nuri; ____ is my light

____nurkalamur; ____, may I see Thy light

____pashir; ____ loosens

____pirkhililbur; ____, may my offspring grow old

____qarradu; ____ is a hero

____qatasabat; ____, help; ____, succor

____qater, ____qatar; ____ is a rock

____qusurani; ____, preserve me

____ra'imsharru; ____ loves the king

____resh-ishi; ____, lift up my head

____re-u; ____ is shepherd

____re'uni; ____ is our shepherd

____rikhtusur; ____, protect the remainder

____rimanni; ____, have mercy on me

____risua; ____ is my helper

____sabatani, ____sabatanni; ____ succor me

____salim; ____ is merciful; popular

____shadua, ____shadu; ____ is my mountain

____shaiqbuulini; ____ has not altered His promise

____shakinbalatu; ____ provides life

____shakinremu; ____ effects mercy

____shakinshum; ____ effects a name

____shakni; ____ is my governor

____shallim; ____, keep safe; popular

____shallimanni; ____, keep me safe

____shallimsharru; ____, keep the king safe

____shamshi; ____ is my sun

____shaquinamati; ____ is exalted in the country

____sharibni; ____ has created the king

____sharrani; ____ is our king

____sharru; ____ is king; popular

____sharusur; ____, protect the king

____shezib, ____shezibbi; ____, deliver from peril

____shii; ____ is my friend

____shimanni; ____, hear me

____shulumamur; ____, I saw safety

____shumeresh; ____ has planted a name; popular

____shumiddina, ____shumiddin; ____ has given posterity/a name

____shumiqisha; ____ has presented posterity

____shumkittilishir; ____, may the true son succeed

____shumlibur; ____, may the name grow strong

____shumukin; ____ has estab-
lished the name
____suusur; ____, protect the path
____taar; ____ is merciful
____tab, ____tabu; ____ is good
____taddin; ____ has given
____taklak; in ____ I trust
____talimusur; ____, protect the
sibling
____tappa; ____ is companion
____tiparii; ____ is my torch
____tuklatsu; ____ is his help
____uballit; ____ has called into
life

____ukinni; ____ has established
me
____upakhkhir; ____ has strength-
ened
____usala, ____usalli; I implored
____
____ushabshi; ____ has called into
existence
____usippi; to ____ I prayed
____usur; ____, protect
____yababi
____zakirshum; ____ proclaims
posterity

AKKADIAN

Old Akkadian is the Semitic language spoken in Mesopotamia alongside and
to the north of Sumerian. In most cities of the middle ground the population's
names will split between Sumerian and Akkadian pretty evenly. Farther south,
the Akkadians thin out; in the north, Sumerians disappear.

Most male names are theophoric. Women primarily use profane, that is,
non-theophoric, names. Do not take ones like (GEME____) Amat____, "female
slave of ____" too literally: GEME-Enlil and GEME-Sin were queens out of the
highest nobility. GEME merely indicates that that syllable was written in Sumerian ideographs rather than Akkadian.

DEITIES AND OTHER BLANK FILLERS

Note that Ishtar's name is often plugged into male as well as female constructions: "Ishtar-is-my-father" as well as "My-mother-is-Ishtar," "Ishtar-is-a-
lion" as well as "Ishtar-is-a-lioness." When a culture considers You Ruler of
Heaven, Judge of Battles, Giver of Law, Creator of Kings, etc., you never take
second place.

Interestingly, many of the more ancient war-words are feminine. Those new
high-tech weapons, swords, are masculine, but axes, maces, archery, and chari-
ots are all feminine.

FILL THE BLANKS WITH THESE

Abba
abi — my father
abil — the man
abu — father
Adad, Addu — storm God
akh, akhu, akham — brother
akhatum — sister
Alla — Goddess
alum, alu — the city
Amar-Sin — God
amu — paternal uncle
Amurru — God
Apih — God
Asar — God
Ayya — Goddess
Baba — Goddess
Baza
belatum — lady
beli — my lord; or My Lord
belum — lord
Bibi
Dagan — grain God
Damkina
Dumuzi — post–Sargonic
Ea — also just E, esp. before a vowel
elak — your God; often LAK after a vowel
Enlil — sky God
Gura — God
Haia — Goddess
Hansha
Harim — God
Ilaba — God
ilak — your God; often LAK after a vowel
ili — my God; often IL before a vowel, or LI after one
Illat — Goddess
ilshu — his God
iltum — Goddess
ilum — God; often LUM after a vowel
Inanna, Nanna — occ. used instead of Ishtar
Irra — God
Ishar, Isharra
Ishtar, Eshtar — "the Righteous One"; the Goddess
Ishum — God
Kabda — God

khal — maternal uncle
Kubum — God
laba — lion
labat — lioness
Laz, Laaz — God
Malik — counselor
malkat — princess
Mama — Goddess
mani — beloved
Mer — God
Meslam — God
Nani
Ningal — Goddess
Ninshubur
Nirah
Nisaba
Numushda
Nunu
nur — light
nuri — my light
Padan — God
pu — word
pusu — His word
puzur — protection
puzursu — His protection
Rasap — God
Rimush — God
Shahan — God
Shamagan — God
Shamash — sun–God
shar, sharrum — the king
Shara — Goddess
sharrat — the queen
-shu — His
Shulgi — deified ruler
Shullat — Goddess
Shumuqan — God
si — she; or She if you use for a Goddess
Sikkur — God
Sin — moon–God
sumu — the progeny
Tishpak — God
Tutu — God
Ulmash — God
umme — mother
ummi — my mother
Wer — also Wir; God
Zikir — God

FEMALE NAMES

Akati-waqrat
Akhulit — woe!
Allasharuum
Amat_____ — slave (fem.) of _____
Arbat — fourth
Aruqtum — green
Arwit — gazelle
Ashlultum — carry away
Balukhtum — feared
Barag-gigalara
Barag-irnun
Barag-lu
Barag-rana-amat-ubkugga
Barnamtarra
Bashtum — vigor; female organs
Bizua
Dabatum — goodness
Daguna
Dariishmatum — the Eternal One has
   heard
Dimmuzi
Dimtur
Dudittum, Dudat — a pectoral orna-
   ment
Enarit — to smite
Erubatum — a festival
Gartum — strong
Gibutum, Kibutum — to trust
Gishgal-irnun
Gudatum — baby
Halati
Hegirnuna
Heshaga
Impae
Ishpatum — arrow-case
Kallatum — bride, daughter-in-law
Kamkammatum — ring
Kaspitum — silver
Kharshitum
Khasastum — to think or remember
Khassat, Khazit — axe (for wood)
Khidutum — joy
Khultum — mouse
Khurat, Khurastum — gold
Kittum — justice
Kubatum — heavy
Kugsigpadda
Kusiptum — cake, pastry
Laqatum — to tear out

Libittum — brick
Lilishshtum — musical instrument
Litum — strength
Lutumuat — may thou be conjured
Mammitum, Mammit — oath
Manat — to love
Marat_____ — daughter of _____
Marat, Merat — daughter, girl
Markhushat — a precious stone;
   turquoise?
Matqutum — sweet almond; sweet-
   ness
Menit — love
Mirit, Miritum — musical instrument
Mittum — war-mace
Mushaltum — mirror
Mushtum — night
Naaqit — to lament
Na'ashrum — to live
Nabalkutum — to revolt
Nadit — to praise
Nakhiashtum — rich, wealthy
Nakhutum — rest
Namrirutum — shine
Namurtum — shining
Namzarutum — a sword
Naplaqtum — war-axe
Naramtum — beloved
Narat — river
Narkabtum — chariot
Natit, Natitium — to throw
Nin-igi-annakezu
Nirtum — smiter
Nuartum — singer
Nukhsit — prosperity
Nurit — light
Nurmtum — pomegranate
Pashtatum — flax, linen
Pirkhashtum — flea
Pizitum — white
Puzuntum — veiled; born with a caul?
Qishtum — gift
Rabatum, Rabbatum — light, soft
Raumtum — beloved
Ribatum, Ribatim, Ribaat — com-
   pensation
Riishtum — rejoicing
Rikhatum — rest
Rintum — love

Rubatum — princess
Sarpanitum — silvery
Shamsatum — disk of the sun
Shat____ — the one of ____; = masculine Shu____
Shelibutum, Shalibutum — fox
Shibtum — old (woman)
Shimtim, Shimtum — destiny
Shinitum — a kind of cloth
Shu'atum — lady
Shuilat — carry away
Shulputum — to ravage
Shumuntum — fat
Sibit, Shibit — seven
Simtum — jewel
Subitum — prayer
Suhush-ki-in
Tabtum — good
Tamshilsit — image, likeness
Tarishaam — to rejoice
Temitum — weaver
Ti'amtum, Tiamat — the sea

Tishtum — rejoicing
Tukin-khatti-igrisha
Udaadzenaad
Ummanum — army (a feminine word)
Urenuntaea
Waqartum — dear, precious
Washtum — powerful
Watartum
Zagaanbi
Zakhutum — oil-presser
Zalimtum — black
Zarmu
Zazaru
Zazatum, Sasatum — moth
Zelitum — shade, protection
Zikiltum — acquisition
Zukhartum, Sukhartum — servant girl
Zummatum, Summatum — pigeon
Zuraritim — lizard; quick, agile
Zurmu

____abi — ____ is my father
____duri — ____ is my wall
____natum

____simti — ____ is my ornament/dignity

MALE AND NEUTER NAMES

A'ar____ — young man of ____
Aba____ — the father is ____
Abi____ — my father is ____
Abil____ — man of his Deity, ____
Abu____, Abuum____ — father is ____
Akhu____ — brother is ____
Akhuma, Akhumma — it's a brother!
Ali____ — where is ____?
Ama____ — paternal uncle is ____
Ami____ — my paternal uncle is ____
Amiir____ — one looked upon by ____
Amur____ — I saw ____
An____taklaku — I trust in ____
Anaah____ — I am exhausted, ____!
Aradmu
Arshi____ — I have acquired ____
Arwija — gazelle
Atanaah — I have had enough
Bal____ — without ____ ....

Bani____ — creator is ____
Beli____ — my lord is ____
Dad____ — beloved is ____
Dalim____ — twin is ____
Dan____ — mighty is ____
Danki____ — mightiness is like ____
Ela____ — a God indeed is ____
Eli____ — my God is ____; can use Goddess
Enbi____ — my fruit of ____; can use Goddess
Enbu____ — fruit of ____; can use Goddess
Enentarzi
Enna____ — mercy, ____
Ennam____ — mercy, my God ____
Enni____ — mercy, my ____
Ennum____, Enum____ — mercy, ____
Epiir____ — ____ has provided

Erreshum
Eshme____—____ heard
Esur____, Eshur____—____ pro-
tected him
Etelalpu____, Etepu____— noble is
the word of ____
Gablulu
Gari____—(who is) the opponent
of ____?
Haablum — the one treated violently
Habil — he has been treated vio-
lently/unjustly
Habilkin — the just one has been
treated unjustly
Habilum — he has been treated
unjustly
Hal____— maternal uncle is ____
Heduut____— the joy of ____
Husus____— remember, O ____
Ibi____—____ has named
Ibni____—____ has created
Ida____—____ knows/is concerned
for
Idin____—____ has given
Idum____— the strength of ____
Ikrub____—____ blessed
Iku____—____ has proven true
Ili____— my God is ____; can use
Goddess
Iliish, Elish — in God (trust)
Ilumma — it's the God!
Imdi____— my support is ____
Imi____, Imid____— the support
of ____
Imlik____—____ has come to a
decision
Imni____—____ loved
Inin____— grant a favor, ____
Ipiq____— grace of ____
Iplu____—____ looked graciously
Ipqusha — Her grace
Ipti____—____ has opened
Iptu____, Iptur____—____ has
ransomed
Ipu____, Ipul____—____ has
answered
Iram____—____ has shown love
Ire____, Iri____—____ shepherded
Irib____—____ has compensated
Irriib____— he has compensated
Isar____— righteous is ____

Ishim____—____ has decreed
Ishku____—____ has provided
Ishma____—____ has heard
Ishni____—____ for a second time
Ishtup____—____ preserved
Ishur____—____ protected
Itur____—____ has returned
Kalab____— hound of ____
Kali____— my all is ____
Kasid____— he has arrived, ____
Kazuhara-kal
Kin____— preserve him, ____
Kuru____, Kurbi____
Kurub____ — worship ____
Laba____— a lion is ____
Libur____—____, may he stay in
good health
Lipit____— handiwork of ____
Lu-Nanna
Lugalanda
Lushalim — may he be well
Maki____ — who is like ____?
Mani____— beloved of ____
Manki____, Manumki____
Masiam____— enough for me,
____; can use Goddess
Mat____— when, ____?
Megir____— the favored one of ____
Meru, Maru — son, boy
Mesi____— enough, ____!
Mihirsu, Mahirsu — who is his equal?
Mika____— who is like ____?
Minarni — what is my sin?
Mittasu — war-mace
Mushium — night
Mushulum — mirror
Nabi____— named by ____
Nada — praise
Namer____, Namiri____—____
shines
Namzaruum — a sword
Naplis____— look, ____
Naram____, Narame____—
beloved of ____
Nashir____— protected by ____
Nawir____—____ shines
Nuh____, Nuhi____— calm down,
____
Nuid____— praise ____
Nur____— the light of ____
Paluh____— awe-inspiring is ____

Pasha____, Pasah____ — become tranquil, ____

Pu____ — word of ____

Puzur____ — protection of ____

Qur____, Qurdi____ — heroism of ____

Qurad____, Quradi____ — a hero/warrior is ____

Ra____ — shepherd is ____

Rabi____ — great is ____

Raim____ — beloved of ____

Rimi____, Rim____ — gift of ____

Ris____ — a helper is ____

Rish____ — rejoicing ____

Risi____ — my helper is ____

Risu____ — his helper is ____

Salim____, Shalim____ — well is ____

Sari____ — breeze of ____

Satpi____, Shatpi____ — one preserved by ____

Sha____ — the one of ____

Shar____ — a king is ____

Shu____ — the one of ____; very popular

Shum____, Shumu____

Silla____, Silli____ — shade of ____

Sillus____ — his shade is ____

Sumid____ — support him, ____

Sumu____, — progeny of ____

Ta____, Tab____ — good is ____

Tadi____, Tadin____ — ____ has given; can use Goddess

Takil____ — one who trusts in ____

Tamshilsu — image, likeness

Tura____, Turam____ — return to me, ____

Ubil____ — ____ has brought

Uli____, Ulid____ — ____ has begotten

Ummi____ — my mother is ____; use Goddess

Utul____ — bosom of ____

Waqar____ — precious is ____

Watar____ — preeminent is ____

____a'ah, ____aha — ____ is brother

____aal — ____ is the city

____a'ar, ____ajar — ____ is young man

____aba — ____ is the father

____abi — ____ is my father; used by women

____abushu — ____ is his father

____ahi — ____ is my brother

____alsu, ____alshu — ____ is his city

____alum — my God, ____, is the city

____ama — ____ is paternal uncle

____ami — ____ is my paternal uncle

____amrani — look on me, ____

____aqar — ____ is precious

____ashrani — ____, take care of me

____asi — ____ is my doctor

____baashti — ____ is my dignity

____bani — ____ is creator

____banika — ____ is your creator

____baqar — ____ is precious

____bela — ____ is lord

____beli — ____ is my lord

____bilani — ____, bear me

____dad — ____ is beloved

____dadi — ____ is my beloved

____damiiq, ____damqu — ____ is gracious; use only God

____damqaat — ____ is gracious; use only Goddess

____dan — ____ is mighty

____dannaat — ____ is mighty; use Goddess

____dari — ____ is eternal

____dugul — ____, look

____dumqi — ____ is my good favor

____duri — ____ is my wall; for women, also

____eli — ____ is my God

____elum — ____ is God

____ennu, ____ennum — ____, mercy

____erish — ____ has requested

____gabar — ____ is strong

____gamil — ____ is one who spares

____gashir — ____ is strong

____habiit — ____ prevails

____hasis —____ is thoughtful

____idi —____ is my strength

____iksur —____ has compensated

____il —____ is indeed God

____ili —____ is my God; used by women

____illaat —____ is the clan

____illasu —____ is his clan

____ilshu —____ is his God; can use Goddess

____ilum —____ is indeed God

____imdi —____ is my support; can use Goddess

____imitti —____ is my right hand; can use Goddess

____ipqi —____ is my grace

____iquisham —____ has presented to me

____isar —____ is righteous

____ishmani, —____ heard me

____ishmeni

____kabtum —____ is honored

____kali —____ is my all

____kam

____kiabi —____ is like my father

____kiah —____ is like my brother

____kibri —____ is like my friend

____kili —____ is like my God

____kilili —____ is my garland

____kimaat —____ is the family

____kin —____ is true

____kina —____ is true

____kiti —____ is my justice

____kurub, ____kuruba —____ worship

____laba —____ is a lion; can use Goddess

____labat —____ is a lioness; can use Goddess

____lamahar —____ is without equal

____lat —____ is the clan

____li — uncertain

____lishim, ____limshim — may ____ decree

____mahri —____ is before me

____malik —____ is counselor

____malkat —____ is princess; can use Goddess

____malki —____ is my counselor

____misar —____ is justice

____mishar —____ is righteous

____miti —____ is my right hand

____muda —____ is wise/concerned

____mutabil —____ supports/directs

____muti —____ is my mate

____nada —____ is praised

____napashti —____ is my life

____nashir —____ is protector

____nawir —____ shines; can use Goddess

____ni — uncertain

____nishu —____ we have a brother

____nuhsi —____ is my prosperity

____nuid —____ praise

____nuri —____ is my light

____nurmatishsu —____ is light to his land

____palil —____ is leader

____paluh —____ is awe-inspiring

____qarad —____ is a hero/warrior

____qurad — his God, ____, is hero/warrior

____rabi —____ is great

____rabiat —____ is great; can use Goddess

____ram, ____rama — love ____

____risi —____ is my helper; can use Goddess

____risu —____ is his shepherd

____sad —____ is a mountain

____saliq —____ cuts

____shamsi —____ is my sun

____shar —____ is king

____sharrat —____ is queen; can use Goddess

____sharrum —____ is king

____shuqir — honor ____

____silli —____ is my shade

____sillum —____ is shade

____silul, ____siluli —____ is protection

____simti, ____simtum —____ is my ornament/dignity

____ta, —____ is good

____taba, ____tabi, ____tab

____tabat —____ (fem.) is good; use only Goddess

____takal, ____tikal — trust in ____

____tar —____ is eternity

____tukulti —____ is my trust; used for women, too

____turam —____, return to me

____umme —____ is mother; use
only Goddess
____ummi —____ is my mother;
use only Goddess
____wabil —____ is one who

bears/carries
____waqar —____ is precious
____wusum —____ is especially
suitable

OTHER SEMITIC

Just like Africa and North America, this is the "assorted and miscellaneous" section for the ancient Mideast. Here you may find just the group you need. They are all single-namers, who will add an eke-name (Handada the Rotund, or Handada the Potter), a place-name (Handada from Byblos), or a patronymic (Handada son of Attametu), sometimes a matronymic (Handada son of Indibii).

• EARLY ARABIC •

There was an Arabia before Islam. These are the simple personal names you will find there. Sources range from cuneiform to records of the opponents of Mohammed.

FEMALE NAMES

Adiya	Hind al-Hunud	Salaym
Afra	Kaula, Khawlah	Samsi

MALE NAMES

Abiyate	Khazailu	Yalu
Amma-ba'li	Mosaylima, Moseilema	Yarap
Geshem	Odomera	Yatama
Imaldue	Te'eri	Zobeir, Zubair

• ELAMITE •

FEMALE NAMES

Indibii

MALE NAMES

Amba-abba
Attametu
Chedorlaomer
Handada
Huddana
Imba-appi
Indabigash
Ituni
Khumbaigash
Kudur-Mabuk
Kudur-Nakhundi
Makishtarra
Maukka

Maumishsha
Menanu
Minana
Mishparra
Mishtatta
Mistashpa
Mitarna
Nutiutbeul
Paru
Pirrada
Pirrumartish
Shutruk-Nakhundi
Tammaritu

Teumman
Umbadara
Umbakhabua
Umman-menanu
Umman-shibar
Ummanaldash, Umanal-
   dash
Ummanamni
Ummannish
Undasu
Urtaki
Urtaqu
Zinieni

• HITTITE •

FEMALE NAMES

Gilu-Khepa, Gilukhipa
Ilani-irinna
Pudu-Khepa, Pudukhipa
Sin-Teshup-ash

Tatu-Khepa, Tadu-Khepa, Dadu-
   Khepa
Tawashshi

MALE NAMES

Abbi-Teshub
Akhsheri
Aki-Teshup, Akia
Alakshandu
Alarandu
Ambaris
Ammikhatna
Anuwanza
Arame
Arandash, Arandas
Arnuanta
Artatamash
Asiri
Aulkia
Bakhianu
Bit-Burutish
Biyassili
Burutash, Purutash
Dudkhalia, Dudkaliya,
   Tudkhaliya
Dushratta, Tushratta
Erisinni
Etaqama

Gil-Teshup, Kil-Teshup
Giliyash
Gunzinanu
Ishganshar
Kali-Teshup
Karparuna
Khalpashshulubis
Khapashshubilish
Khattushar
Khulli
Kielranu
Kili-Teshup
Kilundu
Kundashpi
Kurirpa
Kuruntash
Kushtashpi
Lutipri
Manapa-Teshup
Murshil
Murshilish
Mutallu, Muttallu
Pappash

Pikkandu
Pilandu
Pisandu
Pisiris, Pisirish
Qatazilu
Sangar
Sardur
Shadi-Teshup
Shama-Teshup
Sharkenkate-Ashir
Shaushkash
Shipa
Shirindu
Shubbiluliuma
Sin-Teshupash
Surash
Surri
Sutarna, Sutatarra
Tarkhundapi
Tarkhundaraba
Tarkhundarabush
Tarkhuntash
Tashshu-Dasha

Te-Teshub	Ullusunu	Ushkhitti
Teti	Uriah, the Hittite	Zurashar
Ualli	Urikki	
Uassurme	Urimme	

SUMERIAN

Sumerians use many fewer theophorics than Semitic Mesopotamians. Often, the God-blank (_____) can be filled with other phrases or ideas. You might have a military champion called Meslugal, "hero of the king," a prince named Enzagesi, "master who fills the sanctuary," or Egaltum, "worthy of the palace," and a farmer called Agana, "son of a plot of land." No one actually used these names, but they are perfectly possible.

Also, Sumerians seem to have had a cheery relationship with their Gods and the world. None of the theophoric names indicate guilt, sin, lamentation, or the anger of the Gods.

The Sumerians only rarely gendered names. Those few have been listed at the top, and the rest lumped together. Sure, Gudea was a famous prince of Lagash, but you could just as well use it for the heroine's mother-in-law.

If your Sumerian tale is really epic, with scores of characters, you can eke this selection out with "names in translation" such as are often used for Native Americans and Chinese — Yellow Stone, Mountain, Gazelle. If you use all translated names, you can use fairly long ones. But if you mix translated ones with those in Sumerian, keep the translates short, one word, very occasionally two. Use them mostly for tertiary characters, and a couple of secondary characters just for transition. Actual Sumerian is best for the major players, because the reader will see the names so often repeated that they get accustomed to them. For someone who has a walk-on, you want something less unfamiliar.

Pronunciation

Fear not. The lists below do not have all the Sumeriologists' diacriticals and hyphens. Most historians, as opposed to archaeologists, ignore the diacriticals, and read as if written in Italian.

If you care:

The simple consonants are B, P, D, T, K, Z, S, SH, R, L, M, and N. The CH is the uvular fricative, like the Scottish pronunciation of lo*ch* or the Yiddish of *ch*ayim. There are two G's: a hard G as in gun, and a G with the back of your tongue closing off your throat, as in lung.

There are three "open" vowels, which are sometimes indicated as umlauted A, plain E, and O with a circumflex. The three close (not closed) vowels A and

E with a line above each, and U with an umlaut. These six are elided, or skipped through, either at the end of words or between consonants. There are other vowels, like circumflex E, I, etc. Additionally, any consonant is silent at the end of a word, unless the next word begins with a vowel. It's as if in English "bad man" were pronounced "ba' ma'," but "bad ax" were "bad a'."

So with all these "sometimes yes, sometimes no" vowels and consonants, there is ample opportunity to misunderstand overheard conversations, where the eavesdropper mistook a word from missing the part where the speakers made the subject clear among themselves.

Sumerian Basics

First, there is no language related to Sumerian. While it has structural similarities to extent languages, there is no kinship or descent. So when I say Sumerian is *like* this language or that, I do not mean it as I would if I said Spanish is a lot like Portuguese. It is instead similar to saying Mandarin Chinese is like English, in that both are positional languages.

Sumerian is an agglutinative language, so if you speak Turkish, Hungarian, Basque, or Finnish, or any of a number of North American languages, you already have this concept down. To indicate plurality, they used reduplication; that is, while *nitah* means "man," *nitah-nitah* means "men." Clues gasped by the dying may be confusing as to number, depending on whether they get out the repeat, or try twice to say the singular. Roots of meaning are monosyllabic, but many constructed words are polysyllabic.

There is no grammatical gender, but instead there is a division between the "animate" and "inanimate." Since animals grammatically are "inanimate," this should really be considered a difference between "persons" and "things."

There were several dialects. The two most notable in the tablets discovered are Emegir, the "princely tongue," and Emesal, used for the speeches of women and female deities, also eunuchs. So while names are not specifically gendered in any way obvious, any writing will be according to the sender's gender. This is like the different vocabularies in Japanese for men and women to use.

Sumerian is short on adjectives. Instead, genitives or possessive phrases are used. That is, instead of saying, "golden ring" they would say, "ring of gold." Equally, if you are trying to catch the mood in English, instead of "the Larsan king's marble palace," you would write "the palace of marble of the king of Larsa." Overdo this, though, at your story's peril. It's a good note for dialogue.

FEMALE NAME FORMULAS

Gan____ — maidservant of ____ | Geme____ — slave (fem.) of ____

Male Name Formulas

Arad____ — slave of ____
Ur____ — warrior of ____

____lu — man of ____
____ta-lu — man from ____

Neuter Name Formulas

A____ — child of ____, strength of ____

A____nepadda — child chosen by ____
A____ta — by the strength of ____
Aa____ — parented by ____
Aba____gim — who is like ____?
Abba____ — (the child's) father is ____

Ahi____ — my sibling is ____
Ama____ — mother (of the child) is ____

Amar____ — calf of ____
Dugga____ — the word of ____
En____ — master is ____
En-shakush____ —
Giri____ — I seized (the foot of) ____
Giri____idab — I seized the foot (asked a boon) of ____

____aa — ____ is the parent (of this child)
____aamu — ____ is my parent
____abbamu — ____ is my parent
____adah — ____ is help
____admu — ____ is my parent
____ak
____alsag — ____ is favorable
____ama — ____ is mother (of the child)
____ama, ____amah — ____ is exalted strength
____amamu — ____ is my mother
____amu — ____ is my parent; ____ is my strength
____andul — ____ is protection
____anne-mundu
____azu — ____ is doctor
____baanshag
____bad — ____ is a wall
____badmu — ____ is my wall
____banda — ____ is shepherd
____baragesi — ____ fills the throne
____bashag — ____ has shown

Hala____ — portion of ____
Igi____she — before ____
Inim____ — word of ____
Ki-tush____ — residence of ____
Ku____ — ransom of ____
Lu____ — person of ____
Lu____rakam — this the person belonging to ____
Lugal____ — a lord is ____
Mes____ — hero of ____
Mes____nepadda — hero chosen by ____
Mes-kiag____ — hero beloved of ____
Nin____ — the lady is ____
Sag____ — servant of ____
Sha____ — the heart of ____
Shesh____ — a brother is ____

favor
____bataabe — ____ has gone out
____dalla — ____ is brilliant
____dammu — ____ is my spouse
____dikud — ____ is judge
____dingir — ____ is deity
____dingirkalamma — ____ is Deity of the land
____dingirmu — ____ is my Deity
____dirig — ____ is pre-eminent
____dugga — ____ is good
____engar — ____ is the farmer
____ennu — ____ is guardian
____galzu — ____ is wise/concerned
____gina — ____ is sure
____girgal — ____ is proud
____gugal — ____ is foremost is rank
____gula — ____ is great
____gumu — ____ is my canal bank (preservation)
____hegal — ____ is abundance
____hili — ____ is splendor (Nanna or Utu only)

____hilianna — ____ is splendor of heaven (Nanna/Utu only)

____hursag — ____ is a mountain (refuge, fortress)

____igidu — ____ is leader

____inzu

____izu — ____ knows this one

____kalagga — ____ is mighty

____kalam-dug — ____ of the good land; use son, hero, etc.

____kalla — ____ is precious

____kam — this belongs to ____

____kiag — beloved of ____

____kinishe-dudu

____kuli — ____ is a friend

____kurmah — ____ is a lofty mountain

____kuzu — ____ is wise

____la — one of ____

____ludug — ____ is one who is good

____lumah — ____ is the exalted one

____lumu — ____ is my man (patron)

____lusag — ____ is one who is favorable

____maanba — ____ has presented this child to me

____maangi — ____ has answered me

____maansum — ____ has given this child

____maba

____magi

____magurre — ____ towards the boat (draws near)

____masu — ____ is leader

____masum

____melam — ____ (has, is) super-

natural splendor

____merkar

____muhdadah — ____ has helped me

____muhdah

____mutum — ____ has brought (the child)

____nepadda — chosen by ____

____ninam — ____, it is a sister

____nirgal — ____ is prince

____pae — ____ is shining

____ra — of ____

____resilimmu — before ____ is my salvation

____shagga, — ____ is favorable

____shag

____shesh — ____ is a brother

____sheshmu — ____ is my brother

____sig — ____ is gracious

____silimmu — ____ is my salvation

____sipa — ____ is shepherd

____sisa — ____ is just

____sukkal — ____ is messenger

____tum — worthy of ____

____ur — ____ is warrior

____urmu — ____ is my champion

____ursag — ____ is a favored warrior

____urumu — ____ is my city

____ushumgal — ____ is predator/ferocious fighter

____utumu — ____ is my sun

____zagesi — ____ who fills the sanctuary

____zi — ____ is faithful

____zimu — ____ is my life

FILL IN THE BLANKS WITH THESE

a — parent

Alla — Deity

Damu — Deity

dingir — Deity in the abstract, very common in names

e-gal — "big house," palace

en — master

ensi — "prince," later "governor"

lugal — king

me — "powers inherent in nature and institutions"

mes — hero

nin — lady, princess, queen

uku` — The People

FEMALE DEITIES

Ama — "mother" used for the God-
dess
Anzud
Baba
Ba'u
Damkina
Erishkigal — Goddess of death, rarely

used
Inanna — often "-anna" in a name
Lama
Lum-ma
Nammu
Nanshe
Ningal

MALE DEITIES

Abba — "father" used for the God
An
Dagan
Dumuzi
Ea
Enki
Enlil
Nanna
Nergal

Ningirsu
Ningishzida
Ninurta
Shara
Shulutul, Shul-utul
Shumuqan
Tishpak
Utu

OTHER SUMERIAN

When using the following vocabulary, double-check your gender stereo-types. Does the heroine have to have a pretty-sweet name, or the hero a strong-tough one? There is no reason why Heron, or Smoke, or River should be specifically masculine or feminine. There is every good reason why your foppish nobleman could be named Incense of Flowers, or your tough washerwoman, Stone.

"Relative names" are given to commemorate family members. For example, naming a child Sheshamana may be done in remembrance of its dead or departed uncle. These can also be plugged into formula names.

This list will also include the non-formula names.

Aaa — grandfather
Abba — father
Abbagula — father is great, grandfa-
ther
Abzu — sweet waters
Agga
Amagula — mother is great, grand-
mother

Amar — calf
Badmu — my wall
Banda — shepherd
Damgar — merchant
Dikud — judge
Dingir — Deity but also star
Dubsar — scribe
Dudu

Enakalli
Engar — farmer
Enmerkar
Entemena — lord of the (temple)
  platform; ensi, Lagash
Gal — big, great
Galzu — wise
Gishma — fruit aroma
Gudea — the one called (to power);
  ensi of Lagash
Hili — splendor
Hilianna — splendor of heaven
Id — river
Ittidu — a kind of bird (of prey?)
Kash — beer
Kur — mountain
Kuzu — wise
Lula, Lulamu — fox
Melam — supernatural glory
Meskiaggasher
Mi — black
Nar — singer
Nin — sister, also lady, queen
Ninabba — father's sister
Ninamuna — mother's sister

Ninbanda — lady shepherd
Puabi
Sar — writer
She, Sheh — barley
Shesh — brother
Sheshadda — father's brother
Sheshamana — mother's brother
Sheshanni — his brother
Sheshgal — eldest brother
Shum — onion, garlic
Siduri
Sukhush — root
Tabba — comrade
Ti — arrow
Ubartutu
Udkabar — bronze; no iron or steel in
  Sumerian period
Unzi
Ur — dog, warrior; masculine
Ursag — hero; masculine
Uruinimgina
Urukagina
Utu
Ziusudra
Zuzu

ANCIENT CHINA, A NOTE

You may use the usual Chinese chapter, and you will probably be as accurate as you can be. Just omit family names for many.

Problem is, Chinese writing is ideographic. We cannot say for certain the sounds used to speak those ideas, just as Cantonese and Mandarin will use different sounds for the same concept. Possibly earlier forms of Chinese were not tonal or monosyllabic. It may have been a bit more like Mongol, or Sumerian, or Basque.

Keep your eye out for the latest scholarly publications on the subject while researching. Sometimes a section of linguistics or onamastics undergoes a tremendous revolution in five or ten years.

Best bet: use translation names, and don't say a word about the language being singsong, guttural, or anything else. How often do you comment about your own language when your characters are speaking it?

INDUS VALLEY, A NOTE

Not so long ago, and in some books still published, the language of the inhabitants of Mohenjo Daro and Harappa is catagorized as a complete mystery.

Actually, there is every evidence that they spoke an early form of Dravidian. Dravidians have always been considered to have occupied northern India until driven south by the Indo-Aryans. Occam's Razor demands that a mystery-language group not be invented or assumed, just because early archaeologists had an undeservedly low opinion of Dravidian peoples.

As a fiction writer, it may mean everything to your plot that Harappans be immigrants from Mars. Okay, so early Dravidians are Martians. Everybody's got to come from someplace.

Just remember that while writers in earlier decades could legitimately treat the Indus Valley as a great unknown to be embroidered by their imaginations, you do not have quite the liberty. Yes, you may write the same tales, but you must be willing to say to your readers, "Scientists know better, but accept this as an historical fantasy." Otherwise, the real Mohenjo Daro fans, your best audience, will consider you just another exploitation author, whose research consisted of a couple of hours of "Ooooh, lost cities!" videos.

Names
Without Languages

If you wish to write a murder-mystery or a swashbuckler set in Minoan Crete, you have a problem. Archaeologists do not know even what kind of language the Minoans spoke. A few names may survive in Greek myths, and points of culture may be derived from the Semitic mainland, but they did not speak Greek, and may have spoken something more like Basque than a Semitic language.

Prehistoric sagas also require you to invent a list of names for your characters. You might sit down and study some books on the reconstruction of Indo-European, *if* your chalcolithic heroes are Indo-European. In far ages, the tongues of humanity were as numerous as those of North America before the European invasion. Your story may even take place before Indo-European developed.

If you are setting your story in the Fourth Sector of the Galactic Confederation, or in the wizardly domain of ... um, well ... you see how soon you have to start inventing names. Not only personal names, but place-names, too.

You do not want your characters to be one more crew of Og, Thak, and Theera, nor Zendor, Kobar, and Elissa. Flexibility of length and sound are important, *especially* when the names are strange to the reader, simply so your audience can tell everyone apart. Yet you want the names you have to have a consistent flavor, like real ethnic names.

Lin Carter wrote a chapter of *Imaginary Worlds* on the art of inventing names — "neocognomina" he called it. Other than to warn against over-dosing on names that begin with S or K, he leaves it a matter of the poetic ear of the writer. As he points out, one reason Lord Dunsany or Clark Ashton Smith may be considered superior fantasy writers to, say, Robert E. Howard, is that the latter had some good names in his work, but a lot of clunkers and swipes that detract from the atmosphere. The other two writers were original and euphonious throughout.

Even in the most contemporary of fiction, the choosing of the perfect name off a list takes that same poetic ear. What you need now is a list of names that *might* be Minoan, or lists for all the cultural groups in that galactic sector.

In the late 1970s, I finalized a decade of work on this, originally for fantasy fiction, finally for adventure-gaming. With a few days' work, you can build the basis for a "shadow language" that exists only in its names and a few phrases. Building the name list can be done with a deck of cards; or with a randomizing program if you can program a computer. All the guidelines you need, follow.

SHADOW LANGUAGES

When you go to create the illusion of a living world with unearthly languages, it is not necessary to go into heavy linguistics and create grammars. The languages can be as illusory as the world: shadow languages.

Consider the world in which we live. You do not speak all its languages. Yet you can probably give a good guess as to from what part of the world a person hails, if his or her name has a kind of sound distinctive to that area. For example, there are relatively few speakers of Celtic languages, but places beginning with Caer- are Welsh, with Strath- are Scottish, and Bally- are Irish. When these show up in other parts of the world, you can bet the early settlers were Gaels, as in America or Australia. In the same way, distinctively Welsh names begin with Gw- or Ll-, Scottish with Mac- or Mc-. Irish also use Mc/Mac (Scotland was colonized by the Irish), but are better known for O'-.

There are clues for other languages. The complicated consonant groups at the beginning of Middle European and Slavic languages — prz-, vl-, sht-, or zdr- — are different from the bw-, mb-, or ngw- that scream "Africa!" to the American eye. In the same way, the "simple" monosyllables of Chinese were formerly very distinctive: Yang-tze, Mao Tse-tung, Kai Lung (these look simple until you start adding marks to indicate tones).

You can do the same for the neo-languages of your fictional world(s). For each language you will develop a table of allowable sounds. From this you will build a simple vocabulary that will let you name places and people. Thus, in a crowded cosmopolitan port, an overheard name can be located by characters because they can figure in which ethnic quarter to start looking. Readers will enjoy the extra texture, and pride themselves on recognizing that So-and-so is probably X-ish because he or she (or it) has an X-ish name.

Remember that an area may have place-names with roots in more than one ethnic tradition. This happens if it has been occupied by several linguistic groups in succession, like the mix of Celtic, Anglo-Saxon, Norse, and Norman names in England, or if it has been settled by diverse people, like the United States.

Our lists of vocabulary are based on the roots that appear most often in name books, and in atlases. You can say a lot about a people by their names. There may be several different words for "battle" depending on whether or not the speaker started it, and who won. A people given to "nature names" might need a heavy list of animal and plant names. You may need lists of deities or the attributives of a single deity if a people are given to theophoric names in the Semitic tradition.

Don't forget the possibility of "translating" names. This is best used when

characters have been learning the language involved. This like the old habit of translating Asian names rather than rendering them as sound groups — White Lotus, Jade Cloud, Victorious Pheasant, etc. This is especially good when you have created something really foreign that does not stick well to the English-speaking mind, like <*}%${*>.

Using the Sound Tables

It would be nice if everyone out there read the International Phonetic Alphabet, and our word-processors were set for that as well as ASCII. Instead, here is a set of tables of ways to spell out sounds, which we will refer to as "ASCII Standard Transliteration."

These are not to be confused with how anybody writes their language. "Quick" would be rendered as kwik, "Jeannot" as Jhenno, "Loch Ness" as Lokh Nes, etc.

The tables are for English speakers. They do not contain all possible sounds, because some are too close for most people to tell apart, or sound apart. Everyone will consider some unusable, but they may be someone else's favorite, whether the aspirates (sh, bh, ph, etc.) or the African initial groups (mb, gp, nk, etc.) or vowel strings. When possible I have given examples in English; otherwise I list one possible foreign source. Please note that while English speakers are taught to treat some Greek-derived words (pscudo, pterion) as if the initial p were silent, your original urge to use the P in a compound consonant sound was correct in Homer's time.

In the ASCII Standard Transliteration, there are no silent letters. Instead, i a "spacer" is needed, we use a hyphen. There are ways to differentiate a long vow from a short vowel so there is no need for a silent e at the end (back when th words were first written down, the silent letters often were not silent). We do use under- or over-marks like accents, cedillas, umlauts, or circumflexes. vowels, we do use after-marks, rather than vowel groups (diphthongs) to cate the fifteen major vowel sounds. This makes vowel-stringing easier t so that "Aiea" comes out I'a'a.

SETTING UP A SHADOW LANGUAGE

First, you must decide on a list of allowable sounds. No langu? sounds, and if yours does, it will be so amorphous as to have no self-c

First, choose your vowels, anywhere from four to ten.

Syllables are determined by vowels. A syllable can be:

1) a vowel standing by itself;

2) a vowel followed by a consonant

3) a vowel preceded by a consonant

4) a vowel with a consonant both before and after. For e title of this section:

1) *A*
2) *Up*
3) *Sha*dow
4) *Set*ting

For short, we will call these:

    1) V — vowel only
    2) VC — vowel-consonant
    3) CV — consonant-vowel
    4) CVC — consonant-vowel-consonant

Many real languages get along nicely with only V and CV, like Hawai'ian. Some add a rare VC or CVC, the way Japanese allows only N as a terminal consonant. Many languages use all. You may decide that some consonants can be used only to start a syllable and others only to finish one. While many African languages think nothing of an initial ND, in English it is confined to the *end* of syllables.

Which consonants depends on your taste, entirely. Whatever you do, make a written list. Choose fifteen minimum, up to thirty or so.

Now, from allowable sounds, you will create legal syllables for your shadow language. Set up a table of 13 by 13 squares, or 169 syllables. If this seems too daunting, start with 13 by 4, or 52 syllables.

If you like — and it's optional — use the section on Shadow Roots to help you figure what different syllables should mean, based on the culture you're creating. On the 13 by 13, some of these spaces can represent specific root words, two syllables long. You do not have to do it all at one sitting. It is the sort of task to take to waiting rooms and laundromats, or to do during commercials or while waiting for the kids or the traffic to move.

To use the 13 by 4, pick a card. Its number determines the 13, its suit the 4. If you are using 13 by 13, pick two cards, using their values only.

If you have 20-sided dice around the house, a 20 by 20 matrix will give you 400 roots for people and places. If you have some weird odd number of roots, write them on the backs of old business cards (or halved 3 by 5 cards) and pick them at random out of a fishbowl.

You are now ready to begin the name list for your shadow language.

Names generally run two or three syllables long, with some four and still rarer five-syllable names. Single-syllable names come straight off the table. Make up a sheet of names all the same length at one time. Randomize each syllable in turn and finish a name, rather than doing all the initial syllables, then the second, etc.

Some of these will be real clunkers, but keep going. When you have filled a sheet, go back over the names and try to pronounce them. Scratch the losers. As you go, if a name "looks" or "feels" like a special use — a tropical city, an ominous mountain, a frivolous noble — write that down next to it. Never waste a moment's imagination. It may not strike again, and by tomorrow you will have forgotten it, like any passing image you don't record immediately.

In a short while you can have a list of several hundred names, which is as good as many of the real-world offerings in this book. They will be wholly original to you, neither swiped from Albanian nor Gaelic, with a consistency of sound and meaning that should enmesh your reader in a web of authority and pull them right into the tale.

THE SOUND TABLES
VOWELS

Sound	as in:	Sound	as in:
A	h*a*t	O'	b*oa*t
E	h*e*t	U'	b*oo*t
I	h*i*t	A"	f*a*ther, b*o*ther,
O	h*o*t		British v*a*se
U	h*u*t	E"	f*eu* (French)
A'	b*a*te, d*ay*	I"	f*ew*
E'	b*ee*t	O"	s*aw*, c*au*ght
I'	b*i*te, d*y*e	U"	b*oeu*f (French)

English speakers use a large range of vowels, and spell them a huge number of ways, because these are loan words from other languages. Many languages have only five vowels.

CONSONANTS

Sound	Initial	Terminal
B	*b*in	ca*b*
BD	*Bd*itelny (Russian)	sob*bed*
BH	*Bh*arata (Hindi)	du*bh* (Gaelic)
BHR	*Bh*rastaka (Sanskrit)	
BL	*bl*ind	
BR	*br*ick	
BW	*bw*ana	
BY	*by*elo (Russian)	
BZ		ca*bs*
CH	*ch*in	su*ch*
CHK	*Chk*alov (Russian)	
CHL	*chl*eb (Polish)	
CHW	*Chw*e (Korean)	
D	*d*am	ma*d*
DH	*dh*arma	
DHR	*Dhr*uvasandhi (Sanskrit)	
DHV	*Dhv*ana (Sanskrit)	
DJ	*Dj*idade (Fulani)	e*dge*
DM	*Dm*itri	
DR	*dr*aw	
DT		sta*dt* (Norwegian)

Sound	Initial	Terminal
DV	*Dv*imidha	
DW	*dw*ell	
DY	*dy*ekuyih (Czech)	
DZ	*dz*al (Fang)	a*dz*e
F	*f*an	cu*ff*
FL	*fl*ing	
FN	*fn*escial (Etruscan)	hrae*fn* (Anglo-Saxon)
FR	*fr*ame	
FS		cu*ffs*
FT		ha*ft*
FTH	*Phth*isis (Hellenic)	fi*fth*
FW		
FY	*fy*ord (Norwegian)	
G	*g*one	ba*g*
GB	*gb*elanga (Mende)	
GD	*gd*e (Croatian)	e*gg*ed
GH	*gh*arb (Arabic)	ga*gh* (Ibo)
GHR	*Ghr*ita	
GL	*gl*ass	
GN	*Gn*assingbe' (Togo)	
GP		
GR	*gr*in	
Gth		
GW	*Gw*en	
GY	*Gy*ozo (Japanese)	
GZ		sa*gs*
H	*h*ot	ha*h*
HL	*hl*okomela (Sotho)	ko*hl* (Arabic)
HR	*hr*eade (Anglo-Saxon)	
HS	*hs*ia (Chinese)	
HV	*Hv*ass (Norwegian)	
HW	*wh*at	
HY	*Hy*ang (Korean)	
J	*j*am	
JH	*j*amais (French)	ra*j*
JY	*Jy*amagha (Sanskrit)	
K	*k*iss	si*ck*
KG	*Kg*otso (Sesotho)	hri*cg* (Anglo-Saxon)
KH	*kh*amsa (Arabic)	an*kh*
KHR	*Khr*yse (Hellenic)	
KHT		Bre*cht* (German)
KL	*cl*ing	he*ckle*
KN	*Cn*aeve (Latin/Etruscan)	
KP	(*Kp*elle)	
KR	*cr*ush	fia*cre* (French)
KS	*Ks*ema (Sanskrit)	sa*cks*
KSH	*ksh*atriya (Hindi)	lo*ksh* (Yiddish)
KT	*kt*ora (Polish)	se*ct*
KW	*qu*ick	
KY	*Ky*oto (Japanese)	

Sound	Initial	Terminal
L	*l*et	ca*ll*
LB		a*lb*
LD		ho*ld*
LDZ		ho*lds*
LF		she*lf*
LH	*Ll*yr (Welsh)	Howy*ll* (Welsh)
LJ		bu*lge*
LK		bu*lk*
LM		e*lm*
LN		ki*ln*
LP		he*lp*
LS		e*lse*
I.SK		Komsomo*lsk* (Russian)
LT		ha*lt*
Lth		hea*lth*
LV	*Lv*ov (Russian)	she*lve*
L/	Ł*uba* (Slavic barrel L)	
LZ		she*lls*
M	*m*an	a*m*
MB	*mb*u (Ibo)	ia*mb*
MBR		so*mbre* (French)
MF	*mf*uga (Swahili)	hu*mph*
MFW	*mfw*ene (Luba)	
MG	*mg*eni (Swahili)	
MGB	*mgb*e (Ibo)	
MJ	*mj*i (Swahili)	
MH	*mh*aill (Gaelic)	
MK	*mk*ono (Swahili)	
ML	*ml*uvte (Czech)	
MN	*mn*ikati (Swazi)	li*mn*
MP	*mp*uku (Luba)	li*mp*
MPF		ka*mpf* (German)
MPS		lu*mps*
MPT		pre-e*mpt*
MR	*mr*ityu (Hindi)	
MS	*Ms*iba (Swahili)	
MT	*mt*u (Swahili)	Gli*mt* (Norwegian)
MW	*mw*ana (Ruanda)	
MY	*My*ongo (Swahili)	
MZ	*Mz*ungu (Swahili)	ha*ms*
N	*n*ot	i*n*
NCH		i*nch*
ND	*nd*erit (Albanian)	la*nd*
NDZ		e*nds*
NF		fu*nf* (German)
NG	*ng*iyei (Mende)	si*ng*
NGH		shaa*ngh* (Kpelle)
NGth		le*ngth*
NGW	*Ngw*ato (Tswana)	
NH	*nh*amo (Shona)	

Sound	Initial	Terminal
NJ	*nj*oru (Nyanja)	hi*ng*e
NK	*nk*okon (Fang)	thi*nk*
NKR	*Nkr*uma (Akan)	
NR	*Nr*isad (Sanskrit)	
NS	*ns*iesi (Kongo)	expa*nse*
NSK		Mi*nsk* (Russian)
NT	*nt*ambo (Luba)	be*nt*
Nth		te*nth*
NTJ	*ntj*a (Sesotho)	
NTS		pa*nts*
NTSW	*ntsw*aki (Sesotho)	
NY	*ny*et (Russian)	compa*gne* (French)
NZ	*nz*ila (Kongo)	pi*ns*
P	*p*an	ta*p*
PF	*pf*eferlingen (German)	ko*pf* (German)
PH	*ph*al (Hindi)	lta*ph* (Arabic)
PHR	*phr*al (Romany)	
PL	*pl*ease	
PN	*pn*eumo (Classic Greek)	
PR	*pr*esent	
PRZ	*prz*epraszam (Polish)	
PS	*ps*eudo (Greek)	ca*ps*
PT	*pt*eros (Greek)	a*pt*
PW		
PY	*Py*on (Korean)	
R	*r*an	ca*r*
RB		cu*rb*
RCH		a*rch*
RD		ha*rd*
RDZ		ca*rds*
RG		be*rg*
RH	*Rh*iannon (Welsh)	
RJ		su*rg*e
RK		a*rk*
RL		cu*rl*
RM		wa*rm*
RN		ea*rn*
RP		*h*a*rp*
RS		wo*rse*
RSHT		bo*rsht*
RST		wo*rst*
RT		hu*rt*
Rth		ea*rth*
RV		cu*rve*
RY	*ry*orya (Japanese)	
RZ		sta*rs*
S	*s*it	ye*s*
SB	*Sb*icca	
SD	*Sd*erzhanny (Russian)	
SG	*Sg*eimsolas (Gaelic)	

Sound	Initial	Terminal
SH	*sh*ut	cru*sh*
SHK		
SHN	*Shn*orig (Armenian)	
SHR	*shr*ink	
SHT	*shr*ik (Yiddish)	ha*sht* (Persian); ma*shed*
SHV	*Shv*eta (Sanskrit)	
SHY	*Shy*ama (Sanskrit)	
SK	*sk*ill	a*sk*
SKR	*scr*ipt	
SKW	*squ*irrel	
SL	*sl*ing	
SM	*sm*all	
SN	*sn*ail	
SP	*sp*in	ha*sp*
SPL	*spl*int	
SPR	*spr*ing	
SR	*Sr*oda (Ghanese)	
ST	*st*ing	mu*st*
STH	*Sth*aga (Cherokee)	
STR	*str*ing	
SV	*Sv*en	
SW	*sw*ing	
T	*t*op	si*t*
TCH	*Tch*aikovsky	ha*tch*
TH	*th*en	ba*the*
th	*th*in	ba*th*
thR	*thr*ow	
TL	*tl*ameha (Sotho)	(Nahua*tl*, aka Aztec)
TR	*tr*im	
TS	*ts*ar	hi*ts*
TSH	*Tsh*epe (Sesotho)	
TSW	(*Ts*wana)	
TV	*Tv*astadhara (Sanskrit)	
TW	*tw*itch	
TZ		are*tz* (Yiddish)
V	*v*an	re*v*
VD	*Vd*okhnovenny (Russian)	sei*ved*
VH		
VL	*Vl*ad	
VN	*Vn*esapny (Russian)	
VR	*vr*ai (French)	Le Ha*vr*e
VSK		Petropavlo*vsk* (Russian)
VY	*vy*arateye (Rundi)	
VZ		re*vs*
W	*w*in	ne*w*
Y	*y*es	sa*y*
Y/	*ll*ama (Spanish)	
Z	*z*ipper	ra*zz*
ZB	*Zb*igniew	
ZDR	*zdr*avlyeh (Croatian)	

Sound	Initial	Terminal
ZH	Zhivago (Russian)	gamboge
ZHD	Zhdanov (Russian)	gamboged
ZL	zlato (Croatian)	
ZM		chasm
ZN	znati (Croatian)	
ZR		
ZV	Zvi (Yiddish)	
ZW	Zweiback	
ZY		

Shadow Roots

Consider these guidelines, but by no means limits. A people in volcanic country will likely have different names for fumaroles, hot springs, geysers, hot mud flats, calders, vents, and even different types of lava flow, like the Hawai'ian *pahoehoe* (fast lava) and *a'a* (slower, thicker lava). Eskimos have a vast number of discriminating terms for ice and snow. English is thick with color names. And so forth.

Geographics

Geographic roots are most important for place-names, which can become personal names when someone is "of" or "from" or "owner of" a place.

If a people deal a lot with some aspect of geography, they may have many words that make fine distinctions, like mountain-dwellers who distinguish a high-altitude narrow glen from a high but broad dale from a low-altitude broad valley and narrow canyon. On the other hand, inland desert dwellers may have one word they use for stream, river, lake, or sea.

Direction

east (sunrise-ward)
west (sunset-ward)
north (to the left facing sunrise)
south (to the right facing sunrise)
high or up
low or down
near
distant
behind, in back of
before, in front of
upstream
downstream
towards mountains; upland
towards shore; downslope

Land Features

mountain or mountains
cliff
big rock
hill
valley
lowland, depression
pass
plain
meadow
plateau, highland
butte, mesa
volcano, volcanic area
field

Water Features

sea
bay
strait
lake
river, stream
well, spring, oasis
geyser
swamp
beach
harbor
island
isthmus
cape, headland
canal
ditch
pool

Manmade

house
wall
farm
fortress
village
town
city
country, region
port, harbor
gathering place, market
political divisions of the area (prefect,
    province, see, etc.)

Weather and Sky

rain, drizzle, downpour
clouds
fog
snow
ice
heat
cold
wind
sky
sun
moon
star
rainbow
aurora
planet
meteor, shooting star
comet

Other

forest
woods
grassland
desert
semi-desert
rocky, badlands

Descriptives

These are the adjectives you hang onto other roots. Besides the ideas below, this should include numbers, depending on the speakers' number system (base ten, twelve, three, etc.) and what numbers are important, magical, or lucky.

Color

dark
light, bright
white
black
red
yellow
green
blue
orange
violet
grey
dim
golden
silvery

General

ancient, old
new, young

beautiful
good, fortunate
ugly
bad, unlucky
holy, sacred
damned, forbidden
large, great
small
famous, notable
hidden, secret

Personals

happy
sad, serious
scholarly
wary, careful
wise
energetic
free
brave
shy
powerful, mighty
weak

Relations

Relational roots are generally used for people, but sometimes places are named in memory of people, either directly, like various U.S. towns named Lincoln, or indirectly, like one that might be translated as "[place of] the Ruler of Rivers," so that relationals do creep onto the map.

Familial

This is affected by how complicated people get in designating their relatives: do they count four different kinds of cousins in the first degree, and work out from there?

mother
father
daughter
son
first ancestor, grandparent
spouse, attached person
unmarried or unattached person
suitor, lover
brother
sister

guardian
counselor
judge
teacher
friend
master
servant
slave
freeman
landholder
holy person
giver (of something)
member (of a group)
follower (of someone or something)

Other

ruler (king/queen, chief, lord/lady)
princess/prince (ruler-to-be, precious
person)

Attributions

These roots can be attached to geographics, descriptives, or relationals. They will vary with your flora and fauna, under the Tangibles.

Occupations

sailor
traveler
farmer
smith
herder
dancer
singer
harper, musician

horse
tiger
other animal names
flowers
fruits
trees
gem, treasure
crown, emblem of rule

Intangibles

love
vision, reverie
story, legend
admirable
summons
death, deadly
life, life-giving
safety
will
gift

Martials

battle, combat
battlefield
armor
shield
helmet
warrior
weapon
spear
sword
victory
defeat
protection
danger
war

Tangibles

eagle
wolf

An Example of a Shadow Language

Always remember that any shadow language is only a sample of the represented language. If you really wanted to build a full one, you would have to aim at a vocabulary of about 5,000 words, minimum.

For this one, I filled a 20 by 10 matrix on a single sheet of lined paper with single and double syllables that sounded consistent, noting in the margin which letters or sounds were showing up. When filling the blanks got difficult, those notes built other logical candidates.

The meanings were assigned later, with the roots on index cards so I could look at them in different relations. There was a lot of back and forth correction, as when changing the meaning of a single syllable might change double syllables with that sound. Also, assigning meaning to one root might imply things about a cluster of six.

The odd number of roots reflects both a natural growth of words from meanings, and a change of technology: I went from rolling dice to randomizing on a computer.

Meanings reflect technology, philosophy, and culture. There are words for the soft metals and bronze, but not for iron or steel. The concept of "everything" is a single world, not a universe. Many battle words reflect a culture long in turmoil from the conquest and fragmentation of a vast empire. An ancient starfaring culture should have a different set of meanings, with words for other substances, energies, flight, speed, and astronomical structures.

208 ROOTS

Spelled	Meaning	Spelled	Meaning
A	beauty (soft)	DUMEO	night
AGNU	death	DUMIS	black
AI	light	E	cold (temperature)
AKHAR	red	EDAR	enduring, sturdy
ANU	fleeing	ELE	wonder; glory
AP	seven	ELKI	magic [ELE-KHI, glory-bold]
ARIE	jewel, gem		
ASH	clothing	ELOR	famed
ATL	fresh water	EMAE	sad, hurt
CHAK	world; everything	EPO	dwelling
CHEL	stone (carryable)	ERA	outcry, vocal noise
CHETH	holy, pious	ESHU	ice [E-SHUA, cold-blue]
CHETLI	hunter	ETHA	strength
CHEZMI	sunset	GA	wanderer, stranger
CHI	cloud	GAE	lively
CHIDIS	dance (impromptu)	GAMI	three
CHOG	devour, destroy	GAR	copper; metal in general
CHOL	parent	GATH	young
CHUGIS	menace	GEQUU	legend, fame
CHUSHE	life	GET	delving
CHUSI	cute, cuddly, appealing	GIEX	fish
DAD	dull; brown	GIR	six
DAI	two; paired	GIVU	brave
DAZU	enemy, opponent	GOL	smith, maker, creator
DEIX	winter	GOQUO	judge [from GOS-QUAZ]
DEL	building	GOS	wise, wisdom
DICH	twisted	GULTE	happy
DRETH	dirty	I	fang; sharp
DRISAN	sailor	ICHAL	biter; pack predators
DU	sky; space	IKHA	beautiful (piercing)

Spelled	Meaning	Spelled	Meaning
ILKO	fountain, spring	LUNI	dance (stately)
ILU	star	MAKYU	bow
IMAL	sword	MASHU	vision
INOR	lover	MELNI	sweet
IOD	piercing	MIEX	increasing in number
IS	thread, filament	MOTLI	lake
ISHAR	holy, full of power	MUKHI	fierce [MUZ-KHI evil
ITH	doer		bold]
JHADIS	white	MUZ	bad, evil, foul
JHAS	cold (personality)	NAL	guardian
JHIGAR	bronze [JHIL-GAR help-	NEGI	rough, scratch
	metal]	NIKHU	lone hunting predators
JHIL	help, aid	NO	quick
JHOR	world, place	NOCH	settlement
JHOTI	ford, passage	NOCHI	summer
JHU	old, ancient	NOKRI	blow, strike
JHUED	home	NOKTHA	blast, destroy
JHURU	noble [JHU-RU ancient	NOVI	five
	child]	NUTAL	fortress
KAD	dry	O	growth
KADIEX	desert, dryland	OKI	victorious [O-KHRI bold
KAN	most, great, superlative		growth]
KAR	shield (related to KIR)	OLUR	nine
KETLU	deep (related to KHELU)	ONIEX	woods [growing place]
KHA	gold	OSHU	fog, smoke (related to
KHATI	gilt, gold-imitating		OZO)
KHELU	hidden	OTA	one
KHI	bold	OTHUS	center; start of growth
KHIEL	flower [KHI-ELE bold	OZO(KRA)	movement; river
	wonder]	PAI	negatory; no, not
KHIOL	study, learning	PATIL	yellow
KHIR	purple (the bold color)	PETKA	travel
KHISHU	sun; praise [KHI-SHUA	PETLU	distant
	bold-sky]	PEZ	town
KHIT	torch	PICHE	rain
KHOSMA	fiery	PIEX	rejoicing
KIR	protecting	PIRI	waterfall, cascade
KORIS	contest	POPLI	precious
KOS	warlike	PU	lone
KRANI	chill	PUSHAD	island
KRI	danger	QUAZ	builder
KUSRI	clear, transparent	QUE	colored, painted
LA	song, vocal music	QUITI	embellished
LAIS	graceful, proper	RAEL	gift
LEMA	rapids, cataract	RAIKO	mount; riding animal
LIAKE	glittering	RAKMU	spear
LIO	master	REP	stone (surface, immov-
LIZAE	peculiar, strange		able)
LOTLI	feather	RIAKHI	rider
LUKE	sober, grave	RIET	cliff

Spelled	Meaning	Spelled	Meaning
RIJH	gate, door	U	large
RIN	bridge	UCHORO	storm
RIS	path	UDRO	face
RO	eye, eyes	UKOT	strife
RU	child	UOL	defeat
RUKU	follower	USHAZ	dim; grey
SARUZ	pure	USI	tree
SEPO	belly, body	UTHLI	ruler
SHEN	changing	UVA	tall, high
SHENCHA	moon; silver [SHEN-CHAK changing world]	UVLE	rising
		VAR	four
SHEX	ship, boat	VASU	frost
SHI	ever, eternal	VEI	smooth
SHIOR	mountain [SHI-O ever-growing]	VELO	hand (related to ELE+O, wonder-growing)
SHUA	blue	VET	farm
SID	witty	VICHO	counsel
SIUL	slick, oily	VIETH	friend, ally
SULA	voice	VIEX	falling
TAOZ	dawn	VO	small, fine
TAZ	green	VOIS	hair, crown
TEO	running	VOUZ	music, instrumental
THAE	soul	ZA	ten
THAL	bay, harbour	ZALTI	rotted
THI	hot, fire	ZETA	long, tall
THU	helm, precaution	ZIETI	bad, sick, unfortunate
TIMA	hill	ZIOD	salt water
TOR	eight	ZIZAE	valley
TZIO	spring-time	ZOU	prey; cattle
TZUL	flying	ZUJHU	breeze (onomatopoeic)

Numbers

one	OTA	six	GIR
two	DAI	seven	AP
three	GAMI	eight	TOR
four	VAR	nine	OLUR
five	NOVI	ten	ZA

People, Places, and Things

Most of these were picked off randomized lists. Some were purposely created for their meanings. They are best appreciated if you sound them aloud, hearing them as a foreign language, rather than a strange string of letters.

PLACE-NAMES

Achi — beautiful cloud; a mountain town
Chelziod — rocky sea
Chezmimashu — sunset vision; western or west-facing
Idel — sharp building, place of the tower
Ilkothal — fountain harbor
Ketluepo — deep dwelling
Khelunutal — hidden fortress
Lotlirin — feather bridge

Petka'a — beautiful to travelers; on a rough route
Shenchathal — silver bay
Shexnutal — ship fortress; a port
Taozrael — dawn's gift; eastern or east-facing
Udrorijh — face of the pass
Ukotzizae — strife valley
Ziodmotli — salt lake
Zizaota — valley of one
Zizaris — valley path

PERSONAL NAMES

Aro — beautiful eyes
Ashriakhi — cloaked rider
Asula — beautiful voice
Chinochi — cloudy summer
Chogimal — devouring sword
Dazujhilith — traitor; "enemy help maker" (three elements, for variety)
Edar — enduring
Ethadazu — strong enemy
Ikharo — piercing eyes
Inormotli — lover from the lake

Iodvasu — piercing frost
Kankhosma — most fiery
Khativois — bleached hair
Khavois — golden hair
Mashuoki — dreaming victory
Mukhiele — fierce glory
Nochilotli — summer bird
Rokmuoki — spear victory
Rokmuokith — spear victory maker
Tazliake — green glitter

ETHNIC GROUP USING NUMBER NAMES

Daiolur — second nine
Imalvar — sword four
Inornovi — loving five
Nokthaza — blasting ten

Novinor — fifth lover
Olordai — ninth pair
Varimal — fourth sword
Zanoktha — tenth blast

ANIMAL NAMES

elemukhi — wondrous ferocity
eppoketlu — dweller in deep places
ichaluva — "wolf" of the heights
imalchog — sword-devourer
jhotilo — fording bird (words can get shortened in use, so use it for variety)

rinlotli — bridge bird
shenichal — silver "wolf" (pack hunting predator)
shennikhu — silver "cat" (lone hunting predator)
usiemae — tree-hurting
uvaichal — tall "wolf"

PLANT NAMES

akharusi — crimson tree

chelchog — stone-eater; wasteland scrub

dumeagnu — black death; a poisonous plant

emae'usi — sorrow tree

inoris — lover's thread

motlinor — lake-lover; aquatic

quitiudro — embellished face; a showy flower

udroque — face paint; a dye plant used in cosmetics

vasiod — frost-piercing; an early plant or flower

Annotated Select
Bibliography

From tiny baby-name books bought for change at the supermarket checkout, to philological tomes inches thick, the books on names are almost innumerable. Below are the publications from which I gathered most of the names and language material in this book. Note that many would be found in the genealogical or historical sections, rather than onomastics.

Asante, Molefi K. *The Book of African Names.* Trenton: Africa World Press Inc., 1991.

Baines, John, and Jaromír Málek. *Ancient Egypt.* Oxford: Equinox Ltd., 1990.

Barber, Henry. *British Family Names: Their Origin and Meaning.* Baltimore: Genealogical Publishing Company, 1968.

Bardsley, Charles Wareing Endell. *A Dictionary of English and Welsh Surnames, with Special American Instances.* Baltimore: Genealogical Publishing Company, 1901.

Benz, Frank L. *Personal Names in the Phoenician and Punic Inscriptions.* Rome: Biblical Institute, 1972.

Bisson, Thomas N. *The Medieval Crown of Aragon: A Short History.* Oxford: Clarendon Press, 1986.

Budge, Sir E. A. Wallis. *Egyptian Language: Easy Lessons in Egyptian Hieroglyphics.* London: Kegan Paul, Trench, Trubner, 1910.

Bullfinch, Thomas. *Bullfinch's Mythology.* New York: Thomas Y. Crowell Company, 1940.

Byock, Jesse L. *The Saga of the Volsungs: The Norse Epic of Sigurd the Dragonslayer.* Berkeley and Los Angeles: University of California Press, 1990.

Carter, Lin. *Imaginary Worlds.* New York: Ballantine Books, 1973.

Catalogo Alfabetico de Apellidos. *Catalogo Alfabetico de Apellidos, transcribase este decreto con el catalogo de apellidos y modelo del padron, etc.* Manila: (Philippine) Government Printing Office, 1973.

Catlin, George. *North American Indians: Being Letters and Notes on Their Manners, Customs, and Conditions, Written During Eight Years' Travel Amongst Them.* New York: J. Grant, 1903.

Chadwick, John. *Reading the Past: Linear B and Related Scripts.* London: Trustees of the British Museum, 1987.

Chuks-orji, Ogonna. *Names from Africa: Their Origin, Meaning and Pronunciation.* Chicago: Johnson Publishing, 1972.

Conquest, Robert. *The Great Terror.* Oxford: Oxford University Press, rev. 1990. Yielded a good number of Russian and other Eastern European names.

DiVito, Robert A. *Studies in Third Millennium Sumerian and Akkadian Personal Names: The Designation and Conception of the Personal God.* Rome: Roma Pontifico Instituto Bialico, 1993.

Dix, Helmut. *Die Etruscanische Cognomen [The Etruscan Cognomen].* West Germany: publisher unknown, 1967.

Dogra, Ramesh C., and Urmila Dogra. *A Dictionary of Hindu Names.* New Delhi: Aditya Prakashan, 1992.

Durant, Will and Ariel. *The Story of Civilization.* New York: Simon and Schuster, 1935.

The Encyclopedia Americana. New York: Americana Corporation, 1959. While I did use the articles on names, nicknames, etc., and various linguistic articles, primarily I combed page by page through all the volumes, recording names in use. This older edition is naturally poor in modern biography and science, but much richer in older biography, whether Classical, 19th century, or somewhere between.

Evans, D. Ellis. *Gaulish Personal Names: A Study of Some Continental Celtic Formations.* Oxford: Clarendon Press, 1967.

Ewen, Cecil Henry L'Estrange. *A History of Surnames of the British Isles: A Concise Account of Their Origin, Evolution, Etymology, and Legal Status.* Baltimore: Genealogical Publishing Company, 1931.

Fowler, Murray, and Richard George Wolfe. *Materials for the Study of the Etruscan Language.* Rome: Edizioni dell'Ateneo, 1974. Also known as the *Corpus Inscriptiones Etruscorum Wisconsinensis.*

Fucilla, Joseph G. *Our Italian Surnames.* Baltimore: Genealogical Publishing Company, 1949.

Gandhi, Maneka. *The Penguin Book of Hindu Names.* New Delhi, India: Penguin Books, 1992.

Gelb, Ignace J. *Glossary of Old Akkadian.* Chicago: University of Chicago, 1957. Lists names using a word as a root.

Gillis, Irvin Van Gorder & Pai Ping-Ch'i. *Japanese Personal Names.* City: Edwards Brothers, 1943. Two volumes, for telegraphers, one for personal and one for family names.

Gourvil, Francis. *Noms de famille de Basse-Bretagne, materiaux pour servir à l'étude de l'anthroponymie bretonne.* Paris: d'Artrey, 1966.

Graves, Robert. *The Greek Myths.* New York: Penguin Classics, rev. 1960.

GTE Telephone Directory: Honolulu. Used to evaluate frequency of both Japanese and Filipino personal names, and as a source of some Hawaiian names not in Root.

Guamán Poma de Ayala, Felipe. *Letter to a King: A Peruvian Chief's Account of*

Life Under the Incas and Under Spanish Rule [Primer nueva coronica i buen gobernadoro, etc.]. New York: Dutton, 1978.

Helias, Pier. *The Horse of Pride: Life in a Breton Village.* New Haven: Yale University Press, 1978.

Hoffman, William F. *Polish Surnames: Origins and Meanings.* Chicago: Polish Genealogical Society of America, 1993.

Hutson, Arthur E. *British Personal Names in the Historia Regum Britanniae.* Folcroft, Pennsylvania: Folcraft Library Editions, 1974.

Keenan, Jeremy. *The Tuareg, People of Ahaggar.* New York: St. Martin's Press, 1977.

Koul, R. K. *Sociology of Names and Nicknames of India, with Special Reference to Kashmir.* New Delhi & Bombay: Utpal Publications, 1982.

Lansky, Bruce. *The Baby Name Personality Survey.* New York: Meadowbrook Press, 1990.

Lawner, Lynne. *Lives of the Courtesans: Portraits of the Renaissance.* Rizzoli, 1987. For female Italian Renaissance names.

Levi, Peter. *The Greek World.* Oxford: Equinox Ltd., 1986.

McManus, Seamus. *The Story of the Irish Race.* Old Greenwich, Connecticut: The Devon-Adair Company, rev. 1966.

Miller, Donald Earl, and Lorna Touryan Miller. *Survivors: An Oral History of the Armenian Genocide.* Berkeley and Los Angeles: University of California Press, 1993.

Names, the Journal of the American Names Society. Quarterly since 1953. Every article scanned for possible material; especially useful for Indian, Provençal, Sesotho, Lenne Lenape, Lakota, Baltic, Ukrainian.

Nguyen Trieu Dan. *A Vietnamese Family Chronicle: Twelve Generations on the Banks of the Hat River.* Jefferson, North Carolina: McFarland, 1991.

Osuntoki, Chief. *The Book of African Names.* Baltimore, Maryland: Black Classic Press, originally 1970.

Pacific Islands (Trust Territories) Office of the Staff Anthropologist. *The Use of Names in Micronesia,* 1958.

Powell, Peter J. *Sweet Medicine.* Norman, Oklahoma: University of Oklahoma Press, 1969. For Cheyenne and Lakota names.

Price, Roger, and Leonard Stern. *What Not to Name the Baby.* New York: Price, Stern, Sloan, 1960.

Qazi, M. A. *What's in a Muslim Name.* Chicago: Kazi Publication, 1990.

Rantala, Judy A. *Laos: A Personal Portrait from the Mid–1970s.* Jefferson, North Carolina: McFarland, 1994.

Reader's Digest Association. *Who's Who in the Bible.* Pleasantville, New York: Reader's Digest, 1994.

Roesdahl, Else. *Vikings.* New York: Penguin Books, 1987. Norse, Saxon, and Frankish, in text. Mentions naming practices, also different popularity of names used by the East-Norse.

Rony, A. Kohar. *An Analysis of Indonesian Name Pattern: A Preliminary Investigation into the Problem of Establishing an International Code for Indonesian Names to be Used by International Libraries.* Washington: Catholic University, 1968. Photocopy of typescript; Thesis (M.S.L.S.).

Root, Eileen. *Hawai'ian Names, English Names.* Kailua, Hawaii: Press Pacifica, 1987.

Rowse, A. L. *Names for the Cornish: 300 Cornish Christian Names.* Cornwall: Lodenik Press, 1970.

Salmonson, Jessica Amanda. *The Encyclopedia of Amazons: Women Warriors from Antiquity to the Modern Era.* New York: Paragon House, 1991.

Sawyer, P. H. *Kings and Vikings: Scandinavia and Europe 700 AD–1100 AD* [sic]. New York: Barnes & Noble, 1994.

Schele, Linda. *A Forest of Kings: The Untold Story of the Ancient Maya.* New York: Morrow, 1990.

Scott, Sir James George. *The Burman, His Life and Notions, by Shway Yoe (pseud.).* New York: Norton, 1963.

Siebs, Benno Eide. *Die Personennamen der Germanen [Personal Names of the Germanic Peoples].* Wiesbaden: M. Sandig, 1970. For Frankish, Saxon, Anglo-Saxon, and Norse names; superb pick-lists.

Sims, Clifford Stanley. *The Origins and Signification of Scottish Surnames, with a Vocabulary of Christian Names.* Baltimore, Maryland: Genealogical Publishing Company, 1968.

Steinkeller, Piotr. "More on the Ur III Royal Wives." *Acta Sumerologica* 3 (1981).

Stewart, Julia. *African Names.* New York: Citadel Press, Carol Publishing Group, 1993.

Stieglitz, Perry. *In a Little Kingdom.* Armonk, NY: M.E. Sharpe, 1990. For Laotian names.

Suetonius Tranquillus, Gaius. *The Twelve Caesars.* Translated by Robert Graves. New York: Penguin Classics, 1957.

Tallqvist, Knut Leonard. *Assyrian Personal Names.* Chicago: University of Chicago, 1966.

Thai personal names: chiefly taken from cremation volumes in the National Library of Australia = Nam bukkhon : Suanyai luak chak nangsu ngansop th MA i m MA iyu nai Hosamuthaeng Chat, Prath MA et Australia. Compiled by Kannikar Linpisal. Edited by Songsri Shinn. University of Sydney, 1985.

Timmons, Boyce D., and Alice Tyner Timmons, ed. *Authenticated Rolls of 1880, Cherokee Nation, Indian Territory.* Unknown: Chi-ga-u, Inc., 1978.

Unbegaun, Boris Ottakar. *Russian Surnames.* Oxford: Clarendon Press, 1972.

Velze, Jacob Antoon van. *Names of Persons in Early Sanscrit Literature, etc.* Utrecht: Utr. typ. ass., 1938.

Weekley, Ernest. *The Romance of Names.* New York: Benjamin Blom, 1914.

White, G. Pawley. *Cornish Family Names.* Cornwall: Dyllansow Truran, 1972.

Woods, Richard Donovan. *Hispanic First Names: A Comprehensive Dictionary of*

250 Years of Mexican-American Usage. Connecticut: Greenwood Press, 1984. Large listing, but the historical derivation is often poor, and the author groups some names too enthusiastically as merely variants when they are separate names built off similar Gothic roots.

Woods, Richard Donovan. *Spanish Surnames in the Southwestern United States: A Dictionary.* G. K. Hall, 1978.

Woulfe, Patrick. *Irish Names and Surnames.* Baltimore, Maryland: Genealogical Publishing Company, 1967.

Yamamoto, Shigeru. "The lú-KUR₄-dab₅-ba People in the é-mí-é-ᵈBa-Ú in Pre-Sargonic Lagash." *Acta Sumerologica* 3 (1981).

Zawawi, Sharifa M. *What's in a Name? Unaitwaje? A Swahili Book of Names.* Trenton, New Jersey: Africa World Press, 1993.

Index